The
COMPLETE WRITINGS
and
SELECTED CORRESPONDENCE
of
JOHN DICKINSON

Volume One • 1751–1758

The
COMPLETE WRITINGS
and
SELECTED CORRESPONDENCE
of
JOHN DICKINSON

Volume One • 1751–1758

Editor
Jane E. Calvert

Assistant Editor
Nathan R. Kozuskanich

UNIVERSITY OF DELAWARE PRESS
DISTRIBUTED BY THE UNIVERSITY OF VIRGINIA PRESS
2020

University of Delaware Press
© 2020 by Jane E. Calvert
All rights reserved
Printed in the United States of America on acid-free paper

First published in 2020

ISBN 978-1-64453-183-9 (cloth)
ISBN 978-1-64453-184-6 (e-book)

Library of Congress Cataloging-in-Publication Data is available for this title.

Frontispiece. Courtesy of the Library Company of Philadelphia

CONTRIBUTORS

Editor
Jane E. Calvert

Assistant Editor
Nathan R. Kozuskanich

Transcribers
Alicia K. Anderson
Ellen M. Pawelczak

Editorial Assistant
David R. Hoth

Legal Consultants
Christian G. Koelbl, III
Matthew Mirow
Simon Stern

Digital Assistant
Erica Cavanaugh

Graduate Research Assistants
Mary Osborne
Peter A. Palmadesso
Christine M. Pavey
Joshua M. Powell

Undergraduate Interns
Kelly Coffman
Abigail Mortell

Advisory Board
Kenneth R. Bowling
William C. deGiacomantonio
Randy J. Holland
John Van Horne
Richard Leffler

Preparation of this edition is made possible through the support of

The American Philosophical Society
The Lynde and Harry Bradley Foundation
The William Nelson Cromwell Foundation
The Earhart Foundation
The Friends of the John Dickinson Mansion
The General Society of Colonial Wars
The Library Company of Philadelphia
Mutual Mt. Airy
The National Endowment for the Humanities
The National Historic Publications and Records Commission
The Society of Colonial Wars in the Commonwealth of Kentucky
The State of Delaware
Private Individuals

To
THE AMERICAN PEOPLE

CONTENTS

Acknowledgments

With a project of this magnitude, one incurs many debts, most of which will never be adequately repaid. There are numerous people without whom this edition would not exist at all, and many others without whom it would not exist at the highest standard.

It has been my honor to work with colleagues across many disciplines, whose expertise and professionalism has astounded, instructed, and inspired me. The project launched with the help of Mark Lauersdorf, who patiently tutored me in the art of federal grant writing. With success on the first try, the first JDP team member to be hired, Alicia Anderson, did more than anyone to establish the project on a firm footing by helping to set editorial policy and provide uncannily accurate transcriptions of JD's heretofore inscrutable handwriting. Ellen Pawelczak, a stellar paleographer and proofreader in her own right, took over where she left off. In the early days, as we were struggling to find a way forward with inadequate technology, graduate assistant Peter Palmadesso invented genius solutions to advance transcription and cataloguing efforts where purported experts failed. Later, Erica Cavanaugh at the University of Virginia brought the cataloguing system into the twenty-first century. One of the best decisions I made was to invite Nathan Kozuskanich to join the project. No matter what comes his way, he gamely jumps into the task, even where others give up. If it weren't for him, we would not have produced the first manuscript that got us the publishing contract. If the annotations on these early volumes meet the high standards of other Founders projects, it's because David Hoth came on board with his remarkable ability to unearth details that unfurl the full story of the documents. As challenging as the legal documents are, Nate and I are especially grateful for those experts who lent their time and skill. Chris Koelbl and Simon Stern interpreted the legalese; Chuck Fithian dove into the archives; Dan Gargola translated Latin and gave classical references; and Matthew Mirow, filling the void left by a long string of legal historians, translated the Law French and Neo-Latin passages. Without the commitment of Jennifer Stertzer of the Center for Digital Editing to working with the JDP and publishing the digital edition, the JDP would have folded. Copy editor Jane Haxby cheerfully brought order to the work that will benefit the JDP for the remainder of the project. At the last moment before publication of this first volume, brand new managing editor Christopher Minty stepped in to polish and make final improvements, setting us up for a strong future. What is most remarkable about these individuals is that they performed most of their work in addition to other full-time positions and personal struggles ranging from deaths in the family to debilitating illnesses. And we maintain our resolve amid the alarming new reality of a global pandemic unfolding as this volume goes to press. If there is, as we have joked, a Dickinson curse, we defy it.

The private foundations and organizations that donated to the JDP kept it afloat in the lean years. I am especially grateful to the Bradley and Earhart Foundations, who worked with me during a series of catastrophic family illnesses. Again, the project would have collapsed without them. The folks at the William Nelson Cromwell Foundation have likewise been steadfast partners.

The University of Kentucky provided some funding for travel and in-kind support for editorial assistance, computer hardware and software, and server space. I am grateful to grants officers Mary Boulton and Kyna Estes for working with me on innumerable budgets.

Central to the success of any documentary project are the archivists where the documents are housed. This is especially true when the corpus is as scattered and long-neglected as JD's. Without their knowledge and diligence, many of the documents would not be included. Connie King at the Library Company helped more times than I can count on all manner of requests. Margaret Dunham Raubacher at the Delaware Public Archives was likewise always ready to respond most helpfully, as was the staff at the Delaware Historical Society. Lesley Whitelaw and Barnaby Bryan at the Middle Temple Archives patiently answered every minute query with which David and I pelted them. Most especially, the abilities of Sarah Heim and Steve Smith to navigate the tangled collections at the Historical Society of Pennsylvania and discover long-buried documents never failed to amaze me. These people and others to be acknowledged in later volumes make the edition as complete as possible.

Members of the welcoming scholarly community of documentary editors provided invaluable expertise, advice, and support. Most notably, JDP board members Rich Leffler, Ken Bowling, and John Van Horne, helpfully made connections for funding and read and commented on early drafts.

Playing a seminal role in this endeavor is University of Delaware Press with Julia Oestreich at the fore. I am most grateful that they are not only willing but eager to publish this edition. In an age when print is undervalued and unprofitable, their commitment to seeing this project through is a gift to future generations.

I thank the many strangers I have met throughout my travels who have wished me and the JDP well. Knowing there is a waiting audience for this edition has been a terrific motivator.

I am grateful to Microsoft Word for reminding me on an almost daily basis of the transitory nature of digital media and the limits of human sanity. Thank you for repeatedly undoing my work, compelling my creativity to devise workarounds for your glitches, and thereby insisting on the need for a print edition.

Friends, colleagues, and family, I hope, already know how much their support has meant. Some of them are mentioned above. Additionally, I have valued the encouragement of Jonathan Clark, Jay-Marie Bravent, Abigail Firey, David Olster, Gary Nash, Mark Noll, Jack Rakove, Evelyn Summers, Mark Summers, Tammy Whitlock. The Dickinson Plantation folks, especially Gloria Henry and Vertie Lee, have been partners and friends. Others came serendipitously into my life, such as Anne and Wynn Lee, whose friendship and financial support of the project was an unexpected boost. Without the unwavering love and support of my husband Eric, I would not have made it through the decade it took to produce this first volume. Here's hoping he need not be as stalwart in the next ten. Thankfully, because of Mike Houghton and Governor John Carney, the State of Delaware is giving him respite in the near term with its generous support. My greatest sadness is that one of the JDP's biggest fans and someone who always had faith in JD and me, Delaware's own L.D. Shank III, did not survive to see this moment. I hope it would have made him proud.

Finally, I would like to thank John Dickinson for the devotion to his country that caused him to produce these writings, as well as his particular guidance to me, across the centuries, in pointed directions about not just the need to collect and publish his papers but also how to do it. Yet, knowing him as I now do, I suspect if he knew how we have labored over his "scrawl," he would tell us to spend more time walking, riding, ice skating, or playing badminton instead. "Moderation in every Thing," he tells us from experience, "is the Source of Happiness— Too much Writing, {—} too much Reading…all equally throw Us from the Ballance of real Pleasure."[1] I also thank him for this sound advice and hope one day to be able to follow it.

Where I could not sufficiently express my gratitude, I hope that this edition fills the void.

JANE E. CALVERT
April 12, 2020

---

[1] Doc. 2:42: JD to Thomas McKean, June 8, 1762.

Introduction

By almost any measure, this edition is more than two hundred years overdue. John Dickinson (1732–1808) of Delaware and Pennsylvania wrote more for the American Founding than any other figure, earning him the appellation "Penman of the Revolution."[1] With the publication of his *Letters from a Farmer in Pennsylvania* (1767–68; hereafter *Farmer's Letters*),[2] he became America's first international political celebrity, known around the Atlantic world as the spokesman for the cause in the years leading up to independence. During the Revolution and into the early Republic, Dickinson (hereafter JD) continued to serve his country as soldier, statesman, and author of works that helped establish the basic political institutions of the United States and define the Zeitgeist of the Founding era. He was also unique among the leading figures in his political thought and action.

JD's writings are generally of two sorts. First, he wrote state papers, including most of the issuances of all the first intercolonial and national conventions: the Stamp Act Congress (1765), the First and Second Continental Congresses (1774–76, 1779), and the Annapolis Convention (1786). He also wrote as a colonial Pennsylvania assemblyman (1760s–70s), president of Delaware (1781–82), president of Pennsylvania (1782–85), and president of the Delaware Constitutional Convention (1792). Among these writings are bills, petitions, declarations, addresses, resolutions, proclamations, and constitutions. The second sort of JD's writings are those he addressed to the public, with the intent to inform, engage, and instigate action on the most pressing political issues of the day. He began in the early 1760s to write about free maritime trade, and he progressed over the decades to treat religious liberty, taxation, peaceful political protest, military regulation, the ratification of the US Constitution, public morality, education, science, and foreign relations. Mastering various genres to reach as wide an audience as possible, he wrote newspaper articles, pamphlets, and broadsides; he used forms of epistles, essays, and verse, including America's first patriotic song; he composed serious treatises and biting satire; he wrote under his own name as well as anonymously and pseudonymously as an English Merchant, a North-American, a Farmer, the Centinel, Pacificus, Phocion, Fabius, and Anticipation. In his own day, his contribution was clear. As Benjamin Rush observed, "Few men wrote, spoke and acted more

---

[1] Given by Moses Coit Tyler in his *Literary History of the American Revolution, 1763–1783,* 2 vols. (New York: G.P. Putnam's Sons, 1897), 2:24.

[2] The *Farmer's Letters*, Tyler wrote, "may perhaps fairly be described as constituting, upon the whole, the most brilliant event in the literary history of the Revolution" (ibid., 1:234).

for their country from the years 1764 to the establishment of the federal government than Mr. Dickinson."[3]

For a time, his name and "Farmer" penname were more widely acclaimed than those of any other figures, including George Washington and Benjamin Franklin, and his contemporaries universally recognized him as a leading Founder. Yet today, few Americans have heard of him or know of his contributions. The reasons for his present obscurity are myriad, bound up with, but not restricted to, his controversial decision not to vote on or sign the Declaration of Independence. Had JD not been perceived as the leader of the resistance to Britain, his decision likely would have attracted little notice. Who now recalls that then little-known John Jay made the same decision? But JD disappointed many, and he continued to do so when he resisted persecution by the Pennsylvania radicals during the Revolution. As the documents in this edition suggest, the bitterness from that later, local dispute likely tainted his national legacy far more than his decision not to sign. When ideologically driven whig historians[4] sought fodder to defend their patriotic narratives after the Revolution, they drew on the handiwork of JD's enemies. The radicals' loud libels of treason and cowardice provided a convenient explanation both for why he did not sign and for why he deserved to be written out of history. Still, a few historians mused counterfactually that had JD signed, his power and popularity were such that he would have been America's first president.

Here, then, is the conundrum of JD's legacy. It is improbable that any of the historical factors—JD's actions in his time—would have persisted in obscuring him had his papers been made available for study. His contributions would have been too massive to ignore, his patriotic motives too clear to distort. Yet with the record obscured and partial, undoubtedly these same factors contributed to the disinclination of scholars to attempt a documentary edition, at least for most of the nineteenth century. Failed attempts in the twentieth century cannot be summarized so easily, but they too are tinged with politics. The saga of the attempts to collect and publish JD's writings and correspondence is almost as dramatic as the biography of the man himself.

---

[3] *The Autobiography of Benjamin Rush: His "Travel Through Life" Together with His Commonplace Book for 1789–1813*, ed. George W. Corner (Princeton, N.J.: Princeton University Press, 1948), 154–55.

[4] Whig historians were those writing in the early Republic who sought to create a patriotic narrative surrounding the Revolution, particularly the Declaration of Independence. It was quintessential "winners' history."

The History of Dickinson Editions

In 1801, JD was the first American to publish an edition of his own writings.[5] He seems to have been planning it as early as 1796, when he sent Benjamin Rush a list of the documents he hoped to include. "Though I never aimed at the Character of an Author," he explained, "yet, whenever peculiar Circumstances have compelled Me by a sense of Duty, to publish my sentiments, all my labors have been dedicated to the Interests of Liberty—which always imply a Connection with Virtue and Piety."[6] The idea progressed to reality at the insistence of John Vaughan, a physician in Wilmington, Delaware, and a member of the American Philosophical Society (APS), who acted as JD's literary agent in the 1780s and '90s. The actual plan for publication was laid by Wilmington printers Vincent Bonsal and Hezekiah Niles.[7] JD collected thirteen of his most important works in two volumes and played a great part in their preparation. In his papers as a whole, there is evidence of his sorting through, labeling, and identifying his manuscripts for selection, as well as drafts and notes for the introduction, headnotes, and annotations.[8] Had the opportunity presented itself, he may have included more writings, or different editions of published works. But in the new Republic, they were hard to obtain. For example, of the many editions and copies of the *Farmer's Letters* published, the only one JD could find some thirty years after its publication was the 1769 Virginia edition with Richard Henry Lee's introduction; and JD was not even certain of that authorship. An episode in 1804 highlighted his problem. When, in the second volume of his *Life of Washington*, John Marshall credited Richard Henry Lee with authoring the First Petition to the King (1774), which JD had just published in his edition, JD was furious.[9] "It is my ardent Wish," he wrote to Pennsylvania senator George Logan,

---

[5] *The Political Writings of John Dickinson, Esquire, Late President of the State of Delaware, and of the Commonwealth of Pennsylvania*, 2 vols. (Wilmington: Bonsal and Niles, 1801). A few editions of papers of other figures appeared before JD's: *The Writings of Thomas Paine, Secretary for Foreign Affairs to the Congress of the United States of America, in the Late War* (Albany: C.R. and G. Webster, 1792), though there is no indication that Paine himself initiated or authorized the collection; *The Miscellaneous Essays and Occasional Writings of Francis Hopkinson, Esq.*, 3 vols. (Philadelphia: T. Dobson, 1792); *Works of the Late Doctor Benjamin Franklin: Consisting of Essays, Humorous, Moral & Literary, Chiefly in the Manner of the Spectator*, 2 vols. (London: G.G.J. and J. Robinson, 1793).

[6] JD to Benjamin Rush, Dec. 29, 1796, PCarlD.

[7] R.G. Stone, *Hezekiah Niles as an Economist*, Johns Hopkins University Studies in Historical and Political Science (Baltimore: Johns Hopkins Press, 1933), 52.

[8] The documents JD included will be noted in the table of contents of each volume with an asterisk.

[9] John Marshall, *The Life of George Washington . . .*, 5 vols. (Philadelphia: C.P. Wayne, 1804–7), 2:180.

that the Clerk [at the State Department] may continue his search for that Original Draft, as also for the Original Drafts of the Address to the People of Quebec in the Year 1774—of the second Address to the King in 1775—of The Declaration of the Causes and Necessity of our taking up Arms in 1775—and of the Address to the Several States, on the present situation of Affairs in May 1779. If found in my Handwriting," he reasoned, "they may defend Me against future Misrepresentations." Recognizing the effort this search could entail, JD promised, "The Clerk will be entitled to a Compensation for his extra Labors."[10] These documents eventually ended up in JD's possession, but the misrepresentations, which JD believed were motivated by "party Prejudice," only increased.[11] It is clear that politics, then and now, have determined his legacy more than anything he did or did not do.

The intervening years—almost a century—until the next edition were not kind to JD. Although Wilmington printer Miller Dunott republished his edition in 1814, the prevailing current of whig historiography did not flow in JD's direction. In George Bancroft's famed multivolume *History of the United States*, reprinted many times throughout the nineteenth century, Bancroft treated JD as a personal enemy, eviscerating him with vitriolic abandon.[12] According to Bancroft, if JD were not an overt traitor to the American cause, then he was an effeminate coward who hindered it. The ensuing years of comparative historiographical silence on JD suggest that Bancroft's screed effectively stifled the inclination of other historians to explore his contributions to the Founding.

The next attempt at a JD edition came in the late nineteenth century. As part of the series *Memoirs of the Historical Society of Pennsylvania*, the Historical Society of Pennsylvania (HSP) commissioned *The Life and Writings of John Dickinson*, by Charles J. Stillé. This biography, the first of JD, appeared in 1891; the first volume of the *Writings*, edited by Paul Leicester Ford, appeared in 1895. Ford's edition contained twenty-one of JD's works from 1764 to 1774, most of them published during JD's lifetime and republished in his own 1801 edition. Ford's papers at the New York Public Library reveal that he was working on a second edition, which would, presumably, have extended through 1803, when JD's last pamphlet was published. But before he could finish, Ford was murdered by his brother, Malcolm, at the age of 37.[13]

Ford had been given unlimited access to JD's papers by JD's descendants, the Logan family. After Ford's death, however, the material was scattered. In 1943 and at other points in the 1940s, Robert Restalrig

---

[10] JD to George Logan, Jan. 12, 1805, PHi-Logan.

[11] JD to George Logan, Oct. 11, 1804, PHi-MDL.

[12] George Bancroft, *History of the United States, from the Discovery of the American Continent* 10 vols. (Boston: Little, Brown, & co., 1834–1857), 7: *passim*.

[13] "Paul L. Ford Slain by His Brother; Shot by Malcolm as He Sat at His Desk in His Library," *New York Times*, May 9, 1902.

Logan donated his purportedly reassembled collection of JD papers, splitting it haphazardly between the HSP and the Library Company of Philadelphia (LCP).[14] In short order, scholars began working with the documents and planning documentary editions. By 1946, Delaware state archivist Leon deValinger was contemplating an edition of JD correspondence, and would-be JD biographer John H. Powell, then assistant librarian at the Free Library of Philadelphia, was considering working on an edition of his writings.[15] Powell never finished his biography, nor did he begin serious work on an edition. Rather, H. Trevor Colbourn, then a history professor at Indiana University, took up the latter endeavor.[16]

During the 1950s, the modern discipline of documentary editing was emerging and entering a brief golden age.[17] Beginning with the publication of the first volume of Julian Boyd's *Papers of Thomas Jefferson* in 1950, there was a boom in projects to publish leading statesmen's papers. This development seemed to bode well for a JD edition. In 1954, the new federal agency under the National Archives Establishment,[18] the National Historical Publications Commission (NHPC; now the National Historical Publications and Records Commission, NHPRC) published *A National Program for the Publication of Historical Documents: A Report to the President by the National Historical Publications Commission*, listing JD as someone whose papers were worthy of publication.[19] In 1963, the agency claimed deValinger's project, based at the Delaware Public Archives (DPA), as one of its own. In "A Report to the President Containing A Proposal, by the National Historical Publications Commission," the following appeared in a list of projects:

> *The Correspondence of John Dickinson*, to include letters written both by and to John Dickinson, "The Penman of the Revolution," was formally initiated when, in November 1959, the Public Archives Commission of Delaware and the Friends of the John Dickinson

---

[14] John H. Powell to Dorothy M. Forbis, July 24, 1946, PPAmP-JHPP.

[15] Powell to Forbis, July 24, 1946, PPAmP-JHPP. Another account has deValinger beginning his work in the 1930s, but given the lack of access to the documents, that seems unlikely (see the HSP Feasibility Study, below). See also "DeValinger to Edit Dickinson Papers," *History News* (1950): 50. DeValinger wrote several useful articles on JD. See the bibliography of sources on JD in the Appendix of this volume, 367–72.

[16] Harold Trevor Colbourn, born in 1927 in Australia, died as this introduction was in draft, Jan. 13, 2015.

[17] For a more detailed history of the rise of documentary editing, see Mary-Jo Klein and Susan Holbrook Perdue, *A Guide to Documentary Editing*, 3rd ed. (Charlottesville: University of Virginia Press, 2008).

[18] Since 1985, the National Archives and Records Administration (NARA).

[19] *A National Program for the Publication of Historical Documents: A Report to the President by the National Historical Publications Commission* (Washington, DC, 1954), 47–48.

Mansion, Inc. agreed to cosponsor the project and the latter organization made a substantial grant to finance collecting. Leon deValinger, Jr., State Archivist of Delaware, who had for some years been collecting informally and had acquired the texts of some 3,000 letters at the time of this agreement, was named editor; and the headquarters of the project was established at the Hall of Records in Dover, where the files are maintained.

Supplemental grants have permitted the acquisition of important original Dickinson letters from England and copies of others from widely scattered sources. Collecting has now reached a point where editorial work on the first volume is practicable and is moving ahead.

Meanwhile, by September 1962, Colbourn estimated that he had about sixty percent of the material collected for an edition of JD's writings.[20] But in the course of his work, he committed a scholarly misstep that may have affected both JD editions. In July and October of that year, at the behest of the HSP, Colbourn scooped deValinger by publishing a two-part article in the *Pennsylvania Magazine of History and Biography* containing abridged and edited versions of JD's letters from the Middle Temple in London to his parents in Delaware.[21] This set of letters is undoubtedly the most valuable body of correspondence in JD's papers, both in content and scope. There is no other set so lively, informative, or complete. In a scathing letter to Colbourn, Powell denounced him for a mean-spirited act and an incompetent performance. "Just a few months before [deValinger's] book is to come out," inveighed Powell, "you have published incomplete versions of these letters, with a thin introduction which makes no original contribution to our knowledge of Dickinson, and with notes that do nothing to make the letters more meaningful for us; and in the course of the few notes you do give, you contrive to make errors of commission that reveal you startlingly, surprisingly un-informed about the man whose letters you are editing."[22]

But Powell may have been mistaken on one or more points. Considering that this is the only collection of JD letters that has ever been published, perhaps Colbourn's performance was not as useless as Powell maintained. Significantly, although there was much talk about deValinger's first volume being almost ready for publication, it never

---

[20] Colbourn to Powell, Sept. 20, 1962, PPAmP-JHPP.
[21] See Colbourn in Abbreviations, p. lxxi.
[22] Powell to Colbourn, July 24, 1962, PPAmP-JHPP.

appeared—nor did any further work on JD by Colbourn, who shifted to academic administration in 1967. The remnants of his project reside at the University of Central Florida, where he ended his career as president.[23]

In 1970, at the age of sixty-five, deValinger retired from the DPA and left his JD project to the HSP, hoping that someone would continue his work. By this time, however, scholarly enthusiasm for white, male political leaders was cooling, in favor of social history of unenfranchised minorities and women. In the mid-1970s, as historian Stanley K. Johannesen planned a JD biography and began an edition of the *Farmer's Letters*, he was discouraged in his efforts by Bernard Bailyn, who had given up on his own multivolume edition of American Revolutionary pamphlets after the first volume, and warned that funding for Founders' editions was evaporating.[24]

The next attempt is perhaps the greatest mystery in the saga of JD editions. In 1986, the HSP and the LCP decided jointly to produce a modern, scholarly microfilm JD edition, containing both writings and correspondence, as well as a two-volume print edition of JD's legal papers. With director Peter J. Parker at the helm, the HSP commissioned a Feasibility Study, paid for by the NHPRC and authored by historian and documentary editor Glenn W. LaFantasie. The thorough study "contains an assessment of the need for a microform edition of the Papers of John Dickinson, a review of earlier attempts to edit and publish Dickinson's writings, a report on the survey of extant documents written to and by Dickinson, a definition of the scope of a full-scale documentary project, and a recommended plan of work for the project."[25]

The study began with a strong assertion: "the scholarly neglect that has surrounded John Dickinson, relegating him to the status of a 'forgotten patriot,' is no longer defensible."[26] LaFantasie canvassed major and minor repositories—116 in total—in search of JD documents. He ultimately estimated that there were between eight and ten thousand items extant. The study proposed to build on deValinger's work, arguing that deValinger had failed because "the magnitude of the undertaking clearly exceeded the ability of one person, no matter how devoted to the cause, to complete the necessary work on a part-time basis and on a limited budget."[27] Accordingly, in this new attempt, the project would be supported by an impressive infrastructure: two scholarly institutions—the HSP and the LCP—along with the Friends of the John Dickinson Mansion in Delaware. It was to be housed at the HSP

---

[23] University of Central Florida Office of the President: H. Trevor Colbourn Papers, Special Collections and University Archives, University of Central Florida, Orlando, Florida.

[24] Stanley K. Johannesen, email message to author, Sept. 1, 2013.

[25] Glenn W. LaFantasie, "The Papers of John Dickinson Feasibility Study" (NHPRC, 1986), 1–2.

[26] Ibid., 5.

[27] Ibid., 9.

and, in addition to two full-time employees, it would be staffed with researchers, transcribers, collators, and editorial assistants through cooperative programs with Temple University and the University of Pennsylvania. The editorial board was equally impressive, including important people in the historical and editing professions and keepers of JD's legacy: Leon deValinger; Richard S. Dunn, then editor of the Papers of William Penn; Barbara Moyne Homsey, then president of the Friends of the John Dickinson Mansion; Barbara Oberg, then editor of the Papers of Albert Gallatin; Richard A. Ryerson, then with the Adams Papers; James Stewart, of the Division of Historical and Cultural Affairs in the State of Delaware; and John Van Horne, director of the LCP. It seemed an auspicious beginning. Yet the project never launched, and all these early attempts at JD editions were forgotten, their physical remnants lost in the archives.

Over the next twenty years, a few JD documents were republished in various editions, and some new ones emerged. In 1987, James Hutson's *Supplement* (Yale, 1987) filled gaps in Max Farrand's *Records of the Federal Convention* (Yale, 1911), which involved transcribing and publishing JD's notes. In 1992, John Willson and Hillsdale College Press reprinted the *Fabius Letters* (1788) with a teachers' guide, and in 1999 the Liberty Fund published an edition of the *Farmer's Letters*, with an introduction by Forrest McDonald. Other major documentary editions underway showed JD to be at the heart of Founding events: the Letters of Delegates to Congress, the First Federal Congress Project, the Papers of Thomas Jefferson, the Ratification of the Constitution Project, and others. But without an edition of his own, scholarship on JD continued to languish. By 2009, only two monographs had been published on him since Stillé's 1891 biography—a partial study of his career by David L. Jacobson in 1965 and a biography in 1983 by Milton E. Flower—along with a smattering of articles.[28]

The Founding of the John Dickinson Writings Project

In 2004, Richard Fonte, then the director of the "We the People" program at the National Endowment for the Humanities (NEH), approached historian Jane Calvert at the biennial meeting of The Historical Society in Boothbay Harbor, Maine, where she had just delivered her first scholarly paper on JD.[29] He asked her if she would undertake an edition of JD's writings.

---

[28] David L. Jacobson, *John Dickinson and the Revolution in Pennsylvania, 1764–1776* (Berkeley: University of California Press, 1965); Milton E. Flower, *John Dickinson: Conservative Revolutionary* (Charlottesville: University Press of Virginia, 1983). For a complete bibliography of works published on JD, see the Appendix, 367–72.

[29] Jane E. Calvert, "Liberty without Tumult: Understanding the Politics of John Dickinson," *PMHB* 131, no. 3 (2007): 233–62.

Calvert, who did not envision a career in documentary editing, declined. Fonte then emailed links to the NEH application instructions, and Calvert received invitations to serve on panels reviewing proposals for the NEH Scholarly Editions Grant. As she continued to work on her monograph, *Quaker Constitutionalism and the Political Thought of John Dickinson* (Cambridge, 2009), and realized the great magnitude of JD's writings—both in volume and import—for the Founding, Calvert decided an edition must be undertaken.

The initial plan for the John Dickinson Writings Project (JDP), begun in 2009, was simply to produce an updated version of JD's and Ford's editions—namely, two or three volumes restricted to JD's best-known published works. But further research into his papers in the archives uncovered a wealth of valuable material that could reveal not only significant information about this unique and misunderstood figure, but also an alternative vision for the founding of the Republic. It was not just the drafts of heretofore unknown JD publications that were exciting but also the vast number of unpublished manuscripts.

By this time, however, both the NEH and the NHPRC were struggling to survive, their funding having stagnated at 1970s levels. Bailyn's concerns about the opportunities for Founders' projects were being realized: the academic political climate was such that white, male political leaders were significantly lower priority for funding—unless, that is, they were already known. In 2008, NARA, the parent agency of the NHPRC, published "The Founders Online: Open Access to the Papers of America's Founding Era: A Report to Congress," which outlined "a plan to provide online access, within a reasonable timeframe, to the complete papers of America's Founding Fathers." The report defined "Founding Fathers" as John Adams, Benjamin Franklin, Alexander Hamilton, Thomas Jefferson, James Madison, and George Washington. Now JD was officially, by definition of the federal government, not a Founding Father. Nonetheless, in 2010, the JDP received an endorsement from the NHPRC (which had no money for new projects at that time) and a two-year NEH Scholarly Editions Grant.

It was not until Calvert was several years into collecting documents that she happened upon archival papers that hinted of previous work. Powell's correspondence at the APS alerted her to deValinger's project, but the whereabouts of that project's papers were unknown. At the University of Delaware Special Collections, she discovered the 1986 HSP Feasibility Study, confirming that transcriptions and some photocopies from microfilm of JD's papers were at the HSP. Most of the facsimile originals used for the transcriptions, Calvert later learned, were at the DPA.

The prospect of building on deValinger's work to accelerate the JDP was exciting. But that hope was quickly dashed when the battered boxes emerged from the vault. There were nine, most containing rough typed transcriptions of correspondence, held together with paper clips rusted to the pages, usually without facsimile originals or complete citations. The quality of work was such that it would be of minimal use to the current project. Thus the other great mystery was, if this was as far as deValinger had gotten with his work—about where it had been in 1963—why did he represent to Powell and the NHPC that his first volume was within a few months of completion? Was it wishful thinking? Or is there more polished work missing from the boxes? We may never know.

On balance, rather than advancing the JDP, the reemergence of the earlier projects slowed efforts by providing more documents—facsimile originals and transcriptions—to sort and more incomplete citations to hunt down. Motivated both by the hope of rediscovering lost documents and the fear of having missed even one, JDP staff processed these duplicates, multiplying their time on this tedious task without significant return.

For the early years of the present project, the challenges remained the same as or greater than they were in the 1960s, with additional difficulties brought on by the digital age. Far from the plan outlined in the HSP study, in its first seven years, the JDP was not formally supported by any institution. None of the institutions or groups that had committed to sponsoring and supporting a JD project in the 1950s, 1960s, or 1980s expressed interest in doing so again in a sustaining way. It was staffed by one historian-turned-editor, who worked on the project full-time only when she could obtain funding to buy leave time from teaching. When there was funding, the project employed on a part-time or contractual basis two transcribers and a graduate student assistant. An assistant editor worked on annotations, but only when he found time away from his other academic duties, and a volunteer donated his time.

New challenges of the digital age presented themselves as well. The field of documentary editing was quickly evolving away from traditional analog practices and publication, but without fully functional digital tools to take their place—or at least not for those who were not technically inclined. In addition to word processing programs being unreliable, in the rush to embrace the latest technologies, federal funding agencies were inclined to downplay the slow, meticulous, and expensive work that must form the basis of any scholarly edition, print or digital. Their demand to add digital processing and open-access publication on top of existing work was effectively an unfunded mandate. Few historians possessed the technological skills necessary to craft a true digital edition (i.e., something more than work that has been merely adapted to a digital/online environment). Such work requires computer programmers capable of building Web platforms and writing code. To find those individuals, who also must have humanities skills as well as a willingness to work for the pay of a humanist, is nearly impossible. Moreover, few institutions or organizations can afford to offer expensive digital resources for free. Thus the work proceeded in small increments, colored by a constant, looming uncertainty as to how the next phase would be funded.

Stepping into the breach left by federal agencies were private foundations—the Lynde and Harry Bradley Foundation, the Earhart Foundation, and the William Nelson Cromwell Foundation—that helped see the JDP through building the first three volumes. Smaller but very necessary funding came from repeat donations from the Society of Colonial Wars in the Commonwealth of Kentucky and the General Society of Colonial Wars, to ensure editorial assistance. Smaller amounts from organizations and individuals also defrayed the expenses of transcription and travel to the archives. More recently, the Delaware legislature, prompted by Governor John Carney, has provided funding for a full-time managing editor. Donors are gratefully acknowledged on page vi.

In 2016, the JDP gained institutional stability and assurances of digital publication when it officially partnered with the newly founded Center for Digital Editing at the University of Virginia; and in 2017 the JDP received funding from the NHPRC.

Dickinson's Papers: An Overview

The two largest collections of JD's papers, with a combined total of around 6,500 items, are at the LCP and the HSP.[30] They were donated "at various times 1943–49" by JD descendant Robert R. Logan.[31] Most of the papers are political writings and outgoing correspondence. The HSP collection contains a significant number of deeds and indentures from JD's law practice and management of his tenant properties. Not insignificant is the LCP's collection of books belonging to JD, several of which contain his marginalia. The DPA has a few original JD items as well as part of the deValinger project—a large collection of facsimiles of JD correspondence collected from archives around the country. The Dickinson College Library is the only other repository possessing a "Dickinson collection," which contains a small amount of correspondence and a selection of books that JD donated to the College in 1784. Other archives, such as the Delaware Historical Society, the New York Public Library, the New-York Historical Society, the Library of Congress, and the National Archives, have JD

---

[30] Feasibility Study, 10.
[31] John H. Powell and Edwin Wolf, 2nd, "Inventory by groups" of the PPL-JDFP.

holdings, but they are scattered through various collections, which may or may not be identified as containing JD material. The Pennsylvania Historical and Museum Commission in Harrisburg also has substantial material, mostly related to JD's Pennsylvania presidency. Many other repositories in the Philadelphia area and around the country hold smaller amounts of JD correspondence. With the exception of materials from the Middle Temple in London, whose archivist graciously provided help, the JDP has not had the funds or staffing to explore foreign archives.

For a man who wrote so much on public affairs and had such extensive professional and business dealings, there is a surprising dearth of extant papers. There are several likely explanations for this unfortunate fact. First, JD moved frequently among dwellings in the Delaware Valley, creating ample opportunity for papers to be lost. Over the course of his life, he lived in London for three years; he owned several properties in the Philadelphia area at which he resided; he often retreated to his boyhood home, Poplar Hall, in Dover, Delaware; and he retired in Wilmington, Delaware. Second, because he was seen by many as the leader of the American Revolution, he was a special target for retribution by the British and their sympathizers. In 1777, the British burned his primary Philadelphia dwelling, Fairhill, possibly destroying papers he may have kept there. In 1781, loyalist raiders looted Poplar Hall. It is alleged that one party or another stole his papers and scattered them in the streets of New York City, a loyalist stronghold.[32] This may account for why drafts of the *Farmer's Letters* are missing. Third, after his death, his daughters, Sally and Maria, combed through his papers and may have destroyed most of the letters he exchanged with his wife, Mary, as well as other personal items. Finally, because of his status as a "forgotten patriot," archivists have not been as careful to catalogue and preserve his papers together as they have been with the canonical Founders. If JD kept a copybook, it is not extant, and his letters, which were often drafted on the backs of envelopes, are frequently catalogued under the name of the recipient with no indication of the sender. The HSP Feasibility Study made clear that many repositories were unaware that they possessed JD documents. Equally unsettling was returning to some of the same archives that had responded to LaFantasie's query in 1986 to discover that they could

---

[32] In his *Life of James Otis, of Massachusetts* (Boston: Wells and Lilly, 1823), William Tudor explains that "Mr. Dickinson's house on the Delaware, was plundered by the British troops, when they were evacuating Philadelphia, his papers were carried off and afterwards scattered about the streets of New York" (134). Considering the confusion in this account—the British burned Fairhill, which was not on the Delaware; the loyalists plundered Poplar Hall, which was—it is untrustworthy, but at least it provides a possible explanation for why JD's early papers are missing.

no longer find the JD documents they had listed then. Yet others turned up in their stead.

The state of the two Logan collections at the LCP and HSP is uneven. Apart from making the gifts, Robert R. Logan did not do archivists—or editors—any favors. It seems he kept the collection in no particular order and had little idea what he was donating to whom. For example, a single draft of a document might be divided between the repositories, with some pages at the HSP and others at the LCP. It is impossible to know exactly how the papers were (mis)handled during previous attempts at editions, but it does not instill confidence when one finds notes scribbled upon original documents in ballpoint pen—"A splendid state paper by Dickinson"—in what appears to be deValinger's handwriting.

In 2002, when Calvert began working with the LCP collection, the John Dickinson Family Papers had already been processed quite well. There was a 167-page inventory of 411 items, compiled by John Powell, probably in the 1950s, with some additions by Edwin Wolf, 2nd, LCP director, in 1963. In the inventory, some of the items were described and others even transcribed, but they were in no particular order (except possibly the order in which they arrived), making it unhelpful as a finding aid. The documents themselves, in thirteen boxes, had been organized by date and topic. The collection was nicely reprocessed in 2009–10 by the "Cataloguing Hidden Special Collections and Archives Project" under the auspices of the Philadelphia Area Consortium of Special Collections Libraries (PACSCL).

The R.R. Logan Collection at the HSP was only minimally processed when Calvert first explored it in 2002. It was reprocessed in 2006 with a grant from the NEH. The dearth of quality secondary scholarship on JD meant the staff lacked expertise about him, and as a result much of the material was effectively unprocessed or miscategorized with inorrect dates and titles or none at all. There were reams of unidentified and unordered pages, many of them too illegible to sort but highly significant. In 2012, Calvert reprocessed portions of the collection. But the undertaking was limited by time constraints and lack of available work space at the HSP. This partial reprocessing took a month of steady work, in which Calvert also took digital images of the documents. The first five years of the project were devoted to sorting through the images, identifying the writings, and cataloguing them in the JDP electronic files.

Selection Criteria

The selected documents can be described in two ways: type of document (print or manuscript); and category.

The JDP has sought to include all extant published writings. The general rule for the selection of printed texts was to use a first edition of a pamphlet or broadside or the first appearance in a newspaper. The editor deemed it not feasible to find all extant versions, let alone collate them. However, all known editions of major publications that were produced in JD's lifetime are noted. There are circumstances in which the first edition rule is neither possible nor desirable to uphold: for example, when JD stated a preference for a later edition; when he annotated a later edition; when the first edition is no longer extant; or when it is impossible to determine which version was published first. When such an exception occurs, it is mentioned in the headnote to the document.

The selection of manuscript texts was also simple: the edition includes all documents that fall into the categories mentioned below, as well as the odd personal document that sheds light on JD's personality and character.

This edition contains four main categories of documents (print and manuscript): 1) those written by JD on public affairs; 2) public writings to or about JD or in response his writings; 3) JD's private correspondence and miscellaneous private writings; and 4) nontextual representations of JD.

The two main categories of papers omitted from this edition are JD's estate papers and routine legal documents, such as deeds and indentures. Both of these are housed at the HSP. Although no doubt they would shed light on JD and his world, it was not feasible to undertake their processing and editing.

Dickinson's Writings on Public Affairs

The term "public affairs" is meant to encompass a broad scope of writings on a variety of topics, including politics and legislation; civil, criminal, and maritime law; philanthropic activities; and the military. It includes anything that was published under JD's name as an individual or, following other Founders' editions, in committee, but also anything to do with topics concerning the public. Although it is usual to excerpt legal papers and publish them in a separate series, this approach seemed unsuitable to the corpus of JD's work. (See "Dickinson's Legal Papers and their Context," pp. lxiii–lvi.)

JD's public writings have been particularly difficult to work with for several reasons. Naturally, his best-known writings were published and thus relatively easy to collect and transcribe, which is why this was the first, limited goal of the JDP. But those turned out to be just a small fraction of the extant writings. First, there were many unsigned or pseudonymously published works in newspapers, pamphlets, and broadsides, not to mention official state papers that were unattributed or written in a committee. Then there were his manuscripts, which are mainly drafts rather than clean, final copies. JD labored mightily over his public writings, which is apparent from only a cursory glance at his heavily edited manuscripts.[33] These drafts have been the greatest obstacle to completing the project. Among those who have confronted it, JD's handwriting is notoriously difficult to read. It is not merely that his script is often illegible, or that his drafts are messy, cluttered with deletions, insertions, extensive marginalia, symbol note markers, and lines drawn between sections of text. Along with these challenges, JD also often wrote in legal shorthand with Latin abbreviations, or in his own idiosyncratic shorthand with frequent and erratic abbreviations. Transcribing and proofreading these documents accurately have required an unusual degree of paleographic expertise and much time and effort on the part of the small project staff. There is no doubt that his handwriting alone is a major contributor to his writings' having languished in obscurity. They have simply been inaccessible at the most basic level.

Despite the difficulty involved, it became clear early in the project that the drafts should be transcribed and included. In the first place, the content and importance of many of them could not be determined before transcription. The historical significance alone of his state papers is enough to warrant inclusion of all available drafts. Comparing the evolution of the drafts with the final versions of these papers is a particularly helpful way to gain insights into his political thought—how representative it was of his era, or how original or influential—and to see how others changed or preserved his work. For his other writings, the fact that his contemporaries admired his style and held it up as an example ought to compel us to look closely at his process, at his word choice and phrasing, and at what he decided to keep as well as what he rejected. His writing style received accolades from all corners, from friend, foe, and stranger alike. His cousin by marriage, author Deborah Norris Logan, found that he used "language [that] was always impressive, and so pure that it might be taken for a Standard of the highest excellence." [34] Loyalist William Franklin, Benjamin Franklin's son, lamented that the *Farmer's Letters* "being wrote in a smooth, easy flowing stile they pass off very well with great Numbers of the common people in America."[35] Reviewers in England found his reasoning to be "manly and nervous" (i.e., vigorous).[36] Finally, as noted above, JD himself stated that it was his "ardent Wish" that his drafts be made public for future generations.

---

[33] See a sample original manuscript on p. lxvii.

[34] The Diary of Deborah Norris Logan, 1808–1814, Manuscript 14720.Q (uncatalogued), PPL.

[35] William Franklin to Benjamin Franklin, May 10, 1768, *PBF*, 15:121.

[36] Review of JD's *Speech Delivered in the House of Assembly* in *The Critical Review: Or, Annals of Literature*, vol. 18 (London: A. Hamilton, 1765): 316–17.

<u>Public Writings to and about Dickinson</u>

It may seem an unusual decision to include everything written publicly to, about, or in response to JD and his writings. The editors were compelled in this direction for several reasons. First, most of JD's major writings—several in the form of letters—were directed to the public, and the public responded enthusiastically. The publication of his *Farmer's Letters* launched the first and most robust public epistolary exchange in early American history. By mid-1768, entire issues of newspapers were devoted to articles written by JD, either as the Farmer or the Centinel, and by others in response. Therefore, just as modern documentary editions include both outgoing and incoming correspondence, it is not just appropriate, but also necessary, to include the public response in order to understand the scope of the political debate.

Second, the minimal and inaccurate treatment JD has received from scholars over the past two hundred years demonstrates most emphatically their lack of awareness of his public stature in the years surrounding the Revolution. Historians portray the American Revolution, especially in the early years of the resistance, as an amorphous, leaderless movement, and suggest that what leadership there was came from Massachusetts. But the writings here show otherwise. Not just the sheer volume of material, but also its impassioned nature, prove indisputably that contemporaries on both sides of the Atlantic saw JD as the voice of the American resistance to Britain, whether they agreed with his position or not. Those who agreed followed his advice about how to resist; those who did not labeled him a traitor.

Finally, there is precedent: both JD and Ford, as well as editors of smaller volumes, saw fit to include at least some of these "testimonies" about JD's reputation and influence in their editions. Had they had access to the range of searchable sources available today, they might have included more. Investigations of the online databases of American and British imprints and newspapers have uncovered not merely the expected pamphlets and newspaper articles, but also poems, dedications, toasts, songs, and advertisements for products honoring JD and the Farmer, all depicting a frenzy of patriotic sentiment surrounding him. Before the Revolution, no other American dominated the public imagination as did JD. Such was the enthusiasm that it sparked a backlash of satire and ridicule that sometimes took on a life of its own, spinning out so far from JD that it did not warrant inclusion in this edition.

<u>Correspondence and Writings</u>

The decision to include selected correspondence (incoming and outgoing) came a few years into the project, when it became clear that excluding it would greatly impoverish the edition and limit scholarship.

There was too much rich information available—for understanding the context of JD's thought, his character, and motives for writing—to omit the correspondence. This decision was not made lightly, however, because of the extra work it would entail and the impossibility under the existing circumstances of undertaking it as thoroughly as the editor wished. It is important to note from the outset, then, that the limitations of a single individual—devoted to the project but with minimal funding, and living far from the archives—made an exhaustive search for and processing of JD correspondence impossible. Increasingly aware of the likelihood of failure should the project continue too long without issue, the editor was forced to accept these limitations, rather than making the perfect the enemy of the good. The edition therefore includes what has surfaced organically in the process of collecting the public writings. Furthermore, with regard to all the material, writings and correspondence, the print volumes of this edition should rightly be viewed as merely a first edition. The digital edition that will follow will allow supplementation as more letters are discovered, not to mention corrections to existing material. Work on the digital edition will also facilitate subsequent expanded print editions, should there be demand.

There is relatively little surviving correspondence before 1770. During this period, the editors have endeavored to include all extant letters related to JD's political activities and his private correspondence with friends, family, colleagues, and clients. The very limited number of letters inclined the editors to be less discriminating in their selection, their rationale being that even a little partial information is better than none. When there is more correspondence, much of it is related to routine business in his law practice, with rental properties, and regarding other business activities—debt collection, deed or indenture execution, collection of rents, and land transactions. In latter years, therefore, we generally omit correspondence that does not shed light on a larger issue related to JD's politics or personal life.

Finally, there is a very small number of personal writings that demanded inclusion for the contrast they show with the majority of the corpus and the light they shine on JD's inner life. Whereas most of his writings adopt the serious tone befitting politics, law, or the military, a few were discovered that reveal JD's more creative, fanciful side—poems, songs, an outline for a romantic tale, religious musings, and notes to himself that reveal emotional or physical struggles. These items round out his personality.

<u>Physical Representations</u>

A fourth type of nontextual source included in this edition is visual depictions of and material tributes to JD. In the course of research on documents, a number of representations have surfaced, including paintings, drawings, etchings, statues, and an enamel miniature. The edition includes images of all available artifacts with JD's likeness. Unfortunately, it is probably safe to assume that the 1771 gold medal with his bust and the 1772 wax statue did not survive the eighteenth century—contemporary descriptions of them will have to stand in their stead.

Biography of John Dickinson and Overview of the Edition

JD was born on November 13, 1732,[37] to a wealthy Quaker family in Talbot County, Maryland. His father, a plantation owner and judge, moved his family to Dover, Delaware, in 1741. Young JD received tutoring in the liberal arts by, among others, William Killen, later Delaware chief justice and first chancellor of the state. In 1750, at the age of eighteen, JD began his legal training in Philadelphia, reading law with former king's attorney John Moland. The volumes are arranged chronologically and by period in JD's life and in American history; the following division of volumes is subject to change depending on length of documents when compiled and annotated:

Volume One (Colonial Era I), 1751–1758: This, the present volume, begins with the earliest extant JD document, a letter he wrote at age nineteen, and concludes with cases from his early law practice. From 1753 to 1757, he received legal training at the Middle Temple, one of the Inns of Court in London. Upon his return to the colonies, he established a practice in Philadelphia. The documents generally fall into three series. The first is JD's rich and descriptive **London Letters**, correspondence to his parents written from 1753 to 1756. This is the first time this significant trove has been published unabridged and fully annotated. The second series is the **Documents from the William Smith Libel Trial** from 1758. Although copious papers exist on the prosecution side of this case, these papers have never been studied, and scholars were unaware of JD's role as Smith's defense attorney. The third series is **Documents on the Flag-of-Truce Trade**. During the French and Indian War, tensions between the American colonies and Britain arose over whether trade with the French was legal. JD took many flag-of-truce cases before the Vice Admiralty Court to defend mariners facing charges of smuggling or illegal trading.

Volume Two (Colonial Era II), 1759–1763: Here are JD's earliest political documents. Upon his election to the legislature of the Three Lower Counties (Delaware)[38] in 1759, JD entered provincial politics. He was

---

[37] JD's birth date is sometimes noted as November 2, as recorded in the Dickinson family Bible (PHi-Logan). But this date is according to the obsolete Gregorian calendar. When the British Empire adopted the Julian calendar in 1752, JD considered his birth date to be November 13, as evinced in several pieces of correspondence. See, for example, JD to Mary Norris Dickinson, Nov. 11, 1791, PHi-Loudoun.

[38] During the colonial era, the state we now know as Delaware did not exist. That region was part of Pennsylvania, known as the Three Lower Counties Upon Delaware. These counties

reelected the following year and also became speaker of that House. Unfortunately, there are few extant political documents from this period. But after he was elected to the Pennsylvania Assembly to fill a vacancy in a special 1762 election, he wrote numerous bills in that body. An appendix to this volume will detail his activities in the Assembly. Also during this period is JD's earliest extant essay, drawn from his notes on the flag-of-truce cases in Volume One, which gives insight into how he viewed the constitutional relationship between the colonies and Britain. Finally, this volume contains legal case notes; three commonplace books; a small amount of correspondence to family and friends, as well as a few clients; and a variety of other documents, public and private.

Volume Three (Colonial Era III), 1764–1766: During these years, JD quickly moved to the center of Pennsylvanian and American politics. The issues that concerned him in Pennsylvania were the Paxton Riots (1763–64), in which he sought to protect Native Americans from harm by white frontiersmen; and the controversy over royal government (1764–65), in which he sought preservation of the 1701 Pennsylvania Charter of Privileges and protection of rights for religious dissenters. At the same time, he was at the forefront of the resistance to Britain. As the de facto leader of the Stamp Act Congress (1765), JD wrote the Petition of the Stamp Act Congress and its Declaration, and, among others, a pamphlet that caused controversy for its advocacy of rights, *An Address to the Committee of Correspondence in Barbados* (1766). As the documents demonstrate, with these efforts, JD gained international recognition as an able writer, orator, and politician.

Volume Four (Colonial Era IV), 1767–1769: In these years, JD became an international celebrity as the voice of the American resistance to Britain. Against the Townshend Acts, he wrote the *Farmer's Letters*—the most widely read pamphlet in the colonies before Thomas Paine's *Common Sense* (1776)—and "The Liberty Song" (1768), America's first patriotic song. The letters prompted a tidal wave of public response, mostly in favor, but also in dissent. JD's writings unified and mobilized Americans like never before. Not only did colonial assemblies and committees follow his advice for how to resist the British, Americans also made him a patriotic icon. No other American at the time enjoyed such acclaim. Toasts were drunk to him across the colonies, poems were written and dedicated, tributes were made, honorary degrees were bestowed, and his likeness was etched in copperplate. His "Liberty Song" was sung from Boston to Charles-Town. The French claimed that he was more eloquent than Cicero, and John Adams later

---

were, from north to south, New Castle, Kent, and Sussex. Since 1701, however, the region had its own legislative assembly. Therefore, before 1776, when Delaware became a separate state, it may be referred to as the Lower Counties.

complained that the British considered him "the Ruler of America."[39] In the midst of the celebration of the *Farmer's Letters*, JD joined an effort to write a series of letters under the name Centinel on the episcopal controversy, which seemed a ministerial threat to American religious liberty and engaged the public from Pennsylvania northward. During this period, public documents by, to, and about JD flooded the presses, sometimes taking up nearly entire newspapers for weeks at a time.

Volume Five (Revolutionary Era I), 1770–1775: This period begins with JD's marriage to Mary Norris, daughter of Quaker speaker of the Assembly Isaac Norris II. It was a powerful sociopolitical alliance, but also one based on love. As the decade progressed, JD was increasingly influenced by Mary's strong Quakerism, and there is evidence of his growing concern about the injustice and inhumanity of slavery. He remained at the forefront of the resistance to Britain: Americans were loath to act without his approval and sought his assistance when they did and things went badly. The Farmer's admonitions for peaceful protest were referenced in the aftermath of the so-called Boston Massacre (1770); the Rhode Island legislature wrote for his advice after the *Gaspee* Affair (1772); and Arthur Lee implored him to take up his pen in the wake of the Intolerable Acts (1774). His celebrity increased as his likeness was carved in wax and gold, and Americans named their valued possessions after him—taverns, ships, and stud horses. When the First Continental Congress (1774) met, JD was its leader behind the scenes, drafting many of its documents and dictating the tenor of the assembly, despite not taking his seat until near the end. Americans followed his course even after hostilities became open and the Second Continental Congress (1775) met to prepare for defense. In that body, even as his colleagues became impatient with his calls for reconciliation, JD drafted two famous documents, the Olive Branch Petition and the Declaration on Taking Up Arms. JD's copious writings during this era—notes, speeches, pamphlets, and newspaper articles—were a concerted effort not to foment revolution, as many scholars have assumed, but rather to promote peace and reconciliation and avoid war. Yet, significantly, JD raised the first Philadelphia Battalion of Associators to prepare for war. He also wrote the instructions to the congressional delegates from Pennsylvania directing them to reject any move for independence.

Volume Six (Revolutionary Era II), 1776–1779: During this period, even as JD's reputation fluctuated, his influence remained strong. As the debate

---

[39] John Adams, *Twenty-Six Letters, Upon Interesting Subjects, Respecting the Revolution of America. Written in Holland in the year 1780* (New York: J. Fenno, 1789), 25. This paragraph was adapted from Jane E. Calvert, "The 'Documentary Democracy' of the Writings of John Dickinson, Then and Now," *Scholarly Editing* 34 (2013): 1–15, http://www.scholarlyediting.org/2013/essays/essay.calvert.html.

over independence became public with the circulation of Paine's *Common Sense*, JD and the other moderates in the Continental Congress continued to produce writings urging reconciliation. But public sentiment changed quickly in the spring, and soon it became clear to JD that, although many Americans still did not want independence, that was the course that the Continental Congress would take. In June 1776, he wrote new instructions allowing Pennsylvania delegates to approve independence; he also wrote America's first constitution, the Articles of Confederation, with, among other provisions, a clause for a strong central government and another protecting women's religious liberty and public speech. When the colonies declared independence, JD abstained from the vote and did not sign the document. But he was the only member of Continental Congress to take up arms and defend the cause, first as a colonel in the Pennsylvania militia in 1776, then as a private in the Delaware militia in 1777. Of the major Founders, JD is the only one besides Washington to have military papers from the field, but JD's give us more perspective on the rank and file.

It was not JD's decision on the Declaration that damaged his reputation. Rather, upon his return to the Pennsylvania Assembly in the autumn of 1776, JD ran afoul of the radical faction that had taken over Pennsylvania's government. He refused to sanction what he considered to be their illegal constitution because it threatened the civil rights of dissenters. In response, he wrote extensive edits on their Declaration of Rights, as well as an *Essay on a Frame of Government for Pennsylvania* (1776), presenting his alternative vision, which, among other things, prohibited slavery. Eventually, he abdicated his seat in the Assembly in protest. Accordingly, his enemies libeled him in the newspapers, fabricated charges against him, and pursued him as an enemy of the state. As a private citizen, in 1777, JD wrote a manumission deed for his slaves. Following his military service, JD reentered the political arena in 1779 as a Continental Congress delegate from Delaware, where he wrote policy to secure the peace and Britain's recognition of American sovereignty and rights.

Volume Seven (Delaware Presidency), 1780–1782: Remarkably, despite his controversial stances, JD still had the confidence of the people, who elected him first as president of Delaware, then, before he finished his first term there, as president of Pennsylvania for three years. Citizens of both states hoped his moderate stance would help restore order and justice. One of his best received writings was a presidential proclamation against vice and immorality, which resonated in both Delaware and Pennsylvania. JD was the only figure of the era to be president of two states—for a brief time, simultaneously. His papers show that he made notable accomplishments in both positions. In 1780, Delaware was a rapidly failing state: it was in financial disarray, with dysfunctional courts, an undisciplined militia, and

Tories within and outside the borders. In one year, JD reversed all of these problems and rendered Delaware a model for other struggling states.

Volume Eight (Pennsylvania Presidency), 1783–1785: Pennsylvania was a hotbed of radicalism when its people lured JD away from Delaware. Although his ability to effect change was tempered by the still-virulent sentiment that had driven him out six years before, his moderating influence was evident. He first published another proclamation urging religious observance to moderate vicious behavior. Thinking of him as a religious leader, in 1783 Benjamin Rush founded Dickinson College in his honor, hoping his Quakerly presence would give the board an ecumenical bent. JD donated land and books for the cause. Then, in addition to working to reform Pennsylvania's relationship with the Confederation government and advocating a national bank (one of the few leading Founders to do so), JD dealt with several incidents that had implications for the United States, including: the Mutiny of 1783, which, although JD resolved it with nonviolent methods, caused Congress to abandon Philadelphia as the seat of US government; *Respublica v. De Longchamps* (1784), which influenced the creation of the "Law of Nations Clause" in the Constitution; and *Respublica v. Doan* (1784), a capital punishment case in which JD questioned the propriety of English precedents in US law to protect a man from execution without due process.

Volume Nine (Constitutional Era), 1786–1792: This volume encompasses JD's activities as president of the Annapolis Convention (1786); member of the US Federal Convention (1787); and president of the Delaware Constitutional Convention (1792). His contributions were extensive. After he wrote the Report of the Annapolis Convention, JD wrote to Congress, calling for a Federal Convention. Illness forced him to leave the Convention early and designate a proxy, his good friend George Read, to sign for him, but while present, he offered ideas that shaped and advanced the deliberations. First, he presented his vision for the relationship between the states and the federal government using a metaphor that was repeated throughout the Convention—the states as planets orbiting a sun that was the federal government. Second, when the Convention stalled on the quandary of representation, JD's unique position as resident of one of the largest states, Pennsylvania, and one of the smallest, Delaware, enabled him to make a pivotal suggestion—that the people be represented in one branch and the states in the other, what Forrest McDonald called a "crucial conceptual breakthrough" on the problem of representation.[40] Although this is termed the "Connecticut Compromise," the record reveals that it was JD who laid

---

[40] Forrest McDonald, *Novus Ordo Seclorum: The Intellectual Origins of the Constitution* (Lawrence: University of Kansas Press, 1985), 260.

the first stones. He also was one of the few members of the Convention to speak out against slavery on moral grounds, making the motion for the abolition of the Atlantic trade and objecting vehemently when his colleagues sought to obfuscate the language and reality of slavery in the Constitution. And it appears that his language against corruption may have been the foundation for the emoluments clause.

In 1788, he published another series of letters to the American people under the penname "Fabius," encouraging the ratification of the Constitution. He continued his opposition to slavery in the Delaware Constitutional Convention, but found the state stubborn on the matter. Yet his own abolitionism continued. He freed all of his own slaves unconditionally and wrote and petitioned for abolition legislation. During these years, when more correspondence exists, we see a blossoming of the philanthropy that defined his retirement years. He continued funding schools for poor black and white children.

Volume Ten (Retirement), 1793–1808: Despite the claims of many authors, JD did not fade into obscurity or remain silent during his retirement. On the contrary, as the documents show, he continued to be active in politics, philanthropy, and religious study. His main concerns were America's troubled relations with France, the education of American youth, and theology. He led citizens' groups against the Jay Treaty (1795), published pamphlets on foreign relations and education, and even stood for office, once as late as 1807, just months before his death. His correspondence reveals that he acted as informal advisor to some of the most important figures in the early Republic, including President Thomas Jefferson, Senator George Logan, and Attorney General Caesar Augustus Rodney. He was perhaps most active in philanthropy. He funded the establishment of schools, including Westtown School (still one of the nation's premier Quaker boarding schools), and provided reparations for his former slaves. His work on religion was such that Samuel Miller, a New York Presbyterian minister, considered him a leading theologian.

John Dickinson died on February 14, 1808. According to those by his side during his final days, his last fevered thoughts remained on public affairs—worry about the welfare of the nation and the advance of Napoleon.[41] When the announcement of his passing was made in Congress, members resolved to wear black armbands in his honor. Memorials published upon his death show that, despite his controversial career, Americans still considered JD to be one of America's principal Founders. Although he was not formally a Quaker, he was laid to rest in the burial ground of Wilmington Friends Meeting.

---

[41] Diary of Deborah Norris Logan, 1808–1814, p. 90.

Supplement to Volume One (Legal Foundations), 1754–1756: This supplemental volume will include early documents that require more intensive labor to bring to fruition, namely JD's materials from his time at the Middle Temple. Among these materials are five notebooks of legal cases and his annotated three-volume copy of the *Doctrina Placitandi, ou l'Art et Science du Bon Pleading* (1677). The latter was the textbook students used to learn how to plead the common law, and JD's is perhaps the only American-owned and -annotated copy extant. Should documents surface that cannot be included in Volumes One through Ten, they will appear here.

The writings contained in this edition offer a perspective on late colonial and Founding-era America from one of its leading legal and political minds. It is a view that in important ways set the tone for the resistance to Britain and the founding of the Republic, while at the same time offering an alternative vision for the character of the nation. JD thought very much like the other Whig-republicans of his day; yet he also thought like a Quaker, with a more expansive understanding of rights, liberties, and how citizens should engage in the polity to assert those rights and protect their liberties. Arguably, while JD's colleagues were limited to thinking in terms of the rights of Englishmen or natural rights, he thought in terms of human rights.

In addition to JD's political and legal ideas, for the first time in these pages readers will glean a sense of JD's personality and character, public and private. Without access to the full corpus of his writings, authors have portrayed him as the "cool, cool conservative man," moderate to the point of blandness, cautious to the point of paralysis.[42] His detractors have painted him as indecisive and wavering, too timid or nerveless to engage in the raucous and manly business of politics. But the documents here prove otherwise. He was a passionate actor in his political worlds, taking extreme or unpopular positions and jumping into the fray with full awareness of and disregard for the damage he risked doing to his reputation. He confronted his opponents with fierce logic and drew on his sharp wit to diminish them with ridicule and satire. He likewise infected his admirers with a contagion of patriotic emotion. His correspondence reveals a man equally engaged in the lives of those around him. He was a devoted son, a warm and expressive friend, an ardent suitor to his future wife, and, later, a stern but loving father to his two daughters. With these documents at hand, the one-dimensional caricature of JD must fall.

In 1785, the artist Robert E. Pine, who was working on a painting of the signing of the Declaration of Independence, renewed a request to JD to allow

---

[42] From the 1969 Broadway musical *1776* and 1972 movie musical with the same title. The song "Cool, Cool Considerate Men" was written by Sherman Edwards.

Pine to include his likeness. Naturally, JD declined for the obvious reason that he was not present at the signing. And he explained, "Enough it will be for me, that my Name be remembered by Posterity, if [it is] acknowledged, that I chearfully staked everything dear to me upon the fate of my Country," and that he always "endeavor[ed] to promote their Happiness [and] continued faithfully attached to their cause."[43] Posterity has abdicated its duty to this important figure long enough.

---

[43] JD to Robert E. Pine, July 6, 1785, PHi-RRL.

The Legal Papers
and their Context

Although Founders' legal papers are frequently published in separate series, the editors of the present volume have chosen to preserve the corpus of JD's papers as a whole, placing the legal documents, whenever possible, in chronological order with the writings and correspondence. The reasons for this decision are threefold: First, JD was foremost a lawyer. Law was not merely the profession he practiced his entire adult life, from the beginning of his legal training at the age of eighteen through his seventies; it was a calling to do good that was a part of his identity. Second, JD's lawyerly identity and experience shaped his other vocation: statesman. The legal principles and maxims by which he practiced and lived his own life informed his thought and actions as a politician. To excise his legal papers from the main corpus of his writings would be to remove its foundation. Third, it would have been virtually impossible to designate which documents from his public service in the Continental Congresses or in the state presidencies were strictly "legal" and which were "political." Thus his legal documents are presented here interspersed among his other writings, as he generated and disseminated them in his life, forming a richer trove and telling a more accurate story of his career altogether.

JD's legal papers were the most challenging to process for several reasons. In a corpus notorious for illegibility, they are the least legible; they contain little identifying information, such as titles, dates, venues, or even which side JD represented; they are minimally processed in the archives; they contain highly specialized and archaic language; they frequently deal with obscure individuals; and there are few extant supporting records.[1] Despite generosity from donors, these challenges were naturally exacerbated by limited funding. The editors make no pretense of having processed these papers completely or with complete accuracy. The hope is that having some available, albeit imperfectly, will benefit scholarship nonetheless.

In the annotation of these documents, the editors have intentionally intervened more aggressively than with the more accessible documents, in order to facilitate nonexperts' understanding of the cryptic and specialized contents. Research included the usual steps to try to date the documents and identify venues and individuals. To allow the general reader some possibility of following the logic of JD's arguments, when he cited statutes or cases in law books, the relevant passages from those sources are provided, when they

---

[1] The JDP simply did not have the resources to research these documents as fully as possible. On the challenges of working with Pennsylvania legal records, see Marylynn Salmon, "The Court Records of Philadelphia, Bucks, and Berks Counties in the Seventeenth and Eighteenth Centuries," *PMHB* 107, no. 2 (1983): 249–91.

were discernable. The notes go further, then, to speculate, albeit conservatively, on the part JD played, to suggest the significance of his argument, and, where possible, to identify the outcome of the cases.

The translation of non-English terms, phrases, and passages requires a word of explanation. Some of these are in the dead languages of Neo-Latin and Law French, both of which pose particular challenges. If they read Latin, most scholars today know classical Latin, which has been standardized for the ancient period of Greece and Rome. The Latin used in the early modern era was, by contrast, like English—not standardized in spelling, grammar, or word usage. Moreover, it was highly subjective to the context in which it was used, as well as the personal idiosyncrasies of the writer. The language of the law after the Norman invasion of England in the eleventh century was an admixture of English, French, and Latin, known today as Law French. By the seventeenth century, it had fallen out of favor, and in 1731, Parliament ended the use of Latin and French in legal proceedings.[2] JD's law school materials and his citations to case books show that Law French was still used to some extent, even in America. Interestingly, the difficulty of these languages and their use by jurists to exclude nonspeakers from power is one of the reasons JD's Quaker forebears pressed for laws and legal proceedings to be presented in ordinary English.[3] We have attempted to provide readers with accurate translations of both these languages.

For readers unfamiliar with the historical context of JD's legal writings, the following provides a brief overview of the legal world of colonial Pennsylvania and Delaware.[4]

Categories of Law

Early modern legal thinkers believed that the laws and courts were undergirded by a theoretical framework and a divinely ordained hierarchy of laws, with one category informing the next. The various religious traditions (Quaker, Anglican, reformed Calvinist, Catholic, etc.) each interpreted the categories in slightly different ways and placed emphasis on different ones. At various points in his writings, JD referenced each of these categories.[5]

---

[2] Peter Tiersma, *Legal Language* (Chicago: University of Chicago Press, 1999), 36.

[3] Craig W. Horle, *Quakers and the English Legal System* (Philadelphia: University of Pennsylvania Press, 1988), 167.

[4] See also William M. Offutt, Jr., *Of "Good Laws" and "Good Men": Law and Society in the Delaware Valley, 1680 – 1710* (Urbana: University of Illinois Press, 1995).

[5] For a discussion of these categories and legal obligation, see Philip Hamburger, *Law and Judicial Duty* (Cambridge, Mass.: Harvard University Press, 2008). For Quaker attitudes towards and theories of law, see Horle, *Quakers and the English Legal System*; and Calvert, *Quaker Constitutionalism*.

Eternal law is God's law for the cosmos, which is forever and unchanging. Beneath that is the *divine law*, the law given to man from God through Scripture and revelation including, according to Quakers, the Light within, which all humans are capable of accessing under the right conditions. Flowing from this is the *natural law (ius naturale; lex naturalis)*, which is the divine law known to man through his God-given powers of reason. It is independent of any human law and confers certain rights upon the individual. Early Quakers were more skeptical than most of human reason and preferred instead to depend on the Light within for their understanding of the law and their rights.

Quakers believed that the divine law, accessed through God's Light, would allow humans to know the *fundamental* or *constitutional law*. These are the most basic principles of law, sometimes codified in written form, such as the Magna Carta. Unlike most Englishmen, Quakers believed they ought to be written in an amendable document. Following from the fundamental law were the man-made *positive laws (ius positum)*: Statute laws were individual written laws *(lex scripta)*, or the system of laws laid down by a legislature. This category includes Royal Statutes passed by Parliament, which are designated by a regnal year and monarch (for example, 2 Edw. 3 [or III] is a statute passed in the second year of the reign of Edward III).

The other positive law is the *common law*, the unwritten laws *(lex non scripta)* of England enacted by the people from time immemorial, by ancient custom, and administered by the courts. It is also known as *judge-made law* or *case law* because jurists referenced precedents described in commentaries and reports of adjudged cases. Quakers were suspicious of unwritten laws that might be applied against religious dissenters arbitrarily, so in Pennsylvania they sought to write their laws, and they actively adapted the English common law to their own circumstances. In JD's case notes, there is evidence both of the predominance of English common law, marked by his copious citations to myriad casebooks, and of his conviction that the English law must be interpreted liberally for the unique circumstances of Pennsylvania.[6]

Finally, the *law of nations (ius gentium)* is the law governing nations as parts of a common polity. It was derived from natural law and functioned like the common law in that it was based on custom handed down from the ancient Romans. This law came into play most importantly in wartime, but also in commerce, boundaries and sovereignty, and colonization.

---

[6] In the present edition, see doc. 2:16, "Notes for *Lesee of Daniel Weston & Mary Weston v. Stammers & Paul*, [1760]." Citation format is explained on p. lv.

The Judicial System

As in all British colonies, the law and court systems of Pennsylvania and Delaware were a combination of old English principles and traditions and New World practices. Naturally, English settlers brought their traditions with them, most notably the common law, which the English government required they follow. New developments in the colonies were informed by unique circumstances in the American wilderness, prior Scandinavian settlers in the Delaware Valley, and, most significantly, the priorities of the leaders of Pennsylvania, members of the Religious Society of Friends (Quakers), who founded the province in 1681.

Quakers brought with them distinct ideas about jurisprudence shaped by two factors—their theology and their encounters with the English legal system—which determined their governance of Pennsylvania throughout the colonial period. From their inception in England in the 1650s, Quakers had a complicated relationship with the law and judicial system. Their central theological tenet, that God's Light might shine in anyone's conscience and compel him—or her—to follow divine law, set them up for conflict with English law. During the 1660s especially, with the restoration of the monarchy after more than a decade of war instigated by religious zealots, the government sought to make dissenters from the Church of England conform to the established law of church and state. Parliament passed laws particularly aimed at Quakers and inflicted brutal punishments for transgression. Rather than rise up in rebellion, however, Quakers, who were now pacifists, chose to use peaceful measures against their oppressors, including their own invention of civil disobedience, and challenged the government by mastering the very legal system that oppressed them. They thwarted judges with well-reasoned arguments and inspired juries to resist their arbitrary power.

By 1681, when William Penn received the royal Charter to found Pennsylvania, Quakers had definite ideas about how a Quaker colony should function and what sort of laws it should impose. They championed causes such as religious liberty; commitment to the rule of law; preservation of the sanctity of the jury trial; using mediation instead of the law; recording laws and legal proceedings in ordinary English; banning corporeal punishment and the death penalty; and having prisons without fees and with food and lodging included. Quakers attempted to put these ideals into practice in Pennsylvania with mixed success and much adaptation.

Ultimately, with the Quakers' primary concern being the preservation of religious liberty, their overarching goal was to maintain control of their colony. This meant not just installing themselves and their allies in seats of power, but also doing whatever was necessary to preserve that power, even if it meant sacrificing lesser principles for the greatest one. Throughout the history of the province, Quakers clashed with those who threatened their power, and they showed remarkable political and legal acumen in their ability to adapt, innovate, and manipulate to secure their mandate, even as they became a minority in their own colony. Their efforts were marked by resistance to the powers above them (i.e., king, Parliament, proprietors, governors) and domination of those below them (i.e., non-Quaker constituents).

Although Quakers preferred to resolve conflicts through arbitration, upon arriving in Pennsylvania, they quickly established a system of common-law courts so that the colony would be guided by the rule of law. Although, as noted above, Quakers distrusted the English common law because it was unwritten, and thus potentially arbitrary, they nonetheless embraced it in Pennsylvania where they could adapt it for their purposes. Because common law and rule of law tend to protect those with wealth and power, Quakers, who controlled both, could be assured that the system worked for their interests. They also established a correspondingly robust legal profession and extensive common-law forms and procedures, which encouraged uniformity throughout the region. With Philadelphia as the center, lawyers effectively rode circuit, traveling to the outlying counties for court with their legal forms, law books, and clerks in tow.[7] In law school, after JD obtained a standing desk and began taking long walks for his health, he joked that he was now a "peripatetick lawyer."[8] But this was just the beginning of a nomadic life, divided between two colonies, then two states, Pennsylvania and Delaware. If his commuting between homes and legislatures in the Delaware Valley did not keep him on the road, his lawyerly profession did.

Despite the rapid establishment of the court system, Pennsylvania was unsettled during its first twenty years as a colony. It was torn by constant, vitriolic struggle between the Quaker Assembly, on the one hand, and on the other, William Penn, his executive council, and whatever unfortunate deputy governor he tried to install to control his brethren. There was a constant turnover of constitutions, with each giving more power to the Assembly. Ultimately, the Assembly prevailed with the 1701 Charter of Privileges, which nullified Penn's power and that of his executive council, making Pennsylvania the only large colony with a unicameral legislature.[9] Significantly, it also provided that persons may only be sued in a court of law. At a time when the governors and councils typically acted as appellate courts, Pennsylvania became the only colony in which there was a separation

---

[7] William E. Nelson, *The Common Law in America: Volume II: The Middle Colonies and the Carolinas, 1660 – 1730* (New York: Oxford University Press, 2013), 101–07.

[8] Doc. 1:34: "To Mary Cadwalader Dickinson, March 17, 1756."

[9] Calvert, *Quaker Constitutionalism*, ch. 2.

between the executive and judicial branches.[10] With the ratification of the 1701 Charter, the newly empowered Assembly passed the "Act for Establishing Courts of Judicature in this Province and Counties Annexed," which was to create a new judicial system for the colony.[11] But the act was disallowed by the Crown in 1705, and a struggle ensued between Governor John Evans and the Assembly for new legislation that would allow one or the other to control the courts. The Quakers' solution was to pass bills establishing courts and then wait the full five years allotted by Great Britain to send them for approval. When they were inevitably disapproved, the Quakers had a new bill for the same system ready for the next five-year period.[12] Ultimately, the Judicial Act of 1722 stabilized the situation and provided a more permanent settlement of the judicial system, many aspects of which remained in place beyond the Revolution.[13] Delaware established its courts separately from Pennsylvania's sometime between 1728 and 1736.[14]

Another challenge to the Quakers' ongoing control of their colony was their minority status vis-à-vis their non-Quaker constituents. Yet over the first half of the eigtheenth century, although non-Quaker immigrants dwarfed the Quakers in terms of proportion of the overall population, Friends maintained an average majority in the Assembly of 66.4 percent; they solidified their control by, among other strategies, gerrymandering voting districts and allying themselves politically with other pacifist sects.[15] They took a similar approach in the courts by controlling and disempowering juries. Initially, they packed juries with Quaker jurors. But when that was impossible or ineffective, they essentially nullified juries by various means. Quakers in England had championed the power of juries to resist arbitrary judicial power, most notably in Bushel's Case;[16] by contrast, in Pennsylvania, they preferred "government by judiciary." Here juries were relegated from finders of law and fact to merely finders of fact, while judges determined the law. Judges could control juries and their verdicts by various means, including fining, setting aside verdicts and

---

[10] Erwin C. Surrency, "The Courts in the American Colonies," *The American Journal of Legal History* 11, nos. 3 & 4 (1967): 253–76 and 347–76, at 269.

[11] 2 *SALP* 148.

[12] William H. Lloyd, *Early Courts of Pennsylvania* (Boston: The Boston Book Co., 1910), 82.

[13] G.S. Rowe, *Embattled Bench: The Pennsylvania Supreme Court and the Forging of a Democratic Society, 1684–1809* (Newark: University of Delaware Press, 1994), 65.

[14] *Laws of the Government of New-Castle, Kent and Sussex, upon Delaware* (Philadelphia: B. Franklin, 1742), 39–49.

[15] *LLP*, 2:132, 20–29; Liam Riordan, *Many Identities, One Nation: The Revolution and Its Legacy in the Mid-Atlantic* (Philadelphia: University of Pennsylvania Press, 2007), 29.

[16] See doc. 1:62, n. 12: "Draft One of Notes for *Spring & Kemp v. Ospray & Elizabeth*, [c. 1758]."

granting new trials, and overturning verdicts in courts of equity;[17] likewise, lawyers could employ a variety of legal devices, including demurrer to the evidence, the writ of error and bill of exceptions, and the motion of arrest of judgment. Delaware followed Pennsylvania in these practices.[18]

In JD's day, the Pennsylvania court system was composed of the following elements:[19]

The highest court in Pennsylvania was the **Provincial Court**, which was established in 1684 and renamed the **Supreme Court** in 1711. Although its early decades were marked by instability and a struggle for legitimacy, it evolved over the eighteenth century. Its authority and efficiency increased, and it gained an interest in the results of government prosecutions and a greater concern for individual rights in criminal cases. By the time of JD's birth in 1732, the Supreme Court had entered a new phase of power and prestige, even as it struggled to keep pace with Pennsylvania's burgeoning society.

The **Court of Common Pleas** was a common-law court where individuals could seek redress for civil grievances against one another. It was divided into courts of law and courts of equity. Courts of law handled actions involving monetary damages over forty shillings, personal injury, and breaches of contract. Courts of equity handled matters of legal relief, such as disputes over land. Judges in these courts were appointed and commissioned

---

[17] Nelson, *Common Law: Vol. II*, 99–110.

[18] William E. Nelson, *The Common Law in America: Volume IV: Law and the Constitution on the Eve of Independence, 1735–1776* (New York: Oxford University Press, 2018), 43. There is evidence that throughout JD's career, he continued to maintain the sanctity of the jury, dominant legal culture notwithstanding. See doc. 1:46: "Expanded Rough Notes for Opening Arguments in the Smith Libel Trial, [January 17], 1758," in which he declares that "it is the undoubted right of Englishmen to be tried by their peers"; and in 1788, when he calls the jury a "heaven-taught institution" (Fabius [JD], "Observations on the Constitution Proposed by the Federal Convention: No. IV," *Pennsylvania Mercury, and Universal Advertiser*, April 19, 1788).

[19] Information on the various courts is drawn from the following sources: Paul Crawford, "A Footnote on Courts for Trial of Negroes in Colonial Pennsylvania," *Journal of Black Studies* 5, no. 2 (1974): 167–74; Frank M. Eastman, *Courts and Lawyers of Pennsylvania: A History, 1623–1923*, 3 vols. (New York: American Historical Society, 1922); Lawrence Lewis, Jr., "The Courts of Pennsylvania in the Seventeenth Century," *PMHB* 5, no. 2 (1881): 141–90; Lloyd, *Early Courts of Pennsylvania*; Jack D. Marietta and G.S. Rowe, *Troubled Experiment: Crime and Justice in Pennsylvania, 1682–1800* (Philadelphia: University of Pennsylvania Press, 2006); Rowe, *Embattled Bench*. Although this last work gives a useful overview of the Supreme Court, the indexer mistook Jonathan Dickinson (1663–1722) for JD on several occasions. Other sources consulted include Surrency, "The Courts in the American Colonies"; David R. Owen and Michael C. Tolley, *Courts of Admiralty in Colonial America: The Maryland Experience, 1634–1776* (Durham, N.C.: Carolina Academic Press, 1995); Michael Watson, "Judge Lewis Morris, the New York Vice-Admiralty Court, and Colonial Privateering, 1739–1762," *New York History* 78, no. 2 (1997): 119; and Carl Ubbelohde, *The Vice-Admiralty Courts and the American Revolution* (Chapel Hill: University of North Carolina Press for the Institute of Early American History and Culture, 1960).

by the governor or deputy governor. The many cases of land ownership and debt recovery JD took were tried in these courts.

Only Pennsylvania and Delaware had formally established **Orphans' Courts**, which were courts of equity for matters of probate. They were held by judges of the county courts and were originally established "to inspect and take Care of the Estates, usages, and Employment of Orphans…That Care may be taken for those, that are not able to take care for themselves."[20] They broadened to hear disputes about not just guardianships for children and incapacitated persons, but also estates, trusts, and other civil matters pertaining to agents under power of attorney. With much of his work settling estates, JD spent significant time in this court. One leitmotif of his notes concerned the challenge of interpreting the last wishes of those whose ignorance of the law prevented them from writing a clear last will and testament. He repeated the common-law maxim that the testator's intent was always his "pole star."[21]

The **Register's Court**, composed of the register of wills and the judges of the Court of Common Pleas, sometimes vied with the Orphans' Court for jurisdiction over proving and administering wills. It was an appeals court that heard cases decided by the register of wills.

Criminal law in Pennsylvania also developed along a peculiarly Quaker path. As pacifists, Friends did not believe in capital punishment. And unlike Puritans, they did not believe in original sin or predestination; instead they held that people might sin and still be redeemed, which inclined them to favor rehabilitation and reform. Their experiences with the injustice and brutality of the English criminal and penal system shaped their criminal code in Pennsylvania. Thus, although they they prosecuted morality crimes vigorously, they resisted the severest remedies, capital punishment and banishment. For the first forty years in Pennsylvania, there were only two capital crimes—murder and treason—and during this time, only two men were convicted and executed.

In 1718, however, this lenient code changed because of another key Quaker principle—the refusal to swear oaths, which were considered blasphemous. In order to hold any public trust, Quakers required an alternative legally binding affirmation instead. This exemption from the oath was at risk when Anglicans in Pennsylvania pressed for disapproval by the Crown. Without permission to take the affirmation, Quakers would not be able to vote, hold office, sit on juries or the bench, or serve as witnesses; in other words, they would lose control of the province. In exchange for having

---

[20] *Charter to William Penn, and Laws of the Province of Pennsylvania: Passed Between the Years 1682 and 1700* (Harrisburg: L.S. Hart, 1879), 131.

[21] See Volume 2 of the present edition for documents on this topic.

the affirmation secured, Governor William Keith implemented the harsh English criminal code the Crown desired both in Pennsylvania and Delaware. If Pennsylvania attracted more than its share of unfortunate souls as "the best poor man's country," it also had more than its share of crime.[22] Far from Penn's original aspirations for Pennsylvania as a "Holy Experiment," the province evolved into one of the most crime-ridden in British North America. It appears JD did what he could to try to mitigate the effects of both poverty and the harsh criminal law, taking cases of poor people accused of heinous crimes, such as murder and infanticide. A refrain in these cases was that his honor would not permit his representing a guilty client.[23]

There were several courts for criminal proceedings in Pennsylvania and Delaware. The **Courts of Quarter Sessions** were common-law courts held four times per year. They took place at the county seats and heard less serious cases from cursing to fornication. Presided over by justices of the peace, they also dealt with public matters such as construction of roads and buildings, acknowledgment of deeds, and naturalization of aliens. **Courts of Oyer and Terminer**, from the French "to hear and determine," were authorized to empanel grand juries to inquire into serious crimes to be tried at period courts called **Courts of Assize**, which were held by the justices of the Supreme Court.

Thus far, there is no indication as to whether JD worked in two other courts. One was the **Mayor's Court** in Pennsylvania, which was presided over by the mayor, aldermen, and recorder of the City of Philadelphia, who had justice-of-the-peace powers. The court heard and inquired into crimes ranging from drunkenness to treason. Another was the **Courts for the Trial of Negroes**, which were in both Pennsylvania and Delaware. These were specifically for trying black people charged with "high and heinous enormities and capital offenses," which included not only murder, but also burglary, buggery, and attempted rape. Although Quaker Pennsylvania was a much milder environment for slaves and free blacks than many colonies, especially those to the south, and it was the birthplace of the abolition movement in America, its justice system was not color-blind. Notably harsher than courts for whites, this court imposed the death penalty for the crimes mentioned, and punished lesser crimes by whipping, branding, and castration.

A **Court of Chancery** was where individuals turned to receive justice denied them in the common-law courts. It was a court based on natural law, with jurisdiction over matters of equity, established to soften the often harsh and rigid common law. JD referred to courts of equity as clothing English

---

[22] James T. Lemon, *The Best Poor Man's Country: Early Southeastern Pennsylvania* (1972; rpt. Baltimore: The Johns Hopkins University Press, 2002).

[23] See Volume 2 of the present edition for documents mentioning this matter.

law in "Beauty & Harmony."[24] With the king or, in the colonies, a provincial governor presiding, it had more legal remedies and latitude to overrule decisions by justices and juries in the common-law courts. JD believed that this court embodied the legal maxim "equality is equity," meaning, the law will not play favorites.[25] Because of the Quaker animus against proprietary power and executive authority, Pennsylvania had a Chancery Court only briefly from 1720 to 1736. At other times, matters of equity were undertaken in the other courts. JD affirmed in 1756 that "Every Court there is a Court of Equity."[26] Appeals instead went from the Supreme Court to the Privy Council in England. Delaware, by contrast, established a Court of Equity when it separated its courts from Pennsylvania's.

At least in his early years of practice, JD also took cases heard in the **Vice-Admiralty Court**. Based on the common law and the law of nations, these courts were established during the eighteenth century to handle maritime disputes in the colonies, when it was difficult or impossible for the matters to be handled by the Admiralty Court in Britain. By 1763, Vice-Admiralty Courts existed in nine of the thirteen mainland colonies and had three levels of jurisdiction—local, imperial, and international. Local matters included disagreements between sailors and merchants, such as wage and contract disputes, insurance claims, salvage cases, and collisions and accidents at sea. Imperial cases included matters related to royal fisheries and trees and contraventions of the Navigation Acts resulting in forfeitures and penalties. International jurisdiction occurred during wartime and concerned matters of prizes, or the seizure of enemy ships and cargo. Although in the early years of his practice, JD considered the Admiralty to be a court of equity, "establishd on the generous principles of Humanity & Publick Good," even ignoring differences of race and religion,[27] these courts became unpopular as tensions between the colonies and Britain rose in years before the Revolution. If JD's work in Admiralty cases can be generalized, he tended to represent the seamen against the merchants and the merchants against the British government.

The Legal Profession

As JD entered the legal profession in the mid-eighteenth century, the practice had professionalized and expanded significantly over recent decades. Whereas in the seventeenth century there were few trained lawyers and no profession to speak of, in JD's era, lawyers were a rising elite, increasingly oriented towards imperial standards and committed to increased formalism.

---

[24] See doc. 1:40: "To Samuel Dickinson, August 2, 1756."

[25] See doc. 2:6: "Set Two of Notes for *William Paxton v. Vandyke*, [1759]."

[26] See doc. 1:40: "To Samuel Dickinson, August 2, 1756."

[27] See doc. 2:17: "Notes on a Libel in the Admiralty on behalf of some Danish Sailors, [1759]."

Still, compared to the mother country, legal training in the colonies was primitive; most young men's families could not afford to send them to London's Inns of Court or support them while they established themselves in practice. Thus most had little training and scant education. During the eighteenth century, only around 150 Americans joined the Middle Temple.[28]

In England, lawyers specialized as barristers (i.e., courtroom advocates) or solicitors (for transactional legal work) and had subordinates for clerical work, but in the colonies, there was not enough business to support these divisions, and American lawyers frequently had to take all cases and play all parts themselves. Once established, JD was successful enough to have clerks and students, including Jacob Rush, Benjamin Rush's brother, and James Wilson, later an associate justice of the United States Supreme Court. Still, like other colonial lawyers, he took all types of work. His practice concerned predominantly solicitor work—writing and interpreting wills, drawing up bonds and indentures, dealing with property transfers, and pursuing debtors. The barrister work likewise included everything from mundane trespasses, ejectments, and replevins to murder cases. He frequently represented the weaker party against the stronger—the apprentice against master; the mulatto servant woman against the king; the seaman against the merchant; the merchant against the government; the poor widow against the township.

Nor was the practice of law especially profitable. Legislatures set the fee schedules, which were low, and young men who aspired to raise their social status through the profession were disappointed as they pursued mostly menial work, such as debt collection. Cases in the Admiralty Court, where lawyers were called "proctors" and the initial actions were called "libels," were the few that brought substantial fees from expensive cargoes and prize cases. Most lawyers thus did not support themselves solely in practice. JD, for example, became one of the wealthiest men in the Delaware Valley through his vast landholdings and tenant properties.

Then, as now, lawyers in America were frequently derided as liars, manipulators, and individuals who needlessly complicated and obfuscated business to the detriment of their clients. JD's Quaker sensibilities impelled him to work contrary to these stereotypes. He had the highest reverence for the law and viewed it as an instrument for doing good. While at the Middle Temple, he explained to his parents, "I find no Consideration of equal Weight with defending the Innocent & redressing the injurd."[29] He saw his role as

---

[28] This section draws on the following sources: Eric Stockdale and Randy J. Holland, *Middle Temple Lawyers and the American Revolution* (Eagan, Minn.: Thomson West, 2007); *Lawyers in Early Modern Europe and America*, ed. Wilfred Prest (New York: Holmes & Meier Publishers, Inc., 1981).

[29] See doc. 1:24: "To Mary Cadwalader Dickinson, October 9, 1754."

discerning the wishes and best interests of his clients and facilitating access to legal remedies for all inhabitants of the colonies, regardless of socioeconomic status.

Dickinson's Cases in Dallas's Reports

America's earliest legal casebooks reporting decisions from the Supreme Court included cases from the Pennsylvania courts and were compiled by Alexander James Dallas. JD was involved in at least seven cases included in the first volume, *Reports of Cases Ruled and Adjudged in the Courts of Pennsylvania, before and since the Revolution* (Philadelphia: T. Bradford, 1790). Although none of JD's notes are extant for the cases in 1773, those for the cases in 1784 and 1786 will appear in subsequent volumes of *The Complete Writings and Selected Correspondence of John Dickinson*:

1 Dallas 3–4: *Stevenson v. Pemberton* (1760)
> This case was in the Pennsylvania Provincial Court with Benjamin Chew and John Moland for the plaintiff, and JD and Joseph Galloway for the defendant. A party known as "C" paid Pemberton for a debt in rum, which Pemberton would have to convert to currency. Stevenson was suing Pemberton, claiming that he had a right to the rum since he (Stevenson) had already obtained a judgment against C for a debt. JD argued that C sent the rum to Pemberton as a security and C's debt to Pemberton must be paid before Stevenson's. Judgment was unanimous for the defendant. This case was cited as precedent for the judgment that property given to one party in payment of a prior debt is not subject to attachment by creditors of the first party.

1 Dallas 4: *The Lessee of Ashton v. Ashton* (1760)
> This case was in the Pennsylvania Provincial Court with Chew and Moland for the plaintiff and JD for the defendant. At issue was the intent of a devisor, who left real estate to "the *first Heir Male of I.S.*," and whether the devisor meant the son of I.S. or a more distant male relative. JD argued the son should not receive the property for three reasons: 1) the son did not exist either when the will was written or at the time of the devisor's death; 2) any future devise had to take effect no later than nine months after the death of the devisor, lest the devise establish a perpetuity. If I.S. had a daughter, for example, then the devise would pass only if she had a son who would be the first male heir of I.S.; 3) since I.S. was still alive, his son could not technically be an heir. Judgment was for the plaintiff. This case set the precedent that "heirs" means "children."

1 Dallas 5–6: *The King v. John Lukens* (1762)

This case, an indictment against Lukens by a grand jury for a nuisance, most likely was heard in the Pennsylvania Supreme Court. The question was whether the prosecution could proceed without the endorsement of the prosecutor. JD argued for the defendant that an endorsement was required under a 1705 statute before Lukens should have to plead. Attorney General Chew argued the contrary, claiming that because many cases came before grand juries and justices of the peace without a prosecutor, this interpretation would allow offenders to escape justice. The court found for Chew. This case was cited as precedent in 1914.

1 Dallas 18: *The Lessee of the Proprietary v. Ralston* (1773)

In this ejectment case by the lessee of the Penn family, JD and Edward Tilghman were for the plaintiff. The plaintiff offered letters to prove that a grant to Ralston's ancestors was conditional. These were rejected, and the plaintiffs lost every point but won the case.

1 Dallas 86–98; Appendix 495–99: *Respublica v. Doan* (1784)

Aaron Doan was attainted for outlawry and sentenced to death. As president of Pennsylvania, JD objected in correspondence with the court that Doan had not received a fair and open trial and could thus not be justly executed. The matter extended beyond the issue of Doan and his crimes to the functions of government and the roles of the various branches in a republican system. It pitted JD, advocating for trial by jury, against his longtime friend, Chief Justice Thomas McKean, who had for years been working for separation of powers in Pennsylvania.[30]

1 Dallas 95–109: *Talbot qui tam &c. v. the Commanders and Owners of Three Brigs* (1784)

Heard in the High Court of Errors and Appeals in Pennsylvania regarding a decree in the Admiralty Court, this cause was a marine trespass involving a significant amount of property. Four questions were decided: 1) that owners of letters of marque (ships with license to attack merchant ships) were liable for injuries committed on the high seas by the captains of those ships; 2) that third parties witnessing captures had no right to any prize by virtue of being witnesses; 3) that Pennsylvania Admiralty Court judges may legally assume cognizance in similar cases; 4) that appeal to the High Court of Errors and Appeals was regular. JD delivered the resolution of the court.

---

[30] G.S. Rowe, "Outlawry in Pennsylvania, 1782–1788 and the Achievement of an Independent State Judiciary," *American Journal of Legal History* 20, no. 3 (1976): 227–44, at 239–40.

1 Dallas 111–16: *Respublica v. De Longchamps* (1784)

French national Charles Julian de Longchamps was indicted in the Court of Oyer and Terminer for twice assaulting French Secretary to the Legation François Barbé-Marbois. A physical assault occurred on a public street, which clearly violated Pennsylvania law. The second, verbal assault occurred in the hotel room of French ambassador Anne-César, Chevalier de la Luzerne. JD, president of Pennsylvania, pressed France's request that Longchamps be returned to France for trial, but the judges denied the request. The jury determined that the assaults violated the law of nations protecting diplomats, because the domicile of a foreign minister was considered to be foreign soil. After the verdict, JD asked the judges to consider whether Longchamps could now be returned to France for punishment, whether he could be imprisoned at the pleasure of the king of France, and whether the Pennsylvania Supreme Executive Council could facilitate his imprisonment. The judges answered all in the negative. This case was the origin of the law of nations clause in the Constitution.[31]

1 Dallas 180–86: *Purviance et al. v. Angus* (1786)

This case from the Admiralty Court, concerning the same malfeasant shipmaster involved in the 1784 *Three Brigs* case above, was appealed in Pennsylvania's High Court of Errors and Appeals. This court overturned the Admiralty's rejection of a claim for indemnification brought by the owners of the brigantine *Hibernia* against the captain for his malfeasance, which caused them to pay damages to a third party. The court found that the master of a vessel is indeed liable to the owners for damages when his misconduct has caused injury to another, regardless of whether the error was willful or not. JD's role in this case is not yet clear; his term as president of Pennsylvania ended before the case was heard.

---

[31] G.S. Rowe and Alexander W. Knott, "Power, Justice, and Foreign Relations in the Confederation Period: The Marbois-Longchamps Affair," *PMHB* 104, no. 3 (1980): 275–307, at 286; Richard Tuck, *The Rights of War and Peace: Political Thought and the International Order from Grotius to Kant* (Oxford: Oxford University Press, 1999).

EDITORIAL METHODOLOGY

This edition seeks to provide the reader with documents that appear as true to the original as possible while also being accessible and a scholarly apparatus that gives the reader the historical and literary context to understand the import of the documents, both individually and collectively. The aim of this edition is not to put forth the definitive interpretation of JD's writings, but rather to facilitate new conversations on topics beyond what the editors might imagine. The editors have therefore consciously avoided imposing an overly interpretive framework on the documents. Likewise, annotation does not include historiographical debate or secondary sources, unless they provide specific factual information that is not generally known.

Document Presentation

The documents are arranged chronologically. Unless content dictates otherwise, documents with the same date are organized alphabetically by author or title. Multiple documents from the same newspaper are placed together in the order in which they were published. Undated documents are placed as closely as possible to when they might have been written or published. If only their month can be determined, documents appear at the beginning of the month. If no month can be determined, documents appear either at the beginning or end of the year, depending on context. Documents that could have been written at any time within the span of the volume are placed at the end of the volume.

Documents in the edition are referenced with volume and document number in this format: doc. X:XX. Each document forms a unit with the following components:

A *header* preceding each document contains a document number corresponding with its order in the volume, a title and publication information (if any), and date. Any speculative information is placed in square brackets. Where possible, the document title is the actual title used by the author, though in the cases of lengthy legislation, the title may be shortened or abridged. When the document is untitled, a title is supplied that captures the essence of the document.

Headnotes to the individual documents give general context, when known, for how the document fits into the larger narrative of events, including what prompted the author to write, the reception of the document if it was published, and whether the document caused any shifts in public attitude or policy changes. Responses that appear later in the volume are identified, except for the *Farmer's Letters*, in which case readers are referred to the index. Headnotes also explain physical aspects of the document, including anything of interest about the handwriting or factors that compromised accuracy of transcription, such as damage. If the document is undated, the headnote explains reasons for its specific placement.

The *document text* comes next, beginning with the full title as it appears in the original. It was not uncommon for JD to add a title and date to his documents at the bottom of the text or in a margin. It is impossible to know whether he did this at the time of the creation of the document, or when he was sorting them in anticipation of his 1801 edition. Regardless, these were moved to the top of the document. For correspondence, placement of such elements as salutations, closings, paragraph indentations, and postscripts is regularized; and original signatures are in boldface type. Because all documents do not have docketing information or accompanying envelopes identifying sender and recipient, this information is omitted from the transcription except when it provides significant information. When there is uncertainty about authorship, sender, recipient, or version of a document, it is indicated in the header and headnote.

Document type and *location of original* are noted with abbreviations at the bottom of the document text. See **Abbreviations** below, p. lxix.

Endnotes after each document give the reader support for the specific content and individual features of the document. Readers should be aware that where the text is in columns, the endnotes run first down the left-hand column and then continue at the top of the next.

Annotations are provided according to the following guidelines:

- References to historical events, legislation, figures, and literary references are identified, and, when necessary, a citation is given and the significance to the text briefly explained.

- When an author cited a work only partially or omitted a citation, notes include, when possible, a full citation either to the edition the author probably used or to a first edition. Citations for JD's quotations are to the edition he owned, when known. It should be noted that, according to eighteenth-century practice, passages in quotation marks were often not verbatim and were sometimes only loosely paraphrased. Annotation does not include all the variances between the original sources and the quotations from them. When a series of quotations come from the same page of the source text, only the last quotation in the series is noted.

- In legal documents, titles and dates of royal statutes are given; JD's citations to court cases are updated and supplemented with quotes from that source when doing so can illuminate his reasoning process.

- Wherever possible, individuals are identified briefly with life span, occupation, position, and relevant contributions. When no identifying information was available, the name is passed over silently. Full information is given at an individual's first appearance or when the individual first figures prominently in the text.

- Foreign and archaic words and phrases are translated or defined. If a phrase comes from a work of literature, that text is identified.
- References for classical works are standard abbreviations from the *Oxford Classical Dictionary* and other reference works without specific edition or translation.
- Quotations from classical sources, when in Latin, rely on the originals, with their titles abbreviated as noted below; translations are as cited or by editors.
- References to Bible verses are to the King James Version.
- Correct information is provided for errors in historical fact (e.g., names, dates, or numerical data).
- Names of individuals are spelled correctly in the editorial apparatus, regardless of how they are spelled in the original text. Variations are noted.
- In terms of appearance of the original manuscripts, the editors have attempted to represent the texts—in description and layout—as closely as possible to the originals within reason; anomalies in the text are noted when they interfere with transcription or otherwise compromise its clarity, as in the case of a tear or fading.
- When a draft precedes a printed final version, annotations appear in the final version; only passages not in the final version are annotated in the draft.

The *index* includes persons, places, events, and concepts. The pages in which an individual is identified are in boldface type.

Transcription Policy

The guiding principle of the JDP transcription policy is to render the documents as closely as possible to the originals. JD was a meticulous writer who, even in his messiest drafts, crafted his prose with conscious intent. Rather than second-guessing his authorial and editorial decisions, the editors feel obliged to reproduce them faithfully. Thus, with a few exceptions noted below, the edition preserves the general physical layout of the text, as well as the exact spelling, grammar, punctuation, capitalization, cancellations, emendations, and slips of the pen. Yet, because some aspects of the documents, especially the manuscripts, make them difficult for readers to decipher or would create an excessive amount of extra work or technological difficulties with no meaningful benefit to the reader, a very few changes and modernizations were made. In outlining the policy, it is useful to distinguish among manuscripts, printed documents, and printed documents with handwritten notes.

<u>Manuscript Documents</u>

Transcribing JD's manuscripts has been the single most challenging aspect of this project. Indeed, the illegibility of JD's writing is notorious among scholars who have attempted to work with his documents and has undoubtedly contributed to his writings not being used in their raw form. They have been inaccessible in the most basic sense of being unreadable even by seasoned historians. Even JD himself seemed burdened by his own drafting process. "Whenever Health [per]mits write," he urged, "Tho[ugh] an afflicted Heart pours forth its Sensations without Art, while an aching Head is incapable of the Labor of Correction."[1] JD's editors know the source of the headaches and shared in them. The JDP was thus fortunate from the beginning to engage two of the best paleographers in the country, Alicia Anderson, former assistant editor with the Papers of Benjamin Franklin, and Ellen Pawelczak, her successor at the Franklin Papers. Without these two experts, there would not be an edition, or it would be hopelessly unreliable. Although it is impossible to avoid mistakes in such an endeavor, the manuscripts in this edition are as true to the originals and as accurate as is humanly possible.

Again, the goal was to render the transcriptions as true to the originals as possible. It was sometimes necessary, however, to interfere with the text slightly so as to make it legible and useful. Technology would have allowed replication of the documents almost exactly as they appear on the manuscript page, but then they would have remained inaccessible, forcing readers still to decipher deleted words, order sentences with multiple insertions and deletions, hunt down sentences that continued in the margins of later pages, and guess at cryptic abbreviations. Therefore, while retaining most of JD's idiosyncrasies, this edition remedies these conditions. Throughout, editorial decisions are distinguished from those of JD.

---

[1] JD, Notes for *An Essay on the Constitutional Power of Great-Britain over the Colonies in America* (Philadelphia: W. and T. Bradford, 1774), PHi-RRL.

Basic Editorial Devices

Word inserted by author: {Government}

Word deleted by author: ~~Government~~

Word in a hand different
from main author: [*JD*:] <Government>

Editorial notes in brackets
and italics: [*illegible*]; [*see left margin*:]

Illegible word deleted by author: [~~*illegible*~~]

Word added by editors, very certain: [Government]

Very unclear word, guess by editors: [Government?]

Unclear word inserted
and deleted by author: {[~~Government~~]}

Abbreviated word,
expanded by editors: Gov.^t *becomes* Gov[ernmen]t

When letters or words have been
cancelled by a new letter or word
written over the original, there is
no space between the cancellation
and the insertion: ~~g~~{G}overnment

Other Conditions

- The general physical appearance of the text has been reproduced, including blocks of text, columns, indentations, and blank spaces. To preserve original formatting, manuscript texts are aligned left. This also distinguishes them from printed documents, which are justified. Lines and other drawings on the page, such as hand-braces, insertion symbols, or boxes drawn around words or paragraphs, are reproduced as near to the original as is technologically possible. Where a feature is not reproduced visually, a descriptive editorial note is added.

- Marginalia and other inserted words and sentences are placed in the text either where JD indicated they belong or where the flow of the text dictates. Either way, if the text to be inserted appears far from its intended insertion point (e.g., in the margin, on another page, or on a separate scrap of paper), an editorial note states where it actually appears in the original.
- When edits to a document have been made in an unknown hand or hands, this fact is mentioned in the headnote.
- Underlinings are retained as written. Where underlines exceed two, an endnote specifies how many times.
- Catchwords (the dangling word at the bottom of a page, repeated at the top of the next) are omitted in correspondence but retained in draft manuscripts where they aided editors in determining order of pages.
- Single hyphens replace double hyphens.
- A single em-dash is used for all dashes, regardless of length or number.
- Text written larger or darker for emphasis is rendered in **boldface** type.
- Original signatures are rendered in **boldface** type; copied or proxy signatures are in Roman.
- Abbreviations are expanded except in common titles (e.g., Mr., Mrs., Dr., St.) and numbers (e.g., 4th, 2.^{d}). In expansions, periods are removed, superscript text is lowered, and the missing letters are supplied in square brackets. In cases where there could be either a British or an American spelling (e.g., fav[o]r or fav[ou]r), we followed the conventions of the author in that particular document. When there was no model, spelling follows British conventions before 1776 and American afterward, following the evolution of JD's spelling habits.
- Contractions are retained as written, with or without an apostrophe; "ed" words without the "e" or an apostrophe are not changed.
- Archaic letters and abbreviations are modernized or expanded, and rendered in brackets: the long "s" (∫) is made short; the per sign (℀) is expanded as [per], [pro], [pre], [præ], or [pri], as appropriate; the thorn is rendered as [th] (e.g., [th]e, [th]at), except in the case of "ye" for "you."
- When a dash is used instead of a period at the end of a sentence, a space is left between it and the following word.
- Authorial errors or slips of the pen are not corrected or marked with [*sic*], except where they might be mistaken for an editorial error,

such as a repeated word. Misspelled words that might be confusing are provided with an endnote.

- Capitalization is retained. Typical of the age, however, some letters, including "p" and "s," had middling cases, neither capital nor lowercase. In those instances, which could be decided either way, capitalization follows the conventions of the author in the text or the general usage of the period.
- When multiple words or lines are illegible, they are noted as [*illegible words*]. If the words or lines are illegible because of deletion by the author, they will appear thusly: [~~two illegible lines~~].
- Lacunæ are represented with a descriptive note: [*torn*], [*ink spot*].

It must be acknowledged that readers initially may find it difficult to read the transcribed texts with editorial "barbed wire," but those with complaints might refer to the sample original document on p. lxv, and trust that diligent attention to the editorial methodology will facilitate access.

Printed Documents

JD managed to make even his published writings more difficult for an editor than most, using all manner of textual effects to emphasize his points. One opponent criticized JD for his willingness to "blazon [his ideas] forth with *Italics*, SMALL CAPITALS, and CAPITALS without number, that they might make the greater impression on his readers."[2] Indeed, each one of these features added to the work of transcribers capturing the words and of proofreaders reading them aloud. Nevertheless, these features are preserved not merely for the sake of historical accuracy but also because of JD's clear intent in using them to express his opinions and emotions. The rendering of printed documents departs from the originals in the following ways, many of which are similar to the conditions described above for manuscript documents:

- Columns in newspaper articles are not preserved.
- Page breaks are not noted; catchwords are omitted.
- The long "s" and the ct ligature are not retained.
- Multiple dashes or hyphens between words or sentences are replaced with an em-dash.
- Single hyphens replace double hyphens in hyphenated words.
- In quotations running multiple lines, the quotation marks at the beginning of each line are omitted.

---

[2] A Countryman, "To the Printer of the Pennsylvania Chronicle," *The Pennsylvania Chronicle, and Universal Advertiser* (Philadelphia), August 1, 1768.

- Drop caps at the beginning of documents are omitted; variant text sizes are regularized to a single uniform size.
- Spaces between the ends of sentences and punctuation are omitted.
- Obvious typographical errors, such as an upside-down letter or transposed letters, are silently corrected. Other errors that might compromise textual clarity, such as missing closing quotation marks, are corrected in square brackets; [*sic*] is used only when an error in the original might be mistaken for an editorial error.
- In foreign-language documents, the same general rules apply as above, except that archaic Latin ligatures and abbreviations with no modern counterpart are reproduced as closely as modern technology permits; and in German documents, the superscripted postvocalic-e convention (a small "e" placed over a vowel) is changed to an *umlaut*.
- Errata are silently included, except where there was confusion on the part of the printer, in which case a note is given to clarify.

<u>Printed Documents with Handwritten Portions or Notes</u>

JD wrote in printed works, his own and those authored by others, to edit and comment. These documents are treated like manuscripts in that JD's handwritten notes are inserted in the text where he intended them to appear. When he was commenting, they are treated more like printed documents, with the comments appearing as marginalia. Occasionally there is a bond, certificate, or other printed document with handwritten portions. In all instances, the transcription of handwriting follows the protocol above for manuscripts. To distinguish the handwritten text from the typeface, the former is rendered in a different font.

A Note on Technology and Work Process

The JDP managed with equipment and software already in place or that could be purchased on a very small budget and with limited institutional support. Support increased over the years as the JDP partnered with the Center for Digital Editing at the University of Virginia.

Document Collection

In most cases, images of manuscript documents were taken in the archives under existing lighting with a Fujifilm Finepix digital camera with 12.0 megapixels. A "text" setting allowed for superb resolution of lettering. Each page was imaged in its entirety, and then in segments, depending on how difficult it was to read. The worst documents required up to ten images per page. Most printed documents were downloaded as PDFs from various online databases. Occasionally the situation was reversed, where manuscripts (almost exclusively correspondence) were downloaded, and printed documents were captured in the archives. In very few instances, a repository would send digital images *gratis* upon request. Except in special circumstances, the JDP has not had funding to pay repositories for searches or digital imaging of documents.

Document Storage, Access, and Management

The JDP project files were initially stored on the server of the Collaboratory for Research in Computing in the Humanities (RCH) at the University of Kentucky. The JDP team members, at various institutions in the United States and Canada, accessed the files remotely. Records of the documents and their stages in the editing process were initially stored in a FileMaker Pro 12 database, which also allowed linking to the various iterations of the documents (facsimile original, transcription, proofed transcription, etc.) on the RCH server. After production of the first three volumes, the JDP files were transferred to the University of Virginia's Center for Digital Editing, where the remaining volumes would be produced.

Document Transcription

The JDP initially set out to prepare the print and digital editions simultaneously. The majority of the printed documents were initially transcribed in XML and marked up in TEI Tite by a document transcription service. Manuscript documents were first transcribed into Microsoft Word then converted to XML-TEI. By enlarging the image and adjusting filters and contrast in Microsoft Office Picture Manager, the manuscript transcribers were able to decipher almost every intentional mark in a document. But when the project advanced to the annotation stage in 2013, and there proved to be no viable software solution that allowed editors to work easily with the documents in XML, the dual-edition approach was abandoned. They then struggled to work in MS Word, which was inflexible and increasingly unstable, causing staff to redo work multiple times, until the JDP transitioned to the Classical Text Editor (CTE), version 8.08, in 2015. This program promised to allow the complicated formatting required, and to enable the documents be marked up with XML tagging in preparation for digital publication. But ultimately, the JDP was compelled to return to Word. The digital edition, which will launch within a year of the print publication, will be built and hosted by the University of Virginia.

Transcription Verification

All documents received repeated checks against the originals for different features at each of four stages: 1) After initial transcription, there were three proofreadings. The transcriber reviewed her work twice, and members of the JDP team tandem oral proofread to verify the entire document with focus on the words—deletions, insertions, emphases, unusual spellings, abbreviations and their expansions, and so on. 2) During formatting, editors checked overall textual structures, including indentations, block text, columns, and unusual features such as lines or circles drawn around text. 3) During digital markup, editors had the facsimile originals open next to the transcriptions to check abbreviations and features such as underlining and deletions. And 4) in copyediting, editors spot-checked for spelling and irregularities in the text at all levels, from individual letters/characters/symbols to formatting issues.

Sample Original Manuscript: JD, Draft of "Letter the 10th," [1794]. PHi-RRL. Image courtesy of the Historical Society of Pennsylvania.

ABBREVIATIONS AND SHORT TITLES

Editorial

ALS	autograph letter signed by the author
DS	document signed
Lat.	Latin, to indicate that the language used is Latin
LFr.	Law French, to indicate that the language used is Law French
Ms	manuscript—a handwritten document other than a letter
Rpt	reprint from an edited volume or other printed secondary source

Repositories and Collections

When a document resides in a named collection within a repository, its source is cited in annotation in the following form: XXX-YYY, where XXX is the repository or institution, and YYY is the named collection. Thus, for example, the John Dickinson Family Papers collection residing in the Library Company of Philadelphia is cited as PPL-JDFP.

De-Ar	Delaware Department of State, Division of Historical and Cultural Affairs, Hall of Records, Dover, Del.
DeHi	Historical Society of Delaware, Wilmington, Del.
DLC	Library of Congress, Washington, DC
GAC	Simon Gratz Autograph Collection, Historical Society of Pennsylvania
JDFP	John Dickinson Family Papers, Library Company of Philadelphia
JDP	John Dickinson Plantation, Dover, Del.
JHPP	John H. Powell Collection of John Dickinson Research, American Philosophical Society
Logan	Logan Family Papers, Historical Society of Pennsylvania
Loudoun	Loudoun Papers, Historical Society of Pennsylvania
MDL	Maria Dickinson Logan Collection, Historical Society of Pennsylvania
NN	Theodorus Bailey Myers Collection, Series XI, Pennsylvania Assembly (1754–1759), New York Public Library, New York
Norris	Norris Family Papers, Historical Society of Pennsylvania
Norris/Fairhill	Norris of Fairhill Manuscripts, Historical Society of Pennsylvania
PCarlD	John Dickinson Papers, Dickinson College, Carlisle, Pa.
PHi	Historical Society of Pennsylvania, Philadelphia
PPAmP	American Philosophical Society, Philadelphia
PPL	Library Company of Philadelphia, Philadelphia
PU-Ar	William Smith Papers, University of Pennsylvania Archives and Records Center, Philadelphia
RRL	R.R. Logan Collection of John Dickinson Papers, Historical Society of Pennsylvania
TMP	Thomas McKean Papers, Historical Society of Pennsylvania
UkLoMT	Middle Temple Archive, Honourable Society of the Middle Temple, London, UK

Published Sources in *Volume One*

AL
American Literature.

Am. Weekly Merc.
American Weekly Mercury. Philadelphia.

Anderson, *Crucible*
Fred Anderson. *Crucible of War: The Seven Years' War and the Fate of the Empire in British North America, 1754–1766.* New York: Vintage Books, 2000.

ARGII
Anno Regni Georgii II. Regis, Magnae Britanniae, Franciae & Hiberniae, Vigesimo Nono. At a General Assembly of the Province of Pennsylvania, begun and holden at Philadelphia . . . Philadelphia: B. Franklin, 1755.

Arist. *EN*
Aristotle. *Ethica Nicomachea (Nicomachean Ethics).*

Bacon, *Cases*
Matthew Bacon. *A General Abridgment of Cases in Equity, Argued and Adjudged in the High Court of Chancery, &c.* 4th ed. 2 vols. London: H. Lintot, 1756.

BG
Boston Gazette.

BLD
Black's Law Dictionary.

Brownlow
Richard Brownlow. *Reports of Divers Famous Cases in Law* . . . 2nd ed. 2 vols. London: H. Twyford, 1675.

Burnet
Gilbert Burnet. *Bishop Burnet's History of His Own Time. From the Restoration of King Charles II, to the Conclusion of the Treaty of Peace at Utrecht, in the Reign of Queen Anne.* 4 vols. London: A. Millar, 1753.

Burrow
James Burrow. *Reports of Cases Adjudged in the Court of King's Bench, since the Death of Lord Raymond.* 5 vols. London: His Majesty's Law-Printers, 1766–80.

Carthew

Thomas Carthew. *Reports of Cases Adjudged in the Court of King's Bench, From the Third Year of King James the Second, to the Twelfth Year of King William the Third.* London: E. and R. Nutt, and R. Gosling, 1728.

Chandler

Richard Chandler. *The History and Proceedings of the House of Commons from the Restoration to the Present Time.* 14 vols. London: R. Chandler, 1742–44.

Cic. *Cat.*

Cicero (Marcus Tullius). *In Catilinam.*

Cic. *Phil.*

Cicero (Marcus Tullius). *Orationes Philippicae (Orations, The fourteen orations against Marcus Antonius; Philippics).*

CLE

William Blackstone. *Commentaries on the Laws of England.* 4 vols. Oxford: Clarendon Press, [1765]–69.

Clerke

Francis Clerke. *The Practice of the Court of Admiralty of England, Written Originally in Latin.* London: D. Browne, 1722.

Coke, *Institutes*

Edward Coke. *Institutes of the Laws of England.* 4 vols. London: M. Flesher, 1628–44.

Coke, *Reports*

Edward Coke. *The Reports of Sir Edward Coke, Kt. In English, in Thirteen Parts Compleat.* 13 vols. London: E. and R. Nutt, and R. Gosling, 1738.

Colbourn

H. Trevor Colbourn. "A Pennsylvania Farmer at the Court of King George: John Dickinson's London Letters, 1754–1756," *PMHB* 86, no. 3 (July 1962): 241–86; and no. 4 (Oct. 1962): 417–53.

Collection of Charters

A Collection of Charters and Other Publick Acts Relating to the Province of Pennsylvania. Philadelphia: B. Franklin, 1740.

Croke

George Croke. *The Reports of Sr George Croke Kt.: Late One of the Justices of the Court of Kings-Bench, and Formerly One of the Justices of the Court of Common-Bench.* 3rd ed. 3 vols. London: W. Rawlins, S. Roycroft, and H. Sawbridge, 1683.

CRP

Colonial Records of Pennsylvania. 16 vols. Harrisburg: T. Fenn, 1838–53.

DH

Delaware History.

Dull

Jonathan R. Dull. *The French Navy and the Seven Years' War.* Lincoln: University of Nebraska Press, 2005.

Dyer

James Dyer. *Cy Ensuont Ascuns Novel Cases, Collectes per le Jades Tresreverend Judge, Mounsieur Jasques Dyer, Chiefe Justice del Common Banke.* London: R. Tottelli, 1585.

EAL

Early American Literature.

Finch

Henry Finch. *Law, or a Discourse Thereof in Four Books.* London: H. Lintot, 1759.

Flower

Milton E. Flower. *John Dickinson: Conservative Revolutionary.* Charlottesville: University Press of Virginia, 1983.

General

A General Treatise of Naval Trade and Commerce, As Founded on the Laws and Statutes of This Realm. 2nd ed. 2 vols. London: H. Lintot, 1753.

Gilbert

Geoffrey Gilbert. *The Law of Evidence, by a Late Learned Judge.* London: H. Lintot, 1756.

Grotius, *Rights* (1738)

Hugo Grotius. *The Rights of War and Peace, in Three Books; Wherein Are Explained, the Law of Nature and Nations, and the Principle Points Relating to the Government ... to Which Are Added, All the Large Notes of Mr. J. Barbeyrac.* London: W. Innys and R. Manby, J. and P. Knapton, D. Brown, T. Osborn, and E. Wicksted, 1738.

Hale, *Pleas*

Matthew Hale. *Historia Placitorum Coronae: The History of the Pleas of the Crown.* 2 vols. London: E. and R. Nutt, and R. Gosling, 1736.

Hawkins
> William Hawkins. *A Treatise of the Pleas of the Crown: or, a System of the Principal Matters Relating to that Subject, Digested under Their Proper Heads.* 3rd ed. 2 vols. London: E. Richardson and C. Lintot, 1739.

Hobart
> Henry Hobart. *The Reports of that Reverend and Learned Judge, the Right Honourable Sr Henry Hobart Knight and Baronet, Lord Chiefe Justice of His Majesties Court of Common Pleas; and Chancellour to Both Their Highnesses, Henry and Charles Princes of Wales.* London: J. Flesher, 1658.

Hor. *Ars P.*
> Horace. *Ars Poetica.*

Hom. *Od.*
> Homer. *Odyssey.*

Just. Code
> Justinian Codex Constitutionum.

Just. Digest
> Justinian Digesta.

Justice[*]
> Alexander Justice. *A General Treatise of the Dominion of the Sea. And a Compleat Body of the Sea-laws: Containing What Is Most Valuable on That Subject in Antient and Modern Authors . . . To Which Is Subjoin'd, an Appendix Concerning the Present State and Regulations of the Admiralty and Navy . . . And a New Appendix Containing Several Eminent Lawyer's Opinions in Important Marine Cases.* 3rd ed. London: T. Page, W., and F. Mount, 1724.

Keble
> Joseph Keble. *Reports in the Court of Kings-Bench at Westminster, from the XII to the XXX Year of the Reign of Our Late Sovereign Lord King Charles II.* 3 vols. London: W. Rawlins, S. Roycroft, M. Flesher, 1685.

Keilway
> Robert Keilway. *Relationes Quorundam Casuum Selectorum ex Libris Roberti Keilwey Ar'.* London: A. Islip, 1602.

---

[*] JD regularly cited Justice as Molloy ("Moll." or "Molloy"); the correct citation to Justice is inserted in the notes.

Levinz

Creswell Levinz. *The Reports of Sir Creswell Levinz, Knt., Late One of the Judges in the Court of Common Pleas at Westminster.* 2nd ed. 3 pts. Translated by Sarjeant Salkeld. London: E. and R. Nutt and R. Gosling, 1722.

Lex Parl.

Lex Parliamentaria: or, a Treatise of the Law and Custom of Parliaments: Shewing Their Antiquity, Names, Kinds, and Qualities. London: H. Lintot, 1748.

Littleton

Thomas Littleton. *Littletons Tenures in English.* London: R. Tottle, 1592.

LLP

Lawmaking and Legislators in Pennsylvania: A Biographical Dictionary. Edited by Craig W. Horle et al. 3 vols. Philadelphia and University Park, Pa.: University of Pennsylvania Press and Penn State University Press, 1991–2007.

Modern[†]

Modern Reports: or, Select Cases Adjudged in the Courts of King's Bench, Chancery, Common Pleas, and Exchequer. 3rd ed. 7 vols. London: E. Nutt and R. Gosling, 1720–33.

Modern Cases in Law and Equity. In Two Parts. Containing I. Reports of Special Cases Argued and Adjudged in the Court of King's Bench, in the VII, VIII, IX, X, XI, and XII Years of King George I. II. Cases Argued and Decreed in the High Court of Chancery, in the VIII, IX, X and XI Years of King George I. To Which Are Added, Some Special Cases on Appeals. Vols. 8 and 9. London: E. and R. Nutt, and R. Gosling, 1730.

Cases in Law and Equity, Chiefly during the Time the Late Earl of Macclesfield Presided in the Courts of King's-Bench and Chancery. Vol. 10. London: E. and R. Nutt, and R. Gosling, 1736.

Cases Adjudged in the Court of King's Bench, from the Second Year of King William III to the End of His Reign. Vol. 12. London: E. and R. Nutt, and R. Gosling, 1738.

Molloy. *See* Justice.

[†] For these related works with the same abbreviation, readers are advised to note the volume number in the citation in order to identify the full title here. They may also consult the index of subjects (373–439).

Montesquieu
> Charles Louis de Secondat, Baron de la Brède et de Montesquieu. *The Spirit of the Laws*, transl. Mr. Nugent, 2 vols. London: J. Nourse and P. Vaillant, 1752.

Moore
> Francis Moore. *Cases Collect & Report per Sir Fra. Moore Chivalier, Serjeant del Ley*. 2nd ed. London: G. Pawlet, 1688.

Newcastle
> Thomas Pelham-Holles. *The Duke of Newcastle's Letter, by His Majesty's Order, to Monsieur Michell, the King of Prussia's Secretary of the Embassy, in Answer to the Memorial, and Other Papers, Delivered, by Monsieur Michell, to the Duke of Newcastle.* London: E. Owen, 1753.

OCD
> *Oxford Classical Dictionary.*

ODNB
> *Online Dictionary of National Biography.*

OED
> *Oxford English Dictionary.*

PA
> *Pennsylvania Archives*. 9 ser. Edited by Samuel Hazard et al. 114 vols. Philadelphia and Harrisburg: 1852–1935.

PAPS
> *Proceedings of the American Philosophical Society.*

Pargellis
> Stanley McCrory Pargellis. *Lord Loudoun in North America, 1756–1758*. New Haven, Conn.: Yale University Press, 1933.

Parl. Hist.
> *The Parliamentary or Constitutional History of England; Being a Faithful Account of All the Most Remarkable Transactions in Parliament, from the Earliest Times. Collected from the Journals of Both Houses, the Records, Original Manuscripts, Scarce Speeches and Tracts; All Compared with the Several Cotemporary Writers, and Connected, Throughout, with the History of the Times.* 24 vols. London: T. Osborne and W. Sandby, 1751–61.

PBF
> *The Papers of Benjamin Franklin*. Edited by Leonard W. Labaree et al. 43 vols. to date. New Haven, Conn.: Yale University Press, 1959– .

Peere

William Peere Williams. *Reports of Cases Argued and Determined in the High Court of Chancery, and of Some Special Cases Adjudged in the Court of King's Bench.* 2 vols. London: E. and R. Nutt, and R. Gosling, 1740–49. Vol. 3. London: H. Lintot, 1749.

Petyt

William Peyt. *Miscellanea Parliamentaria: Containing Presidents 1. Of Freedom from Arrests. 2. Of Censures.* London: T. Basset and J. Wickins, 1680.

PG

Pennsylvania Gazette. Philadelphia.

PH

Pennsylvania History: A Journal of Mid-Atlantic Studies.

PJ

Pennsylvania Journal. Philadelphia.

Plowden

Edmund Plowden. *The Commentaries, or Reports of Edmund Plowden, of the Middle-Temple, Esq.; An Apprentice of the Common Law.* London: C. Lintot and S. Richardson, 1761.

Plut. *Luc.*

Plutarch. *Life of Lucullus.*

PMHB

Pennsylvania Magazine of History and Biography.

Pope, *Odyssey*

Alexander Pope, transl. *The Odyssey of Homer.* 5 vols. London: B. Lintot, 1725–26.

Postlethwayt, *System*

Malachy Postlethwayt. *Great-Britain's True System.* London: J. Whiston, B. White, and W. Sandby, 1757.

Pufendorf

Samuel Pufendorf. *Of the Law of Nature and Nations.* 4th ed. London: J. Walthoe, R. Wilkin [et al.], 1729.

PWP

The Papers of William Penn. Edited by Mary Maples Dunn and Richard S. Dunn. 5 vols. Philadelphia: University of Pennsylvania Press, 1981–87.

Q. Horatii Flacci, *Ep. Lib.* 1
Quintus Horatius Flaccus. *Epistularum Liber Primus* (Horace, *Epistles*, book one).

Rapin
Paul de Rapin de Throyas. *The History of England*. 3rd ed. 4 vols. Translated by Nicholas Tindal. London: J. and P. Knapton, 1743–47.

Raymond, *Cases*
Thomas Raymond. *Reports of Cases Argued and Adjudged in the Courts of King's Bench and Common Pleas, In the Reigns of the Late King William, Queen Anne, King George the First, and His Present Majesty*. 2 vols. London: H. Lintot, 1743.

Raymond, *Special*
Thomas Raymond. *The Reports of Divers Special Cases Adjudged in the Courts of Kings Bench, Common Pleas & Exchequer, in the Reign of King Charles II*. London: Assigns of R. and E. Atkins, 1696.

Read's Weekly
Read's Weekly Journal, or, British-Gazetteer. London.

SAL
The Statutes at Large, from Magna Charta, to the End of the Eleventh Parliament of Great Britain, Anno 1761, Continued. Edited by Danby Pickering. 46 vols. Cambridge: J. Bentham, 1762–1807.

Salkeld
William Salkeld. *Reports of Cases Adjudged in the Court of King's Bench, with Some Special Cases Adjudged in the Courts of Chancery, Common Pleas and Exchequer; from the First Year of K. William and Q. Mary, to the Tenth Year of Q. Anne*. Vols. 1 and 2. London: E. and R. Nutt, and R. Gosling, 1721. *Reports of Cases Adjudged in the Court of King's Bench; Together with Several Special Cases Adjudged in the Courts of Chancery, Common Pleas, and Exchequer; from the Revolution to the Tenth Year of Q. Anne*. Vol. 3. London: E. and R. Nutt, and R. Gosling, 1724.

Sall. *Cat.*
Sallust. *Bellum Catilinae*, or *De Catilinae Coniuratione*.

SALP
The Statutes at Large of Pennsylvania. Compiled by James T. Mitchell et al. 18 vols. Harrisburg: State Printer, 1896–1915.

Saunders

Edmund Saunders. *Les Reports du Tres Erudite Edmund Saunders . . . des Divers Pleadings et Cases en le Court del Bank le Roy en le Temps del Reign sa Tres Excellent Majesty le Roy Charles le II.* 2nd ed. 2 vols. London: E. and R. Nutt and R. Gosling, 1722.

Siderfin

Thomas Siderfin. *Les Reports des Divers Special Cases Argue & Adjudge en le Court del Bank le Roy, et Auxy en le Co. Ba. & l'Exchequer en les Primier Dix Ans apres le Restauration del Son Tres-Excellent Majesty Le Roy Charles le II.* 2nd ed. London: J. Nutt, 1714.

*State Trial*s

Sollom Emlyn. *A Complete Collection of State-Trials, and Proceedings upon High-Treason, and Other Crimes and Misdemeanours; from the Reign of King Richard II to the End of the Reign of King George I.* 2nd ed. 6 vols. London, 1730.

Strange

John Strange. *Reports of Adjudged Cases in the Courts of Chancery, King's Bench, Common Pleas and Exchequer, from Trinity Term in the Second Year of King George I, to Trinity Term in the Twenty-First Year of King George II.* 2 vols. London: H. Lintot, 1755.

Style

William Style. *Narrationes Modernae, or, Modern Reports Begun in the Now Upper Bench Court at Westminster in the Beginning of Hillary Term 21 Caroli, and Continued to the End of Michaelmas Term 1655 . . .* London: F.L., 1658.

Tac. *Ann.*

Tacitus. *Annales.*

Tac. *Hist.*

Tacitus. *Historiæ.*

Vaughan

John Vaughan. *The Reports and Arguments of That Learned Judge Sir John Vaughan Kt., Late Chief Justice of His Majesties Court of Common Pleas.* London: T. Roycroft, 1677.

Ventris

Peyton Ventris. *The Reports of Sir Peyton Ventris, Kt., Late One of the Justices of the Common Pleas.* 2 vols. London: E. and R. Nutt, and R. Gosling, 1726.

Verg. *Aen.*

Publius Vergilius Maro. *Aeneid.*

Vernon

> Thomas Vernon. *Cases Argued and Adjudged in the High Court of Chancery.* 2 vols. London: E. and R. Nutt and R. Gosling, 1726–28.

Viner

> Charles Viner. *A General Abridgment of Law and Equity.* 23 vols. Aldershot, England: C. Viner, 1742–53.

Votes

> *Votes and Proceedings of the House of Representatives of the Province of Pennsylvania.* Philadelphia: B. Franklin et al., 1730–75.

Votes, supp.

> *Votes and Proceedings of the House of Representatives of the Province of Pennsylvania. Beginning the fourth day of December, 1682.* 3 vols. Philadelphia: B. Franklin, 1752–54.

WEP

> *Whitehall Evening-Post; Or, London Intelligencer.*

WMQ

> *William and Mary Quarterly.*

Wood

> Thomas Wood. *A New Institute of the Imperial or, Civil Law. With Notes Shewing in Some Principal Cases amongst Other Observations, How the Canon Law, the Laws of England, and the Laws and Customs of Other Nations Differ from It.* 3rd ed. London: W.B., 1721.

Chronology of the Life of John Dickinson

1731	**Nov. 4**: Samuel Dickinson (b. 1689) married Mary Cadwalader (b. 1700)
1732	**Nov. 13 (Nov. 2**, old calendar): John Dickinson born at Crosia-doré in Talbot Co., Md.
1734	**Oct. 4**: Brother Thomas born (died young)
1739	**April 5** (old calendar): Brother Philemon born
1741	**Jan. 18**: Samuel Dickinson moved family to Poplar Hall near Dover, Del.
1740s	Tutored by James Orr and William Killen
1750–53	Read law in Philadelphia in the office of king's attorney John Moland
1753–57	Studied law at Middle Temple, Inns of Court, London; certificate issued March 14, 1757
1757	Began law practice in Philadelphia
1759	**Oct. 1**: Elected to Del. Assembly as representative from Kent Co.
1760	**July 6**: Father, Samuel Dickinson, died **Oct. 1**: Reelected to the Del. Assembly; chosen speaker of the House
1761	Served in Del. Assembly
1762	**May 14**: Elected to Pa. Assembly in special election as representative from Phila. Co. **Oct. 1**: Elected to Pa. Assembly in regular election
1763	**March**: Elected a director of the Library Company of Philadelphia **Oct. 1**: Elected to Pa. Assembly
1764	**June**: Represented the Moravian Indian Renatus in his murder trial; Renatus acquitted Published: *A Speech, Delivered in the House of Assembly* 　　　*To the King's Most Excellent Majesty* 　　　*A Reply to a Piece Called the Speech of Joseph Galloway* 　　　*"Last Tuesday Morning..."* 　　　*A Receipt to Make a Speech* 　　　*A Protest Presented to the House of Assembly*

A Protest Presented to the House of Assembly
Oct. 1: Elected to the Pa. Assembly

1765   **Oct. 7**: Served as delegate to the Stamp Act Congress
Published: Declaration of Rights of the Stamp Act Congress
Petition to the King from the Stamp Act Congress
The Late Regulations
"Friends and Countrymen"

1766   Published: *An Address to the Committee of Correspondence in Barbados*

1767–68   **Nov.–Feb.**: Published: "Letters from a Farmer in Pennsylvania" serially in newspapers

1768   Published: "The Centinel," nos. 6, 7, 8, & 16 serially in newspapers
A Copy of a Letter from a Gentleman in Virginia
To the Public
"The Liberty Song"
Elected member of American Philosophical Society

1769   **Sept. 29**: Awarded an honorary degree from College of New Jersey (later Princeton)

1770   **July 19**: Married Mary Norris (b. July 17, 1740)
Oct. 1: Elected to Pa. Assembly

1771   Published a Petition from the Pa. Assembly to the king protesting the tea tax
Dec. 10: First child, daughter Sarah (Sally), born

1772   **Oct. 1**: Candidate for the Pa. Assembly (against his wishes); not elected

1773   Published: *A Letter from the Country, to a Gentleman in Philadelphia*
"Extract of a Letter [on the Tea Tax]"

1774   **May 7**: Second child, daughter Mary, born
May–June: Published: "Letters to the Inhabitants of the British Colonies"
May 20: Appointed to the Pa. Committee of Correspondence
July 15: Appointed to committee to draft instructions for Pa. delegates to the First Continental Congress

Sept.: Published: *An Essay on the Constitutional Power of Great Britain*
Oct. 1: Elected to Pa. Assembly
Oct. 15: Added as a delegate from Pa. to the First Continental Congress
Oct. 17: Took seat in the First Continental Congress
Oct. 21: Added to the drafting committees, which produced:
    To the Inhabitants of the Colonies
    Bill of Rights and *List of Grievances*
    Petition of Congress to the King
    A Letter to the Inhabitants of the Province of Quebec
Nov. 12: Elected to serve on a Committee for the City of Phila., the Northern Liberties, and Southwark
Dec. 5. Appointed to a Committee of Inspection and Observation
Dec. 15: Appointed delegate to the Second Continental Congress

1775
Feb. 19: Chosen for the Secret Committee of Correspondence
May 5: Daughter, Mary, died
Spring: Raised First Philadelphia Battalion of Associators and commissioned as colonel
Served on Pa. Committee of Correspondence
Served on Pa. Committee of Safety
May 10: Delegate to Second Continental Congress, which produced:
    Olive Branch Petition
    Declaration on the Causes and Necessity of Taking Up Arms
Oct. 1: Elected to Pa. Assembly
Nov. 9: Wrote instructions to Pa. delegates disallowing them to vote for independence

1776
Feb.–March: Worked with members of Congress for reconciliation with Great Britain and to secure military aid from France
March 22: Mother, Mary Cadwalader Dickinson, died near Trenton, N.J.
May: In Dover, Del.
June 8: Wrote new instructions to Pa. delegates allowing them to vote for independence.
June 12–17: Head of committee to draft the Articles of Confederation
July 1: Speech in the Second Continental Congress against the Declaration of Independence
July 2: Abstained from vote on independence
July 10: Joined battalion at Elizabethtown, N.J.
Sept. 1: Returned to Phila. with battalion
Sept. 30: Resigned commission in Pa. militia
Nov. 5: Elected to Pa. Assembly

Nov. 27: Abdicated seat in Assembly in protest over the new Pa. constitution
Published: *Essay on a Frame of Government for Pennsylvania*
Dec.: Accused by Pa. Council of Safety of treasonous activities

| 1777 | **May 12**: Manumitted all his slaves conditionally |

May 12: Manumitted all his slaves conditionally
Summer–Fall: Served as private soldier in Del. militia
Sept. 26: Received commission as brigadier-general in Del. militia; did not act on it
Oct. 30: Dickinson family escaped Phila., joined JD at Poplar Hall (Dover, Del.)
Nov. 22: Fairhill (Phila.) burned by the British
Dec. 19: Resigned commission in Del. militia

1778 **June 29**: Affirmed (rather than swore) fidelity to the State of Delaware
Aug. 19: Third child, son John, born
Sept. 2: Son, John, died

1779 **Feb. 1**: Appointed by the Del. Assembly to serve in the Continental Congress
Published: "To the Inhabitants of the United States"
July 5: Fourth child, a son, stillborn

1780 **April 12**: Declined seat as delegate to the Continental Congress from Del.
Nov. 28: Elected to the Del. Assembly for New Castle Co. in special election

1781 **Aug. 10**: Poplar Hall (Dover, Del.) plundered by loyalists
Sept. 21: Manumitted some slaves unconditionally
Oct. 20: Elected to Del. Executive Council
Nov. 6: Elected president of Del. for a term of three years (served 1)
Published: *For the Use of the Militia of the Delaware State, an Abstract of the Regulations for the Order and Discipline of the Troops of the United States*

1782 **Nov. 7**: Elected president of Pa.
Dec.–Jan. 1783: Attacked by "Valerius" serially in the newspapers; published response
Served as *ex officio* member and president of the board of trustees of the University of Pennsylvania

1783 **Jan. 14**: Resigned as president of Del.
June: Mutiny of 1783, removal of US capital from Phila.

Sept. 9: Founding of Dickinson College by Benjamin Rush; JD donated 600 acres and books; served as president of the board of trustees
Oct. 15: Elected honorary member of the Society of the Cincinnati
Nov. 6: Fifth child, daughter Maria, born
Nov. 7: Reelected president of Pa.

1784   **Nov. 3**: Reelected president of Pa.

1785   **Oct.**: Established permanent residence in Wilmington, Del.

1786   **May 11**: Manumitted remaining slaves unconditionally
Sept. 11–14: Served as chairman of the Annapolis Convention
     Published: *The Report of the Annapolis Convention*
     Presented bill for emancipating slaves in Del.
     Donated funds to found the Society for Alleviating the Miseries of Public Prisons

1787   **Feb. 3**: Declined to serve as delegate to the Confederation Congress from Del.
Feb. 21: Congress read and approved JD's letter from the Annapolis Convention proposing a Federal Convention in Phila.
May 29–Sept. 15: Served as delegate from Del. to the Constitutional Convention
Published: *Fragments on the Confederation of the American States*

1788   Published the first *Fabius Letters* advocating ratification of the US Constitution
April 16: Appointed judge in the Del. appellate court

1791–92   **Oct. 10**: Resigned as judge in the Del. Chancery Court
Nov. 29: Attended Del. Constitutional Convention
Dec. 7: Elected president of the Convention

1792   Served as judge of Del. Court of Appeals
Sept. 15: Put forth as candidate for senator from Del.; preemptively resigned

1794   Donated funds to found the Wilmington Academy for the education of poor children

1795   **Aug. 5**: Led Del. protest against the Jay Treaty

1796   Published: *A Fragment* on the education of youth

1797	Published: "Ode, on France" *Fabius Letters*, a second set in support of France
1798	Published: *A Caution; or, Reflections on the Present Contest between France and Great-Britain* "Ode, on the French Revolution"
1799	Donated funds to Quakers to found Westtown School (Pa.) Donated land for the Brandywine Academy (Del.)
1800	Asked to run for Congress; declined
1801	Published: *The Political Writings of John Dickinson, Esq.* Asked to run for governor of Del.; declined
1803	**July 23**: Wife, Mary Norris Dickinson, died, aged 63. Published: *An Address on the Past, Present and Eventual Relations of the United States to France*
1807	**Oct.**: Del. Republicans nominated JD for election to Congress; not elected
1808	**Feb. 14**: Died, aged 75; buried at Wilmington Friends Meeting burial ground

The
COMPLETE WRITINGS
and
SELECTED CORRESPONDENCE
of
JOHN DICKINSON

Volume One • 1751–1758

1
To Nicholas Ridgely, September 6, 1751

Philad[elphi]a Sept[ember] [th]e 6[th] 1751

Honoured Sir,[1]

Your favour of the 26[th] of last Inst[ant] I Rec[eive]d Yesterday, & am Oblig'd to You for the Confidence You are so Good as to Repose in me; Every thing Sir, in my Power to do for Master Charles[2] You may Depend on, & any services I can do for You in this Place, shall be perform'd with the Greatest Pleasure, by

Your h[um]ble Serv[an]t
John Dickinson

P.S. Please to Present my Service to Your Respected family & Mr. Vining & his Lady[3]

ALS (De-Ar)

---

[1] Nicholas Ridgely (1694–1755) was a planter in Dover and justice of the Delaware Supreme Court. He was also a guardian of JD's close friend and neighbor, Cæsar Rodney (1728–1784).

[2] Charles Greenberry Ridgely (1737/38–1785) was the son of Nicholas and Mary Middleton Ridgely. He later served in the Delaware Assembly from 1776 to 1780.

[3] John Vining (1724–1770) was speaker of the House of Delaware, and chief justice from 1764 to 1770. Rachel Ridgely Vining (1715–1753) was his first wife.

<h1 style="text-align:center">1753</h1>

2

To George Read and Samuel Wharton, [October 1753]

George Read (1733–1798) and Samuel Wharton (1732–1800) were two of JD's lifelong friends. Read, of New Castle County, Del., also studied law with John Moland in Philadelphia and was admitted to the bar in 1753. Read went on to become a leading statesman in Delaware. He was with JD at the Stamp Act Congress, a signer of the Declaration of Independence, president of Delaware, delegate to the Federal Convention and signer of the Constitution, and a US senator. He also signed the Constitution on behalf of JD. Wharton, who was from Philadelphia and later Dover, was a merchant, land speculator, politician, and judge. He and John Baynton founded a successful mercantile firm (see doc. 2:63).

This letter, quoted in Flower's biography of JD and cited as being in the Richard S. Rodney Collection at the Historical Society of Delaware, is not there. Nor has it turned up in searches at other archives. We produce the quoted passage here, in which JD anticipates his trip to London and beginning his legal study at the Middle Temple. Further evidence of the existence of this letter is found in *The Life and Correspondence of George Read*, wherein the author describes it thusly:

> Mr. Dickinson takes a most affectionate leave of his late associates. He is evidently much excited and elated by the prospect of his voyage, and if passages of the letter be written with undue levity, his youth, and circumstanced as he was, almost unavoidable exhilaration may excuse it, and a warm and kindly feeling for Mr. Read and other friends pervades it, which exhibits him very advantageously. He begs to be remembered to Groves, Oldman, and other friends who may inquire for him, and especially to Mr. Moland and family; and in the postscript asks his friend to order the printers boy to leave his paper with the "sheriff."[1]

"I am now preparing for my voyage to another world not with the Common apparatus of coffin, winding sheet, etc., but with a cag[2] of good spirits, a fine featherbed, gammons[3] and fresh provisions—quantum sufficient—and I believe few Christians expect their departure with more resolution and alacrity."

Rpt (Flower)

2

[1] William Thompson Read, *Life and Correspondence of George Read, A Signer of the Declaration of Independence, with Notices of Some of His Contemporaries* (Philadelphia: J.B. Lippincott & Co., 1870), 12.

[2] That is, keg.

[3] Gammon: "The ham or haunch of a pig, or (occasionally) other animal" (*OED*).

The London Letters

In 1753, JD embarked on a two-month journey across the Atlantic to London to study law at the Middle Temple, one of the four Inns of Court established to train English barristers.[1] He was among those colonials wealthy and connected enough to attend school across the ocean—a group that also included his mentor, Philadelphia lawyer and king's attorney to Pennsylvania, John Moland. For JD's parents, Samuel Dickinson and Mary Cadwalader Dickinson, his two-year absence was surely a cause for worry. Samuel lost his three eldest sons from his first marriage while they were abroad, at least two of them while they were in London.[2] JD wrote regularly to assure his parents that he was in good health, or was recovering quickly and fully when illness did strike.

JD did not face London alone, but was supported by a community of family and friends built in part by his father's participation in Quaker merchant networks. Closed membership excluded Quakers from the joint stock companies that engaged in trade regulated by the state through various navigation acts, leaving unregulated American trade as the only option for members of a religious sect also excluded from ecclesiastical, political, and legal professions in England. Intermarriage strengthened the ties among Quaker merchant families who tended to live close to one another in London, and who used family connections and apprenticeships to expand their networks.[3] Before his first marriage in 1710, Samuel lived in London for a year apprenticing with two Quaker tobacco merchant families, the Hanburys and the Barclays. JD's first stop when he arrived in the city was John Hanbury's splendid house on Great Tower Street. By the 1750s, Hanbury was London's foremost tobacco import merchant, and his dealings with planters in Virginia and Maryland meant that his political connections were as strong as his economic ones.[4] JD spent time with the Barclay family socially, and he also kept his father informed of the status of the accounts the Barclays managed that made his education possible.

JD was in London during a time of political turmoil brought on by the death of prime minister Henry Pelham on March 6, 1754, and George II's declaration of war against France on May 17, 1756. Pelham strove for political stability, and the peace and prosperity that followed the end of the War of the Austrian Succession in 1748 made that goal attainable. That peace, however, came at the expense of the relationship with his older brother, Thomas Pelham-Holles, duke of Newcastle, who had served as defense minister since 1739. The two clashed over foreign policy, and after the war, Newcastle became increasingly jealous of his brother's power. They were also at odds over Newcastle's plan as foreign minister to use subsidies to secure foreign alliances. Although Pelham wanted to reduce government spending to ensure domestic support, he acquiesced to his brother's wishes, knowing that a public rift would seriously damage the Whig party.

For JD, young and idealistic, the mechanics of the 1754 election stood in sharp relief to the principles espoused by the Whig lawyers he was studying at the Middle Temple. By the 1750s, it seemed that those calling themselves Whigs had compromised Parliament's victory over royal authority in the Glorious Revolution through bribery and rampant corruption. JD wrote about the election with references to both English and ancient Roman thinkers.

Pelham's death shifted power to his indecisive older brother, whose missteps hastened war with the French. Britain's inability to defeat the French in the Mediterranean, combined with news of war in the American colonies, caused JD concern at the conclusion of his stay in London. He returned home before Pelham's administration fell apart and William Pitt assumed power in November 1756.

Even as JD watched English politics with consternation, he kept an eye on political developments in Pennsylvania, which were tumultuous enough to come under discussion in Parliament. The onset of the French and Indian War in 1754 roiled Pennsylvania at all levels. The pacifist Quaker Assembly's refusal to raise a militia to defend the western frontier created rifts between politicians and between the Assembly and its constituents, the consequences of which reverberated for the remainder of the colonial era. JD would have had a keen interest in attending the arguments before the Lords of Trade about the Pennsylvania situation (doc. 1:33), where the debate concerned whether the Penn family, with whom he was friendly, would retain proprietorship of the province.

In addition to the vivid description of English politics, these letters also provide readers an intimate view into JD's relationship with his parents and life at the Middle Temple. They likewise give us the most complete picture, of any set of JD's writings, of his character and personality.

---

[1] The Inns of Court are a group of four London institutions for legal education: Middle Temple, Inner Temple, Lincoln's Inn, and Gray's Inn. Exactly when they were founded is unknown, but they have existed at least since the Middle Ages and focus on training students in English rather than Roman law. Not all students were called to the bar; some did not qualify and some had other interests. Very few Americans attended, and they usually went to the Middle Temple.

Before 1815, only around 200 Americans were admitted to any of the Inns of Court. See Eric Stockdale and Randy J. Holland, *Middle Temple Lawyers and the American Revolution* (Eagan, MN: Thomson West, 2007).
[2] JD's half brothers, William (1711–1732) and Walter (1713–1728), both died while in London, and Samuel (b. 1715) is noted in the family Bible (PHi-Logan) only as having died abroad.
[3] Jordan Landes, *London Quakers in the Trans-Atlantic World: The Creation of an Early Modern Community* (New York: Palgrave Macmillan, 2015), 84–85, 104.
[4] See *ODNB* and Jacob M. Price, "The Great Quaker Business Families of Eighteenth-Century London: The Rise and Fall of a Sectarian Patriciate," in *The World of William Penn*, ed. Richard S. Dunn and Mary Maples Dunn (Philadelphia: University of Pennsylvania Press, 1986), 379.

3
To Samuel Dickinson, December 18, 1753

A portion of the page is missing, torn down the right side. The probable characters have been supplied in square brackets.

London Dec[embe]r 18[th] 1753

Honoured Father,[1]

I have the happiness to acquaint You of my safe Arrival in London this day, in good health & well recoverd from the fatigue of Our Voyage, tho[ugh] very much reduc'd with the first part of it. In Six weeks We got within Seventy Leagues of the Mouth of the Channel, but were taken with Easterly Winds that kept Us out Eight Days; attended with such foul thick Weather that We run up as far as Beachy-Head[2] without Seeing Land, which was the first We made, the thirteenth of this month. Yesterday We came by Gravesend;[3] this morning to Woolwich,[4] & to day about three a'Clock I got to Mr. Hanbury's,[5] from whence I now write— I was receivd by him, with that Humanity & Kindness, which distinguish the Character of that Gentleman: He has been so go[od] as to promise Me all ~~the~~{His} Assistance in transacting my Affa[irs] which ~~is~~{th}ere is no doubt of his performing, & to Me will be the greatest Obligation— He just now informd Me of this Opportu[nity] which is the most acceptable in the world to Me, as it affords Me the Power of quieting the fears of the best of Parents[—] It shall be, Honoured Father, my Constant Study & Endeavour, to ans[wer] all your Expectations, & my Dear Mother's,[6] & to satisfy all your desires, which I hope You will believe, I Esteem the chief Happiness of my Life— It will give Me the greatest Delight at this distance [to?]{fre}quently to hear from You, & beg that You will believe Me Honoured Parents to be with the greatest Sincerity

Your most Dutiful & most Affectionate Son
John Dickinson

P.S. Please to give my [*illegible*]{L}ove to my Dear Brother[7] & desire him to be industrious—
Please to excu[se] this scrawl, for I write i[n a gre]at hurry—

[*Samuel Dickinson*:] <from John Dickinson in London Dated the 18:th of Decem[be]r 1753
Rec[eive]d the 10:th of March 1754 / Decemb[e]r the 18:th 1753— The Day he Gott to Lon[don]>

To / Charles Goldsborough Choptank Maryland[8] To the particular Care of D Wolstenholme In Annapolis[9]

ALS (PPL-JDFP)

---

[1] Samuel Dickinson (1689–1760) was a planter and jurist born in Talbot Co., Md. He inherited 2,500 acres of land from his father, William Dickinson (1658–1718), and by the time of his death owned 9,000 acres in Maryland and over 3,000 acres in Delaware. He never received formal legal training, but studied the law on his own and served as both a justice of the peace (i.e., a judge in a trial court) and a judge of the Court of Common Pleas. He married JD's mother in 1731 after the death of his first wife, Judith Troth, in 1729 (*ODNB*).

[2] Beachy Head is a chalk headland in East Sussex.

[3] Gravesend is about twenty-five mi. east of London on the River Thames.

[4] Woolwich is about ten mi. east of central London on the River Thames, and is now part of the London metropolitan area.

[5] John Hanbury (1700–1758) was a Quaker tobacco merchant with a firm on Great Tower Street who worked as a commission merchant for prominent Virginia planters and independent merchants in Maryland. He was very close with the governors of both colonies, as well as with key figures in the Pelham and Newcastle ministries (*ODNB*).

[6] Mary Cadwalader Dickinson (1700–1776) was born in Marion, Pa., to a Quaker family that had emigrated from Merioneth Co., Wales, for religious liberty. Her father, John Cadwalader (1677–1734), had been a schoolteacher but moved his family to Philadelphia in 1700 and later became a dry-goods merchant. He also served as a tax collector, on Philadelphia's Common Council, as a judge for the Court for the Trial of Negroes, and five terms as an assemblyman (*LLP*, 2:249–53). Her younger brother was the physician Thomas Cadwalader (1707–1779). She married Samuel Dickinson on Nov. 4, 1731.

[7] Philemon Dickinson (1739–1809) was JD's full brother. He became a general in the New Jersey militia during the Revolutionary War, a Continental Congress delegate from Delaware and New Jersey, and a US senator from Pennsylvania from 1790 to 1793. JD's other full brother, Thomas (b. 1734), is noted in the family Bible (PHi-Logan) as having "died young."

[8] Charles Goldsborough (1707–1767) was a Maryland lawyer and large landholder who held many offices, including serving on the governor's council from 1762 to 1767. He married JD's half sister, Elizabeth Dickinson (1721–1748), on Aug. 2, 1739, in an Anglican ceremony, causing a rift between Samuel Dickinson and the Society of Friends. Choptank is a port town on the Choptank River in present-day Caroline Co., Md.

[9] Daniel Wolstenholme (d. 1795) was an Annapolis merchant. He later moved to St. Mary's Co., which he represented in the Maryland Assembly, 1765–66 and 1768–70.

1754

4

To Samuel Dickinson, January 18, 1754

London Jan[uar]y 18[th] 1754

Honoured Father,

It is with the greatest Happiness that I can acquaint You with my Arrival in England—A Happiness which arises infinitely less from a Sense of my own Safety, than from the Ease and Delight, which I am certain it will give to the best and tend'rest of Parents. As I knew the fears and Apprehensions, your Affection would subject You to on my Account; I seizd an Opportunity that offerd itself the first day I came to London, of Writing to You; but as the Ship went to the Western Shore of Maryland, and the Letter may miscarry; I now can inform You with more Certainty, that I arrivd in this City on the 18th day of December, after a passage of Eight Weeks and three days, quite hearty and well. The Sea as I expected, disagreed with Me very much, and kept Me confind for five weeks to the Cabbin and mostly to my bed. For the first two weeks, We had excessive bad Weather off the Coast of America, which was succeeded by fair Winds for a Month; and then at about Sixty Leagues from the mouth of the Channel, We were taken with Easterly winds, that kept Us plying off for Eight Days; When it came about to S[outh] W[est] by W[est] with such dark thick fogs that We run up as far as Beachy-Head, before We made Land.

I left our Vessel at Woolwich; took water there with Capt[ain] Hill to Blackwall,[1] & from thence walkd to [*illegible*]{L}ondon: Where the Capt[ain] conveyd Me to Mr. Hanbury's. That Gentleman receivd Me, with all the Kindness I could wish for: And promisd Me all the Assistance & Advice in his power, which his Character is a Security of his performing. He knew the Relationship between Robert Goldsborough,[2] & said he supposd it would be very agreable to Me to see him, and that as I was to Settle in the same manner with him; He could inform Me of all the Steps to be taken better than himself. This was extremely agreable to Me, & as there was A Gentleman in his Compting House,[3] then going to the Temple, I waited on him; and to my great Joy soon found Robert. No person could be more rejoiced than We both were to find an old Acquaintance at such a distance from the rest of Our Friends. He very generously made Me an offer of part of his Bed—till I could procure Chambers of my own; which was too acceptable for Me to refuse— Thus by his Goodness I became immediately settled as agreably as I could wish. I immediately enterd myself in the Middle Temple as he had done.[4] By this means I became introduc'd to Mr.

7

Hopkins Treasurer of the [*page break*] Temple;[5] A Gentleman of great Politeness, and Knowledge in the Law; from whose Acquaintance I hope for many Advantages. He has been so kind as to promise Me all the Assistance in his Power; & I am now intimate with him. The Letting of the Chambers belongs to his Office; & by his Advice I have a taken a Sett.[6] He was so good as to let Me have them at £12 [per] Ann[um] tho[ugh] the constant Price had been £15:[7] And besides he has orderd them to be new floord, & fitted up in the genteelest manner. I expect to be in them in March, for as they must be whitewashd and new painted, I must stay till they are quite dry'd: Till then I shall continue with my kind Friend; so that by the time I remove, this way of Life, which would otherwise have been very strange, will be familiar to Me, as indeed it is already. Every person lives without Controul in his Chambers; & according to his Disposition, may either prosecute his Studies with the greatest Quiet, in them, or employ them to the worst Purposes. A Laundress attends by seven in the Morning, lights your fire, brings Us Bread Milk & Butter, & puts on our Tea-kettle. We wait on Ourselves at Breakfast, which is no manner of Trouble: And after that She returns, makes our Beds, & sweeps the Rooms. We then follow our Studies till three or four o'Clock, which in Winter is just dark: then We go to a Chophouse & dine; after which We step into the Coffeehouse, & in a little time return to our Chambers for the Evening. This Account of one day will serve for all the rest; except the occasional breaks of Visits Business &c This manner of Living is very far from being so agreable as the delightful time I have spent with You; but I like it much better than Lodging in any family; and I believe it is as cheap; but with the greatest Care, it will be expensive in London. Mr. Hanbury at my first Arrival, askd Me, if you were acquainted, with the Expense of living here. I answerd that You were not certain, but that You were of Opinion I might live on £100 [per] Ann[um].

He said Robert Goldsborough livd as frugally as any Young fellow, to make any genteel Appearance, & that he could not do with less than £120 a year: besides the Cost of the first Outset, which will amount to forty Pounds more.[8] I thought it my Duty to acquaint You immediately with these things, as they are a little different from what We imagind: But this I beg, Honoured Father, You will believe, that all the Care in my Power shall be taken in every step; that I always shall preserve the warmest, the gratefullest Remembrance, of the innumerable Blessings your unequald Goodness has bestowd: I pray You to be [*page break*] Assur'd that no distance can obliterate, my Sense of my Duty; no Temptations damp my earnest Endeavours to answer your Expectations. That pleasing Prospect, can afford Me Comfort even here, gives new Life to my Industry, & makes London agreable: But never shall I feel that calm, delightful Happiness I have enjoyd, till I see You again. As to the Dangers, A Youth is expos'd to; they depend entirely on the Choice of One's Company. I am only acquainted with Robert, Mr. Hopkins, & some few others, who are very sober & industrious, & at the same perfect Gentlemen: I{A}nd I will venture to affirm, that any person who procedes with the same Caution, will find no more dangers in London than elsewhere. Virtuous Company is the strongest Guard to a person's Morals; he not only reaps a benefit from their Conversation; but by them he is preservd from falling into bad, & defended from Attacks on his Innocence: And I hope to return to You, not only pure in my Morals, but improvd in every thing You desire: Especially in my Business. I have not yet seen any of the Courts, but this month a Term begins, which I design to attend: I am sorry I could not bring my Books with me: for as I am now to polish myself for the last time, to make my publick Appearance; I am resolvd to omit nothing in manner or Substance, that can contribute to my service: And it will be impossible for Me to read to such advantage, in a single Author, as where I have an opportunity of searching all the References, & examining every point of Law through all its stages: therefore if You approve of it, I shall be glad to have my Books transmitted to me by the first Opportunity; and I dare say they will suffer more in Philad[elphi]a lying loose, than well packd in a trunk at Sea: but this I entirely submit to your better knowledge.

I am sorry that I can give You, but a poor account of Tob[acc]o Mr. Hanbury tells me, there never was so great a Glut. Some of the best Tob[acc]o has been sold at a penny 5/8[ths] But there is very little demand for that—So that the Merchants are waiting for the French buying in the Spring, which may give some rise to the Price.[9] I should be extremely glad that what Tob[acc]o You have, may be consignd to Mr. Hanbury. No man can treat Me more kindly than he does, & he professes great Esteem for You. I believe Success has made no alteration in him; he says the obligations he lyes under to You, entitle Me to more Services than it will be in his Power to perform: And I am sure he will do Me all the favours he can. I am grievd Honourd Father to think myself at so great a distance from such dear persons, but I beg You will [*in left margin:*] frequently remember Me, & let Me have the Happiness of hearing from You, And I hope in whatever part of the world I may be, I shall always approve Myself your most Dutiful & most Affectionate Son

John Dickinson

P. S. Please to remember Me to all that Enquire.

[*in left margin of second page, Samuel Dickinson:*] <Jan[uar]y the 18:[th] 1754 to me>

ALS (PPL-JDFP)

---

[1] Captain Hill was master of the vessel on which JD had traveled from America, the *Scipio*, which sailed regularly between England and Maryland or the Capes of Virginia. Blackwall is an area along the River Thames in the east end of London. "To take water" is a now-obsolete usage meaning to take a boat on the Thames (*OED*).

[2] Robert Goldsborough (1733–1788) was Charles Goldsborough's son and JD's half nephew. He came to the Middle Temple in 1752, later served as a delegate from Maryland to the First and Second Continental Congresses, and helped draft that state's 1776 constitution.

[3] Counting house, where accounting and correspondence were undertaken.

[4] JD was admitted to Middle Temple on Dec. 21, 1753. See John Dickinson Admission in "Admissions to House and Chambers, 1737–1758," UkLoMT-MT.3/AHC/3.

[5] Charles Hopkins (c. 1717–1776) was actually under treasurer. He was the Middle Temple librarian, 1750–52, and under treasurer from 1752 until his death. The treasurer was not merely a financial officer but actually the principal officer of the Temple "in whom is lodged the power of executing all Laws and Orders, and the care of the House during his Treasurership." Where the treasurer was elected annually, the under treasurer, whose position was more permanent, had significant duties. He "transacts all affairs of the House under the direction of the Treasurer, enters all Admissions both to the House and Chambers." Charles Worsley, *Master Worsley's Book on the History and Constitution of the Honourable Society of the Middle Temple* (London: Chiswick Press, 1910), 166, 175.

[6] JD took "that Chamber with its Appurtenances Situate in the Middle Temple Lane No. 2. four pair of Stairs on the North side of the Stair Case together with the Chamber consolidated therewith on the South side of No: 1." (JD's surrender of chambers, Feb. 9, 1757, UkLoMT-MT.21/1/94/2/11).

[7] Even Hanbury's adjusted numbers put JD's expenses lower than those of most colonial students, who budgeted between £250 and £300 a year. See Colbourn, 1:251, n.22.

[8] The cash books of the Middle Temple Treasurer's Office record that on Jan. 3, 1755, they received 9 pounds 9 shillings from JD for "three Quarters Rent of his Chamber," UkLoMT MT.2/TCB/18.

[9] Maryland planters experienced the boom and bust cycle of the tobacco economy. Records from America, where tobacco prices presumably mirrored London prices, indicate that in 1751 or 1752, tobacco reached its highest price ever to that date. Perhaps predictably, 1753 saw a high in tobacco imported to Great Britain, mostly from Maryland and Virginia. The period from 1753 to 1756 saw a substantial drop in tobacco prices and imports, with prices losing at least a quarter of their high value by 1755 and imports dropping by almost half to a low in 1756, before both began to rebound. By the 1750s, around 80 percent of the American tobacco imported to Great Britain was re-exported. See, for example, *Historical Statistics of the United States: Colonial Times to 1970* (Washington, DC: US Dept. of Commerce, Bureau of the Census, 1975), 1162–63, 1166–67, 1189–91, 1197–98.

5

To Mary Cadwalader Dickinson, January 19, 1754

London Jan[uar]y 19th 1754

Honoured Mother,

    When I take my Pen to write to You, I am fixd in Doubt, what to say, or not to say. To pour out the Tenderness of my Soul is impossible; and I know not what to omit. I am now removd at a vast Distance from You, but so far from feeling any Slackness in my Affection, that it glows if possible, with encreased Warmth: Either because that my Attention now comprehends in one View, that continual Series of Actions, which before engagd my Love and Admiration separately; or that my Mind now incapable of making Returns of Duty in those Offices, which I shall ever esteem it the Supreme Happiness of my Life to discharge, exerts itself in an unbounded Flow of silent Gratitude & Rapture: Since then my Circumstances deny Me so delightful an Employment, the only Comfort I can enjoy, is that You will believe Absence alone prevents it; And that my Heart regrets the Necessity, that deprives Me of so great a Pleasure. This Favour I expect more from your generous Kindness, than my own merit; for the fondest Reflection can inform me, how infinitely short I have fallen of the Sum of my Duty to such unparalleld Goodness: But need I promise that my Life shall be devoted to the Recompense?

I have been greatly uneasy at the Terrors, with which I know your Tenderness has been alarmd on my Account: And am very sorry if this is the first News of my Safety. By Divine Providence I have been landed in Security these four weeks; & have since enjoyd my Health very well, except a Cold I catch'd for a Seasoning but that I shook off in Eight days; and am now very hearty. And I may say of London, it has been rather troublesome than unkind to Me. At first entring {it,} I found myself in a Social Wilderness; as much at a loss, amongst Houses and Men, as in the strangest Forest: And in a much more disagreable Scituation; for instead of Peace & Quietness, I was surrounded with Noise Dirt & Business, all equally inconvenient;{:} and for which I believe London may vye with any place. The Streets are crooked, & many of them narrow, but they hardly have Justice done them by Travellers; for by common Fame, one would imagine there were nothing but dark alleys, with difficulty to be squeezd thro[ugh]; Whereas a great Number of them are very wide, & some extremely beautiful: But I can{not} say I have met with any thing very surprizing: I was tir'd with the vast extent of the City, & puzzled with the winding of the Streets; but as I {had} heard or seen particular Descriptions of every thing, Nothing excited my Admiration, but only confirmd or lessend, as it frequently happend, my former Notions: Though there certainly are many grand and Noble Works. The two bridges,[1] St. Pauls[2] & some others are prodigious things, but in my Opinion, they are less astonishing, as they seem necessary, and proper for the Glory of so great a City, & in some [*page break*] Measure do but answer, what one might expect from its Magnificence.

I have not yet been any further in the Country, than the Park,[3] which at this Season affords no very pleasant Scene; It is adornd by the Mall, Canal, Buckingham & St. James's;[4] but receives no great Embellishment from the last, which does not answer the Dignity of its Owner. I had a diversion here which I did not expect of Skeeting[5] in some late hard Weather, on Rosamond's Pond.[6] You will not imagine I have been a Stranger at the Play Houses, but have found nothing so striking as Report feigns. Some Actors, especially Garrick & Mrs. Pritchard,[7] are exact Pictures of Life, & easily perswade You they are the very persons they represent: but far the greater number have something so stiff, & affected about them, that they are disgustful to the least Nicety. But these Diversions are too high seasond for Me; they g[r]{l}are agreably for a time, but they blunt the Sight to more lasting, more sincere pleasures: Nor do I think I shall ever find in England, that calm, that peaceful Delight, I have so often enjoyd in Kent:[8] But I should be the most ungrateful Creature in the world, if the Hospitality of its Inhabitants, did not render London agreable. I think I never was treated with more Tenderness & Kindness, by my nearest Friends, than I have been by perfect Strangers to Me. Professions of Friendship seem made here with Sincerity; & kept with Truth. When You are invited to be free at a house, it is expected You will be so: And that Affectation of Appearance, so common with little Breeding and great Pride, and so destructive of Familiarity is here abolishd. Those re-repeated Apologies for Dinner, that great Uneasiness least a guest should be starvd, are quite out fashion: You are welcome to what is found, & if the Lady wishes for any thing better; She is too well acquainted with the world, to render it more disagreable by her Concern. At Mr. Hanbury's I am entirely at home, for so he commands Me to be, & he would not like it, if I were to stand on Ceremony. I drop in at Dinner, Tea or Supper, & pass away two or three hours with the greatest Happiness. Mr. Hanbury, I really believe is one of the best of Men, & his Wife[9] of Women. They are as free & sociable with me, as their Son; they are extremely kind, & am now quite familiar with them. They both [*page break*] Possess a great Share of open Generosity and Goodness. They ha[ve] a Son, with whom I am well acquainted, about my Age; and a Daughter who is married.[10] I have also had the Happiness of meeting with Mrs. Anderson:[11] She heard of my being in Town, and sent Me an Invitation to Dinner on Christmass day; She was exceeding glad to See Me, & receivd Me with the greatest signs of Joy and regard. We had a great deal of Conversation together, and She enquird very affectionately after You. Mr. Anderson receivd Me very politely; they live very genteely, & have a pretty family of Children.[12] She seems to be in a poor State of Health, but is a fine agreable Lady. I frequently go to see them, & am quite intimate there. I have been introduc'd by a Letter I had from Mr. Moland[13] to A Sister of his, married to a rich Banker: I am treated there with the greatest Kindness, & I often visit them. They have a pretty Country Seat, about five miles off, where I expect to spend some very pleasant Days in the Spring & Summer, for they have given Me a very warm Invitation. Thus I have got acquainted in as many families as I wish for, &

with persons of Fashion & Politeness, from whose Conversation I hope for the greatest Advantages. Anthony Bacon[14] has given me a very kind Invitation to make free at his House: And Elias Bland[15] has offerd Me all the Services in his Power. I meet with a great many old Acquaintance here. Robert Goldsborough reads hard, & will make a very pretty figure at the Bar: He behaves with all the Affection of a Brother towards Me; & is{I} shall stay with him, till I get into my own Chambers. I frequently See Nichee Hammond;[16] he is very hearty, but his Uncle has disappointed him; for on his Arrival, he found him just married. He just now informd me of Mr. Wynkoop's Death;[17] for which I am much concernd. Dr. Morris[18] is not yet saild from hence; he treats Me with the greatest Kindness. I frequently visit him; and he has introducd Me to some of his Acquaintance, very agreable, sensible Men: He is not desirous of returning, but will be oblidgd to it, in the Spring.

This moment I rec[eive]d a Letter from my Honoured Father, [per] the Beulah Capt[ain] Richey;[19] with a{A} delightful Account of your health; & as I have finishd my Letter to him, I must beg leave to answer it here: The letter by Coward I have not rec[eive]d but my heart [*page break*] Swells with Transports of Gratitude, to find I am so often rememberd by You: Nor ever will I forget my Duty to such tender & indulgent Parents. Nothing shall be wanting on my part to answer your fondest Hopes, & convince the world, that many advantages are to be acquird in London. Labour is the Path to Glory; & by Divine Command, "In the Sweat of the Brow"[20] are the Goods of Life to be purchas'd. With Patience and Resolution I submit to the Task, no longer dreadful, while such bright Rewards appear. beyond: Can I madly break thro[ugh] the bonds of Duty; bonds tied with such uncommon Goodness; Can I forfeit the Happiness of all my Life, to the dull, the stupid Pleasures of a dreamy Idleness, or the wild gusts of racking Guilt? There needs but Thought to be secure. I beg I may hear frequently from You: that I may often Enjoy that rapturous Entertainment, every Repetition of your Kindness kindles in my Souls{:} that glorious Prospect of my [*illegible*]{Honour, &} your Happiness. Your Wishes reckond my Voyage too fast. We did not get out of the Capes of Virginia, till the 27th of Oct[obe]r— The 25th We got opposite to Hampton, but the wind being ahead, We were oblidgd to run into Hampton Roads, where We lay till Saturday the 27th When We left the Road in the Afternoon, & at night run out. We then had excessive bad Weather for a fortnight; that We made very little way, lying to, most of the time; & consequently rolling [*illegible*]{at a} great rate: So that by the 15th Nov[embe]r the date of my Honour'd Father's Letter,[22] We were about halfway, When You imagind Us [*illegible*]{two thirds} over. The bad Weather reducd Me so low, I did not recover it all the way over, but the two last Weeks, I walkd the Deck pretty well. What made the Sea more agreable to one so weakly, was the most uncommon Care & Tenderness of the Capt[ain] It was even beyond belief: He not only endeavourd to divert Me with Chat, but condescended to the meanest Offices; nor could I prevent him. He is a man of as much Honesty & Goodness, as ever I knew—the more I knew him, the more I likd him. He introducd Me to Gale & Bell, where often visit & who are very kind. I should have been very glad the 14 hog[shea]ds had come to Hanbury.

I have rec[eive]d a [*illegible*]{p}retty Letter from my dear pretious Brother.[23] Do encourage him, & write by every opportunity to him. I know by Experience the Effect of repeated Admonitions, & how soon advice is blotted from young minds, unless again & again inculcated. The dear fellow is ambitious, but the Levity of Childhood will get the better of Glory, unless supported by Incitement. He tells Me, he has been head of the Class, ever since I left Philadelphia. Do encourage the Pretious fellow, his Happiness depends on it.

[*in left margin:*] I could write Honoured Mother, to You much longer, but as I shall have many Opportunities, I will now conclude with prayers for the Happiness of You & my Honoured Father, Your most Dutiful and most Affectionate Son

John Dickinson

[*in top margin of second page, Samuel Dickinson:*] <Jan[uar]y the 19.[th] 1754 to <u>Mamey</u>>

ALS (PPL-JDFP)

---

[1] London Bridge and Westminster Bridge, which finished construction in 1750.

[2] St. Paul's Cathedral finished construction in 1710.

[3] St. James's Park in Westminster was created under James I's (1566–1625) direction, and later remodeled during the Restoration (1660) under Charles II (1630–1685).

[4] The mall is the road that runs east from Buckingham House and borders the north side of St. James's Park. A canal 2,560 ft. long and 125 ft. wide, lined on each side with avenues of trees, is the centerpiece of St. James's park (under Charles II's redesign). Buckingham House (purchased by George III [1738–1820] in 1761 and later reconstructed into Buckingham Palace) lies west of the park, and St. James's Palace (George II's residence) is north of it.

[5] That is, skating. Author Jonathan Swift (1667–1745) noted in 1710 that "Rosamond's Pond [is] full of the rabble sliding and with skates, if you know what those are" (*OED*).

[6] Rosamond's Pond (which no longer exists) sat at the west end of the park, near Buckingham House.

[7] David Garrick (1717–1779) was an English actor and manager of the Theatre Royal in Covant Garden. Hannah Pritchard (1711–1768), an English tragic and comedic actress, was a member of his company.

[8] Kent Co., Del., where Samuel and Mary Dickinson lived.

[9] Anna Osgood Hanbury (1705–1754).

[10] The son, Osgood Hanbury (1731–1784), continued his father's business but reduced Chesapeake trade during the imperial crisis and American Revolution. In 1770, he helped found the London bank of Hanbury, Taylor, Lloyd, which ultimately became Lloyds Bank (*ODNB*). He later served as attorney for the Norris family, into which JD married in 1770 (see James Pemberton to Capel and Osgood, Sept. 19, 1766, PHi-Logan). The daughter, Anna Hanbury Barnard (1732–1792), was the wife of Thomas Barnard.

[11] Rebecca Covington Lloyd Anderson (1713–1774) of Somerset Co., Md., was the wife of wealthy London merchant William Anderson (c. 1709–1771). Her father was Maj. Gen. Edward Lloyd (1670–1718), who served as royal governor of Maryland from 1709 to 1714.

[12] Rebecca Covington Lloyd Anderson had five children at this time: three sons, James Anderson (c. 1744–c. 1785), Edward Anderson (d. 1774), and William Anderson, and two daughters, Sarah (Sally) Anderson and Marion (Mazey) Anderson (d. before 1788). Her youngest daughter, Harriot Rebecca Anderson, was apparently the child that Rebecca was expecting in 1756 (see 1:34 below).

[13] JD's mentor, John Moland (c. 1700–1761). See doc. 2:25, Obituary of John Moland.

[14] Anthony Bacon (c. 1717–1786) was born in England but raised in Talbot Co., Md. He moved to London in the 1740s and became a tobacco merchant and later a military supplier. As a member of Parliament from 1764 to 1784, and as a pamphleteer, he supported the government's full authority over the colonies but argued that taxing them was inexpedient. On May 3, 1754, he, along with London apothecary William Campbell, cosigned JD's bond to the Middle Temple in the amount of £20 (see doc. 1:12, below).

[15] Elias Bland (d. 1780) was a London Quaker merchant recently returned from Philadelphia, where he had been trying to resolve his debt issues.

[16] Nicholas Hammond, Jr., (c. 1733–1783) was the son of Nicholas Hammond (1695–1736) and Mary Dyer Hammond (d. 1778). Although Nicholas, Jr., was born in Philadelphia, his father was from the Isle of Jersey, and Nicholas, Jr., returned there.

[17] Abraham Wynkoop (1703–1753), a Sussex Co., Del., planter and merchant, married Mary Dyer Hammond, his second wife, and thus became Nicholas Hammond, Jr.'s, stepfather.

[18] Possibly Robert Hunter Morris (1700–1764), who departed London in June to serve as deputy governor of Pennsylvania from 1754 to 1756, although there is no indication that Morris was a doctor of any sort.

[19] John Richey (Ritchie) was captain of the ship *Beulah*.

[20] Gen. 3:19.

[21] Hampton Roads is a channel at the mouths of the James and Elizabeth Rivers in the Cheasapeake Bay.

[22] Not found.

[23] Philemon Dickinson.

6

To [Richard Peters], January 22, 1754

Honoured [Sir],[1]

I lately receivd a Letter from my Uncle Cadwalader, inclosing one from You to Mr. Penn, in my favou[r.][2]

I return You Sir, my sincere thanks for this Kindness, and hope my future Conduct will engage the Continuance of your Regard. This I shall account a great Happiness, and shall constantly endeavour to deserve.

I am Sir, Your most Obedient humble Servant
John Dickinson

London
Jan[ua]ry 22.^d 1754

ALS (PHi-Logan)

---

[1] Richard Peters (c. 1704–1776), an Anglican minister, served as secretary and clerk of Pennsylvania's Provincial Council from 1743 to 1762.

[2] Second son of William Penn (1644–1718), Thomas Penn (1702–1775), governor of Pennsylvania, served as proprietor of the colony along with his brothers, John (1700–1746) and Richard (1706–1771), from 1746 to 1771, and then alone from 1771 to 1775. Cadwalader's letter to JD has not been found; JD quoted Peters's letter to Penn of Oct. 1, 1753, in doc. 1:7, below.

7

To Mary Cadwalader Dickinson, March 8, 1754

London March 8th—1754

Honoured Mother,

As I know the great Pleasure, You always receive in hearing of my Health; and as I sincerely participate in your delight, I cannot neglect any Opportunity of Writing, tho[ugh] I can say nothing worth your seeing. I have not yet got into my own Chambers, but still continue with my kind Friend: I grow heartier every Day, & am in great Hopes, not only of enjoying my Health, while here; but that my Stay in England will strengthen my Constitution, & confirm it, for the future part of my Life. There are numberless Instances of it, in my Countrymen, even within the Temple; Who have come here, in a much worse State, than I did, & in two or three Years, have become different Persons: Indeed I begin already to hear some Jests on the difference between Roast Beef, & Hominy.[1]

London is now grown much more familiar to Me, & as Spring approaches, more agreable; the Streets are more dry & clean, which makes much better Walking. The Gloominess of Winter going off, & the Sun making more frequent & friendly Visits, the City is much more pleasant: For most of the Weather, since I have been here, has been so dull & foggy, that We scarce ever saw his face; but now all things begin to look lively, & I have taken several Walks about the Suburbs, & a little Way into the Country, which is extremely beautiful. The fields beyond St. James's towards Kensington,[2] are inconceivably delightful: The Serpentine River glides through them, whose Banks are coverd with Grass, & Regular as the Nicest Parterres.[3] In a fine Day, those fields are filld with People in Coaches, on Horseback, and on foot, rambling about for an Airing. The Mall though, is the most frequented Walk, & is crowded with a gay Assembly, amongst whom, it is very agreable to mix, & Saunter an hour, before Dinner; this is an Entertainment I often indulge

Myself in; not only because it is very diverting, but useful; As Walking is almost the only Exercise I use; And to recreate the Mind, at the same time, We refresh the body, is doubly beneficial. But not all the Diversions of London, shall make Me forget my [*page break*] Duty, and what I owe to You, & Myself. As to the Vicious Pleasures of London, I know not what they are; I never hear of them, & never think of them. Good Company is the Bulwark of Virtue; I have been so happy as to get into a Set of Acquaintance, who know their Interest, & are resolvd to prosecute it. We never go into the way of Vice, & therefore are never injurd by her; for in contending with her, the greatest Cowardice is the Noblest Courage, & the most precipitate flight, the bravest Resistance.

> "Vice is a Monster, of so frightful Mien,
>
> As to be hated, needs but to be seen;
>
> Yet seen too oft; familiar with her face,
>
> We first endure, then pity; then embrace.["] Popes Essay on man.[4]

Fear & Diffidence being the greatest {Security,}, & my mind fully perswaded, {of} it, I think without paying Myself a Compliment, I may say I am in as little Danger, as most. Besides, No one can be more convincd of the Worthlessness of Vice, & the Eternal Consequence it is attended with, of tarnishing & destroying all real Pleasures: It dulls the Soul, to every thing, but its own Object, & tantalizes Us with Vain empty Preachings, amidst the Joys of a Paradise. From hence I conclude, that Vice is folly; Virtue, Wisdom; that Disappointment & Remorse; this, Success & [~~illegible~~]{Delight;} the first, Misery; the Latter, Happiness: This is the Voice of Reason, which Religion confirms by pronouncing, the one Heaven, the other, Hell. May I be able to preserve these Sentiments, & give them Life, by Practize.

I lately rec[eive]d a Letter from Uncle Cadwalader, inclosing a Letter from Mr. Richard Peters to Mr. Penn, in my behalf; A Copy of which follows:

Honourd Sir,

Mr. John Dickinson, Son of Justice Dickinson of Kent County, who has studied the Law, under Mr. Moland, went to London this Summer to compleat his Education, & thinking it to be his Duty, to wait on You, desird my Recommendations, which I very gladly give him, for I know him to have excellent Parts, and a sweet Disposition, and I believe will prove an useful Person to the Counties,[5] or any other place, where he shall think proper to settle. I am

Your Honour's most Obedient humble Servant

Richard Peters Philad[elphi]a

1st—Oct[obe]r 1753— [*page break*]

I have not yet had time to wait on his Honour, but shall in a day or two. I returnd my Compliments to Mr. Peters for his favour, in a Letter.[6] For [*illegible*]{w}hatever Reason, Mr. Peters may be pleasd to entertain so kind an Opinion of Me, it shall be my Endeavour, not only to preserve it, but if in my Power to encrease it. Indeed what little Reputation I have been so happy as to acquire in my Native Country, I shall always look upon as a Pledge of my good behaviour: I am not so unknown, but many Observations will be made on Me; and perhaps People's Expectations may be raisd, by the Pains that have been taken to Usher Me into the World: Let Me be ever so insensible to the Call of Honour, intoxicated with Pleasure, or bewitchd by Idleness, I cannot be so unfeeling of Shame, as to encounter publick Infamy, which surely attends neglected Opportunities of Improvement. No! I am resolvd to return with Credit, or Never: Shall every one's Eyes be fixd on Me for a Month, & then drawn off with a Sneer for their Mistake: Gazd at a While, & neglected & despised the Rest of my days: I dread these things more, than to neglect the Means of avoiding them: And tho[ugh] no Child, Honoured Mother, can have so affectionate, so respectful a Tenderness for any Parent, as I have for You, & my Honourd Father, & tho[ugh] I declare amidst all the Pleasures of London, I have not known a thousandth part of the Joy, I feel with You, Yet I stay here most willingly, as I hope it will enable Me to return to your Happiness.

I expected, My Honourd Mother, before this time, to have receivd a Line from You, & if You knew how highly I value such a favour, I am sure I should not have expected in Vain.

Mr. Hanbury & his Lady, continue the same Goodness towards Me, & ever will, for it is in their Nature. I have as large an Acquaintance as I wish for: & these quite agreable. About a week ago, at the Tragedy of Venice Preservd[7] I saw his Majesty.[8] He is a small Man, but has a very grand walk. He has Nothing else that is remarkable, except that he had the most chearful face in the whole house. The Moment he came in, he clapt up his Glass, & took a Survey of all the Boxes, but did not bow to any, tho[ugh] I observd, he did to some Noblemen that came into his box, a little While after him. At the End of every [*page break*] Act, he got up with all the Liveliness of a Man of Forty, & stood for eight or ten Minutes, till the next Act. He was receivd & dismist with a great Clap, & Nobody sate coverd all the time.

I heard lately by a Gentleman, who was informd by Mr. Groves, that Mr. Chew[9] is coming for England. I should be very glad to see him, but should be sorry to be oblidgd to so unhappy an occasion for it. If he is not come away, please to present my best Compliments to him, & his Lady.[10] I am very much grievd to hear of Mrs. Vining's death;[11] My Compliments to the good family; and to all my friends in general.
One of the Pimples is gone, & the other is going.

Honoured Mother, I beg that You will remember Me, & be assurd I desire no greater happiness in this World, than to be esteemd,
Your most Dutiful and most obedient Son,

John Dickinson

P.S. Please to remember my Love to my dear Brother, & tell him to write to Me by all Opportunities.

[*in top margin, Samuel Dickinson*:] <March the 8:th 1754 to Mamey—>

ALS (PPL-JDFP)

---

[1] Hominy: "Maize or Indian corn hulled and ground more or less coarsely and prepared for food by being boiled with water or milk" (*OED*).

[2] Kensington Palace is about two mi. west of St James's.

[3] Parterre: "A level space in a garden occupied by an ornamental arrangement of flower beds" (*OED*).

[4] Alexander Pope, *An Essay on Man* (London: J. and P. Knapton, 1753), 50.

[5] The part of the Penn proprietorship that became Delaware was known as the Three Lower Counties (New Castle, Kent, and Sussex) on Delaware, which had a separate legislature and courts since 1704.

[6] Not found.

[7] *Venice Preserv'd; or, A Plot Discover'd. A Tragedy* was a 1682 play by English dramatist Thomas Otway (1652–1685). It was performed at the Theatre Royal in Covent Garden on March 2, 1754 (*Public Advertiser* [London], March 2).

[8] George II (1683–1760) was crowned king of Great Britain and Ireland in 1727.

[9] Possibly Benjamin Chew (1722–1810), who was a Quaker-born Delaware planter with land adjacent to the Dickinsons' Poplar Hall. He concluded his education at the Middle Temple in 1744. At this time he represented Kent Co. in the Delaware Assembly, where he was the speaker. He became a Pennsylvania lawyer, legislator, and judge. Before the Revolution, he was attorney general and chief justice of the Supreme Court; afterward he was appointed president of the High Court of Errors and Appeals. There is no indication that Chew traveled to England around this time.

[10] Mary Galloway (1729–1755), daughter of John and Mary Galloway of Maryland's Western Shore, married Chew in 1747. After her death, Chew married Elizabeth Oswald (1734–1819).

[11] Rachel Ridgely Vining died in November.

8

To Samuel Dickinson, March 8, 1754

London March 8th—1754

Honoured Father,

A Duty is never so willingly performd, as when it is dictated by Inclination; And therefore, though I am under a filial Obligation to give You the Satisfaction of hearing from Me; Yet the inexpressible Pleasure, with which I assume my Pen, proceeds more from the Delight I take, in conversing tho' in so distant a manner, with a Person so dear & so honourd. I wrote to You last by the Myrtilla, but I cannot neglect any Opportunity of testifying my Affection,{.} I am now thoroughly convincd, that the Unhappiness of many People in this Life proceeds from the Excess of their Happiness. The Narrowness of the Human Mind, permits Us to Judge of Things only by Comparison; and where that cannot be made, We know things but very slightly: The Hearty & the Wealthy are in a great measure, ignorant of the Blessings they enjoy, because they are unacquainted with the Miseries, which they avoid, & which the Sick & Poor are subject to: So I now deplore the Want of your Company, when the loss of it, discovers its Value: You have always treated Me, Honoured Father, not only with the Goodness of a Parent, but the freedom & Tenderness of a Friend; the Bonds of Gratitude, have been added to the Ties of Nature; and I am indebted to You, not only for my Life, but for all the Blessings of it. For Me, Your Cares & Labours have been employd; and to You I owe that Knowledge (whatever it be) that must guide Me thro[ugh] the World. The kind affectionate Manner, in which it has been conveyd, shall stamp it on my Mind, & direct all my Actions to answer your Expectations, & fulfill your Desires. Your disinterested Wishes are only to See Me crownd with Happiness & Glory; and to disappoint them, will always be accounted by Me, not only Inconceivable Madness, but a Crime of the deepest Dye,{.} You on your part have given Me all the Advantages necessary, and now by Your Generosity I am placd, where all the Benefits to be acquird in my Profession, are to be reapd. I dayly behold Objects which call me to my Duty: Here may I be fird with Ambition at the Honours which are paid to deceased Merit: Here I view the Glory to which Industry exalts itself. I tread the Walks frequented by the Antient Sages of the Law; perhaps I Study in the Chambers, where A Coke or Plowden has meditated:[1] I am struck with Veneration, & when I read their Works, by these familiarising Reflections, I almost seem to converse with them. When I view the Hall, where the most important Questions have been debated, Where a Hampden, and a Holt[2] have opposd encroaching Power, and supported declining Justice, in short upon whose Judgments, the Happiness of a Nation has depended, I am filld with Awe & Reverence. When I see Men advancd by their own Application, to the highest Honours of their Country—My breast beats for Fame! Such are the Rewards of Diligence: The same means are in my Power: Why do I loiter? I sicken at their Glory, I turn [*page break*] from their{S}ight, I fly to Books, to Retirement, to Labour, & every Moment is an Age, till I am immersd in Study,

"And e'er he starts, a thousand Steps are lost"[3]

I now have an Opportunity of seeing and hearing the most learned Lawyers & the finest Speakers. Since my last, I have heard some of the greatest Men in England, perhaps in the World. The Lords Commissioners for Appeals for{rom} the Plantations, sit at the Cockpit,[4] once or twice a week: and Causes are managd there by the best Lawyers at the Bar. There I have heard the great Murray, Hume Campbell, Yorke and Forrester.[5] I might call my own Judgment in question, should I dare to disapprove of the Sollicitor's Eloquence, and perhaps such an Universal Character may influence Me, in his favour; but whatever be the Cause, I cannot forbear subscribing with all my heart to his establishd Fame: He enjoys from Nature, all the Advantages an Orator can wish for; His person is very good, and his Voice is Musick itself. His Language is not only easy & flowing, to captivate the Ear, but so refind as to delight the Mind, & his Arguments so nervous,[6] as to force the Assent of the Judgment. His Speeches don't please only, while warbled from his Tongue, but have such Purity & Strength, that they would bear the strictest Examination of the Nicest Criticks, & just as they are deliverd by him, would prove delightful; but not so delightful, as when enforcd by his engaging Address. In this, he undoubtedly has attaind the Height of Perfection: Every Motion speaks, Every Attitude has a Charm. His Action has nothing affected, nothing forcd in it; but seems a Confirmation of his Words; & if I may use the Expression, they are Twins. The Eye & Ear, are absolutely his Captives: And even in a bad Cause, the Judgment with difficulty rejects what is so powerfully recommended; & can scarce perswade itself, he is in the Wrong. And now Honourd Father, since I have fallen upon the Law, & its Professors; th{W}ith which, of all things, I am most Conversant, & may perhaps be most agreable to You; I must beg Leave to Entertain You a little longer on this Subject. Hume Campbell is a strong manly Speaker, but his Language is not so flowing, as the Sollicitor's, nor his manner so pleasing, but he is an Excellent Lawyer. Mr. Yorke, the Chancellor's[7] Son, is a Young Man, in great Business; but Whether he is a Man of great Abilities, is doubted by many People; Who do not allow him all the Merit, which perhaps he deserves, but Say, that such a Father may push a Son of no great Worth, with Eclat into the World. He speaks a little effeminately & is too tedious. Forrester is A Speaker of great Regularity & Exactness, but I do not think these last equal to the former two, nor are all equal to them. Hillary Term[8] came on the 23.ᵈ of January, when I had an Opportunity of seeing the Grandeur & Solemnity of the Courts of Law. The very Appearance of Justice is aweful, & the Dress of the Judges is calculated to inspire Respect; but how trifling, how despicable are these things, Compard with their Wisdom & Knowledge: The Badges of their Dignity are forgot in the Consideration of their Merit. At this Term I heard some of [*page break*] The most learned Arguments, disposd with the greatest Art & Method: Amongst others I heard one Sergeant Poole,[9] who is reckond as good a Special Pleader, as any in England, but {is} the most wretched

Speaker. He quoted numberless Authorities, & took the nicest Distinctions; but in the very words of the Books, which if ever he was oblidgd to quit, he seemd out of his Element, usd the oddest Terms, & with Repetitions & Questions spliced it out, till he came to another Authority. Many of his Brethren are like him, so that their heads are a kind of Index's to all Law books in general; And are Instances of the Necessity of a Lawyer's not confining himself barely to acquiring Knowledge, but of qualifying himself to communicate it to others: for as the clearest Ideas lose all their force by bad Expression, consequently the Art of Speaking is not beneath his Notice. Even some of the Judges themselves are Examples of this Truth; Which I had an Opportunity of observing in a Cause removd from the Exchequer[10] to the House of Lords, wherein they were calld upon to give their Opinions. I{O}n these Occasions, the House is open, as a Court of Justice. This Noble Assembly has not the Awefulness I expected: They meet [~~illegible~~]{in} a Room much inferior to that appointed for the Representatives of Pensilvania. And as it was not any solemn Occasion, they were drest in their common Cloaths, which were mostly plain, & some quite indifferent. The Nobility in general, are the most ordinary Men, I ever saw: And if there is any Judging by the Heaviness, & Foppery of their looks & behaviour, Many of them are more indebted to Fortune, than their Worth, for a Seat in that August Place. However, When I considerd the Power, with which they were vested, & that they were the Supreme Judicature of my Country, I could not forbear looking on them with Veneration. The Lord Chancellor, deliverd his Opinion, after the Judges, in one of the Clearest, Strongest Speeches, I ever heard. There was Nothing Rhetorical in it, but sound Reasoning, & good Law; In short, it was [~~illegible~~]{a Speech} fit for a Chancellor: His Opinion was for confirming the Judgment of the Exchequer, upon which, they all cryd **Confirm, Confirm**, & Run out as if they wanted their Dinners, for it was nigh five 'Clock. In these Employments, Honoured Father, & in my more retird Studies, I wear the Time, till I return to your Arms; and even this Absence is agreable, as it promises that to be to your Happiness, & my Glory: But I beg You will be perswaded, That Nothing can contribute more to my Comfort in the meantime, than frequently hearing of Your Health; And that Nothing can enforce my Duty, so much as Your Admonitions. The very Thoughts of my Parents, their Expectations, their Desires, Engrave it anew in my Heart: This is the Anchor, that keeps the Giddiness of Youth from Shipwre[~~illegible~~]{ck}.

Your kind favour by Coward, I have Rec[eive]d[11] & hope before this comes to hand, You will have Receivd the Particulars of my Voyage, by the Myrtilla.[12] [*page break*]

Old Mr. Berkley[13] had been at the Point of Death, for some time, so that I did not think it a proper time to enquire [~~illegible~~]{A)bout the Account Sales; but he is now recovering, & shall acquaint You by next opportunity.

I am sorry to give such wretched Accounts of Tobacco. The Market is so everstocked, that Mess[ieu]rs Gale & Bell, sold a considerable Quantity of their best for 1¾—but they have some prospect from Holland, of its rising to 2½. Mr. Hanbury tells Me the same.

The Court is all in Confusion, & this Metropolis plunged in Politiks, on the death of the Right Honourable Henry Pelham Esquire,[14] which happend the day before Yesterday. This Accident falls at the most Unlucky Crisis, it possibly could; just before the Election: For No new Minister can be able in so short a space of time, to concert a Plan, & prepare every thing for that great Event, which no doubt Mr. Pelham had all ready. But a fever has blasted the most mature Councils, & alterd perhaps the face of {affairs throughout} the Nation. How Honours & Glory fade away at this grand Catastrophe, & the Picture that lately glowd with such enchanting Colours, placd in this Light, scarcely affords One pleasing Ray. A Porter now would not exchange fates with the Prime Minister of England;

> Fain would I see that Prodigal,
> Who his to morrow, would bestow,
> For all old Homer's[15] Life,
> E'er since he livd, till now. Cowley.[16]

It is suppos'd, He will be succeeded, as Chancellor of the Exchequer (which is a synonimous Term with Prime Minister) either by Arthur Onslow Esquire, Speaker of the House of Commons, or by Mr. Fox,[17] Secretary at War, a great Orator in the House.

I beg that I may hear from You by every Opportunity, & am Honoured Father, Your most Dutiful & most Affectionate Son

John Dickinson

[*Samuel Dickinson*:] <March the 8ᵗʰ 1754 to me>[18]

ALS (PPL-JDFP)

---

[1] Sir Edward Coke (1552–1634), lawyer and judge, was author of *Institutes of the Laws of England* (1628–1644). Edmund Plowden (1518–1585) was a legal scholar and author of *Commentaries, or Reports* (1571).

[2] John Hampden (1594–1643) was an English politician whose opposition to Charles I and death at Chalgrove Field during the English Civil War (1642–51) solidified his status as a patriot. John Holt (1642–1710) served as lord chief justice of England from 1689 to 1710.

[3] The line is, "And e're he starts, a thousand steps are lost." Alexander Pope, "Windsor Forest," *The Works of Alexander Pope, Esq.* (London: B. Lintot, 1751), 1:55.

[4] The Cockpit was the nickname for an anteroom of the Privy Council chambers in Whitehall Palace previously used for cockfighting.

[5] William Murray (1705–1793), later Lord Mansfield, served as solicitor general from 1742 to 1754, attorney general from 1754 to 1756, and chief justice from 1756 to 1788. Alexander Hume Campbell (1708–1760) was a Scottish lawyer who served in Parliament from 1734 until his death. Charles Yorke (1722–1770) served as solicitor general from 1756 to 1761. Alexander Forrester (1711–1787) was an English barrister who served in Parliament from 1758 to 1774.

[6] Nervous: "Of an animal or person, etc.: sinewy, muscular, strong; vigorous, energetic" (*OED*).

[7] Philip Yorke, first earl of Hardwicke (1690–1764), was a lawyer and close ally of Thomas Pelham-Holles, first duke of Newcastle. He served as lord chancellor from 1737 to 1756.

[8] The English legal year is divided into four terms: Hilary (early Jan. to mid-April), for the feast day of St. Hilary of Poitiers; Easter (late April to late May); Trinity (early June to late July); and Michaelmas (early October to late December). These are abbreviated, respectively, as "Hil.," "East.," "Trin.," and "Mich.," and used to date legal records and royal statutes.

[9] Most likely David Poole (d. 1762), who became king's serjeant on June 29, 1747. See Colbourn, 1:259, n.38.

[10] The government office responsible for managing tax revenue.

[11] Captain Coward's ship *Integrity* arrived at Dover from Maryland around Feb. 18 (*Public Advertiser* [London], Feb. 20, 1754).

[12] Capt. Richard Budden's (1706–1766) ship *Myrtilla* sailed from England for Philadelphia around Feb. 9 (*Public Advertiser* [London], Feb. 11, 1754), apparently carrying JD's letter to Samuel Dickinson of Jan. 18. Budden transported the bells for Philadelphia's Christ Church from Whitechapel bell foundry in 1754 on the *Myrtilla*.

[13] Most likely a reference to Quaker merchant and banker David Barclay (1682–1769) of the firm David Barclay & Sons. See Colbourn, 1:260, n.40.

[14] Henry Pelham (1696–1754) was chancellor of the Exchequer and Britain's third prime minister, serving from 1743 until his death.

[15] Homer, an ancient Greek poet, is the presumed author of the *Illiad* and the *Odyssey*.

[16] This is a version of Abraham Cowley's (1618–1667) poem "Life and Fame." Cowley's original reads "ere since he Dy'ed, till now." See Abraham Cowley, *Poems written by A. Cowley* (London: H. Moseley, 1656), 40.

[17] Arthur Onslow (1691–1768) was unanimously elected speaker in 1728. He was unanimously reelected to that office in 1735, 1741, 1747, and 1754. He retired from Parliament in 1761 and holds the record for length of service as speaker (*ODNB*). Henry Fox (1705–1774), first baron Holland of Foxley, served as secretary of war from 1746 to 1755.

[18] The same docketing appears on the second page in the top and left margins.

9

To Mary Cadwalader Dickinson, March 29, 1754

London March 29th—<u>1754</u>

Honoured Mother,

When I reflect on the many & great Obligations, under which I lye to You, I cannot think my whole Life sufficient to make {a} Recompense: And therefore consider Myself as indispensably bound to neglect no Opportunity of testifying my Gratitude: But I have another very engaging Reason, for so frequently writing; for when I am thus employd, I seem in some manner to be conversing with You, I am transported to Kent, & tho[ugh] so far remote in person, my Soul and all its faculties are with You: How blest am I in Memory?{;} by her favour & Assistance I wing myself to peaceful Plains, the dear House, and all the sweet domestick Pleasures I have enjoy'd; Chearful Days, quiet Nights, delightful Converse: By her kind Offices, I see, I hear, I talk with my Honoured Mother. Of what Nature is our mind? That Oceans swell in vain, & Storms & Tempests yields it way. Three thousand Miles to it, are but a Span, & a Moment wafts it across the Globe! Well may Philosophers say, That he lives twice, who lives well: I subscribe to their Doctrine, for I have experiencd its Truth. With Delight I recall, I dwell upon those chearful happy Scenes I have spent with my Honourd Parents: Like Roses, they Preserve their Sweetness, tho[ugh] faded, and entertain in Idea, as they once diverted in Reality. Tho[ugh] past, they are not forgot, & as long as they are remembred, they will be pleasing. These Reflections at {once} [*page break*] soften and harden Me. They soften Me, as I know I am so far & so long removd from the like Pleasures; that so many tedious slow Days must revolve, before I can return to them: But they harden Me, as they fill Me, with a Resolution to employ this Time well, & confirm all my Endeavours that my Return may be Honourable. Those charming Scenes afford Me, no more Happiness, that calm, that Darling Retreat has no more Joy in Store for Me; Unless I entitle myself by this Absence. Thus, Honoured Mother, I comfort myself for what most grieves Me, & draw some Relief from the Circumstances which afflict Me, for really I do not{, &} believe I n{n}ever shall know any Happiness equal to that of being with You. My Chambers are now fitted up, & are very genteel, & I expect to be in them, in a few Days. I have spoke for Furniture, & by Mr. Hanbury's Advice, for very good— The Chairs Tables &c are to be Mahogony. His Maxim is, that those things are cheapest that are best. If I buy indifferent Stuff, he says, I can get nothing for it, when I leave England, & it will not be worth the Expence of taking with Me, so that it will be just so much Money lost: But if I buy the best, they will not only be useful here, but will serve Me, all my Lifetime. My furniture with Tea things, & every Untensil for my Chambers, with the Fees and Perquisites i{o}n entring them, will come to Forty pounds.

I am now grown quite hearty, & fill in flesh every Day. London did not agree with Me, very well at first, when I was prodigiously weak with the fatigue of the Voyage: but [*page break*] I soon recoverd, by retiring for a month to a Country Village, calld Clapham, about four miles from London: It is remarkable for its pure Air, which quickly recruited Me, & on my Return to the City, the Smoke of it was not all offensive, I got a fine Appetite, which has made as hearty as when I left home, & now I bear London as well as any Cit.[1]

When I waited on Mr. Penn,[2] he was very inquisitive about the fruits of the Lower Counties, & to know how Orchards succeeded with Us: I told him, Our Soil was suitable for any thing, & that We had very fine Apples. He keeps all kind of fruits almost, with Pictures of Birds, Animals, &c that are found in Pennsylvania, to shew his Friends; & therefore I imagine a Present of Our best Apples would be acceptable. I should be extremely oblidgd to you for a Couple of Barrels of these, with Eight or ten of our hams; they dry their bacon so little here, that I cannot eat it, for when You cut it, the Juices run out of it, as they do out of a piece of fresh Beef. If it would not be convenient to send them by the way of Philadelphia, Capt[ain] Hill will bring them with the greatest Pleasure. Mr. Penn was very much pleasd to hear, that We could make Tob[acc]o in the Lower Counties.

Be pleasd to give my most affectionate Love to my dearest Brother; desire him to behave himself so, that I may see him with Pleasure, that I may be [*page break*] Proud to acknowledge our Relation, & not ashamd that We came from the same Parents. Let Us be a Credit to Each other, & the Delight & Honour of Our tender Father & Mother: Let him know what You expect from, what he owes to himself. To observe his duty he must frequently hear it; the dear fellow will listen to Advice, but the Tenderness of his Years must make him a little heedless. He has engag'd his Honour to Me, to be in the head Class at my Return: Let him constantly Remember this solemn Obligation, & let him ever consider, what a mortifying, what an unhappy Disappointment it will be to Me, & how shameful, how ignominious to himself.

I beg, Honourd Mother, that You will not fatigue yourself too much in the Affairs of the Family. I think You always gave yourself too much trouble. My Honourd Father in one of his Letters, says, You are indifferent well: I cannot describe the alarm that word gave Me: if you are unwell, pray let Me hear particularly: I know the Aversion You have to white Maids, but I {can't} forbear thinking it possible to get some good Sort of an elderly body, who might ease You a good deal in the management of the family: I am sure there are many who would be glad of such a Post, on what terms You please. I cannot bear the thoughts of such Journies as You take, in all Weathers. Please to let Me know how You go on in building, & every thing.

Believe most Honoured Mother to be with the greatest Love and Respect, your most Dutiful & most Affectionate Son,

John Dickinson

P.S. Last Tuesday Mr. Hanbury had the unspeakable Misfortune of losing one of the best Wifes that ever liv'd. She dischargd all the Offices of Life, as Wife Mother, Friend, & Woman, with as much Humanity, Sweetness, & Tenderness, as ever I beheld. She died of an Asthma: and leaves a most disconsolate Husband.

[*Samuel Dickinson*:] <March the 29th to Mamey— March the 29.th 1754 to his Mamey—>

ALS (PPL-JDFP)

---

[1] Cit: "A citizen (in various senses). Usually used more or less contemptuously, for example to denote a person from the town as opposed to the country, or a tradesman or shopkeeper as distinguished from a gentleman" (*OED*). See also doc. 1:17, below.
[2] See doc. 1:15, below, for JD's listing of his expense to hire a coach to visit Thomas Penn on February 22.

10
To Samuel Dickinson, March 29, 1754

London March 29th 1754

Honoured Father,

I wrote last by Capt[ain] Richey, & before that by Mesnard[1] & Budden, & now take this Opportunity by Shirley[2] to acquaint You—that I continue in Health, that London agrees with Me better than it did at first, and that I want nothing to make Me quite easy, but more frequently hearing of your Wellfare. I entertain Myself with endeavouring to persue those measures, which it is your wish & my Interest I should. I hope I shall be able to satisfy your Desires, & to convince people, there are Advantages to be acquird here, & that the time & money I spend, are not quite thrown away: It shall be my Care, Honoured Father, that your Kindness & Indulgence, shall not be expos'd to the Sneer of the malicious, & your Honour & Happiness shall be the important Trust, with which I charge myself. With so great a debt to be dischargd, can I be idle? Or can I neglect so sacred a Deposit: My warmest prayers are, that I may be able to perform my Duty, & my only wish, that You would be perswaded, that Nothing in my power shall be wanting.

At present, I am wholly taken up with Reading—for as it is Vacation, there is nothing going on, in the Courts, except in the Circuits: And I have the pleasure of finding A person may be as industrious here as any where— And a little Prudence in our first Steps, with Resolution in the pursuit, will have the desird Success: Good Company is a better Security to our Morals— than Guards to a King. [*page break*] But the misfortune is, that Youth & Inexperience have so little Judgment in distinguishing the good from bad— & so many Rascals appear in the Character of Gentlemen, that no wonder the Ignorant & unwary are so often betrayd by the villainous & deceitful: And when once they are embarqu'd on the Stream of Vice & folly—they may view the Banks of Peace & Happiness, but the rapidity of the Current prevents their gaining them, & hurries them to destruction: But I hope, I shall escape those Snares, not from the Strength of my own Virtue, but thro[ugh] my good Fortune, in the gaining of my Acquaintance. Not that I disclaim all Endeavours of my own, or throw up the Reins of my Conduct. If Indolence & Pleasure, attempt to sooth & soften Me, I look forward to the Consequence, & ask myself, Whether they will be always thus engaging, & what are their Rewards— When Virtue & Industry offer themselves to my View, I consider what glorious Prospects they present: They are the Paths to Credit and Happiness, their Beauty alone knows no decay; Contempt & Misery fly far from them; and Time the insatiable Devourer, of all things else, continually weaves new Laurels for their brows— Every Day is a further Step to their Goal; for they cannot be miserable, who approve their own actions, nor can they be calld old, who are crownd with fresh & blooming Honours.

These Reflections can recall the Fancy from the Starts of Youth, subdue even the Dangers of London, and render the most knotty Points of Law agreable: And with the Blessing of that Divine Being, who has hitherto preservd & favourd Me, I hope, I shall be enabled to perform my Duty to [*page break*] Him, and to You.

Since my Last, I have waited on Mr. Penn; and was receivd by him, with the greatest Affability & Goodness. He rememberd You, & enquird very kindly after You; and then renderd himself very sociable & agreable, by a great many Enquiries of Pennsylvania & the Lower Counties: He was very glad to see Me take such pains in qualifying myself for Business, promisd Me, Every Service in his Power, & invited Me to Dinner a day or two after. I went, & dind with him, his Lady,[3] [*illegible*]{A} Member of the House of Commons, & William Peters[4] of Philadelphia: My Lady is a fine Person, & one of the most agreable Women, I ever knew; She preserves the Dignity of Birth, but with so much Ease, Good nature & Affability, that You would dislike her, did She forget it more. We had a very elegant Dinner, & Mr. Penn dismist Me, with new Expressions of his Respect. He has converst so much with the great, that he seems perfectly to have acquird the Art of rendring himself, agreable, & tho[ugh] I may never have any favours to Request of him, yet I shall endeavour to cultivate his Esteem: And I shall always scorn that Brutal Mean false Pride of some People, who because they are Independant, think no Oblidgingness, no Honour, due to any Person.

I have {been} with Mess[ieu]rs Barkley,[5] according to your Command, & they tell Me they have sent a full Account of the Reason, why You have had no Accounts Sales. I was very much alarmd at the beginning of the Story, but they assurd Me, as they Say they have done You, that they [*page break*] will have 20s[hillings] in the Pound. Tob[acc]o rises very little, but still the Merchants are in hopes from Holland— Ours that came over with

Me, turns out very dry, & so does the whole Cargo, except a little that was damnified in very bad Weather.

The Affairs of State are now pretty well settled, & the Places that were vacant by Mr. Pelham's Death supplied. The two great Offices of First Lord of the Treasury, & Chancellor of the Exchequer, ~~are~~{tha}t were united in him, are now divided. The Duke of Newcastle is advancd to the first, & One Legge to the other.[6] The Earl of Holderness succeeds the Duke of Newcastle, as Secretary of State for the Northern Department, & Sir Thomas Robinson, late Envoy at Vienna, is promoted to the Southern.[7] The Chancellor wanted to bring in One of his Sons, but could not succeed— He himself is to be created an Earl—by the title of Clarendon.[8] It is a most remarkable thing, that Mr. Pelham died so universally belovd & lamented, that not a Single Pamplet or Line has appeard against him; A fate that never befell any Minister in Europe before; & which I think a greater Honour to him, than any Action of his Life. The Parliament will be dissolvd soon, & then his Majesty visits his German Dominions.[9]

Honoured Father, I beg that You will remember Me by every Opportunity, & let Me have the delight of hearing of your health, as often as possible.

I am with the greatest Affection & Respect, your most dutiful & Loving
Son,
John Dickinson

[*in top margin, Samuel Dickinson*:] <March the 29:ᵗʰ 1754 to Me— March the 29:ᵗʰ 1754>

ALS (PPL-JDFP)

---

[1] Capt. Stephen Mesnard carried numerous letters from Benjamin Franklin (1706–1790) on his ship *Carolina* in the 1740s and '50s.

[2] Capt. James Shirley's ship, *London*, is recorded as having docked in Philadelphia on May 23, 1754. See *PG*, May 23, 1754.

[3] Lady Juliana Fermor Penn (1729–1801) was the wife of Thomas Penn (1702–1775).

[4] William Peters (1702–1789) was a Philadelphia lawyer and judge, and the older brother of Richard Peters.

[5] The merchant firm David Barclay & Sons.

[6] Thomas Pelham-Holles (1693–1768), duke of Newcastle, was the older brother of prime minister Henry Pelham. Henry Bilson Legge (1708–1764) served as chancellor of the Exchequer until dismissed from the post in November 1755. He later served under the Pitt administration, and once more when Newcastle returned to power in 1757.

[7] Robert Darcy (1718–1778), fourth earl of Holdernesse, served as secretary of state for the Northern Department from 1754 to 1761, except for June 9–29, 1757, when he resigned temporarily. Sir Thomas Robinson (1695–1770) helped negotiate the Treaty of Aix-la-Chapelle of 1748 and an end to the War of the Austrian Succession. He served as secretary of state for the Southern Department until November 1755 and refused an offer to resume that

post in 1757. Before 1782, these two cabinet positions were divided geographically, with the Northern Department being the junior office covering the Protestant states of Northern Europe, and the senior office of the Southern Department covering the Catholic and Muslim states of Europe. After 1782, the functions of these two offices were merged in the Foreign Office.

[8] In early March, British newspapers printed reports that "the Right Hon. the Lord Chancellor will be Earl of Clarendon, that title being extinct in the late Family" (*WEP*, March 7–9, 1754). However, on April 2, the chancellor, Philip Yorke, was commissioned first earl of Hardwicke instead (*London Gaz.*, March 30–April 2, 1754).

[9] George II remained elector of Hanover, the place of his birth, and returned there frequently, but not at this time. The proclamation dissolving Parliament was issued on April 8 (*Parl. Hist*, 15:293), and the king soon left to spend the summer at Kensington Palace (*WEP*, April 20–23, 1754).

<h1 style="text-align:center">11</h1>

<h2 style="text-align:center">To Samuel Dickinson, April 22, 1754</h2>

London April 22^d—<u>1754</u>

Honoured Father,

This comes by Capt[ain] Hill, who says, he will deliver it himself: It gives Me great pleasure to know, that You will have the Satisfaction of hearing the Particulars of Our Voyage, & seeing a person who so lately saw Me, & can give so circumstantial an Account of Me. But as I know the Capt[ain] will be silent as to the Obligations he has laid Me under, I think it my Duty, & a piece of Justice to him, to discover & acknowledge them. His behaviour to Me, all the Passage over, was not only civil & polite, but extremely tender & affectionate[.] I had the Cabbin boy, always to wait on Me; & the Capt[ain] would sometimes condescend even to Services, I was ashamed to accept of— Indeed he treated Me with all the Goodness of the nearest Relation. I made him a present of five Guineas.

I wrote to You last by Shirley, acquainting You of my being in Health, & of my going on in the Prosecution of those things, which have bro't Me to England, that is, Your Satisfaction, & my own ~~Glory~~ {Credit} & Happiness; & I now take this Opportunity to inform You, of my continuing by the favour of Divine Providence, still hearty, & of my Resolution to persist in every action that will be pleasing to You, & advantageous to Myself: This Conduct, no doubt is what all men in their Senses aim at, or wish for, & yet so unaccountable is the frailty of Human Nature, that few attain it; at least, few practize it, without many blots, & Inconsistences: We know what is good & proper, but regard it only enough, to impute the neglect [*page break*] of it to Us, as a Crime: What We admire, We reject; What We fear, We trust; What We love, We shun; What We hate, We embrace; Pleasd with his shining folds, & speckled Scales, We take a Serpent into Our bosoms, tho[ugh] We know he will sting Us to death: We weep at the Grief

& Anguish that will infallibly succeed, [And?]{Yet} plunge into Enjoyments, that are the Roads to them. "Oh! We are fearfully made."[1]

From these thoughts, which I purposely indulge sometimes, I emerge, & transport Myself triumphant over Vice & folly, to the Virtuous Arms of my most Honourd Parents, their Expectations answerd, Myself prepard to begin my Course thro[ugh] the World, belovd by my friends, & esteemd & approvd by all good Men. While these Prospects swell upon my Sight, still enlarging & brightning, Guilt and Indolence with all their Train fade away, & lessening & removing to a greater Distance, at last vanish into empty Air.

But I do not lose the present time in forming these imaginary Scenes, or foolishly look for that Joy to morrow, which I have not found today. When I paint this Happiness to Myself, it immediately & naturally begets this Enquiry, How is it to be attaind? I am instantly convincd that the Means are in my hands, & that my fancy is not greater than my Power. A few days of Care & Labour now, will repay Me with a Harvest of Honour & Pleasure for Years; and this is a labour too, no ways ungrateful; The surmounting of Difficulties always [*page break*] Affords an agreable Sensation to a generous mind; & I may say, without boasting, I have taken as much Pleasure in unravelling an intricate Point of Law, as a Florist receives, When he sees some favourite flower, which he has long tended himself, at last unfold its glowing Colours, & breathe its sweet Perfumes. Besides there is great Variety & Entertainment in the Study of Our Profession: Especially in England; We see how the Courts of Justice are crowded, by people who know nothing of the Law; how much more agreable then must it be to Us, who understand every thing that is said. Here We are not always plodding over books: Westminster Hall[2] is a School of Law, where We not only hear what We have read, repeated, but disputed & sifted in the most Curious & learned Manner; nay frequently hear things quite new, have our Doubts cleard up, & Our Errors corrected. The Barr is a perfect Comment upon the Written Law, & every great Man at it, is in some Measure a Master & Instructor to these young Students, who have the Wisdom to attend there.

During this Vacation, there h{w}as a great Change happend in the Offices of the Law. A Week or two ago died, Lee L[or]d Chief Justice of the Kings Bench.[3] He is succeeded by Sir Dudley Rider, late Att[orne]y General[4] Murray late Soll[icit]or General, is made Att[orne]y General; & Sir Richard Lloyd is advancd to the Sollicitorship.[5] These Promotions are thought very just: Sir Dudley Rider being a very great Lawyer, & the Attorney's place, too fatigueing for him, as he is now advancd in Years. [*page break*] It is supposd, Murray has now got to the Top of his Glory; for as his Family & Education are not approvd of, it is imagind, he never will preside in Law or Equity.[6] Sir R. Lloyd is a man of vast fortune, & a great Lawyer & Orator; he was promoted without any Interest or [illegible]{Appl}ication made. It is said, he will be Speaker of the House of Commons, on the Death or Resignation of Onslow.

The whole Nation is now taken up with Elections; You see, You hear Nothing else.[7] The{y} have several Rules for fixing the day in different Places; & therefore they are not all on the same.[8] The Westminster Electors are now polling, but as there is no opposition they go on pretty quietly. There are very hot Contests in many parts of the Kingdom, & it is thought the greatest will be in the City of London. There has been above £1000000 drawn out of this City already "for useful Purposes at Elections": & at one borough in the North, the Candidates have set out with two hundred Guineas a man to the Electors. It is astonishing to think what Impudence & Villainy are practizd on this Occasion. If a man cannot be brought to vote as he is desird, he is made dead drunk, & kept in that State, never heard of by his family or friends, till all is over, & he can do {no} harm. The Oath of their not being bribd, is as strict & solemn, as Language can form it,[9] but is so little regarded, that few people can refrain from Laughing, while they take it: I think the Character of Rome will equally suit this Nation, "Easy to be bought, if there was but a Purchaser."[10]

I beg, that I may hear frequently from You, & am, Honourd Father, with Prayers for your health & Happiness, your most dutiful & affectionate Son,

John Dickinson

[*in top margin, Samuel Dickinson:*] <Aprill the 22.[d] 1754 To Me—>

ALS (PPL-JDFP)

---

[1] Probably an allusion to Ps. 139:14: "I will praise thee; for I am fearfully *and* wonderfully made."

[2] Westminster Hall, built in 1097, is the oldest building on the parliamentary estate. At this time, it housed the courts of Chancery and King's Bench, and the Court of Common Pleas was held just west of it.

[3] Sir William Lee (1688–1754), who had studied at the Middle Temple, became a justice of the King's Bench in 1730.

[4] Sir Dudley Ryder (1691–1756) served as chief justice of the King's Bench from 1754 to 1756.

[5] Sir Richard Lloyd (1696/7–1761) served as solicitor general from 1754 to 1759. He became a bencher at the Temple in 1738 and served as treasurer in 1747. He was knighted in 1745.

[6] William Murray was not yet at the "top of his glory." When Ryder died in 1756, Murray became chief justice, and he was named first earl of Mansfield the same year.

[7] As Colbourn and Peters write, "The elections of 1754 were widely regarded as a costly farce; the opposition had been paralysed since the death of Frederick, Prince of Wales, in 1751. Only forty-two seats were contested. Even William Pitt owed his place in the Commons to Newcastle's pocket borough of Aldborough." See Colbourn, 1:268, n.58.

[8] The election took place from April 18 to May 20.

[9] The 1729 "Act for the More Effectual Preventing Bribery and Corruption in the Elections of Members to Serve in Parliament" required would-be voters to swear, "I have not received, or had by my self, or any person whatsoever in trust for me, or for my use and benefit directly or indirectly, any sum or sums of money, office, place or employment, gift or reward, or any promise or security for any money, office, employment or gift, in order to give my vote at this election" (2 Geo. 2, c. 24 [1729]).

[10] A reference to Sallust's depiction of the declining Roman republic in *Bellum Iugurthinum*. Thomas Gordon translated the original line about Rome, "o urbem venalem et mature perituram, si emptorem invenerit" as "a city abandoned to venality; and ripe for perdition, whenever an able purchaser appeared." See *Works of Sallust*, trans. Thomas Gordon (London: T. Woodward and J. Peele, 1744), 193–94.

12
Bond of JD, May 3, 1754

Those admitted to the Middle Temple were expected to give security for the due performance of the duties of membership by providing two sureties bound with person admitted. The duties, financial and otherwise, are described in the second page of the bond below. Although the student ledgers of the time reveal that some individuals were excepted from this requirement, the vast number supplied such securities, calling on family members, London merchants, and sometimes fellow students to act in that capacity.

Know all Men *by these Presents, That We* John Dickinson *of the* Middle Temple Gent. Anthony Bacon *of* Thread-Needle Street *in the City of* London Merchant *and* William Campbell *of* Tower Royal *in the said City* Apothecary *do Stand, and are firmly Bound unto* John Hervey Esquire *Treasurer of the said Society,* Sir John Strange[2] Knight Master of the Rolls Sir James Lowther[3] Baronet Sir Richard Lloyd Knight & Francis Eld[4] Esquire *of the Middle-Temple, aforesaid, in Twenty Pounds of Lawful Money of Great-Britain, to be paid to the said* John Sir John Sir James Sir Richard and Francis *or any of them, their, or any of their Executors, Administrators or Assigns: To which Payment well and truly to be made, We bind us and every of us, our, and each of our Heirs, Executors, and Administrators, firmly by these Presents. Sealed with our Seals. Dated this* third *Day of* May *in the* twentyseventh *Year of the Reign of our Sovereign Lord* George the Second *King of Great-Britain, France* and *Ireland, Defender of the Faith, &c. and in the Year of our* LORD, 17 54

John Dickinson *[seal]*

Sealed and Delivered

In Presence of **James Horsfall**[5]   **Antho: Bacon**[seal]

Cl[erk] ad Sub-Thesaur[6]   **William Campbell**[seal]

(No: 7985) [page break]

The Condition of this Obligation is such, That if the within Bounden John Dickinson do from Time to Time, during all such Time as he shall continue, and be One of the Society and Fellowship of the Middle-Temple, London, usually resort to Divine Service and Sermon, in the Temple-Church, and communicate there, so often as by the Law of this Land he ought to do. And also Satisfy and Pay to the Cook of the said Middle-Temple, for the Time being, all such Sum and Sums of Money, as shall become due from him to the said Cook for his Commons, within three Weeks after the same shall be due, and every Term pay the antient and accustomed Duty or Sum of one Shilling and eight Pence, for his Pensions: And also, Satisfy and Pay, all such Debts, Duties, Charges, and Things which by Usage, Order or Custom of the said Society, now are, or hereafter shall become Due and Payable by him, within three Weeks after the same shall be Due. And also, Observe, Perform, Fulfil and Keep all such Orders as are, or shall be made, for the good Government of the said Society, and shall not, during his Continuance in the Middle-Temple aforesaid, Practice as a common Attorney or Solicitor, in any Court of Justice in England, then this Obligation to be void, or else to remain in Force.

DS (UkLoMT-MT.3/CBB)

---

[1] John Hervey (1696–1764) became a bencher at Middle Temple in 1745 and served as treasurer from 1753 to 1754. He represented Reigate in Parliament from 1739 to 1741, and represented Wallingford from 1754 until his death.

[2] Sir John Strange (1696–1754) became a Middle Temple bencher, or elected official, in 1736. He served as solicitor general from 1737 to 1742 and was knighted in 1740. In 1750 he became master of the rolls, which by this time entailed being a judge of the Chancery Court and member of the Privy Council as well as a keeper of public records. He represented Totnes in Parliament from 1742 until his death, having previously represented West Looe from 1737 to 1741.

[3] James Lowther (1673–1755), fourth baronet since 1731, became a bencher at the Temple in 1714. He served almost sixty years in Parliament, representing Carlisle, Appleby, and at this time Cumberland. He was a fellow of the Royal Society.

[4] Francis Eld (Elde; 1692–1760) became a bencher at the Temple in 1728 and served as treasurer in 1744. He was a master in Chancery and briefly represented Stafford in Parliament from late 1724 until he was expelled in early 1725.

[5] James Horsfall (d. 1785), clerk to the under treasurer of Middle Temple, Charles Hopkins. Admitted to the Middle Temple bench in 1767 when he became keeper of the Temple Library,

Horsfall resigned that position in 1776 when he succeeded Hopkins as under treasurer of the Temple. He was a fellow of the Royal Society.

[6] Thesaur: "treasury" (*OED*).

13
To Mary Cadwalader Dickinson, May 25, 1754

London May 25[th]—1754—

Honoured Mother,

Tho[ugh] I have not yet rec[eive]d an Answer to any of my Letters, I still continue Writing; so constant, so affectionate is my Remembrance of You: The dear Reflection, nor Absence Pleasure or Business can drive from my mind: And the highest Satisfaction I can attain to, will be to convince You from the whole Tenor of my Life, that I equally desire your Peace & Happiness as my own. This I shall constantly aim at, & is what I now think myself in a likely way to attain— I am agreably & entirely settled; and am prosecuting with as much Vigour as I can, the Studies of my Profession. I now have an Opportunity of joining Reading & Study together; from which I have no doubt of gathering the finest Fruits, if they have time to ripen. I have acquainted My Honourd Father, with my Reasons for thinking it necessary to make a longer Stay in England, than was designd: With Hopes that You will join in an Opinion about a thing that seems of such Importance to Me: And I woud only say again, that I hope I am not so unhappy in your Opinion of my Prudence, that You will imagine this Desire proceeds from any other motive than a Sense of my Interest: And I assure You, no greater wrong can be done to my Affection for You, than such a Supposition: And that nothing but the Hopes of returning to You with more Credit, shoud detain Me one moment from You. Not but that England is a most delightful Country, & I have great Reason to admire it & to be pleasd with it.

I am encreasing dayly in Health here; and I have an agreable Acquaintance, & am particularly happy in [*page break*] the Friendship of Mr. Hopkins, Our Treasurer: He is a man of excellent Sense; but to those that know him, the greatness of his Abilities is lost in the Merit of his Goodness, & Benevolence of his Heart. His Humanity & Integrity procure him the Love & Esteem of every one. My other Acquaintance[s] are Mr. Jennings's Son,[1] two or three Americans,[2] & as many Englishmen, all young fellows of good parts and remarkable Industry— And as We are all engagd in the same Studies, We find great Benefit from Our Acquaintance. Indeed I dont chuse to get too general an Acquaintance, [~~illegible~~] for I find I have so much on my hands, that the more time I have to Myself, the more it will be to my Benefit. As to the Families I converse with, I have mentiond them,

& the more I know them, the more agreable they are. Mr. Penn about a Week ago sent for Me to dine with him: I cannot conceive how he got the Dislike of the Philadelphians so much, for I never conversd in all my Life, with a more agreable affable Gentleman. He behavd with a great Deal of Goodness & Kindness towards Me; and a Young Gentleman that lives with him, tells Me, he often asks him, if he has seen Me, & how I do.

Every thing now is grown pleasant; & Spring has beautified the whole Country: The Ingenuity of Art is added to the Productions of Nature, in many Places, but no where to such Perfection as at Vauxhall—[3] You have heard of these famous Gardens, as the Evening Entertainment of the Gentry in & about London—And they are really very fine. You Enter about Six oClock thro[ugh] a Walk as Elegant as can be formd, while Musick is playing from A Noble Orchestra on the Right hand as You come in, standing in the middle of a Grove. A little beyond that is a Chinese Temple, under which are [*page break*] Seats for distinct Companies; & so there are all over the Gardens— The Whole is laid out into beautiful Walks & the Walks bounded by some fine Piece of Painting on ba{o}ards, or Statues. When it grows Dark, A thousand Lamps that hang on the Branches of the Trees, [~~illegible~~]{a}re lighted up & raise another day— In short nothing I think can be better executed— The first time I went with Mrs. Barnett, Mr. Hanbury's Daughter, A Lady of her Acquaintance, Young Hanbury,[4] & the Attorney General of Virginia,[5] (who is now over here) and spent the Evening very agreably.

But notwithstanding all the Diversions of England, I shall return to America with Rapture. There is something surprizing in it, but nothing is more true, than that no place is Comparable to our Native Country. It is some strange Affection Nature has implanted in Us—for her wise Ends.

America is to be sure a Wilderness; & yet that Wilderness to Me, is more pleasing than this charming Garden: I dont know how, but I dont seem to have any Connections with this Country; I think myself only a Traveller, & this the Inn: But when I think of America; that Word produces a thousand pleasing Images; It is endeard by my past Pleasures there, by my future Prospects: That word includes my Honourd Parents, my dear Relations, my friends & every thing that makes Life valuable. I cant bear a Comparison between it & any other place. Tis Rude,—but is{t}'s innocent. Tis wild— but its private. There Life is a Stream pure & unr[~~illegible~~]{u}ffled—here an Ocean briny & tempestuous. There We enjoy Life, here We spend it. And indeed, till I see it again, I shall not be so happy, as I think it possible to be on Earth: [*page break*] But there it woud be Madness to confine my Views of Bliss to this Ball: Virtue (without which there is no bliss) is only a Preparation for the Highest; & what constitutes the Bliss of Virtue here, is not so much any immediate Sensation of Joy, or Peace of Mind for good

Actions; as the Hopes of Futurity, & an humble Reliance upon the infinite Goodness & Mercy of an All-Gracious & Supreme Being. These when Our Happiness is at the highest flood, bid Us not to rest contented, and yet with the most devoted Gratitude bend in thankful Praises to the Benevolent Author. For my Part, Lips cannot express the thanks due from Me for the unmerited favours showerd upon Me by the Divine Hand; amongst the first of which I count my most Honourd Parents—And as they have contributed so much to my Happiness, may I be enabled to make some Retribution to them.

As I did not know of this Vessell's going till lately, & have been very busy, it being Term time, Please to excuse this haste, for I write now at 11 oClock at Night.

Please to give my sincerest Love to my Dearest Brother, with a great Deal of good Advice, & believe Me to be, Most Honourd Mother, your most
Dutiful and most
Affectionate Son,
John Dickinson

P.S. Please to give my Love to Cousin Watt[*illegible*] [&?] Wife—& Neighbours &c

May 28th
The Vessel dont go so soon as I expected—So have time to inform You, that last night I suppd With Mrs. Anderson, who desird Me to present her most affectionate Respects to You— She is very Well—& so is her family. She has some of the finest Children I ever saw.

[*in top margin, Samuel Dickinson*:] <May the 25.th 1754 To <u>Mamey</u> [*to the right of JD's signature*:] To his Mother May 25:[th] 1754>

ALS (PPL-JDFP)

---

[1] Edmund Jenings (Jennings; 1731–1819), son of Edmund Jenings (Jennings; 1703–1756) of Annapolis, Md. The father served on the Maryland Council from 1732 until late 1753, when he retired to England. The son practiced law in England and wrote *Considerations on the Mode and Terms of a Treaty of Peace with America* (London: Edward and Charles Dilly, 1778).

[2] Among the Americans at Middle Temple in May 1754 were John Blair (1732–1800) of Virginia, later a justice of the US Supreme Court; Charles Carroll (1723–1783) of Annapolis, Md., a delegate to the Continental Congress, 1776–77, and a member of the Maryland Senate; William Drayton (1732–1790), later US district judge for South Carolina; Thomson Mason (1733–1785) of Virginia, a judge and legislator who was the younger brother of George Mason (1725–1792); and William Hicks (1735–1772) of Philadelphia, whose bond to the Temple JD cosigned June 1754 (see doc. 1:16; Students Ledger, 1747–1764, UkLoMT-MT.3/STL/1).

[3] Vauxhall Spring-Gardens, located across the Thames from London in Kennington, came under the management of tradesman Jonathan Tyers (1702–1767) in 1729. He aimed to raise the Garden's profile by offering evening entertainment and keeping prostitutes off the grounds. The Gardens were open to respectable people of all classes, and Tyers gave his visitors an evening's entertainment with a moral lesson. For example, when he relaunched the Garden in 1732, the centerpiece display was five tableaux decrying self-indulgence and intemperance. See David E. Coke and Alan Borg, *Vauxhall Gardens: A History* (New Haven, Conn.: Yale University Press, 2011).

[4] Perhaps JD means Mrs. Anna Hanbury *Barnard*, daughter of John Hanbury.

[5] Peyton Randolph (c. 1721–1775) attended the Middle Temple from 1739 to 1743, and served as Virginia's attorney general from 1744 until his resignation in 1766. He then served as Speaker of the House of Burgesses until 1775, and as the first and third president of the Continental Congress. On December 17, 1753, the Virginia House of Burgesses passed a resolution appointing Randolph as a special agent to present in London their complaint about the governor's proposal to charge a fee for affixing the colonial seal on land patents (H.R. McIlwaine, ed. *Journals of the House of Burgesses of Virginia 1752–1755, 1756–1758* [Richmond, Va.: Colonial Press, E. Waddey Co., 1909], 166–69).

14
To Samuel Dickinson, May 25, 175

London May 25[th]—1754

Honoured Father,

I wrote to You last by Capt[ai]n Shirley, about two months ago, which time seems very long to Me, to pass without the Agreable Entertainment of conversing in the only manner I can with my Honoured Parents: And tho[ugh] I now have an Opportunity by Capt[ai]n Hamilton[1] to inform You, that I am very well, yet I am very uneasy at not having heard from You for Six Months: The only letters I have rec[eive]d were those by Richey & Coward, dated in November, a month before my Arrival. But I am assurd, this proceeds more from want of Opportunities than Affection: Nor am I the least afraid, that You have forgot Me, or remember Me with less Love than [as?] ever.

Inclosd I have sent an Account of the Money I have rec[eive]d from Mr. Hanbury: And I hope My Honourd Mother will not be alarmed at the frequent Rides mentiond in it:[2] When I first arrivd, I was very low in health; and receivd great Benefit from Riding; and tho[ugh] I am now grown hearty, yet as it is a very fine Exercise, & We use very little in the Temple, I still continue it.

I have rec[eive]d £120, which has furnishd Me with Cloaths, supported Me to this time, & settled Me in my Chambers: And on a Calculation I have made, I am certain £110 more, will serve Me, till this time next year: Which is more than any Young fellow I know, woud

38

venture to say; but this I will engage for. But this I do not mention, as if I thought the Sum inconsiderable; I really think £230 a great deal for A Year & a half; [e?]specially when I consider the Care & Trouble it costs the best, the dearest of Parents: but tho[ugh] I endeavour to comfort Myself that I spend it innocently and as I flatter Myself, Prudently, yet I shall never be easy & contented, Unless You think so too. Were it possible for Me to get Money, any other way than [*page break*] From You, I woud not vouch it should be spent so wisely: but When You supply Me, & I know what returns You expect; I am filld with Concern & Care. Nothing woud grieve Me so much as to give any Cause from my Extravagance to suspect, that I had not a due regard to your Honour & Hopes, and a proper Sense of your unequalled Goodness to Me. No Pain coud be so sharp, as that You shoud imagine Me capable of trampling on all your more than Parental Cares & Toils for Me; and that my Duty & filial Affection shoud be swallowd up in a few base, sordid Appetites, or drownd in a thoughtless stupid Indolence: On the other hand, when I reflect on the Expectations, Your Fondness inclines You entertain of Me, & my Power to answer them, I am filld with Pleasure, & enchanted with delightful Prospects: This I have often said before, & pardon my repeating it; for it is the constant Sentiment of my Soul, the perpetual Animates of my Actions— At my Books, it enlivens Me; when from them, it recalls Me; In Company it is not banishd; Tis in my Dreams, Tis in my Prayers. This is the mark, at which ever Act of my Life, shall aim; & this Happiness, I think myself now in the right way to attain; but I am afraid the time limited for my Stay here, is too short; tho[ugh] when I consider the Expence of it, & the great Obligations I already lye under to the best of Parents; I dont know how to request an Enlargement of the Term. One thing I hope my Honourd Father, will not suppose, that my Desire to stay longer here, proceeds from any liking I have taken to this Place: for if my Honour & Veracity are to be depended on, I declare, that setting aside the Advantages I expect here, the next Vessel shoud bring Me to America: so different are my Inclinations to my Sentiments: Nor is this Request sudden or heedless, for never shoud it have come from Me; were I not convincd by the maturest Deliberations I am capable of, that my Wellfare & future Happiness are intimately concernd, & that it was [*page break*] My Duty to mention it to You. It woud be impossible to enumerate all the Benefits to be acquird in London: But it cannot be disputed, that more is learnt of Mankind here in a Month, than can be in a Year, in any other Part of the World; Here a person sees & converses with People of all Ranks, of all Tempers. He acquires an Ease & freedom of Behaviour with his Superiors; Complaisance and Civility to his Inferiors. The Wise are his Patterns to imitate— The weak shew him, as in a Glass, the faults and follies, he ought to avoid— Here a man learns from the Example of others, what in another place, Nothing but his own Sufferings & Experience coud teach him. London takes off the Rawness, the Prejudices of Youth & Ignorance. He finds here that he has been frequently deceivd; he ceases to gaze & stare, & finds at last that Nothing is really admirable but Virtue.

As to the particular Advantages in my Profession: They are so many & so great, that it woud be needless to recount them. If the adding Practize to Study will be more likely to fix the Law strongly & clearly in the Memory, if the seeing & hearing the finest Speakers at the Barr, can contribute any thing to improving & polishing one's Address; & if frequent Conversations in your Studies, with Numbers engaged in the same, will instruct one in Controversy; then those Advantages are to be acquird here. But there are other Considerations which induce Me to think a longer Stay in England necessary. I know that every body's Expectations are raisd very high of young fellows coming to England— They constantly look for something extraordinary for all the Expence & Trouble that has been bestowd on them: This I may depend on it, will be the Case with Me; & as much will be expected from Me in eighteen Months, as if I was to stay twelve months longer—They will suppose Me a Complete Lawyer, or why shoud I return so soon: But I know Myself, that a year more woud make a very considerable Difference— And tho[ugh] next Spring I shall have been here eighteen Months; yet I was so weakly & unsettled for four or five months, that I shall not be at my Business above a Year: But now [*page break*] I am grown hearty; could I prosecute my Studies here for two years longer, I am sure I shou'd find the greatest Profit by it: Besides in that time, my Health wou'd become, I hope, so confirmd, that I should feel the benefit of it, all the Rest of my Life. The Climate here is so much more temperate & regular than Ours, that there are numberless Instances of Americans, who in two or three years have carried away excellent Constitutions for very bad ones brought with them. Nay several Gentlemen of Figure, have told Me, that they never knew a weak Constitution failing with Temperance, to arrive at a great Degree of Strength here.

But another very weighty Reason is, that in two years, I can procure the Degree of a Barrister, which I cannot do by next Spring. Since my last, I have enterd into Commons, that is, Dining in Term time with the Barristers & Students of the Society in the Public Hall. We always have with Us some of the Governors, who are calld—Benchers; and frequently some of the Judges & the greatest Lawyers. Now to obtain the Degree of a Barrister, a person shoud be enterd five Years, & keep his Commons for Two; but Mr. Hopkins, Our Treasurer, Who is so good as to distinguish Me with a particular Friendship; Assures Me, that on keeping my

Commons for the Term prescribd, he will by his Interest procure Me to be calld to the Barr. This is a thing, in my Opinon, not to be despisd, as it will certainly be more to my Credit, to return with a Degree, & a Recommendation from the Society, than in the same Character I came away with.

These Honourd Father, are the reasons, which woud perswad[e] Me to stay any longer from You, but as they appear to Me very considerable, & likely to have some Influence on my future Life, I thought myself under an Obligation to mention them. Indeed the only Objection I know is the Expence—but that is enough; tho[ugh] on reflection is not so great; for as the Expence of first fitting out is now over, there will be nothing but the running Expences of the Year; which shall not be above £120—Which I really think will be of more service to Me now, than ever it will be. [*page break*] I have said thus much, Honourd Father, that You may not imagine it is a thing on which I have spent no thought: And if You should be pleasd to consent to my longer stay here, I should be extremely glad to have my Books here by the first Opportunity, for now I read under the greatest Disadvantages.

At present I am taken up chiefly with tending in Westminster-Hall; it being Easter Term which began about three Weeks ago.[3] At the Beginning of this Term, Sir Dudley Rider took his Seat, as Chief Justice of the King's Bench; which he fills with great Credit. Every Judge must be a Sergeant; so that he was oblidgd to take this Degree upon him:[4] And as it was a Ceremony, which I thought I might never have an Opportunity of seeing again, I prest into the Room, where it was to be performed; but was a little surprized, when I had enterd, to find Myself surrounded by Judges & Sergeants, & not above two or three private Gentlemen with Me. The Ceremony is so very fantastick & monkish, that Willes[5] C[hief] J[ustice] of the Common Pleas, who conferrd the degree on Ryder, laughd very heartily, while he was dubbing him. First Ryder counted a Common Recovery[6] as an instance (I presume) of his knowledge in the Law—but instead of pronouncing it, he held it in his Hat & read it. After this he knelt down on a Cushion before C[hief] J[ustice] Willes, Who took a Cap exactly like a Lady's Night Cap; put it over the back of his Wig; & tied it under his Chin. Then a red Cowl was thrown over his Shoulders; and Willes saluting him by the name of "Brother" told him he was now admitted one of his Majestys Sergeants—Upon which he rose up, & the other Sergeants congratulated their Brother Then he was robed as a Judge; to do which they were oblidgd to take off his Wig, which was very much in the way, & going into the Common Pleas, he counted his Recovery again, & presented Rings to his Brethren; and then he was [*page break*] qualified for his Seat in his own Court, which he did not take till next day. And scarcely was that

Vacancy supplied, when another fell by the death of Sir John Strange, Master of the Rolls— This very great man died about a week ago; & is succeeded by one Clarke,[7] who makes a very considerable figure.

The Elections are now over{,} chiefly, & some of them have been as warm, as if there was a Prince on the throne, from whom every thing was to be dreaded: So that there will be several controverted Elections.

Mr. Hanbury has signaliz'd himself in favour of the Court, as much as any man in England. Mr. Nugent[8] One of the Lords of the Treasury, was invited by the Dissenters who form a party in Bristol[9] to set up there, & they promisd to bear the Expence; but this Engagem[en]t they were not quite hearty in fulfilling, & Nugent declind. Mr. Hanbury, who has a large Interest there, no sooner heard this, but he signd a Paper to Nugent, Who is his intimate friend, promising to bear all Charges to the Amount of £10000—Nugent on this, took the Advice of the Duke of New Castle, & he was so much pleasd with the warmth & Zeal it expressd, that he took a Copy of the Paper, & shewd it to his Majesty, Who was highly satisfied with it. Nugent set up for Bristol, & carried it chiefly by Mr. Hanbury's Interest.[10] Indeed this Electioneering has been of great service to Mr. Hanbury, as it has diverted his Mind from reflecting too much on the loss of so good a Wife.

There has been the longest & severest Winter this Year, that has been since 1739—[11] And tho[ugh] the Cold was more intense then, yet it was not of such a duration as it has been this Winter: However We have fine Weather now, & this will be a very plentiful Year. I long to know how You have past the Winter, & how You are now. I have often wishd to join You at a good chearful fire, & [*page break*] cannot think of the time I have so happily spent with You, without grief. Every moment of it brings to my Memory some pleasing Scene or other. Morning Noon & Night were all Joyful— And I am positive, No Pleasures can compare with Domestick, since none can be so pure, none are so mild & serene: but A Share in those, my present fortunes deny Me, tho[ugh] I have no small Happiness in the thoughts of your enjoying them: And whatever Diversions I find here, lose half their Value, in that You do not partake of them. But Honourd Father I am afraid I shall tire You: When I set down to write you, I{M}y Pen has no more bounds than my Affection; & while I am so agreably entertaind Myself, I forget that I may grow troublesome.

I beg that I may have the Pleasure of hearing from You, very soon, & by every Opportunity And I shall never neglect any of declaring how much how sincerely I am Honoured Father,

Your most Dutiful and
most Affectionate Son,

John Dickinson

P.S. Please to present my Respects to all our Friends & Neighbours
We have it our Papers that Governor Hamilton[12] has resignd & that it is on
some Difference with the Proprietor.

JD.

[*Samuel Dickinson*:] <Johneys Letter by Capt[ain] Hamilton to me—May
the 25th—1754 to me>

ALS (PPL-JDFP)

---

[1] Capt. William Hamilton's ship *Ann Galley* sailed from the port of Deal on June 3 and arrived at
Philadelphia around September 5, 1754 (*WEP*, June 1–4; *PG*, Sept. 5).

[2] See doc. 1:15, below.

[3] Easter term began on May 1.

[4] Sergeant-at-law was the highest rank of barrister. Sergeants had the exclusive privilege of arguing
before the Court of Common Pleas. Until 1873 all common law judges were sergeants. Dudley
Ryder received this degree on May 2, 1754.

[5] Sir John Willes (1685–1761) served as chief justice from 1737 to his death.

[6] "Count" in this context is to plead in a court of law (*OED*). Common recovery: "In conveyancing.
A species of common assurance, or mode of conveying lands by matter of record, formerly in
frequent use In England. It was in the nature and form of an action at law, carried regularly through,
and ending in a recovery of the lands against the tenant of the freehold; which recovery, being a
supposed adjudication of the right, bound all persons, and vested a free and absolute fee- simple in
the recoverer . . Common recoveries were abolished by the statutes 3 & 4 Wm. IV. c. 74" (*BLD*).

[7] Sir Thomas Clarke (1703–1764) was knighted the same day he took Strange's position as master
of the rolls, and in June he became a privy councilor.

[8] Robert Craggs Nugent, first earl Nugent (1709–1788), a member of Parliament from Ireland,
gained his fortune by converting from Catholicism to the Church of England and marrying a
succession of three wealthy widows. Horace Walpole (1717–1797) coined the term "Nugentize"
to describe the process these widows underwent. As he wrote to Horace Mann on July 22, 1744,
"Miss Boyle . . . has thirty thousand pounds, and may have as much more, if her mother, who is a
plump widow, don't happen to Nugentize." See *The Letters of Horace Walpole, Earl of Orford*,
ed. Peter Cunningham, 9 vols. (London: Bickers & Son, 1877), 1:316.

[9] Bristol is a port town in southwest England about 120 mi. from London. In the 18th cent., it was
a locus of Quakerism and a major mercantile center, importing sugar and tobacco from the colonies
and exporting textiles, glass, pottery, and other manufactured goods.

[10] Nugent's second wife, Anne Craggs (1697–1756), introduced him to Philip Stanhope, fourth earl
of Chesterfield (1694–1773), who encouraged his election as member of Parliament for St. Mawes
in 1741. By the 1754 election, Nugent's support of the out-ports, that is, ports outside of London,
and questions in Parliament about trade and navigation regulations attracted the attention of Bristol
and Liverpool merchants, who asked him to stand for election in both their constituencies. With
his St. Mawes seat safe, Nugent capitalized on their interest by securing a £10,000 indemnity from
the Bristol merchants (*ODNB*).

[11] The winter of 1739 was so cold that the Thames remained frozen from Christmas Eve to early
March of 1740. See Tim Hitchcock and Robert Shoemaker, *London Lives: Poverty, Crime and
the Making of a Modern City, 1690–1800* (Cambridge: Cambridge University Press, 2015), 137.

[12] James Hamilton (c. 1710–1783) was lieutenant governor of Pennsylvania in 1748–54, 1759–63, and briefly in 1771. The proprietors instructed Hamilton to resist any bill that taxed the proprietary estate, which sparked criticism that the Penns were unwilling to contribute their share to the common defense during the French and Indian War (1754–63). It also gave the Quaker party the opportunity to shift the blame for the province's poor defense onto the proprietors by proposing militia bills that taxed the Penns' land, knowing full well such bills would be quashed. Hamilton asked the Penns to replace him, which they did with Robert Hunter Morris, who arrived in Pennsylvania in October 1754.

<h1 style="text-align:center">15</h1>

Middle Temple Expenses, January 11, 1754–May 28, 1754

JD included this account of his expenses with the previous letter (doc. 1:14) to his father.

1754	**John Dickinson**	**D[ebi]t**
Jan[ua]ry 11[th]	To Cash rec[eive]d of Mess[ieur]s Hanbury & Co.	£30..00..00
Feb[rua]ry 25[th]	To D[itt]o rec[eive]d of Mess[ieur]s Hanbury & Co.	30..00..00
May 9[th]	To D[itt]o rec[eive]d of Mess[ieur]s Hanbury & Co.	60..00..00
		£120..00..00

	[per] Contra	**C[redi]t**
		£ s D
Jan[ua]ry 21[st]	By Cash p[ai]d Taylor as [per] Acc[oun]t	17..12..10 ½
22[d]	By D[itt]o p[ai]d Stationer for Coke & Hawkins's Ab[ridgmen]t[1]	2..12.. 6
D[itt]o	By D[itt]o p[ai]d Washerwoman	00.. 5..5 ½
D[itt]o	By D[itt]o p[ai]d for Tea Sugar &c as [per] Acc[oun]t	00..17..3
D[itt]o	By D[itt]o p[ai]d for a p[ai]r of Boots	1.. 6..00
D[itt]o	By D[itt]o p[ai]d for a p[ai]r of Gloves	00.. 2..00
23[d]	By 2 Dinners	00.. 2..6
D[itt]o	By Portradge of things to Spread Eagle	00..11..2
D[itt]o	By a Hamper	00..1..4
D[itt]o	By Coach hire to Sp[rea]d Eagle & thence to Clapham[2]	00..3..00
[D[itt]o]	By a Ride to Vauxhall	00..3..00
[*illegible*]	By a Ride to Richmond[3]	00..3.. 6

D[itt]o	By Dinner at the Star & Garter[4]	00..2..6
31st	By Coach hire to London	00..1..00
D[itt]o	By Dinner	00..1.. 2
D[itt]o	By Play	00..3..00
Febr[uar]y 1st	By Coach hire to Clapham	00..1..00
6th	By Coach hire to London	00..1..00
D[itt]o	By Dinner	00..1..4
7th	By D[itt]o	00..1..3
D[itt]o	By Coach hire to Clapham	00..1..00
12th	By Play	00..3..00
13th	By Dinner	00..1..3
14th	By D[itt]o	00..1..3
15th	By D[itto] & Coach hire to Clapham	00..2..3
18th	By a Ride to Twickenam[5] & Dinner	00..5..6
23d	By Lodgings for 4 Weeks at 8 [per] Week	1..12..00
D[itt]o	By Provisions & other necessaries	1.. 16..7
D[itt]o	By Barber & Shoeboy	00..3..00
24th	By Dinner	00..1..4
25th	By Mr. Hanbury's footman twice	00..2..00
D[itt]o	By Coffee house boy	00..2..00
D[itt]o	By a p[ai]r of Silk Stockings black	00..14..00
26th	By Dinner	00..1..4
D[itt]o	By Mr. Blackwells footman	00..1..00
D[itt]o	By Washerwoman	<u>00..2..00</u>
[*page break*]		**£29..14..4**

1754	**Brought forward**	**£29..14..4**
Febr[uar]y 27th	By dinner	00..1..4
28th	By D[itt]o	00..1..3
March 1st	By D[itt]o	00..1..3 ½
2.d	By Washer woman	00..4..1
D[itt]o	By Barber for Cut Wig	1..5..00
D[itt]o	By Dinner	00..1..3
D[itt]o	By Coffeehouses for a Week	00..1..5
3.d	By Dinner	00..1..1
4th	By D[itt]o	00..1..4
D[itt]o	By a Map of London	00..1..00
5th	By a Glass	00..4..00
D[itt]o	By Dinner	00..1..2

6th	By D[itt]o	00..1..2
7th	By D[itt]o	00..1..3
8th	By D[itt]o	00..1..1
D[itt]o	By Coffeehouse for Pamphets	00..1..00
9th	By a Ride & Dinner	00..4..00
D[itt]o	By Coffeehouse	00..1..8
10th	By Dinner	00..1..8
11th	By D[itt]o & Ride	00..6..00
D[itt]o	By a p[ai]r of Gloves	00..1..00
12th	By Dinner	00..1..3
13th	By D[itt]o	00..1..2
14th	By D[itt]o & sack Whey[6] for a Cold	00..2..6
D[itt]o	By a Pen knife	00..1..00
D[itt]o	By Washerwoman	00..3..7
15th	By Dinner	00..1..4
D[itt]o	By Chocolate Pot & Muller	00..1..8
16th	By Washerwoman	00..3..4
D[itt]o	By dinner & sack Whey	00..2..4
17th	By D[itt]o	00..2..4
18th	By D[itt]o	00..2..4
D[itt]o	By a lb. of Chocolate	00..3..6
19th	By a p[ai]r of Shoebuckles & Knee	1..11..00
D[itt]o	By Cash p[ai]d Capt[ai]n Hill	5..5..00
D[itt]o	By Waterman for bring[in]g things up	00..5..00
D[itt]o	By Dinner	00..1..3
D[itt]o	By Coffeehouse	00..2..00
20th	By Dinner & Ride	00..4..2
21st	By Dinner	00..1..8
D[itt]o	By a p[ai]r of Gloves.	00..1..6
22.^d	By 2 sticks of Sealing Wax	00..1..00
D[itt]o	By Coach Hire to Mr. Penn's	00..2..00
D[itt]o	By D[itt]o to Mr. Berkley's	00..2..00
D[itt]o	By dinner	00..1..2
D[itt]o	By Washerwoman	00..2..00
23.^d	By Dinner & Ride	<u>00..4..1</u>
[*page break*]		**£42..7..8 ½**
1754	**Brought forward**	**£53..13..11½**
April 28th	By Subscription to a Library	00..3..00
D[itt]o	By dinner	00..1..2
29th	By dinner & Rides	00..5..6

D[itt]o	By a p[ai]r of Boot Straps	00..1..6
30[th]	By dinner	00..1..2
D[itt]o	By Coach hire to Mr. Anderson's	00..1..6
May 1[st]	By dinner	00..1..8
D[itt]o	By 7 p[ai]r of Stockings	2..9..00
2.[d]	By Dinner	00..1..3
3.[d]	By D[itt]o	00..1..3
4[th]	By D[itt]o	00..1..1
D[itt]o	By Coffeehouse	00..2..00
D[itt]o	By Mr. Hopkins's Clerk[7]	00..5..00
5[th]	By Dinner	00..1..2
6[th]	By D[itt]o & going W[estminster] Hall & returning	00..2..3
D[itt]o	By Washerwoman	00..9..7
7th	By dinner	00..1..00
D[itt]o	By going to W[estminster] Hall & returning	00..00..6
8[th]	By Exceedings[8] at entring into Commons	00..13..00
D[itt]o	By Bond & Recipiatur[9] on the same	00..14..6
D[itt]o	By Butler & for Gown	00..10..00
9[th]	By dinner	00..1..4
10[th]	By Exceedings	00..00..8
11[th]	By China as [per] Acc[oun]t	3..14..6
D[itt]o	By Teakettle Candlesticks &c	2..4..6
D[itt]o	By Exceedings in the Hall[10]	00..1..00
12[th]	By Water Pitcher	00..2..00
D[itt]o	By Mr. Alston's[11] servant	00..1..00
D[itt]o	By a lb of Candles	00..00..7
D[itt]o	By 2 doz[en] biscuit Butter & Cream	00..1..3 ½
D[itt]o	By Porterage	00..1..6
D[itt]o	By Coffeehouse	00..2..2
13[th]	By Dinner	00..1..2
D[itt]o	By 6 lb of Sugar at 10[d] [per] lb	00..5..00
D[itt]o	By a Ride to Hamstead[12]	00..3..00
14[th]	By a p[ai]r of Gloves	00..1..6
D[itt]o	By Frikholder & going to W[estminster] Hall	00..1..8 ½
D[itt]o	By Vauxhall	00..5..00
D[itt]o	By cleaning Windows	00..3..00
D[itt]o	By the Smith as [per] Acc[oun]t	1..17..6
D[itt]o	By Mr. Penns Servants & Coach hire	00..5..6

16[th]	By Mr. Alstons servant	00..1..00
D[itt]o	By a Violin & Book	1..2..6
D[itt]o	By a lb of Tea	00..12..00
17[th]	By Dinner	00..1..00
D[itt]o	By Cream Butter &c for a week	00..1..3
18[th]	By dinner	00..1..2
19[th]	By Exceedings in the Hall	00..1..00
20th	By Washerwoman	00..6..00
21st	By Exceedings in the Hall	00..1..00
[page break]		**£72..1..1½**

1754	**Brought forward**	**£72..1..1½**
May 22[d]	By Exceedings in the Hall	00..1..00
D[itt]o	By Coffee house	00..2..6
23[d]	By Exceedings in the Hall	00..00..8
D[itt]o	By Coach hire from Mr. Bacon's	00..1..00
D[itt]o	By Cream Butter &c	00..1..2
24[th]	By Paper Ink stand Ink &c	00..7..9
D[itt]o	By Brooms Coal Scoop Brushes &c	1..4..4
D[itt]o	By Exceedings in the Hall	00..00..9
25[th]	By D[itt]o	00..00..6
D[itt]o	By Washerwoman	00..2..4 ½
	By Ten Plays this Season	1..10..00
D[itt]o	By Furniture as [per] Acc[oun]t	40..5..00
26[th]	By Cream Biscuit Cheese &c	00..4..5
D[itt]o	By Exceedings in the Hall	00..1..00
D[itt]o	By the ["]Spirit of Laws" A Book[13]	00..12..6
27[th]	By Exceedings in the Hall	00..1..2
D[itt]o	By Mr. Anderson's footman	00..1..00
D[itt]o	By a Note Book	00..2..3
28[th]	By Exceedings in the Hall	00..00..7
		£117..2..1

<I have perused this acco[un]t and do not find in itt any charge that tends to extravagancy, or that could have been saved, in [th]e usuall way of liveing of such as [live as] {are} Students in [th]e Temple—

J Hanbury
May 30: 1754—>

Ms (PPL-JDFP)

[1] JD probably purchased the seventh edition of Edward Coke, *An Abridgment of the First Part of Ld. Coke's Institutes; with Great Additions, Explaining Many of the Difficult Cases, and Shewing in What Points the Law Has Been Altered by Late Resolutions and Acts of Parliament. By William Hawkins, Serjeant at Law* (London: H. Lintot, 1751), the first edition of which had been published in 1711. William Hawkins (1682–1750) attended Inner Temple, was called to the bar in 1707, and became a sergeant-at-law in 1724. He also wrote *A Treatise of the Pleas of the Crown* (1716–21) and an edition of *Statutes at Large* (*ODNB*).

[2] Clapham, now a district within London, was about four mi. from the city in 1754. JD had taken lodgings there in hopes of improving his health. See doc. 1:9, above.

[3] Richmond was the name of the town in the vicinity of Henry VII's (1457–1509) Richmond Palace southwest of London. It is now within the London borough of Richmond upon Thames.

[4] The Star and Garter tavern, opened in 1738, was situated at the summit of Richmond Hill, which was still about ten mi. from London in the mid-19th cent.

[5] Twickenham was a village located on the Thames about ten mi. southwest from central London. It now lies within the London borough of Richmond upon Thames.

[6] This mixture of sherry, whey, and sugar was used as a remedy for various minor ailments, including colds.

[7] JD is presumably referring to James Horsfall.

[8] Exceedings: "Extra commons allowed on festival occasions" (*OED*).

[9] Apparently this Latin term was applied to a fee for entering commons. See *Master Worsley's Book*, 183, 186, 188, 190.

[10] Middle Temple Hall, begun in 1562, is a center of life at Middle Temple, where, among other things, the commons dining takes place.

[11] Possibly William Alston (1728–1799), who was admitted to Middle Temple in 1751 and called to the bar in 1753. He maintained chambers at the Temple at least from 1753 to 1757. Alston later became rector of Lofthouse in Cleveland (Charles Ryskamp, *William Cowper of the Inner Temple, Esq.: A Study of His Life and Works to the Year 1768* [Cambridge, UK: Cambridge University Press, 1959], 50).

[12] Hampstead in the 1750s was a village somewhat noted for its mineral springs. It now lies within the London borough of Camden, about four mi. northwest of Charing Cross.

[13] Charles de Secondat, Baron de Montesquieu, *The Spirit of the Laws*, transl. Mr. Nugent, 2 vols. (London: J. Nourse and P. Vaillant, 1752).

16
Bond for William Hicks, June 12, 1754

William Hicks was admitted to the Middle Temple on June 18, 1753, and JD was one of his securities on his bond. The two men remained friends until Hicks's death, with JD then acting as a guardian for his son.

Know all Men *by these Presents, That We William Hicks of the Middle Temple Gentleman John Dickenson of the same and Charles Whiting of Saint Mary Somerset of Queen Hithe[1] Coal Merchant do Stand, and are firmly Bound unto John Hervey Esquire Treasurer of the said Society,* ~~*Sir John Strange Knight Master of the Rolls Sir James*~~

Lowther Baronet Sir Richard Lloyd Knight & Francis Eld Esquire of
the Middle-Temple, aforesaid, in Twenty Pounds of Lawful Money of Great-
Britain, to be paid to the said ~~*John*~~ *Sir John Sir James Sir Richard and
Francis* or any of them, their, or any of their Executors, Administrators or
Assigns: To which Payment well and truly to be made, We bind us and every
of us, our, and each of our Heirs, Executors, and Administrators, firmly by
these Presents. Sealed with our Seals. Dated this *twelfth* Day of *June* in
the *twentyseventh* Year of the Reign of our Sovereign Lord *George the
Second* King of Great-Britain, France and Ireland, *Defender of the Faith,*
&c. and in the Year of our LORD, 17*54*

Wm Hicks[3] [seal]

Sealed and Delivered
  In Presence of *Ch's Hopkins*   *J: Dickinson* [seal]

Chals Whiting [seal]

(No: 7989) [page break]

*The Condition of this Obligation is such, That if the within Bounden
 William Hicks do from Time to Time, during all such Time as he shall
continue, and be One of the Society and Fellowship of the Middle-
Temple, London, usually resort to Divine Service and Sermon, in the
Temple-Church, and communicate there, so often as by the Law of this
Land he ought to do. And also Satisfy and Pay to the Cook of the said
Middle-Temple, for the Time being, all such Sum and Sums of Money,
as shall become due from him to the said Cook for his Commons, within
three Weeks after the same shall be due, and every Term pay the antient
and accustomed Duty or Sum of one Shilling and eight Pence, for his
Pensions: And also, Satisfy and Pay, all such Debts, Duties, Charges,
and Things which by Usage, Order or Custom of the said Society, now
are, or hereafter shall become Due and Payable by him, within three
Weeks after the same shall be Due. And also, Observe, Perform, Fulfil
and Keep all such Orders as are, or shall be made, for the good
Government of the said Society, and shall not, during his Continuance
in the Middle-Temple aforesaid, Practice as a common Attorney or
Solicitor, in any Court of Justice in England, then this Obligation to be
void, or else to remain in Force.*

DS (UkLoMT -MT.3/CBB)

---

1 Queenhithe is a London ward, bordering the River Thames and south of St. Paul's Cathedral. The parish of Saint Mary Somerset lay within that ward.

2 Strange died on May 18, 1754 (see doc. 1:14). The appearance and then deletion of his name indicates that a portion of this document was filled in before the June date thereon.

3 William Hicks (1735–1772), originally from New York, but then of Philadelphia, was admitted to practice as an attorney before the Pennsylvania Supreme Court in 1768. In 1770, he was appointed prothonotary, clerk of the Orphans' Court, recorder of deeds, and a justice for Bucks Co., Pa. Also a political pamphleteer, he once angered JD with his positon (see vol. 4 of the present edition). But their friendship remained strong, and JD became executor of his will. See Charles P. Keith, *The Provincial Councillors of Pennsylvania: Who Held Office Between 1733 and 1776* . . . (Philadelphia, 1833), 456; John Hugh Campbell, *History of the Friendly Sons of St. Patrick and of the Hibernian Society for the Relief of Emigrants from Ireland: March 17, 1771–March 17, 1892* (Philadelphia: Hibernian Society, 1892), 143–44.

17
To Mary Cadwalader Dickinson, August 1, 1754

———————————————————

London Aug[us]t 1st—1754

Most Honourd Mother,

Your favour by Mesnard[1] I have rec[eive]d with a Joy that can be equalld by Nothing but your Delight in receiving {mine} & I count Myself very happy, in having so carefully seizd every Opportunity of furnishing You with that Gratification: for indeed I am entirely happy, when You are so.

Had I the longest Life of Man to come, it woud be insufficient with the utmost Industry & Attention to discharge that Debt I owe to your Care & Tenderness; & certainly then I will exert my utmost Endeavours to [~~dis?~~]{sat}isfy as much of it as possible. Your kind Admonitions shall be engravd on my Heart, & the constant Rules of my Actions. I will think what You direct, & what I do, & observe the Resemblance; till every action of my Life be such, that Prudence nor Virtue can perceive the least Speck upon them: That I know what is my Duty, You are convincd & indeed it requires no great Wisdom to know that; & I beg You will believe I am determind to put in Practize, every thing I understand in Theory But tho[ugh] this Resolution be taken, Yet the Weakness of Youth may fall a Sacrifice to the Strength of Temptation: This I am aware of, & that very Weakness is my greatest Security, as it puts Me on my guard Milo[2] had never perishd with his hands pinchd in an Oak, had he not confided too much in their Brawn. All Relap[~~illegible~~]{se}'s are worse than the first Disease—And so it is in Vice & Virtue— A fit of Virtue is like Water in a fever, which only encreases its Violence—& a Revolt from Vice is but as a Rebellion in Government; which when subdued, always settles it more firmly: The poor wretch who escapes from Vice for a While, & at last is retaken, finds a great

Discouragment to his future Attempts; & a third or fourth made with the like ill Success, sinks him to the bottom with Despair, & fixes him in a settled obstinate Course of Wickedness.

Sensible of these things, I hope with the Divine Assistance to live in such a Manner, as to procure Me Peace & Happiness, & by the Divine Mercy be advancd to everlasting Joy hereafter: These are thoughts that in the Hurry of Business or Pleasure, will intrude & will be heard; & the only Way to ~~hear~~ {dismiss} them, is to hear them out: No Porters, No Compan[ion?]s can forbid them Entrance, or drive them out: May I then ever hear them [*page break*] & hear them with Pleasure.

I am glad You have got my Letters so readily, & that they serve to convince my Honourd Parents in some faint measure, how much I value their Peace & Quiet. It is impossible, but I should write often, when I think of You always. I knew perfectly what You would think of Mr. Hanbury for his Goodness & Tenderness in acquainting Me with that Opportunity: & indeed You cant conceive too good an Opinion of him.

I am extremely sorry that Brother Henry[3] was not pleasd with my not waiting on him—but I am sure he woud have excusd Me, if he knew the Truth of the Accident. I saw my Brother the beginning of the Week; & promisd to call on him, thursday or Friday: On Monday I was taken with a most violent fit of the feaver & Ague: Tuesday I went to meeting in Mr. Walker's[4] Chaise, & coud not have born the fatigue of going down: Wednesday I had a fit: Thursday Morning I went to Mr. W[illia]m Goldsbrough's,[5] where I was oblidgd to dine; & indeed if I had not—it was too long a Ride to my Brother's, weak as I then was, with two smart fits— from Mr. Goldsbrough's, I went to Pollard Edmonson's[6] to Lodge: & Sent Cato[7] down to Oxford[8] to know, when the Vessel saild—He brought Me Word; I must be down friday Night: I coud not, for I had my fit—& Saturday Morning early—I went to Oxford. As this was the Case, Was there a possibility of my going to my Brothers? I am sure it woud have been a great Pleasure to Me, but know, he would not {have} expected it, had he known how unwell I was—

My Honourd Father, in one of his Letters mentions the receiving mine from Sharp's Island;[9] shoud be glad to know if some Verses (which You commanded Me to leave behind) inclosd in it, got safe to hand.

Mrs. Anderson was very glad to hear of your Health, & desires Me to present her very sincere Love to You & My Hon[ore]d Father: I spend some very agreable Hours there: I think She is one of the finest Women I ever met with. [*page break*]

I am highly delighted with the Account of my dear Brother: Nothing coud charm Me more than to hear of his Improvment, & the Satisfaction he gave You: I have writ to the Pretious fellow, & beg'd of him to miss no

Opportunity of writing to Me: It is certainly some disadvantage to be from You, as he will have nobody to spur him on, unless it be done by Letter, or his good Uncle Cadwalader take that trouble upon him, to whose Kindness I am indebted for a great deal of good Advice, which I think has been of some Service to Me. I shar'd in all the Pleasure of the fellow's Jaunt home, which must have been a very fine one; & wou'd very willingly have exchangd London for it: but I must comfort myself with Prospects of those things hereafter. The pleasantest Way I find here of spending my time is in Books; to which I may say I apply myself pretty closely: I am quite hearty & well: I have a very good Appetite, & grow stronger every day: But the greatest Cordial I can have, is a Letter from home: it enlivens my Spirits & gives them a new flow; but generally gives Me a Holyday; for it brings so many things into my mind, that for a day or two I can do nothing but think of You.

I have not yet seen much of England, but have taken a few Rides within ten or twenty miles of London; which convince Me it is the finest Country in the world. It is not level, nor rough; but consists of fine vallies & gently rising Hills, which constantly vary the Prospect. Sometimes from the top of one of them You look down into a charming Vale, or if it happens to be a little higher than com[m]on Your eye travels over Hills & Dales, without number, & meets with Villages & Country Seats, in almost every Spot. Add to this that the fields are all separated by Hedges & trees, which appear like Lace or fringe, ~~which~~ and give a great Beauty & Regularity to the Whole. The most surprizing thing I have met with, in England, is the universal Elegance reigning thro[ugh] all Ranks of People. One cant go into any village near London, & find out any little hutt or Cottage so despicable or mean, but what You will find something pretty (always extremely neat) & of taste about it— Let them be ever so crowded, they will have a little yard before the Door; & that shall have a gravel Walk, if it is but two foot wide; & the sides of it are always [*page break*] adornd with some flowers, & Vines of some kind running over the Walls or Pales. To see these little Hovels so genteely set off, gives Me more pleasure than a View of the most magnificent Palace, as it convinces Me of the general Politeness of the People: I say Politeness, because Elegance of one Sort brings all her Sisters with her.

You cant conceive how the Citizens are despisd at this End of the town, with Respect to their Politeness. Cit bears the same Signification here, as Clown does with Us, or rather worse; for it means an awkard imitator of Gentility: Nothing within Temple Barr,[10] can be as it shoud be: And indeed there is some ground for these accusations. Finery & Stiffness are the two chief Ingredients of your wealthy Citizens: & when they leave off Business, & imagine their Money will entitle them to respect & the Joys of Life—they are so ignorant of every thing from their Counter, that they are not fit to converse with People of Fashion & Breeding, & are perfect Whales in Company, so clumsy & so unweildy,{!} & all their Mammon cannot support their Spirits under the visible disparity. On the other hand, they are so polite in this Climate, that the Language is not polite enough for their Expression: And they have Phrazes at Court now, that woud not have been understood by Queen Elizabeth's[11] wisest Counsellors—thus the polite manner of praising or dispraising any things, is "It is, or it is not, the thing—with a particular Emphasis on the{E}, which had{s} raisd that diminutive to one of the foremost Places in the English Tongue.

I lately Rec[eive]d a very kind Letter from Brother Goldsbrough, I shall write to him by the first Ship to Maryland. Robert is very well, & presents his Love to You, My Honourd Father & my dear Brother.

I have got rid of my Pimple entirely, but by a painful and expensive way: it was of the nature of Wens,[12] & was encreasing, which woud have made it very ugly, as it woud have grown into an Artery w[hic]h conveys the Spittle just under the Ear; & which did make it a very nice Operation: I therefore applied to one of the first Surgeons in London {one Warner},[13] & for ten Guineas, He cut it out with no Damage in the world. It had grown much deeper into the flesh than it appeard out: It has been well these several weeks—& in six months, it cant be perceivd that there is any scar. When I am writing to You, Most Honourd Mother, I dont know when to leave off, but my Pen & Paper begin to inform Me, that all human [*in left margin:*] things have an End: but my Affection for You shall end only with my Life. I am with the greatest Sincerity & Prayers for your Happiness, Your most Dutiful & Loving Son

John Dickinson

P.S. My Lady Penn i{wa}s deliv[ere]d of a fine Boy[14] the 18th of this month—I am just going to congratulate Mr. Penn on the occasion. Remember Me to all.

[*in left margin of first page:*] {Please to remember some Gammons &c by Capt[ain] Hill.}

[*in top margin of final page, Samuel Dickinson:*] <August the 1:st 1754— To Mamey>

ALS (PPL-JDFP)

¹ Capt. Stephen Mesnard's ship arrived at Dover in early July (*Public Advertiser* [London], July 6, 1754).

² Milo of Croton (or Kroton) was a famous Greek 6th c. BC wrestler who won six Olympic titles, five of them consecutively from the 62nd to the 66th Olympiad. While walking through a forest, Milo came upon a tree trunk partially split by wood cutters and held open with wedges. He tried to split the trunk in half with his bare hands, but in doing so the wedges fell out and the trunk closed on his hands. Unable to escape, he was eventually eaten by wild beasts.

³ Henry Dickinson (born c. 1718) was JD's half brother and only surviving son from his father's first marriage.

⁴ Perhaps a reference to Philip Walker (d. 1776), who was married to Elizabeth Dickinson Richardson (died c. 1755), a daughter of James Dickinson (d. 1738). The couple apparently lived at this time in Talbot Co., Md., although after his wife's death, Walker became an Anglican minister serving parishes in Anne Arundel and Caroline counties.

⁵ Most likely William Goldsborough (1709–1760), brother of JD's brother-in-law Charles Goldsborough. His plantation was located on Island Creek in Talbot Co.

⁶ Pollard Edmondson (c. 1718–1794) was a Quaker planter from Talbot Co. who was married to Mary Dickinson (d. 1765), daughter of James Dickinson. He represented Talbot Co. in the Maryland legislature.

⁷ Cato Dickinson (d. 1807) was JD's slave. Although Cato is not mentioned expressly in any of the extant manumission deeds in 1777 (PHi-RRL) or a 1779 addendum to that deed, 1781 (PHi-Logan), or 1786, he would have received his freedom at the latest in 1786, when JD manumitted the last of the slaves in his possession (Kent County Delaware Deed Book y-1, p. 217, De-Ar).

⁸ Oxford is a port town in Talbot Co.

⁹ Sharp's Island, named after Quaker physician Peter Sharpe (d. 1672), was situated in the Chesapeake Bay at the mouth of the Choptank River in Talbot Co. The island no longer exists, having completely eroded by the 1940s.

¹⁰ Temple Barr: "The name of the barrier or gateway closing the entrance into the City of London from the Strand" (*OED*).

¹¹ Elizabeth I (1533–1603) ruled England as queen from 1558 until her death.

¹² Wen: "A lump or protuberance on the body, a knot, bunch, wart" (*OED*).

¹³ Joseph Warner (1717–1801) was a surgeon at Guy's Hospital and a fellow of the Royal Society and published *Cases in Surgery* . . . 2nd ed. (London: J. and R. Tonson and S. Draper, 1754).

¹⁴ Thomas Penn (1754–1757).

18
To Mary Cadwalader Dickinson, August 15, 1754

London Aug[us]t 15th—1754—

Honourd Mother,

I cannot but wish Peace & everlasting Joy to that Man, Who first invented the Art of Letters, since his Ingenuity & Labours supply Me with such a Constant Fountain of Happiness—Since by his Discovery I am enabled to acquaint the dearest Persons on Earth, with my Health, Employments, Pleasures, Hopes, Fears & Wishes, & in the agreable Recital, almost forget the distance that separates Us.

The present Time if well spent, is a{ple}asant, but never equal to what We exspect from future Views—& yet when these arrive, they are but disappointments, & then We cast our Sight still further; We are again deceivd, & again, till at Length quite tird, We take a greater Assurance, & trust for Happiness in another State,

Hope travels thro', nor quits Us when We die {Pope}[1]

Indeed were it not for those Prospects, Life woud be but a Burthensome Lot; but they like the Sun gild it with a delightful Lustre, & banish all its gloom: Abstracted from this, the most sanguine Views assume a wretched Paleness. Thus I please Myself with the Hopes of making You happy by my Credit, & of living with Reputation & Ease— Alas! Grant Me the Completion of my Wishes; the Measure is no sooner full, but it is leaking out— I divert Myself with the Smoothness of the Surface, but fondly blind, dont observe how it is still sinking, till at last—I am surprizd by the Dregs. If such be Life, What is its Worth? Of itself it is Nothing: But it is a strange kind of Arithmetick, which tho[ugh] a Nought itself derives all its Value from the figures placd <u>after</u> it: It is a Miserable Inn, but a good Road: To the fool it is a rough Diamond, which he flings to the Swine;[2] to the Wise, it is a Pretious Jewell, which hereafter shall be their greatest Ornament: In short, to those who trust their whole Stock in it, it is a Bubble more fatal than the South Sea;[3] And while they count themselves immensely Rich, th' imaginary Sums vanish into Air, & in their Place appear as immense Debts contracted under the unhappy Infatuation. Life then derives its whole Worth from a Knowledge of its Worth, & is [*page break*] of no Value only, when it is valued too much: This Knowledge teaches how trivial is every thing in it: Not that I despise the Goods of this World, Fame, Respect, Wealth: I value them, but as they deserve, & would take the same Care to procure them (only greater in Proportion to the Length & Importance of the Journey) as I woud good Boots, or an easy horse, upon a Journey, which serve to render it more agreable, but are useless when it is finishd. And yet how anxious are men about them? How desirous not only of procuring the Pleasures & Regard of the World, but of engaging a Reverence even to their Names, to Words, to Nothing; there is something in Human Nature repugnant to Dissolution

"For Who to dumb Forgetfullness a Prey,
This pleasing Anxious Being e'er resignd,
Left the warm Precincts of the Chearful Day,
Nor cast one longing Ling'ring Look behind?["][4]

But how vain are all their Labours? How many Grand Monumen{ts} & Pompous Inscriptions have moulderd away in Westminster Abbey?[5] I sometimes walk there, & with a pleasing Awe observe the Ravages made by **Time**, in the Honours of Kings & the most illustrious [~~illegible~~]{F}amilies:

Every Moment steals something from their Titles, & even the newest in a few years may serve for mine. There is something agreably Pensive in rambling thro[ugh] the long solemn Isles & antient Cloisters? What a fine Instruction may one Receive from viewing the Monuments of Our greatest Monarchs—of an Edward Henry or Elizabeth,[6] & reflecting, that such is the meaness of all Worldly Glory, that the most despicable Beggar woud not change his Bread & Water for all the Fame, & all the Honours of the Mightiest Princes.
Tho[ugh] this Place is extremely August, & Noble, & the Use ~~of~~ which ~~it~~ {is} ~~is~~ made of it, inspires One with Respect & Reverence, yet as it is expected to see the Remains of the Great & Honourd, & there are such Numbers of them, None strikes in a particular & affecting manner.

But I was lately at St. Alban's, & in a little Church there calld St. Michaels, I ~~was surprizd to~~ found the Monument of the great Bacon.[7] To see the greatest Man that ever livd, whose Mind was reckond a Counterpart to Nature, Whose Merit raisd him to the highest Dignities of his Country, & whose Discoveries have entaild a debt on all the Human Race, laid in a little Parish Church, in a private Place, & amongst Ploughmen & Labourers, had [*page break*] Something in it inconceivably affecting: I was struck with Awe at entring the Repository of such a man; I was struck with Grief at entring such a Repository of <u>such</u> a man. He has a Statue of Grey Marble erected to his Memory; he is represented in the Dress of the Times, sitting & very gracefully leaning on his right hand, which is supported by the Elbow of the Chair, his left hanging carelessly down by his Side, as if he were in Affliction.

When one contemplates such Instances as these, the world grows diminutively mean, the mind spurns at it, & finds its Thirst unslakd with all its Enjoyments: But yet as We were not designd for Angels here, Our Passions recall us to the Duties {of Humanity}, & Reason teaches Us to make the Passage as agreable as possible that leads to future Happiness—And thus while Each pursues his particular Scheme, he unknowing and undesignedly serves as a Wheel to effect the general Good—[8] Amongst others I am putting in my little Oar, & exerting my small Strength; but what will be the the Event of my weak Endeavours, Time alone can discover: This however I am convincd of, that there cannot be upon Earth, a nobler Employment than the Defence of Innocence, the Support of Justice, & the Preservation of Peace and Harmony amongst Men: These are the Offices of my Profession, & if my Abilities are but equal to my Inclination, they will not be undischa[r]gd by Me.

I am now busily engagd in Reading, which I can bear better than ever: I rise constantly at five, & read eight hours every day, which is as much as I can or ought to do; for greater Application woud not only hurt Me, but woud be of no Service, as it woud fatigue Me too much. I dine at four, & am in bed by ten: In short I live in a manner the most proper to answer the purposes for which I came, & nothing gives Me more delight, than to think I do every thing, which I believe You woud have Me. Indeed by this Studious way of Life, I dont see so much of England, but when I have atchievd the Principal Point, it will be time enough to attend to those more immaterial: Tho[ugh] I dont deny Myself {all} [*page break*] kind of Entertainment: I ride out sometimes, & have lately been at Hampton Court.[9] This a Palace built originally by Cardinal Woolsey, in the Height of his Grandeur, but upon his fall, came to the Crown, & by King William was greatly [~~illegible~~] enlargd & beautified.[10] The old Building, is of an odd kind of Magnificence, which now would be calld Whimsical—and consists of two or three large square Courts built all round—which serve only for Offices—but the Additions, which are the only part, in which the Royal family ever livd, is a fine front of Brick & Stone, which looks down the River Thames.

There are a great Number of fine Rooms in it, but nothing equal to what one would expect for a Monarch of great-Britain. Many of them are adornd with Tapestry workd with the Needle; the Stories are generally taken out of the Scripture; but far the most excellent are the Battles of Alexander:[11] it is {im}possible to excell these with the Pencil—the Colours, the Attitudes & the Design, are so lively, so strong & so proper: Besides several other very rich Ornaments—in this Palace, are the famous Cartoons of Raphael.[12] A Person of so little Knowledge as I am, in Painting, to be sure must be ignorant of a thousand Beauties & exquisite Touches which woud ravish an Artist, or one of more Acquaintance with Performances of this ~~stature~~ {sort:}: However as I am in some manner a Judge of Nature, & those P[eice?]s are exact Copies of her, I was highly charmd with them. Every Passion is expressd on the proper face, as it must certainly have appeard at the time. When Simon the Sorcerer[13] is struck blind, Astonishment, Rage, Shame & Grief are all mixd in his Countenance; & such is the awkard & terrified Projection of his hands, & groping before him, that one believes the fact to have happend that Moment. Here is also a very fine Picture of King William on Horseback, by Kneller,[14] which I admire Prodigiously. When I am writing to You Honourd Mother, I dont know when to end, but please to forgive this long Scrawl, which should have been much shorter, had I but more Time. I beg You woud omit no Opportunity of Writing, for indeed Nothing upon Earth gives Me more Pleasure than receiving your Letters, & hearing of your Health. I am oblig'd to conclude, but [*in left margin*:] while Life & Sense remain, Shall be, & endeavour by every action to approve Myself, Honourd Mother, Your most Dutiful & most Affectionate Son,

John Dickinson

[*in top margin, Samuel Dickinson*:] <August the 15:th 1754 To Mamey>

ALS (PPL-JDFP)

---

[1] Pope, "Epistle II," *Essay on Man*, 54.

[2] A reference to Matt. 7:6: "Give not that which is holy unto the dogs, neither cast ye your pearls before swine, lest they trample them under their feet, and turn again and rend you."

[3] The South Sea Bubble was an investment crash that centered on the South Sea Company (est. 1711). In early 1720, Parliament allowed the company to assume the national debt, causing a spike in the value of its shares and a spate of risky investing. The bubble burst in September of that year, ruining many investors and prompting the House of Commons to investigate. See Richard Dale, *The First Crash: Lessons from the South Sea Bubble* (Princeton, N.J.: Princeton University Press, 2004).

[4] Thomas Gray, *An Elegy Wrote in a Country Churchyard* (London: R. Dodsley, 1751), 9.

[5] Westminster Abbey, located near the Houses of Parliament, now contains over 600 wall plaques and monuments, and over 3,000 individuals are buried or commemorated there.

[6] Among the monarchs' memorials JD might have seen are Edward the Confessor (c. 1003–1066), Edward I (1239–1307), III (1312–1377); Henry III (1207–1272), V (1386–1422), VII; and Elizabeth I.

[7] St. Albans is northwest of London in Hertfordshire. St. Michael's church was built in the late 900s or early 1000s over the site of the basilica, the headquarters of Roman Verulamium. Sir Francis Bacon (1561–1626) was an English philosopher, scientist, and statesman. Knighted by James I in 1603, he was created first viscount of St. Alban in 1621. The monument, which was erected shortly after Bacon's death, is located in an alcove to the left of the altar.

[8] Perhaps a reference to Pope's *Essay on Man* (6), which JD also cited in his first *Farmer's Letter*, *PG*, Dec. 3, 1767 .

[9] Hampton Court is a royal palace southwest of London in the borough of Richmond on Thames.

[10] Thomas Woolsey (1473–1530) was appointed to the position of cardinal in 1515, the year construction on Hampton Court began. When Woolsey fell out of favor, Henry VIII (1491–1547) obtained Hampton Court from him in the late 1520s and promptly began renovations. Shortly after the accession of William III (1650–1702) in 1689, he assigned Christopher Wren (1632–1723) to reconstruct the palace in a more modern Baroque style. Ultimately about half of the old palace survived.

[11] Alexander the Great (356–323 BC).

[12] Cartoon: "A drawing on stout paper, made as a design for a painting of the same size to be executed in fresco or oil, or for a work in tapestry, mosaic, stained glass, or the like" (*OED*). Pope Leo X (1475–1521) commissioned the cartoons depicting Sts. Peter and Paul in 1515 from Raphael Sanzio (1483–1520); the cartoons were to serve as full-scale designs for tapestries to be hung on the lower walls of the Sistine Chapel. The surviving cartoons are now housed in the Victoria and Albert Museum in London.

[13] Raphael's cartoon "The Conversion of the Proconsul" depicts the sorcerer Elymas, whom Saint Paul struck blind for trying to stop the spread of the Gospel (Acts 13:5–12). JD confused Elymas with the sorcerer Simon Magus, who was rebuked for offering Saints Peter and John money so that they would give him spiritual gifts (Acts 8:9–24).

[14] Sir Godfrey Kneller (1646–1723) was a German-born painter who moved to England in 1674 and became the country's leading portraitist. The portrait JD saw hung in the presence chamber and celebrates William III's return from the negotiations that led to the Peace of Ryswick in 1697.

19
To Samuel Dickinson, August 15, 1754

London Aug[us]t 15th—1754

Honourd Father,

    I wrote to You a few days ago by Capt[ai]n Reeve;[1] but as I know I can never write too often for your Satisfaction, or my own Pleasure, I assume my Pe[~~illegible~~]{n a}gain: And though your kind Affection emboldens Me to trouble You with an account of my Affairs, & what I am doing, yet the Nature of them is such, that they can afford little Entertainment in the Recital. I rise, eat, read & sleep, & sleeping, reading, eating & rising repeated over & over, produce that Consumption of Time, w[hic]h is calld Life: Indeed I am like Homer's Heroes, of whom Prior humourously says,

        "The greatest Actions I can find,

        Is that, they did their work, & dind.["][2]

    What will be the Event of my Labours, Futurity must determine but were it not for some Prospects from her favours, this kind of Existence woud be but tolerable: for such is the Natu[re] of our minds, they will be making Ex[cur]sions backwards [and] forwards: sometimes She runs over the uncertain Scenes of Life to come, of which Fancy, Pride, Ambition & other Passions form a strange Picture: after tiring herself with this diversion, She soars into the Skies, & looks at Eternity: She examines it on all sides, admires it prodigiously, & after a thousand fruitless attempts to comprehend it, is struck with Astonishment, & finding it impregnable, drops down again to Earth; and, as She must be employd, Rambles thro' all the Stages of Time past—an Entertainment Productive of all good: When I unbend Myself from Study, this is frequently my Employment; and when I thus compare things past with the present, I seem to Myself to have livd all my Days in a Place, from which I had a view only right before Me; What was above Me, & around Me, I knew little of: But now I am releasd from the Limits which confind Me, & find my faculties more at large: For as Madness proceeds from too close an Attention to <u>one</u> Object, so do folly & Imprudence from a Knowledge of too <u>few</u>. Ignorance is not only the Mother of all Errors—but of all Vices; & as Inferiority teaches Us Submission & Care, so does Equality instruct Us in [*page break*] Humanity & Wisdom Tho[ugh] by Your uncommon Goodness & Tenderness, I had the Happiness of a more Liberal Education, than most of my Countrymen, yet I find a good many Mistakes, which I am dayly pulling up, & which I hope in time to have quite eradicated.   What then must be the Condition of Children brought up & invelopd in Ignorance? Their very Ignorance is their Happiness; for when they come to See the Difference between themselves, & the polite Part of the World, they must be miserable: From hence it happens, that young fellows from America, coming here still aim at the Respect & Place they had at home, & in imitating those so greatly above them, like the Frog in the Fable, burst in the Attempt.[3] I know by Sight half a Dozen of those fellows, now

60

tottring on the side of a Jail.   The Reason of this is easily discoverd by only tracing them to their Childhood. What a Nest of Vices shall We find in the Education of a Gentleman's Son in America? The little mortal can no sooner talk than he is exercising {his Commands} over the black Children about him; no sooner walks, but he is beating them for executing his Orders, too slowly or wrong. What Passions spring up from hence? What Crops of Pride, Selfishness, Peevishness, Violence, Anger, Meaness, Revenge & Cruelty? By governing Slaves from his Infancy, he becomes a Slave himself: From amongst them, he is out of his Element: He dreads the Sight of an Equal; He is Cowardly & Sheepish before Persons of any Fashion; barb'rous & tyrannical amongst Inferiors. What a poor Creature is this to come into the world? And yet this in a great Measure is the Case in the Colonies: By conversing constantly with Slaves, they acquire a mean groveling way of thinking with the utmost Pride & Conceit. But here the first Lesson a Person Learns, is that he is nothing. This brings him insensibly to a Knowledge of himself, & of course, to a just Notion of things. After his D̶{R}ecovery from this mortifying Discovery; he considers the Nature of the things w[hic]h make this difference between himself & others, & since he cant attract the Admiration of Mankind, the same Pride {(}which is now become proper,̶{)} that made him desire it, now prevents his paying it to others— Thus a titled Coward, or a gilded Scoundrel he laughs at & despises. I dont pretend these Inconveniences are peculiar to America— If a person is brought up in a Country place in England, with the same indulgence, he is equally ignorant, equally boorish— But London is the place, where a person may learn Truth, where unless he is an absolute fool, he may see human Nature in all Shapes— The honest gener{ous} mind displayd in a frank chearful Behaviour—the Rascal maskd with Smiles & Kindness—Great Qualities eaten up by Conceit; small Abilities, shining & respected by a Prudent Conduct—A Coward lurking und[er] a fierce Hat, & great [*in left margin:*] Noise—A man of Courage conceald by Silence & good Nature. One learns what Qualifications a man wants by his Affectation of them, & What are his Ends—by his Care to conceal them. In short he learns every thing that will be useful hereafter.

I am Honourd Father, Your most dutiful & Affectionate Son

John Dickinson

ALS (PPL-JDFP)

---

¹ Peter Reeve (c. 1714–1800) was a Quaker ship captain and merchant, who, along with Benjamin Franklin and other investors, established a linen factory in Philadelphia in 1764. His ship, the *Lydia*, arrived at Philadelphia between Sept. 28 and Oct. 3 (*PG*, Oct. 3, 1754).

² Matthew Prior (1664–1721) was an English poet and diplomat who helped negotiate the treaties of Ryswick (1697) and Utrecht (1713). The quotation is from his 1689 poem, "Epistle to Mr. Fleetwood Shephard." See *Miscellany Poems Upon Several Occasions* (London: P.

Buck, 1692), 9. The full verse reads: "Thus, of your Heroes and Brave Boys, / With whom Old *Homer* makes such Noise, / The greatest Actions I can find, / Are, that they did their Work, and Din'd."

[3] A reference to one of Æsop's fables in which a frog tries to inflate himself to the size of an ox but, as JD writes, bursts in the attempt (*Æsop's Fables. With Instructive Morals and Reflections, Abstracted from all Party Considerations, Adapted to All Capacities; And design'd to promote Religion, Morality, and Universal Benevolence* [London, J. Osborn, Jr., 1740], 27–28).

20
To Mary Cadwalader Dickinson, September 6, 1754

London Sept[embe]r 6[th]—1754

Honourd Mother,

I have many Opportunities of Writing to You, I never neglect any of them, & still I am wishing for more, tho[ugh] I am afraid my Letters are sometimes so long & so trifling that they are quite tiresome: However I know whom I write to so well, that tho[ugh] I do trespass on her Patience, I am sure her Goodness will forgive Me: And yet when I take my Pen, I scarce restrain Myself from saying, what I have so often said before, & attempting in vain to declare an Affection, Gratitude & Duty, which never can be exprest: It is as impossible for Me to think of You without being filld with Tenderness, as it is to behold the Sun, without being dazzled The Remembrance instantly melts Me, & the Recollection is so pleasing, that every other thought is swallowd up in it. When I reflect on the Virtues of my Honourd Parents, I love & admire them, but when I think of their Goodness to Me, the Emotion excited in my Breast has no Name. And tho[ugh] it is my Prayer, my Endeavour, that I may be able to make some return for your Kindnesses, yet I am afraid I shall never make such as will satisfy <u>Me</u>. Of all the Advantages that Pope acquird by his Poetry, His Intimacy with the Great, His Fame, His Wealth, I think not in any of them, nay not all of them together, was he so happy, as in the Ability of celebrating & consecrating to Honour the Virtue & Memory of his Parents— [1] And of all the Good Qualities he possest, I esteem him for none so much, as the filial Piety which glows in his Works; and I am convincd, A man whose Soul [~~illegible~~] {containd} so divine a Tenderness, must have been a complete good man.   But as I know You receive some Satisfaction in my Entertainment, I beg leave to acquaint You that since my last I have had a very agreable Jaunt to the Mouth of the Thames— The Company was one Dickinson a Nephew of Jonathan Dickinson whom You knew at Philadelphia, & who now with his Brothers holds 3/4 of the Estate, A Son of Tho[ma]s Hyam A friend & Merchant of great Note, & two Gentlemen their Relations— [2] We went down [*page break*] the River in a Yatcht, & had a most delightful Sail with the County of Kent on one hand, & Essex on the other.

The first is the finest County in England, & the other is very charming—So that We were constantly entertaind with viewing the Villages houses & fields as We went along. When We came down to Sheerness,[3] which is a fortification, We went ashore & examind it, but found nothing extraordinary, So we went on board again, & had another fine Sail up the Medway to Chatham & Rochester.[4] Here We saw a fine Country, but our chief Entertainment was in seeing the Men of War which are brought here about 30 miles from Sheerness, to be in Security, as no Loaded Vessel can {come} up so far.[5] We were on board several Ships of the first Rate, The Royal Sovereign of 112 Guns, the Princess Royal of 90—& many others.[6] And the best Description I can give of them, is the antient one of calling them floating Castles. As to the Accommodations of the Admiral when on board, or the Captain, I was very much deceivd—for they have but one Room, besides their Bed Room & the Room for their Servants, which is a kind of Antichamber— The Rooms are extremely plain, as fine work in an Engagement, but supplies the more Splinters. I saw the Centurion, in which Anson went round the world,[7] but there are not many of the Timbers in her that performd that [*illegible*]{Vo}yage, as She has been since rebuilt— Tis usual, I was told to put the men of War in Docks once in every three Years, so that many of them have been several times repaird, which never were below the Nore.[8] They still go on building Ships dayly, & there lately was one Launchd at Woolwich, at which all the Royal Family except the King were present.[9] There was a Prodigious Concourse of People, for which Reason I did not go. We were on board the Somerset[10] a 70 Gun, in Commission, so that a good many of the People {were on board}, & We saw something of their Management. It is very curious to see how regular & exact every thing is in so large a Vessel. The Officers were very polite & shewd us every hole in her. There was a Lieutenants Lady on board—Who shewd us her little Apartment; & of all the Places I ever beheld, I never saw any thing so neat & pretty.

I think I once mentiond to You, Honourd Mother, how agreable it woud be to Me, to have yours & my Honourd Father's Pictures drawn— Be pleasd to believe, I desire few things more earnestly, & add this one more to the many {obligations} You have conferrd on

Your beyond words Affectionate & dutiful Son
John Dickinson

[*first page, in left margin*:] {I drank Tea with Mrs. Anderson Yesterday— I am never so delighted as when I am there; She has something most surprizingly like You in her manner, & in her person there is a Resemblance only She does not look so well as You. She enquird if I had heard from You lately, & desird Me to present her Love to You. Her two Girls, are both very Sensible & pretty—But the Eldest for Understanding—& the Youngest for Beauty excell every thing I ever saw.}

[*first page, in bottom margin, Samuel Dickinson*] <Sep[tembe]r the 6.th 1754 to Mamey>

ALS (PPL-JDFP)

---

[1] Alexander Pope (1688–1744) is among the most famous British poets. Upon his death, he requested to be laid to rest next to his parents and that a monument be erected in their honor.

[2] Jonathan Dickinson (1663–1722) was a Quaker merchant originally from Jamaica who twice served as mayor of Philadelphia between 1712 and 1719. His nephew Caleb Dickinson (1716–1763), a son of Jonathan's brother, Caleb Dickinson (1670–1728), inherited from his estate. Caleb the nephew was a Bristol merchant. He had two brothers, Ezekiel Dickinson (1711–1788) and Vickris Dickinson (1718–1797). His uncle Thomas Hyam (c. 1679–1763) was a Quaker merchant in Philpot Lane and Fenchurch Street in London. He served as a correspondent for the Society of Friends in Virginia and as a business agent for the Penn family. Which of Thomas Hyam's several sons accompanied JD on this jaunt has not been determined.

[3] Sheerness is on the Isle of Sheppey on the west coast of England in north Kent, at the confluence of the Rivers Medway and Thames. It was first established as a fort in the time of Henry VIII, and was rebuilt after a 1667 Dutch raid.

[4] The River Medway is located south of the Thames in Sussex and Kent counties. Chatham and Rochester are in Kent Co. about a mile apart and about thirteen mi. upriver from Sheerness.

[5] There were Royal Navy dockyards at both Chatham and Sheerness.

[6] HMS *Royal Sovereign* was built in 1701 and broken up in 1768. She was a first-rate 100-gun (not 112, as JD writes) revenge class battleship. HMS *Princess Royal* first launched as HMS *Ossory* in 1682. The ship underwent several name changes, but sailed as *Princess Royal* from 1728 until broken up in 1773. She was a 90-gun second-rate ship of the line.

[7] During the War of Jenkins' Ear/War of the Austrian Succession, Commodore George Anson (1697–1762) embarked on a voyage in 1740 to capture Spanish possessions in the Pacific. He sailed around Cape Horn, up the South American coastline to Mexico, then across the Pacific to China. He returned to England in June of 1744, having circumnavigated the globe. Of the six ships that originally set sail in 1740, only the HMS *Centurion* survived to make the voyage across the Pacific. The *Daily Post* and other London newspapers reported that "The Cargo which Commodore Anson has brought home with him is as follows, viz. 2,600,000 Pieces of Eight (Spanish dollars), 150,000 Ounces of Plate (coin), 10 Bars of Gold, and a large Quantity of Gold and Silver Dust; in the Whole to the Amount of 1,250,000 l. Sterling" (*The Daily Post* [London], June 18, 1744).

[8] The Nore is a sandbank in the River Thames that extends from Shoeburyness to Sheerness. It was used as a fleet anchoring ground.

[9] Located about ten mi. from London, Woolwich Dockyard operated from 1512 to 1869 and was enjoying a booming business during JD's stay in England. JD is apparently referring to the launch of the man of war *Dunkirk* and a smaller vessel there on July 22. According to one report, "Both Launches were very fine, and notwithstanding there were the greatest Number of Boats and Spectators ever seen on the like Occasion, we do not hear of any Accident" (*London Evening Post*, July 20–23, 1754).

[10] HMS *Somerset* was a 70-gun third-rate ship of the line that launched in July 1748. The *Somerset* played a role in the Battles of Lexington and Concord and the Battle of Bunker Hill.

21
To Samuel Dickinson, September 6, 1754

London Sept[embe]r 6th—1754

Honourd Father,

I wrote to You last by Budden,[1] & this is the next opportunity that presents itself, which I take to inform You that I still continue hearty & diligent. I find my Health & Diligence keep Pace together very well, & that the latter does not disagree with the first: So that in my Power & Inclination, I think myself doubly obligd to the Author of all Bounties, as without the one, I coud not be active or useful; & not being so, the other woud be dishonourable & Reproachful: for as the Great Bacon says, "Every man is a Debtor to his Profession, from which as he expects to find Profit & Emolument, So he ought to make Returns of Advantage to the World":[2] And thus by discharging the Duties of his Station, he forms part of that great Chain,[3] which by a Commerce of Services, embraces all mankind, in its be{a}nds.

Whether I shall find those Profits & Emoluments, is something doubtful; but if I do not, there is still the Obligation of a man upon Me; and if I cannot shine amongst the Orators of Philadelphia, I may be a very useful Member of Community in Kent, by prosecuting Debts for Sunday Cloaths. This woud be indeed lessening the Sphere, in which I am expected to move; but woud it not be contracting it to more Security? It woud be retiring from the Censures, Malice & Envy of an ill-naturd World: It woud be taking a Resolution in Youth, which is never thought of till Old Age: And he that never climbs, can never tumble— This is very true, but there is another unlucky Truth, He that never climbs, can never rise. I mention these things ingenuously, because I woud not pretend Myself to be a Wonder of Industry, for I really am sometimes a very lazy fellow, & think as supinely as an Indian about the Honours of Life; & sincerely in my most sanguine Views, When I think of the dear, the Noble Retirement of Kent, I find a great Attraction that way: And tho[ugh] I shall engage in busy Scenes in another Place, Yet when I have acquird Honour enough to shed some few rays of Lustre on Retreat, I am sure I shall turn Husbandman, & till the Bed, which in a short time will receive Me. But {before} I go thus far, I must take care that my first Steps be well planted, & that my Outset be wise, [*page break*] My Course constant & vigilant: So that the Result of all my Philosophy is, the Necessity of being more & more industrious. Nothing is more delightful than this Contemplation of our minds, & examining Ourselves as before A Master. I love to trace my Soul thro[ugh] all her Turns & flights; When She is under the Influence of some Passion, I am pleasd to beat her out of the false Lights & Glosses, which She endeavours to draw over her own desires, & I am never so entertaind as with this Chase of my own Thoughts— They are started perhaps by Reason, perhaps by Folly, then lost in Doubt, Indolence flags, Pride is outrageous, Fear checks, Hope Pants, & Resolution & Industry crown the Labour.

Thus very often a Hint from the Book of Psalms has travelld thro[ugh] a strange confusion of Poets, Historians, Philosophers &c concluded with Galen,[4] "Ars longa, Vita brevis"[5] & been finishd with a large lesson of Coke on Littleton.[6] Indeed let Me think or act as I please, this is generally the End. If I have been industrious, Why i'll be more so, from the Satisfaction it gives Me; If I have been idle, I'll be no more so, from the Uneasiness & Reproaches I give Myself— Besides these, I call in all the Arguments & Reasons I can to my Assistance, for a young fellow is like a Lame person, who ought to use all the Crutches & Aids he can get, to keep him from falling— And tho[ugh] it is a glorious, yet it is a difficult Victory for Youth to perswade itself, that Application is preferable to Pleasure: And no Place abounds more with them than this, tho[ugh] not so much at present: The Nobility & Gentry are not yet come to town, & it is surprising to see what a dead dull place London now is— Most of the Houses shut up, so few Coaches rattling thro[ugh] the Streets or People walking, it seems as if there was some publick Calamity— This is not observable towards the 'Change,[7] where being men of Business, they are oblidgd to be in Town: But presently the tide will turn, & in rush Coaches, Noise, Hurry, Dirt & Confusion, & by the Latter end of November, London will a perfect, or rather imperfect Chaos[:] From which I woud most willingly retire, were it no more profitable & useful, than it is agreable. But yet awhile as it woud be improper to see my Native Country, I can only pray for its Prosperity, & the Happiness of those it contains. Please to remember Me most affectionately to my dear Brother; I have not time to write to him. I am Most Honourd Father, as much as I can be,

Your Affectionate & dutiful Son
John Dickinson

[*first page, in bottom margin, Samuel Dickinson*] <Sep[tembe]r 6:[th] 1754 to me—>

ALS (PPL-JDFP)

---

[1] Richard Budden's ship, the *Myrtilla*, sailed from England on Aug. 23 and arrived at Philadelphia between Nov. 14 and 21 (*WEP*, Aug. 22–24, 1754; *PG*, Nov. 21, 1754).

[2] A version of the opening line of the preface to Francis Bacon, *A Collection of Some Principall Rules and Maximes of the Common Lawes of England* (London: J. Moore Esq., 1630), which reads, "I hold every man a debtor to his profession, from the which, as men of course doe seeke to receive countenance and profit, so ought they of duty to endeavor themselves by way of amends to be a helpe and ornament thereunto." It is unclear if JD paraphrased Bacon himself, or if he copied it from another source. Henry Lintot's 1741 printing of *Lord Bacon's Law Tracts* accurately reproduced the original version. JD's unique formulation, particularly the line that one "ought to make Returns of Advantage to the World," does not appear in any other printed American or British source the editors can find.

[3] A reference to the Great Chain of Being, a complex philosophical understanding of the world, originating in ancient Greece, that everyone and everything was bound together by a series of hierarchical links. See Arthur O. Lovejoy, *The Great Chain of Being: A Study of the History of an Idea*, William James lectures delivered at Harvard University, 1933 (Cambridge, Mass.: Harvard University Press, 1936).

[4] Aelius Galenus (129–c. 200) was a Greek philosopher and physician.

[5] Lat. art is long, life is short. The phrase is originally from Hippocrates' (c. 450–c. 380 BC) *Aphorismi.*

[6] 1 Coke, *Institutes.* The *Institutes* are considered the foundational text for the common law. For Littleton, see doc. 1:24, n. 1.

[7] The Royal Exchange.

22

To Mary Cadwalader Dickinson, October 29, 1754

London Oct[obe]r 29[th]—1754

Honoured Mother,

This Letter comes to You, wrote in part, a considerable time before the Date; for as I very frequently & affectionately remember You, it is impossible for Me to be easy, till I have given some vent to my though[t]s catching them as they flow from the Heart, & this pleases Me for another Reason, as it shews that my Letters are not extorted from Me, but that {I} write what I think, & am not oblidgd to think what I am to write; for indeed, Most Honourd Parent, You cannot conceive how large a Share of my Happiness is formd by the Recollection of You: Every Instant puts Me in mind of You, & my Tenderness is awak{d} by every Incident. The Morning blazes upon Me, & Industry calls me to my Task, while Sleep & Night, with soft & quiet Peace surround You: I cannot but wish that so gently, so free from Care & uneasiness may fly all the Hours of Life. At Evening, I sink to Rest, while You remember Me over your elegant board:[1] I cannot but pray that You may eat the bread of Health, & drink the Wine of Joy; & that long, very long may be the time before You retire to an everlasting Peace.

I sometimes endeavour to divert myself with doing what may employ You at the same time, & I believe it woud give me great Entertainment, to think I was breakfasting when You are; but the silly Whim is impossible— However at last, I comfort Myself with this, That in treading always the Paths of Virtue,

I have You for a constant Companion: This gives even Virtue additional Charms, and [*page break*] even She herself seems to receive new beauty in being practizd by You.

When I write, I find myself always very inquisitive, tho[ugh] nothing woud be a more agreable Employment to Me, than satisfying any Questions You will please to ask Me.   I shoud be glad to know how the Building goes on; or what Hedging is making. My Honourd Father usd to talk of it, & I am very fond of it, since I have been in England: If all the Grounds about our House were enclosd with Hedges, it is not possible to conceive how beautiful they woud look. Woud not two Vistos cut due East & West, Parallel with the Front of our house, the first till it comes to the next open fields, & the other to the Creek contribute much to the beauty of the Place? And I think the charming Walk down to the Wharf, proves that a Visto opposite to the back Door woud be very fine. Please to tell Me, Whether the Yard is alterd: As to the Piazza that was talkd of—the're very uncommon here—& Shells are more usual. The manner of forming Flower Gardens before the Door is this. It[*illegible words*] from the All round close to the Pales,[2] there is a border of about 3½ feet for the flowers, & about four inches deep: There is a walk of Gravel parallel with the house & another down the middle to a folding Gate— The Areas on each Side are grass Platts, with a Statue in the Center of each. If I remember, my Honourd Parents were of Opinion, that ours shoud front the dining room too—& so at the other [ha?] End have a Communication with the back Garden, which woud be very pretty— [*page break*] Forgive Me, my Honourd Parents for giving my opinion on those things, as You have always been so kind as to allow Me this Indulgence; & as it constantly approves of all You do: And I am convincd that when all the Improvements designd in Building, Gardens, Meadows & Clearing, are completed—Poplar-Hall[3] will be a most delightful Spot. The Peach, Cherry & Apple Orchards are true ornaments, as they are agreable to Nature, which in our Climate, requires much fruit & much sh[*torn*] I coud dwell upon these things a long time, so agreable is the Remembrance: And perhaps for the same reason, My Honourd Mother will imagine I now mention Miss [*blank*] for if I am not deceivd, She imagind I had some secret regard for that Young Lady more than She wishd—but really I had not: & I rec[eive]d the account of her intended Marriage, as of any other person that can be mentiond for indeed my Chains were not forgd there.

About the middle of this month, I had a very pleasant Journey to Oxford: I went with Mr. Bell & his Lady Who were acquainted there; So that I was introducd to several Gentlemen of Note in the University— I was treated with the greatest Kindness, & had the Particular favour of dining in one of the publick Halls with the Fellows. Oxford is remarkable for the Prodigious

Number of Noble Buildings, & the Beauty of the Country— And what is still more Remarkable, they have been all [*page break*] built by private Benefactions. Their Halls are noted for Neatness, their Chapels for Elegance, & their Libraries for valuable Collections of Books— Of these last, the Bodleyan Radcliffe's & a{A}ll-Souls are the grandest.[4] In the first I saw a great many Curiosities—A Picture of Tully[5] from an an antient bust: The first Edition of his Offices, which was the first Book ever printed in Europe.[6] Q[ueen] Mary's & Sir W[alter] Raleigh's Prayer Books in Manuscript which for beauty excelld any printing I ever saw:[7] They are adornd with Pictures of the history of the New Testament, exquisitely fine— Queen Elizabeth's Copy-Book, in a very pretty hand—& in a fine method.[8] Close adjoining to this Library, is a Picture Gallery, of all the Great Men these two hundred Years past— There are no books Yet in the Radcliffe Library—in St. John's College they shew a Picture of Charles the first, with the whole book of Psalms wrote in the Lines of his face—[9] From Oxford I went to Blenheim,[10] which is extremely grand within, but without the Height is not proportionable to the vast Extent of it, So that it was truly & merrily said by Pope, To be a Quarry above Ground.[11]

Mrs. Anderson & Family are well— She presents her Love—

Please to write by every Opportunity, for the News of your Health is my greatest Happiness.

Most Honourd Mother, I am & ever shall be
Your most Affectionate & most Dutiful Son,
John Dickinson

P.S. Pray remember
my Love to my dear Brother   **J.D.**

[*in top margin, Samuel Dickinson*:] <Octob[e]r the 29:^th 1754 to <u>Mamey</u>>

ALS (PPL-JDFP)

---

[1] Board: "A table used for meals; now, always, a table spread for a repast" (*OED*).

[2] Pales: "A stake, fence, or boundary" (*OED*).

[3] The Dickinsons' plantation house situated on Jones Neck in Kent Co. Del., built by Samuel Dickinson in 1740 and where the family moved in 1741.

[4] Thomas Bodley (1545–1613) was a scholar and a diplomat who undertook the restoration of the library at Oxford in 1598. The new Bodleian library opened in 1602. John Radcliffe (1650–1714) was a philanthropist and physician who left most of his estate to University College in trust, in part to fund the building and operating of a library, which was opened in 1749. Later merged with the Bodleian Library, the building is now known as the Radcliffe Camera. Christopher Codrington (1668–1710), governor general of the Leeward Islands, bequeathed 12,000 volumes to the library at All Souls College along with money to purchase more books and construct a new library. Erection of the new buildings was completed by 1720, but it was not until 1751 that the interior was ready to accommodate books.

[5] Marcus Tullius Cicero (106–43 BC) was a prominent Roman politician, orator, and lawyer. JD is probably referring to the portrait by an unknown artist that appears in Kenneth Garlick, *Catalogue of Portraits in the Bodleian Library* (Oxford, UK: Bodleian Library, 2004), 70.

[6] Cicero wrote *De Officiis*, which offers ethical guidance for the behavior of would-be public officials, in 44 BC. The volume that JD saw at the Bodleian Library was printed at Mainz by Johann Fust (c. 1400–1466) and Peter Schöffer (c. 1425–1502) in 1465. It may have been the first printed edition of a classical text, although not the first book ever printed.

[7] Mary I (1516–1558) reigned in England from 1553 until her death, overseeing a Catholic restoration. Sir Walter Raleigh (Ralegh; 1554–1618) was a noted courtier during the Protestant reign of Elizabeth I and was at times accused of atheism. Their books of hours remain in the Bodleian Library.

[8] JD is almost certainly referring to a copy book created by Edward VI (1537–1553) in 1548. *A Summary Catalogue of Western Manuscripts in the Bodleian Library at Oxford . . .*, vol. 2, part 1 (Oxford, UK: Clarendon, 1922), entry 3071, p. 582, explains that "When the volume was first referenced (about 1648) it was attributed to Edward vi, but before 1697 a tradition arose that queen Elizabeth wrote part at least of this book, and foll. 73–80 are not unlike her early writing."

[9] Charles I (1600–1649) was king of England and Ireland from 1625 to 1649. As a divine right monarchist, he anger many of his subjects with his affinity for Catholicism and arbitrary and authoritarian policies. With the ascent of Oliver Cromwell (1599–1658) during the English Civil War, he was tried for high treason and executed. The calligraphic portrait in brown ink and metalpoint on parchment by an unknown artist dates from the late 16th cent. and is still part of St. John's collection. The hair spilling over his left shoulder is longer than the hair on the right, and the lines of the hair were made up of the text of the Penitential Psalms. The picture is now too faded to see the text, even under magnification.

[10] Blenheim Palace is an elaborate country house in Woodstock, Oxfordshire Co., built between 1705 and 1722 for John Churchill (1650–1722), first duke of Marlborough, to celebrate his victory at the Battle of Blenheim in 1704. The palace is now a UNESCO world heritage site.

[11] In *Of False Taste. An Epistle to the Right Honourable Richard Earl of Burlington.* (London: L. Gilliver, 1731), Alexander Pope wrote of "*Timon's Villa*" in part: "To compass this, his Building is a Town, / His Pond an Ocean, his Parterre a Down, / Who but must laugh the Master when he sees? / A puny Insect, shiv'ring at a Breeze! / Lo! what huge Heaps of Littleness around! / The Whole, a labour'd Quarry above ground!" Blenheim is one of several sites that have been suggested as the source for Timon's villa.

1755

23

To Samuel Dickinson, January 21, 1755

London Jan[u]ary 21[st] 1755[1]

[*missing pages*] Whom did Me the Honour to be particularly kind in their Notice of Me— I complimented them on the birth of their Son—[2] Mr. Penn desird Me to make some Enquiries about Taylors & Sharp's Islands[3]—what Counties they were in—& was much pleasd with my Answers— He told Me he was renewing the Dispute with L[or]d Baltimore—to which those Questions were previous—He gave Me a very kind Invitation to Visit him at his Country Seat at Maidenhead[4]

I am infinitely obligd to my most Honourd Father for his kind Compliance with my Request to stay a little longer in England than was at first designd—& the particular Goodness which the Manner of it expresses—for Nothing can give Me greater Delight than that Opinion & Confidence which You are pleasd to entertain of my Judgment & Integrity for as I value Reputation above every other human Possess[ion] So I value it more with my Honourd Parents than with all the Rest of the World—

My Mind was before so filld with a Sense of your great favou[r] that it is not possible to give it any additional Impulse to enfor[ce] my Duty— And such a Profusion of Tenderness must certainly make Me a Bankrupt in Gratitude—

I have been some time past employd in Reading—but Hillary Term coming on the 23[d] of this Month—I shall run down to Westminster Hall every Morning by 9 oClock, & shiver in that great open Place till 2 or three—

The Parliament is now setting—but the Ministry seems to be every unsettled since Mr. Pelhams Death; The Duke of New Castle has a great party in the House & yet manages [as] Prime Minister— But he & his Brother disobligd the Princess of Wales & the Duke of Cumberland[5]— the first by restraining her too much in the Act of Settlement on the Prince of Wales death[6] [*page break*] And the other, by concluding the War, when he was at the Head of a fine Army, & flushd with the Hopes of Glory—[7] So that it is said they favour a Party formd by the Duke of Bedford, Duke of Marlborough & Mr. Fox—[8] The Parliament have just done the Common & necessary Business—that coud not be delayd—but I believe most of the Gentlemen in that House, woud be glad to know to whom to bow Restless Ambition harrasses all the Great—who destroy

71

all the Real Means of Happiness—actually in their Power—& are truly miserable through the very Desire to avoid it.

There are above seventy controverted Elections this Parliament.[9] One of the greatest Proofs perhaps of the Corruption of the Age that can be mentiond—Bribery is so common that it is thot there is not a Borough in England—where it is not practisd—& it is certain that many very flourishing ones are ruind, their Manufactories decayd—& their Trade gone—by their Dependance on what they get by their Votes— We have every Day {in Westminster Hall} a case movd to file Information for Bribery— But it is ridiculous & absurd to pretend to curb the Effects of Luxury & Corruption in one Instance or in one Spot—with out a general Reformation of Manners—Which every one sees is absolutely necessary for the Wellfare of this Kingdom— Yet Heaven knows how it can be effected— It is grown a Vice here to be Virtuous— We have a Maxim in the Law that "The People is unhappy—when the Laws are unsettled"[10] But I think with much more Truth it may be said—"When Religion is unsettled" Which Great Britain wretchedly experiences at this time—People are grown too Polite to have an old fashiond Religion, & are too weak to find out a new—from whence follows the most unbounded Licentiousness, & utter Disregard of Virtue which is the unfailing Cause of the Destruction of all Empires for it is as impossible for Publick Dignity & Security to exist w[ith]out private Virtue & Honesty—as to build a strong & complete house at a single Stroke— which must be composd of many Materials—put together with many hands—long time & great Labour— [*in left margin:*] I shall write very soon by the Way of Philad[elphi]a & beg Leave to subscribe Myself now— Most Honourd & Belov'd & Best of Parents,

Your most Affectionate & Duti[ful Son]
Jo[hn Dickin]son}

ALS (PPL-JDFP)

---

[1] The dateline was cut off the first page and has been attached to the remaining pages.

[2] Thomas and Juliana Penn's son Thomas. See doc. 1:17, n. 14, above.

[3] The islands on the east shore of the Chesapeake Bay had been part of the protracted border dispute between the Penn and Baltimore families. The two families reached an agreement in 1732, but a final legal decision did not come until 1750 when Chancellor Hardwicke ruled in the Penns' favor. It took until 1760 for the sixth lord Baltimore, Frederick Calvert (1731–1771), to accept this decision, and until 1767 for Charles Mason (c. 1728–1786) and Jeremiah Dixon (1733–1779) to complete their survey. See Colbourn, 2:420.

[4] Maidenhead is located thirty mi. east of London in Berkshire Co.

[5] At the time of this letter, Augusta of Saxe-Gotha-Altenburg (1719–1772) was the dowager princess of Wales. She had been married to George II's eldest son, the prince of Wales, Frederick Lewis (Friedrich Ludwig; 1707–1751), and was the mother of George III. William Augustus (1721–1765), duke of Cumberland, was George II's only surviving son.

[6] The Minority of Successor to Crown Act (24 Geo. 2 c. 24 [1751]) named Princess Augusta as regent should George II die before her son, Prince George (later George III), became an adult. The act mandated that a Council of Regency, headed by the Duke of Cumberland, who was bitter not to be chosen regent, be established to check Augusta's power.

[7] During the War of the Austrian Succession, the Duke of Cumberland served as commander of the allied forces—Britain, the Dutch Republic, Sardinia, and Saxony—before being recalled to England to suppress the Jacobite rebellion in the Scottish highlands. His victory at the Battle of Culloden in April 1746 earned him the nickname "Butcher Cumberland." He returned to the continent but suffered defeat at the Battle of Lauffeld in 1747. Cumberland did not oppose the peace negotiations that stemmed from his defeat, but the Treaty of Aix-la-Chapelle in 1748 ended any chance of redeeming himself on the battlefield.

[8] John Russell (1710–1771), fourth duke of Bedford, was first lord of the Admiralty (1744–48), lord privy seal (1761–63), and a staunch opponent of Newcastle. He was married to a sister of the third duke of Marlborough, Charles Spencer (1706–1758), who served as steward of the household (1749–55) and lord privy seal (1755). Henry Fox was a firm supporter of the Duke of Cumberland.

[9] It took Parliament six months to settle all of the disputed election returns. See Colbourn, 2:417.

[10] A version of the Latin phrase *Misera est servitus ubi jus est vagum aut incertum*, meaning "It is a miserable slavery, when the law is vague or uncertain." The maxim is mentioned more than once in Edward Coke's reports; see *The Twelfth Part of the Reports of Sir Edward Coke, of Divers Resolutions and Judgments Given Upon Solumn Arguments, and with Great Deliberation and Conference with the Learned Judges in Cases of Law* (London: T.R., 1656), 49, 53.

24
To Mary Cadwalader Dickinson, January 22, 1755

London Jan[ua]ry 22[d] 1755

Honourd Mother,

Your favours of August 24[th] & October 30[th] I have rec[eive]d & am very sorry I have had no opportunity of making any Return for so long a Time— but I have at length thrown Coke aside & begun a more pleasing Employment I read over & over that part of your Letter which mentions your Health being better than it has been for these ten Years & while I read it, I thought I saw my Honourd Mother in Strength & Spirits promising Me the Blessing of her dear Converse these many Years to come— But this Salley of Joy was soon checked by a thousand Tears— I know how much You always exposd Yourself— I am afraid You will venture a little too much now— I shoud be extremely glad to know how this Winter time agrees with You—& hope that the new Kitchen was finishd before the cold Weather set in, that You might not be obligd to go out as much as usual— With submission, I cannot be satisfied with the Arguments ag[ains]t a White Maid—at least my Honourd Mother will permit a Lawyer to altercate a little— I cannot bear to see with what Ease the Ladies here manage their families—while You have so much Trouble—But their Families are not such large ones as Ours: For that very Reason, there shoud be an Assistant. Tis true London Maids are not easily found in America; but there can be no Damage in a trial—& there are very notable Maids in Philad[elphi]a— I woud not have one taken out of Kent indeed, Who is as proud as an Empress, because— She is as poor as a Beggar—

But A Maid will find herself necessary & grow insolent; That, My Honourd Mother's Prudence will prevent; Or if She does misbehave herself; She may be turnd off. But that wo[ul]d be troublesome—to get a new one, more so; to turn her off too, & [*page break*] be constantly employd in doing & undoing woud be worse than never changing—

I have raisd Objections which I believe I may venture to say, never have happened, nor ever will: There are certainly such things as good Nature & Common Sense, in Women—& such a Station in our Family, is too considerable to be slightly thought of, or foolishly forfeited by the Ridiculous Dictates of Ill nature— If I am wrong, permit my Motive to plead my Excuse; for I cannot be indifferent to any thing that concerns your ease & Happiness.

I was highly entertaind with the Account of the charming Evening on your seeing Capt[ai]n Hill— there cant be a worthier Man. I am much obligd to Mr. Chew for his kind & polite Participation of your Joy—& for the Goodness he was pleasd to express towards Me— I am glad You were able to form some Idea of my Situation—& to trace Me to my Elbow Chair, envelopd in Littleton[1] & Plowden— When I fix Myself thoroughly & most quietly musing sometimes, I cant forbear Smiling to think—What Tempests & Wars are breeding in this Calm; & tho[ugh] the Materials are so peaceably acquird—What an Eruption there must hereafter be of Noise, Dispute [~~illegible~~] Confusion. In all the Treatises of Philosophy, I dont think there can be quoted Effects so different from the <u>Cause</u>—

But notwithoutstanding I am preparing for such busy & tumultuous Scenes—Yet I promise Myself the Happiness of Ease & Retirement after all—tho[ugh] this is not the greatest Satisfaction I expect— For when I reflect on the End & Intent of my Profession, & my particular Designs in it, I declare with the Utmost Sincerity that on searching my Heart; next to the gratifying my Honourd Parents I find no Consideration of equal Weight with defending the Innocent & redressing the injurd— That seems to Me the Noblest Aim of Human Abilities & Industry: Many great Men have laid it down [*page break*] as a Maxim that {no} Man can ever make a Figure at the Bar—without proposing these things as the Rewards of his Labour After supposing Myself to have obtain all that Wealth or Fame can give; there still remains a Void in the Breast—& I am ashamd of Myself for having thought so meanly & sillily— They are agreable, they may be necessary—

but they ought to come in obliquely I never can conceive that Divine Wisdom designd such mean partial Objects—for the Motives of Our Actions

       All Praise is foreign but of true desert,

       Plays round the Head, but comes not near the Heart[2]

Such Praise I shall always desire, because I shall always desire to deserve it. And I was very much pleasd with Mr. Hanbury's & Uncle Cadwalader's good Opinion of Me for the Applause of worthy Men is an Evidence of our having behavd well—of which one's own Approbation is not sufficient Proof

My Honourd Mother ever watchful for the Happiness & Reputation of her infinitely obligd Son, is desirous of my obtaining the favour of some Gentlemen here, who have a large Correspondence in Philadelphia— I am in the Esteem of those Gentlemen, I hope—but expect no great Advantage from it; indeed I dont think it in their Power to serve Me for I shoud not chuse my Reputation to precede Me, least I shoud survive it. There is a Disadvantage in having Persons Opinions raisd too high.—& Fame is so much more preposterous in Our Days than in Virgils, "when She stood on the Ground; & hid her Head in the Skies"[3] that I have known her very strong & high in Philad[elphi]a without the least foundation laid in London, by the Person of who[m] She was raisd abroad— I will endeavour to behave so that no Man shall be able to say any ill of Me, & that is the most stable Foundation that can be laid for a lasting <u>Credit</u> [*page break*]

Mrs. Holliday & her Son arrivd here after a long passage of ten weeks[4] They were both very ill, all the Way over, & She after coming ashore But are now very well recoverd, & growing daily better, as every one does by the English Air, wh[ich] is remarkably happy in that Respect—I congratulated Her & Mrs. Anderson in your Name on their Meeting—& dind there with them last Christmas Day—at which time Mrs. Anderson always invites her Country men—

I have chosen my Dear Brother's Cloaths, & hope they will please him, they are fashionable & very neat— As to the Lining for the Summer Coat— White is not put into such lightcolourd Cloth.   I am very glad to hear he lodges with our Dear & good Uncle; He coud not grow up in a better family— Nothing coud give Me greater Delight than this, except the Accounts of his Industry; with what Rapture shall I see a Brother, whom it will be an Honour {to acknowledge}— What an Ornament shall We be to one another? What a Comfort to our most Honourd Parents? And Joy to our friends? Earth does not afford a more beautiful Sight, than two Brothers linkd in Love, & paird in Honour: Please to remember my sincerest & tenderest Love to him, & beg him that I may always continue to hear of him with Pleasure—

I heard of Miss Leeds's Marriage[5] without the Uneasiness which our good Friends suspected; but really I cant tell Who is meant by P.R.

I saw Nickee Hammand the other Day who confirms the Account of Messrs. Vining & Wyncoop making an Exchange   I wish them much Joy— & hope Mr. Vining will not remember his Loss—[6]

Please to Let Me hear very often from You, & tell Me the most trifling Matters—they will {be} very entertaining to Me if penn'd by You— I shall take every Opportunity to [*in left margin:*] declare Myself, Most Honourd & Dearest Parent, Your ever dutiful & most affectionate Son

John Dickinson

ALS (PPL-JDFP)

---

[1] Sir Thomas Littleton (d. 1481) was an English judge and writer. His treatise on tenures, published anonymously shortly after his death in 1481, was known as *Littleton*. It was the first law book printed in England and one of the first books given to a law student.

[2] An excerpt from William Mason, *Musæus: A Monody to the Memory of Mr. Pope, in Imitation of Milton's* Lycidas (London: R. Dodsley, 1747), 16. Mason wrote "to" instead of "near."

[3] Commonly known as "Virgil," Publius Vergilius Maro (70–19 BC) was a Roman poet.

The original line is: "Fama, malum qua non aliud velocius ullum; / mobilitate viget, viresque adquirit eundo, / parva metu primo, mox sese attollit in auras, / ingrediturque solo, et caput inter nubila condit." Verg. *Aen.* 4:174–77. John Dryden renders the lines as: "Fame, the great ill, from small beginnings grows: / Swift from the first; and ev'ry moment brings / New vigor to her flights, new pinions to her wings. / Soon grows the pigmy to gigantic size; / Her feet on earth, her forehead in the skies." Dryden, *The Works of Virgil: Containing His Pastorals, Georgics, and Æneis* (London: Jacob Tonson, 1697), 353–54. In Dryden's version the lines are 4:252–56.

[4] Sarah Covington Lloyd Hollyday (1683–1755) of Somerset Co., Md., was Rebecca Covington Lloyd Anderson's mother. Sarah disapproved of her daughter's marriage to William Anderson, but after her second husband, Col. James Hollyday (1696–1747), died, Sarah came to England in 1754 seeking reconciliation with her daughter. Her son, James Hollyday, Jr. (1722–1786), was a lawyer who represented Queen Anne's Co. in the Maryland legislature, 1751–54, 1762–63, 1765–66, and 1768–70. Although he was already a lawyer in Maryland, he entered the Middle Temple in December 1754 and remained until 1758. Sarah and her son James left Maryland on the ship *Prince Edward* around Sept. 17 and arrived in England the last week of November 1754 (*Maryland Gaz.* [Annapolis], Sept. 19, 1754; *Read's Weekly*, Nov. 30, 1754).

[5] JD may be referring to the marriage of Lucretia Leeds (1728–1789) of Talbot Co., Md., to John Bozman (d. 1767). She was the daughter of John Leeds, clerk of the Talbot Co. Court.

[6] After the death of his first wife, Rachel, in 1753, John Vining married Phoebe Wynkoop (1729–1800) on Jan. 16, 1755. Nicholas Hammond, Jr., of the Isle of Jersey, was a stepbrother of Phoebe Wynkoop (Richard Wynkoop, *Wynkoop Genealogy in the United States of America* [New York: Knickerbocker Press, 1904], 35–36).

25

To Mary Cadwalader Dickinson, February 19, 1755

London Feb[rua]ry 19[th] 1755

Honourd Mother,

Your Letter by Capt[ai]n Budden I have rec[eive]d & am greatly pleasd with the Delight You take in all my little Entertainments—indeed I enjoy them doubly by the generous Satisfaction they afford You— I am always most pleasd when in the Country, because it bears some greater Resemblance to my Dear Home—than this dirty noisy City—the Din & Confusion of which banishes thought & Peace—& takes Me almost from Myself—& the pure Air of the Country certainly is necessary for the Preservation of Health— Mine is very good now & confirming dayly & I hope will be strong enough in time to bear to pass the Atlantick— My Voyage here was far from doing Me that Service I expected—but I am now most thoroughly recoverd— As the Spring is coming on, & the Country will soon be very pleasant & Hillary Term is now over— Robert[1] & I have taken Lodgings on the Banks of the Thames directly opposite to the Park of Hampton Court—about a quarter of Mile from Kingston,[2] & in a most charming Part of the Country— We shall move out the latter End of this Week—& are resolvd to remember We are **Americans**—to live soberly & prosecute our Business— I am determind to follow [*page break*] As I always have endeavourd to do, my Honourd Mother's Advice—& to take the Choicest Care of my Health—& I have always found the least Excursions did Me great Service— I had two fine ones to St. Albans, & up the Medway— In mentioning the first,[3] I forgot one Curiosity—which is the Body or rather now the Bones of Duke Humphry—[4] He is laid in a Stone Coffin which was once filld with a Pickle[5] but after it was once discoverd— so many People went to see him—& brought away the Pickle, & by being exposd to the Air, it lost its Strength so much—that the Flesh immediately rotted & decayd—& now there is nothing but the Bones—though about five & twenty Years ago—I am told—the Flesh was quite perfect—

Amongst the other Entertainments I have had—I believe I have not mentiond my being at Court— On L[or]d Mayor's Day,[6] I receivd an Invitation from the Barclays to come to their house, in Cheapside[7] to see the Procession— When I came there, I found Mr. Penn & his Lady & her Sister—& a great Company besides— Mr. Penn chatted with Me—almost the whole afternoon & amongst other things asked Me if I had ever been at Court—I said No—on which he offerd to take Me with him—on his Majestys Birth Day— I told him I understood the Court dressd very gay that Day & that I had nothing Smarter than what I then had on—which was a plain Suit of Broad Cloth—Oh says he [*page break*] that will do very well— If You'll please to call on Me—by 12 oClock on the Day—I shall be glad of your Company— I thankd him & promisd to wait on hi[m]

After the Procession, which was finishd by 5 oClock—& consists of a great Number of Equipages belonging to the L[or]d Mayor Judges & Aldermen—with the several Companies of the City with their Colours & Streamers— I drank Tea at Mr. Barclay's—& then went to the L[or]d Mayor's Ball at Guildhall[8]—with a Tickett which had been given Me— I was so tird with the Crowd—& nothing in the Universe to entertain one— that I went home with a thorough Resolution never to see ano[the]r Mayor's Ball—which I believe I shall always keep

On the 10[th] of Nov[embe]r N. S.[9] I waited on Mr. Penn—who took Me with him in his Coach to Court— Birthdays are always excessively fine but this exceeded any that has been these many Years—but to describe the Dresses woud be as impossible as "to count the Streamers on a L[or]d Mayor's Day."[10] We enterd into a large Room of the Palace—thro[ugh] Avenues lind with Guards & Spectators—this was the Antichamber—where all the Noblemen & Gentlemen stood—thro[ugh] this, the Ladies passd to another large Room on the Right hand His Majesty's Drawing Room—where he sees Company—was on the left—& that leads to the other Parts of the Palace—but none went into this [*page break*] Room—but Noblemen & Officers of the highest Rank The Gentlemen in the Antichamber—conversd with one another—for about an Hour, when the Door of the Drawing Room was thrown open, & those in the Antichamber were admitted—amongst the Rest I found Myself in the Presence of the Greatest & Best King upon Earth—He was standing up, surrou[nded] by the Prince of Wales, Duke of Cumberland, Prince Edward, L[or]d Chancellor, & all the Stars & Garters— [11] Nobody spoke a word, to the King unless addressed by him He stood with a Gold lacd Hat under his Arm, with all the Modesty of a Woman, & every now & then he said a few words to somebody about him—which I coud not hear—but by the Manner, I am sure were nothing but common Enquiries & Answers—between his Speaking he constantly cast his Eyes on the Ground—in short this seemd so painful a Tax upon Majesty that I <u>pitied</u> him— What is calld paying their Complim[en]ts to him, is getting so near in the Circle as to be seen & then bowing— After ten Minutes spent in this Manner, the King bowd—& movd towards another Room, on which all the Company bowd, & returnd into the Antechamber, except the great Personages I have mentiond— In a quarter of an Hour after, the King came thro[ugh] the Antichamber—& went to the Ladies—in a few Minutes he was followd by the Princess of Wales, led by the Prince of Wales, the Princess Amelia[12] by the Duke of Cumberland, & the [*page break*] Princess Augusta[13] by Prince Edward: then those that woud—went after them—& the Royal Family chatted with the Ladies a little While—& then a most wretched Birthday Ode[14]—was most exquisitely performd by a Band of Instrumental & Vocal Musick— Soon after this was done—they all returnd in the same Order—& then the Court was over— I then went to that Place where all the Ladies get into their Chairs & stood close by the Dukes of Grafton & Marlboro' L[or]d Chamberlain, L[or]d High Steward[15]—whose duty it is to have the Chairs calld—& the Ladies safe in them—& there as they calld for the Chairs I had a fine Opportunity of seeing & knowing all the Ladies— At 3 oClock I went away tird of Grandeur & an empty Stomack—& satisfied in a little Chophouse—the Hunger which I had procurd in a Palace— Mr. Penn dind by Engagem[en]t with the Earl of Granville[16]—or I shoud have gone with him— It is inconceivable what a Ferment this new Scene put my Mind in— Such a Multitude of various contending Thoughts sprung up, vanish'd, returnd dyd—I was fird with Ambition—but the Difficulty of Rising—A 1000 Instances of the Meanest persons—but by Villainy—Only the Envy of the unsuccessful— But what are the mighty Blessings to be attaind by the [*page break*] most happy Ambition? What Rewards—for all its Toils & Cares? What Recompense for all the Peace & Ease forfeited by it's Pursuit? To see a King at a little nearer Distance or to wear a Blue Ribbond—[17] But if my Eyes are good I see as well, & am as happy three or four feet further off—& to a Reasonable Man, a good Broadcloth Coat shoud be much more valuable than a bit of Ribbond— But the World does not think these things so—& Politeness has so far baffl'd Wisdom now that People never enquire Whether things are proper or improper, good or bad in their Nature but What [*illegible*] they are in the general Opinion or Whim—& therefore We see dayly & constantly {Men} sacrificing Virtue Ease & Reason to Vice Disquiet & Folly—to gain those things to which Mankind have falsely annexd confusd Ideas of what is really desirable— In short every one in the Course of Life starts after Good, but the race is so headlong—that they never look behind them, & forever perceive the very prize they are running at, is behind them— Indeed some [*illegible*] highly favour by Divine Providence meet with friendly Enemies who stop their Career, & turn them round—when to their Amazement—they find that Happiness, Lovely Maid, who[m] they so rudely & madly pursued—by the Commands of unbounded Goodness— waiting close behind to revive their [*illegible*] Limbs & jaded Spirits— which they had fatigued in their vain & presumptuous Chace—

Honourd Mother—please to excuse this long scrowl—on this occasion—for really another Birthday woud make [*cont. on sixth page, in left margin*:] Me a Philosopher—. I have not Time to add more—if your Goodness wo[ul]d [per]ermit Me—but shall write soon again— Capt[ai]n Hill is just arrivd—but no Letter from My Honourd Mother[—] I am Most Honourd Parent your most affectionate & most Dutiful Son,

John Dickinson

[*on fifth page, in left margin*:] P.S. I have not time to write to my Dearest Brother, Please to give my sincerest & best Love to him—& tell him that tho[ugh] I cant write, yet the transmitting this present by Our Honourd Mother, puts Me, & I hope will put him in Mind of the dear Relation We stand in to one another— Please to remember Me to all Friends & Neighbours, & Cousin Watte & Wife particularly—& tho[ugh] I cant name all the cast, yet I think of [[th][em]] with Respect

ALS (PPL-JDFP)

---

[1] Robert Goldsborough.

[2] Kingston-upon-Thames is located about ten mi. southwest of central London.

[3] JD discussed his visit to St. Albans in doc. 1:18.

[4] Humphrey, duke of Gloucester (1390–1447), was the youngest son of Henry IV (1367–1413) and served as protector of England during the minority of Henry VI (1421–1471). He is often called Good Duke Humphrey.

[5] That is, a preservative.

[6] Nov. 9 was the day of the inauguration of the lord mayor of London, complete with a pageant known as the Lord Mayor's Show.

[7] Cheapside is a street in the financial district of London.

[8] Guildhall, located on Gresham Street, dates from 1411 and remains a center of London's government.

[9] New-Style. The old-style Julian calendar did not accurately mimic the solar year, by the 1750s it was off by eleven days. The Gregorian calendar adopted by the Catholic Church in 1582 had fixed this problem by altering the number of leap years, but Britons did not correct their calendar until 1751–52, when Parliament adopted the Gregorian calendar and, to account for the eleven days, declared that in 1752 the day following Sept. 2 should become Sept. 14 (20 *SAL* 186–211, 368–70). Although the king's birthday was Nov. 10, newspaper reports indicate that the reception JD describes was held on Nov. 11, perhaps because Nov. 10 fell on a Sunday (*Public Advertiser* [London], Nov. 11, 1754).

[10] Quoting Matthew Prior, "A Letter to Monsieur Boileau: Occasion'd by the Victory at Blenheim, 1704," in Matthew Prior, *Poems on Several Occasions* (London: Jacob Tonson, 1709), 191: "'Tis mighty hard: What Poet would essay / To count the Streamers of my Lord Mayor's Day?"

[11] The prince of Wales at this time was George William Frederick (1738–1820), the eldest son of the deceased former prince, Frederick Lewis. He succeeded George II as king in 1760 and ruled Great Britain as George III until his death. Prince Edward Augustus (1739–1767) was Frederick's second son. He later became duke of York and Albany. The British Order of the Garter was the highest level of knighthood, the medal for which was shaped like a star.

[12] Princess Amelia (Emily) Sophia Eleanora (1711–1786) was the second daughter of George II. She was born in Germany but moved to England with her parents in 1714 when her grandfather, George I, acceded to the throne.

[13] Augusta Frederica of Great Britain (1737–1813) was the daughter of Princess Augusta and Frederick, Prince of Wales, and granddaughter of the king.

[14] For the text of the ode, which was written by the dramatist Colley Cibber, see *London Evening Post*, Nov. 9–12, 1754.

[15] Charles Fitzroy (1683–1757) was second duke of Grafton and lord great chamberlain since 1724, a hereditary office of state responsible for the parts of the Palace of Westminster not

assigned to Parliament. The office of lord high steward was generally left vacant, except for special occasions.

[16] John Carteret (1690–1763) was second earl Granville and lord president of the Council from 1751 to 1763.

[17] The blue riband associated with the British Order of the Garter is a 4-inch-wide sash worn from the left shoulder to the right hip.

26
To Samuel Dickinson, February 19, 1755

London Feb[rua]ry 19[th] 1755

[*Samuel Dickinson*:] <Mentions Courts not Duly and Justly kept—>

Honourd Father,

Your Letter by Capt[ai]n Budden I have rec[eive]d—a little before which I had wrote by one Capt[ai]n White who sails into Maryland—[1] Mr. Hanbury had a Letter by the same Opportunity, which he was so good as to shew Me—& I was very much pleasd that he shoud know the Sense & Gratitude I have for his Favours to Me—

I am very sorry to hear My Honourd Father is so weakend by the Gout— but when I recollect the Peace that must flow from a well spent Life—the Calmness & Glory of an Honourable Age—infinitely improvd & sweetend by the Cares & Fondness of My Dearest Mother—it woud be foolish & criminal to indulge my Grief— For if Virtue Love & Happiness are upon Earth, they must dwell with my Parents—I am greatly delighted to find that my Actions & little Adventures make up some part of your Entertainment— by a chearful fire—but these domestick Reflections (if that term may be usd) are too affecting to dwell upon— How much more preferable are these pure & noble swellings of the Heart—in the indulgence of some virtuous—some pious Affection—to all the eager pursuits & pamperd Enjoyments of the Senses—or of the Imagination— I take more Pleasure in one Hour's Sorrow that I am not with You—than I have receivd from all the Diversions of London, all the Time I have been in it. [*page break*]

I am very much obligd for the Accounts You are so good as to give Me of the State of the Law— Laws in themselves, certainly do not make Men happy— they derive all their force & Worth from a vigorous & just Execution of them—& where there is any Obstruction to this, from Ignorance, Villainy or Cowardise—People are just in the same Condition {as if they had no Laws}—& the preserving the forms of Judges Juries, Sheriffs or without Knowledge, Honesty & Resolution is like a Mill, which after a material Wheel is broken, may run giddily round—but will never

81

make a Grain of Flour—   This I really believe to be the Condition of our County at present—& I cant well see how it can be remedied—unless they grow honester, than they are—for suppose there were two Lawyers of equal Abilities—they never woud be a Match—unless they were equal Rogues too— For all the Law of Coke & the Eloquence of Cicero—can never influence Men who dont understand You, or if they do, were determind in their Opinions—before they heard You—

I declare, I dont know Whether to Laugh or be angry—at the ridiculous Folly of Men—who make themselves Slaves for the Priviledge of setting four foot above other People—or rather of shewing to all the World what Asses & Scoundrels they are—But I have the Wellfare & Honour of my Country so much at Heart—that sincerely I am afraid "the <u>Nobility</u> of Kent" will be a Nickname among the Nations—for persons every way despicable & shameful [*page break*]

As to the Lawyers in Kent, their <u>Numbers</u> are really terrifying—& they are still encreasing— I was very much diverted with my Honourd Mother's designing to add to the Students of this Profession; & greatly pleasd with the Entertainment You find in the Chancery[2] Books—& I shall always reckon it one of the greatest Losses, that part of America & myself in particular ever met with, that these Books did not belong to my GrandFather,[3] rather than to Me— The universal Opinion is that Vernon & Peere Will[iams] Who were men of great Abilities & Learning—far exceed the Chancery Cases or Precedents, or any of these anonymous Reports—[4] I wish I could possibly study with You, it woud be the most engaging Employment—& when I return to America I hope to present You with two or three Volumes of Reports by Myself—[5] I have almost compleated one already by the Notes I have taken in Westminster—but they are not designd pro bono publico[6]— tho[ugh] I shall be often oblidgd to quote them in Court—if I can obtain the favour—for the Advantage of them is inconceivable— I have a great many Points resolvd—which I have not met with elsewhere—& a great many I have met with, are in these contradicted & denied— the latest Determinations in the Law for some time before I come into Business—will evidently be very serviceable— Inclosd I have sent [*page break*] two or three Speeches made by some of the greatest Men in Westminster Hall[7]—just to give You some idea of that Species of <u>Humour</u> which is usd there— As it was only a Motion for Judgment—on which the Merits of the Case—& not any matter of Law was considerd—I did not take Notes of it—but when it was over, I thought there was Something so odd in it, that it woud be entertaining to You—& immediately set down to recollect it—but I have not done Justice to the Gentlemen—for I was so hurried in Term with taking Notes, & since with writing them off—that I believe I have forgot some things—& am obligd to send the first rough Draught—

I have not mentiond the Speeches of Prime the K[ing]'s Prime Serjeant[8]—nor Sir Richard Lloyds—because that Strain which the others indulgd—did not become their Dignity—& was not usd by them, tho[ugh] they said a great deal very much to the Point— To explain part of Mr. Pont's[9] Speech {it may be necessary} to add that Prime has a very fine hand—of which he is not a little vain—& he & Sir R[ichard] Ll[oyd]—& Mr. Pratt are King's Counsel,[10] & set within a Barr by themselves—& all Barristers, not King's Counsel set behind— I shall be very glad if this trifle affords my Honourd Parents any Entertainment—or if it does not, I hope they will excuse Me, & believe that was the sole Reason of my troubling them with it—
I am most Honourd Father, Your most dutiful and [*cont. in left margin:*] most affectionate Son,

John Dickinson

ALS (PPL-JDFP)

---

[1] Richard Budden's ship *Myrtilla* left Philadelphia for London the week of Dec. 26, 1754, and arrived at Deal in England on Feb. 12, 1755 (*PG*, Dec. 26, 1754; *Read's Weekly*, Feb. 15, 1755). Samuel Dickinson's letter has not been found. JD's letter sent by Capt. White was probably his letter to Samuel of Jan. 21, 1755.

[2] The Chancery Court was "the court of the Lord Chancellor of England, the highest court of judicature next to the House of Lords . . . It formerly consisted of two distinct tribunals, one ordinary, being a court of common law, the other extraordinary, being a court of equity. To the former belonged the issuing of writs for a new parliament, and of all original writs. The second proceeded upon rules of equity and conscience, moderating the rigour of the common law, and giving relief in cases where there was no remedy in the common-law courts" (*OED*).

[3] It is unclear whether JD meant William Dickinson or John Cadwalader.

[4] Thomas Vernon (1654–1721) was a successful and wealthy chancery lawyer who had studied at the Middle Temple in the 1670s. *Cases Argued and Adjudged in the High Court of Chancery* was published after his death. Law reporter William Peere Williams (c. 1664–1736) and lawyer William Melmouth (1665–1743) served as the editors. The volumes were so riddled with errors that a new edition was published in 1806. The chancery cases collected by William Peere Williams were published by his son, William Peere Williams, Jr., (born c. 1701), as *Reports of Cases Argued and Determined in the High Court of Chancery, and of some Special Cases Adjudged in the Court of King's Bench*, 3 vols. (London: E. and R. Nutt and R. Gosling, 1740–49).

[5] JD produced five sets of notebooks, three dated 1754, 1754–55, 1755–57, and two undated. These, along with his three-volume, annotated copy of the Samson Eure, *Doctrina Placitandi, ou L'Art et Science de Bon Pleading* (London: R. and E. Atkins, 1677), will be published in a supplemental volume of the present edition.

[6] Lat. for the public good.

[7] Enclosures not found.

[8] Sir Samuel Prime (1701–1777) was a lawyer who became a serjeant-at-law in 1736, king's serjeant in 1738, and king's first serjeant in 1749. He retired in 1758.

[9] Possibly Samuel Henry Pont (d. by 1765), who attended Lincoln's Inn, one of the Inns of Court, was called the the bar in 1735, served as recorder of Cambridge from 1742 to 1757, and acted as chief justice for the Isle of Ely from 1748 until at least 1753.

10 Charles Pratt (1714–1794), first earl Camden, was named king's counsel in 1755 and later served as attorney general and chief justice of the Court of Common Pleas.

27
To Mary Cadwalader Dickinson, April 8, 1755

London April 8th <u>1755</u>

Honourd Mother,

I take this opportunity by good Capt[ai]n Hill,[1] with the greatest Pleasure to inform You of my continuing in Health, improving in Knowledge, & doing every thing which You wish Me to do, & which it gives You Delight, to think I do— I dont know Whether other People are actuated in the same Manner, or Whether it is some more than common Reverence impressd on my Mind—by the great Virtue & Goodness of my Honourd Parents—but I think if all other Obligations were taken off—the Destinction of Good & Evil [*page break*] with Rewards & Punishments, quite obliterated; Prospects of Advantage or Disadvantage removd & all Sense of Shame & Honour, extinguishd—Yet the Desires of my Parents woud be a sufficient Motive for the Regulation of my Actions—for if I was to do a thing now—which is contrary to their Will—my Mind would be torturd with a second kind of Conscience, tho[ugh] it were impossible they could know anything of the Action— You will pardon, my Dearest & most Honourd Mother, these Speculations on my Duty, when the Distance I am from You, cuts Me off from the performance of it, in those Offices I coud wish—

I have given my Father an Account [*page break*] of Robert's Marriage—[2] His Father knows nothing of it, & Mr. Hanbury did not think it worth while to stay for his Consent—as he thought the Match very advantageous— But in an Affair of so much importance I should think Myself obligd to have the Consent of my Parents—nothwithstanding the Uneasiness which my Honourd Mother expresses on a certain Occasion— I really think that young Lady very worthy, & agreable—but I declare the Ideas of Miss J—l & Marriage never were in my head at one time— I took great Pleasure in her Conversation, & admird her more than any Lady of my Acquaintance [*page break*] But that Admiration or Esteem would never have grown to the Height of Matrimony—at least I am sure, it never will now, as my Notions of Life have receivd some pretty considerable Alterations—& at present, I solemnly declare I dont know a Woman upon Earth, for whom I have had a single thought as a Wife—but am as free from any Engagement of Affection that way, as the Instant, I was born—

Pray be so good as to give my most affectionate Love & good Wishes to my Dear Brother—& desire him to write often—

I am most Honourd Mother,
your most affectionate & most
Dutiful Son,
John Dickinson

[*in top margin, Mary Cadwalader Dickinson:*] <to Me April [th]e 8th 1755>

ALS (PPL-JDFP)

---

[1] Capt. Hill's ship, the *Scipio*, did not leave England for Maryland until May 28 (*Read's Weekly*, May 31, 1755).

[2] On March 27, 1755, Robert Goldsborough married Sarah Yerbury (1734–1787). The *London Evening Post*, March 27–29, 1755, described the bride as "a beautiful young Lady of 5000 l. Fortune." According to JD in doc. 1:29, below, she had a fortune of £4,000, half of which became Robert's after the marriage.

28
To Samuel Dickinson, June 28, 1755

London June 28[th] 1755

Honourd Father,

I have rec[eive]d your favour and my Honourd Mother's [per] Capt[ai]n Hargrave[1]—& am greatly obligd to my Dearest Parents, who are constantly showering their Kindness in Obligations on a Son who if not worthy of them, is at least earnestly desirous of making some Return to them.

The great Comfort & Delight of my Life is that I shall be able by the Blessing of Providence & my own Industry to do this in a very acceptable manner—though I have receivd a great Interruption of late— [*page break*] I went on all last Winter very briskly with Reading & taking my Notes, which I find to be the most profitable way of Study I ever was in—till about the Beginning of March I felt myself attackd by an Uneasiness in my Breast, with which I usd to be troubled in Philadelphia— In a little time it grew very troublesome, & was attended with fevers, upon which by Mr. Hanbury's Advice I applied to Physicians of the first Rank in London— They immediately orderd Me to intermit all manner of Study, to get into the Country & use Exercise— Upon this Robert & I took Lodgings together at Kingston— & I receivd [*page break*] Relief directly—& am now quite recoverd from my Complaint, tho[ugh] not altogether recruited in Strength But I am daily growing stronger & have all the Assurances human Knowledge & Foresight can afford, that by the End of the Summer I shall be heartier than ever—

My Honourd Mother enquires so very anxiously after my Health, that I am afraid She will be discontented with this Account, & think Me still worse than I say—but if She will please to consider That I might have said nothing about it, I hope She will trust to my Honour, which always [*page break*] compells Me to act openly & fairly with the best of Parents—& as I know the Cruelty of flattering You with accounts of great Strength & Health & then disappointing You— But I know my Honourd Mother magnifies every Danger according to the Distance I am from her, & things that would be trifles in Philad[elphi]a are dreadful in London, & woud be twice as terrible in the East Indies— As for Myself, I am only concerned at my Loss of Time, & the Expence I shall be put to—the first of which I hope to redeem by my Application—& for the other I rely on the kind Assurances of my Honourd Parents—

The Remonstrance of the Pennsylvania Assembly is rejected by the L[or]ds of Trade[2] &c

I am Honourd Father Your most Dutiful & affectionate Son
John Dickinson

ALS (PPL-JDFP)

---

[1] Charles Hargrave was commander of the brigantine *Mercury*, which left Philadelphia in early April and arrived in England on June 9 (*PG*, April 10, 1755; *WEP*, June 7–10, 1755).

[2] The remonstrance was the result of Gov. Robert Hunter Morris's rejection of the Assembly's December 1754 bill to raise £20,000 to aid Gen. Edward Braddock's (1695–1755) campaign against Fort Duquesne, Pa. Morris argued, "I cannot by any Means agree, as I am forbid, by a Royal Instruction, to pass any Law for creating Money in Paper Bills, without a suspending Clause, that it shall not take Effect till his Majesty's Pleasure be known." See *Votes* (1754), 24. The ensuing debate was informed more by the ongoing battle over taxing the proprietor's estate to raise money for defense than by the suspending clause, and in early January 1755 the Assembly resolved to send an address to the king "to testify the Affection and Loyalty of the People of this Province, and to represent the Difficulties we Labour under by Reason of Proprietary Instructions, &c." See *Votes* (1755), 60, 64. For the remonstrance, see 6 *CRP* 448–50). The remonstrance was referred to the Board of Trade on April 15; for their report of 30 May rejecting the address, see 6 *CRP* 505–10.

29
To Mary Cadwalader Dickinson, August 12, 1755

Kingston upon Thames <u>Aug[us]t 12th 1755</u>

Most Honourd Mother,

I rec[eive]d lately the dear Account of your Health in my Honourd Father's Letter, but should have been glad to have seen it {in} your hand & think I have some cause to complain of the Reason, that my Dear Mother was so employd with her other Son, that She had no time to bestow on him that was absent— Pardon Me, for indeed I cannot but quarrel with any occasion that deprives Me of your Conversation—

86

My last Letter was an Account of my recovering from a severe fit of Illness, which I am afraid, made You uneasy, but I was apprehensive, least You shoud hear of it some other Way, & my not mentioning it might make You imagine Me, still worse than I was— I wrote You then, I was [*page break*] quite hearty, & so I continue, only returning every Day nigher & nigher my former State of Health— I beg my Honourd Mother to be easy— & believe the Protestations of filial Duty which cannot think of deceiving, that I am as much out of Danger as ever I was—

I take all kind of Diversions— I go afishing & Riding every Day—for the Thames is not forty feet from our Door—& at home I am very happy with Gouldsborough & his Wife— I am very sorry to hear my Brother[1] disapproves of it but hope he will be reconcild when he receives Mr. Hanburys Letter, & knows it was done by his Consent. You judge very rightly that it was a sudden Affair— G___[2] was not acquainted with the Lady above three {months}—& at the time of our taking Lodgings, did not expect to be married so soon—for he was desirous to get his Father's Consent, & Sh[e] not thinking it proper to stay for it—just at that [*page break*] time We took Lodgings— Afterwards She agreed to stay, & then G. mentiond it to Mr. Hanbury to get him to write in favour of it, to his Father— Mr. Hanbury approvd of it, & did not think it necessary to stay—upon wh[ich] they were married— My Dear Father says my Brother wrote immediately by the way of Philadelphia, he supposes to stop any further Allowance— I shoud be glad to know whether he mentiond any such thing, & what he says on receiving Mr. H's Letter— When G. first mentiond to Me, his marrying without his Father's Consent I told him it was not what I shoud chuse to do—& that Parents had a Right to be consulted—if not implicitly obeyd in that important Affair of Life— But finding it was settled, I did not urge Arguments which might injure Me, but I found woud profit nobody else—[*page break*]

Mrs. Goldsborough's fortune is £4000 Sterling; 2000 of which are settled in such a Manner as not to be disposd of— I believe it is settled on her for Life then to her Children, & if She dies without Children—to her Relations— The other 2000 belong absolutely to her, & consequently by the Marriage to her Husband.

I am very glad I think so much like my Honourd Parents with respect to Marriage I never shall think I am at Liberty to dispose of myself, without their Consent who gave Me Being—And if I shoud ever be so mad as to d[o] it, tho[ugh] you shoud forgive Me, I shoud never forgive Myself—

I am glad to hear Miss Vining[3] is going to Philad[elphi]a. I hope her Charms will procure her a Husband worthy of them—

I am very much afraid, I shall grow one of those foolish fellows—who have annexd so many fine Qualities to the Ladies that shall enslave them,

that they never find any possest of one half & Loiter away Life in expecting a Dulcinea[4] that exists no [*cont. on third page, in left margin:*] Where but in their own Imagination— There are so many Defects in Human {Nature} that a Man may think of five hundred, which are not in the Woman he admires, upon wh[ich] he thinks himself secure, but afterwards discovers some one that in so great a Number escapd his View, & is miserably convincd that 99 Blows avoided, are no shield against the hundredth—
[*on first page, in left margin:*] Honourd Mother, I constantly Remember You, & wish You all the Happiness this World & the next afford, which is the fervent Prayer to the Author of all Goodness, of your most Affectionately Dutiful Son

John Dickinson

ALS (PPL-JDFP)

---

[1] Charles Goldsborough, JD's brother-in-law and Robert Goldsborough's father.
[2] Robert Goldsborough.
[3] Mary Vining (c. 1734–1764) was the sister of John Vining. She married Anglican minister Charles Inglis (1734–1816) in 1764.
[4] In Miguel de Cervantes's *Don Quixote* (1605, 1615), Dulcinea del Toboso is Don Quixote's imagined mistress for whom he fights.

30
To Samuel Dickinson, August 12, 1755

Kingston upon Thames <u>Aug[us]t 12</u>[th] 1755

Most Dear & Honourd Father,

I have rec[eive]d your Letter of 15[th] of June by Shirley, with the very agreable Account of your Health: I wrote to You lately acquainting You with the bad State of my Health this Summer, & my Recovery—but as I know You will be uneasy; I take every Opportunity to inform You of my growing better daily— The Complaint in my Breast with the fever, have both entirely left Me, & I never have the least Return of either—So that I have no manner of Sickness, & have nothing to do but to recover the Strength I had lost, & that by the Blessing of my All-Gracious Maker and [*page break*] Preserver, returns like a Flood Tide— I can walk four or five Miles, & ride twelve or fifteen, & scarce feel the least fatigue—& I am sure by the End of the Fall, to be as stro[ng] as ever I was—

I am extremely sorry to hear such bad Accounts of Crops, & to know that Tob[acc]o bears so poor a Price, especially as my Health has put Me to Expences I coud not avoid. Mr. Hanbury has behavd with his usual Kindness to Me, & frequently calld upon Me at Kingston, & once upon my saying, I did not know how I shoud do, if Tob[acc]o was so low—he tol[d] Me I might draw on him for whatever Sums I pleasd— He is certainly the most worthy M[an] living— [*page break*]

Nothing, Most Honourd Parent, can equal the Uneasiness I feel from the Necessity of being idle— It is such an Interruption to a glorious Course of Study, I cannot bear to think on it.

Absence from the best of Parents, the Pains & Danger of so long a voyage {taken in vain} & Disappointment after all, really almost flings Me into Despair—but still the Love of You, the Expectations of my friends, & the useful Dignity of my Profession, buoy up my Soul, & fill Me with the Hopes of a noble Race if not a long one—   I have so much been accustomd to entertain Myself with glorious Prospects to come, that I cannot bear my Expectations to flag— Short (says Virgil) is the Date of every man's [*page break*] Course here, but to extend his Fame by his Actions, this is the Work of Virtue"[1]—and Life without Honour is the only Death I dread— To leave this world is the Lot of Hum[an] Nature, fixd by the Decree of our Creator, but to continue here ignobly, is the voluntary Choice of a mean Mind.

I encrease so fast in Strength, that I hope by the Blessing of God & my own Industry, I sha[ll] succeed in my Endeavours, & enjoy the Compan[y] of my Honourd Parents with all the Delights of an honest & active Life—

The French are actually afraid to declare W[ar—] Sir Edw[ar]d Hawke is saild from Spithead with 20 Ship[s] of the Line[2]—but no one, except the Regency know[s] his Design—[3] No Secretaries are trusted— Sir Tho[ma]s Ro[binson] in the Council, & L[or]d Anson in the Admiralty, wrot[e all] the Dispatches— We have 20 Ships of the Line no[w] at Spithead, since Hawke's Departure, ready for the [Sea,] [*cont. on first page, in left margin:*] while all the Endeavors of France cant put 20 to Sea, tho[ugh] they have been preparing ever since the last War; We not above 7 months— But what most evidently proves our Superiority, is, that two State Lotteries being set up {for £100000} one in London, the other in Paris, Ours 22 [*cont. on third page, in left margin:*] Blanks to a Prize, theirs very Advantagious to the Subscribers—[~~illegible~~]{Y}et We had [~~illegible~~]{£} 4000000 subscribd by the City of London alone, in five Days—while the whole Kingdom of France was six Months in compleating theirs—the glorious Effects of Freedom & miserable Consequences of Slavery[4]

I am, most Honourd Father, Your [most] Dutiful [& affectionate Son
John Dickinson]

ALS (PPL-JDFP)

---

[1] The original line is: "Stat sua cuique dies, breve et inreparabile tempus omnibus est vitae: sed famam extendere factis, hoc virtutis opus." Verg. *Aen.* 10:467–69. Dryden renders the line as,

"Short bounds of Life are set to Mortal Man, / 'Tis Vertues work alone to stretch the narrow Span." Dryden, 567. In Dryden's *Works of Virgil* the lines are 10:657–58.

[2] Edward Hawke (1705–1781), first baron Hawke, was a vice admiral. Spithead is a roadstead at the entrance of Portsmouth harbor, Hampshire Co., but the term is sometimes applied to the entire channel between the Isle of Wight and the Hampshire mainland. Because of its natural protection from the winds and its proximity to the naval establishment at Portsmouth, it has been a favorite point of rendezvous for the British fleet. *Read's Weekly*, July 26, 1755, listed twenty ships of the line and one sloop that had sailed from Spithead under the command of Hawke and another admiral on July 21. However, Hawke's line of battle for that date listed only sixteen ships, and he had then not received his instructions, dated July 22, to cruise between Ushant, France, and Cape Finisterre, Spain, with a fleet of sixteen ships of the line plus frigates (Ruddock F. Mackay, ed., *The Hawke Papers: A Selection: 1743–1771*, Publications of the Navy Records Society [Brookfield, Vt: Gower, 1990], 129:121–25). The fleet left for France on July 28 (Dull, 38).

[3] With George II in Hanover, Newcastle and Cumberland argued over a course of action against the French. Cumberland favored an immediate declaration of war and an attack on French commerce, while Newcastle urged caution. In a compromise, Hawke was given approval to capture ships of the line but not smaller warships or merchant ships. Eight days later, the inner cabinet authorized the capture of privateers and merchant ships, and then larger warships by the end of August. See Dull, 38.

[4] The British lottery was authorized by 28 Geo. 2 c. 15: "An Act for granting to his Majesty the Sum of one Million, to be Raised by a Lottery," approved in April 1755, the money granted in order "to enable your Majesty to augment your Forces by Sea and Land, and to take such Measures for the Security of your Majesty's Dominions, as may be necessary in the present Conjuncture" (21 *SAL* 275–81). Subscriptions opened on April 15, when, it was reported, "The Crowd was so great . . . at the Bank, to subscribe for Lottery Tickets, that the Counters were broke by the Eagerness of the People in pushing forward. The Subscription closed at Five in the Evening" (*WEP*, April 15–17, 1755). Until 1769, when the English state lottery changed from an annuity to a revenue lottery, holders of blank tickets received a percentage payout per year from the government, albeit a smaller one than for a prize ticket. See Neal E. Millikan, *Lotteries in Colonial America* (New York: Routledge, 2011), 13. French lotteries also expanded in the 18th cent. and for similar ends, but they were tightly controlled by the monarchy, in regulation as well as operation, becoming an integral part of the royal fiscal apparatus. See Robert D. Kruckeberg, "The Wheel of Fortune in Eighteenth-Century France: The Lottery, Consumption, and Politics" (PhD diss., University of Michigan, 2009).

31
To Samuel Dickinson, September 30, 1755

Most Honourd Father,

I have not yet left my Lodgings at Kingston, but coming to Town Yesterday, & hearing of this Opportunity, I have just Time to pour out the most sincere Declarations of unfeigned Duty & Affection, & to inform the kindest & best of Parents of my Health

I am now grown extremely strong & hearty & have begun my Reading again— I shall return to the Temple—the first of Nov[embe]r which is

Michaelmas Term[1]—& am not the least Doubtful of prosecuting my Studies with the greatest Success—

The Price of Tob[acc]o is now very good but Mr. Hanbury desird Me to come & look at some of Ours which came last from Philad[elphi]a. Six hog[sheads][2] of which have been so excessively ill managd, that he does not think they will pay the freight—& Six more are very indifferent— The Packers have been very careless or else it has been hurt in the House— [*page break*]

Please to excuse this hasty Scrawl—I write in another Gentlemans Chambers, & in the greatest Hurry—but expect another Opportunity soon to write more at Large—

> Please to present my sincerest Love &
> Duty to the Dearest Best of Mothers
> & accept the same from,
> Most Honourd Father,
> Your most Affectionate, & dutiful Son
> **John Dickinson**

London Sept[embe]r 30[th] 1755—

ALS (PPL-JDFP)

---

[1] Michaelmas is "the feast of St Michael (St Michael and all Angels), one of the quarter days in England, Ireland, and Wales; the date of this, 29 September" (*OED*). Michaelmas term began after that date and continued until near Christmas.

[2] A hogshead was a large barrel, approximately 48 in. long and 30 in. in diameter at the head, designed for the shipment of tobacco. One hogshead contained about 1,000 lbs. of tobacco.

1756

32

To Samuel Dickinson, January 8, 1756

[*on third page, in left margin*:] London Jan[ua]ry 8[th] 1756—
Most Honourd Father,

It is a long time since I have had the Pleasure either of hearing from You, or of Writing to You: I am in some Uneasiness as to the first because several Ships have arrivd lately from Philadelp[hi]a & I have been debarrd of the other by Want of direct Opportunities, & tho[ugh] the present is not one, Yet I cannot refrain from paying my Duty, as Mr. Williamson a Young Clergyman promises to give this the best Conveyance he can.

My last Letters informd You of my Recovering from a severe fit of Sickness, which by a Fever weakend Me very much: By the Blessing of Almighty Providence My Strength recruited so fast that I returnd to Town the latter End of October, & have ever since found London to agree with Me perfectly well. I am now so hearty that for some Months I have studied not idly, & have attended Westminster Hall except in bad Weather So that I hope to improve my Time to the best Advantage

As I have great Reason to believe that my Disorder proceeded from my bending to write, I now read & write at a high Desk at which I am oblidgd to stand: This was a little troublesome at first, but Custom has reconcild Me so [*page break*] Well to it now, & it agrees with Me, that I have not the least Uneasiness in my Breast, & doubt not but by this means entirely to avoid the Inconveniences I usd to find in Study

I am indeed so perfectly recoverd now that all the Disadvantage I lye under from My Sickness, is Loss of Time, & the Want of that confirmd Strength & Constitution which I might have expected but for this Interruption However I have Hopes now that with Care I shall still be a robust fellow: I am particularly enjoind Exercise & tho[ugh] I cant have as much in Town as in the Country, Yet I find that Fencing & even Shuttlecock can give Me a good Breathing Spell.

I wish I could have the Happiness of hearing that You are near so hearty as I am: I seem to want Nothing to compleat my Health, than to Spirits elevated, & a brisker flow communicated to them by the Delightful Accounts of Your Health, My most Honourd Mother's & my Dearest Brothers— Please to present my most Affectionate Duty Love to them, & assure My Beloved Mother that I am prevented from Writing to her now by the Shortness of Time I have, but that there will be an Opportunity soon [*page break*] to Philadelphia, when I shall write quite fully— For the same Reasons

92

Honourd Father I am obligd to be more short at present, but cant conclude without mention[in]g a Catastrophe, in Europe, of which I suppose some Accounts as well as some Signs have already reachd Your World.

The first of November, the City of Lisbon was utterly destroyd by an Earthquake & a Conflagration ensuing the fall of the Houses—[1] The Shocks, Most astonishing & dreadful,{!} continued for almost two Months—by which every Town in Portugal, has been almost ruind

To pretend to give any Account of this Misfortune, would be to lessen it all I can. The Curious & Learned have their Compassion swallowd up in fresh Enquiries, Whether these Dreadful Events, are the Directions of Providence particularly to punish Mankind, or proceed from Natural Causes—But Great God! May not the same Instructive Lesson be learnt from Either, That Humanity is Uncertainty—and **ab hoc momento pendet Æternitas**—[2]   By the very smallest Computation 20000 Lives are lost. The Richest Prince[3] in Europe more wretched than a Bankrupt— Accounts are just [*in left margin*:] arrivd that his Army are turnd Dissolute & Lawless, & plunder the miserable Remains of his Subjects—

Be pleasd to Remember Me to the Best of Women, & the best of Parents
I am Honourd Father Your most Affectionate & most Dutiful Son
John Dickinson

ALS (PPL-JDFP)

---

[1] Scholars estimate that the Lisbon earthquake was between 8.5 and 9.1 on the moment magnitude scale, one of the strongest in recorded human history. Three separate underwater tremors resulted in three tsunami waves. See Mark Molesky, *This Gulf of Fire: The Great Lisbon Earthquake, or Apocalypse in the Age of Science and Reason* (New York: Vintage Books, 2016), 70–71.

[2] Lat. on this moment hangs eternity.

[3] José I (1714–1777), king of Portugal, had just finished the opulent Casa da Ópera in spring 1755 to celebrate Portugal's fortunes.

33

Transcription of a Hearing "Before the Lords of Trade & Plantations," February 26, [1756]

In early 1756, the quarrel between the Pennsylvania Assembly and the governor over the defense of the province reached the Lords of Trade, and JD was present to take notes. At issue was the right of Quakers to liberty of conscience, balanced with the duties of subjects to obey royal instructions to defend the king's colony, and of elected representatives to attend to the safety of their constituents. The matter arose first in 1689 when the Lords of Trade successfully asked that William Penn's proprietorship be revoked for refusing to supply men or money to help fight King William's War (1689–

97). By the 1750s, the Penn family had converted to the Church of England and struggled against the Quakers and their allies in the Assembly to raise military funds and personnel. In past wars, the threat of invasion was minimal, but George Washington's defeat at Fort Necessity unleashed a flood of petitions to the government and essays to the newspapers reporting violence in the western counties and asking for guns and a militia.[1] Public outcry only heightened the urgency of the situation and the animosity between the governor and the Assembly. One petitioner was Chester County justice of the peace, William Moore, whose November 5, 1755, petition asked that the Assembly "by reason of their religious scruples, [no] longer neglect the defense of the Province."[2] Moore was ultimately arrested, jailed, and charged with libel against the Assembly. Also arrested was his political ally and future son-in-law, William Smith, whom JD defended in his 1758 libel trial (see docs. 1:44 through 1:57). Now disgruntled constituents in Pennsylvania petitioned the king himself, decrying their "naked & defenceless State," and requesting that he remove Quakers permanently from the seat of power.[3]

JD was present when the counsel for the constituents made their case before the Lords of Trade. His transcript provides valuable detail to enhance the scant notes in the *Journals of the Board of Trades and Plantations*.[4] He reproduced this detailed account from his draft notes, which are in the last of his five Middle Temple legal notebooks, covering the years 1755 to 1757 (DeHi), to be published in a supplementary volume to the present edition. It is likely he fleshed out the notes from memory immediately after the hearing and subsequently made more than one draft. The title and introductory note appear to have been written at a separate time from the main text.

Arguments before Lords of Trade on Pennsylvania Law[s][5]

I took Notes of these Arguments, & sent them to Uncle Cadwalader—at last they got into the Hands of some Assembly men—and are printed in a Volume of the Votes—[6] **JD**. [*page break*]

Thursday Feb[rua]ry 26
At the Cockpit   Before the Lords of Trade & Plantations

One of the Petitions from the Inhabitants of the Province of Pensilv[ani]a {be[in]g {was} read} setting forth the Defenceless State of that Colony, the Cruelties & Ravages daily committed w[ith]in it & the {further} Danger to wh[ich] it is exposd by the Inactivity of the Assembly, & praying his Majesty to take these things under his Wise & princely Consideration & to ~~prov~~ afford them such Relief as to his Wisdom shall seem proper

Mr. Yorke[7] began to speak.   My L[or]ds   I am of Counsel with the Inhab[itan]ts of Pensilv[ani]a Who have at last thrown themselves upon their Mother Country for Protection, after fruitless Attempts to [pro]cure it amongst themselves. The Petition now read, is one of many from the Inhab[itan]ts of this [Pro]vince, of Every Sort, ~~Religious~~ Perswasion, & Nation: & these Petitions are most remarkable for their Extraordinary Nature, as well as the extreme Distress of the Unhappy Petitioners; for these are Petitions My L[or]ds ag[ains]t a Majority of their Assembly, who contrary to their Allegiance, to Laws of Nature, & the Opinion of the most sensible of their own People both in England & America refuse to discharge the Duties of those Offices to wh[ich] they are constantly aspiring—

Y[ou]r L[or]dships are too well acquainted with the Situation & Importance of this [Pro]vince, for Me to dwell upon them; for nothing is more evident than if it is neglected, that the French may pour down from that Chain of Communication they have on their Barks[8] by the Lakes, & thus obtain an easy Passage into all the other Colonies

{* I shall Divide} [*in left margin:*] {* What I have to trouble Y[ou]r L[or]dships with into 3 Parts— I shall first Consider the Behaviour of the Quak[ers] in some former Affairs of Gov[ernmen]t [~~T~~{& t}]hen in the late Transactions, & lastly shall say someth[in]g of the Remedy that may be nec[essary]}

I shall beg Y[ou]r L[or]ds[hi]ps Leave then to lay down some facts, wh[ich] are ~~well known before this Board on~~ {manifest from} Papers laid before this Board, at the time they passd, wh[ich] will clearly prove how constantly the Sect of People calld Quakers, ~~have ex~~ by their Seats in Assembly, have exposd this most Valuable Part of his Majesty's Dominions to the Greatest Danger, & by the whole Tenor of their Conduct have shewn their Incapacity for the Duties of Governm[en]t & on these facts We hope We shall obtain some Remedy agreable to the Constitution of Our Mother C[oun]try & of this [Pro]vince [*page break*]

In the Spanish War[9] in the Year 1740 ~~Gov[erno]r Thomas~~ Instructions were sent to the Gov[ern]ors of the sev[era]l Colonies to raise what forces & Money they could for his Majesty's Service, & amongst the rest Gov[erno]r Thomas[10] rec[eive]d Orders upon this Head.[11] He immed[iate]ly laid them before the Assembly & [*illegible*] {de}sird them to {exert themselves on their part to} raise Men & he wo[ul]d heartily concur with them in all Measures for that Purpose. They absolutely refusd to raise a Man.[12] He then attempted to [pro]cure some Money from them; & after long Delays, & tedious Disputes, wh[ich] they knew very well how to begin & {to} protract, at last they did grant some Money, but their Altercat[ion]s had continued so long that the Grant was of No Use.[13]

~~After~~ When the French began to invade this Part of his Majesty's Dominions,[14] the Assembly was calld upon to do someth[in]g in Defence of their Province: Their [Pro]prietaries made them Generous Offers to build Forts at their own Expence, & to give £100 A Year for maintain[in]g them,[15] but this Kindness coud not engage them to the least Act of Defence tho[ugh] they were to reap the Benefit of it.[16] Gov[erno]r Hamilton[17] early in the Year 1754 laid before them Letters wh[ich] he had rec[eive]d from the Secretary of State[18] ~~to re~~ requir[in]g him to use the force of the Province to remove the Incroachm[en]ts of the Enemy—[19] Y[ou]r L[or]dships will please to observe what were their Answers to Mr. Hamilton's Message[20]

In Gov[erno]r Thomas's time their Papers were f~~u~~{i}lld with Conscience & Religious Perswasion & Scruples of bear[in]g Arms— But now ~~when they imagind that the Absurdity of this Strange Doctrine wo[ul]d be too glaring~~ {for some} Reason or ano[the]r they thought [pro][per] to renounce those prior pretences & shelter themselves under an Exemption claimd by the Royal Instruct[ion]s & insisted that on a very nice Calculation the Enemy were a few Miles out of the Bounds of the Province & therefore they were restraind from doing any thing[21]

However some Gentlemen in the house movd for [~~20~~{15}?]000 to be granted for his Majesty's Use— [~~On~~?] [t?]{T}his [*illegible*]{w}as carr[ie]d by a great Majority in the Negative wh[ich] was repeated on sev[era]l other Sums down to 5000[22] This they thought [pro][per] to grant,[23] but at the same time took care to annex such terms to it that the Gov[ern]or found it inconsistent with his Duty to pass it.[24] Mr. Hamilton find[in]g that they were obstinately bent on Clamour & Disputation, & that he co[ul]d not enjoy his Post with Ease & Harmony, resignd it with Dignity & Honour[25] [*page break*]

Then Gov[erno]r Morris was appointed. The Borders of Pensilv[ani]a be[in]g ravagd with the greatest Cruelty & Devastation & Sir Tho[ma]s Robinson[26] ~~that~~ writ[in]g to Mr. Morris that a Number of forces were to be sent over, & requir[in]g him to raise Men & Money in this [Pro]vince, he laid these Orders before the Assembly.[27] Instead of comply[in]g with his Request, their Business was to send over Petitions ag[ains]t the Gov[ern]or These came before this Board & as Y[ou]r L[or]dships were pleasd to leave them as they came, I am at liberty to say they were frivolous & groundless.[28] The State of the [Pro]vince grow[in]g now more desperate, most unheard of Barbar[itie]s be[in]g daily committed—Our Indian Allies came to town begg[in]g Assistance ag[ains]t [the?] Common.[29] Petitions were sent to the Assembly by the Inhabit[an]ts of all Sorts & Nations entreat[in]g them to discharge the Offices to wh[ich] they were chosen {& to afford them Protection} Nay it was demanded as it really was, their Right by all Laws Divine & hum[an]

But my L[or]ds there came in a Petition too from a few Quakers, not from that People in General but from a very small Number of the most Zealous & bigotted, setting forth {what they call} their peaceable Testimony & begg[in]g that it might not be violated[30] This Peaceable Testimony prevaild, [*?] {tho[ugh] they passd a Money[31] & Militia Bill,[32] Yet as th[e]y are so lame as to answer no purpose—} We are obligd to resort here for that Defence wh[ich] has been cruelly denied Us at home.

We therefore are to desire Your L[or]dsh[i]ps that You will advise his Majesty to have these 2 bills set aside as Evasive {trick[in]g} & Vain.[33] Your L[or]dships will be convincd of this from consider[in]g the[2?] {se} Bills— As to the Money Bill, At first they ins[iste]d strongly on tax[in]g the [Pro]prietaries Estate, wh[ich] by an act of Assembly[34] is exempted from the Power of the Assessors: & besides the Gov[erno]r did not look upon himself to be authorizd to lay any Burthen on the [Pro]prietaries Estate; This Dispute however was ended as soon as heard of by the Proprietors, & instead of 500 wh[ich] was the utmost the Tax on their Estate woud amount to they made a Generous Present of 5000[35]

This Obstacle be[in]g removd the Bill passd: But the same Spirit wh[ich] elogd {retarded} its [Pro]gress clogd its Execution: Y[ou]r L[or]ds[hi]ps will observe that after enact[in]g that 55000[36] shall be raisd, & p[ai]d into the hands of the respective County Treasurers, it shall be transmitted by them into the hands of the Provincial Treasurer of the Loan Office[37] & the[re?] it s[h?]

[*blank lines*]

& then follows a Clause recit[in]g the Gift of the [Pro]prietaries & g[*illegible*] order[in]g their 5000 to be p[ai]d to the Comm[itt]ee to be by disposd of for{by} {for} his Majesty's Use: So that this 5000 is the only Sum wh[ich] is actually to be disposd, but the other is artfully dropd in the Loan Office & there it is left.

[*blank lines*]

Ano[the]r th[in]g to be taken Notice of is the Purposes to wh[ich] this Money is to be applied to
Purposes quite agreable to the Peaceable Testimony but utterly evasive of their Duty & his Majesty's Instructions [*page break*]

The next thing I woud submit to your L[or]ds[hi]ps Consideration is the Militia Bill, & this will be found still more Elusive & artful than the other— In the first Place it is self-condemnd by the Preamble:[38] In the next—There is not the least [Pro]vision made for Defence but it is so calculated as to be of no Use. & lastly it is contrary to the Constitution of Pensilv[ani]a [~~of~~{by}?] Charter & contrary to the Constitution of England.

It is self-condemnd by the Preamble for it refers to the sev[era]l Petitions wh[ich] entreated their Aid & [Pro]tection,[39] ~~wh[ich]~~ {&} Yet it has not orderd any thing that will contribute to these Ends[;{:}?] but rejects their Distress & directly contradicts the Voice of a whole People, wh[ich] in this Case pray[in]g for Rights of Nature is the Voice of **God**

By this Act, the Officers are to be chosen by the People, & Articles of War framd by those Officers,[40] So that the Powers of Lieutenancy are taken out of the {Pro[p[riet]or?] & his} Gov[ern]or contrary to the Charter, & conferrd upon the People{: & this is contrar[y] to the Cons[tituti]on of Engl[an]d where all military Power is lodgd in the King}

The next Clause is for converting Proselytes to Quakerism[41] for will not every Coward have a Scruple of Conscience when that Scruple will exempt him from Duty: Every Man may shelter himself under that pretence—& there is no Compulsion, if any one makes this pretence, to oblige him to find ano[the]r Man, or to make Satisfaction for his Absence by pay[in]g a Sum of Money; the utmost Caution has been usd that noth[in]g effectual may follow from this Bill.

Then there is a [Pro]viso that no Serv[an]t or Youth under 21 shall inlist[42]— wh[ich] clause extends ~~to the~~ most serviceable part of the People. For the Youth under that age are the very flower & Strength of a Country, & the most [pro][per] for its Defence: Serv[an]ts too in the Colonies are [~~extrem~~?] very numerous, & the act might have provided some Recompense for the Master w[ith]out depriv[in]g the Publick of the Servant
Ano[the]r [Pro]viso is that they shall not march above 3 days out of[43]

From these th[in]gs Y[ou]r L[or]ds[hi]ps will [per]ceive what Defence his Majesty is to expect for this Part of his Dom[inion]s wh[ich] if they are left [~~to~~?]{e}xposd by the Negligence Obstin[a]cy & Undutifulness of this Assembly, must soon encrease the Power of his Enemies, & become a [Pro]vince of France
The Petitioners be[in]g thus cunningly & cruelly trifled with, We are to move Y[ou]r L[or]dsh[i]ps that You will [pro]cure these bills to be set aside & some Remedy adequate to our Distress [pro]vided   As to the Nature of this Remedy, it woud little become Us to pretend to direct your L[or]dsh[i]ps— But I hope by what has been laid before this Board it will appear that the Assembly have [*page break*] have actually abdicated the Gov[ernmen]t by

refus[in]g to discharge the Duties of it, for if the Duties of Gov[ernmen]t be to defend & [pro]tect the People committed to y[ou]r Care, then to deny that Defence & [Pro]tection is an Abdication.

The Relief that We expect We hope will be agreable to Our Constitution What that Const[ituti]on is will appear from the Charter & by that We find their Laws are to be as near as possible to the Laws of Engl[an]d wh[ich] require that every [Per]son to hold an Office of Trust—shall be qualified by tak[in]g [pro][per] Oaths. The first Statute to this Purpose is the Corporation Act in 13 Car. 2.[44] This Charter[45] was granted after that Act. The next Stat[ute]s are those of 1 W. & M. & 7 & 8 W. 3. & these by 8 G. 1.[46] are confirmd & extended to the Plantations for 7 Years: During that Term then it will not be denied, they certainly were in force there{; &} as by their Charter & 7 & 8 W. 3. All {their} Laws contrary to the Laws of England are declard void, they are certainly w[ith]in the Policy of those Laws at this time ~~Mr. Penn's~~ It may now be [pro][per] to enquire what Claims they have for this Priviledge of hold[in]g Offices under their Charters. Mr. Penn's first Charter[47] takes no Notice of it—tis true he mentions it in ~~that of~~ 1701[48] But in that he refers to 2 Acts of Assembly wh[ich] were afterw[ar]ds rejected by the Crown[49]

* So that the foundation on wh[ich] that [G?]{L}iberty is ~~gr[an]ted~~ {built} is destroyd & consequently the Grant void.

In 1704 They passd a{n} ~~Law~~ {act}[50] in favour of themselves wh[ich] was neither rej[ecte]d or approvd by the King, & therefore tis true it has the force of a Law.

But Yet if they are bound by the Acts of Parl[iamen]t before ment[ione]d requir[in]g Oaths this cannot exempt them from that Obligation.

What My L[or]ds might make the Gov[ernmen]t here more easy during the Adm[inistrati]on of these Peaceable Gentlemen, was perhaps that no Man coud ever imagine ~~that~~ these Principles of Meekness wo[ul]d be carried into Practize, when Disputes arose between them & the Enemies of their {King &} Country & when every thing that all Nations thro[ugh] all Ages have constantly agreed to hold invaluable, was at stake   Every one thought that these [~~illegible~~]{O}pinions related to private Malice & Revenge, & this was the more [pro]bable as many [Per]sons who were not Quakers held the same: & I cant believe My L[or]ds that the Quakers now understand their own Principles: for all these Notions sprung up in the Reign of Charles the first,[51] but the[y?]{N}on Resistence & Submission then held, was only an extraordinary Charity wh[ich] forbad the Resentm[en]t[s] of trifling Injuries: & Gen[era]l Ireton[52] who was as brave a man & as great a Soldier as any in that Age, strictly adherd to this Doctrine [*page break*]

My L[or]d Clarendon[53] tells a Storey of him, wh[ich] is a surprizing Instance of this Gen[era]l Ireton & the famous L[or]d Hollis,[54] then in the House of Commons had a very warm Debate, & as they were coming out of the house toget[he]r [~~Mr.~~?]{L[or]d} Hollis spit in the Gen[era]l's face.[55] The Gen[era]l did not resent it in the least & he was laught at & ridiculd by all the Cavaliers of that time for not challenging the [Per]son who affront~~[in]g~~{[e]d} him & some of his friends tell[in]g him how much his Char[acte]r was injurd by his Tameness, he answ[ere]d that it was inconsistent with his Principles to revenge Private Injuries—

This I say My L[or]ds was certainly the Origin of Quakerism, ~~&~~ {but} liv[in]g in Peace & Quietness for a long time, at last they have degenerated into a Notion that Peace & Quietness is their Religion, & Yet that they never are to exert themselves in defence of them.   In persevering in this strange & unnatural Fancy, they have brought the greatest Miseries on the Provinces— Miseries wh[ich] must continue unless We have a Gov[ernmen]t with different Principles

Your L[or]ds[hi]ps will please to attend to 7 & 8 W. 3. wh[ich] requires an Oath for hold[in]g all Places of [Pro]fit or Trust. A Seat in the Assembly is such beyond Dispute for they have very considerable Wages ~~great enough~~ much greater than what Members of the house of Commons have here: But My L[or]ds if it was not a place of [Pro]fit, can it be conceivd that they are not w[ith]in the Policy of that act? It cant be supposd that Law sho[ul]d extend to serv[in]g on Juries & other inferior Offices & yet not reach to a Seat in the Assembly wh[ich] is one of the highest in a Gov[ernmen]t

They know[in]g of the Restraint of 7 & 8 W. 3.

What renders this Assembly ~~more~~ utterly inexcusable My L[or]ds is that when they might have retird, when no Necessity calld them into that house, when they might have retaind all their Rights, & the [Pro]vince been secure & happy Yet with the greatest Obstinacy & Cruelty they thrusted themselves into Posts wh[ich] has involvd a flourish~~d~~{i}ng People in Discord Misery & Ruin   That People My L[or]ds groaning under Oppression have laid their Dutiful & humble Petitions on the Steps of his Majesty's throne, & hope with Y[ou]r L[or]ds[hi]ps Assistance to [pro]cure some Remedy ag[ains]t the Evils bro[ugh]t upon them by a faction the more pernicious as it stops the very Sources of Government— [*page break*]

Mr. Forrester.   I am of Counsel my L[or]ds with the People of Pens[ylvani]a but as my very Learned friend has so thoroughly & accurately handled the Subject of these Petitions, I shall give Your L[or]ds[hi]ps but little Trouble

The Principles my L[or]ds wh[ich] have occasiond the Miseries We complain of, are so whimsi[cal] & ~~fantas~~ absurd, that really they woud excite Pity to their Assertors did they not affect the Political & Natural Rights of Mankind   Then My L[or]ds they become important, they become dangerous & require not a severe Remedy but a gentle Remedy to a severe Evil   Such every impartial [Per]son will think that wh[ich] has been ment[ione]d & there cannot be any other wh[ich] can go to the bottom of the Wound   This will appear my L[or]ds from consider[in]g the Constitution of this [Pro]vince: for it may appear surpriz[in]g to some {& I beg Y[ou]r L[or]ds[hi]ps Leave} [*in left margin:*] {to address myself now in some Measure to the Audience} why the People shoud chuse Representatives Who act so diametrically opposite to the Wellfare of the [Pro]vince: But a little Information will shew that this Misfortune is involuntary. Pensilv[ani]a is divided into 8 Counties.[56] The whole Body almost of the Quakers live in the 3 inner most, & these 3 chuse 26 Members[57]—the whole house consists but of 36, & consequently the Quakers have always a great Majority. This is a Radical fault in the Constitution & from this fountain flow all the Miseries of that People

When Y[ou]r L[or]ds[hi]ps consider what part of the Gov[ernmen]t has been defective in their Duty, You will find the Blame to lye wholly on the Assembly—   The [Pro][pri][e]tors have nobly generously & repeatedly exerted themselves, & have endeav[ore]d to stir up a Spirit of Zeal & Activity for the Publick Good.

First they made an Offer of very considerable Grants of Lands to those who shoud march for the Defence: & these Grants were to be in the most ample manner they were to be free of Quit Rents for 15 Years   This was ridiculd by the Assembly Then the [Pro][pri][e]tors off[ere]d to give 400 for build[in]g forts & to contribute a £100 a Year for maintain[in]g them This was scornd by the Assembly.   In short my Lords as vigilant & ready as the [Pro][pri][e]tors were to do every thing for the Common Weal, as obstinate & illnaturd was the Assembly to counteract their Designs. Their next step was to vent their Spleen by fall[in]g on the [Pro][pri][e]tors Estate & lay[in]g a Tax wh[ich] amounted to 500 The [Pro][pri][e]tors no sooner heard of it than they sent 5000

Danger My L[or]ds now approachd [*page break*] approachd nearer The People were ~~a larmd~~ {daily} terrified with alarms of Slaughter & ~~fire~~ Ruin. Amongst others Our Indian Allies came to Town, ~~requir[in]g ou~~ acquaint[in]g Us that things were come to a Crisis & that they must take up Arms of one Side or the other: they preferd our antient friendship, & with Our Assistance they woud espouse our Quarrel: find[in]g themselves trifled with by the Assembly, & urgd by Necessity they demanded a Categorical Answer, Whether they wo[ul]d do ~~any~~ th[in]g for their mutual Defence.

Receiv[in]g no Answer, they went back, leav[in]g them to their fate, an{s} an infatuated People

Soon after the Gov[ern]or gave them Notice that these Indians had taken up Arms{X} {& prest them earnestly to think of some Measures for our [Pro]tection—} The Insolence & Stupidity of their Answer is inconceivable— They desire the Gov[erno]r to inform them whether these Indians had not been [pro]vokd by an Imposition in a [Pro][pri][e]tary [Pur]chase   As if when a Mans house is in flames & he runs out to beg his Neighbours Assistance, they shoud cruelly insult his Distress, by enquir[in]g whether the fire [pro]ceeded from a Candle, or a Coal drop[pin]g on the floor or what other Accident.   For such purposes do these Men force themselves into the Assembly, & when they might stay out & enjoy their Principles in Quiet—Still will they exclude others only to expose, not their Conscience or their Obstinacy, but their **mulishness**.

Did I know a harsher Term I wo[ul]d use it!   Indeed I beg Y[ou]r L[or]ds[hi]ps Pardon for my Warmth, & hope Your L[or]ds[hi]ps will ~~for[g]~~ think it excusable on such a Subject as this: if ever it is, it must be when the Rights & Liberties of Soc[ie]ty are sacrificd by ~~the Intrigue~~ Wickedness of faction—& I have great Reason to think it will not be treated with less Warmth in ano[the]r Place—

At last When ~~the~~ [A?]{H}uman Nature coud no longer bear this Treatment & the Assembly found themselves under some force from the just Resentm[en]ts of the People, they did pass the 2 Bills now before this Board

The Militia Bill, I will venture to say is the most extraordinary thing I ever beheld with my Eyes. In the first place it is an Invitation to the whole World to attack them, by declar[in]g that they will resist Nobody

Then it gives Leave to those who will to associate: But there is not the least Direction how this Association is to be formd. The People are to ~~be~~ meet by Chance   Nobody appo[inte]d to preside; by Chance they are to Chuse their Officers, & then the Act goes thro a Number of [Pro]viso's & Restrictions, wh[ich] it wooud be needless to repeat, as Y[ou]r L[or]ds[hi]ps must be convincd by ~~what has been said~~ {barely read[in]g them} that they never were designd to answer any [Pur]poses of Self-Defence, nor ever can— It is most unjust & Partial, & instead of injoin[in]g Compulsion, in wh[ich] the very Nature of these bills consists it absolutely [pro]hibits it, & leaves Room for every one creep out of it who chuses. Those who have a Scruple of [*page break*] Conscience are not to contribute the least to the Means of Defen[ce] but are to be [pro]tected ~~by~~ at the Danger & Expence of those who are are too honest ~~& s~~ to make the same Pretence: So that where all are equally concernd, "Et quod omnes tangit, ab omnibus ferri debet[";][58] Yet the

Burthen will fall only on a small Number, & these the Virtuous, active & brave.

Another thing I woud observe on this Bill My L[or]ds is that it is directly inconsistent with his Majesty's Prærog[ative]   It is depriv[in]g him & his Deputies of the Powers of Lieutenancy & & sets up a Democratical Army in Oppos[itio]n to his Authority. The King by the English Constitution is the head of all Military Power & to him the Supreme Commond belongs. This Power he has gr[an]ted to the [Pro][pri][e]tors, in the [Pro]vince of Pens[ylvani]a & they have transferrd it to Y[ou]r Gov[ern]or   But by this Act it is divested out of him, & bestowd upon the People.

Under the same force, My L[or]ds wh[ich] [pro]ducd the Militia Act they passd the money Bill. By this they pretend to grant 55000 wh[ich] they boast of, as a [pro]digious Effort—But I am informd that if the [Per]sons who signd these Petitions, had been in the Assembly, they wo[ul]d have gr[an]ted at least 4 times as much.   ~~After~~ In fact this Grant is only nominal: for the Money can never be disposd of. It is lodgd in & there is no Authority given to draw it out.

Having thus My L[or]ds shewn the Chicanery & Evasions of the {i} se ~~People~~ {Assembly} I think it must be manifest, that they have renouncd the Duties of their Off[ice]   Magestrates were appointed to [pro]cure the Happiness of a People & to [pro]tect their[s?] & if these have been neglected, then the Magestracy has been neglected, & those possessd of it have forf[eite]d their Posts

As to the Priv[ilege]s claimd by the Quakers, it woud be An Absurdity to Enquire Whether they ever had such Grants, when those Priv[ilege]s are in their Nature destruct[ive] of Society: It wo[ul]d be burning a Candle at Noon to attempt to [pro]ve that all such Priv[ilege]s must be ipso [f?] jure nulla. I ~~shall~~ This strong & evident Truth is laid down in Antonine's Rescript[59] & [*illegible*]{ca}rries Conviction & Author[ity] in ~~the~~ {its} Terms, "**That all Grants to** [par][ticu]lar Members of a Society inconsistent with the Good of {that} Society in General are void of themselves for Salus populi **suprema Lex**"—[60]

Mr. Henley[61]   My L[or]ds—I am of Counsel with the Assembly of Pens[ylvani]a wh[ich] has existed as the Representatives of the Dissenters of that [Pro]vince ever since it was settled, & ~~they~~ {We} now attend this Board to prevent Y[ou]r L[or]ds[hi]ps Advice to his Majesty to abridge these Priv[ilege]s wh[ich] hitherto have been inviolated & I must say that consider[in]g their Importance, they are now contend[in]g [pro] Aris & focis.[62] The Ends designd by these Petitions are so violent that they {are} [*page break*] to avow them, but by What has been said on the other Side, they are no less than to turn out of all Power the Old Inhab[itan]ts of this [Pro]vince, by whose Wisdom & Care it has become the most flourish[in]g in all his Majesty's Dominions & to make Room for the Natives of Salk[s?]burgh & Augsburgh[63]

This Attempt My Lords is not only contrary to the Nat[ure] ~~& Spirit~~ of this Gov[ernmen]t but is destructive of those Priviledges, wh[ich] have been securd ~~to Englishmen~~ by the Toleration Act: It militates ag[ains]t the very Spirit of that Noble Statute.

This Gov[ernment]t was designd & calculated for the Ease & Service of Dissenters— It was settled in Car. 2 time When by the Ecclesiastical Power Acts of Uniformity[64] were cramd down the Throats of the whole Nation In this Period of Persecution & Violence the Quakers & other Dissenters flew to the Wilds of America, to enjoy that Liberty of Conscience ~~wh[ich] made~~ in the Poss[essi]on of wh[ich] they found even Desarts delightful & it will appear beyond Contrad[ictio]n that the Gov[ernmen]t of Pens[ylvani]a was formd for the Benefit of these People from the Words of the Royal Charter & that the Church was barely to be tolerated there. The Words of that Charter are that Will[iam] Penn shall **permit** 20[65]

~~As the Quakers~~ By Mr. Penn's Charter that Liberty of Conscience was to remain inviolable to all future Ages.

As the Quakers are a People of the greatest Industry Prudence & Virtue So they are a Sect of the greatest Wisdom of any I know in his Maj[es]ty's Dominions, & the most ready to support a Gov[ernmen]t agreable to the true Constit[uti]on of England.

By their Care the [Pro]vince of Pens[ylvani]a has been modeld in Imitation of their Mother Country. It is divided into Counties Cities & Boroughs. The People are represented by [Per]sons chosen annually to serve in their Assembly: ~~There they m~~ & as Wisdom will ever be respectd & have deservd Regard paid to her, it is remarkable that the Assembly has always consisted of Quakers: Nor have they ever disappointed the good Opinion of their Constituents, but have managd with so much Integrity & Discretion— that the Publick Treasure has not been wasted & Yet thro[ugh]out the last War this [Pro]vince was safe, while England was spend[in]g immense~~ly~~ Sums, & running [pro]digiously in Debt

But now My Lords, a Heavy Charge is laid upon & they are accusd as the Authors of the present Calamities: However We hope to [pro]ve that they have [pro]ceeded more from indirect Practizes in the Gov[erno]r or his Ignorance [*page break*] Of the Constitution of that Country, & such means have been usd to ~~exp[ose] them to a publick~~ {raise a popular} Clamour ag[ains]t them that I think it my Duty to detect such Artifices wherever I can & to expose them as I shall now endeavour to do

It is well known that the Quakers by their Construction of the new Testament are principled ag[ains]t Self-Defence: & tho[ugh] these Opinions might be im[pro][per] for the Legislature of a Mother Country Yet they are very cons[isten?]t with the Gov[ernmen]t of a Colony. The Prop[rie]tor is Captain Gen[era]l by the Charter & may levy Troops[66] & do every thing that is necessary of that Nature; & therefore Mr. Hamilton's Complaint was not that they wo[ul]d {not} raise Men but that they wo[ul]d not raise £20000—For on consider[in]g the Gov[ern]or's power the other ~~seems~~ appears to be needless: But the [pre]sent Gov[ern]or tho[ugh] he knew it was contrary to their Principles to raise forces, Yet to throw an Odium on them insisted on their doing what they coud {not}, & wh[ich] was unnecessary, if they coud As to Money I must say My L[or]ds that they have from time to time offerd Bills for such Sums as were requisite, wh[ich] have been pertin[a]c[ious]ly obstinately & sillily rejected by the Gov[ern]or: I say sillily, Unless We consider the Design with wh[ich] they were rej[ecte]d that is, to drive these People out of all Power; in that respect it was crafty & artful

First the Gov[erno]r pretended that the Money must be sunk in 5 Years, as if the Law relat[in]g to the 4 New England Colonies extended to this. The Assembly insisted there was No Obligation upon them to do this, that it was contrary to the{ir} constant Practize, & {wo[ul]d be} an Infringem[en]t of their Rights

Some time after in hopes of end[in]g these Disputes, they off[ere]d a bill in a diff[eren]t form for 55000 to be sunk in so short a Space as 4 Years But they happend to be {so} very unreasonable as to tax the [Pro][pri][e]tors Est[ate] to contrib[ute] to the Defence of the [Pro][pri][e]tor's [Pro]vince. This was so extravag[an]t & illnaturd a Charge that the Gov[erno]r refusd to agree to it, & claimd an Exemption for the [Pro][prie]tors wh[ich] the King himself does not enjoy for his fee-farm is always subject to Taxes   The [Pro][pri][e]tors however on Cond[itio]n the Assembly wo[ul]d not insist on this Demand, gave 5000, & then the Bill passd

Hav[in]g at last accomplishd what they were so long opposd in, its now obj[ecte]d that this Bill can never answer any purpose. It is a Bill for strik[in]g 55000, & on the Strik[in]g, the Sum [o?]{i}s raisd: then it goes on, & [reci]ting the [Pro][pri][e]tors Gift of 5000, it gives the Disposal of the whole Sum, the whole Sum My L[or]ds [*blank?*] by this Bill to the Com[mitt]ee   ~~They~~ {Assembly} have more honesty than the Gentlemen of the other Side will [all[ow]?] them & have not savd their Money, at the Expence of the [Pro][pri][e]tors   It is said too that the Services [to?] wh[ich] the Money is to be applied are all peaceable as [*blank?*]

But these are only Part of the Serv[ice]s & then follows a Gen[era]l Clause & other Services for his {Majesty's Use} [*page break*] I expected to have heard it [pro]vd, to justify the Extraordinary Request now made to your

L[or]ds[hi]ps that a great Body of French were fallen upon this Province, were likely to conquer it & so overrun all the Rest— But it seems now the Truth is discov[ere]d that all this Noise has arose from the straggling Incursions of the Delaware Indians on the Borders. These People it is supposd with great Reason were [pro]vokd to these Outrages by a flagrant Imposition upon them in a [Pro][pri][e]tary purchase:[67] In order to remove all Animosities, the Assembly were for enquir[in]g into this Affair, & I confess I cant see the Absurdity of enquir[in]g into the Cause of Inconveniene{t}~~es~~ Conseq[uence]s in order to put an End to them.

However to ~~p~~{m}ake what [Pro]vision they coud ag[ains]t these Misfortunes, {at the Desire of their Const[ituen]ts} they passd a Militia Bill. This is said to be quite imperfect: that may be, for I never saw one in my Life that was not so. All these kind of Bills are vain & foolish Attempts, & I may affirm that there never will be one framd to answer all the Purposes that may be expected from them: But this My L[or]ds seems as [pro][per] as any can be for that [Pro]vince.   It is obj[ecte]d that the People are not to march above 3 Days out of the [Pro]vince. Y[ou]r L[or]ds[hi]ps will please to observe that in the Charter to W[illiam] Penn he is enabled to lead the People 3 Days out of the [Pro]vince:[68] In Mr. Hamiltons Instructions, he is to do noth[in]g but w[ith]in the [Pro]vince: Surely these woud be suff[icien]t Answers to this Obj[ecti]on: But if they are not, I will assert one th[in]g wh[ich] I know will not be denied Me, & that is

{That} No Assembly can make a Law to bind out of their own Colony—

As to the Obj[ecti]on of the People's chus[in]g their own Officers, there certainly cannot be a greater Encourag[emen]t for inlist[in]g, tha~~t~~{n} that they will be commanded by [Per]sons known & esteemd by them.
If Articles of War are to be framd, None can be so [pro][per] t{f}o{r} that Purpose as Officers, who are supposd to be best acquainted with those things

These My L[or]ds are the Consid[eration]s wh[ich] occur to Me & are worth mention[in]g on these 2 Bills—& ~~tho[ugh]~~ We {hope} have shewn that if there have been any Delays, We have not causd them, & therefore are not answerable for the Consequences, nor shall feel those Violent Measures wh[ich] have been ~~re[q?] desird~~ {ment[ione]d}.   The Remedy now desird, is not ag[ains]t the Miseries of the Province, but is levelld at the Assembly who are falsely supposd to be the Authors of them. A Test Act is requird as agreable to the Constitut[ion] of Pens[ylvani]a & England. The Const[ituti]on of Pens[ylvani]a most evidently appears to be an Exemption from all Restraint of Conscience. The Time & Manner of its Settlem[en]t {&} the Principles of its Inhab[itan]ts, shew that it was for the Enjoym[en]t of this Liberty they removd to it.

Can it be Policy then, can it be Wisdom or Justice to introduce the Doctr[ine] of Cha[rle]s 2[d's] time from wh[ich] these People fled, & to force down Oaths & Forfeitures wh[ich] hitherto they have happily avoided— Suppose these People driven {out} [*page break*] Suppose these People driven out, & their Se[a]ts left empty, their worthy Successors will be the Scum of Germany. These p[eo?] no doubt will raise an Army, but Experience will shew that they will contribute no more to the Peace & Safety [*illegible*] of Pens[ylvani]a than the pres[en]t Assembly.

Such a Remedy as this wo[ul]d be but partial, it wo[ul]d be a Revenge taken on a Set of Men who do not appear to blame—But the most adeq[uate] & useful {full} Relief wo[ul]d {seems to} be, to make all the Colonies raise such Sums as they able, & to pass a Gen[era]l Militia Bill to operate in all of them   We hope Y[ou]r L[or]ds[hi]ps will think someth[in]g of this Nature a more mild & Suitable Remedy for the Distress of this [Pro]vince.

Mr. Pratt.   My L[or]ds—I am concernd on the same Side with the Gentleman who spoke last: & after what has been already said, I hardly know how to [pro]ceed:{,} for We are to arg{n}swer in an Instant, to most ingen[ious] Argum[en]ts, composd at Leisure & with Art, & of wh[ich] We coud not have the least Notice till they were deliv[ere]d for the Petitions are very [illegible] {dont express} the least of their Designs, wh[ich] in fact are to depose{,} to tumble down from all Authority the very Fathers of this Country: & to strip {G[entlemen]} of those Rights to wh[ich] they are entitled by the Laws of Nature & Society

The Charter to Mr. Penn, shews in the strongest & clearest Manner that in the {birth in the} very Concoction of this Colony its Gov[ernmen]t was to consist of Quakers & other Dissenters. By their Constit[uti]on they are entitled to all the Priv[ilege]s necessary for the Members managem[en]t of a free State. These Priv[ilege]s they have always enjoyd, & by Acts of Assembly confirmd {approvd} by his Majesty they have been confirmd.
They have held all kind of Places & Offices; they have set on Juries of Life & death, & by the Nature & Spirit of their Const[ituti]on, Aff[idavi]ts have the same force with Oaths.   Their Assemblies too have always consisted of Quakers & by their wise{d}om, Pens[ylvani]a in Wealth, Trade {Commerce}, Popularity {Numbers} of Inhab[itan]ts & in every other Respect, has become the most flourish[in]g of all his Majesty's Dominions: they are grown so considerable that I am told their Trade, to their Mother-Country alone amounts to 300000 a Year.[69]

Every thing that coud be requird from a [pru]dent Adm[inistrati]on has been [per]formd by this People: Tis true they never have exerted themselves in any Military Operations: but it is true too that this was needless

All Military Power is lodgd in the [Pro][pri][e]tor of Pens[ylvania]a as here it is in the Crown: The Assembly there may be compard to Our 2

Houses of Parl[iamen]t & what is their Authority or Concern in things relat[in]g to War? No more than this that they have the Wealth of Kingdom, ~~the Sinews of~~ in their hands, & his Majesty must apply to them for the Sinews of War, & they are the Great Counsel of the Land whose ~~Opinion~~ {Advice} he takes in Matters of Publick Importance. Why then has not the Gov[ern]or exercisd [*page break*] the Authority legally vested in [~~illegible~~] him: I shall be answerd [per]haps out of my own Mouth, for want of Supplies from the Assembly

Now it is not suggested My L[or]ds that the Quakers are Principled ag[ains]t pass[in]g money Bills. This has never been said, it cant be said with any Regard to Truth: If then the Gov[ern]or {had} discharges his Duty, the Quak[ers] might have filld their Offices of Representatives, as well as completely as if they had been of a different [Per]swasion. This My L[or]ds brings Me to the only Point in Dispute, Whether the Quakers are to blame in Relation to the Money Bills.

The craftiness of all Rulers have taught them, that times of great Distress & Publick Unhappiness are the lucky Periods for extort[in]g from their People, any Priviledges, wh[ich] they are ~~des[irous~~?] {lust[in]g} to usurp. Your L[or]ds[hi]ps well know the Policy of King Cha[rle]s the first, Who was constantly alarm[in]g & terrify[in]g his Parl[iamen]t with Acc[oun]ts of the Irish Massacre & Rebellion,[70] to force Gr[an]ts from them inconsist[en]t with the Liberties of Englishmen. This {Mother} Worthy Example has been followd by the Pertinaceous Gov[ern]or of Pens[ylvani]a. He insisted on mak[in]g Amend[men]ts to Money Bills & [re?]sink[in]g the Sums in 5 Years Because he thought the Assembly so frightend, they coud not observe the Imposition, or woud not dare to take Notice of it: But they convincd this Gentleman, that they had more Sense & Resolution; & instead of a base Compliance, they exposd the Weakness & Injustice of ~~their~~ {his} ~~C[illegible]~~ Pretences.
In hopes to avoid these Snares, calculated to raise a Clamour ag[ains]t them, they offf[ere]d a Bill in ano[the]r ~~Way~~ {manner}, to raise Money by a Tax: However here again, the Ingenuity of their Gov[ern]or ~~found~~ laid an Obstacle in their Way. Mr. Penn may be very great in the [Pro]vince of Pens[ylvani]a he is certainly invested with large Powers, for Civil Adm[inistrati]on: But I never can look upon in any other Light than as a fellow Subject {with the Rest of the Inhab[itan]ts} when the Common ~~cause~~ Int[eres]t of all are concernd: He indeed did not justify the Gov[ern]or's Conduct, & I am sure if he [~~illegible~~]{h}ad been on the Spot himself, he never woud have cavilld about 500 when the Gentleman's heart was so large as to grant 5000
On this trifling unjust Obj[ecti]on then of the Gov[ern]or's the [Pro]vince was left defenceless, & the whole Load of Calumny is thrown upon the

Assembly because they woud not surrender up their legal & most Valuable Rights, upon the first Arbitrary Demand their Gov[ern]or was pleasd to make of them.

At last they overcame all Objections, & [*page break*] And 2 Bills were past, & what is most surpriz[in]g, is that tho[ugh] not a Word was said ag[ains]t them in America, Your L[or]ds[hi]ps are now desird to have them annulld

This{e} {1ˢᵗ} Obj[ecti]on to the Money Bill is a most extraordinary one that it locks up the Money in the Loan Off[ice] It is hardly worth while shew[in]g the Mistake of the Gent[lemen] in this Point. The Money is lodgd in the Loan Office tis true but & so it always is, in every Case where Money is raise, & all the Comm[itt]ee has to do is to draw for it as they have Occasion: On this it issues, & this is the only Power they have over 5000

But the Grand Obj[ecti]on if they woud but speak out of the other Side, is not that the Money cant be disposd of but that it is not to be disposd of by the Right [Per]sons: They have no lik[in]g to the Comm[itt]ee, & in their Eyes, the Gov[ern]or is the Man, into whose hands every th[in]g shoud be thrown, All Power all ~~Money~~ {Wealth} shoud center there, his Pleasure shoud ~~Rule~~ {sway} all, his Wisdom shoud guide the Whole.

These Petitions say, there are great Numbers of brave Resol[ute] ~~Souls~~ Men} in the [Pro]vince, ready to seize their Arms, & breath[in]g noth[in]g but Slaughter & Revenge; Heroes animated by the Injuries of their C[oun]try & ardently wish[in]g to meet their Enemy; How strange then My L[or]ds is a Complaint that there is no Compulsion enjoind by this Law: Suppos[in]g the Courage of those Petit[io]ners to be really coold, Yet Compulsion is inconsistent with the Nature of our Gov[ernmen]t   There is indeed One Instance of it {rem[ainin]g} amongst Us, but Compress[in]g in the Land Service was never heard of but in Cases of the utmost Extremity

For these Reasons My L[or]ds & others still more frivolous, for all the Conseq[uence]s of the Gov[ern]or's Obstinacy & wrangl[in]g Your L[or]ds[hi]ps are desird to prevent any Advantages aris[in]g from these Bills & {as a} further Remedy to [pro]cure a Test Act for turn[in]g out the Assembly. This be[in]g a most astonish[in]g {Request} it has been softend by pretend[in]g it is agreable to the Constit[uti]on of England & Pensilv[ani]a   The Arg[umen]ts on this head are really very ingenious: It is agreable to the ~~Laws~~ {Const[ituti]on} of Pens[ylvani]a because their Laws are to be as near as possible to the Laws of England. What is this My L[or]ds but say[in]g that by the Const[ituti]on of Pens[ylvani]a its Const[ituti]on is destroyd: [~~illegible~~]{[Can?]} it ever be conceivd that all the Laws in force here are to be universally & strictly extended there: This woud be such an extravagant Supposition, it requires no Answer but itself.

This Rem[edy] as it is calld, is a weak & insuff[icien]t one. Let it be imag[ine]d that the Quakers are excluded: Their Int[eres]t will not be destroyd [*page break*] Their Connexions will not be broken: ~~& all the Conseq[uence]s that will follow, will be that~~ {So that} [Per]sons will be chosen by the Quaker [Par]ty, & must follow their Instructions, & I dare engage that While the Gov[ern]or [*illegible*] {[acts?]} as he has hitherto done, he will not find the swearing Assembly a jot more Complais[an]t to him than the affirm[in]g

But My L[or]ds there are more fatal Consequences than these to be apprehended; the destroy[in]g ~~antient~~ Priv[ilege]s ~~wh[ich] have existed~~ {antient as the} be[in]g of the [Pro]vince will turn it from its found[atio]n & shake it into Dissensions Confusion: It will raise a kind of Civil War between th[*illegible*]{os}e who [caus{'d}?] & those Who suffer by the Alteration: They already feel the Miseries of Discord, but this will be add[in]g fuel to the flames, & will only imbitter their Quarrels & encrease their Distractions May not these People with Justice complain that the Publick has broke their faith with them: & that after they by their Toils & Industry, have settled im[pro][ve]d & inrichd the Country, Germans are calld in to thrust them from their Rights & to batten on their Wealth & Labours.

The Conseq[uence]s may be that exasperated by thei~~r~~{se} Injuries, & stripd of their Rights & Honours, they may Retreat to some other Climate in hopes to [*illegible*] enjoy ~~what~~ {those Bless[in]gs of wh[ich]} Injustice [to?]{h}as stripd them—

Mr. York in Reply.   My Lords. All the facts necessary for our [Pur]poses are manifest & have not been in the least contrad[icte]d   The Province is defenceless & ravagd in a most cruel Manner by the French allied Indians: & the Question now is Whether this Board will give Ear to these Petitions wh[ich] speak the voice of Reason [*illegible*]{o}f Duty & of their Cons[tituti]on or to these New Priv[ilege]s set up by the Quakers: I call them New for it does not appear that they have been entitled to them from the Settlem[en]t of this Country. It has been ins[iste]d on that the Remedy [We?] require is inconsistent with the Charter on wh[ich] their Const[ituti]on is founded. The most plausible Pretence for this Priv[ilege] {that has been mentiond} is the Clause by wh[ich] Leave is gr[an]ted to any 20 Pe[r]sons peti[ti]on[in]g to have a Pre[ac]her from the Bishop of London,[72] Who shall be unmolested

This I believe My L[or]ds is no Peculiarity in this [Pro]vince more [th][a]n others for I take that Dissenters were the founders of all the Colonies & that they all equall~~d~~{y} owd their Settlem[en]t to the Persecut[ion] in England It was very well known too that these Dissenters had not much more Charity than those of whom they complaind, & all the Diff[erence] was that One had Power & the other had not   It was therefore very likely that the Church of

England wo[ul]d meet with little Quarter in Pens[ylvani]a & the King did very prudently, in mak[in]g a [Pro]vision, he foresaw they wo[ul]d stand in {need of—} [*page break*]

But all these Dissenters were not Quakers, & therefore they are not to be lookd upon as the Sole Object of the Charter: & to require an Oath from those Who hold Offices is far from introduc[in]g the Doctrine of Cha[rle]s 2[d's] time—but is [per]fectly agreable to the Spirit & freedom of the Toleration Act—[72] The Difference is very great & very manifest. If the People who removd to America had staid in England at that time they wo[ul]d have regarded in Law as Popish Recusants Convicts, & subject to all the Penalties of those Statutes, all wh[ich] they avoided by this favourable Grant of the King So that they avoided all the Hardships & Inconven[ience]s they were liable to here but it never was designd to annex new Rights & Powers to them in ano[the]r Country; All their Liberties were safe, their Conscience unfetterd, they ~~ha~~ enjoyd every th[in]g necessary to Freedom but not to Ambition. ~~This~~ However what they desird they seizd, & they have now poss[esse]d it so long that they not only think themselves entitled to Power, but they imag[ine] that Power of so high a Nature, as to be entirely independ[en]t of every th[in]g else: They have paid the least Respect to his Majestys affectionate Remonstr[ance?] & Unless some Legislative Act be passd here to enforce them, this Assemb[ly] is no longer under the Influence of his Majestys Authority.

It has been said that no Military Power is lodgd in them, but in the [Pro][pri][e]tor   That my L[or]ds is only in Time of War; & in Times of Doubt and Uncertainty The Gov[ern]or must in the greatest Confusion w[ith]out the Assistance of the Legislature: This they have confessd by the Prov[ision]s in their Militia Bill wh[ich] tho[ugh] however imperfect, yet shew that they knew someth[in]g of that Nat[ure] was to be done on their Part. Money especially is requisite & that must come from them; this it has been said the Gov[ern]or [per]tinaceously refusd   But that Matter has been so fully handled I shall not trouble y[ou]r L[or]ds[hi]ps any more on that Point Only I woud just observe that g[ran?]t[in]g what they ins[iste]d upon ~~to belong to them, it is~~ was so inconsiderable & trivial, compard with the Dreadful Miseries, & utter impending Ruin to wh[ich] they exposd their Country, that their Pretences can never just[ify] their Conduct.

I beg Leave My L[or]ds to mention one th[in]g more to shew how [pro][per] our Appl[icati]on to this Board now is, even in the Opinion of the very Founder of this Province. It is an Observ[atio]n I found in a Copy of a Manuscript that belong[d] to the late L[or]d Somers, & was burnt with his House.[73] The Author of it was [~~Mr.~~?]{Old} Mr. Penn, who is universally allowd to have been a Man of ~~Universal~~ great Abilities. It appears from this Manuscript that he was the Original Planner of this very board {wh[ich] was afterw[ar]ds compleated on his Model}: & in his [Pro]positions to the King he delivers a great many things, of strong Sense, but in very odd & [par][ticu]lar Expressions: Amongst other Advantages that will [*page break*] Result he says from such an Authority as this, One will be, "That the Power of this Board & their Particular Attention to {& Superintendence over} the Affairs of the Colonies, will [pro]mote a kind of Artificial Virtue amongst them & will gently compell them to be Just to one another {& faithful to the Ends of Government}, & thus to do that by the force of Law, wh[ich] they ought to do from Principle.

One can hardly forbear think[in]g My L[or]ds that this Wise Man actually foresaw what wo[ul]d be the Conseq[uence]s of the Doctrines amongst his People, & therefore prudently endeav[ore]d to establish a Jurisd[icti]on here that might correct the Errors they might afterw[ar]ds fall into.

We Rely upon Y[ou]r L[or]ds[hi]ps Goodness & Wisdom & hope We shall soon obtain a full Relief to the many Miseries We now Labour under.

Ms (PHi-Logan)

---

[1] See, for example *PG*, Sept. 19, 1754, in which an anonymous essayist wrote that the French were "daily plundering our back inhabitants, and spoiling and laying waste to our borders," and that it was "high time to look around us, and unite as with one voice to elect such men as are able and willing to defend themselves and country from so violent an enemy."

[2] *Votes* (1756), 13.

[3] The petition along with an accompanying "brief" can be found in Charles J. Stillé, "The Attitude of the Quakers in the Provincial Wars," *PMHB* 10, no. 3 (1886): 283–315.

[4] "Journal, February 1756: Volume 63," in *Journals of the Commissioners for Trade and Plantations, from January 1754 to December 1758*, ed. K.H. Ledward (London: His Majesty's Stationery Office, 1933), 208–18.

[5] Lords of Trade and Plantations was an administrative body established in 1675 by Charles II to oversee relations between the colonies and the Crown.

[6] It does not appear that these notes were reproduced in any edition of *Votes*.

[7] Charles Yorke, lord chancellor, served as solicitor general from 1756 to 1761.

[8] Bark: "A small ship; in earlier times, a general term for all sailing vessels of small size" (*OED*).

[9] The War of Jenkins' Ear (1739–48).

[10] George Thomas (d. 1774), first baronet, served as deputy governor of Pennsylvania from 1738 to 1747.

[11] Gov. Thomas sent an extract of the king's instructions of April 2, 1740, to the Pennsylvania Assembly on July 2, 1740. The instructions asked that the Assembly "provide Victuals, Transports, and all of Necessaries, for the Troops to be raised" for the expedition against Cartagena led by Vice Adm. Edward Vernon (1684–1757). *Votes* (1740), 76.

[12] The Assembly replied that "we cannot preserve good Consciences, and come into the Levying of Money, and appropriating it to the Uses recommended to us . . . because it is repugnant to the religious Principles professed by the greater Number of the present Assembly, who are of the People called Quakers." *Votes* (1740), 78.

[13] The Assembly, under the speakership of Quaker lawyer and attorney general John Kinsey (1693–1750), battled with the governor and the proprietor until early September, when the 1739–40 legislative session came to a close. The Quakers were victorious in the following election, and Kinsey was easily reelected speaker when the new Assembly met on Oct. 14, 1740. The Assembly promptly opened an inquiry into the seven volunteer companies Thomas had raised in April, demanding to know "the number of servants taken out of this Province on the late expedition for the *West-Indies.*" *Votes* (1741), 13. It was not until October 1741 that the Assembly resolved "that the Sum of *Three Thousand Pounds* . . . be paid for the Use of the King . . . to be applied to such Uses as he, in his Royal Wisdom, shall think fit to direct and appoint." *Votes* (1742), 7.

[14] George Washington's (1732–1799) defeat at Fort Necessity on July 3, 1754, opened western Pennsylvania to attack, a situation made worse by Braddock's defeat at Fort Duquesne in July 1755.

[15] In an Aug. 13, 1751, message to the Assembly, Gov. Hamilton related the proprietors' "Offer of contributing to the Expense of Erecting and supporting" a "strong Trading House on the River *Ohio.*" *Votes* (1751), 82.

[16] The Assembly rejected the offer to build a fort, arguing that "we have always found that sincere, upright Dealing with the *Indians,* a friendly Treatment of them in all Occasions, and particularly in relieving their Necessities at proper Times by suitable Presents, have been the best Means of securing their Friendship," and inviting the proprietors to "join with us in the Expence of those Presents." *Votes* (1751), 82.

[17] James Hamilton was lieutenant governor of Pennsylvania at this time.

[18] Robert Darcy, fourth earl of Holdernesse, served as secretary of state for the Southern Department from June 1751 to March 1754.

[19] Hamilton sent Holdernesse's letter of Aug. 28, 1753, to the Assembly on Feb. 14, 1754. Holdernesse asked the government to "draw forth the armed forces of the Province, and to use your best Endeavours to repel Force by Force" should the French "erect Forts on his Majesty's Lands, or commit any other Act of Hostility." *Votes* (1754), 16.

[20] For the Assembly's reply, see *Votes* (1754), 24–25. Hamilton responded on March 1, 1754, and again on March 2. See *Votes* (1754), 26–31; 33–35. In response, the Assembly voted on "whether the Papers and Evidences, sent down and referred to by the Governor, do make it clearly appear that the Subjects of a Foreign Prince have erected Forts within the undoubted limits of this Government." The motion passed in the negative. In their message to the governor, the Assembly argued that the royal orders "precisely set forth" in Holdernesse's letter "differed from the Governor's Sentiments, or the Words of his Message to the House." *Votes* (1754), 40.

[21] The Assembly asserted that "it appears to us the Government is enjoined, by the Royal Orders, not to act as a Principal beyond the undoubted Limits of his Government, and as by the Papers and Evidences sent down, and referred to by the Governor, those Limits have not been clearly ascertained to our Satisfaction; we fear the altering our Connections with his Majesty's Colony of *Virginia,* and the precipitate Call upon us, as the Province invaded, cannot answer any good Purpose at this Time." *Votes* (1754), 41.

[22] The first motion to raise £20,000 was defeated by 25 nays to 8 yeas. The next motion for £15,000 was defeated 23 to 10. The next motion for £10,000 was defeated 11 to 2. After adjourning for the night, the Assembly spent the following day debating the sum. The motion for £5,000 the next day was defeated 22 to 10. See *Votes* (1754), 47–49.

[23] On May 8, 1754, the Assembly finally agreed to raise £10,000 (not £5,000) in a vote of 15 nays to 17 yeas. See *Votes* (1754), 55–56.

[24] The Assembly proposed raising the money by extending the excise act on spirituous liquors (Act of May 26, 1744: 4 *SALP* 395–407) for ten years. The governor argued that four years was long enough. "If the Governor is restricted by any Instruction from passing this Bill," the

Assembly retorted, "it must be by some Instruction which he has never been pleased to lay before this House." *Votes* (1754), 65.

[25] Hamilton tried to resign in February 1753 after secret proprietary instructions required him to reject any excise bill that did not give him a veto over its proceeds. Those same instructions prevented him from agreeing to the Assembly's 1754 bill to raise money for the king's use. He successfully resigned and was replaced by the time the new Assembly met on October 14. See *ODNB*.

[26] Sir Thomas Robinson replaced Holdernesse as secretary of state for the Southern Department in March 1754 and served until November 1755.

[27] Morris sent Robinson's letter of July 5, 1754, to the Assembly on Dec. 3, 1754. Robinson chastised the assemblymen for their "total Silence" on the instructions in Holdernesse's letter and asked that they "act vigorously in the Defence of the Government under your Care" and to assist "his Majesty's other *American* Colonies, to repel any hostile Attempts made against them." *Votes* (1755), 15–16.

[28] JD mentioned the conflict between Morris and the Assembly in doc. 1:28.

[29] The common enemy: the French. Gov. Morris met with Scarroyday, an Oneida chief; Jagrea, his son-in-law; and Aroas, a Seneca warrior, on Dec. 19, 1754. See 6 *CRP* 194. He met with Scarroyday and Jagrea again, along with representatives from the Six Nations, Aug. 15–22, 1755. See 6 *CRP* 523–91.

[30] On Nov. 7, 1755, the Assembly considered "[t]he Address of Some of the People Called Quakers," that expressed concern that "raising Sums of Money, and putting them into the Hands of Committees, who may apply them to Purposes inconsistent with the peaceable Testimony we profess." See *Votes* (1756), 14.

[31] The Assembly passed "An Act for Re-Emitting and Continuing the Loan of the Bills of Credit," as amended by the governor, on Nov. 22, 1755. *Votes* (1756), 37.

[32] The militia provisions passed in Pennsylvania before the American Revolution did not compel service. For example, the bill Benjamin Franklin introduced and the governor eventually assented to in 1755 was titled "An Act for the Better Ordering and Regulating Such as are Willing and Desirous to be United for Military Purposes Within this Province." See *Votes* [1756], 31; Act of Nov. 25, 1755 (5 *SALP* 197–201). Morris did not like the bill, but was "desirous of doing any Thing that has even a Chance of contributing to the Safety of the People and Province." *Votes* (1756), 37.

[33] The king vetoed the militia bill on July 7, 1756.

[34] Previous taxation acts expressly exempted the estates of the proprietor and governor from taxation. For example, a Nov. 7, 1696, act stated that "our Chief Proprietary and his Deputy in Government shall not be assessed by virtue of this act" (1 *SALP* 226).

[35] Gov. William Denny's refusal of the Assembly's bills, according to Thomas Penn's secret instructions, turned public opinion against the proprietor in both Pennsylvania and England. Penn therefore offered £5,000 for the province's defense. The funds were raised from past-due quitrents extracted in part from frontier settlers unable to farm because of the increasing violence. See J.A. Leo Lemay, *The Life of Benjamin Franklin, Volume 3: Soldier, Scientist, and Politician, 1748–1757* (Philadelphia: University of Pennsylvania Press, 2009), xviii.

[36] In response to Penn's offer of £5,000, the Assembly passed a bill to raise £60,000 for the king's use. See Act of Nov. 27, 1755 (5 *SALP* 201–12).

[37] Beginning in 1723 under "An Act for the Emitting and Making Current Fifteen Thousand Pounds in Bills of Credit" (Act of March 2, 1723; 3 *SALP* 324–38), Pennsylvanians could get loans from the Public Loan Office, whose profits paid for roads, waterways, welfare, and defense. See Terry Bouton, *Taming Democracy: "The People," the Founders, and the Troubled Ending of the American Revolution* (Oxford: Oxford University Press, 2007), 37–38.

[38] The preamble stated that compelling Quakers to bear arms would "violate a fundamental in our constitution and be a direct breach of our charter of privileges." Act of Nov. 25, 1755, 5 *SALP* 197.

[39] The relevant portion of the preamble is: "And whereas a great number of petitions from the several counties of this province have been presented to this house, setting forth that the petitioners are very willing to defend themselves and their country and desirous of being formed into regular bodies for that purpose, instructed and disciplined under proper officers with suitable and legal authority; representing withal that unless measures of this kind are taken, so as to unite them together, subject them to due command and thereby give them confidence in each other, they cannot assemble to oppose the enemy without the utmost danger of exposing themselves to confusion and destruction." 5 *SALP* 197–98.

[40] The relevant portion is: "That from and after the publication of this act it shall and may be lawful for the freemen of this province to form themselves into companies, as heretofore they have used in time of war without law, and for each company by majority of votes in the way of ballot to choose its own officers." 5 *SALP* 198.

[41] The relevant portion is: "That nothing in this act shall be understood or construed to give any power or authority to the governor or commander-in-chief and the said officers to make any articles or rules that shall in the least affect those of the inhabitants of the province who are conscientiously scrupulous of bearing arms, either in their liberties, persons or estates, nor any other persons of what persuasion or denomination soever who have not first voluntarily and freely signed the said articles after due consideration as aforesaid." 5 *SALP* 200.

[42] The relevant portion is: "That no youth under the age of twenty-one years nor any bought servant or indented apprentice shall be admitted to enroll himself or be capable of being enrolled in the said companies or regiments without the consent of his or their parents or guardians, masters or mistresses, in writing under their hands first had and obtained." 5 *SALP* 200.

[43] The relevant portion is: "That no regiment, company or party of volunteers shall by virtue of this act be compelled or led more than three days' march beyond the inhabited parts of the province, nor detained longer than three weeks in any garrison, without an express engagement for that purpose first voluntarily entered into and subscribed by every man so to march or remain in garrison." 5 *SALP* 201.

[44] 13 Car. 2, St. 2, c. 1 (1661): "An Act for the Well-Governing and Regulating of Corporations." The act was a test act designed to keep Catholics out of public office by requiring elected officials to receive communion from the Church of England and swear a number of oaths to the monarch and Protestant doctrine.

[45] Charles II granted William Penn the Pennsylvania Charter on March 4, 1681.

[46] 1 W. & M., c. 8 (1688): "An Act for the Abrogating of the Oaths of Supremacy and Allegiance, and Appointing Other Oaths."

7 & 8 Will. 3, c. 34 (1695): "An Act That the Solemn Affirmation and Declaration of the People Called *Quakers*, Shall be Accepted Instead of an Oath in the Usual Form." The only exception was when qualifying for an office of profit from the Crown.

8 Geo. 1, c. 6 (1721): "An Act for Granting the People Called Quakers, such Forms of Affirmation or Declaration, as May Remove the Difficulties Which Many of Them Lie Under."

[47] William Penn drafted Pennsylvania's First Frame of Government, which went into effect May 5, 1682. See *PWP*, 2:211.

[48] William Penn signed the Charter of Privileges, which went into effect Oct. 28, 1701. *PWP*, 4:104–09.

[49] The 1701 Charter of Privileges referred to "An Act Directing the Attests of Several Officers and Ministers" (2 *SALP* 39–42) and "An Act to Ascertain the Number of Members of

Assembly and to Regulate the Elections" (2 *SALP* 24–27). Both were repealed by the Queen-in-Council on Feb. 7, 1706.

[50] In 1704 the Assembly asserted its legitimacy to pass laws and of its Quaker members to serve. On April 24, the Assembly prepared a bill "for the Confirmation of the said Charter of Privileges; as also to declare, that the Actings and Proceedings of this Assembly shall be deemed, adjudged and taken to be valid." *Votes*, supp. (1752), 2, pt. 2:5. A month later, the Quakers sent a petition to Queen Anne (1665–1714), asking her to "grant that the Affirmation prescribed by Act of Parliament in *England*, to be taken by the *Quakers*, may be allowed here to all Persons." *Votes*, supp. (1752), 2, pt. 2:7. The Charter bill was finally agreed to and sent to the governor in October, along with a bill for "Affirmations to Pass in Lieu of Oaths." See *Votes*, supp. (1752) 2, pt. 2:22.

[51] George Fox, *A Declaration from the Harmless & Innocent People of God, Called Quakers, against All Plotters and Fighters in the World* (London, 1660), is the most obvious, but not the earliest, manifestation of Quaker pacifism. Eliding the fact that early Quakers fought in Cromwell's army, Fox claimed that Quakers had "from the earliest days . . . renounced violence" and "maintained a testimony against offensive violence" that "gradually coalesced into a set of principles concerning peace, which became known as the peace testimony." See Meredith Baldwin Weddle, *Walking in the Way of Peace: Quaker Pacifism in the Seventeenth Century* (New York: Oxford University Press, 2001), 3–4.

[52] Henry Ireton (1611–1651), Oliver Cromwell's son-in-law, served as a general in the Parliamentary Army during the English Civil War.

[53] Edward Hyde (1609–1674), first earl of Clarendon, was a royalist knighted by Charles I in 1643 and appointed to the Privy Council.

[54] Denzil Holles (1598–1680), first baron Holles, was one of the five members of Parliament who tried to arrest Charles I in the House of Commons on Jan. 4, 1642.

[55] Edward Hyde wrote that Holles challenged Ireton to a duel outside of the House of Commons, and Ireton declined for reasons of conscience. Holles, "in choler, pulled him by the Nose; telling him, 'if his conscience would keep him from giving men satisfaction, it should keep him from provoking them.'" See Edward Hyde, *History of the Rebellion and Civil Wars in England, Begun in the Year 1641*, 6 vols. (Oxford: J. Batley, 1720), 3:58.

[56] The three original Pennsylvania counties established in 1682 were Philadelphia, Bucks, and Chester. Lancaster was established in 1729, York in 1749, Cumberland in 1750, Berks and Northampton in 1751.

[57] The 1701 Charter of Privileges provided that "the Inhabitants of each of the *Three* Counties of this Province, shall not have less than *Eight* Persons to represent them in Assembly, for the Province; and the Inhabitants of the Town of *Philadelphia* (when the said Town is incorporated) *Two* Persons to represent them in Assembly." *Collection of Charters*, 46.

[58] Lat. That which touches or concerns all ought to be supported by all.

[59] Antoninus Pius (86–161) was emperor of Rome from 138 to 161. Rescript: "A reply sent by the emperor to an appeal for guidance, esp. one from a magistrate on a legal point" (*OED*).

[60] Lat. The welfare of the people should be the supreme law.

[61] Robert Henley (c. 1708–1772), first earl of Northington, was lord chancellor from 1761 to 1766.

[62] Lat. for God and country; or, more literally, for altars and hearths.

[63] Salzburg in Austria and Augsburg in southern Germany. German migration to Pennsylvania increased from the 1720s to the 1750s, reaching a peak from 1749 to 1754, when almost 35,000 immigrants came to Philadelphia. See Simon J. Bronner and Joshua R. Brown, eds., *Pennsylvania Germans: An Interpretive Encyclopedia* (Baltimore: Johns Hopkins University Press, 2017), 25.

[64] 14 Car. 2, c. 4 (1662): "The Act of Uniformity" was part of the Clarendon Code, legislation directed at religious dissenters, especially Quakers, to enforce adherence to the Church of England and punish those who worshipped differently and refused to take oaths.

[65] The 1681 Pennsylvania Charter from Charles II allowed for an Anglican minister to be sent to Pennsylvania should twenty or more inhabitants of the province request one from the bishop. See *PWP*, 2:73.

[66] The Pennsylvania Charter from Charles II gave the proprietor the power to "Levy, Muster & Train, all sorts of Men, of what Condition soever or wherever born, in the said province of *Pensylvania*." *Collection of Charters*, 7.

[67] The Delawares' resentment towards the proprietors originated with the fraudulent 1737 Walking Purchase, for which Thomas Penn hired three runners to sprint, not walk, as the treaty stipulated, for a day and a half to define the boundaries of a gift of land to the proprietors.

[68] The Pennsylvania Charter from Charles II did not specify a number of days, but it did allow Penn to "make war even without the Limits of the said Province." *Collection of Charters*, 7.

[69] Pennsylvania's main export was grain, and in particular wheat flour. Pennsylvania and New Jersey also exported corn and peas, and the value of the two colonies' exports totaled £300,000 by 1760. See Richard Middleton, *Colonial America: A History, 1565–1776*, 3rd ed. (Malden, Mass.: Blackwell Publishing, 2002), 207.

[70] As many as 12,000 Protestant settlers were killed in the failed Irish Rebellion of 1641 in which Irish Catholics in Ulster attempted a coup against the English administration. See John Marshall, *John Locke, Toleration and Early Enlightenment Culture* (New York: Cambridge University Press, 2006), 58, n. 10.

[71] Thomas Sherlock (1677–1761) served as bishop in the Church of England from 1748 until his death.

[72] 1 W. & M., c. 18 (1688): "An Act for Exempting Their Majesties Protestant Subjects, Dissenting From the Church of England, From the Penalties of Certain Laws." The act allowed freedom of worship to most Protestant nonconformists.

[73] John Somers (1651–1716), first baron Somers, lost his papers in a fire at Yorke's law office on January 27, 1752.

34
To Mary Cadwalader Dickinson, March 17, 1756

London March 17[th] 1756

Dear & Honourd Mother,

I have rec[eive]d your Letter dated in November, with My Honourd Father's, & I must be so free as to say I had the greatest Pleasure from the last, which informd Me of your very good Health:

Besides I am very much disturbd with my Dear Mother's Apprehensions of my Health, & Return to America: Permit Me Dearest Parent to entreat You, not to alarm your Mind with Dangers that do not exist

I find by both Letters that my Return is expected in America this Summer, & I am afraid of giving new Uneasiness by saying it will be better to stay a little longer The Reason is, that my Health is dayly encreasing & growing better & with the Blessing of Almighty God I hope some more Time & Exercise will make Me heartier than ever I was: But there might be some little Danger, in going to Sea, before I have gaind a sufficient Stock of Strength to bear a Voyage: The Difference is, if I shoud come this Summer, I probably shall be much longer in recovering the Voyage; & if I come the Spring after, I shall come very hearty.

What gives Me great Encouragement is, that I dont feel the least Return of the Complaint in My Breast: & as I use more Exercise & a different Way of Reading, I fancy it [*page break*] It was a Neglect of these that bro[ugh]t it upon Me: I have been advisd to stand at a High Desk to read & write, & that coming to the upper part of my Breast, keeps Me necessarily Erect & in the easiest Posture. This agrees with Me extremely well, & tho[ugh] it was a little troublesome at first, Yet I can now stand two Hours together without any Trouble; So that I do every thing on my Legs, & may properly enough be calld a Peripatetick Lawyer: & tho[ugh] no great adept in Natural Philosophy, if ever I shoud be inducd to scribble on that Science It shall be on the Benefits of keeping on Our Legs, which Nature certainly designd to be usd more than they commonly are by People of any Fashion in Life: I am sure I have found very great Advantages from it.

I cannot express the Pain I felt from the Account of that dreadful Midnight[1] I tremble for the Consequences of such a Shock to such a delicate Frame as My Dear Mother's: But I hope there never will be such another: I pray to God, there may not I cannot imagine that Kent is in the least Danger; it is quite removd from it, & defended by Nature from Incursions & the other Inner parts of the Province must be secure too, at least now, when something has been done by the Legislature.[2]

The Government here are taking the [*page break*] Most vigorous Measures for Our Assistance & Protection. L[or]d Loudon, Who distinguishd himself in the late Rebellion so much, will sail in a fortnight for America, to take upon him the Command in Chief[3] His L[or]dship's Character is such as fills every Body with the greatest Expectations. He is a Complete Soldier, & a fine Gentleman: Has a sound Judgm[en]t Great Coolness, & a most engaging affable Behaviour. So that his Authority & Prudence will very probably prevent any ill Consequences from the Pride & Folly of the other Officers & the Governors.

The Government have already taken up Transports for 2500 Men, which will sail with his L[or]dship Some of these will be the best Troops in England It is said there will be 3 or 4 Regiments more raisd in America on the English Establishment; & his Majesty has obtain a very large Sum of Money from the Commons to reward & give further Encouragement to the Colonies Who have distinguishd themselves.[4] All these things will undoubtedly make Our Affairs bear a very agreable face this Summer; Especially considering the present Circumstances of things in Europe. Whether War will be declard or not, is as uncertain as it was a Year ago: & it is not likely France will be very forward to do it. She will have no Allies. Spain has declard her Neutrality: Hanover is secure [*page break*] By a Treaty with Prussia:[5] So that if We do engage it must be with Our own Powers & at Sea, & We are so superior on that Element, that for France to declare War, will be only to declare her own Weakness: She is very sensible of this, & therefore will not suffer the least Act of Hostility in Europe, while We are every Day taking their Vessels: So that they Exclaim ag[ains]t our Perfidy, & woud perswade the World, that it is their Faith, the Observance of Treaties, & Love of {Publick} Peace that ties their Hands, & not the Want of Power; which specious Excuse wo[ul]d be lost by a Declaration of War: For as We have nothing he can fall upon, on the Continent, the Grand Monarch's Arms, long as they are, cant reach over the Channel.

The French have but 59 Ships of the Line, & We have 150. The Difference of lesser Vessels, is much greater; We have 10000 Men more for the Sea Service, than We had either in Queen Ann's War, or the last:[6] & so many of these are already on Board, that it is an undoubted Truth, Our Fleet is better man'd <u>now,</u> than it was at the <u>End</u> of the last War: I have this from several Gentlemen of the Navy; & at the End of last War, We had the finest fleet England ever knew; & Yet our Compliment of Sailors is not yet full. Our Officers were all traind up last War, & are excellent Ones. The Whole Kingdom are in great Spirits, & highly approve of the Conduct of the Ministry: On the other hand the French are prodigiously dissatisfied, their Trade will be utterly ruind in Another Year, the poor Wretches have not yet recoverd [*page break*] The Miseries of the last War, while the Pride & Ambition of their Monarch devours the Ease & Happiness of his Subjects: His Taxes flea[7] the poor Sheep that can afford No more Wool.

Their Fleet is a sad Condition We have above 10000 of their Sailors, which is a very considerable Number: & they want both Cannon & Cordage, which they generally have from Sweden, Denmark &c & We take Care to leave no probability of their being supplied from these Places: But above all, they want Money, so well known to be the Sinews of War: The King has made a Lottery, which fills very slowly & leisurely. We had one, opend, subscribd, & ended at the same Instant almost. He squeezes his Officers, by pretence of borrow[in]g; but what kind of Loan is that, Where the Creditor dare not demand & the Debtor is not obligd to pay. They hardly will venture to encrease their Wretchedness, by plunging into further Expences: They have made a great many Offers His Majesty tells the Parliament in his Speech, but none such as are consistent with the Dignity of his Crown & the Security of his People:[8] & his Majesty, the Ministry & the Whole Kingdom, are so convincd of the Great Advantages We have over Our Neighbours, that Peace will never be concluded but on such Terms as are highly for Our Honour & Safety: They must agree to such as We think proper, & I hope the

Ministry will Act with the same [*page break*] Spirit, they have begun. Surely Our Superiority will prevent their getting over any more Men to Canada, & then We probably shall be more than a Match for them there; if the Provinces can be inducd to do their Duty. The Agents of the Several Colonies were calld before the L[or]ds of Trade & Plantations, to be informd of the Condition they were in, & what they had done: L[or]d Halifax[9] said some of them had contributed more than they were able to bear, & others who were very able had done nothing at all: Rich[ar]d Partridge[10] who knew very well that Pennsylvania was included amongst the last, began to defend the Assembly, & represent the Conscientious Perswasion they were restraind by, for the peaceable Enjoyment of which they removd to that Province, then a Desert, in hopes to live undisturbd under it; Upon which L[or]d Halifax replied, that if they were left to themselves, they were not like to live, but to dye under it, if they were left to themselves: But yet it is not certain Whether any thing will be done here, to put the Province in a better State of Defence.

I fancy the Government will not be very forward in exerting the Power they are possessd of, in any uncommon manner.

Francis[11] has been over here these several Months, he supd with Me some time ago, & told Me, he never designd to practize the Law any more: What he does design I believe nobody but himself knows: but he is entirely on the Side of the Assembly, & there have several things come out in the Publick Papers, in their Favour, which I am [*page break*] Sure are the Offsprings of his Pen. He speaks in Conversation with great Warmth of the Settling the Ohio Lands & I fancy he has some Scheme or another in his head, in which he expects to be of Use to the Ministry: He hinted, dropd in a half-careless, half-important Manner, that he had been let to know that Mr. Secretary Fox woud be glad to speak with him, but finding on Enquiring that he woud have nothing to do but to answer such interrogatories as shoud be asked him & that he would not be at Liberty to harangue at Liberty, he declind the Honour. I thought this some Discovery of his Intentions. Speaking of the Advantages of living in London, he said it was the best Place in the World to teach a Man the Knowledge of himself, & the folly of Pride & Haughtiness: I confess this put Me in Mind of Dionysius at Corinth.[12] Uncle Cadwalader advises Me to be cautious of what I say to him: but before I rec[eive]d his kind hint, I never mentiond a Word of Pensilvania, & my Silence has been so strict, that he can imagine Nothing but that I look on him as a Statesman in Disgrace, & tenderly avoid the mention of his fall. He lives in an odd manner, I don't hear of his going any Where but to Barclays: He has never yet been to Mr. Anderson's tho[ugh] frequently invited by him Mrs. Anderson attributes it to some Quarrel between him & Mr. Allen,[13] Whose family are her particular Friends. [*page break*] I dind with that good Lady on Christmas Day, according to Custom, when She desird Me as often as I wrote to remember her sincere Love to You: She spoke of You as one of her Dearest & most Valuable, & I was in Raptures to hear her give in a large Company, so just & great a Character of my Honourd Mother. She is big with Child again, when I believe, it was little expected, but I never saw her look so well.[14] Mrs. Goldsborough has a fine Boy,[15] & they are both very hearty.

I am delighted to hear of the good Behaviour of my Dearest Brother, and almost envied him his Strawberry Time.[16] I hope We shall both prove a Comfort & Ornament to Our Most Honourd Parents: I beg that You will be so good as to omit no Opportunity to write; it is my greatest Pleasure to hear from You, & the most trifling things will be vastly agreable.

Please to remember Me to our good Neighbours that shall enquire: I wish I was amongst my Gallant Countrymen with a Musket on my Shoulder, but I wish too, that the Operations of their Campaign may never be more dangerous than the Chusing their Officers.

I am, Most Honourd Mother,
Your most affectionate & most Dutiful Son
John Dickinson

ALS (PPL-JDFP)

---

[1] In November 1755, *PG* printed a letter from Maryland reporting that "At Day-break on Monday, the third Instant, Messengers arrived here from New-Castle County (confirming Expresses sent in the Night from elsewhere) giving dismal Accounts, how 1500 French and Indians had burnt Lancaster Town to the Ground, and were proceeding downwards, driving all before them; so that the Inhabitants were in great Distress." See *PG*, Nov. 20, 1755.

[2] On Nov. 2, 1755, Gov. Morris sent a message to the Assembly concerning "Intelligence that a Party of *French* and *Indians* had destroyed some of the Settlements nigh the River *Susquehanna*, killed a Number of the Inhabitants, and carried others off as Prisoners." (*Votes* [1756], 10). He asked that the Assembly prepare a militia bill and a paper money bill. The Assembly replied on Nov. 5 that "great Care and Judgment in conducting our *Indian* Affairs" was needed "at this critical Juncture" (*Votes* [1756], 12, 13). The Assembly passed a bill to raise £60,000 for "the King's Use" to be "struck in Paper Bills of Credit, and sunk by a Tax of *Six-pence per* Pound, and *Ten Shillings per* Head, yearly, for four Years, on all the Estates, Real and Personal, and Taxable, within this Province" (*Votes* [1756], 13, 15). Morris rejected the bill because it taxed the proprietary estate, leading to a protracted and bitter dispute with the Assembly. The Assembly also created an associator movement with the passage of "An Act for the Better Ordering and Regualating Such as are Willing and Desirous to be United for Military Purposes within this Province" (*Votes* [1756], 31; Act of Nov. 25, 1755, 5 *SALP* 197–201).

[3] John Campbell (1705–1782), fourth earl of Loudoun, had raised a regiment of loyal highlanders during the Jacobite rising of 1745. When the inner cabinet decided to recall William Shirley (1694–1771) as commander of British forces in America and send a new lieutenant general and two major generals to oversee military affairs in the colonies, Newcastle selected Loudoun to serve as lieutenant general and governor of Virginia. He arrived in New York on July 23, 1756.

[4] The British inner cabinet meeting on Jan. 20 decided to grant £120,000 to the northern colonies in recompense for their initiative in raising an army in 1755. They also decided that the colonies should be asked to recruit four battalions of 1,000 men each (Pargellis, 41).

[5] In the Jan. 16, 1756, Treaty of Westminster, George II, in his capacity as elector of Hanover, and Frederick the Great of Prussia (1712–1786), promised that neither party would "attack, or invade, directly or indirectly, the territories of the other" and that they would mutually ally against any effort by a foreign power to attack. See Clive Parry, ed., *The Consolidated Treaty Series*, vol. 40, *1753–1757* (Dobbs Ferry, N.Y.: Oceana Publications, 1969), 291–99.

[6] Queen Anne's War was fought between Britain and France in North America from 1702 to 1713, at the same time as the War of Spanish Succession in Europe. King George's War was fought in North America from 1744 to 1748, as the American theater of the War of the Austrian Succession in Europe.

[7] A now obsolete use of "flea" to mean "flay."

[8] In his speech for the opening of Parliament on Nov. 13, 1755, George II asserted that he had "been always ready to accept reasonable and honourable terms of accommodation, but none have been proposed on the part of France" (*Parl. Hist*, 15:528).

[9] George Montagu Dunk (1716–1771), second earl of Halifax, was president of the Lords of Trade.

[10] Richard Partridge (1681–1759), a London merchant born in New Hampshire, had served as Pennsylvania's colonial agent in England since 1740. He also represented a number of other colonies at various times.

[11] Tench Francis (d. 1758) was a prominent lawyer trained at the Middle Temple who represented Talbot Co. in the Maryland legislature before moving to Pennsylvania, where he served as attorney general from 1741 to 1755.

[12] Dionysius II (Dionysius the Younger; c. 397–343 BC) ruled Syracuse in Sicily, from 367 to 357 BC and from 346 to 344 BC. His second reign ended when he surrendered to the Greek general Timoleon of Corinth, and he spent the last year of his life in an unhappy exile at that city.

[13] Possibly William Allen (1704–1780), who was a wealthy Pennsylvania merchant, land speculator, and iron master who served in the Assembly for twenty-nine years and presided as chief justice of the Pennsylvania Supreme Court for twenty-five years, from 1751 to 1774. See *LLP*. 3. pt. 1, 231–80.

[14] Evidently Harriot Rebecca Anderson, Rebecca Covington Lloyd Anderson's youngest daughter.

[15] Charles Goldsborough (1755–1758), son of Robert and Sally Yerbury Goldsborough.

[16] Perhaps a reference to a first courtship by seventeen-year-old Philemon.

35
To Samuel Dickinson, April 1, 1756

London April 1[st] 1756

Honourd Father,

I have rec[eive]d your Letter of 16[th] Dec[embe]r mentioning the Receipt of mine of 30[th] Sept[embe]r in wh[ich] You apprehend I have been in a worse State of Health than represented, but that is really a Mistake, for I dont know any Reason why I shoud not confess the worst, when its over. I am convincd my Illness proceeded from the Inclination of my Breast & too close

Confinement, for as I ment[ione]d in my last, by a contrary Practize I find Myself quite relievd from it: The Winter has been extremely fine, & has agreed with Me perfectly, & the Summer I dont doubt will be of the greatest Service. I design to take some small Journies, which will be very improving in Point of Knowledge, & serve to confirm my Health still more: All the time my Constitution woud allow, I am satisfied has been spent as it [*page break*] ought, & my Hopes of making this appear, is the highest Delight I feel in the most disagreable Absence from the best of Parents.

What thanks shall I return for your kindest Attention to every thing that can be of Service to Me? I shall endeavour to get the Management of any Business from London that may fall within my Practize; & if any thing is intended to be done in those particular Instances You mentiond, I am pretty sure of being employd. At present it is my utmost Endeavour to qualify Myself to do Justice to those, who shall hereafter rely upon Me; I have been this Winter engagd in a very laborious Business in transcribing three Manuscript vol[ume]s In large Quarto,[1] of the **Art of Pleading**,[2] wh[ich] my Lord Coke says is the very Life of the Law:[3] These Books were compild by a great Man at the Barr[4] for his own Use, & he giving Copies of them to his particular Friends, they have at last travelld into my Hands, & I think they are a valuable Treasure. I have found great Benefit [*remainder missing*]

ALS (PPL-JDFP)

---

[1] Quarto: "The size of paper obtained by folding a whole sheet twice, so as to form four leaves" (*OED*).

[2] The textbook for how to plead the common law, Samson Eure's *Doctrina Placitandi, ou L'Art et Science de Bon Pleading* (London: R. and E. Atkins, 1677) was originally published in one volume, but for law students, it was bound in three volumes with many blank pages for notes.

[3] JD is apparently misremembering Edward Coke's statement that "Reason is the Life of the Law; nay the Common Law itself is nothing else but Reason." See 1 Coke, *Institutes* 97 b.

[4] Sampson [Samson] Eure (Evers; c. 1592–1659?) served in Parliament, was attorney general for the Council in the Marshes (Wales) from 1622 to 1640, and served as a king's serjeant from 1640 to 1649.

36
To Samuel Dickinson, May 10, 1756

London May 10th 1756

Honourd Father,

I wrote lately by Mr. Walker but think it my Duty to take every Opportunity of informing You of the Continuance of my Health growing better every Day: As I mentiond in my last, I have been so well as to attend my Studies pretty assiduously—& think I have employd this Winter to more Purpose, than any Time, I have been here.

The Publick Affairs of Europe continue as they have been a great While, that is, Many things talkd of, but nothing done. People are employd at present, with a Supposd Expedition from Toulon against Port-Mahon;[1] but if any such thing is designd, it is certain We have a very Considerable Force in the Mediterranean: There are several Fleets now at Sea, but no news of any thing performd by them, & if they dont utterly prevent the Enemy's sending the least Reinforcements to [*page break*] America, I dont know the least Service the Ministry can shew for the immense Expence the Nation has been put to.[2]

In Times of open War, the Advantage made of a Superior Naval Force, is to destroy the Enemy's Coast, to alarm & distract their Counsels, & fatigue & wear out their Troops; this is what one woud expect now, but perhaps there may be some Politick Reason, which may restrain the Ministry from these Extremities of War, before a Declaration: & this induces Me to believe, that the French will hardly set a Precedent by attacking Minorca, which may be retorted upon them all round their Coasts; or if they do, I hope We shall see our Ships do something else besides going to Brest,[3] eating up their Provisions, & coming back again for more.

It woud be very natural to imagine that a greater Grant than ever was made by an English Parliament, woud produce something, at least equal to what has been done on much smaller, but there is little probability that 50000 Seamen will do any thing, but furnish some Gentlemen [*page break*] with an Opportunity of handling so many more Millions. I think it must be evident We have it in our Power to distress the French Settlements, especially in the West Indies, & that must necessarily confuse & weaken them—& it is certain while things are in their present Situation, the French have not one Single Object to which they are obligd to direct their View, but to America, & Common Sense, must tell them that they can have no possible Counterballance for our Advantages, but vigourously pushing Us there; and it woud be the height of Stupidity to imagine they will not exert every Engine of Craft & Power to effect it.

There were two Vessels lately sent into Plimouth, designd for America with Arms &c and 180 Officers;[4] which proves what has been often said that by every private Ship that Sails, their Colonies receive a Military Supply, & with what constant & careful Attention, their Government regards them. L[or]d Loudon is not saild, but the [*page break*] Transports are.[5]

The Ship I now write by, belongs to Mr. Bell, who designs to continue the Business he has been engagd in: In a former Letter I mentiond my Intimacy with this Gentleman, & how well qualified he was for this Business in every Respect: I am confirmd in my Opinion by a long Acquaintance, & his General Character; he has always treated Me with the greatest Kindness & I shall look upon it as an Addition to the many Obligations I lye under to You, if You will please to do him all the Service that lies in your Power.

I shoud be extremely glad to hear from You; there was a Vessel lately arrivd from Philadelphia, but I had no Letters—

I am, Honourd Father,
Your most Dutiful & most
Affectionate Son,
John Dickinson

ALS (PPL-JDFP)

---

[1] Toulon was a military port city on the Mediterranean in southern France. Port Mahon was the major harbor on the island of Minorca. Its garrison had only 3,000 men, but it was protected by the 800 cannon of Fort St. Philip. On April 17 the French landed twenty-five infantry battalions and a battalion of artillery on the west coast of Minorca with no resistance. British Lt. Gen. William Blakeney (1671–1761) retreated into Fort St. Philip to wait for reinforcements. See Dull, 50–51.

[2] Only twelve of the warships docked in English ports were ready for deployment, and recent discharges and attacks of typhus and scurvy left the British navy as a whole short some 15,000 men. See Dull, 51.

[3] Brest is an Atlantic port city in northwest France about 150 mi. across the English Channel from Plymouth that was, along with Toulon and Rochefort, one of France's three major naval bases.

[4] *Read's Weekly*, May 1, 1756, reported from Plymouth, April 22: "This day was sent on shore from his Majesty's ships Monarque and Ipswich, and committed to prison, 180 French soldiers, who were destined for America, and about 40 French sailors, who were likewise committed to prison, taken by his Majesty's fleet under the command of Admiral Hawke."

[5] The transports carrying troops to America sailed from Plymouth on April 15. Lord Loudoun did not leave from Portsmouth until May 20 (Pargellis, 45, 50).

37
To Mary Cadwalader Dickinson, June 6, 1756

London June 6th 1756

Honourd Mother,

I wrote lately by the way of Maryland to my Father,[1] & as I was a good deal hurried at that Time, coud not write to You, & tho[ugh] in the midst of Business that seemd a pretty good Excuse, Yet I have been repenting of it ever since, & shall not be able to forgive Myself, till I know that You do; but of that from Your great Goodness, I have great Hopes.

My Health has been so very good that I have reapd more Benefit from my Studies in these six Months past, than I ever did in the space of any part of my Life: & Permit Me, Best & Dearest of Parents, to pour out the little swell of a heart, conscious of a well-performd Duty, & tasting as it were, the Sweets of Good Fame: Nor can this be calld vainglorious, since confind to this single Sheet.

Necessity has taught Me a Method of Studying, which I have communicated to several Gentlemen, with no little Approbation of the [*page break*] Design & the Frankness of the Intelligence. I have always accustomd Myself to taking Notes, but I found that very often by setting down Single Points of Law, I was at a great Loss when I referrd to my Notes for forming an Opinion: For this Study consists of so many Distinctions, & so many Exceptions, all intimately related & mutually dependant on each other, that it was quite impossible to collect all the different Members (as I may call them) of an Opinion scatterd in so many Places, Or to perceive the very nice Connexion between them when separated at such a Distance: To remove this Inconvenience, I have endeavourd to throw the Law relating to each head together, & to marshall them in such a Manner, that Some Maxim or General Principle shall seem, as it were, the Trunk of the Tree, the Larger Divisions the Branches, & all the little Niceties & Minutenesses the Twigs & Leaves. One's Knowledge may be said to flourish, when digested in this manner, & this Regularity frees one from a thousand Errors, Confusd & Undistinguishd Reading produces: Besides it really saves a great Deal of Labour, & keeps Our Learning like a Sword always bright & ready to be drawn, Whereas if a Man after laboriously studying a Point, & turning [*page break*] over a Multitude of Books, contents himself with barely noting down the Result of the Whole, without remarking the Particular Circumstances which lead to it, in a little time they will rust in his Memory, & he must go through the same Drudgery again {to revive them}, besides the Danger he runs that when such Niceties are forgot, he wont have the least Suspicion that there {are} such: How then can he communicate them to others? Or if sets them down singly & Each by itself, how will he be surprizd when he quotes it as a General Rule before Judges, to hear his Antagonist say, This grows out of such a Maxim, it extends only so far, & then divides itself into two Parts, one of which is exactly our Case.

In short I am convincd by Experience that a Person must be led into Endless Mistakes, Unless he has the Substance of his Knowledge disposd in a Regular Manner: & I am also convincd from my little Attempts, that something like the Way I have got into may be of Service; & I will spare no Pains to make mine so to Me. [*page break*] Perhaps if this Letter shoud fall into the hands of some People, they might think it a little odd to talk so much to You about the method of Studying Law, but they woud excuse it, if they knew the Tenderness with which You regard every thing that [~~regards~~]{concerns} Me, & how little Pleasure I take in any thing unless sweetened by a Consciousness of Your Knowledge & Approbation of it.

126

I have by the Blessing of Divine Providence such good Health that I flatter Myself with the most agreable Hopes of returning to my Native Country with some Share of Reputation, that is, with Proofs of not having mispent my Time, for if I am not capable of greater Improvement, it is my Misfortune & not my Fault, & I hope my Friends & Myself will find sufficient Satisfaction in my having dischargd my Duty according to my Abilities, if not according to our Wishes. How much I desire to shew Myself worthy of their Goodness, is easier to be conceivd by a generous Mind, than describd by the most Ingenious Pen. [*page break*] I quite long to begin the "Militia Forensis"[2] but I must confess, that my Courage I believe is a little false like a Young Soldier's in his first Regimentals, & I fancy I shoud be apt to tremble at the Signal of Battle. However I must comfort Myself that a little Cowardice has been the fault of the greatest Orators.

"So were I equalld with them in Renown." Mil.[3]

As to Publick Affairs, there is nothing new except his Majesty's Declaration of War against France on the 18th of last month,[4] which has not made & is not likely to make the least Alteration in the face of Affairs: There are about 8 thousand Hessians & 3 or 4000 Hanoverians landed here for our Defence in Case of an Invasion:

This is a Piece of Policy that has disobligd the Nation extremely, for instead of raising a Certain Natural & sufficient Power by a Militia, a Whole People are to depend for Protection on the Precarious External & Slender force of Foreign Troops, Who must be instantly recalld, if the Politicks of Germany shoud [*page break*] take the least Turn—& if they stay here, must be very disagreable to all men Who value their Liberties & Constitution, by setting a Precedent, which in Cases of the Crown has ever been found an immutable Law, for the Increase of the Regal Powers: The Strides of which since the Revolution have been Gigantick. Rapin says with a grave Face, what no man in these times can read without a Smile, "That Charles the Second to make the People <u>sensible</u> of the <u>Slavery</u> that was imposd on them, resolvd to review his Troops, which by the Return of the Garrision of Tangier, amounted to <u>no less</u> than <u>four thousand</u> Men effective & well armd["][5]

The Standing Forces of this Kingdom in time of profoundest Peace {are 20000 Men}, & these by the bare Magick of the word **Invasion** are multiplied to 40000, tho[ugh] the French dare not look us in the face at Sea, & notwithstanding their Agility cannot yet skip from Calais to Dover.

There cant one Single Reason be assignd Why England shoud look for her Security ashore, rather than on that Element which Nature has so kindly spread round her; or if She should make so absurd a Choice, Can one Single Reason be assignd, why that impor[*page break*]tant Trust shoud be committed to Slaves & Foreigners rather than to Freemen & Natives, but that it pleases the King; Nor can the most ingenious Artists in cloathing Imperial Desires with Specious Pretences [~~illegible~~] give one Reason for its pleasing, but such a one, as even their Modesty will never suffer them to give; <u>That it will encrease his Power.</u>

When Concessions are made to Princes, tis as ridiculous to think of Stopping, as for a Master of a Ship to guess at the Depth of Water in an Ebb Tide, which every Moment decreases, till he is convincd of his Folly by ~~Striking a Rock~~ {running aground}: [~~illegible~~] {There indeed} the Comparison ceases, for the Vessell, if She does not split with Striking, will be relievd with the next flood—But there is no Flood in Power: When it has got a Turn one way, there is no means in Nature for altering its Course but Violence: & I think a moderate Acquaintance with the English History, will teach one this Truth: & also that most of our Civil Wars have been Claims {& Complaints} made in the Field in a Lump together—which had either been given up singly or winkd at in Parliament: So dangerous is what Some People call [*page break*] Complaisance & Trust in their Prince. For my part I confess I have not the most remote Suspicion of his present Majesty's most gracious & hearty Affection for the Wellfare of this People & Constitution, & (as Bolingbroke[6] says) I dare engage that all our Posterity will repose the same Confidence in **Every** Prince of the same Royal & Illustrious House.
I hope My Honourd Mother, will excuse my Politick if She cant approve them, & will forgive my dabbling in them, as the English Constitution & the English Laws are strictly united.

I dind with Mrs. Anderson the other day & She repeated her Request to be always rememberd to You: I am always delighted to hear her speak of You because I think She almost does Justice to You: We dind on a fine Ham sent her by Mrs. Allen,[7] & rememberd Our Country-folks very affectionately.

I am Honourd Parent,
Your most Dutiful & most Affectionate Son
John Dickinson

P.S. Please to remember Me to my Dearest Brother: & Pardon this Scrawl I have not time to transcribe it.

ALS (PPL-JDFP)

---

¹ See doc. 1:36, above, the possible reference to Philip Walker of Talbot Co., Md.
² Lat. the battle of court debate.
³ JD quotes the poet John Milton (1608–1674). See Milton, *Paradise Lost. A Poem, in Twelve Books* (Berwick upon Tweed: Robert Taylor, 1754), 67.
⁴ The declaration was signed on the 17th but proclaimed in London on the 18th.
⁵ Paul de Rapin de Thoyras (1661–1725), a former army officer, was a French historian. This section is informed by his *History of England* (1724), but it is not a direct quotation. After first

discussing how Charles II spent 1684 "establishing the King's acquired absolute power" in part through "the augmentation of the Forces by the Garrison of *Tangier*," Rapin writes, "To make the people in some measure fully sensible of their new slavery, the King affected to muster his forces, which from one regiment of Foot, and one troop of Horse-guards, (raised by himself, with the murmurs of many of his Subjects) were increased to four thousand compleatly trained and effective men." See Rapin, 2:733–34.

[6] Henry St. John (1678–1751), first viscount Bolingbroke, was a politician and diplomat. After George I's ascension to the throne and a Whig victory in the 1715 election, Bolingbroke fled to France in March 1715 to avoid arrest by a Parliament looking to uncover political misconduct in the late administration. He joined the Jacobite cause as James II's (1633–1701) secretary of state but was dismissed in 1716. He then tried to negotiate a return to Britain in exchange for betraying his former allies. He finally returned to England in 1725. In his writings during exile, he rejected absolute monarchy in favor of limited monarchy balanced by the landed classes in Parliament.

[7] Possibly Margaret Hamilton Allen (c. 1709–1760), wife of William and daughter of Andrew Hamilton (1676–1741), a Scottish lawyer best known for his defense of John Peter Zenger (1697–1746), who was on trial for libel in New York.

38
To Samuel Dickinson, June 6, 1756

London June 6th <u>1756</u>

Honourd Father,

I wrote lately by Captain Gordon to Choptank, acquainting You with the daily Encrease of my Health & Strength which by the Blessing of Almighty God still continues: The Town agrees with Me so well, that I dont think of leaving it till the Terms are over, which will not be these five or six weeks: The Gentlemen of the long Robe have been put into a very warm ferment by the suddent death of L[or]d Chief Justice Ryder.[1] The Vacancy is not yet filld up; & there are great Doubts, Who will be appointed: Murray, the Attorney General stands next in place, & there can be no Objection to his Merit But yet there are two reasons against his Promotion to this Post—One is the great Loss he will suffer by accepting it, as the Salary is but £4000 a Year & his Practize amounts to more than Eight: The other Reason is, that the Ministry cant well spare him out of the House of Commons, where he is the only Match they have for One Pitt, a Discontented Statesman [*page break*] Who is the Patriot of the Times, & gives them a good Deal of Trouble.[2] If Murray however is appointed—tis very probably Sir Rich[ar]d Lloyd will succeed him & Mr. Yorke, a Son of the Chancellor be made Sollicitor General.

I hope I am something Excusable in beginning with News which arise as it were, in my own Province—tho[ugh] they are less important than those of Kingdoms & States: The Name of War was given {to} the Military Operations of Us & Our Enemies the 18th of last Mo[nth]. A Ceremony I was glad to see once, but considering the Subject, I think the seeing once, very sufficient to gratify the most Eager Curiosity:[3] We have no Accounts Yet of France having declard War: But their Hostile Invasion of the Island of Minorca, is mentiond by his Majesty as the more immediate Cause of his Declaration.

You must by this time have had very full Accounts of this Expedition: Its fate is not yet determind—tho[ugh] People's minds are wound up to the highest Pitch of Expectation & Advice is lookd for every Moment— The last Accounts to the Government & which may be depended on are, That Admiral Byng left Gibraltar the 8th of May with 13 Ships of the Line & 3 or 4 Frigates, with 1000 on Board [*page break*] for the Reinforcement of Fort St. Philip, the only Fortification that can possibly hold out against the Enemy: that Byng had a fair Wind for four Days after leaving Gibraltar, in which time the Voyage from thence to Port Mahon is generally performd, & that the Garrison of St. Philip tho[ugh] closely beseigd held out till the 11th when the last expresses saild.[4]

The Beseigers are protected by a Fleet of 11 Line of Battle Ships & some Frigates, & as Byng according to the highest Degree of Probability must have arrivd at Minorca the 12[th5]—there must either have been an Engagement, or the French have retird: Which of these has happened—is utterly unknown:[6] But under the Cloud of this Uncertainty, a Crop of Lies springs up every Moment: I was in the City Yesterday & heard from <u>indubitable Authority</u> that Byng had beat the French, & the French had beat [~~illegible~~] Byng—that Byng had run away with{out} fight[in]g & that the French had run away without fighting [*page break*] In short that there had been no fight, or if any like that in the old Song, "And We ran & they ran &c"[7]

Amidst these clamorous Falsehoods, which are generally urgd with the more Noise, as there is the less Reason in them, Men of Sense & Moderation argue from the Certainty of known facts, to the Probability of doubtful Consequences, & upon Cool Reflexion find no very strong Reasons to be under any great Apprehensions.

St. Philip coud not be taken ~~be taken~~ before Byng's Arrival— If the Enemy declind an Engagement by Sea the Garrison woud be reinforcd, & the Beseigers very much distressd— If the Enemy fought us, there is Ground to hope from our Superiority, from the Eagerness with which Byng solicited this Command & the Spirit of our Sailors, that We shall have the Advantage. If We have, the French must be just in the same Condition the Poor Spaniards were upon the Island of Sicily—when their Fleet was demolishd by this Byng['s] Father in the Beginning of George the first's Reign.[8] Whatever is the Event of these things, it is certain the Ministry have disgusted the Nation extremely in [*page break*] their Conduct of this Affair:

They had receivd Intelligence, of the Destination of the Armament at Toulon, Nay it was known all over the Kingdom, a great While before they thought of sending a fleet into the Mediterranean, & when began to talk of it they were so dilatory in their Preparations, that at last the Fleet seemd to be driven away by the Complaints of the People.[9]

The fault is generally laid on the Duke of New Castle, who enterd very unwillingly into this War, & that Pitt I have mentiond has declard, if Port Mahon is taken he will impeach his Grace.   The Ministry have given great Offence too—by rejecting a Militia Bill—for putting this Kingdom into a State of Defence by an Internal Power; I was in the house of Lords when it was thrown out by a Majority of 59 to 23—tho[ugh] it had passd <u>unanimously</u> in the house of Commons.[10] The Earl of Halifax distinguishd himself very much in a Speech for the Bill,[11] & the L[or]d Chanc[ello]r said as much against it [*page break*] as coud be said: But I confess some of the Arguments made use of against it, I was astonishd to hear from Englishmen. The Earl of Granville set out professedly against all Militias, condemning them as weak & fruitless Attempts: The Chanc[ello]r did not begin on so large a Foundation, & Said He desird it might not be understood as if he was prejudiced against all kinds of Militias, or was willing to perpetuate the Necessity of our being defended by mercenary & foreign Troops as We now are: but when he was entred into the Warmth of Argument, he forgot the bounds he had prescribd himself & his Opinion was full as extensive as Granville's—for he laid great Stress on this that a Militia woud introduce a Military Spirit, woud destroy that Commercial one, which is now become a Part of the English Constitution—& in a little time, it woud be necessary to make Laws for suppressing it, as We lately were obligd to do for Scotland.[12]   If this is not perpetuating the Necessity of our Defence by foreign Troops—I dont know what is. But such is the Complacency these great Men have for the Smiles of their Prince, that [*page break*] they will gratify every desire of Ambition & Power, at the Expence of Truth, Reason & their Country: So ridiculously weak are we with all the Means of Strength in our hands—that as the Earl of Bath[13] said—it is a Common Expression in France "That when they want to give Us a Sound Fright of an Invasion, they have nothing to do but to white-wash St. Germans,[14] & the Preparations for this Affair will do the Job effectually.["]
The other Powers of Europe seem very inclinable to preserve a strict Neutrality & there is not the least Whisper of the French Intrigues succeed[in]g in any Court: So that the two Nations will very Probably be left to try their own Proper Strength

This Affair of Minorca being so near seems to have driven America out of People's heads, but I wish very much to hear from You: We have had no Accounts a good While, & I imagine Something must be done by this Time on one Side or the other. L[or]d Loudon will arrive long before this, & I hope a great Deal from his Prudence & [*page break*] Conduct: Our new Gov[ern]or will sail soon too, & being a Military Gentleman—will perhaps overcome that Lethargick Quietism, which hitherto has cast such a Gloom over Us:[15] But I have from very good Authority that Mr. Penn has been obligd to give up all Disputes about the Land tax & Paper Money:[16] So that on the Whole, Neither he nor the Assembly have any great Reason to boast. The Quakers Yearly Meeting is now setting, & I suppose they will now appoint Deputies to their Pensilvanian Brethren, to sail immediately after it is over.[17]

Tench Francis has had a Violent fit of Sickness, but is now very well recoverd: I think from what I can gather from him, he came over for the Government, I am apt to think he relied on the Quaker Interest.

Most Honourd Father, I long to hear from You: Unless I receive Your Commands to sail sooner, Next Spring I hope to embrace the best of Parents, & that from the Improvem[en]ts—I have made in my Profession, You will say, I am Your most Dutifu[l] & most affectionate Son

John Dickinson

[*in left margin of fifth page*]: P.S. This Instant there is Advice of Admiral Boscawen's taking 13 Martineco Men & two East India Ships.[18]

ALS (PPL-JDFP)

---

[1] Gentlemen of the long robe: members of the legal profession (*OED*). Dudley Ryder was appointed chief justice in 1754.

[2] William Pitt (1708–1778), the Elder, became first earl of Chatham in 1766. He had benefitted from Newcastle's patronage in the past: Newcastle secured the seat from Seaford, East Sussex, for him in the 1747 election, and later the seat from Aldborough, Yorkshire Co., in 1754. But with Henry Pelham's death, Pitt galvanized parliamentary opposition to his former patron and called for a war against France in the name of the "long forgotten people of America" (*ODNB*).

[3] At about noon on May 18 at St. James's Palace, the king "appeared with his Sword drawn at the Window of the Room over the Gateway, while Garter Principal King at Arms" read the declaration. Meanwhile, at about 11 a.m., the lord mayor, aldermen, and sheriffs had proceeded from Guildhall to Fleet Street and at the Temple Bar "caused the City Gate to be locked up." A procession consisting of two troops of horse guards escorting the kings of arms and other officers marched to Charing Cross, where the declaration was read and proclaimed. From thence they moved to the Temple Bar and, after obtaining admittance to the city, read and proclaimed the declaration at the end of Chancery Lane. Then the official procession, followed by the city procession, continued through the city to read and proclaim the declaration at the end of Wood Street and at the Royal Exchange (*London Evening Post*, May 18, 1756; *London Gaz.*, May 15–May 18, 1756; *Public Advertiser* [London], May 19, 1756).

[4] John Byng (1704–1757), admiral in the Royal Navy, set sail from England on April 6, but bad weather meant he did not reach Gibraltar until May 2. A messenger arriving at the Admiralty Office with dispatches on May 31 confirmed that Byng's fleet of thirteen ships of the line and three frigates left Gibraltar with a fair wind on May 8 (*London Gaz.*, May 29–June 1, 1756). The *Gazetteer and London Daily Advertiser*, June 1, estimated that Byng would

arrive at Port Mahon by May 13 and reported "that St. Philip's fort still held out the 11th, so that there is some reason to hope Admiral Byng may not arrive there too late."

[5] Byng reached Minorca on May 19.

[6] The better ships and captains had been assigned to Hawke's expedition, and Byng's undermanned squadron was unable to defeat the French in battle on May 20. Blakeney finally surrendered on June 28. See Dull, 52; Anderson, *Crucible*, 171.

[7] The song "We Ran and They Ran" is attributed to Murdoch McLennan of Crathie, Scotland, when it appears in *The Works of Robert Burns; Containing his Life; . . . Select Scottish Songs of the Other Poets . . .* (New York: Leavitt, Trow, and Co., 1849), 129–32.

[8] George I (1660–1727) reigned as king of Great Britain from 1714 until his death. George Byng (1663–1733), first viscount Torrington, was an admiral in the Royal Navy and father of John Byng (see n. 4, above). He commanded the British fleet that defeated a Spanish fleet at the battle of Cape Passaro in August 1718.

[9] Since January, Cumberland had been arguing with the inner cabinet to reinforce Minorca, but Anson thought the activity in the Mediterranean was a distraction from a larger invasion of England. In consequence, the cabinet did not order Byng's small fleet to the Mediterranean until March 9, and it was only after news of the April 17 French landing reached London on May 6 that the government deployed additional ships to reinforce Byng. When Newcastle appeared in public after the fall of Minorca, the public threw mud at his carriage. See Dull, 51–54.

[10] On Dec. 8, 1755, Pitt moved that the House of Commons should form a committee of the whole to consider the militia laws. After a postponement, Commons on Jan. 21, 1756, resolved that a bill should be brought in to improve those laws. The resulting bill was presented on March 12 by George Townshend (1724–1807), member of Parliament for Norfolk, and after amendments was passed on May 10. On May 24 the bill was debated at length in the House of Lords and rejected by the margin JD states (*Parl. Hist.*, 15:704–69). For an example of the resulting criticism, see *A Modest Address to the Commons of Great Britain, and in Particular to the Free Citizens of London; Occasioned by the Ill Success of Our Present Naval War with France, and the Want of a Militia Bill*, 2nd ed. (London: J. Scott, 1756), which argues, "The A[dministratio]n strengthens itself by collusive practices with the worst and weakest of men, and sets up for some a real, for others an imaginary interest, which is distinct from, or contrary to the public good" (4).

[11] The report of the debate in *Parl. Hist.* does not record any speech by the Earl of Halifax, although it does include speeches in favor of the bill by Philip Stanhope, second earl Stanhope (1714–1786), John Russell, fourth duke of Bedford, and William Talbot (1710–1782).

[12] For the speeches of the Earl of Granville and the lord chancellor, see *Parl. Hist*, 15:714–19, 724–40. For the law about Scotland referenced by the chancellor, see "An act for the more effectual disarming the highlands in Scotland" (19 Geo. 2, c. 39 [1746]; 18 *SAL*, 519–31).

[13] William Pulteney (1684–1764) was a persistent critic of the Walpole ministry both in print and in parliamentary debate.

[14] The Château de Saint-Germain-en-Laye is a royal palace west of Paris that was the home of the exiled James II after the Glorious Revolution. With the Jacobite uprising of 1745 still fresh in British memory, French interest in the House of Stuart was not to be taken lightly.

[15] Thomas Penn had appointed William Denny (1709–1765), a captain in the British army, as the new lieutenant governor for Pennsylvania. The king approved his appointment in May 1756, and Denny arrived at New York on Aug. 15. Also in May, Denny was commissioned as lieutenant colonel for America only.

[16] Pennsylvania had issued paper money since the Assembly's first passage of a paper money act in 1723 (Act of March 2, 1723, 3 *SALP* 324–38). Paper money had been a contentious issue throughout Gov. Hamilton's tenure. When Parliament passed the Currency Act of 1751 (24

Geo. 2, c. 53) it failed to restrict specifically the issuing of paper currency in the colonies outside of New England, so the Assembly passed an act to raise £40,000 in paper money on Feb. 25, 1752 (*PA* 4:3493). Hamilton rejected it on the basis of secret instructions from Thomas Penn, who believed that such bills usurped his executive power unless he could control how the money was spent. These instructions hampered Hamilton's ability to raise provincial defense funds with the outbreak of the French and Indian War, a problem his successor inherited. In the wake of Braddock's defeat in July 1755, the Assembly passed a bill to raise £50,000 in paper money funded by a general land tax that did not exempt the proprietary estate (*Votes* [1754], 118–20). Gov. Morris vetoed the bill. Penn subsequently donated £5,000 to the war effort to calm outrage, and the Assembly exempted the proprietary estate from its future paper money bills. See W. Shirley and James H. Hutson, "Benjamin Franklin and Pennsylvania Politics, 1751–1755: A Reappraisal," *PMHB* 93, no. 3 (1969): 303–71.

[17] In 1756, the Yearly Meeting of the Quakers was held at London from June 7 through 12. For the epistle issued by the meeting, see *Epistles from the Yearly Meeting of the People called Quakers, Held in London, to the Quarterly and Monthly Meetings in Great Britain, Ireland, and Elsewhere; From the Year 1675, to 1759, inclusive* (London: Samuel Clark, 1760), 261–64. British Quakers had heard that there was a move in Parliament "for totally excluding our Friends in Pensilvania & other parts of America from having seats in any Provincial Assembly by imposing an Oath," based on reports that the Pennsylvania Assembly could not defend the colony against the French and Indians because of its Quaker principles. According to a report on the matter in April, they had succeeded in preventing any parliamentary action for the moment, "But it is fully expected that our Friends will not suffer themselves to be chosen into assembly during the present disturbances in America." Two or more delegates should be sent "to explain the present state of affairs, and what is expected from Friends in those parts." The Yearly Meeting adopted the recommendations and appointed John Hunt (1712–1778) and Christopher Wilson (1704–1761) as delegates (Isaac Sharpless, *A History of Quaker Government in Pennsylvania*, 2 vols. [Philadelphia, T.S. Leach & Co., 1898–99], 1:250–54).

[18] Vice Adm. Edward Boscawen (1711–1761), a career naval officer, was at this time in command of a squadron stationed in the English Channel, off Ushant. He wrote his wife that his ships had captured two French vessels "from Martinico, laden with sugar" on May 27 and 28 (Peter K. Kemp, ed., "Boscawen's Letters to His Wife," *The Naval Miscellany*, Publications of the Navy Records Society 4, no. 92 [1952]: 213). *WEP* reported the capture of two "French India Ships" in its issue of June 5–8. Martinico is the island of Martinique.

39
To Mary Cadwalader Dickinson, August 2, 1756

London Aug[us]t 2^d 1756

Honourd Mother,

It is a great while since I have rec[eive]d a Letter from You, but had the Pleasure of hearing from my Dear Brother the other day that You were well: I have often said, & if I speak from my heart, I must often repeat it, that to hear of your happiness is an Addition to mine; & if mine on the other hand, as your Tenderness has always taught Me to believe, contributes to yours, I am sure I shall constantly exert every faculty & Power I am possest of in the Discharge of so amiable a Duty; & I bow in humble Gratitude to my Creator & Preserver for his infinite Mercy in restoring Me to so firm a State of Health.

I have told my Honourd Father of my Industry, & now permit Me to inform You of my Diversions: I have not taken many, but as this is the last Summer I shall be in England, I design to take a Jaunt to Bristol, & I advisd to drink the Waters as very [*page break*] serviceable to Persons of a thin Constitution:[1] This will be the only opportunity I shall have of seeing any thing of the Country Parts of England: Towards Winter I shall return to my Studies, & "cum hirundine prima"[2] take my Flight for America. There certainly will be a Convoy in the Spring, & there are so many French Sailors taken that all the Rest are on board the King's Ships, & there will be but few Privateers;[3] So that I am under no manner of Apprehensions about being taken.   The Brest Fleet has been blocked up all this Summer & has not yet stirr'd out;[4] but Byng has tarnishd all his Father's Laurels in the Mediterranean.[5]

I hope our Affairs in America will be managd better this Year than were the last, & that by this time You begin to find the Advantage of having a Supreme Commander, whose Authority Knowledge & Address may turn out united Force against the Common Enemy. I wish L[or]d Loudon had saild sooner, but if he had, he probably woud have found himself a General without an army, or perhaps an army without ammunition: For there was such unaccoun[*page break*]table Negligence & Mismanagement in the Preparations that his L[or]ds[hi]p was heartily tird of His Command before he left England,[6] & was obligd to complain to his Majesty.

I am extremely sorry to find such violent Animosities & heats as appear in the Pens[ylvani]a Papers: It is really melancholy to think of returning to one's Country groaning under the double Miseries of War & Discord—Fire & Slaughter raging round, & Parties & Dissensions weakening & distracting Us within.[7] How soon do men lose sight of Publick Good, when under the Influence of Private Passion—or which Side shall an honest Man espouse where both are in the wrong, as constantly is the Case when such Passion is raisd. Tench Francis is still in London, & I can perceive very plainly that he is no friend of the Governors Party: He does not talk so positively of never practizing again as he usd to do. [*page break*] Francis seems to Me to be a man who has read too much: His Notions are extremely confusd—by perpetual Altercation he has got a knack rather than a method of arguing— he has such an important way of hesitating & travelling round a thing, that if he spoke less, he woud speak better, but if he spoke better he woud not appear so wise to common People as he does: He is [~~illegible~~]{far from being a Lawyer} without his Books, with them he must have merit to be sure from the figure he has made: He has read the Roman History but does not understand any thing of the Civil La[w] nor of their Customs. He values himself on being a Classick, & I happend one day to say I had read Tacitus[8] this Winter, which seemd to surprize him very much; he said there were but

3 or 4 men in Philad[elphi]a coud read it; however to try my Knowledge I believe he artfully mentiond Sallust,[9] of whom I profest Myself an Admirer; he said he had just bought one & down he brout it (We were at Mr. Bacon's where he lodges) & We turnd to Cæsars famous Speech for the Conspirator[s][10] but We soon differd in our Paraphraze & an Argument [beg]un on the Roman Laws, in which your Son "omne [*cont. on first page, in left margin:*] tulit punctum"[11] & tho[ugh] I had manifestly the Advantage of him, Yet I observd so well the Respect due to his Age, that I afforded him a decent Retreat, & he said after I was gone, that I was the most Polite Scholar of my Years he had met with. I am Honourd Mother,

Your most Dutiful & most affectionate Son,
John Dickinson

ALS (PPL-JDFP)

---

[1] Bristol is a seaport city about 120 mi. west of London at the confluence of the Rivers Avon and Frome. By the mid-18th century, the reputation of the hot water spring there was sufficient to attract the attention of doctors. See Patrick Keir, *An Enquiry into the Nature and Virtues of the Medicinal Waters of Bristol, and Their Use in the Cure of Chronical Distempers* (London: R. Willock, 1739), and George Randolph, *An Enquiry into the Medicinal Virtues of Bristol-Water: and the Indications of Cure which it Answers* (Oxford: J. Fletcher, 1745). Both found the waters useful for the treatment of a variety of chronic conditions, although Randolph thought they had little effect on healthy bodies and might actually be harmful to "all cold watry phlegmatick Constitutions" (29).

[2] Lat. with the first swallow.

[3] Privateer: "An armed vessel owned and crewed by private individuals, and holding a government commission known as a letter of marque authorizing the capture of merchant shipping belonging to an enemy nation" (*OED*).

[4] Beginning in January 1756, a series of British admirals positioned British fleets off the coast of France to blockade the small French fleet at the port of Brest, which resulted in heavy shipping losses to France from British privateers and warships. See Dull, 60.

[5] Adm. John Byng became the scapegoat for the loss of Minorca and was executed on March 14, 1757.

[6] For an account of the administrative delays that kept Loudoun from sailing for the colonies in a timely manner, see Pargellis, 45–79. He finally landed in New York on July 23, 1756, too late to save Oswego from capture by the French.

[7] Gen. Edward Braddock's defeat and death in July 1755 shifted the theater of war from Pennsylvania to New York, which meant removing British troops from the province and exposing the western counties to attack. Increasing violence revived the perennial debate between the governor and the Quaker Assembly about a militia law. "The removal of the army from the frontiers will leave the back settlements entirely exposed to the incursions of the French and Indians," Gov. Robert Hunter Morris warned the Assembly on July 28, "I lay these matters before you, that you may, as soon as possible, fall upon measures for the protections of the western frontiers." See *PG*, Aug. 14, 1755.

[8] Publius Cornelius Tacitus (c. 56–c. 120) was a Roman historian. Only half of the thirty volumes of his *Annals* and *Histories* survive.

[9] Gaius Sallustius Crispus (Sallust; 86–c. 35 BC) was a Roman historian whose works included a history of Cataline's conspiracy, *Bellum Catilinae.*

[10] Gaius Julius Caesar (100–44 BC) became emperor of Rome, but in 63 BC, he was a senator accused by some of involvement with the plot of Lucius Sergius Catalina (108–62 BC) and by others of conspiring to overthrow the Roman republic. Caesar's speech suggesting a less draconian punishment for the five conspirators who were executed is recorded in *Sall. Cat.* 51.

[11] Lat. carried every point.

40
To Samuel Dickinson, August 2, 175

London Aug[us]t 2[d] 1756

Honourd Father,

I hope my last by Capt[ai]n Vaughan[1] has given You the Satisfaction of knowing the Continuance of my Health: I am daily growing stronger; & what I think almost of the same Importance, more learned: I read, I write, I attend as much as either my Body or Mind can bear, for I dont know what Vision haunts Me, & is perpetually pointing out the Paths of Glory, tho[ugh] I despair of ever reaching her Temple, but

"In such attempts, 'tis glorious e'en to fail"[2]

This Summer I have confind myself chiefly to the reading Chancery Reports, which I look upon in some measure as the winding up the Course of one's Studies; that is, not as finishing them, but giving such a complete Acquaintance with the whole Body of the Law, that afterwards a Man's reading is like travelling again in the same Road. [*page break*] The Laws of England abstracted from the Courts of Equity are like a Body consisting only of Bones & Muscles strong & hardy in the greatest Degree, but void of that Beauty & Harmony it has when cloathd with flesh, which in adorning it, does not detract in the least from its former Qualities. The most fond Admirer of our Common Law must allow, {~~Perhaps some may~~} that there are some Cases in which the Severity of its Rules, requires some little softening: In short that the Necessities of Human Nature are greater than our Foresight, & that the most excellent Institutions may be extrememly just & reasonable in Ninety nine Instances, & quite defective or improper in the hundredth. Then arises the Clamour, & innumerable Benefits, the Result of the highest Wisdom cant atone for a single Error

. . . . Quam aut Incuria fudit,

Aut humana parum cavit Natura. Hor.[3]

So much more inclinable are We to Malice than Gratitude. It woud be both inconvenient & unbecoming for the Courts of Common Law to relax any thing of their Firmness, as their{re} are a thousand Duties of Sovereign [*page break*] Power, incompatible with the Royal Dignity to execute.

Perhaps it may be said that the Chancery Law is unnecessary for a Practizer in Pensilvania where there is no Court of Equity; but I think it woud be much properer to say, Every Court there is a Court of Equity, for both

Judges & Juries think it hard to deny a Man that Relief which he can obtain no where else: & without reflecting that Equity never intermeddles, but where Law denies <u>all manner</u> of Assistance, Every Judgment, Every Verdict is a confusd Mixture of private Passions & Popular Errors; & Every Court assumes the Power of Legislation.

The Inconvenience of this extensive & arbitrary Authority is severely felt already, & will hardly decrease till the Source is stopd. However as a Man may shew his Learning without success, I shall continue my Application that I may be able, when a wrongful Judgment is given against Me to produce Coke, Plowden, Ventris,[4] Salkeld[5] &c & shew

<u>Diis</u>   <u>Catoni</u>

"Victrix causa illis placuit, sed victa peritis"[6]

That tho[ugh] they gave Jud[g]ment for the Plaintiff, Yet all the Learned were of Opinion with the Defendant. [*page break*]

Publick Affairs are managd in such a manner that it is disagreable saying any thing about them: The Ministry pressd by the loud & perpetual Murmurs of the People at last sent a Fleet to the Relief of Port-Mahon: but its Force & Commander occasioned as much Discontent as the Delay: However the Place might have been relievd but for the infamous Conduct of Admiral Byng: He met the French Fleet off Minorca the 20th of May & tho[ugh] superior to them by one Ship of the Line, he only permitted some of his Vessells to cannondade, keeping himself at a very secure Distance: & then under pretence of the Intrepid's being disabled, by a most notorious Act of Cowardice retreated to Gibraltar: For St. Philip being thus deserted & reducd to the greatest Distress, after a most Gallant Defence of two months to the immortal Honour of General Blakeney, surrendered the 20th of June to Marshall Richlieu:[7] Byng is come home under an Arrest,[8] & instead of being tried by a Court Martial, to satisfy the Resentment of the People who suspect some Villainy in the Ministry, it is said he will be impeachd by the house of Commons, & the Parliament will set for that Purpose—[9]

[*in left margin:*] I am Honourd Father,

Your most Dutiful & Affectionate Son

John Dickinson

ALS (PPL-JDFP)

---

[1] Probably Edward Vaughan, captain of the ship *Swanzey*, who left London on June 21 and arrived at Philadelphia on Sept. 1 (*PG*, Sept. 2, 1756).

[2] A version of this adage appears in William Smith, trans., *Dionysius Longinus on the Sublime*, 3rd ed. (London: B. Dod, 1752), 12: "They are mindful of the maxim: 'In great attempts, 'tis glorious e'en to fall.'"

[3] Lat. "which either carelessness produced or human nature inadequately protected against." Hor. *Ars. P.*, 352.

[4] Sir Peyton Ventris (1645–1691) was a judge and politician who rose to prominence after the Glorious Revolution, representing Ipswich in Parliament from January 1689 until his appointment as justice of Common Pleas in May of that year. His *Reports of Cases Adjudged in the Courts of King's Bench and Common Pleas* "endure as among the most important written during the Restoration" (*ODNB*).

[5] William Salkeld (1671–1715) was a serjeant-at-law and law reporter whose *Reports of Cases in the Court of King's Bench, 1689–1712* "became the standard work for that period" (*ODNB*).

[6] Lat. "The victorious cause pleased the gods, but the conquered cause pleased Cato." Marcus Annaeus Lucanus, "De Bello Civili," or the *Pharsalia*, ln. 128. JD changed the line to read: "The victorious cause pleased them, but the vanquished cause pleased those who had perished."

[7] Marshal of France Louis-François-Armand Vignerot du Plessis (1696–1788), third duke of Richelieu, was in command of the French fleet in the Mediterranean.

[8] Byng arrived home in England in July 26, and was promptly arrested and incarcerated in an upper room in Greenwich hospital.

[9] In the six months between Byng's arrest and trial, the Newcastle ministry fell and the public debated Byng's guilt via pamphlets. He was tried by a court martial (not Parliament) which started on Dec. 28, 1756, and ended on Jan. 27, 1757.

1757

41
John Spelman, Certificate of John Dickinson's Call
to the Bar at the Middle Temple, March 14, 1757

**Middle
Temple**   **These** are to certify That John Dickinson Esquire second Son[1] of Samuel Dickinson of Delaware in the County of Kent in the province of Pennsylvania in America Esquire was specially admitted of the Honorable Society of the Middle Temple on this Twenty first day of December One thousand Seven hundred and fifty three was called to the Degree of the letter Barr on the Eighth day of February One thousand Seven hundred and fifty seven and was published in the Common Dining Hall of the said Society on the ninth Day of the same Month and year and hath paid all Duties due to the Society and the Officers thereunto belonging In Testimony whereof I have hereunto set my Hand and Seal of the said Society this fourteenth day of March in the Thirtieth Year of the Reign of our Sovereign Lord George the Second by the Grace of God of Great Britain in the Year of our Lord One thousand Seven hundred and fifty seven.

John Spelman
Treasurer [*seal*]

<Witness
　　Ch's Hopkins Sub Trea[sure]r>

Ms (PPL-JDFP)

---

[1] JD was the second living son, the first being his older brother Henry.

42
To Thomas McKean, October 20, 1757

D[ear]r Sir—[1]

　　As I flatter myself that We are to look upon Ourselves as friends to each other throughout Life, I hope You will not expect any declaration{s} of my Esteem, but will be convinced by all my actions & the unaffected freedom of my Behaviour towards You, that it is very great: As an Instance of this, I beg You will give Yourself the trouble to take out a Capias[2] on the inclosd Declaration against Hackett who lives at the Trap.[3]

I suppose You have heard that our Supreme Court[4] was interrupted by Mr. Allens having the Gout: Coupland[5] is dead, & Growdon[6] deaf, [so] that We are to have almost a new bench; may perhaps entirely, for **it is said** the Assembly design to appoint the Judges. I hope your house will treat the Governor[7] with more respect than ours, & shew the world You have at least more good-manners if not more Christianity than We peaceable people.[8]

Please to present my Comp[limen]ts to Miss McKean[9] & believe Me

Your sincere friend

& very h[um]ble Serv[an]t

John Dickinson

Philad[elphi]a [~~illegible~~] {Oct} [obe]r 20[th] 1757

ALS (PHi-TMP)

---

[1] Thomas McKean (1734–1817) was one of JD's lifelong friends. Like JD, McKean served both Delaware and Pennsylvania throughout his career. He was first elected to the Assembly of the Three Lower Counties in 1762, where he served for the next seventeen years. He represented the Lower Counties in the national congresses before and during the Revolutionary War, at which time his attentions shifted to Pennsylvania. McKean and JD were united on every major political issue except the question of independence, which McKean favored. Together he and JD opposed the state's 1776 constitution, and they continued to work together in Pennsylvania politics during the 1780s, when JD was president of the state and McKean served as chief justice of the state Supreme Court. They both served as delegates from Delaware to the 1787 Constitutional Convention and then worked together on the Delaware constitution in 1792. Their rich correspondence continued until JD's death in 1808. At this time, McKean was deputy attorney general for Sussex, the southernmost of the Three Lower Counties.

[2] A capias warrant is issued for the arrest of a named person.

[3] The Trap, now known as the Comdr. Thomas MacDonough House, is near Odessa in New Castle Co., Del.

[4] That is, the Delaware Supreme Court.

[5] Caleb Coupland (Cowpland, 1692–1757) was a Quaker cordwainer who immigrated to Pennsylvania in the early 17th cent. A wealthy and prominent member of the community, he served as the Chester Co. justice of the peace for twenty years. See *LLP*, 2:289–92.

[6] Lawrence Growdon (1694–1770) of Bucks Co., Pa., was a substantial landowner who served in the Assembly and as secretary of the Land Office. While serving on the Pennsylvania Supreme Court, he held numerous other positions, including prothonotary of the Court of Common Pleas, clerk of the Orphans' Court, and recorder of deeds for Bucks Co.

[7] Thomas Penn.

[8] That is, the Quakers. Although JD identified strongly with Quakers, and did so increasingly over the course of his life, the tinge of sarcasm in this remark is suggestive of the differences he had with them that prevented him from becoming a member of the Society of Friends.

[9] Dorothea McKean (1737–1776) or Susan McKean.

43
Notes for *Elizabeth Taylor v. William Empson*, [1757–58]

These notes refer to a "feigned action sur wager" to determine the validity of John Taylor's will, dated November 11, 1755. A feigned (or sham) action sur wager is one in which there are dummy parties set up by the plaintiff and defendant, sometimes with obviously fictitious names, so that the actual persons involved in the dispute can see what a court would decide, without making themselves liable. When the facts were in dispute, it was a method to move fact-finding from Chancery to common-law courts for a jury trial.[1] This happened especially in certain types of real estate disputes. When Taylor's will was submitted to the county register, petitioners raised caveats, claiming that the "writing purporting to be the will of the said John Taylor was obtained by fraud and also that the said John was not of sound and disposing mind and memory at the time of executing the same." On March 10, 1756, the Register's Court directed that the facts "be tried at Common Law upon a feigned issue to be joined between the parties." The result of that trial was summarized in a letter from William Plumsted to Joseph Parker of May 1, 1758: "the writeing said to be the last Will of John Taylor is reversed and by that he died intestate."[2]

The notes summarize testimony on behalf of the parties to the lawsuit. Unfortunately, it is not clear from the notes what JD's role, if any, was in the lawsuit. Perhaps he was working with Moland; perhaps he and Moland were opposing counsel in the lawsuit; or perhaps he was simply observing and taking notes on the lawsuit. Records indicate that despite accusations by Taylor that his wife Elizabeth was extravagant and neglected his affairs, she nevertheless received her share of his estate, which she controlled for the remainder of her life.[3]

The pages of this document were folded lengthwise down the middle, with text written down each length as though it were a full page. When the pages are opened up, the text appears in two long columns per page. Initially, JD would have read it like a bound booklet, turning the pages. When the pages were stored opened up flat, the beginning of the document appeared on the second page in the second column. The columns and pages have been put in proper order here. Much text has been lost: half of one full page and some columns have been intentionally cut or ripped out. There is also some age-related damage.

Eliz[abeth] Taylor—[4]

v

W[illia]m Empson[5]

Feignd Action sur W[a]ger to try the Validity of a Will

Issue— Whether John Taylor[6] did duly execute & at his decease leave a
Will dated the

11[th]– of Nov[embe]r 1755.

Jos. Vernon.[7] Saw John Taylor sign the Will shewn him—& also the other
Witnesses sign.

Crossex[amine]d   Understood it was an Add[iti]on to J[ohn] Taylor's
Will—on Acc[oun]t of some mills he had built that Summer.
Thought Taylor was right in his Senses—did not see him walk or
rise from his Chair—
The Writ[in]g was exposd to view some part of the [time]   Taylor told
[his] Wife— where to get the Will {in a Drawer}   Taylor askd him to
sign the Will—

Samuel Mendenhall.[8] Saw John Taylor sign the Will— Subscribd it as a
Witn[ess]—
Taylor said he sent for him to sign the Will—& he signd it at his
Request.

Crossex[amine]d. Five [Judges]   Taylor se[nt for] him & 2 others to sign
a Will he had made on his Son's death[9]—he shewd the Will & signd it   Said
no man shoud know what was in it while he livd: Declard it to be his last
Will & Testam[ent]   He & the other Witn[esse]s signd it

6 Weeks before the signing this last Paper—Taylor sent his Negro boy for
[him?]{Me}—he went—was in Taylor's Room alone with him— Taylor
said he had made some Alter[ati]on in his Estate since his last Will—wh[ich]
made some Add[iti]on to his Will necess[ary]
Opend the first Will—saw [my?] [*illegible*]{[*illegible*]} to it—Saw
he had Sent for it from Branton's[10] th[at?]{is} day. S[ai]d he did not design
to make ano[the]r Will—nor ever wo[ul]d but only an Add[iti]on— Else
Part of his Estate wo[ul]d come to those he did like. Askd Me when Id come
to sign the Add[iti]on or Codicil—for that this [*text cut*] the old Will be[in]g
provd tog[ethe]r wo[ul]d do as well as a new Will. I told him any time.

6 Weeks after this Dan[iel][11] [*blank*] came for Me— Taylor told Me he had
sent for Me to sign the Add[iti]on or Cod[ici]l he had talkd of to
Me before. Bid his Wife bring the Writ[in]g She had put by— She
bro[ugh]t it—& laid it on the Table— By _it_ he means the Paper
here signd [*illegible*]   He signd it—s[ai]d he was afr[ai]d he

co[ul]d not write it so well—as to be read— Said something about his Eyesight— [*page break*]

[*top half of page cut away*]
A very little time from bring[in]g it into the Room till signing— A Piece of Paper over the Writ[in]g Part at the signing—<u>but</u> the Will was bro[ugh]t in <u>open</u>— The Paper was bro[ugh]t in with the Will.

Taylor did not seem to be of sound dispos[in]g mind & Memory—tho[ugh] as well that Night as for some time before— I believe it was ow[in]g to the Influence of Liquor— [It] was [long] [arg[ue]d?] with him—often saw him in Liquor— I judgd from his Speech & Looks— Heard no complaint about his health—but believe it was impaird by drinking—

Q[ues]tions by Mr. Moland. Did Taylor talk. What? Answer— He did not
> say any th[in]g senseless—but he seemd in Liquor— Dont remember any th[in]g incoherent— He talkd about a young Couple th[at] were married in an airy light manner—
> He committed High Treason—i.e. clipt the King's Eng[lish] i.e. did not sp[ea]k plainly—

The Will was not read.
At Jos[eph] Talbot's,[12] he seemd to be in great [*illegible*]
> He s[ai]d he was in great Sorrow— He s[ai]d th[at] You my Fr[ien]ds & the World know the Cause— I am grow[in]g old—& if I live long I am afraid I shall come to want— thro[ugh] the managem[en]t of Dan[iel] Calvert & my Wife who destroy my Estate so fast.[13] They have less[ene]d my Estate £600 [agt.?] these 7 years past—th[at] Dan[iel] had not a shill[in]g but What he gets from Me—

He wo[ul]d not talk of his Aff[air]s before his Wife   My Uncle was left Executor— [*column break*]

[*top half of page cut away*]
Rich[ard] Parkes[14] Saw John Ta[ylor] [sign] the Will—
> John Taylor req[ueste]d me to sign—& the other 2. Did not call it his Will—but a Cod[ici]l or Add[iti]on
> Taylor told me aft[erwar]ds he had signd a Will—but not his own—

bro[ugh]t his Wife's & Dan[iel] Calvert's Will—
Testor was very much in Liquor—for he s[ai]d th[in]gs about the Young Couple wh[ich] he w[oul]d not have s[ai]d if Sober.
Will was signd immed[iate]ly after my Com[in]g

The Writ[in]g part was cov[ere]d with a Paper—   His discourse was
not insensible—only as it was light & [*unfit?*] for him [*torn*] a
Neighb[o]r's Son— He did not pronounce clearly—
Talkd sensibly about an A[rre]st—
Testor s[ai]d he did not know—if his Name co[ul]d be read
Bid Calvert sign his Name— Did not [bid?] him take away the Will—
El[izabeth] Taylor [& Dan[iel]?] [took] the Paper & laughd
[*remainder of column torn away*] [*page break*]

[*top half of page cut away*]
S[ai]d he had made a Will 5 Years before wh[ich] no one knew the Contents
of.

Askd Me if I knew what I signd— I s[ai]d he told Me—it was a Cod[ici]l to
his Will— He s[ai]d No—it was A Will— Not his Will—but his Wife's &
Dan[iel] Calvert— S[ai]d his Wife had maint[aine]d Calvert 7 Years out of
his Est[ate] at not less than £100 a Year.
S[ai]d he was obligd to sign for fear of his Life for that his Wife had
threatend his Life about the Will.
He bid Me declare all this—if Ever I was calld upon.
He s[ai]d he took the Paper he signd for a Cod[ici]l & did not discover it was
a Will 'till next day. [Then?] it was sent to Plumstead—
S[ai]d he wo[ul]d go to Chester & get Jos. Parker[15] to make his Will—& if
he died—he bid Me tell Empson to put in [Caveats?] for his Children— For
they wo[ul]d be ruind—if this was a Will.
[*remainder of column cut away*] [*column break*]

[*top half of page cut away*]
The Girl had fits—he askd if I co[ul]d keep her for £20 a year— I s[ai]d I
co[ul]d if She grew no worse— He s[ai]d he had tho[ugh]ts of leav[in]g her
20 or 24 a year—
___ Nobody present dur[in]g this Conv[ersati]on—
==
==

John Williamson.[16] From 3 weeks before Taylor's death— I was with him
he s[ai]d he had settled his Affairs & lodgd them in a safe hand   Well
in his Senses.
___
==

Thomas Downing.[17] Taylor told Me he had settled his Affairs—had made
A Will & wo[ul]d send it to Philad[elphi]a
This was in Nov[embe]r Believes Taylor told him that Plumsted[18] was
Ex[ecut]or   Heard him sp[ea]k in Dan[iel] Calvert's prais[e.]
___
==

William Plumstead.

> This Will came to my hands in this Paper with a short Letter wh[ich] I took to be his hand— Taylor had often req[ueste]d Me to be Ex[ecut]or 2 Letters— One from Taylor—the other from Plumsted—about his be[in]g Ex[ecut]or   Plumstead adv[ise]d Taylor's Wife sho[ul]d be Ex[ecut]or

Taylor told Me he had not a Child he co[ul]d repose the least Trust in— S[ai]d his W[ife] was a loose Woman—[*page break*]

I tho[ug]t him touchd in his Senses When he turnd his Wife out of Doors— by his Violent Passions   Never compl[aine]d of Calvert
On the Reconcileation he spoke very much in Praise of his Wife—never heard him say any th[in]g ag[ains]t her after the Reconc[iliati]on   ==
S[ai]d Calvert was very useful to him.

M. Lovell.[19] In the Summer 1755 Taylor shewd Me a Letter to Plumstead desir[in]g him to be an Ex[ecut]or—& req[ueste]d my Interest with Plumstead.
I carried it to Plumstead—he declind—I prevaild—& told Taylor—
He said he **woud** make his Will—& bid Me tell Plumstead— Who afterw[ar]ds told Me he had it.
Never heard Taylor talk of a Cod[ici]l or Add[iti]on or any other Will Believed he had none th[at] he designd shoud Subsiste—
Taylor often spoke of Calvert as an honest Man & recommended him to me—& that Taylor generally employd him[.?] Calvert subservient to Taylor—

Never saw Taylor & his wife quarrel but [once] or twice when he was much disguisd[20] —& then he begd Pardon of Me in the Morning.

John Ellison. Taylor told Me he had made his Son his serv[an]t to [pre]vent his spend[in]g Money & th[at] he had not a son fit to leave a foot of Land to.[21]

W[illia]m Nob[lett]. Sons had bad Characters & [foolish?]   He told Me he wo[ul]d [~~let?~~]Make one of my Sons Heir of his Books—if I wo[ul]d let him have him Early in the Morning.
Taylor often sent for Daniel—& calld him his friend Daniel.

John Hanley.[22] Heard Taylor tell Dan[iel] while he had a Groat[23] in the World—he sho[ul]d not be put upon, upon enq[uirin]g about the

Aff[ai]r between Dan[iel] & Old Tenors S[ai]d it was the same Acco[un]t Dan gave him— [*column break*]

Told Dan[iel] not to mind People's Reflections   He had put his Business into Dan[iel]'s hands & he ought to do it—as he had no Clerk Calvert desird Me to charge my memory with this Discourse—

[*torn*] **Shewd** a Power of Att[orne]y to Calvert **irrevoc[able] & w[ith]out Account**—

Will read—

[*illegible*] Not much more than a third given the Wife—& £150 to Dan[iel] Who [did?] many Services to Taylor—

Many Letters to prove th[at] Calvert was in great confidence with Taylor & managd all his Affairs

Aff[i]d[avi]ts taken before the Register offerd in Evid[ence]—but obj[ecte]d to: Because taken in a spiritual Court, wh[ich] cant [pro]ve Wills relat[in]g to Lands—as this Will is. 6 Co. 23.[24]

Answ[er]   This is not relat[in]g to any thing relat[in]g to any Thing relat[in]g to [*torn*] [*illegible*] of that Cod[ici?][l] but [to] a [Collateral] Point to wit the Man's Credit— Besides the   Dep[ositi]ons   were regularly taken.

For Defendant

Depos[iti]on of Jo. Talbot taken by Consent   Proves Taylor to have been very uneasy & jealous of Calvert

Hen[ry] Hale Graham.[25] Thinks the Will to be Calvert's hand—& the Interlineations to be Taylors—
[Hence] was in doubt Whether the Dr.'s hand was Calverts.

Jos. Gilpin[26].
Taylor s[ai]d all the Diff[iculties] his Mill wo[ul]d make—wo[ul]d occasion his add[in]g a Cod[ici]l to his Will.

Hannah Talbot.[27]
In July 1755 Taylor s[ai]d his Wife was always teaz[in]g & plague[in]g about his Will & underst[an]d[in]g {He} had lodgd it in

Brinton's hands   She went to Brinton—to know what Leg[acy] was left her—but Brinton wo[ul]d not tell as it was seald: She went then to a Lawyer Who told her Noth[in]g co[ul]d be done in his Lifetime [*page break*] She then req[ueste]d Him to make his Will anew. He seemd to assent—& Dan[iel] began to write   He bore it some time—& then told them he wo[ul]d never sign any th[in]g they writ— His Wife then flatterd—Askd him what woud become of his Children– He told her he woud leave some body to take Care of them & her t[oo?].

Edw[ar]d Brinton.

Three or 4 y[ear]s ago Taylor bro[ugh]t a Will to Me & left it with Me—till his death

This was since the Reconcileation— El[izabeth] Tay[lor] even talkd to him about the Will—

The Fall he died—he sent for the Will—late in Oct[obe]r   By a Note in the Doctor's handWriting—

{Told how he woud dispose his Estate}

Saw the Dr. the latter End of Nov[embe]r   Spoke about his Will & She [demurs?]—coud not understand—

Jos. Hempfield. Heard Taylor say he designd to leave his Estate to his Gr[an]dChildren for he had not a son th[at] ought to have a Groat

6 Co. 25. Marq[uis] of Winchester's Case—[28]
2 Vern. 76.   Stiles 427. 2 P. Will. 205—[29]
[*line of text torn out*]

Ms (PHi-RRL)

---

[1] See John H. Langbein, Renée Lettow Lerner, and Bruce P. Smith, *History of the Common Law: The Development of Anglo-American Legal Institutions* (New York: Aspen Publishers, 2009), 375–76.

[2] *Chester County Wills*, Item 1720, Wills, 1659–1790 (microfilm), Chester County Archives and Records Service, Chester County Estate Papers, 1700–1820, Chester County Archives, West Chester, Pa.

[3] Joseph Smith Harris, *The Collateral Ancestry of Stephen Harris, Born September 4, 1798, and of Marianne Smith, Born April 2, 1805* (Philadelphia: G.F. Lasher, 1908), 92.

[4] Elizabeth Taylor (died c. 1772) was the second wife of John Taylor. They married on Oct. 11, 1734 (see n. 6, below). See Harris, *Collateral Ancestry*, 89, 92.

[5] William Empson, the son-in-law of John Taylor, married Taylor's daughter Martha Nov. 29, 1738. See Martha Taylor's marriage certificate, Taylor, Harris, Roman, Frazer, and Smith Families Papers, Chester Co. Historical Society, Chester, Pa.

[6] John Taylor (c. 1697–c. 1756) of Chester Co., Pa., was a prominent Quaker physician, planter, and surveyor. He also held many public offices, including sheriff of Chester Co., member of the Assembly, and justice of the peace. He was disowned by the Society

of Friends in 1745 or 1746, possibly for transgressions related to the manner of his marriage. See Harris, *Collateral Ancestry*, 90–91.

[7] Possibly Joseph Vernon (d. 1762) a Quaker yeoman of Lower Providence Township, Montgomery Co., Pa.

[8] Probably Samuel Mendenhall (1722–c. 1787), a Quaker and yeoman, of Concord in Chester (now Delaware) Co.

[9] John Taylor's son Philip died in 1754.

[10] Almost certainly a reference to Edward Brinton (1704–1779) of Birmingham Township, Chester Co., a justice of the peace who served as an administrator of John Taylor's estate.

[11] Daniel Calvert was Elizabeth Taylor's friend and later beneficiary of her estate. See Harris, *Collateral Ancestry*, 93. He was a farmer of Thornbury Township.

[12] Joseph Talbot (1711–1783), a Quaker yeoman, apparently resided at this time in Middletown Township, Chester (now Delaware) Co. He lived in Aston Township at the time of his death.

[13] Here on the page there are some calculations appearing under and between the text. Most likely they were already present and JD merely wrote over them.

[14] Possibly Richard Parks of Thornbury Township (now Delaware Co.), Pa.

[15] Joseph Parker (d. 1766) of the borough of Chester, was clerk of the court and deputy register for Chester Co.

[16] Most likely John Williamson (1690–1760), a yeoman and Quaker minister of Newtown, Chester Co. (now Newtown Square, Delaware Co.), or perhaps his son John Williamson (1728–1794), of the same place.

[17] Thomas Downing (1717–1772) was a Quaker miller and businessman after whom Downingtown in Chester Co. is named.

[18] William Plumsted (Plumstead; 1708–1765) was register general for the province of Pennsylvania. He also served as mayor of Philadelphia in 1750, 1754, and 1755. The Plumsted family was one of the wealthiest Quaker families in Pennsylvania.

[19] Possibly Michael Lovell (d. 1758), a Quaker merchant of Antigua and Philadelphia.

[20] Disguised: an archaic slang term for intoxicated (*OED*).

[21] John Taylor was referring either to John Taylor, Jr., (1721–1761), or to Jacob Taylor.

[22] Most likely John Hanley (d. 1769), a tavern keeper in the borough of Chester in what is now Delaware Co., although possibly John Hanley (died c. 1771), a yeoman of Londonderry Township.

[23] Groat: "The English groat coined in 1351–2 was made equal to four pence" (*OED*).

[24] 6 Coke, *Reports* 23, "Pawlet *Marquess of* Winchester's *Case*," Trin. 41 Eliz., B.R. (1598). The case addressed the last will and testament of the late William Paulet (1532–1598), third marquess of Winchester, who, it was argued, "was not of sane and perfect Memory, such as the Law requires at the Time of the Making of the said supposed Will."

[25] Henry Hale Graham (1731–1790) was a judge in Chester, Pa.

[26] Probably the Joseph Gilpin who lived near Concord.

[27] Hannah Baker Talbot (1713–1759) was the first wife of Joseph Talbot (see n. 12, above). She was a daughter of John Taylor's first wife, Mary Worrilow Baker, by her first marriage.

[28] JD is mistaken in his citation. It should have been 6 Coke, *Reports* 23.

[29] 2 Vernon 76, *Belson* v. *Oldfield*, Trin. (1689), a case in the Court of Chancery concerning "Mrs. *Bettinson* travelling into *France* for her Health, and there falling into Company with the Plaintiff, who having the young Lady under Power, prevailed so far upon her, as to make Mrs. *Bettinson* solemnly swear to make her Will, and thereof to make the Plaintiff her Executor, and to give her all her Estate." The court dismissed the

case and referred it to the Ecclesiastical Court.

Style 427, *Hacker v. Newborn*, Mich. (1654): "If a Man make his Will in his Sickness, by the over importuning of his Wife, to the end he may be quiet, this shall be said to be a Will made by constraint, and shall not be a good Will."

2 Peere 205, *Clarkson v. Hanway* & al., Mich. (1723) in the High Court of Chancery. The plaintiff brought a bill to set aside the defendant's conveyance "by Indentures of Lease and Release . . . in Consideration of an Annuity of 20 l. to be paid to the said Simon Hanway for his Life, and a Fine was levied to the Uses of the Deed" (203). The court suspected fraud, arguing that Hanway "intended to sell this Estate" and that it was "a very weak Bargain, to sell an Inheritance of 40 l. per Annum for an Annuity of 20 l. per annum" (205).

1758

Documents from the William Smith Libel Trial

Violence wracked western Pennsylvania after the fall of Fort Necessity in July 1754 and Braddock's defeat and death at Fort Duquesne a year later. The Pennsylvania Assembly, controlled by pacifists and their allies, disputed over how best to provide for the common defense. The Assembly had long fought with various governors over militias and defense, but in late 1755 a new figured moved to the center of the controversy: William Moore, a justice of the peace from Chester County. In early November 1755, he sent a petition signed by himself and thirty-five others asking the Assembly to, "by Reason of their religious Scruples, [no] longer neglect the Defense of the Province."[1] Before adjourning for Christmas, the Assembly dismissed Moore's petition as "founded on mistakes and misapprehensions of facts and circumstance."[2] They had, after all, just passed the province's first formal militia law on November 25.[3] The province's increasing militarization convinced six pacifist members to abdicate their seats in June 1755 to save "the reputation of our religious professions."[4] For those seeking to end Quaker party rule, the upcoming October elections held much potential.[5]

William Moore joined with William Smith in fall 1756 to campaign actively against the Quaker party. Smith, provost of the College of Philadelphia (1755–79 and 1789–91) and an Anglican minister, was called before the Assembly earlier in the summer to answer for the "libelous, false, and scandalous assertions" he allegedly printed about the government in London's *Evening Advertiser*.[6] Smith was no stranger to the Assembly, having published in London in 1755 and 1756 two pamphlets highly critical of Quaker rule.[7] Moore's and Smith's efforts did not result in a defeat for the Quaker party, but shortly after the election, three more pacifists vacated their seats so they could be "filled by members of other denominations, in such manner as to prepare, without any scruples, all such laws as may be necessary to be enacted for the defense of the province."[8] One of the men elected in the ensuing by-election was Moore's nemesis, Isaac Wayne (1699–1775), who, Moore was convinced, had led a campaign in fall 1756 to tarnish his reputation by organizing multiple petitions to be sent to the Assembly accusing Moore of various breaches of judicial ethics.[9] The Assembly formed a committee to inquire into the accusations in April 1757, and set a date of August 25 for Moore to appear before them to answer for his alleged misconduct.[10]

Rather than answer in person, Moore drafted a memorial to the Assembly on September 22, entitled "The Humble Address of William Moore, one of the Justices of the Peace for the County of Chester."[11] The memorial was later published with a preface arguing that Moore "did not fail on all occasions to discover his zeal for a well-regulated militia, for the protection and security of this distressed province" and thus "was marked out by [the Quakers], as an object to execute their resentment upon."[12] Moore also sent an address to Lieutenant Governor Denny on October 19, which he subsequently published in the *Pennsylvania Gazette* and *Pennsylvania Journal*.[13] Moore denied the Assembly's public accusations against him and traced their apparent vendetta to his November 1755 petition. "Will not the Perusal of such virulent and malignant Papers," Moore asked, "induce the World to think, that Pennsylvania is no longer the Land of brotherly Love, Forebearance and Meekness, but of the most bitter Persecution, and severe Calumny?"[14] Moore also decried the Assembly's abuse of power by denying him a jury trial. "Trials by our Peers (and not by the Parties against us) I take to be one of the highest Privileges of an Englishman," he wrote.[15] Smith, a trustee for the Society for Promoting Religious Knowledge and the English Language Among the German Emigrants in Pennsylvania, asked Johann Friedrich Handschuh (Hanshaw) to translate the "Address" and Anthony Armbruster to publish it in his German newspaper, *Die Philadelphische Zeitung*.

When the Assembly convened in January 1758, the members turned their attention to Moore's now-public "Address." They were convinced that Smith was the true author and issued a warrant to bring him before the Assembly. He was arrested on January 6, 1758, and questioned for publishing Moore's "Address," which the Assembly determined to be a seditious libel.[16] He refused to apologize and was accused of contempt and denied habeas corpus. When Moore appeared before the House on January 11, he acknowledged himself as the sole author of the "Address." However, he refused to answer the many petitions against him, "believing the House had not cognizance of such matters."[17]

On the morning of January 13, the Assembly called Smith before them. Smith complained that he had not been charged with any crime, nor had he been present at the examination of evidence against him. That afternoon, he informed the Assembly he wanted Benjamin Chew as counsel. The Assembly replied that because Chew was a king's attorney, Smith must choose other counsel.[18] The same day, Denny, who was sympathetic to Moore, presented the Assembly with a lengthy missive, admonishing them to "take Care to confine yourselves within the Limits by which it is circumscribed" by the constitution of the province.[19] On January 17 the Assembly challenged Denny to remove Moore from his office and then considered two resolutions that would guide their proceedings against William Smith. The first was "Whether the Council for said *Smith* shall be allowed to dispute the Power and Authority of this House to enquire into, and punish Persons guilty of, Libels against the Government?" The second was "Whether the said Council shall be allowed to shew the Address of *William Moore* to the Governor is not a Libel, in Contradiction to the Judgment and Resolves of this House?" Both passed in the negative.

With Chew's services denied, Smith relied on Philadelphia lawyer John Ross[20] and twenty-five-year-old JD, recently returned from the Middle Temple, to defend him.[21] Although Ross was JD's senior by many years, with extensive experience at the bar and in the Assembly, it quickly became clear that he could not, or would not, mount a robust defense. When Ross cheerfully acquiesced to the Assembly's resolutions, Smith objected and turned to JD to represent him instead (doc. 1:48).

JD's notes for the opening arguments (docs. 1:45, 1:46) mainly focus on whether the present Assembly, elected in October 1757, could prosecute a perceived libel on the former Assembly, elected in October 1756. Certainly the House of Commons had punished members for publishing libels, but JD contended that such cases had always been linked to contempt or a member's breach of privilege. JD also questioned the Assembly's power to imprison people, particularly past the time of their adjournment. If an adjourning assembly did not have to free the people in their custody, then those people could be perpetually incarcerated. Finally, in his arguments, JD sought to define what a libel was according to English law. When the Assembly ruled that Smith's lawyers could not question their authority to try the case, or argue whether the "Address" was in fact a libel, JD focused on the fact that Smith was being denied trial by jury, and that the Assembly was prosecuting him for something that was actionable under common law. JD reinforced the point that what the Assembly was doing to his client was contrary to legal precedent and English rights stretching back to the Magna Carta. With the original defense strategy blocked, and the patience of the Assembly running thin, JD tried logic. Printer to the Assembly David Hall had sought the advice of Joseph Galloway and Isaac Norris before printing of the "Address" in the *Pennsylvania Gazette*, and they did not object. Smith had merely facilitated a German translation of the "Address," so surely Galloway and Norris could not object to his actions if they approved Hall's. They certainly did object, and Smith was found guilty in the Assembly by "*a great majority.*"[22] "Our old inveterate scribbler has at length wrote himself in a jail," Isaac Norris wrote to Benjamin Franklin, then watching the proceedings from afar, in London.[23]

JD, Ross, and Smith were called before the Assembly on the afternoon of January 25 to hear the verdict that committed Smith to prison until he gave satisfaction to the House. Pounding his breast, Smith complained that he had been "singled out as the peculiar Object of their Resentment," and "assured them, no Punishment they could inflict, would be half so terrible to him, as the suffering his Tongue to give his Heart the Lie."[24] As he finished his speech there was "tumultuous Stamping of Feet, Hissing, and Clapping of Hands" so loud that the chair demanded the doors to the Assembly be shut and the clappers seized.[25] The Assembly spent the next few days trying to determine the identity of the clappers while Smith sat in jail with Moore. Unwilling to give the Assembly the satisfaction of an apology, both men remained there until April 8, probably visited by family, when the Assembly recessed and released them on a writ of habeas corpus. In June, Smith married Moore's daughter, Rebecca, at Moore Hall in Chester County.

Smith petitioned the King-in-Council for relief; upon receiving the petition on April 1, the Privy Council ordered a hearing for Smith's relief. Benjamin Franklin represented the Assembly and Thomas Penn represented Smith. In Pennsylvania, Joseph Galloway worked on behalf of the Assembly, and JD and John Ross worked for Smith. The ongoing dispute between the governor and the Assembly meant that Moore and Smith remained free because the arrest warrant the Assembly drew up was never served. The issue was far from over, however. After a new Assembly took their seats in October 1758, the Committee of Grievances ruled on November 17 that Moore's petition was "scandalous and seditious libel" and that he and Smith be incarcerated until "they should make satisfaction to the House."[26] Smith set sail for London to argue his case before the Privy Council, which agreed on July 26, 1759, that although Moore's "Address" was a libel on the 1756 Assembly, no future Assembly had the right to prosecute that libel.[27] The trials of William Smith were now concluded.

Critics of the Quaker party tried to capitalize on the trial and its outcome to discredit the Quaker party, in part by criticizing them for curbing freedom of speech and the press. In a sentiment borrowed from JD's arguments at trial, proprietary party supporter William Bradford wrote, "[w]e hope . . . it will soon be understood what the LIBERTY OF THE PRESS is amongst us, and whether there be any power in a *free* government that can *license* that in one PRESS which is *punishable* in *another*."[28] In the January 1758 edition of his *American Magazine* Bradford mentioned the "alarming" actions of the Assembly, and followed that in the February edition with a more comprehensive history of the Moore saga put together by Moore himself.[29] The introduction let readers know the stakes were high, for at peril was nothing less than the "enjoyment of *civil* and *religious* LIBERTY; the unalienable rights of *private Judgment*; the security of *property*; freedom of *Speech* and *Writing*; *Trials* by JURIES, and a *Government* by *known* LAWS, not by the arbitrary decisions of those who may be our judges."[30] He also published a series of essays in the *Pennsylvania Journal* by "The Watchman," who looked to the lessons of ancient and English history to critique the Quaker party. His first installment invoked John Trenchard and Thomas Gordon's *Cato's Letters*: "Freedom of speech is the great bulwark of liberty; they prosper and die together."[31] Thinking "Watchman" to be Smith himself, critics accused him of being the "author or promoter of almost every virulent and false libel that has been published here or in Great Britain, against the constitution, and good people of this province."[32] For the Watchman, the trial had exposed the Quakers' true intention to quash the speech of those who disagreed with them. If they had their way, "Every word will be termed '*seditious*;' every truth '*libellous*.' To tell, what you know, will be call'd '*false*;' to speak what you think, '*villainous*.' When matters come to this pass, *Genius* will be depressed, *Freedom* of *Speech* and writing banished, *Honesty* tongue-tied; and then commences all the political process of *seizing, examining, imprisoning, burning*, and what not."[33]

JD's documents for this case are typical of most of his extant legal and political papers—they are mostly undated, inconsistently numbered, in no discernable order in the archives, and extraordinarily messy with heavy edits. These papers were particularly challenging to transcribe and order, and much deduction was required, based on the verifiable facts of the case as well as clues within the documents themselves, to determine their chronological placement. Adding to the difficulty was that frequently one set of pages might contain three discrete documents. In the headnotes, we have attempted to be as clear as possible about the physical appearance of the documents to explain the placement and the original presentation of each item. Although there are multiple drafts of the same arguments, because there was no definitive final version of any document, we annotated each item at first mention. The exception to this rule is the pair of documents giving a timeline of the trial. In these the fully annotated version is the second one. Also readers may find it helpful to review that second timeline, which was written at the end of the proceedings, first for the chronology of events.

Of the several types of documents in this series, three deserve mention: First, there are *notes* that seem to have been made during the proceedings or as preliminary ideas for future writings. These tend to be cryptic and messy, as though scribbled in haste, possibly during the proceedings themselves. Second, there are neater but still heavily edited draft prose *arguments* that JD may have planned to make at a later time. Finally, there are other documents that appear to be draft *transcripts* of how the arguments and debates actually unfolded. These sometimes heavily edited texts, likely drawn from memory, are distinguished by different speakers being identified. We must wonder if JD intended these, which he wrote in the third person, for publication at some later point.

The labelling of the documents as "opening" and "closing" arguments is slightly misleading as it suggests that there were arguments in between them. But these were the only arguments offered. Between them there was testimony from witnesses and requests from Smith's attorneys for time to prepare. The "closing" arguments were actually the main ones in the case.

Also important to note is that none of the extant secondary sources or other documentary editions relating to the Smith trial mention JD as a participant.[34] These documents, then, represent a significant cache of new information on this interesting moment in early American history, which ought to be counted with the 1735 New York libel trial of John Peter Zenger as an important colonial case for freedom of the press and also one that raises the question of the separation of governmental powers. Moreover, this highly public and controversial trial, with JD at the center, undoubtedly served as a dramatic introduction of the young lawyer to the people of Pennsylvania and contributed to his electoral success a few years later in 1762. Likewise, this episode foretells his willingness to challenge the entrenched leadership in the Assembly in the next significant political drama, the 1764 campaign for royal government, led by two of the same men JD confronted here, Joseph Galloway and Benjamin Franklin. Finally, it also should be observed that, although JD's relationship with his future father-in-law, Isaac Norris, had a contentious beginning during this trial, before Norris died in 1766, he and JD had become political allies.[35]

---

[1] *Votes* (1756), 13.

[2] *Votes* (1756), 54.

[3] "An Act for the Better Ordering and Regulating Such As Are Willing and Desirous To Be United for Military Purposes Within this Province," Nov. 25, 1755.

[4] *Votes* (1756), 104. The members were James Pemberton (1723–1809) of Philadelphia Co., Joshua Morris (1713–1802) of Philadelphia Co., William Callender (1703–1763) of the City of Philadelphia, William Peters of Chester Co., Peter Worral (d. 1786) of Lancaster Co., and Francis Parvin (c. 1700–1767) of Berks Co.

[5] The Quaker party consisted of more than practicing Quakers. Members of the Society of Friends were able to maintain power by forging alliances through "civil Quakerism." Non-Quakers appreciated the Quakers' commitment to "Pennsylvania's unique constitution, liberty of conscience, provincial prosperity, loosely defined pacifism, rejection of a militia, and resistance to the arbitrary powers of proprietors," and joined with them to protect this ideology. See Alan Tully, *Forming American Politics: Ideals, Interests, and Institutions in Colonial New York and Pennsylvania* (Baltimore: Johns Hopkins University Press, 1994), 258; Jane E. Calvert, *Quaker Constitutionalism and the Political Thought of John Dickinson* (New York: Cambridge University Press, 2009).

[6] *Votes* (1756), 119. The Assembly noted the issue as no. 334, April 17 to April 20, 1756.

[7] William Smith, *A Brief State of the Province of Pennsylvania* (London: R. Griffiths, 1755); Smith, *A Brief View of the Conduct of Pennsylvania, for the Year 1755* (London: R. Griffiths, 1756).

[8] *Votes* (1757), 5. The members were Mahlon Kirkbride (1703–1776) of Bucks Co., William Hoge (d. 1789) of Bucks Co., Peter Dicks (c. 1690–1760) of Chester Co., and Nathaniel Pennock (1712–1774) of Chester Co.

[9] See William Moore, *A Preface to a Memorial Delivered in to the Assembly of the Province of Pennsylvania, September 22, 1757* (Philadelphia: J. Chattin, 1757). James Chattin (b. 1726) partnered with Benjamin Franklin in 1751 to establish a press in Lancaster Co. See James N. Green, "English Books and Printing in the Age of Franklin," in *A History of the Book in America, Volume I: The Colonial Book in the Atlantic World*, ed. Hugh Amory and David D. Hall (Chapel Hill: University of North Carolina Press, 2009), 272.

[10] *Votes* (1757), 106, 140.

[11] *Votes* (1757), 153. The minutes note that the Assembly read the memorial but do not reprint its content.

[12] Moore, *A Preface* (1757).

[13] See 7 *CRP* 765; *PG*, Dec. 1, 1757. *PJ*, Dec. 1, 1757.

[14] *PG*, Dec. 1, 1757.

[15] *PG*, Dec. 1, 1757.

[16] See the transcript of the questioning, "In Assembly, January 6th, 1758," in PHi-Logan.

Seditious libel was a criminal offense under the common law, whereby a written statement was considered to be intended to undermine or overthrow the existing governmental or ecclesiastical authorities. Unlike the modern understanding of libel, in which the written statement must be false, in seditious libel, the statement against the government or government officials might well be true. Whether an author was found guilty of seditious libel often depended on the whim of the judge who heard the case. So prevalent was prosecution for this crime and so severe the punishment—life in prison—that authors usually hid their identities with pseudonyms and omitted letters from key words so as to have plausible deniability if charged. See Leonard W. Levy, *Emergence of a Free Press* (New York: Oxford University Press, 1985).

[17] *Votes* (1758), 17.

[18] Ibid., 21.

[19] Ibid., 21.

[20] John Ross (1714–1776) was a prominent Anglican lawyer from New Castle Co., Del., who clerked for Andrew Hamilton (*LLP*, 3, pt 2: 1257).

[21] JD's call to the bar is dated March 14, 1756 (doc. 1:41), and his letter to Thomas McKean on Oct. 20, 1757, was written from Philadelphia (doc. 1:42), so JD returned from London sometime between these two dates.

[22] *Votes* (1758), 29.

[23] Norris to Franklin, Feb. 21, 1758, *PBF*, 7:385.

[24] *Votes* (1758), 33.

[25] Ibid., 33.

[26] *Votes* (1759), 8–9.

[27] See *Acts of the Privy Council of England: Colonial Series, Vol. IV, 1745–1766* (Hereford: Hereford Times Limited, 1911) 374–85.

[28] *American Magazine and Monthly Chronicle for the British Colonies* (Philadelphia; Feb. 1758), 214.

[29] *American Magazine* (Jan. 1758), 199; see "Debates in Pennsylvania: Case of William Moore, Esq.," *American Magazine* (Feb. 1758), 210–27.

[30] *American Magazine* (Feb. 1758), 210.

[31] *PJ*, Feb. 23, 1758. See Letter no. 15, "Of Freedom of Speech: That the same is inseparable from publick Liberty," in *Cato's Letters; Or, Essays on Liberty, Civil and Religious, And Other Important Subjects*, 4 vols., 4th ed. (London: W. Wilkins, T. Woodward, J. Walthoe, and J. Peele, 1737), 1:96–103.

---

[32] *PJ*, March 9, 1758.

[33] *American Magazine* (July 1758), 495. The Moore-Smith trial also prompted the publication of a broadside in 1758 titled *Labour in Vain: or, an Attempt to Wash the Black-Moor White* (Philadelphia, 1758), made up of an engraving and 120 lines of verse. The engraving depicts Moore as a North African Muslim in the center of a stage, stripped to the waist and sitting in a large wash bucket, while his supporters look on or help wash him. The image of trying to wash away blackness reaches back at least to Æsop's fable of washing the Ethiopian (or Blackamoor) white, in which a slave tries to scrub away his skin color. Richard Peters, who worked with Smith to replace Franklin as president of the Academy's board of trustees, and Attorney General Benjamin Chew, who ran on the proprietary ticket in York Co., Pa., in the 1756 election, stand on either side scrubbing Moore with brushes. Proprietary party supporter and William Allen's law partner, Joseph Turner (1701–1783), pours a bucket of water onto Moore, while William Smith brings another. Phineas and Thomas Bond, key witnesses in the proceeding, stand to the side, observing the scene, as does Gov. Denny, seated in an armchair. The attached verses depict Moore as a corrupt judge with a "cruel and rapacious hand," aided by his accomplices in his scheme to undermine the Assembly.

[34] See "Documents on the Hearing of William Smith's Petition, [27 April 1758]," *PBF*, 28–51.

[35] In addition to these documents in JD's papers, there are five other significant collections dealing with the Smith trial. They are the Papers of William Penn at the Historical Society of Pennsylvania; the William Smith Papers at the Penn University Archives and Records Center at the University of Pennsylvania Archives; the Papers of the Pennsylvania Assembly at the New York Public Library; and there are some in the Penn Papers at the Historical Society of Pennsylvania and a few others in the Boston Public Library.

44
Timeline Notes of Pennsylvania Constitutional History
for the Smith Libel Trial, [c. January 17, 1758]

This brief outline of Pennsylvania's constitutional history logically appears first as necessary legal background for understanding the Assembly's powerful role in the colony as well as a key point of contention between the Assembly and Smith's counsel—whether the Assembly had cognizance (i.e., jurisdiction) to try a libel case when the provincial courts were in session. This very question was on the minds of many people, as evinced by Governor Denny's message to the Assembly on January 13, in which he observed that Pennsylvania was "so widely differing in its present Frame and Constitution from that of our Mother Country, especially in the Branches of the Legislative Body."[1] As the only major colony in British North America with a unicameral legislature, created by the implementation of the 1701 Charter of Privileges after a long contentious process, the Assembly wielded more power than most, and critics of the Quakers had long complained that the colony was "ungovernable."[2] Here JD focuses on the power of the Assembly in relation to the power of governors and the rights of prisoners, suggesting his disapprobation of the Assembly's behavior in this case.

This and the following document were written on the same set of pages.

April 25[th] 1782[3] Orig[ina]l Frame of Governm[en]t	Assembly shall sit till such time as Gov[e]r[n]ors Council shall declare, they have & approbation: & that declaration shall be a dismiss[al] to the General Assembly for that time; which General Assembly shall be notwithstanding capable of assembling together, upon the summons of the [Pro]vincial Council at any time during that Year[;] if the said [Pro]vincial Council shall see occasion for their so assembling.[4]
Dec[embe]r 1682.[5]	**Confirmd** by act of **Settlement**, only the time of meet[in]g changd from 20[th] of April to the 10.[th] of May.[6]
April 2.[d] 1683[7]	The same clause— Number of Rep[resenta]tives lessend.
Second Frame of Governm[en]t	Accepted by great Numbers.[8]
Nov[embe]r 7[th] 1696.[9]	Number still lessend & qualif[icati]ons regulated.[10]
Third frame of Governm[en]t by way of Act of Assembly.	The <u>power</u> of <u>Representatives</u>—to [pro]pose needful bills shall sit on their own <u>Adjour[n]m[en]ts</u> <u>and</u> Committees & continue in order to prepare bills, redress grievances, & impeach Criminals—**<u>until</u>** the Gov[ern]or & Council for the time being shall dismiss them: but capable of assembling on Summons by Gov[ern]or & Council. Therefore these clauses thought consistent.[11]
May 1697	**Confirmd** by act &c.[12]
28[th] Oct[obe]r 1701.[13]	Recites the Surrender of the Frame in 83. State of Laws alterd. Article of Conveience added. Election of Sheriffs & Coroners by the Freemen. $^2/_3$ to have the power of an Assembly. Criminals to have all advant[age]s of [Pro]secutors.
Judges of the Qual[ificati]ons & Elections of	

<table>
<tr><td valign="top">their own &
members</td><td>The power of the Assembly given in the same words as before only that "till such time as Gov[ernmen]t & Council &c. omitted.[14]
==</td></tr>
</table>

No [Per]son shall or may at any time hereafter be obligd to answer any Compl[ain]t matter or th[in]g whatsoever relat[in]g to [Pro][per]ty—
before the Gov[ernmen]t or in any other place—
but in **ord[ina]ry courts** of Justice—
Take care of [Pro][per]ty & neglect Liberty—

[*in right margin:*] Law of [A[ppro][pri]ation?] [*page break*]

Stat[utes] for benefit of Subj[ec]t receive large Constr[uction] West. 2. c. 26.[15] ext[en]ds to all Just[ices] tho[ugh] it mention only Just[ices] Itiner[an]t

A Stat[ute] shall extend to Every one who app[ear]s to be grieved— tho[ugh] it app[aren]t the Remedy only to some [Par][ticu]lars

Royal Charter to make Laws for rais[in]g money or other use for the publick peace State safety of the Province or private utility of [par][ticu]lar [Per]sons.[16]

Grant they can commit for Cont[em]pts or impeach—yet they cant [pro]ceed as here.

[*bottom left, upside down:*] Libel &c

Ms (PHi-RRL)

---

1 *Votes* (1758), 22.

2 Blackwell to Penn, May 1, 1689, *PWP*, 3:243.

3 JD intended to write 1682.

4 1682 Frame of Government, § 19: "THAT the General Assembly shall continue so long as may be needful to impeach Criminals fit there to be impeached, to pass Bills into Laws that they shall think fit to pass into Laws, and until such Time as the Governor and Provincial Council shall declare that they have nothing further to propose unto them for their Assent and Approbation: And that Declaration shall be a Dismiss to the General Assembly for that time; which General Assembly shall be notwithstanding capable of Assembling together upon the Summons of the Provincial Council, at any Time during that Year of the said provincial Council shall see Occasion for their so assembling." *Collection of Charters*, 16.

5 The first Pennsylvania Assembly convened at Chester in December 1682.

[6] 1682 Frame of Government, § 14: "Free-Men shall yearly chuse Members to serve in a General Assembly as their Representatives, not exceeding Two Hundred Persons, who shall yearly meet on the Twentieth Day of the Second Month, which shall be in the Year *One Thousand Six Hundred Eighty and Three*." *Collection of Charters*, 15. Before the switch to the Gregorian calendar in 1752, Britain and its colonies used the Julian calendar and considered March to be the beginning of the new year. Thus, the "Second Month" was April.

An Act of Settlement, Made at Chester, 1682: "[T]he said Members elected to serve in the General Assembly, shall yearly meet and assemble, on the *Tenth* Day of the *Third Month*, to the End and Purposes declared in the Charter, at and in such Place as is limited in the said Charter, unless the Governor and Provincial Council shall, at any time, see Cause in the Contrary." *Collection of Charters*, 27.

[7] The Second Frame of Government was agreed to on April 2, 1683.

[8] The 1683 Frame of Government § 13 allowed each of the three original counties (Bucks, Philadelphia, Chester) and three lower counties on the Delaware (New Castle, Sussex, Kent) to "yearly chuse out of themselves *Six* Persons . . . to serve in Assembly." Sec 15 allowed for population growth: "AND that the Representatives of the People in the Provincial Council and Assembly, may in after Ages bear some Proportion with the Increase and Multiplying of the People, the Number of such Representatives of the People, may be from time to time increased and enlarged, so at no time the Number exceed *Seventy-two* for the Provincial Council, and *Two Hundred* for the Assembly." *Collection of Charters*, 31.

JD could be referring to the fourteen members of the Council, forty-three members of the Assembly, and four inhabitants of Philadelphia listed as present when the frame was agreed to. See *Collection of Charters*, 34.

[9] When William and Mary restored William Penn's proprietorship in August 1694, he appointed his cousin, William Markham (1635–1704), as lieutenant governor. The Assembly demanded Markham accept a new constitution which gave it the power to propose legislation, i.e., "prepare and propose to the Governor and Council, all such bills and other matters, that may be from to time presented by the Assembly." 1 *CRP* xlv–lxvi. It was adopted on Nov. 7, 1696, without proprietary approval.

[10] The 1696 Frame of Government provided for "four persons out of each of the . . . counties to serve as . . . representatives in Assembly." 1 *CRP* xlii.

[11] 1696 Frame of Government: "And be it further enacted . . . that the Assembly shall sit upon their own adjournments, and committees, and continue in order to prepare and propose bills, redress grievances, and impeach criminals, or such persons as they shall think fit to be there impeached, until the Governor and Council for the time being shall dismiss them; which Assembly shall notwithstanding such dismiss, be capable of assembling together upon the summons of the Governor and Council, at any time during that year." 1 *CRP* lxvii.

[12] 1 *SALP* 236: "The Law for Ratifying and Confirming the Acts & Proceedings of the Assembly in 1696," passed on May 1697. The act assuaged any fears that the "dissolution of the Councill and Assembly, in October 1696" had made "all the laws past in the Last Assembly . . . void," including the "Act Past at the Said Last Assembly Intituled the frame of the Government of the Province of Pennsylvania, And the Territories Thereunto belonging."

[13] The 1701 Charter of Privileges was agreed to on Oct. 28, 1701.

[14] 1701 Charter of Privileges § 2: "[T]here shall be an Assembly, yearly chosen by the Freemen thereof, to consist of *Four* Persons out of Each County. . . . Which Assembly shall have the Power to chuse a Speaker and other their Officers; and shall be Judges of the Qualifications and Elections of their own Members; sit upon their own Adjournments; appoint Committees; prepare Bills in order to pass into Laws; impeach Criminals, and redress Grievances; and shall have all other Powers and Privileges of an Assembly, according to the Rights of the Freeborn Subjects of *England*, and as is usual in any of the King's Plantations in *America*.

"AND if any County or Counties, shall refuse or neglect to chuse their respective Representatives as aforesaid, or if chosen, do not meet to serve in Assembly, those who are so chosen and met, shall have the full power of an Assembly, in as ample Manner as if all the Representatives had been chosen and met, provided they are not less than *Two Thirds* of the whole Number that ought to meet." *Collection of Charters*, 43–44.

"V. THAT all Criminals shall have the same Privileges of Witnesses and Council as their Prosecutors." *Collection of Charters*, 45.

"VI. THAT no Person or Persons shall or may at any Time hereafter be obliged to answer any Complaint, Matter or Thing whatsoever, relating to Property, before the Governour and Council, or in any other Place, but in the ordinary Course of Justice, unless Appeals thereunto shall be hereafter by Law appointed." *Collection of Charters*, 45.

[15] 13 Edw. 1, st. 1 (1285): "The Statute of Westminter the Second." The citation appears to be in error because the only mention of "itinere Justiciariorum" is in c. 10, not c. 26.

[16] Charter of Pennsylvania: "We . . . do grant free, full, and absolute power . . . to him [Penn] and his heirs . . . to ordain, make, and enact and under his and their Seals to publish any Laws whatsoever, for the raising of Money for public Uses of the said Province, or for any other End, appertaining either unto the publick State, Peace, or Safety of the said Country, or unto the private Utility of particular Persons, according unto their best Discretion." *Collection of Charters*, 3.

45

Initial Notes for Opening Arguments in the Smith Libel Trial, [c. January 17, 1758]

This set of notes, drafted on the verso of the previous document, presents the basic defense JD and Ross hoped to make on Smith's behalf the afternoon of January 17. Most of the remaining documents repeat and elaborate on the points here.

1.st Po[in]t.   Whether the house has Cognizance?
1 Lev. 165. Pritchard for cont[emp]t to house of L[or]ds—disch[arge]d by Hab[eas] Corp[us]. 1 Sid. 245. Raym. 120. (1 Keb. 888. matter of cont[emp]t is disch[arge]d by session of Parl[iamen]t (a multo fortiori)[1] by dissol[utio]n) Lev[inz] says for fear the Subj[ec]t sho[ul]d be always impris[one]d)[2]

==

2.^d   If they have Cognizance, if this be a Libel? No false or scandalous matter contain'd in a [Pro]ceed[in]g in a Regular course of Justice—will make a Libel. 1 Lev. 240. 1 Sid. 414. 1 Saund. 131. 2 Keb. 854. 4 Co. 14. b. Dyer 285. Pl. 37.[3] tho[ugh] the Court hath no Jurisd[icti]on 832.[4] But not [*torn*] of that obj[ecti]on here, because this house is of opinion—the Gov[ern]or has that Superlative power of

Judg[in]g on an imp[eachmen]t[5] {{No libel without [[par?][ticu][lar]] [&?] [*illegible*]} All this is by way of [[Pro]se[cuti]on?] here Mr. M[oor]'s[6] was se defend[end]o[7]—but gr[an]t it a Libel—then the C[our]ts of Law are open— }[8]

3.[ly]

If Mr. Smith[9] be guilty?
Mr. S[mith] overlookd as a friend.

==

The transl[at]or was only
publish[in]g a publick th[in]g—

==

Assemb[ly] printer had publishd.[10]
A Member of parl[iamen]t denied
his priv[ilege] because he was
~~chosen~~ {arrested} before he was
chosen. Moor 340. n. 461. Lex.
parl. 384.[11]

Algernon Sydney[12]

==

Hawk P.C.[13]

==

Nevil's case 16 Car. 1.[14]

Raym[ond]
rem[arka]ble Wise &
good men[15]

==

Courts of Com[mon] Law always
[pro]ceed after prorog[ations] or
dissolutions.

Mem[ber]
committed for ever

==

Raym[ond] 381. Earl of Stafford's
case—[16] Referrd to a Comm[itt]ee
to consider, Whether Appeals
given into last parl[iamen]t were
of force to be [pro]ceeded on
now— Declard that App[eals] &
writs of Error were in force.

Petition in course of
Just[ice] & seven
bishops.
{no offence to
assist—}

==

No friendship—no
[trust][in]g walls.
[Cr?]

==

Precedaneous—[17]

==

V[ide] The address call[in]g a
Libel—

No crime to address

==

==

Law of the Ægyptians[18]

Sublato principali—tollitur adj[unctu]m[19]

==

Mr. Hamilton[20]   Morris—[21]
Last September[22]

House of Commons can take notice of th[in]gs only as Contempts or Crimes. this not a contempt, & if {a} ~~Contempt~~{rime} they dont [pro]ceed regularly.

When the Gov[ern]or has so much power.

==

It is a Crime <u>or</u> it is not. if it is a Crime the courts of Law are open: if it is not a Crime this house cant, will not take notice of it:

==

It is not a **contempt** that is not pretended—the reason then of this house tak[in]g notice of it must be because it is a ~~Crimes~~ & yet dont [pro]ceed on it as a **Crime**

== [*page break*]

Att[orne]y Gen[era]l[23]
{Submission} Judges in their own Cause

==

Bail at Com[mon] Law none here
✓ No appeal in case of mist[ake?] {at least in this Province—}

———

And Assemb[ly] composd of Indiv[idua]ls who may mist[ake?]— not infallible.

———

✓ High treason as well [&c?]

———

No injury to enquire if this house has Cogniz[ance]

———

The other side—

[*text upside down:*]

Colpeper disch[arge]d because he coud not be pun[ishe]d by the house[24]
== {Blood on his head}
Cont[em]pt & Breach may Comm[it] members or others— but someth[in]g added to the word Libel
== as well ag[ains]t a stranger
But Comm[itmen]t for Libel is only pun[ishmen]t & then twice

==

Parl[iamen]t sitt[in]g <u>and</u>[25] Reflect[in]g on the ~~powers~~ Rights & Priviledges of Parl[iamen]t

164

———

Imprisond forever

Ms (PHi-RRL)

———

[1] Lat. by far the stronger reason.

[2] 1 Levinz 165, "Prichard's Case," Pasch. 17 Car. 2, B.R. (1665): "On an *Habeas Corpus* for bringing him hither, 'twas return'd, That he was taken by an Order of the House of Peers for a Contempt; and the House of Peers being prorogued, 'twas held by the Court, That their Orders are all at an End."

1 Siderfin 245, *Lee Serjeants at Arms v. Prichard*: "As to the arrest of one that supposedly claims the privilege of a Peer: While the order was set by the Peers before Prorogation, and that it had been ordered that Prichard would surely be taken by Lee, their Serjeant took Prichard 6 days after Prorogation of Parliament and delivered him into Fleete [Prison] until was paid to him some fees, Prichard remained *Habeas Corpus*. And due to the account, and after several days, they ordered that Prichard should be discharged. And several precedents were cited, where parties taken after Prorogation under orders or warrants of Parliament would be discharged, if it is appropriate, so that they could be taken after the dissolution. And Prorogation determines each thing that is not present in a Writ of Errors. And let them know that they can be returned to at the next Parliament, vide 22 E. 3.3. And how if he is to be taken before the Prorogation again, he is able to be bailed, because it is not acceptable that they should be in arrears. And men should not be perpetually restrained of their liberty."

Raymond, *Special* 120, "Pritchard's Case": "The House of Lords, in Parliament, made an order for the apprehending of *Pritchard* to commit him to Prison. Before the Order executed the Parliament was prorogued. The Serjeant at Arms five days after the Prorogation of the Parliament arrested the said *Pritchard*, and had him in custody, and now he brings his *Habeas Corpus*. . . . *Keiling* Justice. If a Man be committed by Parliament which is prorogued, the Court may bail him. Here the return is not sufficient, because no day is mentioned when the Warrant came to the Serjeant at Arms, and therefore the Party ought to be discharged. . . . By the Court he was discharged."

1 Keble 887–88, *The King v. Pritchard*: "I heard it declared, that whatever is done, must at the next Prorogation be begun anew, except in Error, where *Scire facias* [Lat. "A writ directing a sheriff to require a person to show cause why a record should not be annulled or why another person should not have advantage of it" (*OED*)] may be retainable at the next Sessions, being grounded on Judicial Record; But this is but matter of Contempt, which is discharged by the Session of Parliament."

Levinz does not mention imprisonment is his report, but 1 Siderfin 245 notes: "Et coment il ad etre pris devant le Prorogation uncore poit etre Baile, *quia non constat* le quell ils unque meet arrere, Et homes ne serront perpetualment restraine de lour Liberty." [LFr. And although he had been taken before the prorogation, yet he may be bailed because it is uncertain whether they were put in arrears. And men shall not be perpetually restrained of their liberty.]

[3] 1 Levinz 240; 1 Siderfin 414; 1 Saunders 131, report on *Lake v. King*, Trin. 19 & 20 Car. 2, B.R. (1667), a case about a published libel. Levinz notes in the marginalia that "[p]rinting and delivering Copies of a Petition to the Parliament, is no Libel, tho' it tends to scandal."

It is unclear to what JD is referring in 2 Keble 854, which reports on four disparate cases, none of which deal with libel or slander. JD likely meant instead 2 Keble 832, *Lake v. King*: "The Court conceived that printing a Petition to Parliament, with traverse of delivery of it to any else, as here is justifiable, and printing is but a quicker way of writing; and if any thing were irregular, it was punishable in Parliament, not here; and *4 Co. 14. b.* in *Buckly*'s case, notwithstanding what is reported, it was held that want of jurisdiction will not make a Libel."

4 Coke, *Reports* 14 b., is part of a larger section titled, "Actions for Slander," and reports on *Buckley v. Wood*, 33 & 34 E., B.R. (1590). Wood brought forth a bill in the Court of Star Chamber [see doc. 1:46, n. 11) that Buckley was "a Maintainer of Pirates and Murderers, and a Procurer of Murder and Piracies . . . . And it was resolved *per totam Curiam* [Lat. by the whole court] that for any matter contain'd in the Bill that was examinable in the said Court, no Action lies, altho' the Matter is meerly false, because it was in the Course of Justice . . . . It was resolv'd and adjudg'd, that for the said Words not examinable in the said Court, an Action on the Case lies, for that can't be in the Course of Justice."

Dyer fo. 285, *Seignior B. v. Sir Richarde C.*, Trin. 2 E., C.B. (1568). No. 37 concerns *de scandalis magnatum* [Lat. libels upon peers]: "[I]n the Michaelmas Term, in the 13th year of Henry VII, an action of defamation was brought by Lord B. against Sir Richard C. and others in the banking community. The case was that the said Sir Richard had had a forger make a false brief, by which the said Lord B., according to that brief, had been neither judged nor tried. [But] the said Lord B., because of the slander of the said forgery by which he was followed, he brought his said action of defamation, declaring slander on the 12th day of March in the 12th year of the reign of Henry VII. And the defendant justified the said slander, which he had used in the said brief, because it had begun before, that is to say, some day in the 11th year of the King etc., when at the conclusion of his plea, he himself was slandered. And from this better explanation on the judgement of his plea, the matter of justification is good, but beyond the intention of the law and statutes concerning slander. Because nothing punishable could be agreed upon according to the law, except that it had been false and vexatious."

[4] That is, Keble 832, see n. 3, above.

[5] See the Assembly's response to Denny in *Votes* (1758), 23–26.

[6] William Moore (1699–1783) was appointed a justice of the peace for Chester Co. in 1741. He served in the Pennsylvania Assembly from 1733 to 1740, and as a colonel in the Chester Co. militia during the French and Indian War. See Samuel W. Pennypacker, *Historical and Biographical Sketches* (Philadelphia: R.A. Tripple, 1883), 229–39.

[7] Lat. self-defense.

[8] Hilary term had recently started when Smith's case came before the Assembly. For the English legal year, see doc. 1:8, n. 8.

[9] William Smith (1727–1803), a Scottish immigrant, was a minister of the Church of England and provost of the College of Philadelphia (now the University of Pennsylvania). Although he initially came to America at the behest of Benjamin Franklin, among others, he made an enemy of Franklin and the Quaker Assembly with his public criticisms of Pennsylvania's military policy in the French and Indian War.

[10] David Hall (1714–1772), Benjamin Franklin's business partner, published the Address in *PG*, Dec. 1, 1757.

[11] Moore 340 n. 461, "Fitzherbert's Case," Hill. 35 E. (1593): "Note that in the Parliament held in the 45th year of Elizabeth, the case was made that the arrest of Thomas Fitzherbert was fulfilled in the County of Derby . . . . And the lower house of Parliament agree, that as the arrest was made before he was elected Burgess, that he was not able to have the privilege of that House. And Speaker Cooke, the Solicitor of the King, confirmed the case of Thorp, who was the Speaker in Parliament in the time of Hilary [in the] 6th [year of the reign of Elizabeth] adjourned by prorogation; the Speaker's arrest was executed at the behest of the Duke of York. And before Parliament began to meet, again it was determined that the Speaker did not hold privilege, and so they elected another Speaker."

Lex Parl. 384: "The Lower House of Parliament agreed, That in regard one was arrested, before he was chosen Burgess, that he ought not to have the Privilege of the House" (referring to Fitzherbert's Case).

[12] Algernon Sydney (1623–1683) was an English politician and republican theorist executed for plotting against Charles II when he wrote *Discourses Concerning Government* in response to Sir Robert Filmer's *Patriarcha, or the Natural Power of Kings* (1680), which defended divine right monarchy. Sydney became a martyr for the Whig faction, which later overthrew James II in the Glorious Revolution (1688–89). His *Discourses* were published posthumously in 1693 and became an important inspiration for the American Revolutionaries.

[13] Possibly a reference to 1 Hawkins 193, which begins a chapter on libels.

[14] *Lex Parl.* 378–79: "Mr. *Francis Nevill*, of *Yorkshire*, a Member of the House, was, *February* 4. 1640 16 *Car.* I. questioned for *Breach of Privileges* in the precedent Parliament, which met 13 *Car.* 1640. by discovering to the King and Council what Words some Members did let fall in their Debate on that House. Whereupon Mr. *Bellasis*, Knight for *Yorkshire*, and Sir *John Hotham*, were committed by the Council Board. And Mr. *Nevill* being brought to the Bar, was by the House committed to the *Tower of London*; and Sir *William Savill*, touching the same Matter, was ordered to be sent for in Custody."

[15] It is unclear to what JD is referring. The citation suggests Raymond, *Special*, but we were unable to find a reference to "Wise & good men."

[16] Raymond, *Special* 381: "*Memorandum*: The Lord Viscount *Stafford*, upon a *Habeas Corpus* from the Tower, desired to be bailed, being impeached in Parliament by the House of Commons, and by reason thereof had layen in Prison in the Tower for almost two years; but we did resolve, That a Person accused of High Treason, and not within the Act of *Habeas Corpus*'s, is not *de jure* [Lat. by right] to be bailed by this Court, and we did not think fit on Discretion to Bail him; and we alledged the Orders of the House of Lords, though we did not rely thereon, which are as followeth, *viz. Die Martis* II *Martii*, 1671: It being moved, that this House would declare whether Petitions of Appeal, which were presented to this House in the last Parliament, be still in force to be proceeded on." The committee appointed to report on the matter concluded that "[t]hat in all Cases of Appeals and Writs of Error they continue and are to be proceeded on in *statu quo* [Lat. in the former state], as they stood at the dissolution of the last Parliament, without being *de novo* [Lat. from the new], and that the dissolution of the last Parliament doth not alter the state of the Impeachments brought up by the Commons in that Parliament" (384).

[17] Precedaneous: "Happening or existing before something else; antecedent, preceding, previous" (*OED*).

[18] The ancient Egyptians had no code of laws as such but rather based their jurisprudence on the central cultural value of *ma'at*, i.e., harmony, believing if people were at peace with themselves and the community and lived lives of mindfulness and consideration, all would be in balance according to *ma'at*.

[19] Lat. "If the principal be taken away, the adjunct is also taken away" (1 Coke, *Institutes* 389).

[20] Presumably Andrew Hamilton.

[21] Possibly Gov. Robert Hunter Morris, though he left office in 1756.

[22] Probably a reference to Moore's growing troubles with the Assembly. On Sept. 22, 1757, the Assembly first read William Moore's memorial. On the 28th they asked Gov. Denny to remove him from office. See *Votes* (1757), 153, 159–60.

[23] Benjamin Chew served as Pennsylvania's attorney general from 1755 to 1769.

[24] William Colpeper (d. 1726), a poet and Whig politician, was one of five gentlemen who

delivered the Kentish Petition on May 8, 1701, to the House of Commons requesting they turn their loyal addresses into bills of supply so William III could build a standing army. Colpeper, chairman of the quarter sessions at Maidstone, wrote the petition which was subsequently signed by the deputy lieutenants, justices, and grand jurors of Kent. The Tory-dominated Commons deemed the petition insolent and seditious, and imprisoned the five men in the gatehouse until the end of the session when Daniel Defoe (1660–1731) demanded their release in the name of 200,000 people. See *ONDB*; Daniel Defoe, *The History of the Kentish Petition* (London, 1701).
[25] Underlined four times.

46
**Expanded Rough Notes for Opening Arguments in
the Smith Libel Trial, [January 17, 1758]**

JD wrote this and two other documents on the same set of four legal-sized pages, in apparent haste on the day the trial commenced. Although they initially presented as a single document, both the contents and their physical appearance strongly suggest they should be treated as separate but closely related documents. This first item in this subseries expands on JD's arguments in doc. 1:45 concerning the three major points of Smith's defense. He wrote these notes utilizing the front and back of two legal-sized pages. The second document in the subseries (doc. 1:47, immediately below) is notes on the deposition of Thomas Bond. JD wrote these on a single legal-sized sheet in the middle of the set, folded like a booklet into quarto pages. The third document in the subseries (doc. 1:51, below), written on the last page, includes JD's notes for his own arguments before the Assembly, which took place on January 21.

1.ˢᵗ Point   Whether the house has Cognizance {Right of Englishmen to remonstrate when imp[risone]d even to the King. 7 Bishop's Case[1] Read a little. Learnedly & fully touch on Author[ity]— respect & Duty—no other Judges   Wise & good men. [not] pretended}

    Charge loose {**Libel**}: theref[ore] 2 points. 1ˢᵗ How far (V[ide] marg[in)

[*in left margin:*] {[~~illegible words~~] 1. How far this house [h]as Cognizance [~~illegible~~] {{~~illegible~~}} ~~[illegible] to the late house~~ any fact preced[aneou]s to their Existence}

    House of Comm[on]s commit only for breach of of Priviledge[2] {Safety} or contempt {dignity} {or in order to Impeachm[en]t}

    ==

No Instance in Lex parl[iamentari]a but for one of these, & th[at] by the <u>same</u> parl[iamen]t to whom off[ended?], except Nevil's 16 Car. 1.[3]

Pritchard disch[arge]d on Hab[eas] Corp[us] from a Comm[itmen]t by house of L[or]ds for a contempt. 1 Sid. 245. Raym. 120. Levinz 165 says it was for fear the subj[ec]t sho[ul]d be always impris[one]d
{==}
1 Keb. 888. Matter of Contempt disch[arge]d by prorogation: "{Arg[umen]t} a multo fortiori by Dissolution".
{==}
Raym. 381. Earl of Stafford's case— Referrd in house of peers to a Comm[itt]ee to consider— Whether appeals bro[ugh]t in last parl[iamen]t were of force to be [pro]ceeded on now— declard th[at] appeals & writs of Error were in force: Arg[ue]d their doubts in this case where a Jud[icia]l matter was depend[in]g, shews how cautious they woud have been on a cont[em]pt
==

A member of Parl[iamen]t denied his Priv[ilege] because he was arrested before he was chosen. Fitzherberts case. Moor 340. Lex parl[iamentaria] 384.
==

One of my L[or]d Hale's[4] arg[umen]ts in the case of Barnardiston & Soame[5] was th[at] the injury was <u>precedaneous</u> to the parl[iamen]t & theref[ore] no notice coud be taken of it. 2 Raym. 958.[6]
==

{3 Checks in Eng[lish] Const[itution] {Check designd by the wisdom of our Anc[est]ors*
[*left margin*:] {*V[ide] next page {Θ} V[ide] Address 2[ly] how [~~illegible words~~] far this house has Cogniz[ance] if this be a Libel?}
Re[pu]tation. Law of Ægypt[ians]: Scipio Africanus.[7] If thing{s} Assembly can commit, every follow[in]g one may commit, & so a man may be imprisond for ever. ut supra.[8] for if the following Assemblies have the same publick spirit with the present, they will be equally inter[este]d in Reflexions thrown on the dign[ity] & Author[ity] of Parl[iamen]ts {The parl[iamen]t cant lessen the pow[er] of anot[her]} Nor will the Maxim &c {by th[at] means convictions in C[our]ts of Laws} be any barr to them: if one single Instance can be adduced,

where a Judg[men]t of the house of Com[m]ons was ever quoted as a Case wi[th]in that maxim: then I acknowl[edge] no other Assembly can take notice of this fact—but if &c

==

Turning streams of Justice. dont know &c. This act is a <u>Cont[emp]t</u> or a <u>Crime</u>.[9] The first is not pretended—& if the 2.[d] the courts of Justice are open—& it is the undoubted right of Englishmen to be tried by their peers—first by Gr[an]d Inq[uisi]t[o]r & then by a Jury— If it is a Crime, it is an offence ag[ains]t the Laws, & not so much an Insult to this house, which has not the Executive powers in its hands, as to the Courts of Justice. Too well acq[uainte]d with the Rights and Priv[ilege]s of Freemen for me to insist on them. Magna Charta 29—[10]

[in left margin at brace:] {Star Chamber High Comm[ission]}[11]

No freeman shall be taken or impris[one]d or diss[eize]d of his freehold or outl[awe]d or exild or otherw[ise] destroyd, nor will we pass upon him, but by Jud[gmen]t of his Peers or Law of the Land. 30 times confirmd.[12]

Mentiond by the Judges in Paty's Case—Raym. 1105.[13] but referrd in all their Arg[umen]ts to the priv[ilege]s of the house. Lex Parl[iamentaria]

Omnis inn[ovatio] plus novitate [per]turbat quam utilitate [&c?][14] *[page break]*

2.[d] Point. If they have cognizance whether this be a Libel.

I am surprizd to find the word **Libellous** made use of in the messages to the Gov[ernmen]t—because th[at] word implies a motive whi[ch] this house has utterly disclaimd; & th[at] is a Resentm[en]t {&} of some im[portance?] to their Char[acte]r for a Libel is a malicious defamation expressd in print[in]g, writ[in]g, pictures or signs, tend[in]g to blacken the mem[or]y of one who is dead—or the Reput[atio]n of one who is alive, & to expose him to publick hatred, contempt, or Ridicule. Hawk. pl. 6. 193. & 195 he says No writ[in]g can be a Libel, unless it reflect on some [par][ticu]lar [Per]son[15]   Now no [Per]son is reflected on here—but the members of the last assembly: & this house says they do ~~not [look at this?] as a contempt to~~ not consider this piece, as reflexions upon that assembly—but as an insult to the powers of Governm[en]t.

[in left margin:] {V[ide] Address—}

But to pass this, & to suppose notwithstand[in]g the word **libellous**, that this house has no regard to the Reputation of the late Ass[em]bly I conceive this to be no Libel.

==

No false or scandalous matter contain[d] in a petition to a Comm[itt]ee of Parl[iamen]t 1 Lev. 240. 1 Sid. 414. 1 Saund. 131. 2 Keb. 832. **or** in articles of the peace[16] exhib[ite]d to the Just[ice]s of the Peace 4 Co. 14. b. or in any other [Pro]ceed[in]g in a regular course of Justice Dyer. 285. Pl. 37. will make a Compl[ain]t amount to a Libel—for discouragem[en]t tho[ugh] the Court has no Jurisd[icti]on. 2 Keb. 832. **but** we are not afraid of that here &c &c &c &c

[*in left margin:*] {Sublato princ[ipa]le tollitur adj[unctum]} {Law of Ægypt}

==

Those things allowable by way of [Pro]secut[i]on but here Mr. Moor acts se defendendo—they publishd {present} their address[17]—he publishes {present} his memorial {If we are wrong—they are wrong—they run parallel. supp[ose] M[oor] acq[uitte]d of Extort[ion]} but grant it to be a Libel then it is turn[in]g the streams of Justice

[*left margin:*] {Θ ✓ Mr. M[oor]'s subseq[uen]t to the Ass[em]bly}

==

House of Com[mons] cant examine Witn[ess] on oath—

==

{Θ}   The Right of Englishmen to debate of their Constitution

==

Which has been always mend[in]g—Long Parl[iamen]t[18]

==

Trial of Seven bishops— Suspend[in]g penal Laws ag[ains]t Papists.

==

If lawful for Mr. M[oor] to make his def[ense]— Lawful to assist him— Sublato princ[ipa]le toll[itur] adj[unctum]
[*in left margin:*] {X} [*page break*]

[*bottom of page:*]
3 Point   If Mr. Smith be guilty.

Assembly's printer had publishd it. with <u>Leave</u>—Smith [conc[erne]d?]

==

Translation only publish[in]g a publick thing   {Council}

==

Then in the Press—how [pro]mote

Ms (PHi-RRL)

---

[1] In the Trial of Seven Bishops (1688), James II brought charges of seditious libel against seven prominent bishops in the Church of England for defying his second Declaration of Indulgence, which ordered them to read it before their congregations and would have decreed religious toleration. The bishops' acquittal in the Court of the King's Bench encouraged James II's opponents to foment the resistance that led to the Glorious Revolution.

[2] Possibly a reference to *Lex Parl.* 63: "If any Offence whatever be committed in the Parliament by any particular Member; it is an high Infringement of the Right and Privilege of Parliament for any Person, or Court, to take the least Notice of it, till the House it self either has punish'd the Offender, or referred them to a due, or proper Course of Punishment. . . . Their Right and Priviledge so far extends, that not only what is done in the very House, sitting the Parliament; but whatever is done relating to them, or in pursuance of their Order, during the Parliament, is no where else to be punish'd but by Themselves, or a succeeding Parliament, tho done out of the House."

[3] See doc. 43, n. 14.

[4] Sir Matthew Hale (1609–1676) was an English jurist best known for his *History of the Pleas of the Crown* (London: E. and R. Nutt, and R. Gosling, 1736). He served as chief justice of the King's Bench, chief baron of the Exchequer, and chief justice of the Common Pleas.

[5] *Barnardiston v. Soame* (or Some), Mich. 26 Car. 2, B.R. (1674). The case concerned Sir Samuel Barnardiston's (1620–1707) election to Parliament. Sir Stephen Soame, sheriff of Suffolk, challenged the results of the election and filed a second false return to prevent Barnardiston from taking his seat. Parliament punished Soame, so the Court ruled he could not be punished twice and the plaintiff had no actionable offense under the common law.

[6] 2 Raymond, *Cases* 958, *Ashby v. White*, Trin. 2 Ann., B.R. (1703) in which reference is made to *Barnardiston v. Soame*: "Although this matter relates to the parliament, yet it is an injury precedaneous to the parliament, as my lord *Hale* said in the case of *Barnardiston vers. Soame*. 2 *Lev[inz].* 114, 116. The parliament cannot judge of this injury, nor give damage to the plaintiff for it: they cannot make him a recompense."

[7] Scipio Africanus (236–183 BC) was a Roman general and consul who made legendary achievements during the Second Punic War (218–201 BC) and in battles against the Carthaginians. Hailed as a hero by the Roman populace, he provoked jealousy in his fellow patricians, who put him on trial for bribery and treason. Scipio then retreated from public life, disillusioned by the ingratitude of his peers.

[8] Lat. as shown (or described) above.

[9] Contempt: "Disobedience or open disrespect to the authority or lawful commands of the sovereign, the privileges of the Houses of Parliament or other legislative body; and, *esp.* action of any kind that interferes with the proper administration of justice by the various courts of law; in this connection called more fully *contempt of court*" (OED). This JD intends to contrast with what Blackstone would later define as a crime: "an act committed, or omitted, in violation of a public law either forbidding or commanding it" (4 *CLE* 5).

[10] Magna Carta (1225) § 29: "No free man shall *in future* be arrested or imprisoned or disseised of his freehold, liberties or free customs, or outlawed or exiled or victimised in any other way, neither will we attack him or send anyone to attack him, except by the lawful judgment of his peers or by the law of the land. To no one will we sell, to no one will we refuse or delay right or justice."

[11] Court of Star Chamber: "An English court of civil and criminal jurisdiction which developed in the late 15th cent. from the judicial sittings of the King's Council in the Star Chamber at

Westminster, trying especially those cases affecting the interests of the Crown" (*OED*); Court of High Commission: "A court of ecclesiastical jurisdiction commissioned by the crown to try various offences against the ecclesiastical establishment, and to crush any resistance to the supremacy of the crown in these matters" (*OED*).

[12] The assertion that Magna Carta had been confirmed thirty times was a popular refrain for those asserting English rights. For example, Robert Rich, second earl of Warwick (1587–1658), gave a speech in the House of Lords in 1628 repeating this claim: "As to *Magna Charta*, and the rest concerning these Points, they are acknowledged by all to be now in force; that they were made to secure the Subjects from wrongful Imprisonment; and that they concern the King as much, or more than the Subject. . . . [W]e know that *Magna Charta* itself, hath been at least 30 Times confirmed; so that now, at this Time, we have 36 or 37 Acts of Parliament to confirm this Liberty." See *The Parliamentary or Constitutional History of England*, 24 vols. (London: J. and R. Tonson and A. Millar, 1751–63), 8: 69.

[13] 2 Raymond, *Cases* 1105, *Regina v. Paty et alios*, Hill. 3 Ann., B.R. (1704). John Paty sued for being denied his right to vote and imprisoned by the House of Commons. In this important due process case, Justice Holt dissented, arguing that Parliament had no legal authority to imprison, and that the House of Commons could not legislate unilaterally without the House of Lords or infringe on the right to sue.

[14] Lat. Every innovation disturbs more by its novelty than it benefits by its utility. The phrase is: *Omnis innovatio plus novitate perturbat quam utilitate prodest*. This was another common refrain of 18th-cent. political and legal thought, that innovation was a danger to be avoided.

[15] 1 Hawkins 193–96 is a chapter titled, "Of Libels:" "*Sect. 1*. . . . That a Libel is a strict Sense is taken for a malicious Defamation, expressed either in printing or Writing, and tending either to blacken the Memory of one who is dead, or the Reputation of one who is alive, and to expose him to publick Hatred, Contempt or Ridicule. *Sect 2*. But it is said, That in a larger Sense the Notion of a Libel may be applied to any Defamation whatsoever, expressed either by Signs or Pictures . . . . *Sect 9*. However it seems clear, that no Writing whatsoever is to be esteemed a Libel, unless it reflect upon some particular Person."

[16] Articles of the Peace: "A Complaint made or exhibited to a court by a person who makes oath that he is in fear of death or bodily harm from some one who has threatened or attempted to do him injury. The court may thereupon order the person complained of to find sureties for the peace and, in default, may commit him to prison" (*BLD*).

[17] One of Moore's complaints in his "Address" was that the Assembly "order[ed] to be published in the common Gazette, a most virulent and slanderous Address, charging me, in the bitterest Terms, with divers Misdemeanors, and corrupt Practices, in my Office" (*PG*, Dec. 1, 1757). That Address, from the Sept. 26 meeting of the Assembly, concluded that after "having heard the Evidence concerning said Charges and Complaints, and being thereupon fully satisfied and convinced, that the said William Moore, Esq; regardless of the impartial and just Discharge of his Duty in the Said Office, and wickedly and corruptly, thro' an avaricious Disposition, and designedly to oppress and distress the poor Inhabitants of the said County, hath greatly misbehaved himself in his said Office." "An Address to the Governor from the Assembly," *PG*, Oct. 6, 1757.

[18] The Long Parliament was named to distinguish it from the so-called Short Parliament, which sat for only three weeks in 1640. The Long Parliament lasted from 1640 until 1660, encompassing the period of the English Civil War. Although it presided over a period of experimentation with republican government and passed laws protecting basic English rights and liberties, it also executed political enemies, most notably Charles I in 1649. As part of the English Civil War, the Long Parliament changed the constitutional structure of England, either for better or for worse depending on whether one was a royalist or a republican. JD notes in doc. 1:53, the people clamored against the Parliament and so "they were obligd to change their conduct" (p. 215).

47
Notes on Thomas Bond's Deposition in the Smith Libel Trial,
[January 17, 1758]

Although Thomas and Phineas Bond are not mentioned by name in the published records of the Assembly's proceedings, the copy of Thomas Bond's examination (only the cover sheet of Phineas Bond's is extant) in JD's papers is dated January 17, which is also the date of the examination given in the "Minutes of the William Smith Trial, January 17, 1758." Although attached to the proceeding document, this is clearly a separate set of notes, both in content and layout. The page is divided in quarto, like a booklet.

[*left side*]
S[mith]'s Exam[inatio]n   A Copy of <u>an</u> address

Dr. Th[omas] B[ond][1]   Soon after a Visit &c M[oor] shewd & read an Add[ress] to the Gov[erno]r wr[i]t[in]g many of the most material paragr[aphs]—day before present[in]g shewd me an interl[ine]d[2] Copy— askd my opin[ion]   I obj[ecte]d   [that?] even[ing] des[ire]d me to come to my Broth[er's][3] to cons[ide]r of the interl[ine]d add[ress] & a new plan. Exam[ine]d both— M[oor]'s copy best, with some small alt[eration]s then trans[criptio]n by Levers[4]   Interl[ine]d Copy dis[p[ose]d?]
==

Never heard—nor saw Mr. S[mith] write—nor that he woud
==

Did not know S[mith] had any hand
==

[*in left margin:*] {was th[at] Add[ress] publ[ishe]d} ~~I never [hear~~?] had Mr. S[mith] had any hand in advis[in]g—revis[in]g or correct[in]g the address— Mr. S[mith] agreed to M[oor]rs plan

[*right side*]
We were all concernd— No pen put to paper   [More?] amend[men]ts [pro]posd by others than S[mith]   [Were?] those alter[ation]s made [{of?}] subst[ance] they were. {S[mith]'s Am[endmen]ts arose in Conv[ersati]on only—} No Certainty
==

Is th[at] {You saw} the same addr[ess] publishd? {&} now before the house? The same in substance
==

~~What time?~~ Was not the draught adherd to by Mr. M[oor] approvd by Council, & declard by them to contain noth[in]g libellous at the time of Consultation or any time before— Yes—

==

Does not know whose hand the Inter[lining?] was in. {No Crim[ina]l part [pro]vd to be S[mith]'s—}

==

Time {of Conv[ersati]on}—after the Election—

==

[*illegible*] {Dr. Th[omas] Bond} consulted Council th[at] his Add[res?]s was lawful— So did Moor

[*lef side*:]
S[mith] never shewd any forwardness in this affair {M[oor] shewd the paper to S[mith] my brother & myself}

==

{Copied by Levers & pres[ente]d}
Some alter[ation]s [~~pro~~]posd {made} from time to time afterw[ar]ds {but not by any of us}. then publishd
M[oor] out of Town—left care of the press to me—Obs[ervation] here princ[ipal] escapes

==

Found a [pro]of of Mr. Brandf[or]d[5] on the table. Figures did not convey his [*illegible*]   he then cast about for somebody to assist him {&} went to S[mith]—he said D[octo]r can you do this as well as I can. he askd me what paper—I told him the proof of M[oor]'s paper— I **prevaild** on him to overlook it as ~~people~~ {printer} waited—made insignif[ican]t Correct[ion]s I then deliv[ere]d it. Obs[ervation] Concealm[en]t no crime—but in Treason.

==

Saw a manuscript Copy—dont know whether before or after publication—

[*right side*]
Was ~~th~~ Lev[ers's] Copy made from S[mith]'s— No [then?] Obs[ervation] {Saw Lev[er]s transcrib[in]g—was pres[en]t when M[oor] deliv[ere]d.} then Mr. S[mith] not concernd in publ[ishin]g this Libel before the house

==

Was any of the alter[ation]s in th[at] copy wh[ich] Levers copied from—in S[mith]'s hand— No. nor made by him. nor had the least hand in them. said to be ano[the]r [Per]sons.

==

Was any altera[tion]s made by direction of prisoner at the Consultat[ion]s—
No, but believe those proposd were rejected.

==

Don't know S[mith] offerd any. Said least of any them

==

What time was this Consultation? After the last Election.

==

Literal {or figures} Correct[ion]s only by S[mith}   Obs[ervation] man to
be comm[itte]d for a Letter—a single Letter

==

Ms (PHi-RRL)

---

[1] Thomas Bond (1713–1784), a physician who trained in Britain and France, practiced medicine with his younger brother, Phineas, at the Pennsylvania Hospital they helped found with Benjamin Franklin.

[2] Interline: "To insert additional words between the lines of (a written, esp. a legal, document)" (*OED*).

[3] Phineas Bond (1717–1773), was a physician who trained in France. He and his brother, Thomas, were also founding members of the American Philosophical Society.

[4] Robert Levers (1723–1788) was a schoolmaster, a bookkeeper, and a clerk for Charles Brockden (1683–1769), when Brockden served as recorder of deeds for Philadelphia. Brockden introduced Levers to provincial secretary Richard Peters, whose notoriously bad handwriting kept Levers modestly employed until Peters's death. Levers also acted as a proxy for Peters's land speculation deals, and he worked as an assistant to postmaster William Franklin (c. 1731–1813) and as a clerk to the governor's secretary. See Francis S. Fox, *Sweet Land of Liberty: The Ordeal of the American Revolution in Northampton County, Pennsylvania* (University Park: Pennsylvania State Press, 2010), 1–35.

[5] William Bradford (1719–1791), printer of the *PJ*, published Moore's "Address" on Dec. 1, 1757. Bradford was the nephew of printer Andrew Bradford (1686–1742), and grandson of printer William Bradford (1663–1752).

48
Draft Transcript of Opening Arguments in the Smith Libel Trial, [January 17, 1758]

This relatively clean and polished document appears to reflect what transpired in the House of Assembly beginning at 3:00 p.m. on January 17. The tidiness of the script indicates JD wrote it after the fact. We have determined the date of composition based on the document heading, but also from the mention at the very end of the inclusion of Thomas Bond's deposition (see doc. 1:47, above), which occurred on January 17, and other depositions not yet in hand, which were taken on January 18 and 19 (see doc. 1:50, below). It is unclear why JD numbered three pages with (5) and three pages with (7).

The present transcript records two noteworthy turns in Smith's defense. First, when Ross preceded to make the arguments JD had outlined in his notes above, the Assembly informed him that they had that morning passed resolutions barring Smith's counsel from making the first two of those arguments; second, when Ross immediately demurred to the Assembly's authority on the matter, Smith stopped Ross and turned his defense over to JD.

---

(1)

Before the Honourable the Representatives of the Freemen of Pennsylvania, in
Assembly met—

Wednesday 17[th] of Jan[ua]ry 1758—

The Rev[eren]d Mr. Smith was brought to the Barr of the house by the Serjeant {at} Arms; & the Speaker[1] acquainted him from the Chair, That he was brought before the house to answer a Charge of ~~aiding~~ {abetting} & promoting the Writing & publishing a Libel intituld The Address of William Moore Esq[ui]r[e].

> The Clerk[2] orderd to read the Address— (here insert the Address)

Mr. Speaker.   Mr. Smith, this house has thought [pro][per] to make the following
Resolves {in your case} & orders them to be read, that You & your Counsel may not
Meddle with those points which they have already determind.

> Clerk orderd to read the Resolves (here insert them)

Resolvd

1.*[*in left margin:*] {*It is not pretended to give the express words of the Resolves[3] [as?] the house never woud [per]mit Mr. Smith to have a Copy of them.

There were likewise some other Resolves, declaring in general terms that it was highly criminal to reflect on the Assembly or to publish any thing derogatory of their Rights & Priv[ileges] & that the present House had Authority to take Notice of such things & punish those who shoud be guilty of them.} That Mr. Smith or his Counsel shall not be allowd to speak or argue against the Authority or Power of this House to take Cognizance of the Charge against him.

2. That Mr. Smith or his Counsel shall not be allowd to speak or argue that the Addressed W[illia]m Moor Esq[ui]r[e] is not a Libel.

Mr. Ross Counsel for Mr. Smith   Mr. Speaker, I have the Honour to appear before this house as Counsel on behalf of Mr. Smith who stands chargd with abetting & promoting the writing & publish[in]g the Libel that has been read— I Sir, have the greatest Reverence for Parliaments, & for the Constitution of this Gov[ernmen]t. I shoud be very far from encouraging any attempts to injure it, I shall therefore pay the greatest Respect to the Resolves You have been pleasd to have read: tho[ugh]

Indeed they take away the very points we intended to have insisted on: for we designd Mr. Sp[ea]ker to make 3 points in this Case— 1ˢᵗ— Whether this Hon[ora]ble House has Cognizance {of this Cause} even supposing Mr. Moore's Address to be a Libel— 2ˡʸ Whether it be a Libel or no— 3ˡʸ Whether Mr. Smith be guilty as he stands chargd [*page break*]

(2)

These I say Mr. Sp[ea]ker are the points we designd to have insisted on in Mr. Smith's defence, but as this Hon[ora]ble House has been pleasd to make these Resolves, We are debarrd from speaking to any but the last— This Sir lays us under very great Hardships, but to be sure this House is the best Judge of their own proceedings, & their Resolves must be Laws to Us: I shall not say a word Mr. Sp[ea]ker on those points You have determind, but look on Myself to be quite stopt from going any further on them: {I shall not open my Lips about them: I will keep Myself within the Limits which this Hon[ora]ble House is pleasd to set, & shall behave myself with that submission which is due to the Representatives of the Freemen of Pennsylvania; & shall therefore confine Myself entirely to the 3.ᵈ Point—

Mr. Smith.   Mr. Sp[ea]ker, I beg that I may be indulgd for with a few words on this occasion {as} My Counsel has given up points that I never consented to, I hope the House will be so good as to allow me to insist on things of such high Concern not only to me but every man in this province. I shoud be very glad Mr. Sp[ea]ker that this hon[ora]ble House woud be pleasd to give an Instance 1.ˢᵗ This House has been pleasd to make some Resolves in my Case, which have entirely deprivd Me of my Defence: It is impossible Mr. Speaker, for Me to consider these Resolves as Laws; I shoud therefore be very much obligd to the House if they woud for my Satisfaction & that of the Audience shew their Conduct to be Parliamentary, by giving Precedents in support [*page break*]

(3)

> of their Resolves—I shoud be glad Mr. Speaker to have a Precedent
> {to shew} that the House of Commons at home had ever taken upon
> them to try a Man for a Libel w[ith]out remitting to the Courts of
> Law, except the Author had been one of their own Members— 2^{ly}
> To shew that ever a Subsequent House of Commons had taken
> Cognizance of any thing written ag[ains]t a former House—

Mr. Isaac Norris   May it please the Speaker, I think it my Duty to say
> something in Vindication of the Proceedings of this House on the
> present Occasion. They have made several Resolves in this Case,
> wh[ich] are said to deprive them {Gentleman at the Barr} of
> their {his} Defence. I take it May it please the speaker, that this
> house has a Right to Prescribe the Modes of their own Trials; this
> every Court does.
>
> The Points that have now been resolvd, were so clear & evident
> that this House was convincd, they coud be disputed only to protract
> the Cause to an unnecessary Length: Their Reasons therefore must
> {be approvd of} by all unprejudicd People; be approvd of & I
> cannot conceive how it coud be [con?] expected that this House
> woud sit & hear that Authority which "undoubtedly belongs" to
> them, disputed.

Mr. Joseph Galloway—[4]   I believe every worthy Member of this House is
fully ^{X} [*in left margin:*] {X perswaded that the Motives for making these
Resolves were very just & strong—& I dare say they will not condemn them
now by departing from them: if it was necessary & not incompatible with
the Honour of this House, it woud be easy to shew Numberless Instances &
Precedents upon Precedents where [the] House of Commons have
proceeded in this M[ann]er ag[ains]t Criminals}
Speaker.   I wonder how the Prisoner at the Barr can desire that We shoud
> over look our own Resolves, because he is not satisfied: It is beneath
> the <u>Dignity</u> of this House to have their Jurisdiction denied, in Cases
> where they are know it is so plain & theref[ore] I wish He & his
> Counsel woud Proceed accor[ding] to the Directions of the
> House—
Upon this Mr. Smith & his Counsel seemd to be in a good dea[l] of
Confusion— He entreated Mr. Dickinson if it was possible, to bring the
Points determind in the Resolves into the Consideration of the House again.
He answerd it was impossible to attempt it $^\Theta$ [*in left margin:*] {Θ it without
enraging the Memb[er]s   But Mr. Smith persisting with [*illegible*] in his
Request—he began [*page break*]

(4)

Mr: Speaker, I appear before this Hon[oura]ble House, ~~as Counsel~~ to assist Mr: Smith in making his Defence.

We designd to have proceeded Sir, in the manner that has been mentiond by the Gentleman who spoke first in this Cause; ~~and [illegible] that Order~~ but as the House has disapprovd of that Order, We have been {so much} disconcerted ~~& thrown into {so much} Confusion~~, as scarcely to know what Method to pursue.

It woud give Me great Uneasiness to say any thing which shoud not express the respectful Deference I feel for the Determinations of this House; & if I shoud commit any such Error, I hope it will be candidly attributed to the Difficulties I am under & ~~th~~{My} little Experience ~~will~~ {in} the Usages of Parliaments or Assemblies.

On the other hand ~~Sir~~, I shoud think myself ~~justly~~ {greatly} blameable, if I shoud fail in my Duty to Mr. Smith by omitting any thing that may be urgd in his favour when perhaps his Reliance upon Me has prevented his engaging {the Assistance of } others in his Cause.

I hope therfore Sir, that while I endeavour to avoid the Imputation of Negligence, I shall not incurr another Charge that woud make Me equally unhappy; and I flatter Myself that I shall not do this; because I know Mr. Smith's Sentiments, & what he expects from Me on this occasion.

If he entertaind the least Intention of [~~attacking~~] {opposing} your {just} Rights, ~~some other Person than Me {than me} must have had the~~ {I shoud not have the} Honour of addressing You at this time: [*illegible*] ~~I have too} much Reverence for the Representatives of a Free People, to engage in any such Scheme. And permit Me to say, that Mr. Smith [torn] [illegible] such. If indeed~~ {But Sir,[X] [*in left margin:*] {X But Sir, Mr. Smith does not desire Me to engage in any such ~~Scheme~~ {Design—} If indeed he appeald} He appeald to {any} other Authority for Assistance; [~~two illegible lines~~] it might be calld an Attempt to limit your Jurisdiction or if he applied to any other Power for Protection, he might be accusd [*page break*]

(5)

{of derogating from your Dignity. But Sir,}

But Sir, he [~~illegible~~] {does nothing} of this Sort: He desires no other Judges of your Priviledges, but Yourselves.

He submits with chearfulness to your Decision and only {humbly} prays—that You will call your view [~~illegible~~] {upon} some Points of the utmost Importance; which perhaps the Wisdom of this House will think worthy of their Consideration.

It is easy to perceive from the Audience now present that this is a Cause of Expectation, & engages the {earnest} Attention of the People of this Province.

Whether <u>they</u> apprehend themselves to be co[ncer]nd in the Event, I cannot say: But tho[ugh] it seems to be of the greatest Consequence to Mr. Smith, I am convincd the Honour of this House is as much interested, as the Happiness of that Gentleman.

This Opinion is founded on a fact so evident, that it cannot be disputed: [~~illegible~~] {And yet I shoud be afraid to mention ^X [*in left margin:*] {X mention it, if I did not Recollect that Truth exprest with ~~the~~ Decency ~~that becomes Me in this place~~, can never offend good Men. What I woud beg Leave to observe with great Respect, is that the Members of} with great Respect, {is} that the Members of this House now sit as Judges in their own Cause; And tho[ugh] I am perfectly satisfied how well their Integrity will guard against every Insinuation of Prejudice, Yet permit Me with submission to say; It will be more difficult to guard against the Reflections of ~~the [illegible]~~] World

If ~~therefore~~ any Occasion therefore shoud be afforded ~~for~~ {to} the Public to imagine, Mr. Smith has been deprivd of a full Defence; the Justice of this House may receive a perpetual Stain from those Acts, which for one hasty Moment were thought extremely fair & reasonable.

As to the Reverend Gentleman at the Barr, Commitment being your method of Punishment, no less than his Liberty depends on your Determination; and in a Question relating to the Liberty of a Fellow-subject, I dont doubt but this [*page break*]

(5)
House will always proceed with Caution and Circumspection.

What renders these still more necessary in this Case is; that ~~the~~ if any Mistake shoud be ~~made~~ committed, (& with great respect I speak it, Bodies of Men may err as well as Individuals) No Redress of our Grievance ~~coud~~ {can} be obtaind in this Province; for I understand Sir, that You think, persons committed by You, cannot be baild on an Habeas Corpus.

If any Error then shoud happen in this [Pro]ceeding, and Mr. Smith in Consequence of that Error, shoud be deprivd of his Liberty, he must bear the Punishment that follows, {[~~illegible~~]} without a Possibility of Relief; And all his Comfort, <u>if that is any</u>, will be, to know it is **unjust**.

But Sir, I shoud not speak of Mr. Smith alone: This is the Cause of every man in the Province.

This interesting Point is now to be determind, **Whether** this House can try a man ~~for~~ according to the Forms of the Courts of Law, & imprison him for an Offence that is cognizable in those Courts; {which} has ever been decided in them, & is bailable there; that is, if they can thus restrain ~~him~~ {A Man} of his Liberty ~~by~~, when by the **known** Laws of his Country, & in the **usual** way of Proceeding he woud enjoy it.

Much might be said, Sir, of that careful Tenderness with which our Mother-Country has in all ages watchd over her growing Freedom, till it arrivd to its present State of Strength & Security: But I shall not insist on a Subject, which ~~I am {the Conduct of} sure this Hon[oura]ble House must be {has shewn} {it to be} so much {well} better acquainted with than I am.~~ {I am convincd this House must be so well acquainted with——

I woud only observe, that it has ever been a favourite [*page break*]

(6)

Maxim of her Policy, to settle her Rights by public & positive Laws: So that no man coud be deprivd of his Reputation, his Liberty or his Life ~~or his Property~~, but by Rules as clear & indubitable as ~~those by which he held these Blessings~~ {the acknowledgd Values & Beauty of those Blessings}

For this Purpose the Statute of Magna Charta was made; and has been above ~~thir~~{for}ty times solemnly confirmd.   In the 29th Chapter of that Statute[,?] it is enacted "That no Freeman shall be taken or imprisond, or be disseizd of his Freehold, or Liberties or free Customs, or be outlawd or exild, or be otherwise destroyd, nor will We pass upon him nor condemn him, but by lawful Judgment of his Peers, or by the Law of the Land."

This Clause contains the sacred Rules for the Trial of Englishmen: But any Determination of this House {against Mr. Smith} cant be calld the "Judgment of his Peers": The meaning of those important & invaluable Words is too well known.

How far then, can this Proceeding be said to be governd by the "Law of the Land"?

Tis true that My Lord Coke in his Explanation of this Statute, says the Lex Parliamentaria[5] is included therein. Perhaps it was within the Meaning of the Legsilature at that time; for the Jurisdiction of the Parliament might with ~~some~~ propriety be calld the Law of the Land.

The Rights & Powers of the House of Commons in England undoubtedly belong to <u>them</u>, as much as the Right of being represented in Parliament belongs to the People in general; those Rights & Powers having existed as long as the House itself, & being intermixt with the very Constitution of the English Government {; and perhaps the Wit of Man coud invent no other manner of forming a limited monarchy.}

But there never was an Instance where this House has determind on such an Offence as ~~that~~{e present} chargd against Mr. Smith; And how an Authority hitherto <u>unheard of</u> and <u>unexercisd,</u> can be calld the "Law of the

Land" does not seem Easy to be shewn. Especially considering this House has been constituted since the Statute of Magna [*in left margin:*] Charta & by a Charter from the Crown.   Granting however Sir, that this house is invested with all the Rights Powers & Priviledges of the Commons in England, I believe I may venture to say, there is no Example even there of such a Proceeding as this.   I do not remember that the House of {Vide pa. 7.} [*page break*]

(7)

I do not remember that the House of Commons ever committed a man for Writing or publishing a Libel, without alledging it to be a Contempt or Breach of Priviledge: But the warrant for taking Mr. Smith into Custody, the Notice sent him by the Clerk of the House, & the Charge made against him since he came here, only accuse him of writing & publishing a Libel in general, without the least suggestion of those things,which I presume are absolutely necessary to give this house Cognizance.

In ~~the Address of the Lords to Queen Anne in~~ the great ~~Cause~~ Affair of Ashby & White, ~~they expressly declare,~~ {[*illegible words*] the Lords [thou[gh]t?]} that with respect to the ~~Author Jurisdict~~ Authority only of the Commons, "there is a great Difference between Matters **solely** cognizable in Parliament, as Contempts Breaches of Priviledge or things done & movd in Parliament, and **matters cognizable in the Courts of Law**, which might have some Relation to Parliament."[6]

And indeed in the latter Case, there ~~have been~~ {are} several Instances where the Commons themselves have been so cautious of turning the Streams of Justice, as to remit Offenders against their Dignity to the Courts of Common Law, when perhaps by a full Exertion of their {disputed} Power, they might {themselves} have determind ~~[illegible]~~ ~~[It yet?] themselves~~ {the affairs.}

Thus even in their Anger, they have been ~~cautious~~ {prudent,}, & have allowd ~~of~~ such Trials {to others} as they themselves woud ~~chuse~~ wish for, if any thing dear to them was at stake. 🔲[7]

The Power of this Honourable House is undoubtedly ~~very great~~ extensive: ~~Its Dignity is very great: This I shall always respect; & to that I shall~~ {ever} [*page break*]

(7)

~~readily submit.~~   But it cannot be **unlimited**. For an unlimited Power was never heard of under an English Constitution.

Now Sir, this Offence as it is chargd against Mr. Smith, has no more Relation to Parliamentary Proceedings, than Murder or Robbery; and if this House can take Notice of it in this manner, I cannot conceive, why every {other} Crime may not be enquird into & punishd here, ~~and~~ nor why the Power of this House may not be Properly termd **unlimited**.

Mr. Smith desires Me Sir, to inform You & this Hon[oura]ble House, that he looks upon it to be his indubitable Right as an Englishman, if he is tried at all for this supposd Offence, to be tried by his Peers, on an Enquiry by the Grand Inquest of the Country[;?] and he hopes that this House, whose Employment is to preserve the Liberties of the People of this Province, will not be displeasd with his Zeal on insisting on what he apprehends to be his Birthright.

He therefore prays; as such Condescentions have been made by the house of Commons, that he may be remitted to the usual Course of Law.

~~We beg Leave, Mr. Speaker, to submit~~ {Sir}, [*page break*]

(7)

~~Mr. Smith {We} begs Leave, Mr. Speaker, to submit one thing more to the Consideration of this Honourable House.~~

The Fact M.{r Smith} is chargd with, is either a Libel, or it is not. If it is a Libel, {&} ~~Mr. Smith~~ {it shoud provd ~~to be~~{that Mr. Smith} concerted in it, he} may certainly be indicted & punishd for it in the Courts of Law; {for I will venture to say, not ᵒ [*in left margin:*] {ᵒ not a single Instance can be shewn, where a{n} ~~Judgment~~ Order of the House of Commons was pleaded in Bar to an Indictment at Common Law.} ~~t~~{T}herefore if You proceed against him ~~too~~, he will suffer two punishments for one & the same Crime, which our Law justly regards with the utmost Detestation.

Nay Sir, even this may {not} be all he will undergo for this Offence. If this House can punish for "Reflections thrown on the Members of the late House, & for Derogations of the Rights of Assembly in general" ~~which i[s?]~~ ~~[illegible] [description~~?] {as} ~~of~~ this Address {is decsribd} in a Message lately sent to the Governor, Every <u>future</u> Assembly seems to be as much interested in <u>these Points</u>, as the <u>present</u>; & Mr. Smith may be committed during his Life.

This is the very reason assignd in the Lawbooks, Why [~~illegible~~] {a Subsequent} Parliament cannot take Notice of what was done ag[ains]t another , {(}as Levinz pa. [*blank*] expressly says, "for fear a man might be always committed[.]⁸
{This comes in, at the bottom in a Note)}

~~If the~~ If the Fact Mr. Smith is chargd with, is not a Libel, then your Resolve is directly contradicted; & of Consequence We have been deprivd of a free, fair & legal Defence; for We intended to have offerd some Reasons to the House to {have} shewn that Mr. Moore's Address was not a Libel in the Sense of the Law: But We were not permitted.

All therefore that I can now pretend to say, is ~~humbly~~ to desire You & every member of the ~~Honourable~~ House to take into your ~~wise~~ Consideration, the Influence of such a Precedent in times to come. [*illegible words*] ~~A Regard~~ [*page break*]

[*torn; one or more lines of text loss*] [*illegible line*]

The Case now ~~under the Determination~~ pending before the House is an uncommon one: {And tho[ugh]} The Consequences of your ~~Determination~~, {Judgment [*after*?]} are unknown, ~~but~~{Yet} I apprehend, [*illegible*] {*importance*?] {~~which~~} {they are {of} very great Moment}

Your decision is not to be considerd alone, ~~as~~ confind to the Limits of Mercy & Equity, as I am perswaded it will be: But [*illegible*] {I [*illegible*]} {I imagine} Sir, that to form a ~~careful~~ full View of its Importance, We must consider the Pretensions it may hereafter give Rise {to,}, & the extent to which those Pretensions may be carried.   For Sir, a small Acquaintance with History will convince Us, that Acts of power not very alarming in themselves, have afterwards provd Precedents for dangerous Demands & dreadful Determinations.   It must for this Reason be proper, upon such Occasions as the present, to pursue these Reflections with some {degree of} Freedom; & [*illegible*] {permit me Sir, while I} feel the utmost Reverence for the Opinion of this house, to remember that ~~in the Ex[*illegible*] of~~ ~~[*illegible*]~~, Actions [not?] which could scarcely be calld wrong, have become fatal in their Effects to future Ages.

No People ~~Mr. Speaker~~, can {reasonably} expect to enjoy that peculiar Blessing, of which there never has been an Instance in the World; {I mean} of being <u>always</u> governd by wise & good Rulers.

If then Sir, ambitious or wicked men shoud ever have
[*lower third of page blank*]
[*page break*]

(12)
Mr. Dickinson— {Here insert what he said for which Vide page 4.}

Here Mr. Norris & Mr. Galloway {interrupted Mr. Dickinson &} spoke for some time. Mr. Norris insisted that the House was invested with the Rights & Pow[er]s of the House of Commons; that they had often committed [Per]sons for e{C}ontempts & Breach of Priviledges & that the Proceeding[s] of this House were agreable to the Rules of Parliament. {Mentiond some man who was committed by the House[.]}

Mr. Galloway quoted ~~a good~~ several Instances out of the Miscellanea Parl[iamen]taria,[9] when the House of Commons had committed

Persons, & said they were quite similar to the pres[ent] Case. This he calld a great favour, & said it was as absu[rd] & irrigular {to allow} ~~for~~ Mr. Smith & his Counsel to dispute the[ir] Authority, as it woud be in the King's Bench in Westminster Hall, to suffer a Defendant to plead to the Jurisdiction, because the Sum demanded was above £500— That as to remitting to the Court of Common [O] [*in left margin:*] {[O] Common Law it was inconsistent with their Dignity to send down Offenders against them; as if they had not Authority to punish the most trifling Offences—}

Mr. Ross— Here Mr. Ross recited the Substance of the {Abbhorers[10]} Case ~~of the~~ & Colepepers (insert them here in Mr. Ross words) & then offerd to read Burnett & Rapin's History[11] in confirmation of what he had said: But ~~the Speaker~~ Mr. Norris objected to reading them) & the Speaker told Mr. Ross, that they woud hear no Quotations but out of the Parliamentary Proceedings {that their Rules & Proceedings were different from those of the {*} [*in left margin:*] {* Courts of Common Law}}; that they woud not listen to old Histories; that he had read a Book calld Mother Shipton's Tales[12] himself, & he might as well quote that. Mr. Ross told the Speaker, he had an Authority {in Lord Coke's work} to prove that the Law of Parliament coud not be understood without having Recourse to History; but he was not allowd to read either of the Books.

    Here Mr. Dickinson's second speech comes in {for which} Vide pa. 13. [*page break*]

(13)

Mr. Dickinson— Mr.Speaker {I shall be greatly obligd to this Honourable Hou[se]} [*] [*in left margin:*]{ * House, if they will {be} so good as to indulge Me with {~~the Liberty of~~} a few words. ~~I shoud be sincerely sorry, Sir, if I shoud transgress the Rules of this House; &~~ It has been observd by ~~a Worthy~~ Member, "that it woud be as absurd & Irregular to allow Mr. Smith to dispute the Authority of this House, as it woud be in the King's Bench in Westminster Hall, to suffer a Def[endan]t to plead to the Jurisdiction, because the Sum demanded was above £500—" With great Respect to the Opinion of the Member, I beg leave to submit, that the Inconsistency does not seem to <u>Me</u> equally strong in both Cases. The Jurisdiction of the King's Bench has been clearly & completely settled for a long ~~while~~ {time}. It has taken Cognizance of actions {for several hundred Years,}, not only of £500— Value, but of infinitely greater Importance. So that the Man who objects to their [*illegible*]} {The same} worthy Member ~~of this [house?]~~ h[as] been pleasd to favour

186

Us, with several Instances of Commitments by the ~~House of~~ Commons {of England} as similar to our Case. Every Instance that has been quoted (except Colepeper's) was a Commitment of some Member for a Contempt or Breach of Priviledge, by the very Parliament the {person} had offended ag[ains]t—. But Ours ~~is not the Case of~~ Case has no Resemblance to these, in one single Particular. Mr. Smith is not a Member; he is not chargd with a Contempt or Breach of Priviledge, nor is this {the} House ~~offended against.~~ {ag[ains]t which the Offence} [*illegible line*] ~~if any was committed.~~ against which the Offence was committed.

The Power of the House of Commons, is certainly very great: But we find from Colepeper's Case, that when they extended their Power to punish other than their {own} Members, {for things done out of the house} the People of England became alarmed, they questiond their Authority claimd by them; ~~they~~ {Some} refusd to submit to it. In shor[t] the House of Commons grew cooler & wiser, & Remitted Colpeper to the Courts of Common Law.

[*in left margin*:] ~~H. of C[*illegible*][it?]~~ / ~~In[*torn*]~~

However Sir, allowing the Hous[e] [*torn*] has such Power: ~~& that this house has [*torn*] Power with them~~; Yet Sir, {with great subm[*torn*]} I cant thin[k?] [*torn*] Proceedings in Mr. Smith's Case can [*torn*] ~~to~~ {on} any {[*illegible*]} in the House of Commons, [that?] [*torn*]

~~There are several Circumstances [besides?] [*torn*] have~~ {been} ~~mentiond, that [*illegible*] with this Case from any one are cited. Mr. Smith is [formally?] chargd wit[h] [*torn*] [in answer to?] [*illegible*] [& calld to his Defence or in the?] [*illegible*]~~ [*page break*]

(14)

~~Courts of Law, That [*illegible*]ion is a [*illegible*]an Offence punishable at Law without any suggestion of the facts necessary to give this House Cognizance in a Parliamentary way. This House designs to proceed in the trial according to that [*illegible*] of [*torn*]~~[13]

~~Th[*torn*] [*illegible line*] the Proceedings in the House of Commons, that they [*illegible*] to constitute [*illegible*] different Jurisdiction, which being gradually extended, may produce all the Mischiefs Questions to this Honourable House f[*illegible words*]~~]

~~But Sir, the [*illegible*] of this Proceeding is not mor[e][*illegible words*]~~ {the} ~~Authority [*illegible*] [it is had.?]~~

In the first place Mr. Smith is [*illegible*] chargd with "Abetting & promoting the Writing & publishing a Libel" but is not said to ~~have committed~~ {be guilty {of}} any Breach of Priviledge, or ~~to be guilty~~ of any Contempt. One of these things I ~~beg leave to say~~ {conceive}, is necessary to

187

give this House Jurisdiction {<u>in a Parliamentary way.</u>}. Secondly, Mr. Smith's Offence, if it is any, was committed ~~at~~ [a time?] precedent to the Existence of this House, {.} ~~and [illegible] the~~ If we are allowd Sir, We hope to shew, that these are good Objections ~~and~~ to the Proceedings ag[ains]t Mr. Smith. No instance has been mentiond, where the House of Comnmons in England, has taken Notice of any thing that happend in ano[the]r Parliament. {;} ~~except in Colepepper's Case, & there they~~ {~~did not [illegible]~~} ~~[illegible] to a Court of Law.~~

{And} ~~But~~ in our Province Sir, ~~if any Preced[ent]~~ {not a single} Precedent can be shewn, where the Assembly has ~~taken~~ proceeded, upon <u>such</u> a Charge as the present, & undertaken to punish an Offence committed <u>before</u> they were a House * Vide Margin [*in left margin*:] {* Thirdly— This house proceeds according to the exact <u>forms</u> of Trials in a Court of Law, by [~~illegible~~] ~~[for the?]~~ [~~illegible~~] examining the Witnesses upon <u>oath</u>.

These things I beg Leave to say [*torn*] [*torn*]y proceedings [&?] [~~illegible~~] in the House of Commons, I have heard mentiond by the least [*torn*] seem to constitute a new Jurisdiction, which being gradually extended may produce all the Mis[*torn*] [~~illegible~~] some time ago. } [*page break*]

(15)

~~If this be the Case there[,] & with Submission~~ {If the Circumstances of our Case are such Sir, as I have represented them then} I t[*torn*] its [~~illegible~~] the{at the} proceeding ag[ains]t Us is unprecedented, & the Authority, hither to unheard of, & unexcersizd.

I submit [~~to~~] {th} is Cause therefore with great Respect to the Wisdom of this Honourable House[,?] as an Affair of the utmost Consequence to every Man in this Province.

It must be acknowledgd that there are no Examples {amongst Us} of this sort. ~~Our Case is therefore, what the Lawyers call a Case "[Prima] [impressioni]s~~[14] Alterations of every [~~sor~~?] kind, Sir, are dangerous; Perhaps none are more so, than Alterations ~~of~~ in Power. Ours is a Case that will, I hope, deserve the particular Consideration of the House {It is what the Lawyers call a Case "Prima Impress[ionis"} Our Liberty depends on the determination of a New & unsettled Point.

The Courts of Law, Sir, have on many Occasions observd a commendable Caution, when Attempts have been made to introduce new D[*torn*] That a thing has never ~~happend~~ {been done}, has been [*torn*] good Argument that {it} coud not legally [*torn*]

Littleton in his Tenures, speak[s?] [*torn*] {Penalties imposd {on Lords} by the} Statute of Merton,[15] for Disparagemen[t] [*torn*] says that no Action can be brought [*torn*] "Si Parentis conquerantur"[16] because it [never] heard of that any {such} Action was brought.[17]

So in Onslow's Case in Levinz[18] it was determin[d] that no action lay for a double Return to Parliament
[*in left margin:*] {Who objects to their Authority in such a Cause, woud [*illegible*] aim at that [ver]y thing, which We humbly [*illegible*] ~~this House to~~ {[*illegible*] ought now to be} avoid{ed,} that is, the introducing a Novelty. For it woud be as uncommon for that Court to <u>refuse</u> to take Cognizance of such an action, as it is in the present Case, for this House to <u>claim</u> Cognizance. The Difference then between that Case & Ours, is: That there the Jurisdiction is Antient, here quite new: there it {is well known &} never was <u>denied</u>; & [*illegible words*] {here it is unknown & never ~~was~~} <u>demanded</u>. ~~But not withstanding the~~ {Established} [Antiquity] ~~& [Extent?] of [illegible]~~ {But not withstanding the Estab[lished] Extent of that Court's Jurisdiction {[*illegible*]} in Cases where}, [~~the Judges present so much?~~] [*illegible*] ~~in Cases where particular actions [illegible]~~ {particular Actions are given by [*illegible*] [Statutes?]—} the P[[lainti]ffs?] [must?] ~~alledge~~ mention the ~~Stat~~ Act on ~~what~~{which}they are founded; so great is the Reverence preservd, for the ~~Institutions~~ {[Customs} of Antiquity:{; &} The same ~~worthy~~ Member so careful ~~to~~{in} causing the Reasons of a new Authority to appear—} [*page break*]

(16)

by a Sheriff, because there was no account of any such action. What makes this last case the more remarkable, is, that this Custom of making double Returns was become very common, & was a great Grievance: So that there were above 70 double Returns made to one Parliament. Yet notwithstanding the Mischief, the Judges never coud be inducd to depart so much from {the} old Rules {of Law} as to allow of an action for this cause.

At Length by 7 & 8 King Will[ia]m 2.[d] an Action was given for double Returns.[19]
If the Courts of Law have behavd with so much Circumspection, ~~about~~ {in regard to} a doubtful <u>Action</u>; ~~because~~ it seems to be infinitely more necessary, in a debate concerning a New <u>Authority</u>, that [~~will?~~] {not} only deprives One freeman of his Liberty; but affects the Rights of Every Man in Penns[ylvania.]

No Man, I daresay, {[~~Mr. Speaker~~?]} apprehends that this Honourable House will unjustly or oppressively abuse the Power they now claim. But what may be the Consequences of a Change is unknown. [C?] ~~Alterations~~ {Novelties} in every Government produce Contention & Confusion:{:} "Omnis Innovatio plus novitate perturbat, quam Utilitate prodest." Every Innovation does more harm by the Distraction it introduces, than the Evil it is designd to prevent, woud have done by its Continuance. * [*in left margin:*] {* If Sir, as We apprehend, {the Cognizance of} Offences of this ki[nd] ha~~ve~~{d} hitherto always belongd to his Majesty's Courts; [*torn*] [~~*illegible line*~~] {Authority now insisted on may not [only?] [affect]} Not only, [*torn*] of this province [~~*illegible words*~~] ~~the [*illegible*] of their force~~ Its importance {may} extend something [*torn*]ly say, That Power like the Ocean {very dangerous & very [useful?]} never changes its Bounds without Destruction. [~~*several illegible lines*~~] ~~sandy Isla[nds] or along barren Shore.~~ [~~*illegible words*~~] [*torn*] [~~*illegible lines*~~] [*torn*] [~~*illegible*~~] It's Over flowing may drown [~~*illegible*~~] <u>Palaces</u>, Cities & Fields; [~~*illegible words*~~] [*torn*] sandy Isla[nds] or along barren Shore. [*torn*] parts.}

Extraordinary & unusual Methods are certainly to be avoided, where there is a more easy & simple Remedy. If Mr. Smith has been guilty of any Offence, it is punishable in the Courts of Common Law. He entreats this Honourable [*page break*]

(17)

House, that they will allow him that Noble and Inestimable Priviledge, ~~to~~ which he [~~*illegible*~~] {is entituld to by his Birth;} the Priviledge of being tried by his Peers.

I hope Sir, Th~~is~~{at}] [~~*illegible*~~] {Remitting to a Court of Law} will not be thought to interfere with the Dignity of the House, as it has been done by the Commons of England. [*in left margin:*] {Vide page 12.} It cannot possibly look "As if they had not Authority to punish the most trifling Offences": since the more trifling they are, the less worthy they woud be to imploy the Time & Attention of this Honourable House. . . . .

Here Mr. Norris, Mr. Galloway, Mr. Hughes, Mr. Fox[20] & several ~~more~~ {other} Members rose up one after another & desird the House to remember their Resolves; that the Counsel had actually ~~been speaki[ng]~~?] {engagd their Attention} [*torn*] those very Points, which it h[*torn*] they shoud {not} speak on. That the [*torn*] exposd to Ridicule by making Reso[*torn*] they had not firmness enough to [*torn*] their Lenity had extended too far alre[*torn*] as to their Authority, it woud be vain [*torn*] convincing those, who woud not be [*torn*] And in the present Case it was unbecomi[*torn*] their Dignity, to suffer any Enquiries into [th?][*torn*] {their Authori[ty]} Norris said, that the House of Commons had often [*page break*]

(18)

proceeded in the same manner that the~~{is}~~ House had done. That there was an Instance some years ago of one [*blank*] whom the~~{is}~~ House {of Assembly} had committed for a Contempt.[21] That ~~if the~~ the [*torn*] [proceeded?] [*torn*] [to the Petition?] [*torn*] Resolves were binding upon them, till they saw proper to alter them; & if the Counsel proceeded according to the Directions of the House, <u>perhaps</u> they might be so good afterwards as to allow them to speak on those Points that were now to be waivd.

Mr. Galloway said it was derogatory of & destructive to the Rights & the Honour of the House, to permit the Counsel to insist on those Points that were already settled.

~~That it woud be altogether as absurd for the House~~ That it coud not be expected that the [Hou]se woud go into an Enquiry about their Jurisd[iction] in the Prisoner's Case, when they had given the[ir] Judgment in More's: That it ~~coud~~ woud be altogether as absurd, as for a Court of Law to enquire into their Authority, when they were trying an Accessary to a Crime, after they had tried & condemnd the Principal, & he was executed: * [*in left margin:*] {[*torn*] If this has any meaning, Whether [*torn*] ["That] [*torn*] to add Guilt [*torn*]d, than to be [*torn*] that the first [*torn*]} Which he said was such a barefaced piece of [~~*illegible*~~] Folly & Inconsistency as no Court coud be guilty of. [*page break*]

(19)

Upon this {that} House, "[~~*illegible*~~] multâ viâ,"[22] determind that the Counsel shoud not say any more, on the two first Points; but that the Witnesses shoud be calld, & they shoud immediately proceed to {~~taking~~} the Examinations.

Mr. Smith's Examination ~~taken~~ when he was ~~first~~ brought before the House on his being first taken into Custody was read
Here insert Mr. Smith's Examination

After reading this Examination, they calld Dr. Thomas Bond Who was sworn & gave this Evidence
Here Insert Dr. Thomas Bond's Testimony & then all the other Witnesses in their Order—

Ms (PHi-RRL)

---

[1] The Assembly elected Isaac Norris II (1701–1766) to serve as speaker in October, but upon reconvening on Jan. 2, 1758, they received notice that "Mr. Speaker was so much indisposed as to be unable to attend publick Business," and so unanimously chose Thomas Leech (c. 1685–1762) to serve in his stead. *Votes* (1758), 9. Leech was an Anglican merchant and member from Philadelphia Co. who regularly replaced Norris as speaker during Norris's periods of illness, some of which conveniently coincided with politically uncomfortable moments in the Assembly such as the Smith trial. Indeed, Leech's Anglicanism prevented any charges that Quakers were targeting Smith because of his religious persuasion. *Votes* does not indicate when Norris returned to the Assembly, but this document confirms that he was an active participant in the trial.

---

[2] Charles Moore (1725–1801), a physician, was appointed clerk after his twin brother, Thomas, resigned from the Assembly in 1757. He served until 1776.

[3] In the evening of Jan. 11, 1758, the Assembly passed four resolves in regard to Moore's "Address": 1. That to publish a libel on the Assembly's proceedings violated the members' rights; 2. That Moore's "Address" was "a false, scandalous, virulent and seditious Libel;" 3. To claim that the Assembly could not examine complaints into the behavior of public officials "promote[d] and encourage[d] wicked Men in oppressing and distressing the Community"; 4. That Moore delivered a signed copy of the "Address" to David Hall. The Assembly then ordered Moore to be imprisoned, and that the "libelous Address be burnt by the common Hangman at such Time and Place as this House shall hereafter direct and appoint." *Votes* (1758), 18.

[4] Joseph Galloway (c. 1731–1803) was a Quaker lawyer and politician born in Anne Arundel Co., Md., who moved to Philadelphia with his father in 1740. At the age of seventeen, he began practicing law, and before he was twenty, Galloway was arguing cases before the Pennsylvania Supreme Court. He served in the Pennsylvania Assembly from 1757 to 1775, and as speaker from 1766 to 1774. He was a close ally of Benjamin Franklin until they disagreed about independence. Galloway served in the First Continental Congress and proposed a Plan of Union, but after it was rejected, he moved to New York and joined the British army under Gen. William Howe (1729–1814). He returned to Philadelphia when the city was occupied in 1777, and when it was retaken by Americans, he fled to England. The Pennsylvania Assembly convicted him in absentia of high treason and confiscated his estates. In England, he wrote against Howe's prosecution of the war in the mid-Atlantic region, and in later years he turned to religious study (*ODNB*).

[5] Lat. the law of Parliament. 2 Coke, *Institutes* 47: "By the Law of the Land no man can be exiled, or banished out of his native Country, but either by the authority of Parliament, or in case of abjuration for felony by the Common Law: and so when our books, or any Record speak of exile or banishment, other than in case of abjuration, it is to be intended to be done by authority of Parliament."

[6] On March 14, 1704, members of the House of Lords presented Queen Anne with "An Humble Representation and Address" concerning *Ashby v. White* (1704) and the case of the Aylesbury men. This was an action brought by Matthew Ashby and four others, against the constable and others of Aylesbury for rejecting Ashby's vote in a parliamentary election. Ashby prevailed in a suit in the Court of Queen's Bench, but when the Aylesbury men pressed the same cause, they were imprisoned at the pleasure of the House of Commons and denied habeas corpus. The Lords' "Representation" condemned the actions of the House of Commons as unprecedented and unjust and sought redress for the men by the Queen through a writ of error. See Able Boyer, *The History of the Reign of Queen Anne: Digested into Annals, Year the Third* (London: A. Roper, 1705), 3:224–43. 228; and 14 *State Trials* 861–78.

[7] Sibling symbol not found.

[8] See docs. 1:45, n. 2 and doc. 1:46, above.

[9] See for example Petyt 16–17: "*Edward Smalley* upon the Question was *adjudged guilty of the Contempt, and abusing of this House by fraudulent practice, of procuring himself to be arrested upon the Execution, of his own assent and intention, to be discharged as well of his Imprisonment, as of the said Execution. Matthew Kirtleton,* Schoolmaster to Mr. *Hall,* was likewise upon another Question adjudged guilty by this House of like Contempt, and abusing of this House, in confederacy and practice with the said *Smalley* in the intentions aforesaid. 2. Upon another *Question* it was *adjudged* by the *House,* that the said *Smalley* be for his *Misdemeanor* and *Contempt committed* to the Prison of the *Tower.* 3. Upon the like *Question* it was also *adjudged* by this *House,* that the said *Kirtleton* Schoolmaster, be also for his *lewd Demeanor* and *Contempt* in *abusing* of this *House, committed* to the *Prison* of the *Tower.*"

[10] Abhorrer: "Any of those who signed addresses of abhorrence of the actions of those who petitioned Charles II in 1680 for the summoning of Parliament" (*OED*). Here, JD means Lord Chief Justice George Jeffreys (1648–1689), who presided over Algernon Sydney's trial, Mich. 35 Car. 2 (1683). See 3 *State Trials* 710–40 for a report of the trial.

[11] Most likely a reference to Burnet 2:235–39, which discusses Algernon Sydney's trial: "Sidney wrote a long vindication of himself, (which I read,) and summed up the substance of it in a paper that he gave the Sheriffs: But suspecting they might suppress it, he gave a copy of it to a friend. It was a fortnight before it was printed" (238).

Most likely a reference to Rapin, 3:220–21, which discusses Algernon Sydney's trial: "[t]he most urgent proof against him, was a manuscript found among his papers. . . . He said at first that the manuscript was not writ by him, and he could see no reason why it should be ascribed to him. That tho' he was the author, it might be writ many years ago, in answer to Filmer's book, with no intention of publishing it" (221).

[12] Mother Shipton was a witch and prophetess who, according to what is most likely legend, lived in Tudor York (*ODNB*). Her story is told in the pamphlet, *The Prophesie of Mother Shipton in the Raigne of King Henry the Eighth* (London: R. Lounds, 1641).

[13] On this and the next line, there is a repair that obliterates the words.

[14] Lat. on first impression.

[15] The Provisiones de Merton, 20 Hen. 3 (1235), which limited the power of the king, were agreed to by Henry III and the barons of England in the parish of Merton. Ch. 6, "The Penalties for Ravishment of a Ward, Forfeiture of Marriage, or Disparagement of a Ward," stipulated that if a lord married "those that they have in ward to Villains, or other, as Burgess, where they be disparaged," the lord would "lose the Wardship unto the age of the Heir, and all the Profit, that thereof shall be taken, shall be converted to the Use of the Heir."

[16] Lat. if a parent complains.

[17] Littleton, fol. 23 b.: "Also it hath bene a question how these wordes should bee understand. Si parentes conquerantur. &c. And it seemeth unto some that considering the statute of Magna charta Cap. 6. that willeth that heredes maritentur absque disparagatione &c. [Lat. heirs shall be married without disparagement] upon which this sayd statute of Merton upon this point is grounded as it seemeth, and in so much that it was never sene that any action was brought by the action of Merton for suche disparagynge agaynst the wardeine, and if any action may be taken upon such matter, it shal be taken by common presumpcion before this tyme, or at some time to be put in use, that these wordes shal be understand in such manner."

[18] 3 Levinz 29: *Onslow v. Rapley*, Mich. 33 Car. 2, C.B. (1681): "Case for a double return upon an Election of Members for Parliament. The Defendant pleaded, that the Plaintiff was not chosen, and Issue thereupon, and Verdict for the Plaintiff. And now it was mov'd in Arrest of Judgment ["a stay of proceedings, after a verdict for the plaintiff or the Crown, on the ground of manifest error therein" (*OED*)], that no Action lies for a double Return . . . . Judgement was, That the Plaintiff shall take Nothing by his Writ."

[19] JD means William III and is referring to 7 & 8 Will. 3, c.7 (1696): "An Act to Prevent False and Double Returns of Members to Serve in Parliament."

[20] John Hughes (c. 1712–1772) was a representative from Philadelphia Co.; Joseph Fox (1709–1779) was a member for Philadelphia Co.

[21] It is unclear exactly to what Norris is referring. The Assembly did declare members who were elected but did not take their seats to be in "Contempt of the Authority of the House" but did not imprison them. See, for example, *Votes*, supp. (1752), 1:35. It is possible Norris is referring to an episode in 1731 when the Commissioners and Assessors of Lancaster Co., Pa., refused to pay the wages and reimburse the travelling charges of the members elected from the county. The Assembly deemed them to be "in high Contempt of the House" and ordered the serjeant at arms to take the men into custody. *Votes*, supp. (1754), 3:154.

[22] Lat. by a great road, i.e., after much deliberation.

49
Draft Fragment on the Cognizance of the Assembly in the Smith Libel Trial, [January 1758]

Although this fragment relates to a central argument in the case, the Assembly's claim that it had cognizance to try a libel case, which appears in most of the documents in the Smith trial, we place it following doc. 1:48, where JD makes his first and most detailed case against the Assembly's assumption of this power.

The [Pro][pri]ety of the Distinction that has been mentioned will [a]ppear ~~extremely~~ {very} evident, by considering the Confusion and [inj]ustice, which a contrary Doctrine must introduce.

If the House of Commons can take Cognizance of "Matters [cogn]izable in the Courts of Law", because they "may have some [Rela]tion to Parliament", two distinct Authorities would ex[sis?]{is}t, [who]se Determinations in the same Case may be directly [op]posite to each other— ~~What is still worse, if they agree, [a P]erson may be punished twice for the same Offence.~~ {Unhappy Contradictions & Contests [bet]ween the Power of the Crown & the People would probably} [ari]se; and no Man could tell to what Limits the Jurisdiction of the [Co]mmons would extend, if it should include "all Matters that [m]ight have some Relation to Parliament."

On the other Hand, [i]t would be worse, if these two distinct Authorities should [a]gree, for then a Person may be twice punished for the [s]ame Offence.

Ms (PHi-RRL)

50
Notes on Depositions in the Smith Libel Trial, [January 18–19, 1758]

In taking these notes, JD folded most of the pages in a similar way to his notes on Thomas Bond's examination (doc. 1:47): like a booklet in quarto, usually with the pages of writing progressing from the upper left to right, then bottom left to right. Some of the leaves, however, he only folded in half and wrote down one full side. The order of witnesses in JD's notes—Levers, "Hanshaw," "Brandford," Armbruster, and Hall—differs slightly from the order recorded in the Assembly's proceedings: Robert Levers, Johann Friedrich Handschuh, Anthony Armbruster, David Hall, and William Bradford. In a marginal note to doc. 1:54, JD confirmed that his order was accurate when he explained, "The Reason of examining Mr. Bradford before Mr. Hall was that Mr. Smith's Counsel apprehended some of the Members woud have been alarmd at those Questions being put to Hall, which they woud neglect while Bradford was examind" (p. 250). After the depositions, John Ross requested copies of the transcripts, at Smith's expense, because "[JD] had not taken down the several Examinations of the Witnesses at Length."[1] The Assembly consented. In doc. 1:55, JD noted that the clerk transcribed the depositions, and particularly that of Levers, in "words quite different from those of the Witness," and when JD attempted to have the record corrected, he was "treated with the utmost severity; chargd with ~~being~~ {allowing himself to be} ignorant of Parliamentary Proceedings" (p. 274).

---

(1)

Mr. Levers.

    Employd by Moor in copy[in]g an add[ress] to Gov[erno]r Denny.

==

went to Dr. {T[homas]} B[ond]'s {to wait on M[oor]} found there 2 B[on]ds—Moor & Smith {agr[ee]d with M[oor] to copy & then went to} Smith & comp[are]d the copy S[mith] made with D[octo]r's again.
the draught deliv[ere]d
Req[ueste]d by M[oor]

==

In whose hand was the draught deliv[ere]d. dont {cert[ain]ly} know {In whose hand the [one?] part.}—part of it app[eare]d to be in S{a} hand like S[mith]'s—but [~~illegible words~~] {coud have [*illegible*] [in whose}] it was {th[at] he cant be positive [*illegible*]}

==

{Simil[arity] no Evid[ence] in Crim[ina]l matters.}[2] Have copied so often S[mith]'s hand, as to be positive {know} when I see it.

==

some remarks made in Conv[ersati]on, & alter[ati]ons in Consequ[ence]— of those remarks—believe they were—but dont know by whom—cant say any made by S[mith]

==

Who held the paper in his hand—somet[ime]s in M[oor]'s—

==

Never heard S[mith] say any th[in]g abo[u]t it only in the Rem[ar]ks in conv[ersati]on—dont know wh[ich] of them were S[mith]'s: nor what was said by any [par][ticu]lar Gentleman. [*column break*]

(2)

Dont know by whom Alter[ation]s made nor in [pur]suance of whose remarks.

==

Was any alter[ation]s made in [pur]suance of S[mith]'s rem[ar]ks   Dont remember there was one.

==

Who held the paper & made the Alter[ation]s— S[mith] read the paper {to the best of my Remembrance}—dont know—who made Alter[ation]s **Obs[ervation]** a single idea may alter Remembrance {he only read it to those who knew it & had it in their hands}

==

Were the alter[ation]s in the same handw[ritin]g with the other p[ar]ts of the paper   Ans[wer] dont know because he was desird to copy the paper by a [par][ticu]lar time & hurry made me neglig[ent] of tak[in]g Notice in whose hand it was.

==

Why desird to copy   Ans[wer] that it might be presented to the Gov[erno]r by Moor. At 5.

==

Wh[o was] the orig[inal] dra[ugh]t deliv[ere]d to. Ans[wer]. I del[ivere]d to Mr. Will[iam] Moor.

==

Did any body wait on you while You were copy[in]g & who— Ans[wer] Copied it at my own house at 4 or 5   M[oor] & P[hineas] B[ond] came to me, to know how far I had gone. S[mith] never came.

[*bottom half of page*:]

(3)

Mr. Hanshaw.[3]

 After Christm[as] went to S[mith]'s—to fetch the money he had earnd—fo[un]d him sick—in bed—after some few w[or]ds he askd—have You read th[at] piece— I asked wh[ich] piece— ~~he expl[ained]~~ {is it} Mr. Moor's—he answ[ere]d Yes— {I read} 3 sev[era]l times in the news—his qu[estio]n was why did You not transl[ate] it & put it in y[ou]r Dutch Newspaper— My ans[wer] was I did not think it [pro][per]   He then said You have been blamd very much: that You have not trans[late]d it many Dutch people have soug[h]t {it in} y[ou]r news but have not fo[un]d it {The Dutch people near}
Mr. Moor desires to have it in y[ou]r pap[er]   Mr. Moor desires 60 might be pr[int]ed & sent to him. After a few w[or]ds he askd me why I pr[in]ted but one ½ half sheet {some} last week {before}. I said I sh[oul]d have more leisure after Christm[as]   After some

196

[*column break*]

(4)

he desird I wo[ul]d transl[ate] it: & I did it duly with Reluctance; all such strifes & quarr[els] in Gen[era]l are a detestation to my mind.

===

Wh[at] were the Excuses You made   Ans[wer]. {B[*illegible*] &} Because I did not like it.

===

Wh[at] Arg[umen]ts did S[mith]make use of to [per]swade You   Ans[wer]. The desire of the people & Mr. Moor. no other.

===

Did S[mith] dict[ate] any method of publish[in]g it   Ans[wer]. He bid me put some short pref[ace] & the pref[ace] I put was th[at] the people desird it Mr. S[mith] bid me put such a pref[ace] & say the people might Judge of it accord[ing]ly.

===

Obs[ervation] Mr. S[mith] did not give him a Paper. The pref[ace] not part of the Charge ag[ains]t S[mith]   Pref[ace] transl[ate]d & to the [pur]pose above. Did any other th[an] S[mith] desire You to publ[ish] this   No. Who wrote the preface— Ans[wer] I did not write one word—but I made it accord[ing] to his direct[ion]   Was the pref[ace] dictated by Mr. S[mith] the subst[ance] was [*page break*]

[*top half of page:*]

(5)

S[mith] Earnestly desird it might be put in on M[oor]'s acc[oun]t but usd no threats—

==

Who pays You your Salary— Ans[wer]. S[mith]

==

Did Mr. Smith desire You to publish it as a Printer. I am no Printer: I only translate

==

Did You think it might be misch[ief] to transl[ate]& publish it. Ans[wer]. He was afraid it woud—but hopd the truth might app[ea]r

==

What Concern has Mr. S[mith] with your press. Ans[wer] S[mith] is clerk of the T[rus]tees—& he supp[osedl]y has the direction of the press.

==

Who gen[eral]ly bro[ugh]t papers to You to be transl[ate]d & pr[in]ted

Ans[wer]. When I overl[ooke]d pieces in the Eng[lish] Paper S[mith] often
blamd {& said}—they are fo[un]d in the Engl[ish] paper—& are not in
yours.
==

In what Paper—did You first p[rin]t it the [31[st]?] of Dec[embe]r [*column
break*]

(6)

Printer told me S[mith] sent for them
==

Obs[ervati]on. Is this a Publ[icati]on: S[mith] did not give the paper {: but
<u>bid</u> him transl[ate] & <u>bid</u> the printer publish.}
==

Printer bro[ugh]t them to mr. Smith but {Hall publ[ishe]d the act of
publ[ishing] the [Prin]ter's & Smith [bid him?] [*illegible*]} but printer knew
them.}
==

From what paper did You trans[late]   Ans[wer]. From Frank[lin] & Hall's
paper.
==

Did not S[mith] tell You Hall the Assembly's Printer had printed it: & gave
it as a Reason why You might do it   Yes.
==

Did not S[mith] advise th[at] You might print the Ass[embly's] mess[age]
dont remem[ber] a word about it.
==

Did S[mith] ever blame You for omitt[in]g art[icles] in Hall's paper— Yes
often.
==

Did not Mr. Sm[ith] did not say he had come from the Country— Dont
remember
[*end of column*]

[*bottom half of page, reversed*:]

(7)

Did You ever receive money for transl[atin]g this paper. Ans[wer]. Never.
rec[eive]d £50 for gen[era]l Serv[ice]s   No pay for [par][ticu]lar pieces.
==

Mr. Brandford

I printed this paper.
Who bro[ugh]t it. Mr. Will[iam] Moor.
Did You shew it to any body before You ~~shewd~~ printed it. No.

198

Was it in S[mith]'s hand— No. {tho[ugh] I have often seen his hand & know it.}

Did You acq[uain]t any body with the Cont[en]ts & ask them whether You might print it. No.   Dont know what became of the Copy I printed from.
==

Who corr[ecte]d the [Pro]of. P[hineas] Bond came & told me there were one or 2 words amiss—but no matter whether they were alt[ere]d or not. Theref[ore] left them out.
[*column break*]

Armbruster.[4] (8)

Translat[io]n sent to me by Hanshaw: who is employd by a sorty of Gent[leme]n to transl[ate]
==

Mr. S[mith] never gave me any ord[er]s but Copy sent by Hanshaw.
==

Who employd You to print 62 Copies— Ans[wer] There were no gen[era]l Orders— I gen[eral]ly pr[in]t more than enough
==

When You print a paper— Do You send 50 or 60 Copies to Mr. S[mith] No.
==

Why did You send 62 copies to S[mith] of this. I had no orders—but a man came & askd Me if the paper was out: & askd for them—if a man comes for them, must I not send them. I saw this man with S[mith] & therefore thought I might send to S[mith}
==

When did You see this man in Comp[any] with S[mith]   Ans[wer]. A month before at my house. [*page break*]

(9)

Mr. Hall—[5]

Did You print M[oor]'s address
Yes
==

Who bro[ugh]t it to You. Moor
==

Did You shew it to any body before You [pre]sented it. No.
==

Did you acq[uain]t any body with the Contents & ask them if [it] might be safe in print[in]g it

Ans[wer] I deliv[ere]d the Cont[en]ts as well as I coud & askd if I might pr[in]t it
==

Who did You shew it to. Ans[wer]. I cant so well answer th[at] q[ues]tion unless I enter into some Circumst[ances] [previous?] to it.

Some time ~~ago~~ {before} this Paper was publ[ishe]d I believe a fortn[igh]t or 3 w[ee]ks Dr. P[hineas] Bond came to my house & told Me I might remember some time before I had publishd an add[ress] from the Ass[embly] to the Gov[erno]r relat[in]g to M[oor]'s abus[in]g his off[ice] of magest[rate] & desir[in]g Gov[erno]r to remove him th[at] M[oor] & his fr[iend]s thought it hard of the Ass[embly] to publish such an add[ress] in Gazette th[at] wo[ul]d greatly aff[ec]t his family Char[acte]r & C[*illegible*] & Mr. Moor I found was displ[ease]d with me for pr[in]t[in]g it   I told Dr. [*Bond*] M[oor] coud not be angry with me—as I was printer to the [Pro]vince I tho[ugh]t the Ass[embly] had a right to order me to do such th[in]gs   If anything wrong—the Ass[embly] to blame not me   D[octo]r then took the paper out of his pocket—wh[ich] [wh[*illegible*]?] I ~~had~~ read over. I told him it was of such a nature I coud not print it, as I was pr[in]ter to the {Pro]vince   He then s[ai]d someth[in]g about Liberty of the press: but when he went [*column break*] away I s[ai]d I coud not pr[in]t it: he said he wo[ul]d let M[oor] know what I s[ai]d & I did not see him for 10 days— then he came & said he had rec[eive]d an ans[wer] from M[oor] who insisted on hav[in]g it pr[in]ted in the manner it was first sent for th[at] he had del[ivere]d it to the Gov[erno]r in those w[or]ds to be p[rin]ted accor[ding]ly if it was to be p[rin]ted— I told him again, I coud not p[rin]t it.

A few days after I rec[eive]d a Letter from M[oor] in wh[ich] he shewd a good deal of Surprize at my refus[in]g to pr[in]t it after hav[in]g inj[ure]d his Char[acte]r so much; & desird a positive answ[er]   I tho[ugh]t the best advice I co[ul]d have was from some Gent[leme]n of the Ass[embly] & those th[at] were near Town—that is Galloway & Masters   I went to & told them the nature of the paper ~~of~~ as well as I co[ul]d after once read[in]g it over—they told me if it was signd I might pr[in]t it—th[at] the Liberty of the press might be open wh[ich] they desird— So it was pr[in]ted
==

Askd if Dr. Bond did not ~~com~~ {compl[aine]d} mention the Liberty of the press {being denied}— Yes
==

Did You say You were afr[ai]d You might be appreh[ende]d to be under the Influence of the Ass[embly] & of their party
==

Did not the Gent[leme]n of Ass[embly] recomm[en]d it to You to have the Orig[ina]l & signd—th[at] we might come upon them— Yes
Obs[ervation] This wo[ul]d entitle You to come on the author—but not those who foll[owe]d your Example   {Apply the Evid[ence] to the diff[eren]t p[oin]ts   Blind lead the blind. Can any of these members give a vote.}
==

Whether at the last time Dr. Bond was with him he s[ai]d it was a Libel— No—
==

Did You shew M[oor]'s Letter to these Gent[leme]n   Ans[wer]. I did.
==

What Acc[oun]t did You give— Ans[wer] {that} I thought it a very virulent paper, & containd [*page break*]

gross Reflexions on the last Assembly

==

Whether You wo[ul]d have pr[in]ted this paper if these Gent[leme]n had not given you ~~Ca[use?]~~ {consent}   No.
==

Whether we confind our advice to this paper or the Liberty of the press in Gen[era]l   Ans[wer]. You gave the Liberty of the press as a reason why I sho[ul]d pr[in]t it.
==

Did You mention it to any others— Yes—2 others—they told me I sho[ul]d be wary in pr[in]t[in]g it   These two were Robeau & Baynton.[6]
[*remainder of page blank*]

Ms (PHi-RRL)

---

[1] *Votes* (1758), 27.

[2] JD subsequently expanded this argument. See docs. 1:53 and 1:54, below.

[3] Johann Friedrich Handschuh (Hanshaw; 1714–1764) was a Lutheran minister and language instructor at the Philadelphia Academy who translated Moore's "Address" into German. The copy of his deposition in Logan dated Jan. 17, 1758, but *Votes* records it on the afternoon of January 18 (*Votes* [1758], 27).

[4] Anton Armbrüster (Anthony Armbruster; 1717–1796), was a German-born printer who in 1752 assumed ownership of *Die Philadelphische Zeitung*, a German-language newspaper that

did work for the Society for Promoting Religious Knowledge and the English Language among the German Emigrants in Pennsylvania. He partnered with Benjamin Franklin from 1754 to 1758. The Assembly initially questioned Armbrüster on January 18, but his deposition ended with him being taken into custody by the sergeant at arms "for a Contempt to this House, prevaricating in his Testimony, and refusing to answer in a Case wherein he was produced as a Witness" (*Votes* [1758], 27). The following day, he "asked Pardon for his Misbehaviour" and answered the questions. A copy of his deposition is in PHi-Logan.

[5] For versions of Hall's testimony at different levels of detail, see docs. 1:54 and 1:55.

[6] Daniel Roberdeau (1727–1795) was a Philadelphia merchant and member of the Assembly from 1756 to 1761; John Baynton (c. 1726–1773) was one of the men elected to replace the Quaker pacifists who had resigned from the Assembly in 1756.

51
Preliminary Notes for Closing Arguments in the Smith Libel Trial, [January 20, 1758]

JD jotted these notes on the back of a set of notes he took for and during the initial proceedings on January 17 (docs. 1:45 and 1:46). His first point referring to Ross's opening remarks suggests he was reviewing those notes and planned to uses Ross's words as a point of depature for his own arguments on January 21. He and Ross had requested a deferment of their arguments two days in a row, the 18th and the 19th, to "consider and sum up the Evidence."[1] As these notes hint and subsequent documents elaborate, JD took over for Ross on short notice, with only a half day to prepare. The Assembly records show the House met at 9:00 a.m. on Saturday the 21st, which meant JD would have begun his preparations the afternoon of Friday the 20th. The next two documents, docs. 1:52 and 1:53, immediately below, are much expanded versions of this document.

1. <u>Mr. R[oss]</u> so learnedly & fully &c
2. Short time—but have in my Studies read a little &c
3. Treat this affair in such mann[er] as to preserve respect—&
4. Perform the part of an honest Adv[ocate]
5. Doubt not be[in]g heard with Att[ention] & Cand[our]   As we apply to themselves {subm[issive]ly} who are the [Par]ty offended— So that both J[udge]s & Acc[use]rs
6. Sure they will act with great Circumsp[ecti]on in their own cause
7. As wise men [~~fear~~?]{know} & good men fear the partial dictates of their own hearts, on their own Interests
{8. No other Judges in Case of <u>Mistake</u>—therefore cautious—of Liberty}

[*in left margin*:] {Assembl[y] composd of Ind[ividu]als who may mist[ake]}

8{9}. Mr. S[mith] conceives every freeman of &c to be concernd in this Case as it is, Whether a man shall be deprivd of his Liberty, the most valuable of all poss[essi]ons—for an offence wh[ich] is bailable at Com[mon] Law

[*in left margin:*] {Power afr[ai]d to hint &c}

because this house is pleasd to draw it into their Cognizance.

==

10. No stream w[ith]out a fountain—no build[in]g w[ith]out a foundation.

==

11. If any author[ity] it can bear Exam[ination] if Exam[ination] is not allowd—susp[ici]on

==

Great many writs [pro]vided— No Crime but he may be baild. The best way to preserve the Rightful Priv[ilege]s is to abide by those th[at] are known.

Arthur Hall[2]
Infalliable
Omnis Inno[vati]o[3]
{The English Constitution grown old—under the Customs & Laws wh[ich] compose it, & old things cant well be alterd— Experim[en]ts are dangerous—}
Case of £500

Primæ Impressionis
Double Return
Si par parentes conquer[antu]r &c
No Instance of one Parl[iamen]t punish[in]g for ano[the]r quoted but Colepeper's & he remitted—but not one ment[ione]d when there was no Parl[iamen]t

Ano[the]r Parl[iamen]t— A Stranger— A Contempt— New [Jur[is]d[icti]on?] by [date?] Dont [pro]ceed in the way of the House o[f] Com[m]ons

Ms (PHi-RRL)

---

[1] *Votes* (1758), 27 and 28.

---

[2] Arthur Hall (1539–1605) was a translator and member of the House of Commons who was called before Parliament on May 19, 1572, to answer for the content of some of his speeches. He was "brought to the Bar by the *Serjeant*, was charged with several Articles, and confessed his Folly, and humbly submitted himself to the House, and was remitted." In 1580, Hall was in trouble again for publishing a book that "contained Matter of Reproach against some particular Members of the House, derogatory to the General Authority, Power and State of the House, and prejudicial to the Validity of the Proceedings of the same." This time Hall was sentenced to six months in the Tower of London, fined £500, and removed as member of Parliament from Grantham. In 1586 he was barred from ever serving in Parliament again. *Lex Parl.* 136–38.

[3] Lat. Every innovation disturbs by its novelty more than it benefits by its usefulness. The complete phrase is: *Omnis innovation plus novitiate perturbat quam utilitate* (*BLD*).

52
Rough Draft and Notes for Closing Arguments in the Smith Libel Trial, [January 20, 1758]

This and the following two documents share enough similar language and reference each of the deponents in such a way that they all seem to pertain to the same argument, namely the final one that occurred on January 21, after Smith's counsel had made their two requests on January 18 and 19 to review the evidence in preparation for their defense. This set of notes is clearly a draft of the following set, doc. 1:53, and seem to be preparations for arguments yet to be made.

---

(1)

No Lawful Evid[ence] as part[ici]pes Criminis—[1] V[ide] What is be[in]g accessory or aid[in]g or abett[in]g—

=====

1. Apply the Evid[ence] of contriv[in]g & writ[in]g—to that part— {2.} then the Evid[ence] of publish[in]g to th[at] part. 3. Submit the Law aris[in]g & then 4ly conclude.

I appear for S[mith] chargd with advis[in]g [pro]mot[in]g &c a Libel.

This is a cause of utmost import[ance] as Prerog[ative] of Crown—Author[ity] of this house & Liberty of Subj[ec]t concernd: wish I may treat it in [pro][per] manner: My Experience at Barr small—& {there fore} tho[ugh] I have endeav[ore]d by a close applic[atio]n to the studies of my [Pro]fession, & a strict attend[ance] on C[our]ts of Justice to qualify myself for assist[in]g the Innoc[en]t & distrest—I sho[ul]d have been extremely glad to have had an Opport[uni]ty to have [pre]pard myself better for an aff[ai]r of such conseq[uence]: th[at] so my Industry might have aided my Exper[ience] & time & Leisure might have enabled me to speak more fully

& accurately in so weighty a cause before such hon[ora]ble Judges: but ~~however~~ so happ[ene]d {by a mistake} half days notice—& attend[ed] here since—& now disapp[rove?]d— No time for [~~pre?~~] compar[in]g or digest[in]g Evid[ence]: but only such hints as shall occas[ional]ly arise from repeat[in]g them. **But** Sir the gre[a]ter the Advant[age] we thus [lose,?] the gr[ea]ter we doubt not will {be} your Candour & Indulgence to [~~illegible~~]{Us}: th[at] Truth however obscurd, may at length app[ear] & Innoc[ence] be seen {in all its purety.}

Ano[the]r th[in]g wh[ich] might alarm some people, is th[at] Our Judges are the [Per]sons <u>offended</u> by the crime we are chargd with: th[at] the [Par]ties supposd to be injurd, are the [Par]ties to determ[ine] that Inj[u]ry: & that those men are to pass sentence ag[ains]t us, ag[ains]t whom we are said to have comm[itte]d an offence. {Those [Per]sons who be most likely to make [*in left margin:*] {make such Reflections, who are distrustful of popular compassion; comfort or—} People who think in this manner Mr. Sp[eake]r must always have stronger impressions on their mind of your ~~power~~ Author[ity], than of your Justice [*illegible*] & to be sure it is natural for a man who is in the power of ano[the]r to reflect on what he **can** do, rather than what he **ought** to do— But Mr. Sp[eake]r We disclaim these idle appreh[ension]s & left all our fears at the door of this house—because we knew ~~the~~ our worthy Judges wo[ul]d adm[iniste]r strict impart[ia]l Justice & wo[ul]d {relig[ious]ly} guard ag[ains]t & suppress every suggestion of Resentm[en]t {& hear with Indulgence what we offer.}

What still puts us in a worse, ano[the]r unfortun[ate] th[in]g is, th[at] our Plan is alt[ere]d   We designd ut [~~ante~~] post. pa. 3.[2]

[*text continued from missing page:*] {them in cont[inue]d gross reflexions. Ano[the]r th[in]g—our plan alt[ere]d]} [*page break*]

{[Obs[ervation]s?] on Evid[ence]} (2)

Every Evid[ence] is more a Princ[ipal] than Sm[ith][3]   {Every arrow of this [Pro]secution has past thro[ugh] them w[ith]out hurt[in]g them, & is fixd in us: if for the publick} [*in left margin:*] {Good th[at] one man bear the s[u]{ff}[ering]s {af[ron]ts}of the others; Mr. Smith will ~~well~~ chearfully submit, & think himself happy to serve his fr[ien]ds by suffer[in]g for them {then let the [unhurt hart][4] &c}: but allow him to wonder by what strange unlucky fate of his it is decreed, th[at] Crimes in him sho[ul]d be innocence in others.}
==

Happy for P[hineas] B[ond] he is here & not in a Court of Justice: he forcd Sm[ith] for friendsh[ip] a gentle force. {Publisher in the Strongest manner— }Then let the unhurt hart &c

==

A man's Conv[ersati]on to be sifted to see if noth[in]g can be discov[ere]d Next th[in]g will be looks   Turn Disciples of Pythagoras[5]

==

No Certainty of Sm[ith]'s be[in]g concernd.   Smith a Pr[in]ter & Ag[en]t to Moor

==

A [Pri]soner's Exam[inati]on unless signd—No Evid[ence] 9 Mod. 89. Law of Ev[idence] 136.[6] but if it is—only a Copy of <u>an</u> Address. & V[ide] infra.[7]

==

For one Letter or figure {& these left out too by B[on]d's Evidence}—a man is to be deprivd of his Liberty, is to forf[ei]t his share in those invaluable Rights securd to every Englishman by the Hab[eas] Corp[u]s Act[8]   I hope every freeman will blush to think there is any th[in]g in these Evid[ences] wh[ich] ought to deprive a fellow subject of his Liberty.

==

Similitude of hands No Evid[ence] in Criminal matters {Algernoon Sydney-{,} insist on. Sealed with his head the claim of Rights of a freeborn Englishman asserted with the Spirit {&c} & liberties often def[ende]d with tongue & hand.} G[eneral] [Law] of Ev[idence] 54. 55.[9]

==

It hath been said, that he who hath read a Libel by himself, or he[ar]d it read &c & aft[erwar]ds mal[i]c[ious]ly reads or rep[ea]ts part, in the presence of others, is gu[il]ty of an unl[aw]ful publ[icati]on. Hawk. 195. {and he knows it to be a} Libel. if he writes a Copy & does not publish it no Libel. So if he deli[ver]s it to a Magestrate [it was?] history. Concealm[en]t no offence but in Treason. {Sm[ith] did not know it to be a Libel when he gave orders to M[oor], the members allowd it to be pr[in]ted is a Libel—}

==

No Crime so heinous, to put an Englishman in so miserable a situation but he may endeavour to obtain his Liberty by Hab[eas] Corp[us]: & Judges may bail if they see [pro][per]—but if a man thro[ugh] Ignorance or mistake do any act which shall be voted a breach of Priv[ilege]—he becomes in worse cond[iti]on than any felon or traytor. his fr[ien]ds cant apply or breach of Priv[ilege]

==

Best way to preserve Rightful Priv[ilege]s is to abide by those th[at] are known & certain & it is not in the power of one or both houses to make their priv[ilege]s Add[ress] of Peers to Q[ueen] Ann. guard ag[ain]st least

whispering.} Guard[ian]s of the Rights &c. Judges in sua caus[a].[10] Good men [*illegible*] [sans?] know [*illegible*]
Infelix pop[ulus] ubi Jus &c[11] {No marks to guide one, & swallowd in the Gulf of Priv[ilege]s; Scylla & Char[ybdis][12] {S[mith] has not the same Rights with other freemen of the [Pro]vince} {this opin[io]n of Lords—} Meet with safety & preside with dignity—wav[in]g Charter &c—as this the first Instance of Libel &c all those quoted were ag[ains]t own members or others sitt[in]g parl[iamen]t & not only a Libel—but the cause of the Libel expressd as ag[ains]t the house or its members

==

{Twice pun[ishe]d horror, & contrary to the divine Law. Not an Inst[ance] where a Jud[gmen]t of house of Comm[on]s quot[e]d in books tender the maxim th[at] a man cant be punishd twice.}

Mr. Smith not guilty.
Assembly's printer had publishd it with <u>Leave</u> {mak[in]g traps} {How can these Members give a Vote} Smith a printer for [pro]mot[in]g &c Translat[ing] publish[in]g a publick thing {Colepeper's case & Long Parl[iamen]t S[mith] will be as much punishd as Moor.} Council adv[ise]d with Then in the [Press?] Walk free &c No Criminal part [pro]vd on Smith. {This the house of Justice—here She dwells with de[light?]} Mr. Smith must forget he is an Englishman—must forget the Rights and Liberties &c. is born undoubted heir to—Magn[a] Chart[a] Bill of Rights—**because** You command {[he sho[ul]d not enjoy?]} must not lament the loss of Blessings he is entit[le]d to **because** [*torn*] casts his view [*torn*] [*page break*]

(3)

Our Defence changd {Tis your part to command, tis ours to obey. We must make wh[at] defence You will [allow]. [*ink blot*] to have stood on a p[oin]t of the utm[os]t importance.}— 1. Designd to have provd th[at] this house w[oul]d take no Cogniz[ance] of any thing preced[en]t **because** noth[in]g coud be an offence ag[ains]t this house, when there was **no** house to be offended; th[at] this ~~hou~~ doctrine is confirmd by the Practize of Parl[iamen]t & the voice of Law in all ages. 2. Th[at] this house has no power to take cognizance of an offence th[at] is punishable at Com[mon] Law—th[at] this tak[in]g things out of the com[mon] Course of Just[ice] is an infringem[en]t of Magna Charta the found[ati]on of the Rights of Englishmen. {30 times confirmd}—contrary to all the Rule of Law— A Suspension of the Hab[eas] Corp[us] act the bulwark of English Liberty {as no bail here}— Th[at] this is contrary to the spirit of the Rights & Liberty securd by the Bill of Rights— in wh[ich] one of the things complaind of was sett[in]g up <u>new</u> Courts. Th[at] the people of England have always lookd with a Jealous eye upon

Innov[ations] of this sort & history is full of Instances {Star Chamber High Comm[ission]}—& th[at] in the affair of the Kentish Petitions Colepeper's Case—{who [peti[ti]oned] about treaties & committed—} the Conduct of the house of Com[m]ons was universally condemnd by the people—the Pr[is]oners hono[re]d with Visits from {crowds of} persons of highest Rank, City of London was prepar[in]g a petition of Like Nature—& the house of Com[m]ons was not so blindly partial, but th[at] they were convincd they were wrong, & remitted him to— **We** did not only design to shew, we shoud be irrigularly punishd here—but th[at] this Court coud have no Cognizance—bec[ause] such conseq[uences] wo[ul]d follow as the English Law regards with horror, & th[at] is We be pun[ishe]d twice.

~~But~~ Very earnest to have begun here, but must follow the orders of the house as Encouragem[en]t given to hear us on this here after—

Chargd with a <u>Libel</u>.*   Then it is Mr. Smith's business to shew he is not guilty of a <u>Libel</u>. Cert[ain]ly he is to acquit himself from the crime with wh[ich] he is chargd—{& that charge is Libel} & if the Crime with wh[ich] he is chargd is not a Libel, then he is acq[uitte]d from the Charge. Y[ou]r Resolves cant make it a Libel—the Law makes it so. You take away half our defence before we are heard X [*in left margin:*] {X Mak[in]g Votes have the power of Stat[utes] & [per]mit me to say Resolves of &c cant make one tittle of the Law pass away.   We are not allowed to go into the merits—wh[ich] is tak[in]g the Justice of the case—}

*Surpizd to find the word **Libel**—wh[ich] always supposes a [Per]son for its found[ati]on— No Writ[in]g &c—& all the Inst[ance]s the learned member quoted of Libels punishd by Com[mons]—was not simply Libels—but some facts added, as ~~Faults or Cont[em]pts~~ Libels upon the house then sitt[in]g, or some of its members—~~the same~~ but in the address to the Gov[ernmen]t it is calld ~~a~~ scandalous Libel upon the powers of Gov[ernmen]t tend[in]g to destroy the most essential parts of the Constit[ution] This has been confirmd by the same learned member, who insists [*page break*]

(4)

upon th[at] as Mr. S[mit]h's Crime, & not the Reflexions on the late assembly {it is not pretended this Assemb[ly] is the least inter[este]d in the Reflex[ions]}— So th[at] this is a Libel w[ith]out a [Per]son reflected, wh[ich] I say is a Non-Entity—a th[in]g never heard of before

This Libel then wh[ich] is no Libel for the Reason given Mr. S[mit]h is to answ[er] V[ide] antea*.

But it may be proper to relate this aff[air] at large & then Exam[ine] what share Mr. Sm[ith] had in it. Mr. Moor calld up by late Assemb[ly] his Conduct. they make & publish ag[ains]t Moor a most heavy & severe charge on his Reputation. M[oor] actuated {&} though fit to make his defence. He foll[owe]d their steps—they present—he presents they publishd—he publishes—they use severe words—he uses their words— if ~~he~~ was wrong, he was led astray by them; they run parallel from begin[ni]ng to end.   & this in his own def[ense]   Laid down as establishd Doct[rine] {this [Mr Mag[istrate]?] knew well} that no false or scandalous Words containd in a petition to Parl[iamen]t. 1 Lev. 240. 1 Sid. 414. 1 Saund. 131. 2 Keb. 832. &c in Articles of peace exhib[ite]d to Just[ice] of Peace 460. 14. b. or in any other [Pro]ceed[in]g in a regular course of Justice Dyer 285. Pl. 37. will make a Compl[ain]t amo[un]t to a Libel—bec[ause] of the discourt[es]y   Now all this [Pro]ceed[in]g is by way of [Per]secution—but M[oor]'s was in his own defence—& theref[ore] in the course of Justice—**but** the books go so far as to say it is no Libel tho[ugh] the Court has no Jurisd[icti]on. 2 Keb. 832. However this we are not afraid, as we are sensible from late Add[resse]s what {high} opinions this house entertains of the Gov[erno]r's authority.

=====

He went to the Autho[rity] they had establ[ishe]d

=====

Law of Ægyptians—Scipio Africanus {because the Romans were a free Peop[le]}. Checks in Gov[ernmen]t— {Leave to pr[in]t anyth[in]g ag[ains]t late Ass[embly] as th[at] told i[n] Trial of Seven Bishops— Suspend[in]g penal Laws ag[ains]t Papists—great Joy.

If Lawful for Mr. Moor—lawful to assist him— Sublato princ[ipali] toll[itu]r &c

Ms (PHi-RRL)

---

[1] Lat. partner in crime.

[2] See "**We**" at page 3, below.

[3] Principal: "Designating the chief person concerned in some action or proceeding; *esp.* that is the actual perpetrator of, or directly responsible for, a crime" (*OED*).

[4] Reference to line from *Hamlet*, 3.2.271–74: "Why, let the strooken deer go weep, / The hart ungallèd play. / For some must watch while some must sleep. / Thus runs the world away."

[5] Pythagoras (c. 570–c. 490 BC) founded Pythagoreanism, a philosophical school and brotherhood that prescribed a highly structured way of life and the doctrine of metempsychosis—the transmigration of the soul after death to a new body. See Hermann S.

Schibli, "Pythagoreanism," in *Concise Routledge Encyclopedia of Philosophy*, ed. Edward Craig (New York: Routledge, 2000), 728.

[6] 9 *Modern* 89, *King v. Layer*, Mich. 9 Geo (1722): "Then *Mr. Stanian* and *Mr. Delehay*, who were present when the Prisoner was examined before the Council at the Cockpit, offered to give Evidence of the Prisoner's Confession there, but this was opposed by his Counsel, for that he had not signed any Confession, and probably some unguarded Words might drop from him at that Time, which might amount to a Crime, if given in Evidence. Thereupon the Court declared, That it was no Evidence."

"Parol Proof of what a Prisoner confessed before the Council, not admitted except his Confession be signed by himself; and that voluntarily and without Oath." William Nelson, *The Law of Evidence: Wherein All the Cases That Have Yet Been Printed in Any of Our Law Books or Trials, and That in Any Wise Relate to Points of Evidence, Are Collected and Methodically Digested under Their Proper Heads*, 3rd ed. (London: E. and R. Nutt, and R. Gosling, 1739), 136.

[7] Lat. below.

[8] 31 Car. 2, c. 2 (1679): "An Act for the Better Securing the Liberty of the Subject, and for Prevention of Imprisonments Beyond the Seas."

[9] Gilbert 54–55: "But that the Comparison of Hands only should be a Proof in a Criminal Prosecution, was never Law but only in the Time of *K. J.* and the Distinction has ever been taken that the Comparison of Hands is Evidence in Civil and not on Criminal Cases . . . . Now the Comparisson of Hands is no more than a Presumption founded only on the Likeness, which may easily fail, because they are very subject to be counterfeited; therefore when the Comparison of Hands is the only Evidence in a Criminal Prosecution, there is no more than one Presumption against another, which weighs nothing."

[10] Lat. no one should be a judge in his own case. The complete phrase is: *Nemo iudex causa sua.*

[11] Lat. the unhappy people; where there is a right, there is a remedy.

[12] That is having to choose between two evils, or two unpleasant alternatives. In Greek mythology, Scylla and Charybdis were two immortal monsters who lived near a strait that Odysseus had to navigate in Homer's *Odyssey*. Odysseus chose to lose a few men to Scylla rather than face losing his entire crew to Charybdis's whirlpool.

53

**Draft Closing Arguments in the Smith Libel Trial,
[January 20 1758]**

These draft notes are an earlier version of doc. 1:54 below.

(1)

I app[ear] on behalf of Mr. Smith who st[an]ds chargd with advis[in]g [pro]mot[in]g & publish[in]g a Libel.

[*in left margin:*] {Perhaps not im[pro][per] to def[en]d mys[elf] before I att[em]pt to def[en]d my Client—

Nursd in the arms of Liberty for the greatest part of my time spent in this [Pro]vince here learnt the lessons of Freedom—th[at] every man is entitled to the Laws—th[at] no [man should?] be lookd on as guilty till he is condemnd—Some people mistake & I am blamd for do[in]g what I have y[ou]r autho[ity] to do—but great Reflect[ions] wo[ul]d fall on You if every man was deterrd from defend[in]g a [Per]son accusd before You— My first Appear[ance] for a Clerg[yman]}

This is a Cause of utmost import[ance] as [Præ]rog[ative] of Crown Author[ity] of this house & Liberty of Subj[ec]t concernd [if?] [Præ]rog[ative] concernd because it is draw[in]g into this Jurisd[icti]on, an Offence th[at] hitherto has been punishd in the C[our]ts of King at Com[mon] Law: Author[ity] of this house is concernd, because y[ou]r determ[inati]on will settle y[ou]r Jurisd[icti]on in cause[s] of this nat[ure] & the Subj[ec]t is inter[este]d because he is deprivd of his Liberty in an extraordinary manner[. I] Wish I may be able to treat it in a [pro][per] manner. My Experience at the Barr small & theref[ore] tho[ugh] I have endeav[oure]d by a close application to ~~my~~ {the} Studies of my [Pro]fession & in strict attendance on Courts of Justice to ~~qualify myself for assist[in]g~~ {collect some Assistance for} the distrest & Innoc[en]t I sho[ul]d have been extremely glad to have had an opport[uni]ty to have [pre]pard myself better for an aff[ai]r of such Con[sequence] that so my Industry might have aided my Inexperience & time & leisure might have enabled me to speak more fully & accuriately in so weighty a Cause, before such hon[oura]ble Judges.

But it happ[ene]d Sir by a mistake th[at] I had but ½ day's notice before this aff[ai]r came on & Attend[ance] since & now &c &c

But Sir the greater advant[age] I have thus lost, the greater I doubt not will be your Cand[ou]r & Indulg[ance] to me, th[at] thus Truth may be at last disclosd, tho[ugh] long obscurd & **Innocence** at length break thro[ugh] the clouds wh[ich] have surro[unde]d [him.]

There is a [par][ticu]lar Circumst[ance] Mr. Sp[eake]r in this case, wh[ich] might alarm some people—if it was theirs—wh[ich] is th[at] our Judges are the [per]sons offended by the Crime We are chargd with

Th[at] the [par]ties supposd to be inj[ure]d are the [par]ties to deter[mine?] [torn] & that those men are to pass sentencing ag[ains]t Us— ~~ag[ains]t~~ whom w[e] are said to have traducd.

The people most likely to be alarmd in this manner are those Who have reason to ~~appreh[en]d~~ {fear} if they sho[ul]d be unjustly oppressd, th[at] the greater part of their Countrymen woud not pity their misfor[tune]—for to a good man noth[in]g can be more melancholy [torn] [than?] [to be] [~~torn~~ssly injurd] {receive wrongd{s}}, unsoftend with the Compassio[n] [torn] [of the w]orld— Besides these people must [*page break*]

(2)

must always have stronger impressions on their mind of your A[torn] than of your Justice—& to be sure

211

It is natural for a man who is in the power of ano[the]r {who is offended with him,} to reflect on what he can do, rather than wha[t] he **ought** to do. **But Mr. Sp[eak]r**

We disclaim these idle apprehend[sion]s for we left all our fears at the door of this house—**because** we knew our most worthy Judges wo[ul]d adm[iniste]r faithful impartial Justice & [would] [*torn*]gly guard ag[ains]t & [*torn*] every sugg[esti]on of Resentm[en]t.   From this Cause then We have no Uneas[iness] but a very unfort[unate] th[in]g is th[at] Plan of our [Pro]ced[in]g is alt[ere]d by the Orders of this house

We designd to have [pro]vd {1.} th[at] this house co[ul]d take no Notice of any th[in]g preced[en]t to it—**because** noth[in]g co[ul]d be an off[ence] ag[ains]t this house, when there was **no** house to be offended—th[at] this Doctrine is conf[irme]d by the pract[ice] of Parl[iament] & the voice of Law in all ages.

2. Th[at] this house has no power to take Cogniz[ance] of an off[ence] th[at] is pre[se]n[ta]ble at Common Law—that this tak[in]g things out of the Com[mon] Course of Justice is an Infringem[en]t of Magna Charta the Grand Confirmation of the Rights of Engl[ish]men 30 times passd An Oppos[iti]on to all the Rules of Law— A Suspens[ion] of the **Hab[eas] Corp[us]** act {the great Bulwark of English Liberty—} as no Bail here—& contrary to the {[very?]} spirit of the **Bill of Rights**[1] th[at] noble attend[e]r of the ~~glorious~~ {ever memorable} Revolution[2] Th[at] the English People have alw[ays] lookd with a jealous Eye upon Innov[ation]s of this sort— & history full of Inst[ance]s that in the Case of the Kentish Petitioners—when the Colepepers petit[ione]d about treat[ie]s & were committed—the cond[uc]t of the house of Commons was <u>univers[al]ly</u> condemnd by the People the Petit[ione]rs hon[oure]d with Visits from Crowds of Persons of highest Rank—City of London was prepar[in]g petitions [*torn line*] was not so blindly partial but th[at] they were conv[ince]d they were wrong & rem[ande]d Colepeper to Law   wise in their anger.

We did not only design to have shewn th[at] We sho[ul]d be irregularly punishd here—but th[at] this house coud have no Congnizance

Because such conseq[uence]s wo[ul]d follow as the Eng[lish] Law not beholds but thinks of with <u>horror</u>   & that is—a [Per]son may be twice pun[ishe]d   I will allow, if one single Instance can be [pro]ducd where a Jud[gmen]t in the house of Com[mon]s was pl[eade]d in barr to an Ind[ictmen]t ~~below~~ in C[our]ts of Law, th[en] this Conseq[uence] wo[ul]d not, but if [*illegible*] {an} Inst[ance] can be quoted {if [any coud?] &c}, then I assert this Conseq[ence] terrible even in Imaginat[io]n [*page break*]

(3)

Imagination wo[ul]d follow— Argu[in]g upon a P[oin]t so clear so demon[stra]ble is altogether unnecessary; I shall theref[ore] quit it, earnestly {& humbly} beseech[in]g **You Mr. Sp[ea]k[e]r** & every member of this hon[oura]ble house {as Guard[ian]s of the Rights & Priv[ileges] of the Peop[le]}, to take it in to your wise Consid[erati]on, & {be pleasd} reflect if those Rights & Priv[ileges] are not most intimately concernd in y[ou]r determ[inatio]n—.

Upon this po[in]t of the Congniz[ance] we designd to have begun upon this to have insisted—but this was not allowd: {One thing X} [*in left margin:*] {X One thing At Conclusion, Mr. Sp[ea]k[e]r I humbly submit one thing— Tho[ugh] I utterly deny th[at] one parl[iament] can punish for off[ence]s ag[ains]t a late one, even comm[itte]d in the time of the 2.^{d} but gr[an]t it, to end all uneas[iness] about y[ou]r Congniz[ance]— If this house can shew one preced[en]t of the house of Com[mon]s punish[in]g an offence—done—while there was no parl[iamen]t I will give up the Cause} Our Plan was changd, & tho[ugh] we are [per]swaded th[at] ~~your~~ {the} votes {of the hon[oura]ble house} have not the power of Stat[ute] nor th[at] ~~your~~ {their} resolves can make one tittle of the Law {to} pass away—yet Decency obliges us to submit— Tis your part Mr. Sp[ea]k[e]r to command—tis ours to obey—& since we cannot make the defence We intended, We must make the{[at]} {defence} We are allowd.

We are chargd with advis[in]g writ[in]g & publish[in]g a Libel. To clear ours[elves] from the Charge of advis[in]g writ[in]g & publish[in]g a Libel We came here— But when we are here, we find the Case is alt[ere]d & we are to defend ours[elves] from a charge of &c a [par][ticu]lar paper wh[ich] this house has resolvd to be a Libel— The Criminality is determ[ine]d ag[ains]t us before we have app[eare]d—for now instead of clear[in]g ours[elves] from be[in]g Libellers—we are to clear ours[elves] from be[in]g advisers [pro]moters or p[ub]lishers of a certain Paper Mr. Smith und[oubte]dly had a right to acquit hims[elf] from the {crime with wh[ich] he is} chargd, the {crime} Chargd is a Libel, if then the Crime [pro]vd is <u>not</u> a Libel— he is acq[uitte]d from the {crime} chargd. What are the Law books filld with but {1000 of} Disputes whether a fact be H[igh] Treason or Murder or Felony or the like {th[at] is whether [par][ticu]lar facts amo[un]t to the crimes wh[ich] the Law calls by these names.}. 2 th[in]gs then Mr. Smith had a right to dispute—the fact itself—& the Crim[ina]lty of th[at] fact—& conseq[ent]ly ~~by~~ this vote wh[ich] precludes him from disput[in]g the Case has lopt off one half of his defence.

The Law Sir determ[ines] what is a Libel, & th[at] Law is to be fo[un]d in the Law Books—& I hope no Jud[gmen]t of this house will ever call th[at] a Libel, wh[ich] the Law does not call so

213

This Libel then to wh[ich] we are to ans[wer] is an Addr[ess] from Mr. Moor
to Gov[erno]r Denny— And in order more fully to understand this Aff[ai]r
{be able to apply the testimony} it may not be im[pro][per] to relate it at
large—& then examine what share Mr. Smith had in it.   Mr. Moor was
summond [*page break*]

(4)

Summond by the late Ass[embly] to attend them on some Comp[lain]ts
th[at] had been made to them by sev[era]l [Per]sons of his misbehavior in
his off[ice] as a Magest[rate] His conduct. Upon this they [pro]ceded to
exam[ine] Witn[esses] till they had got such Evid[ence] as they tho[ugh]t
wo[ul]d sup[ort] an Add[ress] to the Gov[erno]r they presented an Add[ress]
{sett[in]g forth the Comp[lain]ts} contain[in]g many heavy & severe
charges on his Reputation they likewise publ[ishe]d it.

Mr. Moor actuated by his regard for his Char[acte]r tho[ugh]t fit to make
his defence; he did it indeed with most bitter reflexions on the late
Ass[embly] no doubt he was encouragd to ~~do~~ {give} this vent to his anger—
as his knowl[edge] as a Magest[rate] co[ul]d inform th[at] no scandalous
matter whatever containd in any [pro]ceed[in]g in a Reg[u]lar course of
Justice {*tho[ugh] the Court has no Jurisd[icti]on.}—as in a Petition to
Parl[iamen]t or in an Art[icle] of Peace exhib[ite]d to Just[ice] of Peace—
will make a Compl[ain]t [as not[ed]?] to a Libel—for the discouragem[en]t
wh[ich] might follow.* These th[in]gs are allowd too in the way of
[Pro]secution—but Moor's was in defence of his Reputation—& whatever
part of his Char[acte]r any man condemns—one th[in]g I am sure of, th[at]
they cant condemn th[at] part where he Endeav[ours] to vindicate
[~~illegible~~]{his} Char[acte]r

He went to the Author[ity] the Ass[embly] had estab[lishe]d He followd
their steps—they presented an Addr[ess] to the Gov[erno]r he pres[ente]d
an Addr[ess] to the Gov[erno]r   they publ[ishe]d their Addr[ess]   he
publ[ishe]d his {[*caret*]}—they usd severe words—he uses <u>their</u> words—
He sent his Justif[icati]on thro[ugh] the same channel that conveyd their
charge, th[at] he might pour a balm into the wounds of his Reputation as
soon as possible.

{Law determ[ines] wh[at] is a Libel & th[at] Law app[ear]s in the Law
books} If this attempt of Mr. Moor to vindicate himself however unjust the
Charges are on the late Ass[embly] is not a Libel, I hope no Jud[gment] of
this house will call th[at] a Libel wh[ich] the Law does not call so.

Petition of Seven Bishops; acquitted to great Joy of the People

==

Long parl[iamen]t clamourd ag[ains]t so much while sitt[in]g—th[at] they were obligd to change their conduct

==

Law of Ægyptians   Scipio Africanus calld to an ano[the]r & why Because the Romans were a free people.   Checks in our Gov[ernmen]t Love of Fame one of the best Checks
== [*page break*]

(5)

Now Mr. Sp[ea]k]e]r We come to the third po[in]t [pro]posd— Whether Mr. Smith is guilty of advis[in]g writ[in]g & publish[in]g—A Libel—

On this charge every part by the Rules of Law to be [pro]vd for it is a **Conjunt[ive]** charge,[3] & numberless Cases to this Po[in]t but I am sure it will not be denied— One Instance I will mention—Richmond Park affair.[4]

But so far from [pro]v[in]g all the parts—I beg leave to say there is no [pro]of of one part— The Order Mr. Sp[ea]k[e]r wh[ich] I shall now persue will be this—

1. I shall consider the Evid[ence] th[at] goes to the advis[in]g writ[in]g &c
2. The Evid[ence] th[at] related to the publishing—
3. ~~Submit the Law arising on the Testimonies~~ {The Evid[ence] for Us—}
&

Then conclude.

The first th[in]g th[at] strikes us Mr. Sp[ea]k[e]r in the course of this Evid[ence] is th[at] every man who gives Evid[ence] ag[ains]t us—is more Crim[ina]l than Mr. Smith. Dr. T[homas] Bond was consulted by Moor, ~~Dr. T[homas] Bond~~ was present when Sm[ith] was [pre]sent says all were concernd—& more alt[eration]s [pro]posd by others th[an] Smith Dr. P[hineas] Bond says Smith never shewd any forw[ar]dness in the aff[ai]r th[at] he hims[elf] cons[idere]d Counsel—th[at] he pressd Sm[ith], th[at] he prevaild with him to make the alt[eration]s he did—wh[ich]   only were literal or figures. Mr. Levers transcribd, & Hanshaw Hall & Bradford & Armb[ruste]r {translated &} publishd.

Every arrow of this [pro]secution has past thro[ugh] these witn[esse]s w[ith]out hurt[in]g them, & fixes in Mr. Smith's breast— He becomes the com[mon] Receptacle of Guilt, & the dart th[at] pierces others with its fullest force, leaves not the least mark, but ruins us with its glance.   If this distinction ~~of~~{[*illegible*]} be for the publick good—if the cause of Justice is advanced by it, Smith will {chearfully} submit ~~with~~ & rejoice to save others, tho[ugh] it is by suffer[in]g for them: But [per]mit him Mr. Sp[ea]k[e]r to

<u>wonder</u> **By** wh[at] unknown wickeness it happ[en]s th[at] crimes in him sho[ul]d be Innocence in others   th[at] the nature of th[in]gs sho[ul]d change, when done by him & when done by others. However these th[in]gs are so & it is y[ou]r pleasure we sho[ul]d answer & we obey— [*page break*]

(6)

I shall now pursue my plan & consider the Evid[ence] th[at] goes to the advis[in]g Writ[in]g &c.

1. Mr. Smith's Exam[inatio]n   Obj[ectio]n This I submit is no Evid[ence] unless signd 9 Mod. 89 Law of Evid[ence] 136. Taken only in præparatorio[5]

    But gr[an]t[in]g it to be Evid[ence]—it only amo[un]ts to this— th[at] he took a Copy of an Addr[ess]—but it does not app[ea]r what Addr[ess]—[wh]eth[er] th[at] pres[ede]d th[at] publishd—or some other—however allow[in]g [th?]—{—}for we are so confid[en]t of our Innoc[ennce] th[at] we will allow th[in]gs th[at] I am sure never wo[ul]d be expected from us: allow[in]g the Addr[ess] Mr. Sm[ith] copied from to be the addr[ess] pres[ente]d & publ[ishe]d—wh[ich] is this Mr. Sp[ea]k[e]r to the advis[in]g & contriv[in]g a Libel—is copy[in]g a Libel after it is written—<u>advis[in]g</u> {abet[in]g} & ~~writ[in]g~~ {promot[in]g} it— is this <u>promot[in]g</u> it, to copy it after it is <u>finishd</u>.

[*in left margin:*] {Dr. P[hineas] Bond ment[ione]d it but did not determ[ine] the time so it cant be presumd to be before publ[icati]on—but suppose &c not to others—}

Lambs Case 9 Co. 59[6] expressly in point. V[ide] th[at] part when he **know[in]g it to be a Libel**—writes a Copy—Obj[ection] We did not <u>know</u>—for learned Counsel s[ai]d it was no Libel—Reason why we copied—to write a history & this a h[u]mble th[in]g as it ref[er]s to a dispute ab[ou]t the author[ity] of this hon[oura]ble house—.}

[*in left margin:*] {w[ith]out Intention & w[ith]out Injury}

Besides this copy never publ[ishe]d for tho[ugh] Dr. P[hineas] B[ond] saw it yet he had seen the Orig[inal]—& Lambs Case is express th[at] it must be [lent &c?] read to **others**—Now wh[at] the mean[in]g of this word **others**. but others th[an] those who knew of it—this is Law & this is reason for it is absurd &c

Will find all the other q[ues]tions & answ[ers] explaind by the other Evid[ence]—for Sm[ith] was so little concernd in this aff[ai]r th[at] it app[ear]s he was ignor[an]t of many th[in]gs th[at] the Bonds & other [cert[ain]ly?] knew V[ide] his Exam[inati]on[7]

2. The next evid[ence] is Dr. T[homas] Bond's. V[ide] Depos[itio]n[8] Exact Agreement betw[een] the witn[ess] to the [par][ticu]lars. Letters refer to one another—
3. Dr. Ph[ineas] Bond.[9]
4. Mr. Robert Livers.[10]

This then is the Evidence to [pro]ve our writ[in]g advis[in]g &c this Libel— Evid[ence] so slight & trifl[in]g th[at] ~~I hope every freeman will blush to think any fellow-subject ought to be deprivd of his~~ **freedom** ~~upon it~~ {no man wo[ul]d be convicted at com[mon] Law of this most Unconscionable Tress[pass] upon it}— Shall remarks made in conversat[io]n between five gent[leme]n but not [pro]vd by <u>wh[ich]</u>—shall alt[eration]s {made} in conseq[uence] of those rem[ar]ks, but not [pro]vd by whom—I say shall these th[in]gs deprive an Eng[lishman] of his Liberty, & send him like a Malefactor to a Com[mon] Jayl.   The 3 Evid[ence]s agree th[at] none of them was made by Sm[ith] Mr. Liv[er]s opin[ion] th[at] it was a hand like unto S[mith]'s contra[dicte]d by both the B[ond]'s
{y   y}[11] Dr. P[hineas] Bonds Figures & letters.

(7)

But gr[an]t Levers to be positively sure it is like S[mith]'s hand what is th[at]: is it not firmly settld th[at] Similitude of hands is no Evid[ence] in Crim[ina]l matters.[12]   The best blood in Engl[an]d has been spilt on th[at] vile Doctrine, when Col[onel] Algernon Sydney was put to death by it. This great & brave man, with a Spirit becoming his birth & country oppos[~~illegible~~]{d} & struggled with the unjust Usurp[ation]s of a tyrannical Prince & a wicked sett of Ministers: he gallantly asserted those rights wh[ich] he rec[eive]d with his **Life**, & wh[ich] he was resolvd to keep while he retaind his **Life**: [~~illegible~~]{and} he did: for he seald with the loss of his {head} the claim of those Liberties wh[ich] he had so often so boldly maint[aine]d with [~~illegible~~]{H}is tongue & his hand: He was sacr[ifice]d upon a Charge of H[igh] Treason; where one ov[er]t act was [pro]vd by Sim[ili]tude of hands—a Jud[gmen]t lookd upon with detestation by every Lawyer—& every honest man since: His Att[ainde]r rev[oke]d in Parl[iamen]t 1 Will. & Mary:[13] for ~~Opin[ion]~~ {Jud[gmen]t} of Law V[ide] Law of Ev[idence], 54. 55. 2 Hawk. P. C. 431. Raym. 40.[14]
Very well convincd this house will never revive ~~it~~ an opin[ion] th[at] when alive murd[ere]d the best & bravest Subjects.
But   grant this copy actually to be S[mith]'s—Sm[ith] did not pub[lish] &c even to Mr. Levers—for Moor shewd it Lev[ers] & it wo[ul]d be absurd[ity] to blame Sm[ith] for publ[ishin]g it to Moor who was the

author of it & ag[ains]t Law as I have shewn above of read[in]g or lend[in]g to others.

[*in left margin*:] {But both B[on]ds say Lev[er]s copy was not from Sm[i]t[h]s.

θ It is extremely happy for these Gent[leme]n th[at] this cause is not in a {Com[mon]} Court{se} of Justice—your Rules Mr. Sp[ea]k[e]r are diff[eren]t from those of Com[mon] Law—It is ~~uncommon~~ {unprecedented} there, for a Principal to come & accuse the accessary—for the most guilty to accuse the most innocent.

[*in left margin*:] {θ This comes in at pa. 12.}

{I don't sp[ea]k by way of Accusat[io]n but mention them as extraordinary, & not disagreeable to them.}

Dr. Bond says {*} Sm[ith] was very backw[ar]d to be conc[erne]d but he prest him, he **prevaild** upon him: These Mr. Sp[ea]k[e]r are ungrateful sounds in the Ears of Justice—to [pro]ceed from a Witn[ess] ag[ains]t a [Prisoner]

[*in left margin*:] {* He presided over the press he usd a great many [A]g[en]ts with Bradford—but We none with Hanshaw but th[at] Hall has pr[in]ted it—}

But when he had **prevaild**—wh[at] was it to do: it was to commit the enormous crime of add[in]g {^{X}} a Letter or mak[in]g a figure

[*in left margin*:] {X Besides the Paper was then in the press—& a Proof Sheet[15] only amended.}

And shall a freeman of Pennsylvania be impris[one]d & denied the com[mon] Priv[ilege]s of Light & Air for a Letter or a figure—are all our boasted Rights come to this. {Shall a letter or a figure condemn a man.} Mr. Sp[ea]k[e]r indulge me with your Patience for really it must be almost tir[e]d with {hear[in]g} ~~repeat[in]g~~ {titions of} such ridiculous & trifling testimonies.   This prodigious Crime of add[in]g literal Corrections is entirely purgd away by Bradfords 2.^d Answer, for he says [*page break*]

(8)

Says he left out all the corrections th[at] Dr. P[hineas] Bond had made.[16]

Here then Mr. Sp[ea]k[e]r I will make a pause & beg Your ~~Y~~{th}is hon[oura]ble house to turn back their view & be so good as to observe if yet their app[ear]s the least ~~spark~~ {sign} of Evid[ence] not only of an actual but of an intentional Offence. Mr. Sm[ith] did not form the plan of this Libel— Mr. Sm[ith] did not compose it— There does not app[ea]r thro[ugh] the whole Course of the Testim[ony] even the smallest Spark of Resentment in Mr. Sm[ith's] bosom ag[ains]t the late Ass[embly]

It is not [pro]vd th[at] he went to Dr. Bonds on this aff[ai]r he w[a]s a friend—he was often there. During the [Conversation?] [*torn*] th[at] turnd on the subj[ec]t of the Addr[ess]—how did he behave—As a man of his [Pro]fession ought to do—he s[ai]d least of any body says Dr. T[homas] Bond—he never shewd any forwardness—says Dr. P[hineas] B[ond] ~~Mr. Lev[ers] says to the best of his Rememb[erance] some alter[ation]s were made but he cant say in Conseq[uence] of whose Rem[ar]ks but this [person]~~

In the Course of **Conversation**—while we were talk[in]g of this **Paper**—Mr. Sm[ith] [~~pro]posd~~ {made} some Rem[ar]ks—but neither they nor Le[ver]s can say any alt[eration]s were made in Conseq[ence] of them:

There is someth[in]g Mr. Sp[ea]k[e]r in this Evid[ence] th[at] strikes me with terror, th[at] almost makes me tremble— We appear here to answ[er] for words dropd in the course of Conv[ersati]on, in the {free} familiar intercourse of friendly discourse {Commun[icati]on}.* [*in left margin:*] {* Puts one in mind of terrible times in History—V[ide] pa. 9.}

In a fr[ien]d's house in comp[any] with friends, Mr. Sm[ith] to have av[oide]d this Charge, must have kept a surly silence, or disputed perhaps quarr[ele]d with the man th[at] entert[aine]d him or his father

As little as he co[ul]d he joind with them—he shewd no forw[ar]dness—he said least of any—if he talkd at all, he must have talkd of the Addr[ess], & if he talkd of the ad[d]r[ess]—cert[ain]ly what he [*in left margin:*] {*said must have been remarks upon it.}

If Enquiries of this sort Mr. Sp[ea]k[e]r are to be made—if our Conv[ersati]on is to be sifted—while we indulge the social joys friends[hi]p—& practize the sacred Rules of Hospitality—then Adieu to the best—the dearest of human Enjoyments: If Crimes are to be sought for in the room ~~of [his?]~~ of friendly entertainm[en]t the next step must—be {to} our beds—& even Dreams will be criminal.

Permit me Sir to quit this melancholy subj[ec]t on wh[ich] no man can dwell with the least pleasure, & to comfort my ~~Client~~ {self} with recollect[in]g my Judges—& th[at] You Sir preside in this Cause. When I remember this Mr. Sp[ea]k[e]r I seem to revive, & I will not suffer any gloomy appreh[ension]s to take hold of Me, when I consider to whom I am speaking.

The Evidence [*page break*]

(9)

Permit me Mr. Sp[ea]k[e]r to make one more observation on these 3 Deposit[ion]s of the Bonds & Levers. Their Evid[ence] Sir relates only to the prepar[in]g the Copy for an addr[ess] to the Gov[erno]r so that wav[in]g the weakness & futility of their Evid[ence]—giv[in]g up entirely what they do not [pro]ve to the Minutest degree of [pro]b[abili]ty th[at] Sm[ith] was concernd in [pro]mot[in]g or abett[in]g the writ[in]g ~~& publ[ishin]g~~ this

Libel— **Yet** no man can be so mistaken as to say th[at] there[fore] [*torn*] guilty— There is no diff[erence] between publish[in]g & pr[omoti]ng[.]
[*in left margin*:] {You have resolvd this to be a Libel—but th[at] is one suppos[itio]n th[at] it is publ[ishe]d {for nothing is a Libel till then}. But You have not resovd th[at] present[in]g it to the Gov[erno]r is publish[in]g it—& th[at] is the diff[erence] universally estab[lishe]d in the books—th[at] present[in]g to a Comm[itt]ee of Parl[iamen]t no Libel—but to <u>others</u> is.}

The Ass[embly] had applied to the Gov[erno]r ag[ains]t Moor, he app[eal]s to the Gov[erno]r in his def[ence] in the course of Justice {They present he presents &c}. Ass[embly's] Opin[ion] of Gov[erno]r's Auth[ority] And at this time the Ass[embly] was dead in Law.[17] Most violent & unjust Charges to be sure Moor made upon the last {Ass[embly]}—such charges as must be disbelievd the moment it is known ag[ains]t whom they are made—& the Opin[ion] the freemen of this [Pro]vince have since shewn of those Gent[leme]n's Cond[uc]t plainly discov[er]s how unde[serve]d they were: **But Mr. Sp[ea]k[e]r** however unjust his Charges were upon [Per]sons lately in publick Capac[itiy]— [per]haps noth[in]g is more to be wishd th[an] freedom of censur[in]g Publick Ministers when their Off[ice]s are expird— [*in left margin*:] {Power of the House of Lords.} Their Dignity & the Com[mon] Safety forbid it, while they are in office, but nothing can be better designd—th[an] such a Liberty afterwards.
[*in left margin*:] {Hope this House will not call that a Libel wh[ich] the Law does not call so.}

The wise custom of the Ægyptians; not to bury a King—till his Virtues & Vices have been compard.
Scipio Africanus after he had driven Hannibal from the gates of Rome, & deliv[ere]d Italy from a Burthen under wh[ich] She had been groaning for 16 Years—was sealld to an Acc[oun]t for his Conduct & why **because** the Romans were then a <u>free</u> people.[18]
[*in left margin*:] {[*torn*] the best men in Rome [*torn*]utd off for Libells under th[at] Law. Annals 1. Cap. 72.[19]}

But afterw[ar]ds in the time of the Emp[e]rors[20]—Words & Looks were crimes—& the best man[21] in the Roman Empire put to death—because he was [pre]sent when a fr[ien]d read a Piece in wh[ich] he called **Cassius the last of the Romans.***[22]
[*in left margin*:] {* This was by the Lex lesæ maj[es]tatis[23]—an unknown uncertain Law as Tacitus says—of wh[ich] a man did not know he was guilty till he rec[eive]d the punishm[en]t Formerly says th[at] histor[ian] We had this Law[24]—but diff[eren]t crimes were pun[ishe]d by it—as Crimes ag[ain]st Facta arguebantur, dicta impune erant[25]—but revived by Tiberius[26]—& [18?] }

Long Parl[iamen]t in Cha[rle]s 2.[d's] time so much clam[oure]d ag]ains]t th[at] they were obligd to change their Cond[uc]t & Constit[utio]n sav[e]d by Comp[lain]ts of the people.

Trial of Seven Bishops—Penal Laws—great Joy of the People—
[*page break*]

(10)

Now come to the Evid[ence] about publish[in]g.

1. Hanshaw says Sm[ith] told him to transl[ate] it & gave as a Reason that Hall the Assembly's Printer had pr[in]ted it & th[at] the Dutch People near Moor wanted to see it.[27]

2. Armbruster says Mr. Sm[ith] did not give him order to pr[in]t it {but} & [after?] contr[a]d[ie]ts himself & says Mr. Sm[ith] gave {bid} him orders for an overplus Number of 62.[28]

   The same Rule holds as to these witn[esses] as the rest—they are more Criminal th[an] Sm[ith] but my poor Client seems to be the Common Scape Goat to bear every bodys Offences.

   Many Q[ues]tions askd as if Sm[ith] had usd some unjust means as threats to force these men: but th[at] not the Case, or if he had it is a Maxim of Law—Domino nu parti in illicitis obdur[a]nost

[*in left margin*:] {Speaker / Laying Traps—}

   What Arg[umen]ts {Reason} did he use then—that they might put it because it was pr[in]ted in Hall & F[rank]lin's Paper {the Paper the [f?] source of our Misfort[une]}—for We [*illegible words*] by th[at] have we been deceivd & entrapd into the situation We are now in.

   We argued with Ours[elves] in this manner— Hall cant be so stupid as he is pr[in]ter to the Ass[embly] to publ[ish] such a Paper as this w[ith]out the **Advice & consent** of some Gent[leme]n of the Ass[embly]—& it seems We were not mistaken—but of this hereafter

[*in left margin*:] {In the Common way of Business as Usual / Publick before / Not the Manuscript

Did not send for H[anshaw]

Did not give him {a} Paper

[*torn*] Moor [estab[lishe]d?]

Often blamd him before

Bid H[anshaw] & he bid Armb[ruster]}

   Mr. Sm[ith] is concernd in this press as a **Trustee** for the Soc[ie]ty to [pro]mote the Eng[lish] Language—so th[at] he is actually a Printer as much as Hall Bradford or Armbruster. Noth[in]g more disagreeable to people th[an] to pay for Paper & when they hear th[in]gs talkd of—not to have Acc[oun]ts at the [pro][per] time & theref[ore] Sm[ith] might well chide Hanshaw & tell him [*torn*] many Dutch People compl[aine]d

221

th[at] they had not fo[un]d this Addr[ress] in their Papers: & it was Mr. S[mith]'s **duty** as a **Trustee** to take care th[at] any th[in]g was done to keep up the Cred[ibility] of his Paper: & putt[in]g Hanshaw in mind of his omission, was noth[in]g more th[an] wh[at] we had often done before on neglects of the same nature—

[*in left margin, diagonally*:] {false to his Truth if he had not spoken for 62 Copies.}

Did not send for Hanshaw on this occasion.

Did not give him a Paper—he transl[ate]d from Hall's—the source &c

We Agents to Moor for the 62 Copies—as we told Hans[aw] they were for him & Armb[ruster] was ord[ere]d to charge them to him.

Besides it was publ[ished] when we publ[ishe]d it for it had been sometime in Hall & B[radfor]d's

(11)

One obj[ecti]on on this Evid[ence] At the time we bid him publish this Address—We did not <u>know</u> it to be a Libel {as learned Co[unse]l said not.}—& {*}[29] **know[in]g**{—it to be a Libel,} is necessary to make it an offence. 5 Co. 59. Hawk. P. C. 196. Moor. 813.[30]   **But**

[*in left margin*:] {This agreeable to the Law deliv[ere]d by the Duty th[at] Sins of Ignor[ance] are easily atond for

Levit[icus] 4. 27. 28 And if any one of the com[mon] people [sin] thro[ugh] Ignor[ance] while he [doeth somewhat] ag[ains]t the [Com]mand[men]ts of the Lord—concern[in]g th[in]gs wh[ich] ought not to be done & be guilty thereof;

Or if his Sin wh[ich] he hath sinned com[m]its his Knowl[edge]—then he shall br[in]g his offer[in]g—a kid of the Goats—a female w[ith]out blemish—for his sin wh[ich] he hath sinned.}

The members of this house told Hall if it was Libellous; he might pr[in]t it—but to take care th[at] he co[ul]d [pro]ve the author. This leads Me Mr. Sp[ea]k[e]r to the

3 Point—Our Evidence

1. Bradford not of much Conseq[uence] he only says—the Copy he pr[in]ted from was not S[mith]'s writ[in]g[31]

2. Hall lays open the whole trans[action?] of our Guilt & the fountain of all our misfort[une]s

    Hall says he never wo[ul]d have publ[ishe]d this addr[ess] w[ith]out the Advice &c this leads us into this ~~mistake~~ crime.[32]

    If this Addr[ess] had never been publ[ished] in Hall's paper—We sho[ul]d never have been a [pri]soner at this Bar—& th[at] Addr[ess] had never been publ[ishe]d in Hall's paper w[ith]out the **Advice &**

~~consent~~ {& consent} of three members of this house—of Conseq[uence] theref[ore] we sho[ul]d never have been here, if it had not been for—these three members.

[*in left margin*:] {Owing to—but}

Perhaps I am mistaken when I say they told Hall to take care if it was libelous—th[at] he co[ul]d [pro]ve the author.

[*in left margin*:] {Not for his own [pro]fit but true to his Trust}

Can it be possible th[at] any worthy members of this house, wo[ul]d advise the pr[in]t[in]g of a "Scandelous Libel ag[ains]t the late Ass[embly] & containing gross reflections & tend[in]g to subert {& destroy} the most essential parts of the Constitut[io]n & to take away the most valuable Powers of this house," as it is said to do Mr. Sp[ea]k[e]r in your Addr[ess] to the Gov[erno]r

[*in left margin*:] {Woud they run the Risque of publish[in]g such alt[e]r[in]g only to punish the Author— Mr. Hall's Evid[ence] accesses them not To confine Myself to the words

Don't know now   to blame / Break heads / Stick close as Salvation / Mr. Yorke[33] by way of Mitigation / Serjeant}

Can these Gent[leme]n complain of such a Libel be[in]g publ[ishe]d when it never wo[ul]d have been publ[ishe]d w[ith]out their **adv[ice] & cons[en]t** Or can these Gent[leme]n give a Vote for condemn[in]g a man for an offence wh[ich] they allowd & abetted.

One of the most excellent men of this age Young has said speak[in]g &c

"He that prevents it not when in his power
Supports them in their course of flagr[an]t guilt["][34]

[*in left margin*:] {Unwilling to mention the Nature of the Paper but now}

But this was not only support[in]g us in what we did—it [*page break*]

(12)

It was sett[in]g us an Example—& now   We are condemnd for follow[in]g it.

({[X] infra} Suppose a Case of High Treason—& then sit as Judges.

Liberty of the Press pretended—but not to catch people in Traps— but we can brace the Arg[umen]t—then allow us the same Indulg[ence] as Hall—for We are as much a Printer besides he publ[ishe]d first & We {only re-}publ[ishe]d what was publishd.

[*in left margin*:] {It gives Me great concern}

[*in left margin*:] {If Liberty for them for Us too [*illegible*]}

When Hall came to these Gentl[eme]n he told them &c & they answer[e]d &c

223

[*in left margin*:] {Let not the best of Blessings be usd to destroy Liberty—
wh[ich] used to pre[sume?] it.

If Hall to blame it was owing—but}
This is what they have done—Now **Ill** tell what they have not done.
They did not warn Hall—they did not tell him the Conseq[uence]s
they did not end[eavou]r to prevent a Crime.

Not only this—but tho[ugh] we have been down into what we did
by these Gentl[eme]n They are to be our Judges. No case in point but
&c **Bible.**[35]

Men were frail then—but too much Virtue & Integrity to deal
harder with those they had led astray than themselves.

He did not punish because a [par]ty to the Offence—
[*in left margin*:] {If Criminal for Us Why not &c}
Mr. Sm[ith] did not know this to be a Libel—as Couns[el] denied
it. These Gentl[eme]n told Hall if it <u>was</u> libelous, he sho[ul]d take are
{to know author.} Mr. Sm[ith] pr[in]ted this Addr[ess]—bec[ause] it
was in Hall's Paper.
[*in left margin*:] {for his own [pro]fit / Mr. Smith in Trust}
These Gentl[eme]n allo[we]d it to be pr[in]ted for the Liberty of the
press {it seems}. Mr. Sm[ith] ~~pr[in]ted~~ did only wh[at] these
Gentl[eme]n had allowd to be done.
[*in left margin*:] {Not only this—but Sm[ith] wo[ul]d not have done his duty
to his Majesty & the Society [~~illegible~~] Moor was to pay.
Mr. Sm[ith] is a Printer but these Gentl[eme]n dont pretend to be. [lett?]
wh[ich?]
[Per]haps this house dont [*torn*] **Society.** His Majesty [s?] {Chief Subscriber
& at the head of it— Many R[ight] Rev[eren]d Bishops Sm[ith] a Trustee
under [them?]
They will not be pleasd if it reaches the royal ear—his Maj[esty] will
not be pleasd th[at] his Printer sho[ul]d be treated hardly for ~~doing~~
republishing wh[at] the Assembly's Pr[in]ter had publ[ishe]d with **advice &
consent** of some members}
* What signif[ies] their reasons to us of Lib[erty] of Press & for fear
Mr. Hall sho[ul]d be tho[ugh]t a Partyman—[36] Did we know {co[ul]d
we know} any th[in]g of these priv[ate] aff[air]s

But we knew Hall wo[ul]d never have <u>dard</u> to pr[in]t this addr[ess]
w[ith]out Leave of his masters—& We tho[ugh]t Mr. Sp[ea]k[e]r they
thems[elves] at least wo[ul]d never think it crim[ina]l to do wh[at] they
had allowd to be done—but in this we were mistaken.

⌈ Diff[erence] betw[een] Moor's off[ence] & ours—as his preceded
the leave of these Gentl[eme]n but ours followd & was [pro]duced by
th[at] Leave.

This Mr. Sp[ea]k[e]r is the Evid[ence] ag[ains]t so slight so trifling
so incons[idera]ble th[at] I hope Every freeman will <u>blush</u> to think a
fellow Subj[ec]t sho[ul]d be deprivd of his Freedom upon it

As I said before both the [~~illegible~~] writ[in]g **and** publish[in]g
sho[ul]d be [*page break*]

(13)

[pro]vd—but here I beg leave to say neither is— It is extremely happy
for those Gentlemen &c V[ide] pa. 7 & 8 wh[ich] come in here.

This Sir is the Evid[ence] as to the Writ[in]g—the Evid[ence] as to
the other the publ[ishin]g is still weaker—   [As?] We are **Trustees** for
managing a Print[in]g house—& have done noth[in]g but in the
com[mon] course of our Business th[at] is transcribd from Hall's Paper

[As] Hanshaw [pro]ves to have been always our Custom & th[at]
before now he had been often blamd by ~~us~~ for not do[in]g it. We did not
send for Hans[haw]   We did not give him a Paper for this many People
imagind—No. We only referrd him to wh[at] the Ass[embly] printer
had publishd. If we are wrong—we have been lead wrong by your
Printer & his fault was owing [*blank*] but Sir Ive done on this point.

However this Mr. Sm[ith] prays for th[at] he may be the only man
in Pensilv[ani]a who is bro[ugh]t into this house for an off[ence] he
never wo[ul]d have been guilty of but for some members of this house:
th[at] none but ~~him~~{e} may ever behold those men sit as his Judges who
occasiond his crime.

This cause Mr. Sp[ea]k[e]r as I said at first is of the utmost
Importance not only to Mr. Sm[ith] but to every Freeman of this
[pro]vince—In wh[ich] the Præerog[ative] of the Crown & the ~~Liberty~~
{Rights} of the Subj[ec]ts are equally inter[este]d & I app[ea]r with Joy
in behalf of a man who I am [per]swaded has the Laws of his Country
on his Side

[*in left margin:*] {Suppose an Indifferent impartial [per]son who understood
English and Dutch sitt[in]g down & read[in]g these 2 papers—what
Difference coud he find: I never knew the German to be a wicked Language
before, tho[ugh] rough & coarse.}

~~As for~~ Tho[ugh] I understand I am blamd by many people, Nursd
in the arms of Liberty—for the gr[ea]test part of my time sp[en]t in this
[Pro]vince

Here have learnt the generous lessons of honest Freedom Th[at] no man to be lookd on a guilty till cond[emne]d

Th[at] noth[in]g sho[ul]d discourage a good man from assising an inno[cen]t

Great Reflect[ion]s on this house if nobody wo[ul]d defend those accusd before You. I engage in no [par]ty—but in the cause of Just[ice] & a shame to me & my [Pro]fession—if I did not.

[*in left margin*:] {A Precedent for a good Gov[ernmen]t is a Preced[en]t for a bad Governm[en]t}

A sense of Virtue—as well as your Honour require th[at] there sho[ul]d be [per]sons concernd for Mr. Smith— What serv[ice]s I coud do—I have endeav[oure]d to do—[per]haps might have been able to do him more [*page break*]

(14)

If We had not been so streightend by y[ou]r Resolves

Two thirds of our Def[ence] Cogniz[ance] Libel taken away

Thus those Obj[ecti]ons wh[ich] in Justice to ours[elves] to our Countrymen we designd to have made are taken away

Th[at] noble Priv[ilege] of be[in]g tried by our Peers—on a Charge fo[un]d by the Grand—a Priv[ilege] as old as the English Const[ituti]on & will last as long as the Spir[it] of Freedom remains is denied us

Mr. Sm[ith] must forget he is an Eng[lishman] must forget the Rights & Liberties he is born rend[ere]d heir to Magna Charta, Bill of Rights & all those{e} Securities to those Liberties wh[ich] the Wisdom of our Ancestors has pland, & their blood has ~~pourd to support~~ {purchasd}

[*in left margin*:] {V[ide] pa. 2.}

because You command him

He must not lament the loss of Blessings he is entitled to—

because it is your pleas[ure] he sho[ul]d not enjoy them

This he submits to—but [~~per~~]mit ~~him to~~ {he cant forbear} cast[in]g his view forward when a worse house—for surely a worse house {than this} may succeed, shall govern; [*illegible*] & is afraid this Preced[en]t may hereafter fall heavier on your Posterity—th[at] it can do on him. tho[ugh] that indeed is bad enough—for y[ou]r pun[ishmen]t is Comm[itmen]t & the same for Sm[ith] as for Moor—no [pro]protion.

No Crime so heinous, to put an Englishman in such a miserable situat[ion] but he may end[eavou]r to obtain his Lib[er]ty by **Hab[eas] Cor[pus]** & have the Assist[ance] of Counsel to pl[ea]d his cause before the Court where he is bro[ugh]t—& Jud[ge]s may bail if they see [pro][per]—but if a man does any act [~~act~~?] thro[ugh] ignor[ance] or

226

mist[ake] {wh[ich] shall be votd b[e]c[ause] of Priv[ilege]} as by joining in Conv[ersati]on at P[hinaes] B[ond's] or doing wh[at] the Ass[embly's] Printer has done before, with the **advice & consent** of some of the members—he is put in worse state than a felon or traytor—if his fr[ien]ds appl[y]—b[e]c[ause] of Priv[ilege]

Has any Evid[ence] app[eare]d of a Crime th[at] the most cruel dispos[iti]on wo[ul]d think deserves impris[onmen]t   w[ith]out Bail too—wh[ich] I suppose wo[ul]d be reckond a Breach of Priviledge

But be[in]g ~~deprivd of Trial [and~~?] irreg[ular]ly punishd not all: We may be **twice** punishd—this is tho[ugh]t in Low detestable {& horrible}—& ag[ains]t all reason for the intent of punish[in]g is not to make life miserable by repeat[in]g it—but to discour[age] vice by correct[in]g it. By the Divine Law—even the the murd[ere]r livd—when the price of blood was once dichargd. Quote one Inst[ance] where a Jud[gmen]t by house of Com[mons] pl[ea]ded in barr to an Ind[ictmen]t in the Courts of Law—& I will allow that we cant be punishd twice—but if &c— [*page break*]

(15)

But to make this still plainer—supp[ose] Sm[ith] ~~acq[uitte]d~~ {ind[icte]d} of this Crime ~~by a Trial~~ at Com[mon] Law— He must be either acq[uitte]d or conv[icte]d Take your Choice   If acq[uitte]d will it not be said this house has unjustly deprivd a man of his Liberty w[ith]out legal Evid[ence] of his Guilt— Say then he is condemnd—Will not this house then be the cause of his being <u>twice</u> punishd
Dilemma—insist on it.
On the one side [j]ust[ice]   on the other Dishonour very sev[ere] on Guard[ian]s of the Rights & Lib[erties] of Pennsylv[anian]s
Judges in your own cause—& Wise men know & good men fear the
    partial dist[inction] of their own hearts where their own Int[eres]t is
    concernd; & guard ag[ains]t the least whisper[in]g &c
Infelix populus ubi Jus[s]or &c   A good Comment The L[or]ds addr[ess] to Q[ueen] Ann— "The best & surest way to preserve the **rightful** Priv[ilege]s of Parl[iamen]t is to abide by those th[at] are certain & known & it is not in the power of either or both houses—to create new Priv[ilege]s to themselves: And however it may be seen in the Int[eres]t of the Lords to be silent—while the house of Com[on]s are sett[in]g afoot <u>new pretences</u> of Priviledge because they may share in the advent[age]— Yet we think it our duty & our Inter[es]t to do all we can do to preserve the Constitution entire, & not to sit quiet when we see Innovat[ion] attempted wh[ich] tend to diminut[io]n of the Rights of the Crown—or to the prejudice of the Subject.["]²[37]

[*in left margin:*] {By some [par][ticu]lar fate The same Infallibility now at Rome in Religion that usd to be in Politics has Scripture seald up as the Lex lesæ Majest[atis]}

[*in left margin:*] {Give me one Inst[ance] of call[in]g a man to an acco[un]t for wh[at] was done which no [P]arliament.}

So th[at] att[em]pts have been made by house of Commons unjustly & likewise in Colepeper's Case—V[ide] pa. 2. The house of Com[mons] resol[vd?] [*torn*] had Cogniz[ance] in Ashby & White's case {θ} before they devour [*in left margin:*] {θ but mistaken for Jud[gmen]t for P[lainti]ff in [Dom.¹ [Pro?]ur?]}

Infelix populus &c   No Marks to guide one {Even Scylla & Char[ybdis] give notice} & swallowd in the **Gulf of Priv[ilege]s** before we ~~see it~~ know there is one. Submit if it might not have been d[ishonou]rable to the Freemen of Pens[ylvani]a

This a Cause of Expectation {no doubt People wishd to see their {P[rivilege?]s settled} if I know any th[in]g of their temper}—a will be better pleasd with merciful th[an] severe Jud[gmen]t

[*in left margin:*] {* Pens[lyvani]a[ns] Who are equally concernd in this Cause with Us to be satisf[ie]d as We had Obj[ecti]ons in Law &c}

This the house of Justice—here She dwells with Delight— & while she resides with so much Dignity & Lustre in the other end—I hope the decision of this aff[ai]r will not give occasion

[*in left margin:*] {Lib[er]ty of Speech alw[ays] accomp[anies] Lib[er]ty of [Per]son for by the members of the Body the Tongue & hand—as the Susten[ance] of Life is rec[eive]d by the mouth—& when th[at] is Shut it is equally pernicious to one & the other. Rara tempor[e] &c[38]} {over} [*page break*]

(16)

[*in top margin:*] {but we are denied to speak—whatever we may think—Assertions & Resolves dont give Power tho[ugh] they shew great will[in]gness to receive it. {One tittle to pass away &c V[ide] pa. 3.} When Ja[me]s 2. while D[uke] of Y[ork] went openly to Mass &c And when Cha[rle]s 2.[d] was known to be a Papist—an Act of Parl[iamen]t made &c—[39]}

occasion to any injurious Comparisons: On th[at] decision it will depend whether Mr. Smith shall walk free and to his own house or a [Pri]soner to a Jayl.

{*}Hon[oura]ble Companions.

[*in left margin:*] {* One Petition from Mr. Sm[ith] th[at] all who have shard in the crime may share in the punishm[en]t for it will afford him little comfort in his impr[isonmen]t to think his treatm[en]t like [*torn*] of the Lamb in the fable—[40] {In ~~days~~ time past [&c?]} A Lamb & ano[the]r creature   I have forgot what &c}

at least those who causd his.

Thanks for your Indulgence—first Appear[ance] before such hon[oura]ble Judges—

Hope [*illegible*] every mom[en]ts Juvent[ee][41] will add to my Knowl[edge] th[at] next time I have the honour &c—

Three things distinguish Sm[ith] from those persons who gave Evid[ence] ag[ains]t him: he is a Clergyman, Provost & Writer.

Mr. Dickinson so ill at latter End.

Ms (PHi-Logan)

---

[1] The English Bill of Rights (1689) provided "that excessive bail ought not to be required, nor excessive fines imposed, nor cruel and unusual punishments inflicted."

[2] The Glorious Revolution (1688–89).

[3] A conjunctive charge is when multiple crimes are named and separated by "and" instead of "or," thus constituting a single offense rather than several. A conviction on one of these crimes bars any subsequent prosecution on the others.

[4] In 1751, Princess Amelia became ranger of Richmond Park, southwest of central London. She immediately began denying the public access to the park, which caused an uproar. Members of the public printed pointed essays in the press, particularly in the *London Evening-Post* (see, for example, "To the Author, &c. On Richmond Park" in the issue from Dec. 9, 1752). They drafted a memorial to Amelia, which she refused. It was printed in the *London Evening-Post*, July 16–18, 1752, and JD may have seen the reprint in *The Gentleman's Magazine*, vol. 22 (London: E. Cave, 1752), 380–81. People also sought recourse through legal channels, and a series of judgments between 1754 and 1758 ultimately forced Amelia to grant public access to the park's ancient footways. The first case, *Symonds v. Shaw* (1754), was unsuccessful. In 1757, local brewer John Lewis (1713–1792) sued the gatekeeper for forcibly denying him access to the park. *Rex v. Gray* (1757) came before Chief Justice William Murray, lord Mansfield, at the Summer Assizes in August. The defense produced an anonymous pamphlet entitled, *A Tract on the National Interest, and Depravity of the Times* (London: J. Shepheard, 1757), which attacked Amelia's method of restricting access to favored ticket holders: "Can any man of common understanding be one moment at a loss to see the iniquity of this scheme?" (48). Mansfield stopped the trial to find those responsible for writing, printing, and distributing what he considered a libel to influence the jury. Lewis was immediately suspected, and swore an affidavit that he was not involved. The case eventually continued at the Surrey Assizes on April 3, 1758, before Sir Thomas Denison (1699–1765) and Sir Michael Foster (1689–1763), both of whom had heard the 1754 case (see *London Evening-Post*, April 4, 1758). Lewis won and the verdict restored public access to the park via ladder stiles (see *London Evening-Post*, April 6, 1758). See *ODNB*; Kenneth J. Panton, *Historical Dictionary of the British Monarchy* (Lanham, Md.: Scarecrow Press, Inc., 2011), 45; Mrs. Matthew Hall, *The Royal Princesses of England, from the Reign of George the First* (London: George Routledge and Sons, 1871), 101–03; 1 Burrow 510–13.

[5] Lat. in preporatory (i.e., in preporatory testimony).

---

[6] 9 Coke, *Reports* 59 b., "John Lamb's Case," Mich. 8 Jac. 1 (1610): "if he writes a Copy of it and do not publish it to others, it is no publication of the libel; for every one who shall be convicted ought to be a contriver, procurer, or publisher of it, knowing it to be a Libel."

[7] A copy of Smith's examination is in the Penn Family Papers, PHi.

[8] See "Doct[o]r Thomas Bond's Deposition," Jan. 17, 1758. PHi-Logan and PU-Ar.

[9] See "Doct[o]r Phineas Bond's Deposition," Jan. 17, 1758, PU-Ar. A coversheet for a copy of the deposition exists in PHi-Logan, but the document is not extant. See also *Votes* (1758), 13.

[10] See "Mr. [Robert] Levers's Deposition," Jan. [1]7 & 18, 1758. PHi-Logan.

[11] Perhaps indicating the insertion of "Dr. Bonds Figures & Letters," these marks appear beneath the words "opin[ion]" and "it was" in the line above.

[12] This seems to be the only argument JD made that resonated with the Assembly, who voted unanimously to disregard Levers's testimony about the similitude of hands. See *Votes* (1758), 29.

[13] The 7th Private Act (1688) of the first session of Parliament under William and Mary reversed the charges against Sydney and declared that he had been wrongfully and unjustly convicted.

[14] 2 Hawkins 431: "As to the third particular, *viz.* Whether Similitude of Hands be any Evidence in Criminal Cases: It is observable that this with other Circumstances in *Algernoon Sidney's* Case was ruled to be good Evidence of his having written a Paper charged against him as an Overt-act of High Treason: Yet in the Trial of the seven Bishops, the Court was divided in Opinion, whether Similitude of Hands were Evidence of the Defendants having signed the Paper charged against them as a Libel; and the Parliament having declared an Opinion in the Reversal of *Algernoon Sidney's* Attainder, that Comparison of Hands is no Evidence of a Man's Hand-Writing in Criminal Cases: It seems to have been generally holden since that Time, that it is not Evidence in any Criminal Case, whether capital or not capital."

1 Raymond, *Cases* 40, *Rex v. Crosby* alias *Philips*, Pasch. 7 Will. 3, B.R. (1695): "But the principal point of treason charged upon Mr. *Crosby* being the writing of certain treasonable paper, which the King's counsel endeavoured to prove by comparison of hands, having no other evidence; the prisoner Mr. *Crosby* produced the copy of the act of parliament for the reversal of the attainder of *Algernoon Sidney* Esq.; in which it is declared, that the comparison of hands is not legal evidence. Upon which the jury found the prisoner not guilty."

[15] Proof-sheet: "A sheet printed from a forme of type or printing plate for the purpose of examination and correction before being finally printed off for use" (*OED*).

[16] In "Questions ask'd by the Assembly": "Q. Who corrected your Proof Sheet? A. Doctor Phineas Bond, and when he brought back the Proof Sheet there were some Words mark'd in it, but as he said it was immaterial whether put in or no, I left them out, and corrected what litteral Faults were marked on the Sheet." "William Bradford's Deposition," Jan. 18, 1758, PHi-Logan.

[17] That is, adjourned and unable to act.

[18] In the Battle of Zama (202 BC), Scipio Africanus defeated the Carthaginian army under Hannibal (247–c. 183 BC). His victory ended Carthage as a significant military power in the Mediterranean and brought an end to the Second Punic War (218–201 BC).

[19] Tac. *Ann.* 1.72: "That year triumphal honours were decreed to Aulus Cæcina, Lucius Apronius, Caius Silius for their achievements under Germanicus. The title of 'father of his country,' which the people had so often thrust on him, Tiberius refused, nor would he allow obedience to be sworn to his enactments, though the Senate voted it, for he said repeatedly that all human things were uncertain, and that the more he had obtained, the more precarious was his position. But he did not thereby create a belief in his patriotism, for he had revived the law of treason, the name of which indeed was known in ancient times, though other matters came

under its jurisdiction, such as the betrayal of an army, or seditious stirring up of the people, or, in short, any corrupt act by which a man had impaired 'the majesty of the people of Rome.' Deeds only were liable to accusation; words went unpunished. It was Augustus who first, under colour of this law, applied legal inquiry to libellous writings, provoked, as he had been, by the licentious freedom with which Cassius Severus had defamed men and women of distinction in his insulting satires. Soon afterwards, Tiberius, when consulted by Pompeius Macer, the prætor, as to whether prosecutions for treason should be revived, replied that the laws must be enforced. He too had been exasperated by the publication of verses of uncertain authorship, pointed at his cruelty, his arrogance, and his dissensions with his mother."

[20] Augustus (63 BC–14 AD) ruled as Rome's first emperor from 27 BC until his death. Emperors ruled both the eastern and western halves of the Roman Empire together until the death of Theodosius I (347–395).

[21] Aulus Cremutius Cordus (d. 25 AD) was charged with treason during the reign of Tiberius (14–37 AD). He took his own life by starving himself to death.

[22] Tac. *Ann.* 4.34: "In the year of the consulship of Cornelius Cossus and Asinius Agrippa, Cremutius Cordus was arraigned on a new charge, now for the first time heard. He had published a history in which he had praised Marcus Brutus and called Caius Cassius the last of the Romans." JD is mistaken about the details. Cordus wrote the work in question; he did not merely listen to the reading of another's work.

[23] Lat. law of treason. Literally, the law concerning human digity (i.e., the dignity of the Roman people).

[24] England had several treason acts: 25 Edw. 3, st. 5, c. 2 (1350): "Declaration of What Offences Shall be Adjudged Treason"; 1 Ann., st. 2, c. 21 (1702): "An Act for the Further Security of Her Majesties Person and the Succession of the Crown in the Protestant Line"; 7 Ann., c. 21 (1708): "An Act for Improving the Union of the Two Kingdoms [England and Scotland]." These acts focused on actions (killing royals, levying war, aiding enemies, etc.) and not words.

[25] Lat. Deeds only were liable to accusation; words went unpunished.

[26] Tiberius Gracchus (c. 169–133 BC) was a Roman politician whose reforms led to his assassination.

[27] See "Mr. Fred[rich] Hanshaw's Deposition," Jan. 18, 1758, PHi-Logan.

[28] See "Anthony Armbrusters Deposition," Jan. 18 & 19, 1758, PHi-Logan.

[29] Sibling symbol not found.

[30] JD means 9 Coke, *Reports* 59.

   1 Hawkins 196: "But it hath been resolved, That he who barely reads a Libel in the Presence of another, without knowing it before to be a Libel, or who hearing a Libel read by another, laughs at it, or who barely says, That such a Libel is made upon such a Person, whether he speak it with or without Malice, or who is only proved to have had a Libel in his Custody, shall not in any respect of any such Act be adjudged the Publisher of it."

   Moore 813, Lamb's Case.

[31] "William Bradford's Examination," Jan. 18, 1758, NN: "Q. Was [Moore's Address] in the hand writing of Mr. Smith or whose else? A. It was in a fair round Clerk's hand, I had seen Mr. Smith's hand before, but I don't think any part of it was in his hand."

[32] "David Hall's Examination," Jan. 18, 1758, NN: "Q. Whether without the Advice & Consent of these Gentlemen would you have printed it? A. I think, I should not."

[33] Thomas Yorke, a merchant and later a judge of the Court of Common Pleas for Philadelphia Co. (1759–61), was the representative for Berks Co.

[34] Edward Young, *Busiris, King of Egypt: A Tragedy* (London: J. Tonson, 1722), 53–54.

[35] Possibly 1 Kgs. 21:1–16, the story of Ahab and the vineyard, with JD casting himself as Elijah.

[36] That is, a supporter of the proprietary party.

[37] See Chandler 7:130.

[38] Lat. "These times having the rare good fortune that you may think what you like and say what you think." The complete quotation is: "*Rara temporum felicitate ubi sentire quae velis et quae sentias dicere licet*" (Tac. *Hist*. 1.1).

[39] 13 Car. 2, c. 1 (1661): "An Act for Safety and Preservation of His Majesty's Person and Government Against Treasonable and Seditious Practices and Attempts." The act made it a punishable offence to "publish or affirm the King to be an Heretick or a Papist," and forbade people from "writing, printing, preaching, or other speaking, [to] express, publish, utter or declare any words, sentences, or other things to incite or stir up the people to hatred or dislike of the person of His Majesty, or the established government." Yet the act also affirmed that "Members of either of the said Houses and the Assistants of the House of Peers and every of them shall have the same freedome of speech and all other Priviledges whatsoever as they had before the making of this Act Any thing in this Act to the contrary thereof in any wise notwithstanding." The following year Parliament passed 13 & 14 Car. 2, c. 33 (1662): "An Act for Preventing Abuses in Printing Seditious, Treasonable and Unlicensed Books and Pamphlets, and for Regulating of Printing and Printing-Presses," which forbade any person "to print, or cause to be printed either within this realm of *England*, or any other his Majesties dominions, or in the parts beyond the seas, any heretical, seditious, schismatical or offensive books or pamphlets."

[40] Æsop's fable, in which a wolf catches a lamb and argues to justify killing her. The moral is that innocence is no protection against tyrants. See *Æsop's Fables. With Instructive Morals and Reflections, Abstracted from all Party Considerations, Adapted to All Capacities; And design'd to promote Religion, Morality, and Universal Benevolence* [London, J. Osborn, Jr., 1740], 2–3

[41] A variation on juvant: "*Obsolete*. Youth" (*OED*).

54

**Draft Transcript of Closing Arguments for the
Smith Libel Trial, [January 21, 1758]**

This lengthy document seems to be an after-the-fact reconstruction of JD's actual argument made before the Assembly, and the Assembly's responses. Like doc. 1:48, but unlike other draft manuscripts in this series, it also includes mention of various speakers in dialogue with one another. It shows that JD was able to argue many of the points he intended in his drafts above, several of which were highly critical of the Assembly's behavior and its ignorance of British law and procedure. Certainly a significant reason he wanted to record the proceedings must have been the vitriol directed at him by several members of the Assembly, most notably Joseph Galloway, who became a lifelong political enemy (see doc. 1:55).

It is possible that JD prepared this manuscript for anonymous publication, or at least started revising sections for publication. It reads like a play, complete with stage directions, and is free of the specific references to legal reports and treatises that mark his preparatory notes. On p. 16, JD inserts the first-person voice of an outside observer, a common trope in anonymous publications. Ultimately JD did not join the public debate in the press that followed the trial,

232

nor does it appear that he shared this manuscript in whole or in part with the critics of the Quaker party who did.

---

(1)

Mr. Speaker, [By the Cause] of this Honourable House, Mr. Smith [*illegible words*] to apply to Me [*illegible words with inserted phrase*] [*illegible line*] "abetting & promoting the writing & publishing a Libel [*illegible words*] William Moore Esq[ui]r[e]" {As} I have attended during the{is} Trial [*illegible words*] {I} now appear {{*illegible*}} before this Honourable House to offer [*illegible words*] {to assist Mr. Smith in making his defence, it now becomes my Duty to submit to your Consideration such arguments [*illegible words*] in {his} behalf [of the gentleman] [*illegible words*] as I am {have been [*illegible words*] occurrd to Me from} the Evidence that has been given.

This seems to Me, Sir, a {In a} Cause {Sir} of the utmost {such [Especial]} Importance, and equally interesting to the Prærogative of the Crown {{[*illegible line*]}}, the Authority of this House {Assembly}, & the Liberty of the Subjects, I should therefore have been very glad, [*illegible*] {of} as my Experience at the Bar is but [*illegible words*] of [*illegible*] had an Opportunity {t}of {have} preparing{d} Myself better; {more fully; [*illegible*];} that I might {have} been enabled to [to give] offer [&?] something more worthiness{y of} the <u>Attention</u> of such Honourable Judges, [*illegible words*] {I am [*illegible words*]}] {this House} {in} a Cause {Question} of so much Consequence. {But at [*two illegible lines*]]} {But Sir my being engagd} here in the Examination of the Witnesses & the Badness [*illegible*] the{is} Affair {{ fill it?}} of me of my Health lay Me [*illegible words*] under so many Disadvantages that} [*illegible line*]; and now I find Myself so much [*illegible*] that nothing but Mr. Smith's earnest Entreaties could prevail on {upon} Me to trouble the House on{at} this [*illegible*] {time}.

[*two illegible lines*] {I must beg Leave [*illegible*] therefore Sir, [*illegible*]{to} rely on} your Indulgence & Candour; [*three illegible lines*] and [*illegible*] hope the Inconveniences I labour under, will procure Me your Excuses for any Mistakes or Inaccuracies I may commit. {Indeed Sir, this Affair is of so complicated a Nature that I shall think Myself very fortunate if I com[m]it only a few.}

The Defence of a Fellow Subject must appear to all men, so agreable {{[Honourable?]}} an Office, & so becoming the Duties of my Profession; that it X [*in left margin:*] {X that it [*illegible words*] {does not seem generally} necessary, to assign any [reason] {motive} for undertaking it. But as the G[entle]man [*illegible*] at the Barr, stands accusd of an Offence against the Rights & Dignity of the Representatives of this Province {& I understand, I have been blamd for defending him;}; with your permission, Sir, I will mention the Reasons which have influencd Me to engage in this Cause.

Speaker. We <u>dont</u> want <u>none</u> of your Reasons {nor your Excuses.} Go on with the Prisoner's defence.

Mr. Dickinson then proceeded. There is one {particular} Circumstance &c} ~~There is one particular Circumstance, Mr. Speaker, in our Case, which {that} might alarm some people, in our {{*illegible*}} Scituation[: I] mean, that [*illegible line*]~~

{For the Charge ag[ains]t ~~him~~ the Gentleman at the Barr {in the Notice sent him by your Clerk} is formd in the manner of an Ind[ictmen]t [*illegible*] mean, that [*illegible words*] [com[mon] Law; [*illegible words*] {~~in the Notice sent to him by your Clerk~~} {for} "abetting & [pro]moting the writ[in]g and publishing a Libel".[1] This might perswade {[*illegible*]} [*page break*]

(2)

[*illegible words*] That the parties supposd to be <u>injurd</u>, are the parties to <u>determine</u> that Injury: ~~and that [*illegible line*]~~ But **Just** People {~~But just People [*illegible words*]~~} must have stronger Impressions on their minds of your <u>Authority</u> than of your <u>Justice</u>; and [*illegible words*] {certainly A} man in the Power of another, <u>who is offend[ed] {wit[h] him</u>, is more apt} to reflect on what his <u>Passion</u> may [*illegible words*] {prompt him to do} than what his <u>Reason</u> may dictate. ~~But~~ {However} Sir, We [*illegible words*] {~~[will?] not~~} {have no} Apprehensions {of that sort,}, because We hope [*illegible words*] [*illegible*] {that} faithful impartial Justice, [*illegible words*] {will be administerd, and} every Suggestion of Resentment religiously supprest. From this Cause then, We shall have no Uneasiness; ~~but it is~~ {We are} very unfortunate [*illegible*], ~~that~~ {in having} the Plan of Our Proceedings ~~is~~ alterd by the Resolves of th~~is~~{e} House.

[*in left margin*:] {Us that our Defence was to be formd in the same manner. But since We came here We find that We are to answer a Charge of abett[in]g & [pro]mot[in]g the writing a ~~Paper~~{Part}icular Paper, which the House has resolvd to be a Libel. This Sir destroys our first Expectation, & shews that {however the Charge was formd} the Rules of the Com[mon] Law are not ~~to be followd in these proceedings~~ [*illegible*] {now to govern Us. [*illegible*]} For every man who is acquainted with Law books, knows that they are filld with [*illegible*]{Dictates}, Whether [par][ticu]lar facts amount to the Crimes of wh[ich] the respective [Per]sons are accusd. Mr. Smith therefore in a Court of Law woud have been intituld to dispute two Points—first the fact itself—& 2^{ly} The Criminalty of that Fact: But in obedience to the Resolve We waive this. However We flatter Ourselves [that?] the Wisdom of the House will suggest every Argument on th[is] ~~head~~ {Point} in our favour, & that [their?] (vide Margin of 4[th] Page)} [*page 4, in left margin:*] {Humanity will incline them to [~~consider~~] {weigh} those Arguments relat[in]g to the liberty of a Fellow-Subject with Tenderness.

There was another matter, which one of the Members[2] gave Us Reason to think this Honourable House woud take into their Consider[ati]on after We had done examin[in]g the Witnesses; and perhaps they woud not be unwilling to know just the Heads of what We designd to have offerd— We intended to have} We ~~designd~~ {intended} to have shewn, Sir, 1.[st] That this House coud take no Notice of any thing precedent to it; because nothing coud be an Offence against this House, wh[en] there was **no** house to be offended; {And that} This Doctrine is confirmd by the Practize of Parliament, & the Voice of the Law in all ages. 2.[ly] That this House has no ~~Pow~~ Authority to take Cognizance of an Offence that is punishable at Common Law: That thus taking things out of the Common Course of Justice is an Infringement of the Magna Charta, that grand Confirmation of the Rights of Englishmen; [*illegible*] A Suspension of the Habeas Corpus Act, the Bulwark of English Liberty; {and an Introduction of the greatest Injustice, as a man might be punishd twice for the same Offence.}[3] 3.[ly] That this [*illegible*] House coud not punish any Offences but Contempt & Breaches of Priviledge, which were not allegd to be Mr. Smith's Offences, either by the {[a]}Notice sent by the Clerk of this House to him [*in left margin:*] {a. Vide the Notice page [4]}; or {[b]} by the Charge deliv[ere]d by Mr. Speaker from the Chair, on Mr. Smith's Appearance[4] [*in left margin:*] {b. Vide page [1]} [*page break*]

(3)

[*in left margin:*] {NB. That whenever}
Appearance at the Bar: **Or** if this Offence had been alledgd to be a Contempt or Breach of Priviledge, that it was not cognizable here, being committed out of this House;{,} {by a person not a Member:} That such Acts of Power have always been lookd on with a jealous Eye, by the People of England, when exercizd by the House of Commons; which appears from the Case of the Kentish Petitioners, when the House of Comm[on]s were so wise in their Anger as to remit Colepeper, one of the Petitioners, to the Course of Law.

Mr. Dickinson was interrupted here, & reprimanded with great Anger, for saying any thing about the Authority of the House, when that Point had been resolvd— He then proceeded.

Mr. Speaker, I am very sorry, that any thing I have said shoud displease{.} ~~this Honourable House.~~ I did not design to argue ag[ains]t ~~the Point[s?] of~~ the Cognizance; I only mentiond ~~them~~ {it} to ~~shew {[illegible]} the Inconvenience We sufferd by having [illegible] a part of our Defence taken~~

from [*illegible words*] {to shew the} Importance of that Point, which the House gave Us ˣReason to think they woud take into their Consideration. {; after We {had} done examining the Witnesses.} [*in left margin:*] {x vide page 18}

But since it is their Pleasure, I shoud not ~~so much as~~ mention it, I shall carefully avoid it; {.} [*three illegible lines*]
I shall now, Sir, proceed to the Consideration of the Charge against Mr. Smith. ~~In the Notice deliverd to him [by yourselves,] he is accusd of "Abetting and promoting the Writing & publishing a Libel" and We expected that he was to [illegible words]~~ [*page break*]

(4)
"Abetting & promoting a Libel." But since We have been here, We find the Case ~~is~~ alterd; and We are to defend Ourselves from a Charge of abetting & promoting the Writing & publishing a <u>Particular Paper</u>, which this House has <u>resolvd to be a Libel</u>.   ~~The Criminalty [is] determind against Us before We have been heard and now instead of clearing Ourselves from being {concernd in a} Libelous, We are to clear Ourselves from abetting & promoting a certain Paper. Mr. Smith undoubtedly had a Right to defend himself from the Crime with which he is chargd, & that Crime is a Libel. If therefore he is not permitted to deny it being a Libel, he is deprivd of the Right of defending himself from the Crime with which he is chargd.~~
{The Law:books, Sir, are filld with [Different?] arguments {to shew, what particular Facts amount respectively to} Treason, Murder, {or} Felony. [*two illegible lines*] Mr. Smith then ~~by~~ {in a Court of} Law was entituld to dispute two Points; first, the fact itself, & secondly the Criminalty of that fact: Consequently, the Vote which precluded him from disputing the last, has [lopt?] ~~off~~ {deprivd him of} one half of his defence: But [*illegible words*] {Sir, We submit} {[*illegible*]} {to the order} of the House; ~~We submit [illegible words] Defence We intended [illegible words]~~ {And shall proceed according to their Directions.}
~~By the Rules of the Courts of Law Mr. Speaker~~ {At Law Sir,} every part of this Charge oug[ht to be provd?] for it is <u>Conjunctive</u>[.] Mr. Smith is chargd with "Abetting <u>and</u> promoting the Writing <u>and</u> publishing a Libel. But as this House perhaps may not think the[mselves?] [*torn*] [*illegible words*] {restraind in the same manner} [*illegible*] [*torn*] I shall now consider the Evidence give upon this [ch]arge, & endeavour to shew that not one single [*page break*]

(5)
Part is supported by it.

In order to speak with the greatest Regularity ~~& Clearness~~, by ranging {together} the Facts & the Testimony relating to them ~~together~~, I shall ~~presume this Method. [Sir.]~~

1.st ~~I shall~~ consider the Evidence that goes to the abetting and promoting the Writing.~~-~~{t}he Address.

2.^ly The Evidence that relates to the Publishing{: &}

3.^ly The Evidence adduced for Us~~, [illegible words]~~]

{*()The First thing that strikes Us, Mr. Speaker, in the Course of this Evidence, is, that every Witness against Mr. Smith, confesses himself to be more criminal than the person {accusd.} Dr. Thomas Bond says {^c.}he was consulted by Mr. Moor; that he was always present, when Mr. Smith was present; that all of them were concernd, & more Alterations in the Address {were} proposd by others, than by Mr. Smith.

[*in left margin:*] {c. Vide page 21.}

[*in left margin:*] {*All from hence to the middle of the next page comes in, at the 8.th page at Letter **F**.}

Dr. Phineas Bond says, {^d}Mr. Smith never shewd any forwardness in the Affair; that he himself consulted Counsel, {& overlookd the Press;} that he ~~pleaded~~ {intreated} Mr. Smith, that he prevaild with him to make the Corrections he did, which were only alterations of a Letter or a Figure. [*in left margin:*] {d. Vide page 23.}

Mr. Levers transcribd the Address; and Hanshaw, Hall, Bradford & Armbruster, the rest of the Witnesses, either translated or published it.

Thus Sir, Every Arrow of this Prosecution has past thro[ugh] these men, ~~without their feelings~~{ it}, ~~but fixes fast in Mr.~~ {in its fullest force, unfelt; and without leaving the} [*page break*]

(6)

~~Mr. Smith's breast. He becomes the Common Receptacle of Guilt; and the Dart that pierces others in its fullest force~~ [*illegible words*] {[*illegible*}] the slightest Trace upon them, but ruins Us with [~~its very~~] {it's very} **Glance**.

{Since} ~~If~~{in} this Distinction ~~be found a Public Good, if the Cause of Justice is advanced by it, Mir. Smith~~ {his friends find Safety, Mr. Smith will not repine^5 at their good Fortune, but} will chearfully submit, & rejoice to save others—tho[ugh] by suffering himself: ~~But~~ {However} permit him, Sir, to wonder, ~~by what strange unlucky fate of~~ [his, or?] thro[ugh] what ~~unknown Wickedness~~ {strange fate or} {~~of [illegible]~~] {^X} unknown Wickedness} it happens, that what is Criminal in him shoud prove ~~innocent~~ {blameless} in others; and that Nature of things shoud {seem} changd, when done by him, & when done by those who give Evidence against him.

237

[*in left margin:*] {^X This alludes to Mr. Smith being suspected as the Author of the Brief State & Brief View[6]—the Cause of all the Assembly's Resentment against him.} {)}}

The first Evidence that ~~relates to the abetting & promoting~~ {arises in this Cause Sir, is Mr. Smith's} Examination. The Gentleman who spoke before Me,[7] either forgot this, or past it over as immaterial: But as I have heard some people mention it as strong proof against the Gentleman at the Bar, I beg Leave to ~~trouble You and this Honourable House with~~ {make} some few ~~Considerations~~ {Observations} upon it.

This Examination of the person accusd cannot be legal Evidence, as it is not signd by him. But as it is not our Design to shew Ourselves to be Innocent in the Eye of the Law, so much as in Truth, & the Opinion of every impartial person, {we} grant~~ing~~ it to be Legal {Evidence.} i{I}t amounts {then} to no more than this: That Mr. Smith took a Copy of <u>an</u> Address; but it does not appear of <u>what</u> Address; whether that presented, that publishd, or {of} some Other. [*page break*]

(7)

However allowing ~~still further, for We are so convincd of our~~ {another Point, not in the least provd,} ~~Innocence, that We shall give upon any Points that wo[ul]d not be expected from Us, [I say]~~ [*illegible words*] {that the Address} {from which} Mr. Smith copied ~~from, to be~~ {was} the Address presented & published. [*in left margin:*] {& ~~which~~ {that} he is now chargd [*illegible*] {with} before the House:} What is this ~~Mr. Speaker~~ {Sir,} to the Charge? Is copying a Libel <u>after</u> it is ~~printed~~ {[written?]} written, abetting that Writing? Or is transcribing a Libel <u>after</u> it is <u>finishd</u>, <u>promoting</u> it?

In 9th Coke Lambs Case, It is said, that to copy a Libel is not an Offence, unless the Copier <u>knows</u> it to be a Libel & lends or reads the Copy to <u>others</u>. Now it [~~was~~] {is} certain, ~~We~~{Mr. Smith} did not know Mr. Moore's Address was a Libel, as he had been assurd by several Gentlemen of Eminence in the Law,[8] that it was not: Besides {it does not appear that} Mr. Smith ~~does not appear to have~~ had any malicious design in copying it; but ~~assigns this Reason~~ {only} that ~~as~~ he was collecting Materials for a History of this Province,[9] [~~he~~] {and} thought this Paper relating to a dispute about the Authority of this House, worth his Notice.

It is evident, ~~Mr. Speaker~~ {Sir}, that this was Mr. Smith's sole view in copying the Address, <u>because</u> he never published that {Copy.} Dr. Phineas Bond says indeed that he saw it, but then he had seen the Original, and Lamb's Case is express to this Point, that it must be lent or read to **others**. That word cannot possibly mean any ~~thing~~ {persons,} but "**others** than those

238

who knew of the Libel before." S{For s}urely it woud be absurd to say, that shewing it to those who had seen it before, was publishing it; and it woud be highly unreasonable to punish a man as a Libeller, when in fact he is no Libeller {as ~~which~~ he coud not be w[ith]out writ[in]g or publishing it: Θ Indeed it is said} [*in left margin:*] {Θ Indeed it is said in Hawkins's Pleas of the Crown page 196 "that the having in one's Custody a written Copy of a Libel publickly known, shall be Evidence of the Publication of it."[10]   The meaning of the words is very plain. The admitting such kind of Proof is to discourage Libels; & at best is but Presumptive Evidence, which according to the Maxim, holds no longer, than {till} the Contrary is provd.[11] Now in our Case, the force of this Presumption is entirely destroyd by direct & positive Testimony, that this Address was publishd in another manner. It appears then, Sir, that Mr. Smith neither contrivd this Address, nor knew it to be a Libel, nor publishd it; Unless therefore A Man can &c. Vide next page.} Unless therefore [*page break*]

(8)

A man can be guilty without {any malicious} <u>Intention</u>, & without <u>any Injury</u>, Mr. Smith must be lookd on as Innocent.

All the other parts of Mr. Smith's Examination, Sir, except what relates to this Copy, You will find explaind by the other Depositions; for he was so little concernd in this Affair, that ~~it appears~~ he was ignorant of many things ~~that~~ {{with} which} the Bonds, & the other Witnesses were well acquainted ~~with~~. You will permit Me ~~Mr. Speaker~~ {Sir}, to ~~say~~ {assert} with some degree of **Positiveness**, that he ~~was ignorant of every thing~~ {of which} ~~[illegible words]~~ {{[illegible]}} {with} {knew no more than he has acknowledgd;} as it is a constant establishd Rule in the Construction of an Examination, that equal Credit shall be given to every part of it; & if One part is made use of against the Person accused, any other that favours him, must be regarded. Considering Mr. Smith's Examination in this fair Light, ~~Sir,~~ It must be thought, that instead of containing any thing that can be prejudicial to him, it will rather recommend his Cause{.} ~~to this Honourable House.~~

The other ~~Testim~~ Evidence that related to the Abetting & promoting the Writing, ~~is~~ {consists of} the Depositions of Dr. Thomas Bond, Dr. Phineas Bond & Mr. Robert Levers.[12] It will be unnecessary for Me to read these over at Length, as they have been so often repeated in the Course of this Trial.

I shall confine Myself ~~with making~~ {to the Substance of what they have said concerning Mr. Smith,} {&} such Reflections as naturally arise out of {i}~~the most part of what they have said~~ {F.} [*in left margin:*] {F. All containd within the Parenthesis pa. 5 & 6 comes in here.}[13]

The Agreement of these three Gentlemen ~~Mr. Speaker,~~ {Sir} in those Parts of their Testimony that Affect Us, is very remarkable. They all mention the <u>same</u> times of meeting, the <u>same</u> Company, the <u>same</u> Conversation, the <u>same</u> facts with regard to **Us**: They all say they were [*page break*]

(9)

They were at Dr. Phineas Bond's with Mr. Moore & Mr. Smith [*illegible*] that they talkd of an Address [~~that~~] Mr. Moore designd to present to Governor Denny—that several Remarks were made & some Alterations proposd by the Company in general, but none in particular by Mr. Smith— {Θ (Vide margin)} [*in left margin:*] {Θ It is not provd that he went to Dr. Bonds on this Account; It is not hinted: He was an intimate friend of the Doctor's, & frequently visited him.

As to his part in the Conversation wh[ich] turnd on the Address, he {behavd like a Gentleman,}[{&}?] joind in it: but joind in it in such a manner, as shewd him to be quite unconcernd. Neither the Doctors nor Mr. Levers can say one single Alteration was made in Consequence of what he said.　　Thus far they all correspond.

Mr. Levers indeed is of} [*illegible words*] ~~of any~~ — Mr. Levers {indeed} was of Opinion that the Copy he transcribd from, was in a hand <u>like</u> unto Mr. Smiths,{.}{ ~~but in this he is expressly contradicted by the two~~ {^X}~~Bonds.~~}

[*in left margin:*] {^X Vide page 25.}

{And} Dr. Phineas Bond mentions one Circumstance more that past between him & Mr. Smith ~~alone~~{ly}—that he entreated & prevaild on him to correct the Proof—that ~~which he had~~ {receivd} from the Printer, ~~which he did~~ by adding {some} single Letters and single Figures.

~~This [then] Mr. Speaker is the Evidence to prove no Abetting & promoting the Writing {Mr. Moore's Address　} Evidence so slight so slender {against any but those who [give?] it,} that no man woud be convictd [illegible] on such at Common Law, of the most trifling trespass.~~

{But Mr. Lever's Testimony (Vide next pa. at top}

~~Indeed it is extremely happy for these Gentlemen that this Cause is not [depending?] in the {^Θ} other end of this house.~~

[*in left margin:*] {~~Where the Supreme Court is held!~~}

~~Your Rules Sir, are different from those of Law [it is] unprecedented then, for the Principal to accuse the [Accessory] for the most guilty to accuse the most innocent.~~

~~But even after the {se} Foundations of the Law have been shaken, to search for {this [illegible words]} Testimony {given} against Us What is the E[vent?]? {& [illegible]ent of it?} Shall Remarks made in Conversation between five Gentlemen, but not fixd upon Us? Shall Alterations proposd in~~

240

~~Consequence of those Remarks, but not provd [on] Us? Shall these things[,]~~
~~I say [*illegible*] convict Us of an unpardonable, unbailible Offence?~~
{^X} [*illegible words*] [doom] ~~an Englishmen to a loathsome Gaol~~ [*illegible*
~~words*] [*illegible words*] [*illegible words*] [common Blessings] of Light and~~
~~Air?~~ {~~And Dr. Phineas Bond~~ says Mr. Smith was very backward to be
concernd, but he entreated, he **prevaild** with him [on this?] Mr. Speaker,
[*in left margin*:] {^X ~~This word was not [too] strong for [*illegible*]ts [*illegible*]~~
~~[succeeding?]~~ [*illegible lines*]]} [*page break*]

(10)

[*in top margin*:] {* Mr. Lever's Testimony of his Copying from a Writing
in a hand like Mr. Smith's, is directly contradicted by the two Bonds. This
can fix no Guilt upon Us then: And the ~~Enormous~~ {monstrous} Crime of
adding a Letter or a Figure is entirely wipd}
~~Speaker, are ungrateful Sounds in the Ears of Justice, when proceeding from~~
~~a Witness against a Prisoner. But when he said~~ **prevaild**, ~~what was it to do?~~
~~To commit the~~ enormous ~~Crime of~~ altering ~~a Letter or a Figure —~~
~~And shall an Englishman be doomd to a loathsome Gaol? shall he be denied~~
~~the Common Priviledges of Light & Air for a Letter, for a Figure? Are all~~
~~our boasted Rights reduced to this?~~

~~Mr. Speaker, Be so good~~ {Sir,} ~~as to indulge Me with your Patience, for~~
~~I am afraid You must hear with Reluctance the Repetition of such Ridiculous~~
~~[*illegible*]~~{E}~~vidence.~~ {~~Mr. Lever's Testimony of (vide [*?][*illegible*] pa[.~~
~~?] *)}~~

~~This~~ prodigious ~~Crime of Literal Correction is~~ entirely wipd away by
Mr. Bradfords {^O} [*in left margin*:] {^O Vide page } Answer to the second
Question; for he says, that he left out all the Corrections that were that were
made on the Proof-Sheet when Dr. Phineas Bond returnd it.[14]

Here then ~~Mr. Speaker,~~ {Sir,} ~~I will~~ {Permit Me to} [*illegible words*]
~~entreat You & this Honourable House~~ to [*illegible words*] & observe, ~~if~~
{~~yet~~?] {that} hitherto there {does not} appears the slightest Sign ~~not only~~ of
an actual, ~~but~~ {nor} even of an intentional Offence.

Mr. Smith did not form the Plan of this Libel—he did not compose it—
{he did not write a ~~Letter of it —~~ {word, a syllable, a letter of it}—he did not
interest himself in it— He does not discover thro[ugh] the whole Course of
the Testimony, even the smallest spark of Resentment against the late
Assembly. He shews no Zeal, no Activity in the Affair.

~~It is not provd that he went to Dr. Phineas Bond's on this Account — he~~
~~was an intimate Friend of the Doctor's & often there. During the~~
~~Conversation which turnd on the Subject of the Address he behavd like a~~
~~Gentleman, & joind in it; but joind in it, in such a manner as~~ shewd {provd}
~~him to be quite unconcernd. [He said?]~~

241

[*in left margin*:] {~~Vide page 11. in margin. to be within it"~~. <u>Words</u> ~~became capital Offences, & a chearful Evening spent with ones~~ friend ~~Acquaintance frequently produced an order to die in the Morning. The Historian~~[15] ~~after some mournful Reflections on that unhappy situation of his Country, recollects {the delightful freedom enjoyd under}~~ the [*illegible*]~~d & gentle Government of some excellent Emperors, & breaks out in an Extacy of Joy~~ "**Rara tempora** ~~felicitatis; ubi sentire quæ velis, & quæ sentias dicere liceata~~ {[For?]} {[In?]} ~~Times of uncommon Felicity when men might think~~ [*illegible*] ~~{what they} pleasd, & speak what they thought.~~ ~~By the Goodness of Providence We live in The times of this {"uncommon} Felicity {"}~~ ~~In times when Liberty does not & speech, two principal Boons of Heaven & Nature are not incompatible. That if Mr. Speaker, Enquiries of this sort are to be made &c Vide page 11.~~ [*page break*]

(11)

[*in top margin*:] {~~and least of any body, says Dr. Thomas Bond and and Dr. Ph[ineas] Bond.~~}
{~~In the Course of, Conversation indeed, while they were~~} {~~while the others were~~} ~~talking of the Address, Mr. Smith~~ [*illegible words*] ~~{joind in it~~ [*illegible words*]~~, but} neither the Bonds nor Mr. Levers can say, One single Alteration was made in Consequence of what he said.~~

~~There is something in this Evidence Mr. Speaker, that strikes Me with Terror, & almost makes Me~~ <u>tremble</u>.

~~We appear here to answer for Words dropd in the Course of Conversation, in the free familiar Intercourse of friendly {domestick} Conversation.~~ ~~In a friend's House, in Company with Friends, Mr. Smith to have avoided the Charge now brought against Him, must have kept a sullen surly~~ <u>Silence</u>, ~~or have disputed, perhaps quarreld with the man that entertaind him, or with his Father. [One coud] he was conscious of the Misfortunate~~ [*illegible words*] ~~{[illegible]} for he intermeddled~~ <u>no further</u> ~~than the {[illegible]}~~ [*illegible*] ~~of Civility oblig'd him~~ *~~he shewd no forwardness & said the least of any man present. If this be Libelling, it is scarcely possible to say [what is not a libel~~ [*illegible words*]~~]. We are not to [ᶿ?]~~

{~~Enquiries of this sort~~ [*illegible words*] ~~are to~~} {~~If Enquiries of this sort are to~~} ~~be made~~ ᶿ~~if our~~ <u>Conversation</u> ~~is to be~~ <u>sifted</u> {~~for crimes~~} ~~while We indulge the social Joys {Pleasure} of Friendship~~ ~~and practize the sacred Rules of Hospitality~~ ~~then~~ <u>Adieu</u> ~~to the best the dearest of Human Enjoyments~~

~~If Crimes are to be sought for~~ [*illegible words*] ~~the Rooms of friendly Entertainment {[*illegible*]} {at Firesides & [*illegible*]} the next step must be to our~~ Beds— ~~and our~~ Dreams ~~will be criminal.~~

~~Permit Me Sir, to quit this melancholy Subject on which no man can dwell with the least Pleasure, & to comfort Myself with reflecting; that the Man cannot [hev?] deserve the name of Guilty, when he coud not have been innocent, without tearing the [*illegible*] {breaking the Laws} of Decency~~ [*in left margin:*] {^O ~~not fallen on the~~ Tiberian Age ~~of Roman Servitude, but the~~ happy time ~~of English Liberty, {that} flourish [*illegible words*] [Plant in the rough woods] of Pennsylvania. We know nothing of the Miseries of [*illegible*] Slavery, but what History informs Us of. We read at this Distance, with Relief & Detestation of the~~ unsettled boundless ~~"Law of violated Majesty" that [*illegible*] swept away the best & bravest Citizens {in Rome.} Formerly, says the Historian Tacitus, {{[*illegible words*]}} We had the Lex lese Majestatus, but [other?] Crimes were then punishd by it, [*illegible words*] in the City, a M[utinous] [*illegible words*]~~ **Facta arguebantur, dicta impune erant** ~~—Actions were punishd, what no man sufferd for~~ **—words—** ~~But~~ **now,** ~~that is in the Reign of Tiberius, this Law was grown so~~ extensive ~~&~~ uncertain, ~~that while it was unknown~~ what ~~was [*illegible*] in it, every thing [was] [*illegible words*]~~

~~Vide page 10 in margin[s].~~} [*page break*]

(12)

I beg Leave Sir, to make one more Observation on these Dispositions of the two Drs. & Mr. Levers: Their Evidence relates entirely to preparing an Address to present to the Governor. Waving therefore the Weakness ~~& Futility~~ of their Testimony; & granting, what they do not prove to the minutest Degree of Probability—that Mr. Smith was concernd in abetting & promoting the Writing the Address; Yet I hope Sir, that You & this Honorable House will never think him guilty of any Offence, in promoting it for that purpose.

You have resolvd, that [this?] the Address now before the House ~~& publishd to the World~~, is a Libel: [*illegible*]{This} {comprehends the Address [*illegible*]{in} its present State, as publishd to the World. {but} You have not resolvd that presenting it to the Governor was such a Publication of it, as woud make it a Libel. What I content for then, with submission, is this; that We are not precluded by your Votes from shewing, that Mr. Smith coud not be guilty of any thing libelous, when he was only preparing an Address to the Governor, in the usual method of appl~~ying~~{ication} ~~to the Supreme Majestrate~~.

This Distinction seems to be clearly & firmly establishd in the Law books; where it is held that scandalous matters containd in articles of the

Peace exhibited before a Justice of the Peace, shall not amount to a Libel. {—} So nothing in a Petition to a Committee of Parliament, however severely it may reflect on the Characters of the Persons complaind of, shall make the Petitioner guilty of a Libel: But if he publishes them. to any others than those he applies to for Redress, he is a Libeller.

~~The law assigns a very~~ {There is certainly great} [*page break*]

(13)

~~wise Reason for~~ {great Wisdom in} this Distinction; If Men were to be calld to an Account for attempting to seek Relief; {,} ~~from Injuries~~ instead of <u>protecting</u> them from Injuries, the Law woud only <u>expose</u> them— And the more violently a Man was outragd, the more dangerous it woud be to complain; {,} as in all probability, [*illegible*] {his} Language woud be animated in proportion to ~~the~~ {his} Grievance. The Justice of the Law might therefore be properly arraignd, if its Subjects in endeavouring to procure the Redress of one Evil, shoud fall into another, & perhaps a worse.

How strongly ~~Mr. Speaker~~, {Sir,} does this Doctrine tend to excuse Mr. Smith from ever thing that yet has been alledgd against him?

[*illegible line*]{All the Witnesses agree that Mr. Moore's Address was formd on purpose to be presented to the Governor.} ~~And if the Assembly to attend them on some Complaints that had been exhibited before them of his Misbehaviour as a Magistrate~~

{Then the only Question (Vide next page)}

~~Mr. Moore appeard & deliverd a Paper {in} to the House expressing great Respect for the Assembly, but entreating to allow him the Priviledge which every Englishman was intituld to, of being tried by his Country. The House thought proper to reject his Prayer, & proceeded to examine Witnesses against him on Oath.~~

~~When a great Number had been examind, they proposd an Address to the Governor, setting forth the Complaints against Mr. Moore containing many heavy & severe Charges on his Reputation.~~

~~This Address was not only presented to the Governor but publishd in all the Newspapers for some time.~~

~~Mr. Moore afflictd & astonishd to see his Character branded in the Publick Prints, thought it a duty to~~ [*page break*]

(14)

~~Himself, to his Family, to his Friends, to make some defence~~ [*three illegible lines*]

~~To be sure He must have been a good deal enragd with the Reflections cast upon him in this manner, However he behavd so cautiously, that he seems to have proposd the late Assembly's Proceeding as a Pattern to~~

~~himself; that if ever such should be questiond, he might have~~ [*illegible*] ~~their~~
~~Example to~~ [*illegible*] ~~He precisely followd their steps. They presented an~~
~~Address to the Governor: He presents an Address to the Governor. They~~
~~publishd their Address in the News papers: He publishd his Address in the~~
~~News papers. They usd severe words against him: He turns~~ {[X]} ~~their own~~
~~{words} upon them. In short he sent his Justification thro[ugh] the same~~
~~Channels which conveyd their Charges, that he might pour a Balm into~~
~~{[heal]} the Wounds of his Reputation as far as possible.~~
[*in left margin:*] ~~{x It is Remarkable that the severest part of Mr. Moore's~~
~~Address is when he asks if the words made use of by the Assembly are not~~
~~more applicable to them, than to him, & then repeats them.}~~

~~This Sir, I submit to the House as a true state of the Case between Mr.~~
~~Moor & the late Assembly. The only Question {[~~*illegible lines*~~]} was formd,~~
{The only question} then is, if ~~it~~{this} comes within the Reason of those
Cases I have mentiond where scandalous Matter is contained in Articles of
the Peace &c a Petition to Parliament~~:~~{;} and I hope this Honourable House
will think it does {~~& that this Address [was] made in the~~ the Cause of
Justice}. The late Assembly had ~~desird the Governor~~ {presented a
Remonstrance to the Governor desiring him} to turn Mr. Moore out of his
Office. It was therefore proper for him to answer, <u>where</u> he was accusd, in
order to avoid the Punishment requird: so that We have the sanction of the
late Assembly's Opinion, that his Application to the Governor was right, if
theirs was {right.}. But Sir, We shall not rely upon their Opinion only, for it
appears by a {[X]} Message sent the other Day to the Governor,[16] that this
~~Honourable~~ House thinks him invested {on this occasion} with the Power
& Authority of the {Whole} <u>House of **Peers** in England</u>. It would be
needless {& absurd} to argue
[*in left margin:*] {X Insert this extraordinary Message in a Note.} [*page
break*]

(15)

argue after this, that Mr. Moor's Address was as much in the Course of
Justice, as if it had been to a <u>Committee</u> [~~or~~?] {which is only a} <u>part</u> of the
House of Peers in England.

If it was so, [~~*illegible*~~] & Mr. Moore was justifiable in presenting that
Address, then Mr. Smith cannot be criminal in assisting him to form {it for
that purpose} if he did <u>Assist him</u>: {~~And the Evidence of the Bonds & Mr.~~
~~Levers~~ [*illegible*] ~~only to~~ [*illegible words*] ~~an Address for~~ [~~that purpose~~?]} I
do not pretend Sir, to ~~excuse~~ {justify} the violent Charges made in that
Address upon the late Assembly: The Approbation the Freemen of this
Province have since shewn of those Gentlemen's Conduct at the last
Election, ~~plainly discovers~~ {will have its due Weight in ~~shew~~ proving} how

245

undeservd they were. But Sir, however unjust those Censures ~~were~~ are, upon ~~persons lately in~~ {the behaviour of persons in their late} publick Capacities, perhaps nothing is more to be wishd, than the Freedom of blaming Publick Ministers; when the~~y [illegible words]~~] time for which they were employd is expird. Their Dignity & the Common Safety {may} forbid it, while they are in Office, but nothing can be better designd, than such a Liberty afterwards.

{False Aspersions will *} [*in left margin:*] {* will dye of themselves; but just remarks on Maladministration may teach others if not more Virtue, at least more Caution: And why shoud the Remembrance of an Authority, ~~protect~~ {schreen} Men from being blamd for the Abuse of that very Authority, which was delegated to them for quite different purposes.}

The Human Mind {[*illegible words*] {being formd for Society,} [*illegible*]} naturally desires the Esteem of Mankind, & dreads Shame & Infamy. ~~Whereas~~

Even those Men who have arrivd to a Degree of Power sufficient to protect their persons from the Punishment due to bad Actions, have yet ~~been so far influenced by their Respect for the Judgment of [illegible]~~ ch[*illegible*]{osen} rather to ~~be [illegible]~~ {leave} a Memory grateful to future Ages, than to indulge the{ose} Passions which might have been satisfied with {scandalous} Impunity.

How much stronger then, is the Motive to Virtue in the Publick Ministers, when Dishonour does not loiter till the End of Life, but seizes them at the End of those Employments in which they have misbehavd themselves?

~~Indeed [two illegible lines]~~] [*page break*]

(16)

{Indeed it is altogether improbable that any ~~People will be so [illegible words]~~ {Rulers will ever govern well; Unless they are restraind by some Apprehensions of Disgrace or Chastisement.}} We see therefore that all free & happy Nations have improvd on this Disposition of Human Nature, ~~to avoid Infamy & the dread of Punishment~~ and <u>interwoven</u> as it were, the dread of Infamy & Punishment in their several <u>Constitutions</u>. History is full of Instances from the Earliest Ages down to this time, of the great Care with which every Wise People has examind the Conduct of their Ministers, when their Offices were expird. {~~and [no?] free~~ [X]} [*in left margin:*] {~~X free State ever {has} existed without such a Check upon [illegible words]~~}} The Ægyptians, Who were first remarkable for the Art of Government, & indeed for every other Art, went {carried this policy} so far, that [~~illegible words~~ ~~of their~~ {when any of their} Princes {died}, they denied them the Common Right of Burial, till their Virtues & Vices were compard: Nor woud they suffer their <u>deaths</u> to be honourable, till it was determind that their <u>Lives</u> had been <u>just</u>. Θ

[*in left margin*:] {Θ The force of Mr. Dickinson's Argument was broken by this Interruption: but this was the Scope of it, as I have been since informd. He designd to have shewn from the Examples of the Grecians & Romans, & ~~from several Instances [illegible] own Country~~ that their Liberty was preservd, by their Laws for calling their [~~Ministers~~] {Officers} to an Account for their Behaviour [*illegible*] [~~their Offices expired~~?]; {when they returnd to a private Station;} & after some Instances of the same nature in our own Country, to have drawn this strong & striking Conclusion "That as no <u>free State</u> ever <u>has existed</u> without such a Check upon their Ministers, it was impossible any ever <u>shoud exist</u> without it."}

Here Mr. Dickinson was very violently interrupted & some of the Members observd with great Wrath, that for sometime he had actually been justifying that Paper, which they had resolvd to be a Libel; & was proving it to be no Offence; because it was against the <u>late Assembly</u>, when the present House had determind it to be an Offence. Mr. Dickinson repeated the Distinction which he made before (Vide page 12) & said he was only endeavouring to shew that in ~~Law &~~ Reason & in <u>Law</u>, from the <u>Experience</u> of other Governments, and the <u>Constitution</u> of our Own, It was Allowable & proper to enquire into the Conduct of Publick Officers, at least ~~so far as [illegible words]~~ in an Application to the <u>Supreme Magestrate</u> {whose Authority was acknowledgd}, for Protection from those Officers. But the House grew so extremely warm, that he immediately declind this Point, & told them he ~~woud~~ {thought it his Duty to} avoid a subject so disagreable to them. [*page break*]

(17)

[*in left margin*:]
{Magestrate whose Authority was acknowledgd, for Protection from those Officers. That the same Argument which woud prove it unlawful to censure the Conduct of the last Assembly, [*illegible*]{W}oud prove it equally unlawful to censure the full Assembly of the Province, the Long Parliament of Charles the 2.d or the Parliaments of Henry eighth[17]—and that——}

Mr. Speaker, I now come to the 2.[d] general Point I proposd, & that is, to consider the Evidence [*illegible*] which relates to the "Abetting and promoting the **publishing** Mr. Moore's Address."

It may serve to explain the Testimony on this head, to observe; that there is {a} Society in England formd by several Noblemen & dignified Clergy men, calld "the Society for [*blank*][18]

247

This Society has appointed {Mr. Smith &} some {other} Gentlemen in this Province their Trustees; & has furnishd them with sums of Money to set up a Dutch Press in this City, to furnish those People with any books or Intelligence they shall want in their own Language, & thus carry on the Useful & Charitable Scheme for which they associated themselves. The other Trustees from their Confidence in Mr. Smith's Integrity & Abilities, have devolvd the principal Care of the Trust upon him, so that he is <u>Acting Trustee</u>, presides over their Press, & manages all the other Affairs of the Society.

The two Witnesses Hanshaw & Armbruster, who have been examind to prove Mr. Smith's publishing this Address, are men whom ~~Mr. Smith~~ {he} has employd in this Printing Office—Mr. Hanshaw as Translater, & Mr. Armbruster as Printer.

It was for this Reason, I presume, that when these men appeard, many Questions were askd them, as if Mr. Smith had usd threats or unjust means to force them to print the Address: After the most strict scrutiny however, nothing of this sort appeard.

~~Mr. Hanshaw says that~~ I shall therefore beg Leave to observe ~~with great Deference to this Honourable House~~, that Mr. Smith does not discover in the Course of this Evidence, any more Zeal or ~~Activity~~ Forwardness in publishing the Address, than he had shewn in the forming it.

Mr. Hanshaw says [*page break*]

(18)

says he went to see Mr. Smith; & in the{ir} Conversation about their Business, Mr. Smith askd him, if he had seen Mr. Moore's Address to the Governor. He answerd, he had not: Upon which Mr. Smith told him to translate it, & {give it to Armbruster to} print; for that the Dutch People near Mr. Moore wanted to see it.   He says some days after Mr. Smith saw him again, & enquiring if he had translated the Address, he was angry when he understood it was not done. Mr. Hanshaw excusd himself by saying he was afraid to translate a thing reflecting so much on the late Assembly. Mr. Smith told him he need not have any Apprehensions, for he saw it was printed in Franklin & Hall's Paper <u>who were Printers to the Assembly</u>, & therefore there coud be no Danger. Upon this Mr. Hanshaw translated it, deliverd it to Armbruster & it was printed.

As to Armbrusters Deposition, it is nothing but a Confirmation of Hanshaws, except that he says Mr. Smith gave him Orders for an Over plus Number of 62 Copies. This ~~it~~ seems to be lookd on as a Proof of Mr. Smith's being very earnest to have this Publication encouragd, & therefore I shall speak to that part hereafter.

248

This Mr. Speaker, is the Evidence to suppose the Charge of publishing the Address, against Mr. Smith: And surely when it is considerd, it will be thought there is much greater Reason to pity him, than {to} blame him.

He was unfortunately true to the Trust riposd in him, & is become a Prisoner, ~~while he only~~ {by} indend~~ed~~{ing} to be an honest man. His only ~~Intention~~ {Design} seems to have been, to keep up the Credit of the Press that was committed to his Care. When he blamd Hanshaw he told him, that many Dutch people had complaind, that they had lookd for Mr. Moore's Address in their Papers, but found it was not put in. As nothing is more disagreable to those who pay for ~~P~~{N}ews-Papers, than to hear {of} remarkable things ~~talkd~~ in other Prints, & not have them in such as they take, The Societys Paper must consequently have come into disrepute [*page break*]

(19)

by such Neglects. But beside this Consideration, & beside the profits which were {to accrue} to the Society by a Casual Sale, Sixty two Copies of the Address were actually bespoke by Mr. Moore; for Mr. Smith {^{X}} [*in left margin*:] {^{X} Vide page 27.} told Hanshaw these Copies were for him, and {$^\Theta$} [*in left margin*:] {$^\Theta$ Vide page 33.} Armbruster was orderd to charge them to him. It therefore was Mr. Smith's duty as a Trustee to keep up the Character of this Dutch Paper, & promote the Interest of his Constituents by printing the Address.

But it is said, Mr. Smith was extremely exact in his Directions for printing it; that is, he was extremely exact in his Duty. Was he more ~~particular~~ {earnest} on this Occasion than was usual? By no means. It was very common {*} [*in left margin*:] {* Vide page 28.} for him to order Hanshaw to translate particular pieces to be printed. But he [~~was angry with~~] {rebukd} him, for not obeying! So he [~~alw~~] always did, when he deservd it by the same Omissions, which has {sometimes} happend before. {$^\Theta$} [*in left margin*:] {$^\Theta$ Vide page 28.}

In short it appears evident, that Mr. Smith was no otherwise concernd in this Affair, than in the Ordinary way of his Business, as Trustee. He did not send for Hanshaw— He did not give him a manuscript to translate, he referrd him to the Publick Prints. He usd no force—no threats to induce him {to [*illegible*]}: He usd no Arguments but one, & indeed that was so strong, that all others became unnecessary. He told him it could not displease the Assembly to have the {Address} printed, when it had been publishd by ~~Franklin &~~ Hall their own Printers. ~~You will perceive in that Paper [*illegible words*].~~

Nothing certainly coud be more just than Mr. Smith's Judgment on this subject. He argued with himself in this manner. Mr. Hall is Printer to the

Assembly, & has a great deal of Business from them[:?] he woud not therefore chuse to displease them on that Account. But besides this, he is a Prudent Man & woud not dare to print such a free Paper as the Address, without the Leave of the Assembly, or some of the Members. As he [*page break*]

(20)

must undoubtedly then have some such Authority for what he has done, there cannot possibly be any Danger, in only <u>reprinting</u>, what he had <u>before publishd to the World</u>.

In this manner Mr. Smith reasond, & tho[ugh] he finds he was right as to Mr. Hall's Motives, yet he <u>fatally feels</u> that he was mistaken in ~~the better part of~~ his Conclusion.

This naturally leads Me, Mr. Speaker, to the third General Point I designd to consider, & that is

The Evidence which has been adducd for Mr. Smith.

We have troubld the House with the Examination of two Witnesses only; and the first of these is very short. Mr. Bradford does not say any thing of much Consequence, except this, that the Copy he printed from was not in Mr. Smith's Writing, & that he left out all the Corrections Upon the Proof Sheet Dr. Bond returnd to him.

[*in left margin*:] {NB. The Reason of examining Mr. Bradford before Mr. Hall, was that Mr. Smith's Counsel apprehended some of the Members woud have been alarmd at those Questions being put to Hall, which they woud neglect while Bradford was examind.}

Our next Witness was Mr. David Hall, <u>Printer to the Assembly</u>.[19]

This Gentleman says that when Dr. Phineas Bond brought the Address to him, he did not chuse to print it; and when the D[octo]r urgd the Reasonableness of Mr. Moore's vindicating himself in the same Papers where his Reputation had been attackd, he answerd; that he thought it his Duty to print <u>any thing</u> the Assembly orderd him, & nothing against them. However after much pressing, he thought fit to consult some of the Members. He applied himself to Mr. Isaac Norris the <u>Speaker of the late Assembly</u>, & of of the <u>present at the first Sessions</u>, to Mr. William Masters[20] & Mr. Jos[eph] Galloway two other Members. With the <u>Advice & Consent</u> of these Gentlemen, Mr. Hall printed the Address.

Here Mr. Dickinson was interrupted ~~in the bitterest Language~~ by Mr. Norris & Mr. Galloway, & in the bitterest Language chargd by the Last with "base, mean, scandalous, villainous" Attempts to misrepresent the Evidence. They said he had suppressd the Reason of their allowing Mr. Hall to print [*page break*]

(21)

Print the Address, that is, to prevent Objections that might be made with regard to the Liberty of the Press, in order to throw an Odium upon them. Then they spoke a considerable time in Justification of their Conduct, & said whatever they had done, was with a Design to preserve the Honour of the Assembly; that they might not seem to restrain the Liberty of the Press: If they had errd, they humbly submitted themselves to the Censure of the House.[21]

Mr. Dickinson {being first severely censurd by the Speaker,} was then orderd to proceed.

~~Mr. Speaker, I have [such a] sense of the Respect due to this Honourable House, which [*illegible words*] the Freemen of Pennsylvania,~~. Mr. Speaker, It is with great Concern, I have heard {what has been said} ~~such a Construction [put] {made} on my words, as was never intended;~~ * [*in left margin:*] {* And have receivd such Usage here, as I {never receivd before & I} am apt to think I shall never receive again in <u>any other place</u>.} ~~and~~ I beg leave to observe ~~to~~{with} great respect to the{is} Honourable House, that such frequent Interruptions only break the Sense ~~of~~{,} {of what I am saying,} & afford an Opportunity to put such a <u>meaning</u> on my Expressions as was never <u>meant</u>. It will be utterly impossible therefore, ~~for Me to [ex?]~~ while I am subjected to the same ~~Interruptions~~ {Inconveniences,} to avoid the same Accusation~~:~~{,} unless I coud invent some magic Term, to convey all Mr. Hall's Testimony at one Breath. I hope the~~re~~{n}~~fore~~, this Hon[oura]ble House will not think Me guilty of Misrepresentations, because I ~~dont~~ {cant{n}ot} speak in a manner, [~~that the [*illegible*] of~~ {~~that [*illegible*] of [*illegible*]~~]} {that} Nature will not allow.

I was saying Sir, that Mr. Hall's Apprehensions were removd by his Conversation with Mr. Norris, Mr. Masters & Mr. Galloway~~;~~{ :} & that with their **Advice & Consent** he publishd Mr. Moore's Address.

Now the Reason of our examining Mr. Hall, was to shew that We were not mistaken in our Opinion of his ~~motives~~ {Authority} to print the Address~~;~~{,} & if <u>he</u> was excusd by those Gentlemen's License, We are at least, equally excusable who only followd his Steps. All therefore that related to [*page break*]

(22)

our Justification, was <u>that License</u>: for whatever particular Reasons the Gentlemen might assign for it, the fact is, that Mr. Hall printed the Address with their **Advice & Consent**; & this fact is what We think ourselves excusd by.

Tis true they told him "to print it to prevent any Objections that might be made respecting the Liberty of the Press, which they thought shoud be

251

open" And advisd him "if the piece containd any thing libellous in its Nature, he shoud know the Author & be able to prove him":[22] But does this take away the [~~illegible~~] {Truth} of Mr. Smith's Judgment? Does this destroy Mr. Hall's Authority for printing the Address? If it does not do these things, ~~Mr. Speaker,~~ {Sir,} it does nothing;{:} Mr. Smith's Excuse is built on Mr. Hall's; & this Paper publishd by the <u>Printer to the Assembly</u>, is the source [~~illegible words~~] of all Mr. Smith's sufferings.

Here Mr. Dickinson was interrupted again by Mr. Norris & Mr. Galloway. Mr. Masters rose up with them, <u>but said nothing</u>. The other two accusd Mr. Dickinson {again} of Misrepresenting the Evidences & repeated most of what they had said before. They talkd a long time on the Liberty of the Press, & mentiond the Opinion of Lord Chief Justice [*blank*] with Regard to {it}.[23] They begd the House woud indulge them with time to give them their Sentiments on this head.{,} & said they hopd on hearing them, they woud find nothing in their Conduct to be blamd. They chargd Mr. Dickinson with great Indecency in accusing two of the Members, before whom he was speaking{;} & said it was an Abuse of the Lenity of the House towards the Prisoner at the Bar. ~~He was~~{He was} then allowd to go on.

Mr. Speaker, Tho[ugh] I have heard with great Uneasiness, something affecting Myself from the Worthy Members, who spoke last; Yet it was with the highest ~~joy~~ {Satisfaction} I attended to them, while they pleaded so strongly, so convincingly for my Client. I rejoicd to find the Members of this ~~Honourable~~ House, possest of such noble & just [*page break*]

(23)

just Sentiments of Liberty; {Sentiments} so becoming the honourable Station, to which their Country has calld them.

{X} [~~illegible~~] We join in their Opinion; ~~We~~ embrace {and accept} their Argument. {With what pleasure can I pursue the praises they begun?} The Freedom of the Press is truly inestimable: It is the Preserver of every other <u>Freedom</u>, & the Antidote {t}of every kind of <u>Slavery</u>.[24] By ~~this~~ {the Assistance of the Press}, the Language of Liberty flies like Lightning thro[ugh] the Land {X} [*in left margin:*] {X ~~and when the least Attack is made upon her Rights, spreads the Alarm to all her Sons & raises~~ {and rouses} a Whole people in her Cause. A free Communication of Sentiments, discovers their Agreement, shews their Strength, and produces an Union that renders them irresistable. In short the Freedom of the Press is so opposite & dreadful to the Usurpers of unjust Power & the Enemies of Mankind, that **Liberty** however [~~illegible~~] maimd & wounded **still** breathes & struggles, while <u>that</u> prevails; and {even} **Turkish Tyranny** [~~illegible words; torn~~] {could never give the mortal stroke}, **till Printing** was pu[~~t to d~~?]{nishd} with death.

But Sir does not} But Sir, does not every word that can be said in favour of this ~~Liberty~~ {Freedom}, operate in Mr. Smith's Favour? And while these Gentlemen were so tenderly attentive to the Liberty of Hall's Press, have they not been laboring [in o]ur cause?   Mr. Smith, by presiding over the Society's Press in this City, is to every purpose {as much} a Printer as Mr. Hall; & entitled by the Laws of his Country to the same Protection. This Sir, has not been denied, it cannot be denied.

Then We come to this <u>important Enquiry</u>; How it happens when these two Gentlemen were {in} these Circumstances exactly alike, the <u>same</u> thing shoud prove save to one, & ruinous to the other.

The only ~~Shadow~~ {[*illegible*]} of a Difference that can be pretended, is that Mr. Hall was Printer to the Assembly, & publishd in the English Language; but Mr. Smith was Printer to <u>We know not what</u> Society, instituted for carrying on We <u>know not what</u> {^X purposes,}, & publishd {his paper} in Dutch.

> ^X Note. The purposes of this Dutch Press were suppos[ed] not to be favourable to a certain party.[25]

To draw any Inference from these premisses, Mr. Speaker, against Mr. Smith, which will not hold against Mr. Hall;{,} We must say; That the glorious Protection afforded by the Laws of our Country to the Press, with all the Noble & exalted Sentiments on this Subject, to be found in the Lawbooks & other Writings, were solely calculated to guard the Press of the Assembly of Pennsylvania; or else, that the Dutch is a wicked & detestable Language, & that things which are <u>lawful</u> in English, are <u>unlawful</u> in that. [*page break*]

(24)

If these things do not distinguish Hall's Case from Ours, {in his favour,} Nothing else does:{;} and if it is criminal in Us, it is criminal in him {& in Mr. Bradford—who [*illegible*] ~~printed it [before he did~~?]:} {If} ~~He is~~{They are} innocent, We humbly presume We are infinitely more so. For both of them printed the Address before We did; and Hall's publication, as he was Printer to the [*three illegible lines*] {^X} [*three illegible lines*] {Assembly, actually produced} {^X} [*in left margin:*] {^X Vide page 29. this Reason given to Hanshaw why We might print it with Safety.} producd ours, & was the Cause of all [~~our~~?] {the} Misfortunes, which have since happened {to Us.}. The Loss of Liberty, the Fatigue of a long & troublesome Trial, ~~&~~ {the} Numberless Insults which ~~the Vulgar~~ {are} liberally bestowd on Prisoners— all these Sir, Mr. Smith has sufferd from that Single Step of Mr. Hall. ~~Our Offense was occasiond by his; & the License that was given to him to keep his Press open, have been a fatal to Us.~~

~~But Mr. Speaker, I hope the~~ best ~~of~~ Blessings, ~~which has been so often & so successfully used {employd} in the preservation of Liberty, will not by a surprizing Peculiarity of Fortune, be used~~ made use of to ~~destroy~~ the Liberty ~~of the Reverend Gentleman at the Bar: For that would be the Case, if the Freedom that was granted to Hall, which lead Us into the same Act with him, shoud catch Us as it were in a Snare, & hurry Us into a Gaol.~~

Here Mr. Norris & Mr. Galloway & some other members interrupted Mr. Dickinson {with Vehemence,}, and said he was accusing them. ~~Mr. John Hughes said he stuck to the~~{is} [*illegible*] ~~of the three Gentlemen Point, as if his~~ Salvation & Redemption ~~depended on it.~~ {Mr. Norris said, he still was misrepresenting the Evidence, as they told Hall to take Care to know the Author, & be able to prove him.}

Mr. Norris {& Mr. Galloway} had been very busily in taking Notes {& comparing them,}, all the [*page break*]

(25)

all the {[[*illegible*]]} time Mr. Dickinson {was speaking,}, & now ~~he~~{Mr. Norris} told the House that he had taken down something he had said, at the very instant he had spoke it, that he begd Leave to read to the House; to shew what Liberties Mr. Dickinson had taken & with how much Indignity he had treated the House. He put the House in Mind of the Atrocious Nature of the Address, & that in their Message to the Governor they had calld it "A Scandalous Libel against the Late Assembly, containing gross Reflections upon them, & tending to subvert & destroy the most essential Parts of the Constitutio[n] & to take away the most valuable Powers of this House."[26]

(Quere if these are the express words of the Message—if they are not look for the printed Message & put them in verbatim here.)

He then said, that ~~Mr. Dickinson~~ {the Young Gentleman} had forgot what he himself had been saying sometime before; for he had acknowledgd that the Address containd {[X]} [*in left margin:*] {[X] Vide page 15.} unjust Charges on the late Assembly, & yet afterwards he usd these express Words, which he was sure he coud not be mistaken in, as he had written them down: He then read these words in his Notes {[Θ]} [*in left margin:*] {[Θ] Vide page 19.} **"that it was Mr. Smith's duty to print the Address."**

He enlargd upon these words a long time; to prove the Indecency & Disrespect, with which Mr. Dickinson had treated the House, in saying it was "Mr. Smith's duty to publish a Paper," which was [*illegible*]{so} pernicious a tendency, & had been resolvd by them to be a **Libel**.

When he had done speaking, William Allen Esq[ui]r[e] Chief Justice of the Province, rose up in his place, & said, The Young Gentleman had usd the Words he was chargd with, but if the house observd the Rule of Reason

& Law that was constantly adherd to in every Court of Justice he had ever seen, "Of taking all a man says together"[27] there was nothing [*in left margin:*] {Nothing can be a stronger Proof of the Decency & Respect {with} which this Young Gentleman conducted himself, in the Course of this Trial, than this Charge: for it shews by their fixing on these words only, of all that he said in the warmth of Argum[en]t & he occasionally spoke with great Earnestness, that they thought them most likely to hurt him: though they were sitting cooly to catch any unguarded Expression he should drop.} [*page break*]

(26)

to blame in what had been mentiond. He said Mr. Dickinson had been proving that Mr. Smith was to be lookd on as a Printer, by presiding over the Society's Press: that as the Dutch People complaind of the Address not being in their Papers; & as 62 Copies of it had actually been bespoke by Mr. Moore, it "**therefore** was Mr. Smith's duty as a Trustee, to keep up the Character of the Dutch Paper, and promote the Interest of his Constituents, by printing the Address." This he said, was the Sense, & believed pretty near the Words Mr. Dickinson usd; & as Mr. Smith did not imagine {the printing the Address} to be unlawful, to be sure it was his duty to advance the Benefit of those who intrusted him: That considering what had been said in this manner, he did not see any thing in it liable to Censure.

Mr. Norris & Mr. Galloway both answerd the Chief Justice, & spoke a great While, but the House {in general} was so well satisfied with Mr. Dickinson's behaviour, that he was orderd to go on. He began & said, He thought himself very unfortunate, as he felt the greatest ~~Respect~~ {Reverence} for the House, & carefully endeavourd to observe the utmost Respect for them, to find himself subjected to such severe Reflections......But here the Speaker calld out to him with great Anger, & told him they did not want his Apologies, for he only broke their heads, & then gave them Plaisters:[28] {These were his words.} He bid him go on ~~where he left off~~ with the Prisoner's defence.

Mr. Speaker, I was saying, when I was interrupted, [~~We~~] never ~~shoud have printed the Address if Hall had not first;~~ {that Mr. Smith's Sufferings were owing to the Leave granted to Mr. Hall by the Speaker of the late Assembly, & of the present Assembly, at the first Sessions, & by two other members to print the Address:} & because I shoud be extremely unwilling {again} to incurr the Charge of accusing any Members of this House; whenever I shall have occasion to mention the Evidence relating to them, I shall read it out of Hall's Deposition, which I have under your Clerks hand. [*page break*]

255

(27)

Mr. Hall ~~says~~ {has sworn} that **without the advice & consent** of those Gentlemen of the Assembly, he woud not have printed the Address;{,} [*illegible*] ~~I think fully~~ [*illegible words*] ~~I have said. So that if Mr. Hall had not printed this Paper, he should not; [*illegible*] of Consequences, instead of~~ [*illegible words*] ~~Consequence~~ {[[Gentleman]] ~~at the Barr}~~ ~~conducted thro[ugh] the streets by a Sergeant at arms~~ [*four illegible lines*]] {his printing it, is the Reason We gave to Hanshaw, Why We might print it; and printing it, brought Mr. Smith to this Barr.}

If Mr. Moore's Address then, had never been publishd in Hall's Paper, [~~We~~]{Mr.} Smith had never been a Prisoner at this Bar; and that Address had never been publishd in Hall's Paper, without the **advice & consent** of three Members of this House: It follows then by uncontrovertible Deduction ~~& of necessary Conclusion~~, that without this Advice & consent of thi{e}s{e} Member{s}, Mr. Smith-had-never-been-a-Prisoner-at-this-Bar.

Here Mr. Dickinson was interrupted, & Mr. Norris said it was intolerable Usage of the House, to accuse some of the Members, when the House had not thought fit to Censure them; & when they had {done} nothing, but what they hopd the House woud be perfectly satisfied with, when they shoud please to allow them time to vindicate themselves. {*Mr. Galloway according to Custom raild.} [*in left margin:*] {* There was some talk here of the Serjeant at Arms, in order to intimidate the Young Gentleman; but he proceeded with a Resolution becoming an honest Man engagd in an honest Cause.} Mr. John Hughes said, Mr. Dickinson stuck to this Point as tho[ugh] his Salvation & Redemption depended upon it. {Mr. Jos[eph] Fox said he [~~illegible~~] ought to be stopt, for he did not know if he went on, but he woud be guilty of High Treason.} On his setting down, Mr. Dickinson suddenly begun.

Mr. {Speaker} I have no Intentions of accusing any Members of this ~~Honourable~~ House. I have the Honour of attending here, to defend & not to impeach; & all that I desire, is that I may be allowd to make a full & fair Defence, for the Reverend Gentleman who has requested my Assistance. I say not a Word Sir, relating [*page break*]

(2~~7~~{8})

relating to the Members, but what I find in this Deposition, {under your Clerks hand;{.}} If Mr. Hall does not accuse them, I'm sure I dont. I appeal to the House, if I have blamd them in the least for the Advice they gave to Mr. Hall. Th[ese{y}] must entertain a ~~different~~ {dreadful} Opinion of their ~~own~~ Conduct ~~from what I do, to~~ {who} say I ~~blame~~ accuse them by {barely} mentioning it. I have not condemnd it {[[~~and if any one is against~~]]}; I {have}

only endeavourd to excuse Mr. Smith, by shewing he had done nothing but what the Speaker of the late Assembly & of the present Assembly at the first Sessions had <u>advisd & consented</u> shoud be done, & tho[ugh] that <u>Advice & Consent</u> was not given to Us, that yet it was the real [~~illegible~~]le Cause of our Action; as We shoud not have venturd to do it, without such a Precedent as Hall set Us, & <u>We knew</u> he woud not have venturd to do it, without such a previous Authority as that Advice & Consent gave him.
[*in left margin*:] {[~~illegible line~~]}

I cannot conceive therefore, Sir, how I can be said to accuse these Gentlemen. Does not Hall swear, He woud not have printed the Address {without their Advice & Consent?}? I cannot <u>accuse</u> them then, by ~~repeating~~ {reading} <u>his</u> Words. Does not Hanshaw swear, that the Reason Mr. Smith gave him why they might print the Address {& why he himself consented to print it—} was that Hall had printed it? Surely it is not <u>accusing</u> them, to repeat <u>this</u> ~~testimony~~. {Evidence.} ~~Well~~ t{T}hen ~~Mr. Speaker~~ {Sir}, do I <u>accuse</u> them, when I join these Testimonys together, & [~~illegible words~~] {only give Utterance to a} Conclusion from them, [as?] {which} the Sentences themselves [~~would draw,~~]{.} ~~if they had Tongues.~~{?} {form in the most forcible manner}? "That the Advice & Consent of these Gentlemen producd Mr. Smiths Publication."

One of the Gentlemen[29] has put the House in mind of the {^{X}} [*in left margin*:] {X Vide page 25.} Atrocious Nature of the Address, & ~~that it~~ therefore might imagine I designd to accuse them by mentioning <u>their Advice & Consent</u> to publish a paper of {$^\theta$} [*in left margin*:] {θ Vide page 25.} "such a dangerous Tendency": But the House never heard one word from Me, of the atrocious Nature of that Address; and whoever ~~says~~ {imagines}, that those Gentlemen were to blame in advising **such** a paper to be publishd, will ~~say~~ {imagine} more [*page break*]

(29)

more than I have <u>said</u> throughout this whole Trial.

{**No Sir!**} I [~~illegible line~~] {understand too well I hope the Respect due to the Representatives of the People of Pennsylvania, ~~than~~ to think of accusing any} ~~Every~~ Man who sits in this House{:}~~, than to think of accusing him:~~ I have only attempted, as far as my weak State of Health woud permit, to shew ~~for~~ how Mr. Smith's Conduct was excusd by ~~the~~ what these Gentlemen have done.

It was {indeed} <u>improbable</u> ~~indeed,~~ that <u>they</u> woud **advise** the publishing **such** a paper; but our Defence arose from {our Opinion of} [~~illegible~~] {it's} being <u>infinitely more imprabable</u>, that <u>Hall</u> {who was printer to the Assembly} woud dare to publish it without their **advice**; & from {that} <u>Opinion's</u> proving <u>true</u>.

I have been chargd with ~~for~~ {with accusing these Gentlemen by} suppressing {^X} [*in left margin*:] {X Vide page 24.} ~~One~~ {part} of the Advice the{y} ~~Gentlemen~~ gave to Mr. Hall. Indeed I have hither to past it over in silence, for fear it shoud bear the face of accusing more than any thing I have said.

Mr. Hall says, that the Members told him "they thought his Press shoud be open; but if the piece containd any thing **libellous** in its Nature, he shoud know the Author, & be able to prove him."[30]

At the time of giving this advice, The Address which has been describd to be of <u>such a pernicious Nature</u> was a secret, known but to few persons, & must have crept thro[ugh] the Province very slowly as a Manuscript, transcribd from hand to hand: But on this Permission, it [*illegible words*] & {took Wings &} flew {at once} thro[ugh] the World ~~at once~~. ~~Knowing~~ t{T}he Authors ~~& being~~ {being known &} liable to punish{ment} did not abate its Malignity— But {the} Flagrancy of the Libel as it is calld, encreasing by the Publication, might <u>occasion severer Penalties</u> on him. ~~If~~ ~~[promoting?] [two illegible lines]~~ {*} [*in left margin*:] {* ~~[two illegible lines]~~} The Young {Gentleman} has mentiond facts here, {through necessity,}, that he found he coud not dwell on without seeming to accuse: He therefore quits them with this [*illegible*] transition, & takes that for <u>granted</u>, which no one woud allow from such Premisses: Nor he himself woud have granted, but from his Respect for his Audience. His ~~Conclusion~~ from the Premisses is very remarkable[.]} Granting ~~however~~ {therefore} Sir, that this part of their Advice [*page break*]

(30)

tends to excuse the Conduct of these Gentlemen, which ~~I [illegible]~~ {no man has ever heard me} blamd{e}; Does it operate against Mr. Smith? [*illegible words*] ~~[can think] it does Sir~~; {It is impossible it shoud:} for the Author of the Address printed by Hall, is the Author of the Address printed by [*illegible*]{Mr.} {Smith:} Nay the Author is known, is apprehended & now lies in Confinement for his ~~Offence~~ {Address.}.

The Reasoning {still} turns then {[*illegible*]} with the utmost force in our favour. If [*illegible*]{in the Opinion of these Gentlemen, the Writer's being known & provd, woud excuse Mr. Hall, & his Offences} were to be laid on the devoted Head of this Author; Mr. Smith's Offences are exactly the same, & have the same Atonement

I have now Mr. Speaker, ~~gone thro[ugh] the~~ {Considerd} gone thro[ugh] the Evidence in this Cause in the manner I proposd, & made such Reflections as occurrd to Me, & [ʝ?] appeard necessary.

I first considerd the Testimony which relates to Mr. Smiths "Abetting & promoting the Writing the Address;" and I cannot but believe this Honourable House will think it so slight & inconsiderable, as to pay no manner of Regard to it.

~~It cannot be imagind, that [barely joining?]~~

Mr. Lever's Opinion, that the Copy from which he transcribd, was in {a hand like} Mr. Smith's, [*illegible*] ~~directly contradicted~~ {cant affect him} as the two Bonds have expressly sworn, that Mr. Levers did not transcribe from {a Copy of} Mr. Smith's{.}[31] ~~Copy~~

Mr. Smith's Correcting the Proof-Sheet that Dr. Phineas Bond bro[ugh]t him, can be {of} no weight, as Mr. Bradford has sworn that he left out every one of those Corrections: besides the Address was then printed off, & woud have been finishd in a few hours without these b[eing] made.

Thus all the Evidence on this head, is reducd to what past at Dr. Bonds: {;} And [*illegible words*] ~~persons who are talking of a Libel, without {one particular Word being provd upon him} one single Letter being alterd or added to it in Consequence of what a [Necessary,?] [illegible] calld the "Abetting & promoting the Writing it," Mr. Smith must be looked upon as [certainly innocent?] of this part of the Charge~~ {really Mr. Speaker, there is something} [*page break*]

(31)

And really Mr. Speaker, there is something in this Evidence, that strikes me with Terror, & almost makes me tremble.

<u>**Words**</u> usd in the free familiar Intercourse of <u>domestick Conversation</u> are now summond as Witnesses against Us.   In the house of a <u>Friend</u>, in Company with <u>Friends</u>, Mr. Smith to have avoided the Charge now brought against him, must either have kept a <u>sullen</u>, <u>surly</u> Silence; or have ~~disputed~~ {engagd in a Dispute}, perhaps {a} quarrel~~d~~ with the Man who entertaind him, or with his {^X}Father.

[*in left margin*:] {^X Dr. Ph[ineas] Bond married one of Mr. Moore's Daughters.[32]}

One woud think he was conscious of the Misfortune hanging over his head, for he intermeddled no further than ~~the~~ common ~~Laws of~~ Civility obligd him. He shewd no forwardness. He said ~~the~~ least{ss} ~~of~~ {than} any ~~one~~{man} present— Not one sentence—not one Letter is provd to be alterd or added by him— But [*illegible line*]

If this be Libelling, it is scarcely possible to say what is not Libelling.

As yet Mr. Speaker, the Reverend Gentlemen for whom I am concernd, is not to be lookd on as a guilty person, nor the Evidence against him to be regarded ~~with that Respect it woud~~ as sacred barely because it had been given.

I shall beg Leave therefore Sir, to treat this Testimony as equally disagreable to You, & {to} every man who knows the Inestimable Value of Liberty; and the dangers to which this ~~kind~~ {sort} of Evidence woud expose her.

It is natural when We reflect on these ~~things~~ subjects, to recollect similar Instances in preceding Times; & to judge from the Experience of other Nations what may be the Consequence of Events among Ourselves: And I confess upon this occasion, I cannot drive from my Remembrance, the remarkable Observations of Tacitus, on a kind of Proof surprizingly resembling the present.

The Historian had been describing the Calamities of his Country in the Reign of Tiberius, while the **"unsettled boundless Law of violated Majesty"** swept away the best & bravest Citizens in Rome.[33]

Tis true, says the Noble & Elegant Author, We formerly had the "Lex lesæ majestatis"; But other Crimes were then punishd by it, as Seditions in the City, or Mutinies in the Camp— [*page break*]

(32)

***Facta arguebantur, dicta impune erant"**— <u>Actions</u> were punishd— No man sufferd for <u>Words</u> {θ?} But then, that is under Tiberius, this Law was grown so <u>extensive</u> & <u>uncertain</u>; that while it was unknown to the People, what [~~were~~?] {was} within it, every thing was construed by the Senate to be within it. <u>Words</u> became Capital Offences; and a cheerful Evening spent with one's friends, frequently producd an Order to dye in the Morning.

From this mournful Period, the Historian [*illegible*] {turns} his View with a kind of Rapture on the mild ~~Administration~~ {[*illegible*] during} {Reigns} of some good Emperors, and {mentions [*torn*] as the Standard of perfect ~~Liberty;~~ Freedom;} When Men enjoyd the Uncommon Happiness of thinking as they pleasd—and speaking as they thought—[34]

[*in left margin*:] {Notes. Mr. Dickinson found too great a resemblance between this little extract from the Roman History, & the Proceedings of the Assembly to make any comparison between them; & therefore very carefully confind his allusion to the point of Evidence. But it is impossible to read these Lines without observing that [eve]ry particular relating to the Lex lesæ majestatis; [is] surprizingly applicable to the unknown & boundless Priviledges claimed by the h[ouse] [wh]ich some of the Members said were really **unlimited.** Such was their Notion of their power.}

{In such times Sir We live, and enjoy} ~~B~~{b}y the ~~indulgent~~ Goodness of Providence, ~~Sir, enjoying~~ under the Best Constitution of Government, & the most excellent of Princes, every Felicity that has yet fallen to the Lot of the most favour People {[~~illegible words~~] (Vide ~~some~~ lines at the bottom to come in here*) No one} [*bottom paragraph*:] {* [~~illegible line with~~

260

insertion] {No one surely can} suffer himself to suspect, that the Condition of a Roman [*illegible words*] was {ever} preferable to that of an Englishman at this Day.

No Sir: As long as Political <u>Wisdom</u> {is truly understood,} [*illegible*] Political <u>Virtue</u> [*illegible*] {justly esteemd;} [*illegible words*]; {[*illegible line*]} [So?] long will Posterity reflect with Admiration & Delight, on that perfect beautiful{beautiful &} [*illegible*] {well [*illegible*]conducted} System of Civil & Religious Liberty, that [*illegible*] {distinguishes} with unfading Glory, the pleasing Annals of the present Illustrious Family.

Our good Fortune has thrown Us on an Age & Country} [*illegible words*], where Liberty & Speech, two of the Principal Blessings {[Gifts?]} granted {by Heaven} to Man, are not incompatible. But if, [our Speech?] Our conversation is to be sifted, while We indulge the social Pleasures of Friendship; and practise the sacred Rules of Hospitality; [*illegible*]{if our [*illegible*]{[*illegible*]} must learn the sad lessons of solemn silence, & our Souls, of {be shut up in} [un]chearful Reserve; then} Adieu! to the best & dearest of Human Enjoyments— If Crimes are to be sought for at our {peaceful} {peaceful} Firesides & {social} {social} Tables; the next Step must be to our <u>Beds</u>—and even <u>Dreams</u> will be <u>criminal</u>.

Permit Me Sir, to quit this melancholy Subject, on which no one man can {willingly} dwell{,} without the least and {to} comfort Myself with reflecting; that the man cannot deserve the name of <u>guilty</u>, who coud not have been <u>innocent</u>, without breaking the Laws of Decency. [*page break*]

(33)

In speaking on the other part of this Accusation, I mean "the Publishing" the Address, I shoud have thought it my Duty to have offerd something to the Consideration of this Honourable House, on the Liberty of the Press: but "{in} that Trouble was savd Me {I was prevented} by some worthy Members. It will be unnecessary then {now} for Me to say more than this; that the Laws of our Country are so very indulgent to the Liberty of the Press;{,} that when any thing is publishd, and [*illegible lines with insertion*] [the establishd Religion, the Rights of the [*illegible*], [or?] the [Administration] of Government,] {improper License is taken; if the Printer does not endeavour to screen the Author, & was only concernd in the common way of his Business, he is never treated with any severity: **But** that there never was an Instance in the English Dominions before the present where the least Notice was taken of a Printer for **copying** from <u>another Press</u>, which he had seen publishing for some time <u>with Impunity</u>.

Mr. Smith, Sir, is Trustee to a Noble & Charitable Society at home. His Directions from them are, "that their Press shall be as free & open as any in the Province":[35] He is therefore a Printer; & in obedience to his Instructions,

~~he what other Printers {[did]}. Unhappily for him, he has not found the same Indulgence.~~ {and it was his Duty to this Society, perhaps I shall not go} too far, if I say it was his Duty to his **Gracious Majesty**, who is a Principal Subscriber to this generous Undertaking, to obey the Instructions ~~that were~~ given him{;} [*illegible words*] {and to promote with his most earnest Endeavours}, the Publick-spirited Plan, that {was committed to his Care. It appears from the Evidence,} that he conscientiously attempted to execute the Trust reposd in him and ~~that he~~ accordingly followd the Example of other Printers; but unhappily found ~~that~~ there was not the same Indulgence for him as for the Rest.

{Thus,} Whatever Offence ~~he~~ {Mr. Smith} has committed was [~~owing?~~] ~~to~~ {occasiond by} the [Assembly's] Printer—[*illegible*] [*torn*] [*illegible*] {and any fault that he had been guilty of was} o[win]ng—

—but! Sir I've done on this Subject. [*page break*]

(34)[36]

This Cause ~~Mr. Speaker~~ {Sir}, I said at first was of the utmost Importance not only to Mr. Smith, but to every Man in this Province; and I imagine from the great Concourse of People now attending here, that ~~it~~{th}is is ~~generally thought so.~~ {the General Opinion.} ~~As the Authority of this House, & the Rights of the Subject are equally concernd in your Determination, no doubt [torn] {this [Audience]} been pleasd to have {had} [two illegible lines] and [be?] obeyed.~~

Your Determination, {is no less} to Mr. Smith, than Liberty or Imprison[ment,] and an Imprisonment of a very Particular Nature too.

"There is no Crime so heinous in Law, as to prevent an Englishman's endeavouring to obtain his Liberty by Habeas Corpus, or to deprive him of the Assistance of Counsel, or to hinder the Judge's bailing him if he thinks proper."[37] But as this House claims all the Power of the House of Commons, ~~I suppose~~ {no doubt} it woud be accounted a Breach of Priviledge, to sollicit the Discharge of a Man committed by them, at least during their Sessions.

Therefore Sir, if the Sentence of this House shoud be unfavourable to Mr. Smith, he will {be} reducd to a more miserable sit[uation] than the most profligate & abandond Villain. ~~The Lenity of [illegible] [the greatest Deference] [illegible words] Consideration of this Honourable House if any Offence has been provd [illegible] Mr. Smith of so black [two illegible lines]~~{* [*illegible words*] and stript [*illegible line*] even of the Claim of Liberty.}

[*in left margin:*] {* [~~two illegible lines~~] Permit Me [S]ir, to entreat this Honourable [Ho]use to consider, if any Offence has been provd on Mr. Smith of so black [a] [Nat]ure that he deserves to be placd in these

melancholy Circumstances [*torn*] whilst living, to all the Rights of the
Living; & stript [*illegible*] Even of the <u>Claim</u> of <u>Liberty</u>.}
[*in left margin:*] {^{Θ 38} [*four illegible lines*] Censures will [{[be]}] so severe,
as not only to throw Mr. Smith into Confinement without an Expectation of
Relief, but even to communicate a <u>Taint</u> to those, who [*illegible*]
{charitably} attempt it. ~~The Offen[ce of] [*illegible line*]~~ *}
    ~~If this judgment (Vide p. [*four illegible lines*]~~]
But Sir, this is not all he may suffer from th[is] [*page break*]

(3̶3̶{5})

Judgment. He may undergo such a Scene of Distress as the law justly regards
with detestation{.} ~~& abhorrence.~~ The Intent of punishing is not to render
the Life of a Delinquent miserable, by repeating it, but to discourage Vice
by a proper Correction. But if Mr. Smith is condemnd here, he may be **twice**
punish'd for the same Offence: {Nay, he may be kept in Confinement by
every {^X} succeeding Assembly}
[*in left margin:*] {Notes. ^X For if this Assembly coud confine Mr. Smith for
this fact which happend during the former Assembly, every following
Assembly woud certainly have the same Right to commit him, that the
present {had:}: And this Argument has been [*illegible words*] ~~Weight~~
~~[illegible]~~ {been confirmd by} what has since happend— For every
Assembly since that time has constantly issued Warrants against Mr. Smith
to take him into Custody, & he was obligd to fly to his Sovereign for
Protection.}

    Here Mr. Dickinson was interrupted with ~~ex[cessive] Anger~~ {excessive
Rage} by several [*torn*] to dispute their Authority **again;** ~~by~~ But Mr. Yorke
saying, he thought Mr. Dickinson now made use of this Argument as an
Inducement to **Mercy**, he was allowd to go on again.

    I say Sir, that if Mr. Smith is punishd by the sentence of this House, he
may be subjected to such Distress, as the ~~English~~ Laws of England look
upon with [*illegible*] Detestation[.]

    It cannot be denied, that ~~of~~ Libels are Cognizable in the Courts of
Common Law {& that a Sentence of the House of Commons was never
pleaded {in barr} to an Indictment in these}— [~~disapprove of~~] then Mr.
Smith shoud be indicted ~~then~~ for this Offence— One of these two things
must certainly happen— He will either be acquitted or convicted— If he is
acquitted on a Trial by his Country; Will it not be said; this House has
unjustly deprivd a Man of his Liberty without <u>legal proof</u> of his Guilt? If he
is convicted; ~~this House~~ {your Judgment} will be the Cause of his being
twice punishd for the same Offence.

    Thus Sir, whatever is the issue of this Affair it must be such as no Wise
or good Man can wish to see: For [*page break*]

263

(34{6})

For on the one hand, great ~~Dishonour~~ {Reproach} must fall on this {Honourable} House, & on the other, great Injustice on the Reverend Gentleman at the Bar.

This Consideration shews ~~of how much~~ {the} Consequence of a single Innovation in the usual Methods of Proceeding: And as this is a Cause of great Expectation, in which {the Prærogative of the Crown} the Authority of this House & the Rights of the Subject are equally concernd; [*torn*] here present woud have been pleasd to h[ave?] seen thos[e] [*torn*]ed in which they ~~we~~{a}re so much interested: ~~that We [were?] [*illegible*] to be silent on the [*illegible*] & We obeyd.~~

Here Mr. Dickinson was interrupted again, & it was said he was striving still to break in upon the Resolves & after a good deal of time spent in justifying the Resolves & censuring Mr. Dickinson for every Hint he had given towards them, he was orderd to proceed; but finding himself very [~~unwell~~?] {much fatigud,} he informd the House that he ~~shoud [*illegible words*]~~ had been so much interrupted, that the Method ~~with~~ in which he designd to speak, was broken, & he shoud trouble them no further[÷] ~~[*illegible words*] in the Manner he had intended.~~

(34)

The G[entle]man at the Bar, Sir, is fully convincd [how] much his Happiness is concernd in the Decision of this Cause; but he hopes this House ~~consider~~ {will deliberately reflect} if this Influence may not be much more extensive & important, than he will presume to think any thing ~~relating to~~ {affecting} his ~~Liberty~~ {mself} alone.

If yet he is to be accounted a freeman of this Province, [~~he is yet~~?] there ~~yet~~ {still} subsists ~~a~~ {an intimate} political Relationship between him & this numerous Audience.{,} * ~~He is [protected?] [torn] [illegible words]~~] [*in left margin:*] {[*torn*] Members to consider, if an Offence had been provd ag[ains]t Mr. Smith of so black a Nature, that [h]e deserves to be placd in this melancholy situation; [*illegible words*]] to be made an Alien to the Laws of his Country, & stript not only of Liberty, but even of the very <u>Claim</u> to it.

But Sir, this is not all he may suffer from your Judgment} {and} If hereafter the Sentence of this House shoud prove erroneous, the Injury done to ~~him~~ {Mr. Smith} will give a Wound to the Rights of every man in Pennsylvania [*illegible*]{.} {For so far} it will be [~~so far~~] an Attempt, to destroy those Laws by wh[ich] they are protected.

{That} * Liberty is of a delicate nature, & requires to be treated with a gentle hand, ~~& [illegible words]~~] {and feels her} ~~the~~{Her} whole body disorderd {by the least Hurt in any part, are Truths provd by every Rage in} ~~How far any Mistake in~~ her history[.]

How much S[*illegible*] {The Public} is interested in this Affai[r] will no doubt be tenderly considerd by those, [to?]{W}hom [the?] ~~Public hav~~ {are} constituted it's Guardians: But [*torn*] your Determination ~~shoud prove~~ {be} unfavourable [to] the Rev[eren]d G[entle]man now before You, I sincerely wish he may be the last Man who will ever ~~feel~~ {suffer} the uncom[mon] Hardships that will follow—

I call them uncommon S[ir] because You punish by ~~C~~{I}mprisonment, & [*torn*] woud [ae]count it a Breach of Priviledge {[for a man?] [*illegible*] [*torn*]} to sollicit [*torn*] Discharge of a man committed by You during your {[superscript X]} Sessions. [*in left margin:*] {Notes [superscript X] The Assembly understands the whole year to make one Sessions.}

This stroke sinks him at once below the Cond[uct] of the most profligate & abandond Villain: For there is no ~~C[ause?]~~ {Charge} so heinous in Law, as to prevent an Englishm[an] endeavouring to obtain his Liberty by the Writ of Habea[s] Corpus, to deprive him of the Assistance of Counsel [&?] to hinder the Judges bailing him, if he thin[ks?] [*torn*]

But Sir, Your Censures will be so severe, as not to throw Mr. Smith into Confinement without an Ex[*torn*] of Relief; but even to involve in the same Misfortune th[*torn*] kind friends who charitably attempt it.

Permit Me Sir, to entreat You & these Honourable [*torn*]

Ms (PHi-RRL)

---

[1] The William Smith Papers at the University of Pennsylvania contain two notices from clerk Charles Moore, neither of which contains the language JD quotes here. The first, from Jan. 12, informs Smith that he was to appear at 10:00 a.m. the next day "to answer such Charges as shall then and there be inhibited against you," and therefore to "send for any Evidences" necessary (Moore to Smith, Jan. 12, 1758, PU-Ar). Smith noted that he received the notice at 8:15 p.m., and that it was strange for the "House to desire me to send for Evidences to Charges that either are to be made, or which have been made & never communicated to me." The second, from the morning of Jan. 13, informs Smith, "As the House are uncertain whether they may sit Tomorrow, they have ordered me to acquaint you, that they must know what Gentleman you make Choice of for Council betwixt this of Evening" (Moore to Smith, Jan. 13, 1758, PU-Ar).

[2] Thomas Yorke. See doc. 1:53, n. 33.

[3] The principle of double jeopardy, or being tried twice for the same crime, has roots in ancient Greece and Rome as expressed in Just. Digest 48.2.7: "the governor should not permit the same person to be again accused of a crime of which he has been acquitted." See also Jay A. Sigler, "A History of Double Jeopardy," *American Journal of Legal History* 7, no. 4 (1963): 283–309.

[4] "The Serjeant at Arms attending, according to Order, with *William Smith*, he was called in, and acquainted from the Chair, that he was charged with being a Promoter and Abettor of the

Writing and Publishing a Libel, intituled, *The humble Address of* William Moore, *one of the Justices of the Peace for the County of Chester*" (*Votes* [1758], 20).

[5] Repine: "To feel or express discontent or dissatisfaction; to grumble, complain" (*OED*).

[6] William Smith, *A Brief State of the Province of Pennsylvania* (London: R. Griffiths, 1755); and *A Brief View of the Conduct of Pennsylvania, for the Year 1755* (London: R. Griffiths, 1756). These two pamphlets accused the Quakers of solidifying their political power at the expense of the people's safety: "They are *Rulers, Assembly-Men, Politicians,* and unrighteous *Monopolizers of Power,* pursuing separate Interests from their Country and sacrificing the Majority of their Fellow-Subjects to these dirty interests" (*Brief View,* 85–86). The Quakers were in fact duping their constituents: "It is very plain they have no mind to give a single Shilling for the King's Use, unless they can thereby increase their own power; but they keep continually voting Money in order to keep the People on their Side; who are not well enough acquainted with the Nature of Government to understand why the Money-Bills cannot be passed, think every such rejection of a Money-Bill, a Design against their Liberties, and throw the whole Blame upon their Proprietors and Governors, treating their Names in the most insolent and contemptuous Manner" (*Brief State,* 22–23). *A Brief State* was published in three editions between 1755 and 1756.

[7] Joseph Galloway.

[8] Phineas Bond's testimony revealed that Moore sought legal advice before publishing his Address to ensure there was nothing criminal in his words: "his council told him the old Assembly were a non-entity and you may do it safely, otherwise I am certain he would never have done it" (Examination and Deposition of Phineas Bond, Jan. 17, 1758, PU-Ar).

[9] Smith never published a history of Pennsylvania, but he did work on a manuscript until at least 1772. In an April 3, 1772, letter to John Penn, Smith wrote that "I acquainted your Honour a Year Ago, that I was writing a History of this Province," and asked Penn "to procure me Copies of such [of the Penn Family] Papers as you may think useful, else send the Originals to your Brother [Richard Penn, Jr., (1735–1811), then the lieut. gov. of Pennsylvania], who would give me Leave to copy for myself" (Smith to Penn, April 3, 1772, PU-Ar). Penn replied that he would "endeavor to collect for you myself from his [uncle Thomas Penn's] papers," anything that "shall appear the least necessary for your purpose" (Penn to Smith, June 27, 1772, PU-Ar).

[10] 1 Hawkins 196: "[T]he having in one's Custody a written Copy of a Libel publickly known, is an Evidence of the Publication of it."

[11] "[T]ho' *Presumption* is what may be doubted of, yet it shall be accounted Truth, if the contrary be not proved." See entry for "Presumption" in Giles Jacob, *A New Law Dictionary,* 7th ed. (London: H. Lintot, 1756).

[12] All three depositions can be found in NN.

[13] See pp. 237–38 for text intended here.

[14] "Q: Who corrected your Proof Sheet[?]. A. Doctor Phineas Bond, and when he brought back the Proof Sheet there were some Words marked in it, but as he said it was immaterial whether put in or no. I left them out, and corrected what litteral faults were marked on the Sheet." Deposition of William Bradford, Jan. 18, 1758, PU-Ar.

[15] That is, Tacitus.

[16] On Jan. 17, 1756, the Assembly sent Denny a reply to his message of Jan. 13: "If you have no other Powers of Jurisdiction 'but those which are expressly delegated and granted,' by Virtue of what express Authority or Delegation has your Honour, and your Predecessors,

assumed to yourselves the Right and Power of altering and amending Bills passed by the Assembly, and of putting an absolute Negative on them, with other Powers and Rights, belonging to the House of Lords alone, and no more expressly granted than the Power of Judging on Impeachments?" See *Votes* (1758), 23–26.

[17] The Reformation Parliament sat from 1529 to 1536. When it severed England's ties with Rome and established the Church of England, the Parliament broadened its authority to encompass all aspects of the government of the realm.

[18] The Society for Promoting Religious Knowledge and the English Language Among the German Emigrants in Pennsylvania was formed in the early 1750s, a result of the efforts of Reformed minister and missionary Michael Schlatter (1716–1790) to raise money for charity schools for German immigrant children in Pennsylvania to learn English. William Smith and Benjamin Franklin served as trustees. When German printer Christopher Sauer (1695–1758) criticized the schools, Franklin and the Society established Armbruster's rival press, which printed the *Philadelphische Zeitung* from July 12, 1755, to December 31, 1757. See John B. Frantz, "Franklin and the Pennsylvania Germans," *PH* 65, no. 1 (1998): 24–25.

[19] For JD's notes during the deposition, see doc. 1:50. For his detailed account of a hostile exchange with Galloway during the deposition, see doc. 1:55.

[20] William Masters (d. 1760), a lieutenant-colonel of the Philadelphia City Regiment, was one of two representatives from Philadelphia City, the other being Franklin.

[21] Not surprisingly, the Assembly found these members should be "highly commended . . . for the prudent Caution they had given Mr. Hall . . . and the due Care they had taken at the time to guard against any Encroachment on so useful a Privilege as Liberty of the Press" (*Votes* [1758], 28).

[22] See "Mr. David Hall's Deposition, January 18.th 1758," PHi-Logan.

[23] As both a prosecutor and a judge, Lord Mansfield supported vigorously enforcing seditious libel laws. In the 1752 libel case against printer William Owen, he argued for the government that the jury only needed to decide if the defendant published the pamphlet in question, leaving it to the judge to decide whether it was libel. Charles Pratt, Owen's attorney, argued that libel was a matter of intention on which a jury should decide. Mansfield lost the case. See Jeffrey A. Smith, *Printers and Press Freedom: The Ideology of Early American Journalism* (New York: Oxford University Press, 1988), 82–83. As one critic later wrote in 1771, after the trials of Henry Sampson Woodfall (1739–1805) for publishing the *Letters of Junius* (1769–72), criticizing the administration of George III: "Lord Mansfield has succeeded so far in his vile, his infamous design of destroying the liberty of the press, that there is not one bookseller has now the resolution enough to publish the most trifling essay" (*The Scourge, Number I* [London, 1771], 3).

[24] English law focused on removing prior restraint to printing to ensure freedom of the press. A decade after Smith's trial, William Blackstone (1723–1780) summarized press freedom as follows: "The liberty of the press is indeed essential to the nature of a free state: but this consists in laying no previous restraints upon publications, and not in freedom from censure for criminal matter when published" (4 *CLE* 151).

[25] William Smith was critical of the "*German* Sectaries of various Denominations, all *principled against Defence*" who allied themselves with the Quakers (*Brief View*, 22). He accused the Quaker party of using Sauer's press to sway German pacifists to their party by promising never to pass a militia law. "In consequence of this," Smith wrote, "the *Germans*, who had hitherto continued peaceful without meddling in Elections, came down in Shoals and . . . voted in the County of *Philadelphia*, which threw the Balance in the Side of the *Quakers*" (*Brief State*, 27). His opinion of Germans outside of Philadelphia was not much better: "[O]ur Germans are extremely ignorant, . . . and [t]herefore by sending their *Jesuitical* Emissaries among them, to persuade them over to the *Popish* Religion, [the French] will draw them away

from the *English* in Multitudes" (*Brief State*, 30). Franklin's opinion of the Germans was not any higher, and his recent falling out with Sauer made German loyalty in early 1758 an uncertain thing.

[26] The Assembly resolved on Jan. 11, 1758, "That the Piece, intituled, *The humble Address of William Moore . . .* is a false, scandalous, virulent and seditious Libel, highly reflecting on the Honour, Dignity and Proceedings of the last House of Assembly of this Province" and that "to assert . . . that as Assembly of this Province hath no Right or Power, or is not invested with legal Authority to hear Petitions, examine into and redress the Aggrievances and Complaints of the People against public Officers" subverted "one of the fundamental and most essential Powers of the Constitution." *Votes* (1758), 18. Their subsequent arrest warrant to the sheriff called Moore's address "high derogatory to, and subversive of, the Rights and Privileges of this present House." *Votes* (1758), 19.

[27] It is unclear if JD is referring to a specific source, or just providing a summary of the idea that a witness's testimony should be considered in its entirety.

[28] Plaster: "a solid medicinal or emollient substance spread on a bandage or dressing and applied to the skin, often becoming adhesive at body temperature" (*OED*).

[29] Isaac Norris.

[30] Bradford noted that "without the advice and consent of Mr. Norris, Late Speaker, Mr. Masters, and Mr. Galloway, whom he consulted on that occasion at Mr. Norris' house, he would not have printed it" (*American Magazine* [Philadelphia; Jan. 1758]: 200).

[31] Although JD may not have used the comparison to Algernon Sydney (see docs. 1:45, 1:52, 1:53) the Assembly ultimately was persuaded by his argument and voted unanimously to disregard Levers's testimony about the similitude of hands. See *Votes* (1758), 29.

[32] William Moore and his wife, Williamina (1705–1784), had five daughters: Mary, Frances, Rebecca (b. 1723), Williamina (b. 1722), and Anne (b. 1742). The daughter mentioned here is most likely Williamina, who married Phineas Bond in 1748. Her sister Rebecca married William Smith. See Harrison Dwight Cavanagh, *Colonial Chesapeake Families, Vol. 2: British Origins and Descendants* (Bloomington, Ind.: Xlibris, 2014), 199–200.

[33] JD likely is referring generally to Tac. *Ann* 1.72–74, which discusses Tiberius and his revival of "the law of violated majesty" (1.72). Modern translations render this as "the law of treason."

[34] A reference to the opening chapter of Tacitus's *History*: "I have reserved as an employment for my old age, should my life be long enough, a subject at once more fruitful and less anxious in the reign of the Divine Nerva and the empire of Trajan, enjoying the rare happiness of times, when we may think what we please, and express what we think" (Tac. *Hist.* 1.1).

[35] It is unclear to what JD is referring. In his petition to the Privy Council, Smith noted that he was a trustee for a "private society, in London for maintaining Charity Schools, to instruct German here; and to that End having the Care & Direction of a Printing Press, to furnish them with a News Paper, & other Matters in their own Language." See "The Petition, Complaint & Appeal of William Smith," Feb. 6, 1758, NN.

[36] A revised version of this page comes at the end of this document.

[37] It is unclear to what JD is referring.

[38] Sibling symbol not found.

55

Fragment of Draft Transcript of David Hall's Deposition in the Smith Libel Trial, [January 21, 1758]

This fragment gives a detailed account of a portion of printer David Hall's deposition. For the broader context and long version, see doc. 1:54 above. Like the lengthy version, this seems to have been written after the fact and with an eye toward eventual publication.

The import of this fragment is arguably less about the Smith trial than it is about the beginning of a long and bitter rivalry between JD and Joseph Galloway. Although the two had much in common—they were about the same age, both from Quaker families, and both lawyers and politicians—they could hardly have been more different in temperament, style, and political priorities. They worked side by side in Pennsylvania courtrooms and later the Assembly, but as this document shows, Galloway's resentment of JD was close to the surface. Written almost like a play, this vignette details a contentious encounter between the two during the Assembly's questioning of printer David Hall. Here is colorful evidence of the animosity between them, which would influence both the end of colonial Pennsylvania history and the nascent United States. They clashed repeatedly and publicly in the 1764 campaign for royal government and over resistance to British taxation, until Galloway fled to New York as a loyalist in 1778.

This fragment of a document begins on page 42. Page 41 is blank, and page 40, which was excised with a blade, was filled with writing. It appears from page 46 of the present document that it contained "the Remainder of Mr. Halls Examination." And what what seems to have been page 39 had at least one marginal note marked with an asterisk. Unfortunately, this fragment does not fit neatly with any extant documents, causing speculation that JD wrote much more on this trial than has survived.

---

(42)

Mr. Galloway. May it please the Speaker, that this Question may be askd Mr. Hall, whether ~~he~~ did {You} directly or indirectly explain to those Gentlemen any one Paragraph or Assertion in that Address otherwise than by informing them, that it was a virulent & harsh Paper containing Gross Reflections ag[ains]t the late Assembly.

~~Speaker Let the Clerk~~ The Speaker consented the Clerk shoud write it down as was usual, in order to have it askd— And the Clerk had begun Writing—

Mr. Dickinson. Mr. Speaker . . . .

Mr. Galloway. **Pray** Mr. Speaker, let some Notice be taken of that **Young man**: Was ever such Audaciousness seen? I shoud be glad to know

Whether he is to stop my mouth or I his. I claim the Protection of the house from his Insolence, or I must {go off &} quit my Seat. The **Young man** forgets the Difference between Us: tho[ugh] We may be something upon a footing in the Courts of Law, yet here I am his **Superior**, I am his **Judge**, & I pray Mr. Speaker, that he may be taught a proper Respect for the Dignity of the Members of this house. Never in my Days did I ever see such a **stork** brout into any publick place. I desire Mr. Speaker, that this **Young man** may be obligd to hold his Peace, & that the Witness may answer my Question.

Mr. Speaker. What no Decency, no Decency Young man; Do learn how to behave Yourself, or We must take some other Method. Mr. Hall answer the Question that has been askd You.

Mr. Hall. I shoud be glad to have it repeated.
Then the Clerk read "Whether did You directly or indirectly explain to those Gentlemen any one Paragraph or Assertion in that Address otherwise than by telling informing them, that it was a virulent & harsh Paper containing gross Reflections against the late Assembly["]

Mr. Hall. I did not.

Mr. Speaker. Now Young Gentleman, You have the Leave of the house
[*page break*]

(43)
to say what You want.

Mr. Dickinson. Sir, I humbly thank the Honourable House for their Leave. As the Accusation seems to be turnd from the Gentleman at the Bar upon Myself, I Can hardly express my Gratitude for this Goodness in affording Me an opportunity of vindicating my Behaviour from the Scandal {Misconstructions} which has{ve} been [thrown] {made} upon it.
I shoud think Myself unworthy of the Honour of appearing in this place, if I shoud silently acknowledge the Cruel Aspersions which this House has heard: Nay I shoud imagine, I in some measure deservd them, If I did not feel the just Resentment of Conscious Honesty {Innocence} wounded in the dearest, the   tenderest part— My In Reputation— Forgive Me Sir, if I appear movd— You & every worthy man must be sensible what I suffer on this Occasion, if I am not the abandond shameless Character, I have been represented—

The first part of the Charge indeed, "that of being a **Young man**," gives Me very little Uneasiness; tho[ugh] ~~the Members~~ {something was} certainly meant ~~something~~ extremely reproachful ~~from~~ {by} this{e} frequent Repetition of those words, & the~~ir~~ manner of pronouncing them.

~~I [illegible words] [youth?] [illegible words]~~ {I must confess Myself so unknowing Sir, that I never understood Youth [~~illegible~~] [illegible] dishonourable, nor Age in itself meritorious: [~~My?~~] ~~[illegible words]~~ {[~~illegible words~~]} Nor shall I take upon Myself the unnecessary Care of defending the Determinor of Providence from the hasty charge that now arraigns [Nature?]. It will be sufficient for my Vindication that the same infinite} Infinite Wisdom ~~that gave~~ {which ~~[ascertaind]~~]} {that} {appointed} an earlier ~~Date~~ {Period} {time} for others, was graciously pleasd to ~~Spark Me into~~ {Give Me my} Being, a little later.

~~My Youth~~ ~~therefore~~ {What therefore, I neither occasiond nor could prevent} will never be ~~imputed to Me as an offence~~ {accounted an Offence in Me,} either by the Good or Wise— [*page break*]

(44)

~~But if I [illegible words] that it must be imputed to Me [illegible line] will probably correct it [illegible] will probably correct it~~{—}
{~~But~~ {And} if those to whom it appears criminal, can but ~~for once procure the Happiness of~~ thinking {cooly,} they will know that I am continually subduing this {[~~two illegible lines~~]} {**prodigious involuntary Sin.** Perhaps on this} Reflection such objectors will permit me to say, what I sincerely shoud be glad, they coud with equal Truth repeat,} {That} Every Moment ~~that flies,~~ Carries [away] part of <u>my Guilt</u> on its wings, {[~~illegible~~]} {But {[~~illegible~~]ly wish that} {Sir} till this [~~illegible~~] {**insulted period**} of my Life {ˣ} [*in left margin:*] {X has reachd the Bounds allotted to it by Heaven;} [~~illegible~~] {shall [~~illegible~~]} {had} I can only {[~~illegible~~]} [~~illegible~~]; {My wishes & the [course?]} that when it is ~~gone~~ past; [~~illegible~~] all its Imperfections may be past with it; [~~illegible~~] that [~~Time?~~] ~~[while] [illegible]~~ ~~[take from my Youth & may] add to [illegible words]~~ I may advance in Knowledge {& ~~Virtue~~} while I advance in ~~Age~~{years,} & {that encreasing Infirmities may find some Alleviation from an Increase of Virtue: So that I may} may not ~~drink~~ {partake} the bitter Potion of <u>those</u>; [~~illegible words~~] Who continue * **ignorant** [*in left margin:*] {* The Eyes of the Young Gentleman who spoke, applied these words [~~illegible words~~] ~~for whom~~ {where} they were intended, in a manner that coud not be observd by them who were at a Distance.} [~~in spite of~~] {with Opportunities} of [~~illegible~~]{Instru[ction]} & **obstinately**, {& ~~wickedly~~} persist in Errors, because they once **foolishly** adopted them, & ~~wickedly~~ {weakly} wish for

~~Pleasures~~ {Honours} that wiser Nature long since warnd them to ~~forget~~ {forego}.

The other part of the Charge, Mr. Speaker, is very severe upon Me. I wish the ~~worthy~~ {honourable} Member could have found it <u>consistent</u> with his <u>Duty</u> to the <u>Publick</u>, to have treated Me with a little more Lenity. <u>Audacious</u> & <u>insolent</u> are harsh terms, Sir, even if ~~I had~~ {a **young man** had} inadvertently fallen into a Mistake— ~~and I shoud be [*illegible*] greatly obligd to the Gentleman.~~ I am sure I shoud have submitted to the ~~Instructions~~ {Advice} of my **Superior** with great Gratitude, if instead of punishing Me, he had been pleasd to inform Me of my fault. I dont know what the Gentleman may think of the Imputations he laid upon Me, but I <u>yet</u> feel so much Reverence for Modesty, that [~~a peaceable~~] Life woud be burthensome to Me if I coud imagine that the World woud join with him in {his unkind} Opinion.

[~~Pardon Me Sir for~~] {Please to permit Me then Sir} just {to} mention my Behaviour & the Reasons of it, in order to convince this Honourable House, how much Respect I desire to preserve towards them, & how little I have deservd the Reproaches I sufferd.

~~Mr Galloway~~ {The Member} was dictating a Question to the Clerk, to have it proposd to Mr. Hall. That question did not allude to certain facts, & desire the Witness to tell what they were, ~~but the [*illegible words*] itself~~
[*page break*]

(45)

itself [not?] for the {but [[not?] {[then?]} [forth?]] at Large.} ~~therefore, & nothing was to be done by the Witness, [illegible line with insertion]~~ Instead of relating what past, {t}he {Witness} was only to give an Affirmative or Negative to a Number of particular Circumstances that were suggested to him; which might bear some Resemblance to the Truth, but woud have {an} ~~a vastly different~~ Effect, when laid together in that train, {vastly different} from what they woud have had, if the Story had been artlessly told by the Witness.

This Question therefore was a <u>leading Question</u>, as it is calld in the Courts of Law, & such as they will not allow. The Reason of their discountenancing such Questions holds in every Case, where a fair Enquiry is making; & as I found so many of the forms of the Common Law observd here, I did not imagine but this Hon[oura]ble House woud have indulgd {Us} with all the Rights of a just & legal Defence.

I rose up with a design to request the {per[ogative?] of the} House to have that Question more generally proposd: I stood still in this place, & was so far from interrupting the ~~Speaker~~ Gentleman that I waited till he {had} finishd the whole Question, & was silent. {I appeal to every member who is

near Me for the truth of what I say.} The Clerk was [s?] writing it, & I thought this the proper time to address the House, {when no one was speaking} as{nd} the Clerk woud in a few moments have been ready to read the Question to Mr. Hall. I attempted Sir, to speak, but found Myself subjected to Ind[ict]ment I was sorry {indeed} to receive, but which I shoud have been much sorrier to ~~deserve~~ {or to} {[~~*illegible*~~] ~~the Crime that produed the~~ [~~*illegible*~~]} {give another under the Same Circumstances. For}
  ~~I was not~~ [*seven illegible lines*]
  ~~The Behaviour I have~~ [~~*illegible*~~] ~~Sir,~~ [*illegible words*]

[*recovered fragment*:][1]
sorrier to deserve{,} or to give another under the same Circumstances.   For next to the Misfortune of ~~being obligd to blush for~~ [~~*illegible*~~] {doing} some shameful Action {~~for which I might so blush~~} ~~of my own~~ {myself}, I shall [~~*illegible*~~] {always} count that of covering with Confusion by an unjust Charge an Innocent person, who shoud be in some measure under my Protection[:] {Unless Sir, I live to obtain that firmness of Temper & of pace, [~~*illegible*~~] to which I now find Human Nature may arrive, that having forgot to blush Myself, I become insensible too of the {the [*illegible*] [such] [*illegible*] must give to others} behaviour of [~~*illegible*~~] I have mentiond no[w] producd those violent Invectives against Me (Vide margin) [θ]

[*in left margin*:] {θ violent Invectives against Me. I was interrupted before the house coud understand what I intended; & now it is too late to ~~say more upon~~ {[much] on} it. I designd In the most respectful manner I coud, to have dischargd my Duty to the Reverend Gentleman at the Barr; [~~*illegible words*~~] {[~~& to have~~]} [~~*illegible line*~~] But I was prevented. Thus Sir, I have shewn an honest Regard {I hope} to the Cause I have undertaken, & a Decency becoming Me in this place; & tho[ugh] I have receivd such treatment as I little expected [~~*illegible words*~~] in this Honourable House, Yet I cannot but be pleasd that it was receivd on such an occasion.
  Mr. Galloway's passion at this violation of his **Dignity** still continuing, he replied much in the same manner he spoke before: But the House without passing any Censure on Mr. Dickinson, proceeded to ask the Witness the following Questions {Vide page 40}}[2] [*page break*]

(46)
~~of no Offence, but a Disign to do my Duty; & surely that can be no great Offence, or the other Gentlemen who have spoke in this Cause & Myself woud never have appeard before this Honourable House~~
proceeded to ask the Witness the following Questions

Here comes in the Remainder of Mr. Halls Examination, containd in page 40 Which Sec[tion] 1

Notes.

In the Course of taking these Depositions particularly in taking Mr. Robert Livers's, the Answers were written by the Clerk several times in words quite different from those of the Witness— And Whenever Mr. Dickinson attempted to have any Alteration made, he was treated with the utmost severity; chargd with ~~being~~ {allowing himself to be} ignorant of Parliamentary Proceedings (Vide pa. 4)[3] which was said to be now manifest, & every method made use of to intimidate him, [~~illegible words~~] {from make{i}ng that very defence which they had allowd him to undertake꞉{.} [~~Tho[ugh]?] several of the Members [illegible] with which [illegible words~~]}.

But all these particulars woud have taken up too much Room. However he found that the only way to please—was {tamely} to surrender up a Man, who relied upon him, & who but for that Reliance, might have been provided with other Counsel. This Conscience & Honour forbad him to do.

[*upside down*:] What is contain in these Papers [tackd] together also in the Examination of Mr. Hall—& therefore comes in an[swer][in]g the Depositions—

Ms (PHi-RRL)

---

[1] This fragment was discovered with doc. 1:54.
[2] Page excised with blade.
[3] Presumably of the present document, not extant. Although docs. 1:53, 1:54, and 1:57 contain pages numbered (4), none contain an example of the behavior noted.

56
Draft Summary of the Smith Libel Trial, [January 25, 1758]

JD drafted this summary of events and arguments in Smith's trial on or after the day the Assembly pronounced Smith guilty and remanded him to the jail. A clean, expanded copy with edits is immediately below (doc. 1:57). Only items not appearing in the later version have been annotated.

~~Ŧ~~{W}[iam] Moor, one of his Majesty's Just[ice]s for Chester Country summ[one]d before house of Assembly to answer Compl[ain]ts exhib[ite]d before them by about 30 Inhabitants of low rank in th[at] C[oun]ty—for Misbehaviour in ~~that~~ his Office

==

Moor app[eare]d & by a Plea with advice of Counsel ~~disclaimd their~~ denied their Jurisd[icti]on or Authority to [pro]ceed in this manner

==

Upon this they examind Witnesses upon oath ex parte[1] & then thou[gh]t [pro][per] to address the Gov[erno]r to remove Moor from his Office, charging him with many gross & scandalous crimes
== {The year expird— ~~The~~ {Most} of the same members rechosen.}
They likewise publishd this Addr[ess] in the Publick Newspapers.

==

Moor followd their Example {with advice &c}—he ~~prepard~~ {sented} an Addr[ess] to the Gov[erno]r in his Vindication {Here insert the Address—}—& as they had publishd their Charges ag[ains]t him—he also publishd this addr[ess] in defence of his Character.
== {This was done when there was no Assembly
The Gov[erno]r appointed a day to enquire to justify Moor—but prevented—for}
The new Assembly sent two armd men to bring Moor before them ~~for publis~~ on account of this Addr[ess]— Their orders were executed in a ~~terrible~~ violent manner—& Moor instantly confessd himself the author of that Address—{& was committed to the Common Jayl.}

==

The Assembly then enquird Who had been concernd with Moor in writ[in]g & publish[in]g this Address—& thought they had suff[icien]t Reason to call the Rev[eren]d Mr. Smith Provost of the Colledge in this City before them— ~~What share he had in writ~~ Accordingly he was ~~brought to their Barr &~~ {taken into custody by their Serj[ean]t at Arms—treated &c at length rec[eive]d orders to app[ea]r 24[th] Jan[ua]ry[2] to answer a} chargd{e} ~~with~~{of} being the Abettor & promoter of the Writing & publishing a Libel entituled the Address of W[illia]m Moor Esq[ui]r[e] [*page break*]

When {Mr.} Smith app[eare]d at their Barr—the following Resolves were read over to him

By these Resolves Mr. Smith's Counsel found themselves precluded from speak[in]g to two most material points—The Authority or Jurisdiction of the House of Assembly to take notice of this affair: And the Criminality of that Addr[ess] wh[ich] they resolvd to be a Libel.

Under the first head they designd to have insisted that notwithst[an]d[in]g the Assembly of Pennsylvania claims all the Rights Priviledges & Powers of the House of Commons in England—Yet they are not entitled to them: because the Rights Priviledges & Powers of the house of Commons in Engl[an]d are not derivd from any [par][ticu]lar {positive} Law[s?]{,} which gives them; but naturally {rightfully} & undoubtedly belong to the house of Commons, as much as the Right of being repres[ente]d in Parl[iamen]t belongs to the people in General: {;} & {that} for those Rights &c of the house of Commons have existed as long as the house itself, & are so intermixt with the very Constitution of the Eng[lish] Gov[ernmen]t   That therefore they have power to punish for Cont[em]pts ag[ains]t their Dignity, or for breach of Priviledge, & to impeach Criminals before the house of Lords: **But** that the Powers of the house of Representatives in Pennsylvania, are derivd from [par][ticu]lar Grants & cannot exceed those {what are} mentiond in those Grants—that

The parts of these Grants relat[in]g to the p[re]sent point are the 4th Section of the Royal Charter (which insert here) the 2.d Section of the Charter of Priv[ilege]s gr[an]ted by W[illia]m Penn in 1701 (wh[ich] insert here) & the clause of an act of Assembly passd in 1705, contain[in]g the Powers & Priv[ilege]s of Assembly— V[ide] pa. 72 of the printed Book at bottom (insert this too)[3]

That nothing in these Grants or {this} Law gives them power to punish Cont[em]pts or breach of Priviledge——

But if they had such power{,} that they coud {not} take no notice {Cognizance} of this fact, as it was only an offence against the late Ass[em]bly {precedent to this Assembly—& even} [they?] done at a time when there was no Assembly at all: But granting that they had Authority to punish offences ag[ains]t the [*page break*] late Assembly, or offences committed when there was no Ass[embly]

Yet in the present Case, they were depriving Mr. Sm[ith] of the invaluable Priviledge of an Englishman to be tried by his Peers by {on a Pres[entmen]t by} a Grand Inquest of the Country—for that the crime with wh[ich] he was chargd to [*illegible*] before this house—was an Offence at Com[mon] Law—& ought to be [pro]secuted there: [*in left margin:*] {No appeal ag[ains]t their Resolves— Conseq[uent]ly a Democracy—} & th[at] it was utterly unprecedented even for the house of Commons in England to try a man for a Libel in general—w[ith]out alledging it to be a Cont[em]pt or {a} Breach of Priviledge {but here it was for a Libel V[ide] the Charges}: & that this proceeding Mr. Smith {woud not only be deprivd of his Lib[er]ty for an Off[ence] b[aila]ble at Law but} might be punishd twice—as this was an offence at

Com[mon] Law: therefore he ought to be [~~in?~~]{rem}itted to the Courts of Law

{*} [*in left margin:*] {* That the house of Represent[atives] had no author[ity] to try a man by exam[inin]g Witn[esse]s on Oath—~~&~~ that trying Mr. Smith in this manner for a Libel in Gen[era]l w[ith]out so much as pretend[in]g in their Charge th[at] it was a breach of Priv[ilege] or a Cont[em]pt [w]as a direct breach of ~~M~~ 29 Chapt[er] of Magna Charta ~~& sett[in]g up a Juris~~ was join[in]g {both} the power of the house of Commons at home to impeach & the power of the house of Lords to determine on those imp[eachmen]ts, in themselves~~:~~{;} {&} It will be seen hereafter th[at] even the Præorog[ative] of the King is destroyd by this pretended Author[ity] V[ide] pa.}

The 2.ᵈ Point the Counsel were debarrd from insist[in]g on {by these Resolves} was

That the offence Mr. Smith was chargd with was not a Libel: their reasons were that—Mr. Moor had only followd the example of the Assembly in defend[in]g himself before that Authority wh[ich] they had accusd him before—That whatever he alledgd ag[ains]t the late Ass[em]bly was what he apprehended to be necessary, in order to ~~make his~~ {Vindicate hims[elf]:}

That the Lawbooks are clear th[at] nothing ~~is a Libel~~ {containd in} any [Pro]ceed[in]g in a Regular Course of Justice—will make a Compl[ain]t amo[un]t to a Libel, even tho[ugh] the matter shoud be false or scandalous—As in a Petition to a Comm[itt]ee of Parl[iamen]t & th[at] Mr. M[oor]'s addr[ess] was in the Course of Justice—~~to~~ & not by way of Compl[ain]t—but in defence of his Char[acte]r wh[ich] had been grossly reflected on {& prevent his removal from his post}: Th[at] his Application was [pro][per]—as the Assembly had accusd him to the Gov[ern]or & have lately invested him with the Extraordinary power to Judge on an Imp[eachmen]t presented to him ag[ains]t Mr. Moor.

But these two points as has been said, were determ[ine]d ag[ains]t Mr. Smith before he came to the Barr—

The 3.ᵈ & only Point then th[at] [*illegible*]{he w}as allowd to insist on was, That he was not guilty of {abett[in]g &} [pro]mot[in]g the Writ[in]g & publish[in]g a Paper wh[ich] they had ~~determ~~ resolvd to be a Libel—
[*page break*]
What share Mr. Smith had in this affair—will appear from the follow[in]g Depositions—wh[ich] are taken from the minutes of the Assembly—The Originals under the Clerks hand remain[in]g with Mr. Smith— Here ~~recite~~ {insert} all the Depos[i]t[ion]s.

Upon this Evid[ence] It was observd by the Counsel for Mr. Smith, th[at] there was not a single Evid[ence] ag[ains]t him who was not much more criminal than him: th[at] not one of them [pro]vd the least malice or ill nature in Mr. Smith tow[ar]ds the late Assembly— [*in left margin:*] {Agreem[en]t of the Evid[ence]} Th[at] {the Evid[ence] was only this that} he happ[ene]d accidentally to be on a visit at Dr. Phineas Bond's {the Son in Law of Mr. Moor}—when the Company were talk[in]g of Mr. Moor's addr[ess]—th[at] ~~accord[in]g to Dr. Th[omas] Bond's evid[ence]~~ Smith said least of any— ~~& acco~~ shewd no fondness in the affair: th[at] what he said was only in the course of Conv[ersati]on— th[at] some Rem[ar]ks were made ~~by so~~ & some alter[ation]s in conseq[uence] of those Rem[ar]ks—but not one alter[ati]on [~~*illegible*~~]{[pro]vd} to be made in conseq[uence] of what Sm[ith] said: th[at] as to [Pro]of Sheet wh[ich] Ph[ineas] Bond prevaild on him to correct—He only made some literal Corrections—& th[at] even these were left out in the pri[n]t[in]g as app[ear]s by Br[adfor]d's Deposition.

Th[at] as to the Evid[ence] of publish[in]g—Mr. Sm[ith] coud not be blamd because he is a Trustee to the Society for [Pro]mot[in]g the English Language—That his Gracious Majesty is a large Subs[cribe]r to this laudable & useful ~~Association~~ {Scheme}, [*in left margin:*] {Counsel} & th[at] Mr. Smith had the Directions of his Right Rev[eren]d[4] & Right Hon[ora]ble Constituents, [*in left margin:*] {Ass[embly] Addr[ess] publ[ishe]d} ~~to see~~ that their Press was as free as any in the [Pro]vince—that this Address of Mr. Moor's had been publishd near a month in two English Papers—one of which was printed by Hall Printer to the Assembly— This {the} Reason assignd by Mr. Sm[ith] to Hanshaw for publish[in]g it [*page break*] That Mr. Smith was informd Hall had done this with the Advice & Consent of some principal Members of the Ass[embly]

That this Information was not false as [pro]vd by Hall's Evid[ence]—th[at] he never wo[ul]d have pr[in]ted it w[ith]out the Advice & consent of these Gentlemen
That Mr. Sm[ith] coud not be justly calld to an Acco[un]t for only republish[in]g what had been {first} publishd ~~fir~~ by the Ass[em]bly's Printer with their Leave—th[at] he was lead into this act by their means—& th[at] they ought not to condemn him for an Offence th[at] they themselves had occasiond   For the very Members who advisd Hall to print it sat as Judges on Mr. Smith for hav[in]g it translated {into Dutch} from {[~~to an~~?]} Hall's Paper & republishd: th[at] this was only done in the way of his Business—as Hanshaw says Mr. Smith blamd

him for not translat[in]g it, as he had freq[uen]tly done before for Omissions of the like kind—& th[at] it was in discharge of his Duty to the{e}se Society who had entrusted them with their Affairs—in order to [pro]mote the Credit & [Pro]fit of their of their Press—as the Dutch People complaind this Paper was not translated—& their [Pro]fit—as Mr. Moor had bespoke 62 Copies for himself—

That the reasons what was pretended by the members of the Assembly—about the Liberty of the Press (V[ide] Halls Depos[ition])] held as strongly with regard to Mr. Smith—Who was as much a Printer as Smith Hall—th[at] if it was criminal in Smith—it was crim[ina]l in Hall—& if Hall was innoc[en]t We were much more so—as what We did, was in conseq[uence] of what he had done

People thou[gh]t Smith oppressd[5]

Petition about Bail—[6]

Ms (PHi-RRL)

---

[1] Lat. out of the party, i.e., with respect to only one party.

[2] The trial date was set for Jan. 17, not 24. See *Votes* (1758), 21. JD corrected the date in the next version, doc. 1:57, below, p. 282.

[3] See doc. 1:57, n. 11.

[4] Thomas Sherlock was bishop of London in 1757.

[5] In a letter to his father, Philadelphia lawyer and judge Edward Shippen, Jr., (1729–1806) noted that "the evidence was agreed by everybody out of doors to be very lame." Edward Shippen, Jr., to Edward Shippen, Jan. 28, 1758. PHi-Balch-Shippen Papers, 1:53.

[6] On Jan. 23, 1758, the Assembly received a petition "from sundry Inhabitants of the City of *Philadelphia* . . . praying that *William Smith* may be admitted to Bail, and offering to enter into proper Recognizance in whatever Sum the House on their Wisdom and Clemency shall think it reasonable to demand." *Votes* (1758), 28.

57

Edited Summary of the Smith Libel Trial, [January 25, 1758]

This edited draft of the timeline of the Smith trial is a clean version of doc. 1:56, above. It is mainly in JD's hand; edits in another hand, presumably John Ross's, are rendered with <single angle braces>. A third hand is rendered in <<double angle braces.>>

---

(1)

1757 August	William Moor {First Judge of the Court of the Court of Common Pleas &} one of his Majesty's Justices of {the Peace for} Chester County, [was summoned] {receivd a Notice} to

appear before the house of Assembly, to answer complaints exhibited there against him by about 30 Inhabitants[1] of little or no reputation in that County, for misbehaviour in his Office.

Mr. Moor<e> attended at the day, & [~~put in~~] ~~a Memorial,~~ {deliverd a Paper} with advice of Counsel, denying the Jurisdiction & Power of the House to hear & determine on these complaints<~.~; and soon after delivered a Memorial answering the Charges against him, but still denying the Jurisdiction of the House.>

September — The house however proceeded to examine Witnesses on Oath ex parte, & then thought proper to address the Governor praying him to remove Mr. Moor from his Office, & charg[in]g him with many gross & scandalous crimes.[2]

October 1st — The Annual Election of Representatives came on according to the Laws of this Province, when most of the former Members were re-elected.[3]

About two weeks after this, the Assembly's Address against Mr. Moor was publishd in the News Papers.

Mr. Moor conceiving himself to be much injurd by this Address & Publication, thought it a duty to himself, to his family & friends to vindicate his Character.

He therefore followd the Example of the Assembly, & presented an Address to the Governor, setting forth {everything he thought necessary for} his defence, ~~&~~ [~~illegible~~] & praying his Honour to appoint a day for hearing him & his accusers, face to face. ~~Here insert~~ {Vide the printed Copy of} Mr. Moor's Addres<s~.~, ~~or affix a~~ ~~printed Copy~~.> {annexd.}

The Governor according to Mr. Moor's request appointed a day for the hearing.[4] [*page break*]

(2)

As the Assembly had not only presented but publishd their Address, Mr. Moor thought he had as ~~great~~ {good} a right to vindicate his Character, as they had to traduce it, & that his defence ought to be as publick as their accusation: for these reasons he publishd his Address <as above> in the same [*illegible*] {manner} that the Assembly had done.

December ~~This Publication of~~ Mr. Moor's Address was {~~made~~} {framd} between the late Election & the time appointed by Law for the meeting of the new Assembly—so that at the time of {preparing presenting &} ~~Publishing~~ the Address, there was no Assembly existing; & <*>two eminent Gentlemen of the Law [*in left margin:*] <* ~~One of them the Attorney~~ General.> had [*illegible*]~~d~~ {advisd} Mr. Moor that he coud not be calld to an account by the present Assembly for what he did.

Jan[ua]ry 2.[d]
1758.

However the new Assembly as soon as they met {by Adjourment}, sent two armd men to bring Mr. Moor before them for being the author of this Address.[5] Their orders were executed in a terrible manner; Mr. Moor instantly confessd himself the author of the Address,[6] & was committed to close custody in the Common Jayl<; agreable to the following Mittimus.*>[7] [*in left margin:*] <* ~~Here insert the Mittimus.~~ >
{By these means, Mr. Moor was prevented from making his defence before the Governor at the day appointed.}

~~The Assembly then enquird, Who had been concernd with Mr. Moor in writing & publishing this Address, & thought they had sufficient reason to call the~~ <called> <On the same Day[8] that the Assembly issued their Warrant to take Mr. Moore into Custody, the likewise issued a Warrant for> Rev[eren]d Mr. Smith Provost of the Colledge in this City<,>[9] ~~before them.~~ <on a Suspicion or Information that he had been concerned with Mr Moore in framing the Address.>

<Mr Smith> Accordingly he was taken into Custody by their Serjeant at arms, & not permitted {for some time} to speak with any one but in his presence: At length he was calld to the Barr, & demanded a Copy of the Charge & Leave to be heard by Counsel: these were allowd; & ~~this is~~ the Charge <was as follows>
"Charge ag[ains]t Mr. Smith—

"You are chargd with being a Promoter & Abettor of the writing & publishing a <u>Libel</u>, entituled The Address of William Moor one of the Justices of the peace for the County of Chester."

The 17[th] day of Jan[ua]ry was appointed for Mr. Smiths hearing[10] [*page break*]

(3)

On the 17[th] of Jan[ua]ry when Mr. Smith appeard at the Barr with his Counsel, the following Resolves were read over to him.

Resolvd

1. That Mr. Smith or his Counsel shall not be allowd to speak or argue ag[ains]t the Authority {or Power} of this house to take Cognizance of the Charge ag[ains]t him—

2. That Mr. Smith or his Counsel shall not be allowd to [deny] argue ["?]That the Address af[oresai]d [of] is not a Libel—

{*}

* There were some other Resolves read which cannot be exactly rememberd—but the Substance of them was That it was highly Criminal to write or publish any thing derogatory of the Rights & Priviledges of Assembly & that this{e} {present} house has a Right to take notice of such things & punish those who are guilty of such acts—

By these Resolves Mr. Smith's Counsel found themselves precluded from speaking to two ~~most~~ very important Points— 1. The Authority or Power of the house of Assembly to take Notice of this affair; & 2. The Criminality of that Address, which they had resolvd to be a <u>Libel</u>.

Under the first head, they designd to have ~~d~~ insisted, that notwithstanding the Assembly of Pennsylvania claims all the Rights Priviledges & Powers of the House of Commons in England, Yet they are not entitled to them: Because the Rights Priviledges & Powers of the House of Commons in England, are not derivd from any positive Law, which gives them; but naturally, rightfully & undoubtedly belong to the house of Com[m]ons, as much as the Right of being represented in Parliament belongs to the People in general; for those Rights of the House of Commons have existed as long as the house itself, & are intermixt with the very Constitution of the English Government: That therefore they have power to punish for Contempts against their Dignity, or for breach of Priviledge & to impeach Criminals before the house of Lords.

But that the Powers of the house of Assembly in Pennsylvania, are derivd from particular Grants, & cannot exceed what are mentiond in those Grants—

The parts of these Grants relating to the present point are the 4[th] Section of the Royal Charter to Mr. Penn, the 2.[d] Section of the Charter of Priv[ilege]s granted by Mr. Penn in 1701—& the Clause of an act of Assembly passd in 1705—containing the Powers & Priv[ilege]s of Assembly— V[ide] pa. 72. of the printed Book[11] {all which follow in their [pro][per] order} [*page break*]

(4)

at bottom   All which insert here.

That nothing in these Grants or this Law gives them {Assembly} power to punish Contempts or Breach of Priviledge—& the design of them seems to be, to invest the Representatives with proper Authority to answer the Exigences of Government, & not to erect them into a Court <of Justice> for punishing Offences <[illegible words]>: But if they had such power, that they coud not take Cognizance of this fact, <not only> as it was precedent to this Assembly, & done at a time when there was no Assembly at all <but likewise because they had no Power to examine Witnesses upon oath.>: <[>But granting still further, that they have Authority to punish Offences against the late Assembly, or Offences committed when there was **no** Assembly <and [Power?] to examine Witnesses upon oath>—**Yet** in the present Case, they were depriving Mr. Smith of the invaluable Priviledge of an Englishman, to be tried by his Peers on a Presentment by the Grand Inquest[12] for the Country—for that the Crime with which he was chargd before the house, was an offence at Common Law, & ought to be [pro]secuted there: that by their Proceeding in this manner, & turning the Streams of Justice, Mr. Smith woud not only be deprivd of his Liberty, for an Offence that was bailable at Common Law—but might be punishd twice for the same offence, as he might be indicted—{*} [*in left margin:*] {* That there is a great Difference between matters & causes <u>solely</u> cognizable in Parliament As Contempts—Breach of Priviledge, or {or} matters {things} done & movd in Parliament, and ~~Matters~~ Causes cognizable in the Courts of Com{mon} Law— That in the latter Case there are Instances where the house {of Commons in England} have stopt their Enquiries & remitted the [Per]son accusd to the Courts of Common Law: But that} ~~Besides~~ that it was utterly unprecedented ~~even~~ for the{m} ~~house of Commons in England~~ to ~~try~~ {punish} a man for a <u>Libel in ~~England~~ general</u>, without alledging it to be a Contempt or a Breach of Priviledge—But here Mr. Smith is chargd with abetting & [pro]moting {the writing & publishing} a Libel in general—Vide pa. 2.^d the Charge.{*}—— That the house of Assembly have no right {or Authority} to **try** a Man by examining Witnesses on oath—& that ~~trying~~ {depriving} Mr. Smith {of his Liberty & trying him} in <u>this manner</u> for a Libel in General, without so much as pretending in their Charge, that it was a Breach of Priviledge or Contempt, was a direct & manifest infringement of the 29th Chapter of Magna Charta, & was joining both the Power of the house [*page break*]

(5)

House of Commons at home to impeach, & the power of the house of Lords to determine on those impeachments, in themselves:{;} [f?]{(} {&} It will be seen hereafter that even the Prærogative of the King is destroyd by this pretended Authority. V[ide] pa. [*blank*])

The 2.^d Point the Counsel were debarrd from insisting on by these Resolves, was

That the Offence Mr. Smith was chargd with abetting & promoting, was not a Libel: their reasons were, that Mr. Moor had only followd the Example of the Assembly in defending himself before that Authority, which they had accusd him before: That whatever he alledgd against the late Assembly, was what he apprehended to be necessary in order to vindicate himself: That the Lawbooks are clear, that nothing containd in ~~a Regular~~ {any} proceeding in a Regular course of Justice, will make the Complaint amount to a Libel, even tho[ugh] the matter shoud be false & scandalous—As in a Petition to a Comm[itt]ee of Parliament, or in Articles of the Peace exhibited before a Justice of the Peace: That Mr. Moor's application was in a regular course of Justice, to defend himself from a Charge before an Authority that coud deprive him of his Office, order him to be prosecuted, & by this treatment ruin his Reputation.

But these 2 points were determind against Mr. Smith, as has been said, before he came to the Barr—<, & his Council were not allowed to speak to them.*> [*in left margin:*] <* Mr Smith, himself, did however remonstrate against this as depriving him of his Defence, &

notwithstanding the Resolves of the House (which he said he could not consider as Laws) required for his own Satisfaction & that of the Audience that the House woud shew their Conduct to be Parliamentary, by giving a Precedent{s} ~~in Support of~~ in Support of their Resolves.

1ˢᵗ Precedent asked by Mr Smith was to shew that ever the House of Commons had taken upon them to examine Witnesses upon Oath and try a Man for a **Libel**, without remitting to the Courts of Law{,} [~~or bring~~?] except the Author had been one of their own Members?

2.ᵈˡʸ To shew that ever a Subsequent House of Commons had [~~either~~?] taken Cognizance of any Thing written against a former House?

The Assembly attempted to give some Precedents on these heads, but the Council observing that they were not any how in Point and calling for others it was observed that the house did not come prepared, & the Council were ordered to proceed immediately to the 3ᵈ Point, which was all that they were ~~allowd~~ allowed to insist upon[*torn*]>

~~The 2.ᵈ & only point then that he was allowd to insist on was,~~

  {**3.**ᵈ Point} That ~~he~~ {Mr. Smith} was not guilty of abetting & promoting the writing & publishing The Address of William Moor Esq[ui]r[e] which they had **resolvd** to be a Libel— [*page break*]

(6)

What share Mr. Smith had in this affair, will appear from the following Depositions taken from the Minutes of the Assembly— The Copies under the hand of the Clerk of the Assembly remain in Mr. Smith's care.

Here insert all the Depositions

Upon this Evidence   It was observd by the Counsel for Mr. Smith, that there was not a single Witness against him, who was not much more criminal than him: that not one of them provd the least malice or ~~Ill will~~ Resentment in Mr. Smith ag[ains]t the late or present Assembly—& that the Evidence as to the **Writing** the address amounts only to this

That Mr. Smith happend accidentally to visit Dr. Phineas Bond, & met there Dr. Thomas Bond, {Mr. Levers} & Mr. Moor the Father-in-law of Dr. Ph[ineas] Bond—that the discourse turnd on the Address which Mr. Moor had prepard in order to present to the Governor—& Mr. Smith joind in the Conversation—that some alterations were made in consequence of the remarks made amongst the Gentlemen, but not the minutest Alteration provd to be made in consequence of what Mr. Smith said: The two <Dr> Bonds & Mr. Levers agree expressly in this: Dr. Th[omas] Bond says, Mr. Smith said least of any; & Dr. Ph[ineas] Bond says, he never shewd any forw[ar]dness

285

in the affair— So that what he did say, was only in the course of Conversation amongst the friends of the Gentleman, in whose house he then was.

That as to the Proof Sheet which Dr. Ph[ineas] Bond after much entreaty prevaild on him to correct; What corrections he did make, were only <u>literal,</u> & even these were left out in the printing, as appears by Bradford's Depos[iti]on

That as to the Evidence of **Publishing** the Address;

It appeard that Mr. Smith did no more in this affair than he usually did in others; that is, orderd his Translator[,] Hanshaw, to translate & put in the Dutch Paper what was [*page break*]

(7)

publishd before in the English Papers: that he did not send for Hanshaw on this occasion, but when he came to him for his Salary—told him to translate Mr. Moor's Address, & blamd him for not doing it sooner, as he had often done before for Omissions of the like kind:
[*in left margin:*] {V[ide] Hanshaw's Depos[iti]on pa. [*blank*]}
That Mr. Smith did not know this {Address} to be a Libel, as two eminent Gentlemen of the Law had ~~told~~ {assurd} Mr. Moor it was not— That besides this reason for not thinking it unlawful, Mr. Smith had seen it printed in two Eng[lis]h Papers for a month before; one of which was printed by Mr. David Hall Printer to the Assembly— That Mr. Smith assignd this as a reason to Hanshaw ~~that~~ why it might be safely printed in the Dutch Paper: That Mr. Smith was informd Hall had printed this Address with the <u>Advice & Consent</u> of ~~some {Principal} Members~~ <<the Speaker and some principal Members>> in the late & present Assembly÷{;} that this informat[io]n was not false, as Hall swears that he never woud have printed it, without the <u>advice & consent</u> of these Gentlemen of the Assembly [*in left margin:*] {V[ide] Hall's Deposit[i]on pa. [*blank*]}: That Mr. Smith coud not justly be calld to an Account for only republishing what had been first publishd by the Assembly's Printer with their Leave; that he was lead into this act by their means—& that they ought not to condemn him for an offence which they themselves had occasiond (for the very members without whose Advice & consent Hall woud not have printed it, sat as Judges on Mr. Smith for ordering Hanshaw to translate out of Hall's Paper, & republish it)
That Mr. Smith is Trustee to a Society in England for promoting the English Language <{& Religious Knowlege} among the German Em[i]grants>

That his Gracious Majesty is a large Subscriber to this laudable & useful
Scheme
That this Society has a Dutch Press in Philadelphia to ~~answer this Purpose~~,
~~which {That} Mr. Smith overlooks as Trustee~~ <forward this Design &
publish a News Paper in the German Tongue once every Fortnight.>
~~That he had~~ <That Mr Smith, as a Trustee {& by [Vote?] of the other
Trustees} has the Direction of this Press committed to him and has> the
~~Directions~~ <Order[s?]> of his Constituents at home [*page break*]

(8)
{()among whom are several ~~Bishops~~ {~~Clergymen~~} & Noblemen {&
Clergymen} of the first Rank, <<~~& Clergymen~~ in England>> to take care
that their press shoud be as free as any in the Province—that accordingly he
<had always ordered his Translator> {to re}publishd in the Dutch Paper,
~~almost~~ everything that came out in the English Papers, & amongst the rest,
this Address of Mr. Moors<e>—that he did this in the faithful discharge of
his Duty to the Society at home; in the first place to keep up the Credit of the
Paper, as it appears by Hanshaw's Deposition that the Dutch People
complaind that they had not seen it in their paper [*in left margin:*] {V[ide]
Hanshaw's Depos[iti]on pa. [*blank*]}—& 2$^{\underline{ly}}$ to encrease the profits of the
~~Society~~ {Press} which depended on the Credit of the {Dutch} Paper, besides
that this particular Address was likely to sell well—& Mr. Moor himself had
bespoke 62 Copies<-, & was to pay for them.> [*in left margin:*] {V[ide]
Armbruster's Depos[iti]on pa. [*blank*]}

   That it was cruel to sacrifice Mr. Smith for doing his Duty like an honest
man, & take no Notice of Hall who had publishd first—& to let those men
who advisd that Publication set on ~~him~~ {Mr. Smith} as Judges.
That what was pretended by the Members of the Assembly about the Liberty
of the Press (V[ide] Hall's Depos[iti]on ~~pa.~~ [*blank*]) held as strongly with
Regard to Mr. Smith—for that he was as much a Printer as Hall—& there
was the same reason for the Society's Press being open, as for Hall's or
Bradfords: that if it was criminal in Mr. Smith, it was criminal in Hall—& if
Hall was innocent, Mr. Smith was much more so; as what Mr. Smith did,
was in consequence of what Hall had done—& if the [~~illegible~~] **Advice &
consent** of the members woud excuse Hall, it woud excuse those who
transcribd from him.

After this[13] Mr. Smith, his Counsel & the Audience withdrew—& the
House took several days to consider of this affair—

   In the meantime Mr. Smith's trial became the General Subject of
Conversation, & the whole Town, except [*page break*]

(9)

The most violent on the part of the Assembly, thought Mr. Smith very ill usd, & even persecuted; [~~illegible~~]{the} reason of this treatment was supposd to be, that Mr. Smith was accounted the Author of a {some} Pamphlet{s} publishd some time ago in London, calld A Brief State ~~&c~~ {& Brief View &c} in order to shew the Miseries this Province was reducd to, by the Mismanagement of the Quakers: This renderd him very obnoxious to that party, & the Assembly had calld him ~~before the~~ to their Barr once before, but were obligd to dismiss him, as no Evidence appeard ag[ains]t him: & now it was thought, they were glad of any pretence to get him in their Power—

However when the Evidence on which the Assembly proceeded, became Publick; People in general seem to be very much dissatisfied {that a man shoud be deprivd of his Liberty on such ~~trifling~~*} [*in left margin:*] {* {slight} testimony: besides they thought}, {they} thought that Distinction of Persons in making use of those who were really guilty to accuse a Man, who appeard to have no concern in writing or ~~framing~~ {publishing} the Address, more than in the course of Conversation, & in the way of his Duty, was very unjust.

Accordingly ~~the~~ <a majority> ~~Church Wardens,~~ Vestry-men[14] & a ~~great Number of the~~ <several of the> Principal Inhabitants of Philad[elphia] presented a Petition to the Assembly, offering ~~to give [illegible]~~ <[*caret*]> Bail <{in} any Sums ~~as~~> for Mr. Smith, if he might be allowd his Liberty— No notice was taken of this Petition—

On Wednesday 2~~6~~{5}[th] Jan[ua]ry Mr. Smith was again brought to the Barr when the Speaker deliverd his Sentence in these words,

"Mr. Smith, this house having enquird into the charge against You, have found You guilty of promoting & publishing the Libel entituld The Address of William Moor Esq[ui]r[e] & do order that You be committed to the gaol of this county, until You make Satisfaction to this house." [*page break*]

(10)

Mr. Smith then read & tenderd to the house his Appeal to his Majesty in Council, in these words

"To the hon[ora]ble the Representatives &c
I Apprehend &c— Here insert the Appeal—

Mr. Smith's Counsel in support of the Appeal read the 5[th] C[la?] Section of the Royal Charter to Mr. Penn which insert here

The Counsel then insisted that this was not now Mr. Smiths Case—but that his Majesty himself was concernd, as his Royal Prærogative was now to be determind, & by a Court, that they themselves acknowledgd, was not a Court of Record—
That Appeals lay to his Majesty even upon Laws passd by both parts of the Legislature, & it woud be very odd if they woud not lye from the Judgment of one branch[:?]

That all Appeals were founded on some Error in {matter of} fact or {matter of} Law, & if that was the Case {here}, it woud be extremely hard We coud not apply to our Gracious Sovereing for Redress:

That in the present Case the Assembly had establishd a Jurisd[icti]on never heard of before, which they would not suffer to be enquird into; they they calld a [suffer] Paper a Libel, when the Law does not call {it} so, which they woud not suffer to be disputed; & now gave a Sentence, from which they woud not suffer an appeal; & by the same Doctrine might make themselves absolute masters of the Lives Liberties & Properties of every man in the Province—For they have nothing to do, but what they have done in this Case, to 1.ˢᵗ to resolve that they have Jurisdiction 2.ˡʸ that a particular fact is Murder, Treason or whatever they please to call it & 3ˡʸ [to?] deny an Appeal— [*page break*]

(11)

However the house utterly rejected Mr. Smiths appeal & returnd it to him: On his desiring that the tender & Refusal might be enterd on their Minutes, they askd with anger, if they were to be directed by him how to keep their minutes
The Speaker then read a form of an Acknowledgm[en]t made by the Bishop of Bristol in James 1ˢᵗ time, & insinuated as if the same woud be sufficient from Mr. Smith—[15]
But Mr. Smith told him he was not conscious of having done any offence, & therefore he coud acknowledge none, for he coud never allow his Lips to give the Lye to his heart—<with more to the same Effect, which was so much approved by [the?] {a vast} Audience that the Majority of them signified their Applause by a loud Clap; which the Assembly considering as an Insult upon them hurried Mr Smith to Goal by the following Mittimus without suffering him to open his Mouth, when he attempted to vindicate himself from some unjust Charges alleged against him [after?] on Account of the ~~Tumult among the~~ People.{'s Behaviour.}>

~~Upon this they made out the following Mittimus~~

"~~Philadelphia Ss~~[16]—
<Philad[elphi]a Ss>

To James Coultas[17] Esqr. Sheriff &c

here insert the mittimus

<N.B>Mr. Smith is now confind in Jayl<, and it is remarkable that he is Charged for ~~writing and~~ promoting and abbeting the Writing and publishing a Libel; he is Sentenced for Promoting & Publishing a Libel, & he is committed for More than is contained either in the Charge or Sentence; ~~without~~ and indeed this was necessary, as his [~~illegible~~]{Ch}arge & Sentence were common Law Offences, on which a Committment could not have been founded without adding something more

It is also remarkable that the Sentence finds him Guilty of Promoting &c but the Mittimus only adjudges, without saying either Guilty or innocent, & then adds something never mentioned before about Privileges; but no Contempt alleged.> [*page break*]

Memo[randu]m   An Oath charged in the Bill of Fees—[18]

Ms (PHi-RRL)

---

[1] Three petitions arrived on Nov. 24, 1756; three on Nov. 25; three on Nov. 26; three on Nov. 27; six on Dec. 15; two on Jan. 4, 1757; four on Feb. 16 (one from "divers inhabitants"); one on March 10; and two on April 1 (one from "several of the inhabitants" of Chester Co.). See *Votes* (1757), 32–34, 47, 62, 86, 99, 106.

[2] The 1756 Assembly wrote an address to Gov. Denny on Sept. 30, 1757, asking him to remove Moore "from the Offices of Judge of the Court of Common Pleas and Justice of the Peace, and from all other Publick Offices, Posts, and Employments whatsoever under His Majesty within this Government" (*Votes* [1757], 160). In their Jan. 17, 1758, message to Denny, the 1757 Assembly renewed their request that he "either remove *William Moore* from his public Offices, or permit us to impeach him of the many heinous misdemeanors charged against him, some of which are not cognizable in the ordinary Courts of Justice" (*Votes* [1758], 24).

[3] In the October 1757 election, twenty-seven members were returned (including Thomas Leech, Daniel Roberdeau, and Joseph Galloway) and nine new members joined the Assembly.

[4] Gov. Denny refused to remove Moore from office without an enquiry, and to that end, on Sept. 30, 1757, he asked the Assembly to give him copies of all the evidence against Moore (see *Votes* [1757], 162). On Oct. 20, Moore's Address arrived (see 7 *CRP* 764). To resolve the matter, Denny set Jan. 9, 1758, as the date of the enquiry into Moore. When he arrived that morning to Council chambers, there were "above Twenty Witnesses, on the Part of Mr. Moore and the Petitioners against him with their Witnesses, making above Thirty" (7 *CRP* 777). He

was greeted by William Masters, Galloway, and Roberdeau, who unofficially informed him "that the House would proceed by Impeachment against Mr. Moore," and requested that the hearing be delayed (7 *CRP* 777). The Council was unanimous that the hearing should proceed, but then a letter arrived from Moore, written from prison. "The Assembly knew that this Day was appointed by your Honour to hear my Cause . . . . How far then it may be thought decent to your Honour, for the present Assembly by Seizing my Person to prevent that Hearing" (7 *CRP* 778). Denny canceled the hearing and wrote to the Assembly: "[f]rom the Moment I received the above [Moore's] Address, I determined on a full and close Enquiry into the Charges . . . [a]nd to that End I appointed this Day for hearing all the Proof in the Case, after due Notice being given to the Parties and their Witnesses. . . . I was sincerely disposed to do every Thing in my Power, consistent with the Rules of Justice, in this Matter, and . . . any Delay therein cannot be imputed to me" (*Votes* [1758], 14).

[5] On Jan. 6, 1758, Speaker Leech issued "his warrant to the Serjeant at Arms, requiring him to bring the said *William Moore* forthwith to the Bar of this House, to answer such Questions, touching the said Address, as shall there be put to him" (*Votes* [1758], 12). The Assembly's Jan. 10 message to Gov. Denny noted that "the said *William Moore* was arrested by a Deputy of our Serjeant at Arms, and is now in Custody" (*Votes* [1758], 15).

[6] When Moore appeared before the Assembly on Jan. 11, he admitted that the manuscript the Assembly showed him "was his own Hand Writing, and that he had delivered the same to the Printer for Publication." When asked if he had any assistance, he replied, "'I drew it up myself, Part at my own House, and Part in Town—I did in deed shew it to several of my Friends, who made few or no Alterations in it; I am therefore the Author of it myself'" (*Votes* [1758], 17).

[7] That is, warrant.

[8] The date was actually Jan. 6, 1758. See *Votes* (1758), 12.

[9] JD did not mention Smith's first appearance before the Assembly. Leech issued a warrant for Smith on Jan. 6. He appeared that same day and was "examined, and afterwards committed to the Custody of the Serjeant at Arms, till further Orders from this House" (*Votes* [1758], 12). He was called before them again on Jan. 13 and "charged with being a Promoter and Abettor of the Writing and Publishing a Libel" (*Votes* [1758], 20). Smith asked for copies of the charge against him and his Jan. 6 examination, and to be released from jail to hire a lawyer and prepare for his defense.

[10] Smith, Ross, and JD appeared before the Assembly at 3:00 p.m. on Jan. 17. "The House then proceeded to the Examination of Witnesses before the said *Smith*, and his Council; and having spent much Time therein, adjourned to Ten a Clock To-morrow Morning" (Votes [1758], 26).

[11] Royal Charter, 1681, § 4: "We . . . do grant free, full, and absolute Power (by Virtue of these Presents) to him [William Penn] and his Heirs, to his and their Deputies, and Lieutenants for the good and happy Government of the said Country." *Collection of Charters*, 3.

Charter of Privileges, 1701, § 2: "FOR the well governing of this Province and Territories, there shall be an Assembly yearly chosen . . . [w]hich . . . shall have Power to . . . impeach Criminals, and redress Grievances; and shall have all other Powers and Privileges of an Assembly, according to the Rights of the Free-born Subjects of *England*, and as is usual in any of the King's Plantations in *America*." *Collection of Charters*, 44.

2 *SALP* 218, "An Act to Ascertain the Number of Members of Assembly and to Regulate the Election" (1705) § 5: "And be it further enacted by the authority aforesaid, That the representatives so chosen and met according to the direction of this act, shall be the assembly of this province, and shall have power to choose a Speaker and other their officers, and shall be judges of the qualifications and elections of their own members; sit upon their own adjournments, appoint committees, prepare bills in order to pass into laws, impeach criminals and redress grievances; and shall have all other powers and privileges of an assembly according to the rights of the freeborn subjects of England, and as is usual in any of the Queen's

plantations in America." This act is dated Jan. 12, 1705–06; because of the calendar shift, the year of 1706 when the act was passed, but is retrospectively 1705. The session began in October 1705. For the act, JD is citing *A Collection of All the Laws of the Province of Pennsylvania* (Philadelphia: B. Franklin, 1742), 72–73.

[12] That is, grand jury.

[13] Saturday, Jan. 21, 1758.

[14] Vestryman: "A member of the parochial vestry [i.e., a body elected by members of the congregation of a church and invested with the conduct of its business affairs]" (*OED*).

[15] John Thornborough (1551–1641) was called before Parliament in 1604 to answer for a book he published in that year entitled, *A Discourse Plainely Proving the Evident Utilitie and Urgent Necessitie of the Desired Happie Union of the Two Famous Kingdomes of England and Scotland*. The House of Commons claimed that the book violated their privilege of secret debate. See *ODNB*. He made the following acknowledgment:
"1. I confess I have erred in presuming to deliver a private Sentence, in a Matter so dealt in by the High Court of Parliament. 2. I am sorry for it. 3. If it was to do again I would not do it. 4. I protest it was done out of Ignorance, and not out of Malice, towards either of the Houses of Parliament, or any particular Member of the same; but only to declare my Affection to the intended *Union*, which I doubt not but all your Lordships do allow." See *The Parliamentary or Constitutional History of England*, 24 vols. (London: T. Osborne and W. Sandby, 1751–61), 5:109–10.

[16] Lat. abbreviation for *scilicet*, meaning particularly, to wit, or namely; used to indicate the venue of a legal proceeding.

[17] James Coultas (d. 1768) was a landowner and sawyer. See Robert Patterson Robins, "Colonel James Coultas, High Sheriff of Philadelphia, 1755–1758," *PMHB* 11, no. 1 (1887): 50–57.

[18] The text has been cut out and pasted from another sheet of paper.

Documents on the Flag-of-Truce Trade

The flag-of-truce trade was maritime trade with the enemy during wartime. Flags of truce were passes given by colonial governors that allowed ship captains to enter an enemy port; often these ships were themselves referred to as flags of truce. Ostensibly, the trade was limited to exchange of prisoners; in practice, it flourished in all manner of contraband goods. An intense debate roiled around the legality of the trade, and one's position was seen by many as a reflection of one's patriotism. JD, however, questioned the illegality of the trade on constitutional grounds.

By the time of the French and Indian War, there was increasing scrutiny of colonial trade with belligerent nations, and in particular flag-of-truce trade. In the early 1740s, naturalized French refugees living in the English colonies had facilitated trade with Spain, using their French credentials to gain access to Spanish goods and their English credentials to import those goods into the mainland colonies.[1] For the northern colonies, France's entry into the War of the Austrian Succession in 1740 compromised their access to molasses and sugar from the Caribbean. English law considered provisions to be contraband goods in times of war, so American merchants shipped such goods to the neutral Dutch island of St. Eustatius (or Statia), where the French also shipped their molasses. With the advent of the French and Indian War in 1756, when Parliament authorized the Navy to seize Dutch ships engaged in this trade, Americans sailed instead to the then-neutral Spanish port of Monte Cristi on Hispaniola, present-day Haiti and the Dominican Republic.

Pennsylvania was a main hub of the flag-of-truce trade. The Quakers who controlled the province were arguably the most successful group of merchants in the western Atlantic world, and they had built Philadelphia into the largest commercial port in the colonies. Most colonial governors encouraged the illicit trade by the sale of countless passes to merchants, and Pennsylvania lieutenant governor William Denny was particularly liberal with the passes.[2]

When JD returned from London in 1757 and began practicing law in Philadelphia, tensions between Britain and the colonies on the issue of maritime trade were rising. Contraband trade through free ports in the Caribbean was ongoing, and the flag-of-truce trade was increasing. In 1760 alone, as many as five hundred ships took on cargoes of French molasses. In late August 1760, William Pitt, leader of the House of Commons, was focused on defeating France, and to this end ordered all colonial governors to cease issue of flags of truce and halt all such illegal trade. Accordingly, the Crown attempted to prosecute flag-of-truce traders in the newly established Vice Admiralty Courts. JD, with his eye on the British constitution, law of nations, and the welfare of American trade, represented merchants and captains whose vessels and cargo were seized. Retrospectively, the dispute can be interpreted as one between the nascent capitalist ideology of free trade and the increasingly antiquated imperial mercantile system.

Ultimately, by 1763, the Royal Navy put an end to flag-of-truce trade by the seizing ships and their cargo. The American Duties Act of 1764, known as the Sugar Act in the colonies, was part of Prime Minister George Grenville's (1712–1770) attempt to regulate colonial trade by establishing a Vice Admiralty Court for All America, which signaled to Americans a dangerous turn in imperial policy.[3]

Unfortunately, efforts to annotate these documents were hampered by the lack of extant court records for the Vice Admiralty Court in Pennsylvania.[4]

---

[1] Thomas C. Barrow, *Trade and Empire: The British Customs Service in Colonial America, 1660–1775* (Cambridge, Mass.: Harvard University Press, 1967), 160.

[2] Alan Gallay, ed., *Colonial Wars of North America, 1512–1763: An Encyclopedia* (New York: Garland Publishing, 1996), 706.

[3] Anderson, *Crucible*, 575.

[4] The only collection rendered just over two legal-sized pages for a case in 1758–59. Although John Moland, along with Joseph Galloway, was proctor for the defendant, and the handwriting is similar to JD's, there is no definitive indication of his involvement. See Pennsylvania Admiralty and Vice Admiralty Court Records, DLC.

58
Notes on a Flag-of-Truce Case, [n.d.]

The physical appearance of these notes suggests that JD may have written them while he was at the Middle Temple or otherwise studying. The paper and the writing are similar to those in his legal notebooks from that time. Since these notes pertain to flag-of-truce cases, which he accepted upon his return to the colonies, we have placed them first in this series of documents.

The notes concern a lawsuit involving conflicting claims to an unidentified vessel commissioned as a flag of truce. They open with excerpts from the published reports of court decisions in two English cases, Broom's Case (1697) and *Ewer v. Jones* (1703). The excerpts are followed by a numbered list of legal arguments in support of the "Second Point," which suggests that a first point is missing and that the notes are thus incomplete. The conflicting claims were not, as was frequently the case, between a privateer who had taken a vessel and the owner of the vessel; but rather two conflicting claims of ownership, with one of the claims being based on a determination of a foreign (non-English) court. Also, given the substance of the excerpts from the Broom and Ewer cases and the legal arguments set forth in the notes, it seems clear that JD represented the party in the lawsuit whose claim was based on the foreign court's determination. His arguments refer to earlier cases as precedent for an English court accepting the determination of a foreign court as to ownership of a vessel.

Here and in every subsequent flag-of-truce document, JD represents the side defending the right to the trade. He argues repeatedly that those who engaged in flag-of-truce voyages were, in effect, king's ambassadors who served a vital diplomatic purpose during times of war and therefore were entitled to certain privileges and protections in order to facilitate their missions.

Broom's Case[1]   **Trin[ity] 9 Will[iam] 3. B.R.**

He by Letters of Mart[2] &c from the African Comp[any] took a French Ship in the River of Besaw near Gambore. Broom carryd the Ship to Africa & the Adm[iral]ty there cond[emne]d it as the Kings Prize   After this Broom sold the Ship at Land & applied the money to his own use & came into England & was sued in the Adm[iral]ty here for an Account. After Sentence ag[ains]t him he appeald & then movd for a [Pro]hibition but it was not obtaind for the Suit here is but an Ex[ecuti]on of the first sent[ence] by wh[ich] the Ship is adjudgd the Kings Prize   Now the

Adm[iral]ty having a Jurisd[icti]on that Sentence has bound the [Pro][per]ty & We cannot examine the [Pro][per]ty but must take it according to their Determ[inati]on—wh[ich] cannot be gainsaid till it be repeald on an Appeal—

Trin[ity] Term 2. Anno Regina[3]   2 Raym[ond] 936.[4]

The Sentence of a Civil Law Court in a foreign Realm shall be executed in a Court of the same Nature here & [pro]ceed[in]g after the same Law And no [Pro]hibition because the temp[ora]l Courts [pro]ceed by a due Law & We must give Credit to the sentence as it was adj[udge]d in the time of Cha[rle]s 2d between Hughs & Cornelius:[5] An English Ship was taken at Sea by a French Vessel after the Peace made between Us & the Dutch wherein France was left out & the Ship was carried into France & cond[emne]d there as a Dutch Ship & afterw[ar]ds the Ship came into England & in an Action of Trover[6] brought by the Owner of the Ship ag[ains]t the Vendee it was adj[udge]d that by the Sentence in the Court of France tho[ugh] it was an **unjust** Sentence the [Pro][per]ty was alterd & the Vendee had Judgment. [*page break*]

    Second Point— If She is a Flag of Truce as cannot be doubted— Whether this Claim good?

1. Civil Law now settled—tho[ugh] formerly doubted: 24 hours [pro]portatio &c—[7] Pro[per]ty alterd by being brought **infra præsidia**[8] 4. Ins. 154.[9] <u>2 Raym[ond] 893.[10] 936.</u> Sal. 32. Broom's Case tho[ugh] the King concernd there— Amulto fortiori[11] in case of a Subject 10 Mod. 77.[12] [Pro][per]ty not alterd by being carried into a Neutral Country.

2. The Stat[ute] for **Restitution** can only mean where the Vessel was not cond[emne]d in an Enemy's Port for the first Stat[ute] of this Sort made 4 & 5 W & M.[13] & yet the Civil Law Rule of the [Pro][per]ty being alterd by Condemn[ati]on held in 9 W. Sal. 32 & 2 Anne. 2[14] Raym[ond] 936.

[*in left margin:*] {Must mean only Where it is not a third {[*illegible*]} [Per]son}

3. L[or]d Coke who goes further than any other Writer says th[at] Amb[assad]ors are not bound by any [~~private~~?] Act of Parl[iamen]t Custom[s?] or Law of this Realm[15]

But this Claim is founded on Act of Parl[iamen]t for by the Law of Nations ut supra[16] 2.

4. Natural Laws are misapplied when such Conseq[uence]s are drawn from them as are contrary to Equity. Wood 127.[17]

5. Unless We are adj[udge]d Prize—the Claimers are not w[ith]in the Act of Parl[iamen]t wh[ich] is only designd to Settle the Matter between the Recaptors & former Owners—but if there are no Recaptors the Owners cannot claim—that Stat[ute] plainly designd for th[at] Case alone   The Cases in Sal[keld] & Raym[ond] at least [pro]ve this

6. If She is [pro]tected by her Comm[issi]on from Forf[eiture] ~~ag[ains]t~~ where her Cargo is cond[emne]d   Surely She shall be cleard from a Claim th[at] coud not have been made but for that Commission.
    Here is the most Authentick & Regular Title.
    10 Mod. 77. Not suff[icien]t to recover on a Policy of Insurance
[page break]

So in Reason & Equity— Punish[men]t equal to the Offence   Divine Law of Lex Talionis[18]   Suff[icien]t Discouragement   What Civilians call "Noxæ dedere"[19]   As where a beast does Damage the Master may give him up.[20]
    But let **publick faith** be kept &c[21]

8. Ship restord tho[ugh] carry[in]g **contraband** Goods to the Enemy—on presumption th[at] the Owners were not unacq[uainte]d with the Nature of the Cargo. Answ[er]
of Engl[ish] Lawyers.[22]   Tho[ugh] an Act of **Hostility**.

9. If Vessel condemnd—No Diff[erence] between Flags of Truce & other Captures.

10. Forf[eiture] odious in the Eye of Equity wh[ich] is governd by the Civil Law & theref[ore] No forf[eiture] where Compens[ati]on can be made.

10. Conseq[uence]s of Condemn[ati]on   "Whatsoever Ye woud th[at] Men shoud do unto You do You even so unto them["][23] both moral & Politick. Our poor people there &c[24]
    Rather save one Roman &c[25]

{11. Nemini suum off[ici]um damnosum esse debet.[26] a Maxim. But here the Gold[en] Kindness will hurt him for he must make good to the owners.}

~~11.~~{12.} We have recov[ere]d 20 Subj[ec]ts—a great Benefit—they their Liberty—a greater—& to take their Vessel—woud not be like the Conduct of the generous old Romans to Pyrrhus[27]—&c

Ms (PHi-Logan)

---

[1] "Broom's Case," Trin. 9 Will. 3, B.R. (1697). JD copied the text from 1 Salkeld 32–33.

[2] Letter of mart (or marque): "A government licence authorizing the holder to take reprisals on citizens of a hostile state; (later also) a licence to arm a vessel for the capture of enemy merchant shipping" (*OED*).

[3] The reign of Queen Anne.

[4] The case is *Ewer v. Jones*, Trin. 2 Ann. (1703). JD copied the text from 2 Raymond, *Cases* 935–36.

[5] *Hughes v. Cornelius*, Mich. 32 Car., B.R. (1682). See n. 10, below.

[6] An action of trover is the common-law practice of recovery of damages against one who had found and appropriated another's possessions for his own use.

[7] Lat. declaration; verdict. "Others again are of Opinion, that tho' the Prize has not been carried within the Jurisdiction of the Prince whose Sovereign the Captor is, of there is what they call *a firm Possession*, that is, if the Prize has been 24 Hours in the Power of the Captor, the same cannot be restored by a neuter Nation." Justice 665.

[8] Lat. within the defenses. "The international law doctrine that someone who captures goods will be considered the owner of the goods" (*BLD*).

[9] 4 Coke, *Institutes* 154: "That where the King of England was in league with the King of Spain, and with those of Holland, &c. and one of Holland upon the high sea *in aperto prælio* [Lat. in open battle] took the goods of a subject of Spain, and brought them to England, *infra corpus comitatus* [Lat. within the body of the country], and so the goods were *in solo amici* [Lat. in friendly soil], the Spainiard whose goods were taken libeled for them *civiliter* [Lat. as becomes a citizen] in the Admiralty Court. It was resolved by the Whole Court of the Kings Bench upon conference and deliberation, that the Spainiard had lost the property of the goods for ever, and had no remedy for them in England."

[10] 2 Raymond, *Cases* 893: "In the case of *Hughes* v. *Cornelius*, in which I [Holt] was of counsel with the plaintiff in my lord *Hale*'s time, an *English* ship was taken in the time of the *Dutch* war, and condemned as a *Dutch* ship in the admiralty of *France*, and sold to the plaintiff; and in an action of *trover* brought by him for the ship upon a trial before my lord chief justice *Hale*, the sentence of the admiralty of *France* was produced under seal of the court, and all this matter was found specially; and although the fact was found to be contrary and falsifying the sentence in the admiralty of *France*, yet that sentence was held to bind the property of the goods, and the plaintiff recovered."

[11] Lat. from the much stronger.

[12] 10 *Modern* 77, *Assievedo v. Cambridge*, Hill. 10 Ann., B.R. (1711): "If a ship injured by taken by the enemy, and after a possession of nine days, but before she is carried *infra præsidia* [Lat. completely in the power of the captors] be retaken by an *English* man of war, the property is not changed; but if it be found that the plaintiff in the policy is not *concerned in point of interest*, he cannot recover against the underwriters."

13 4 & 5 W. & M., c. 5 (1692): "An Act for Granting to Their Majesties Certain Additional Impositions Upon Several Goods and Merchandize for the Prosecuting the Present War Against France."

14 That is, *Ewer v. Jones*.

15 4 Coke, *Institutes* 153: "But if a foreign Ambassador being *Prorex* [deputy king or viceroy] committeth here any crime, which is *contra jus gentium* [Lat. against law of nation] as Treason, Felony, Adultery, or any other crime which is against the law of Nations, he loseth the privilege and dignity of an Ambassador, as unworthy of so high a place, and may be punished here as any other private Alien, and not to be remanded to his Soveraigne out of curtesie. And so of contracts that be good *jure gentium*, [Lat. law of nations] he must answer here. But if any thing be *malum prohibitum* [Lat. wrong because prohibited] by any Act of Parliament, private Law or Custom of this Realm, which is not *malum in se jure gentium*, nor *contra jus gentium*, an Ambassador residing here shall not be bound by any of them."

16 Lat. as described above.

17 Wood 127: "If it happens that upon application of a natural Rule to some Case which it seem'd to include, there follows Decision from thence contrary to Equity, we must conclude that the Rule is misapplied, and that this Case must be decided by some other."

18 Lat. law of retaliation. Lex talonis was a principle from early Babylonian law that the punishment for a crime should be the exact damages inflicted on the victim. JD's description of it as "divine" suggests the Old Testament law of an eye for an eye (Ex. 21:24).

19 Lat. surrendering the guilty body.

20 Wood 291: "If a *Beast* . . . doth any damage (call'd *Pauperies*) the Owner . . . may (*Noxæ dedere*) give it alive to the Person injured for the Offence."

21 It is unclear to what JD is referring.

22 Newcastle, 19: "If contraband, the Ship could have neither Freight nor Costs, and the Sentences were favourable, in restoring the Ships, upon presumption, that the Owners of the Ships were not acquainted with the Nature of the Cargo, or Owners thereof." It is likely that JD meant to write "acquainted" above.

23 Matt. 7:12.

24 It is unclear to what JD is referring.

25 "He would rather save one Roman from the enemy than get all that the enemy had." Plut. *Luc.* 8.4.

26 Lat. no one should be damned for doing his duty.

27 Pyrrhus of Epirus (319–272 BC) fought successful but costly battles against Rome; hence the phrase "Pyrrhic victory."

59

"On a Libel Against the Flag of Truce Beaux Enfants," [c. 1758]

These notes relate to a libel—the first pleading of the complainant—in the Vice Admiralty Court to establish rights to a French vessel seized in the Delaware Bay by the *Spry*, a 22-gun privateer piloted at this time by Captain Benjamin Spring. The vessel's commander, Captain Hewet or Huet, claimed it had been commissioned as a flag of truce to carry twenty English prisoners to New York and was forced into the bay by bad weather and a shortage of provisions. He asked Lieutenant Governor William Denny to release the vessel and allow it to proceed to its final destination.

Upon examination, the ship was found to be carrying sugar and other commodities. Suspecting that the vessel was engaged in illegal trade, Denny refused the commander's request and left the issue of whether it had been lawfully seized by the *Spry* to the jurisdiction of the Vice Admiralty Court.[1]

It is unclear from JD's cryptic notes what role, if any, he played in the proceeding, or what role his mentor, John Moland, played. The outcome of the proceeding is also unknown. The argument seems to have been that, even if the vessel's cargo should be awarded to the captain and owners of the *Spry* because the vessel had been engaged in illegal trade and its seizure was lawful, the vessel itself should be returned to its original English owner, Meyler, from whom it had been taken by the French. The intent of many of his notes, especially after the first page break, is unclear, because the notes address an evidentiary issue but do not refer to facts involved in the proceeding. But the following document (doc. 1:60) sheds some light, suggesting that the present set of notes was prefatory to the latter. The notes here outline an argument that to allow the seizure would in effect be inconsistent with the ship's status as a flag of truce. Citing several of the same sources as the prior and subsequent documents, JD argues again that those who engaged in flag-of-truce voyages were, in effect, foreign diplomats.

On a Libel ag[ains]t the Flag of Truce Beauxs Enfans by the Captain[2] & Owners of the Spry Privateer   July 10.th 1758—   & a Claim by One Meyler of Bristol—[3]

Mr. Moland.

> 2 Depositions to [pro]ve the [Pro][per]ty of the Beaux Enfans to have been in Meyler before here taking by the French & was then calld little Jenny &c[4]

10 Mod.[5]

Contrivance of the Enemy to [pro]tect their Vessels— Answ[er:] Is return[in]g Prisoners a Contrivance— M[oland:] Might [pro]tect all their Vessels— Answ[er:] They may be taken at Sea & if Susp[ici]on—sent in. Can see they are loaded— When they arrive safe—still liable if the same Susp[ici]on— What [pro]ves too much [pro]ves nothing—

==

M[oland] French Treatm[en]t   Answ[er] No Recompense to our poor People Ho[gs?]head to fit their shoulders.

==

299

The Man & not the Vessel—the Flag of Truce— Answ[er] Could the Man come w[ith]out? could our Subjects. Reciprocal Obl[igati]ons
==   {This Morality—Christianity goes further.
Ambass[ad]ors   Burlesque[6] to talk of them— Answ[er] Coke speak[in]g synonymously—[7] Their [pro]tection arises from the Nature of things.

Grotius 381.[8] In Notes. Answ[er] Is it abuse to return [Pri]soners.
    Besides is there not a Cartel[9] settled—& is not that the Kings. Faith {Mouths of Kings}?[10] it {not} Well known{?} th[at] no [Pri]soners were restord till the Cartel Settled.
==

Forf[eite]d by Robb[in]g the King of his Duties— Answ[er] That is foreign to this Claim—for then it arises from a Crime & not from [Pro][per]ty
==

She was bound to N[ew] York— Answ[er] Stress of Weather {this app[ea]rs from Exam[inati]on}
Not in this Port. Molloy g{A}pp[[endix][11]
==

Good Prize to the Captors— Molloy[12]   {Goods of c[ontraband]{[Enemy?]}
Good Prize—in a friends Ship. Answ[er] Engl[ish] Lawy[ers] Even tho[ugh] **Contraband** Goods— Yet Ship restord.[13] [*page break*]

Like the Seal of Eccles[ias]tal Court[14]
==

Seal **conclusive** Evidence
==

Diff[eren]t Degrees of Evidence
==

We must have further time &c
Shoud show some Law to the Point.
==

G[rotius][15] Must [pro]duce the best Evidence. [*page break*]

Puff[endorf][16]   Answ[er] of English Lawyers & Burlamaqui[17] all agree—

Sent not receivd
Revolution

Ms (PHi-Logan)

[1] See *PG*, June 22, 1758, and 8 *CRP* 139.

[2] Capt. Benjamin Spring (c. 1730–1776) of Philadelphia commanded the *Spry*.

[3] Probably Richard Meyler, Sr. (d. 1772) or possibly his nephew Richard Meyler (d. 1787). Both were Bristol merchants engaged in the sugar trade with the West Indies.

[4] The *Little Jenny* was a snow, engaged for many years in the trade between Bristol and the West Indies. She was taken near Jamaica by a French frigate in early March. The depositions evidently claimed that snow captured by the *Spry* in mid-June and called the *Beaux Enfants* was the *Jenny* as renamed by the French. See *New Hampshire Gaz.* (Portsmouth), May 12, 1758; *PG*, June 22, 1758.

[5] It is unclear to what JD is specifically referring. See doc. 1:58, n. 12, above, and doc. 1:60, n. 6 and 8, below.

[6] Burlesque: "Droll in look, manner or speech; jocular; odd, grotesque" (*OED*).

[7] 4 Coke, *Institutes* 152–57, discusses ambassadors within the context of c. 26, titled "*De Conservatore seu custode Treugarū, i. Induciarū & salvorum Regis Conductuum.*" [Lat. Of the Observation or Keeping of Truces, Leagues, and Safe Conducts of the King] Coke noted that "it is to be observed that of ancient time, and until latter days no Ambassador came into this Realm before he had a safe conduct. For as no King &c. can come in this Realm without a license or safe conduct, so no *Prorex*, &c. which represent a kings person can doe it" (155).

[8] Grotius, *Rights* (1738) 381: The notes contain an extensive discussion on Christian Thomasius's *Institutionuum Jurisprudentia Divina* (1688) wherein he distinguishes between "*Embassadors, who have done nothing amiss, from those who have behaved themselves ill*; and then such as are sent by one Power to another, with which it is at Peace, from those who *come from an Enemy.*"

[9] Cartel: "A written agreement relating to the exchange or ransom of prisoners, etc.; such exchange itself" (*OED*).

[10] An allusion to a statement attributed to French king John II (1319–1364): "That if Faith and Truth should be banish'd from the rest of the World, yet they ought to be found in the Mouths of Kings." See Laurence Echard, *The History of England. From the First Entrance of Julius Cæsar and the Romans, to the End of the Reign of King James the First* (London: J. Tonson, 1707), 373.

[11] Justice 97–98: "The Lord High Admiral, or Commissioners, to appoint a Commissioner of the Navy, or some one or more Person or Persons, who shall constantly reside at such Place or Places as her Majesty shall appoint; by Virtue of which Appointment, such Person or Persons shall supervise every thing relating to these Cruizers, and take Care that all Necessaries for them be immediately provided, when they come into Port through Stress of Weather, or to careen and rest; and as soon as they are refitted, order them to Sea again."

[12] Most likely a reference to Justice 327–32, a section entitled "Of Prizes." All "Vessels belonging to our Enemies, or Commanded by Pirates, Buccaneers, and others"; all "Vessels fighting under another Flag than that of the Nation whose Commission they carry, or having Commission from two different Princes or States"; all "Vessels and their lading, in which there are no Charter Parties, Bills of Lading, nor Invoices"; and all "Vessels refusing to strike and bring to, upon the Summons of our Ships, or those of our Subjects arm'd for War, may be compell'd thereto by Artillery, or otherwise; and in Case they resist and fight they shall be good Prize." See 327–28.

[13] Most likely a reference to Newcastle, 17–18: "We have subjoined hereto two Lists, tallying those marked A. and B. which were delivered to His Grace the Duke of *Newcastle*, by Mons[ieur] *Michell* . . . From whence it will appear, that as to the List A, which contains 18 ships and their Cargoes, . . . 4 Ships were restored by Sentence, but the Cargoes, or Part of them, condemned as Prize, or Contraband, and are not now alleged, in the Lists A. or B. to have been *Prussian* Property."

¹⁴ It is possible that JD is comparing a customs seal, or the seal of some other official, to an ecclesiastical seal, implying that a seal proved authenticity the way an ecclesiastic seal authenticated a will. See, for example, 1 Strange 671: "The seal of the ecclesiastical court does authenticate the will, for there the will is to be brought in and proved."

¹⁵ Hugo Grotius (1583–1645) was a Dutch jurist whose works contributed to the foundation of the law of nations, based on natural law.

¹⁶ Samuel Freiherr von Pufendorf (1632–1694) was a German jurist and natural law theorist who wrote on history, political philosophy, and economics. JD may have had in mind his work *Of the Law of Nature and Nations* (London: J. Walthoe, R. Wilkin, [et al.], 1729).

¹⁷ Jean-Jacques Burlamaqui (1694–1748) was a Genevan legal and political theorist. His works were *The Principles of Natural Law* (London: J. Nourse, [1748]) and *The Principles of Politic Law* (London: J. Nourse, [1752]), which were published in one volume in 1763.

60
Notes on a Flag-of-Truce Case, [n.d.]

If this set of notes is not for the libel against the *Beaux Enfants*, the same case as the preceding set (doc. 1:59), they are for a very similar case relating to a dispute over the seizure of a ship commissioned as a flag of truce. It seems that the dispute was whether the ship and "Goods of Accession," that is, goods other than the cargo, such as provisions, were subject to seizure to pay debts. The notes, in addition to reiterating familiar themes, also outline an argument that to allow the seizure would in effect be inconsistent with the ship's status as a flag of truce.

Two points   Whether [pro]tected by her Comm[issi]on of Truce & if She
is   Whether this Claim good   As to 1.st
Hull¹ only claimd theref[ore] no dispute now about the Goods—

1. War not the horrid Savage th[in]g it was form[er]ly   Now has its Laws
   Some Rules to mitigate the Misch[ie]fs of our Wickedness.   Captives
   not butcherd except by Indians nor drag on Life in [per]petual Slavery
Country, Friends—Parents &c being dear to all Men by common Consent
   agreed th[at] they shoud not be lost forever. So Exchange of Prisoners
   & Flags of Truce—Wh[ich] restor[in]g Us to every thing sacred &
   dear—justly lookd on as **sacred**.   First calld Heralds— Homer says
   {"dear to Gods & Men"²   Tacitus says} "Sacrum etiam [Ŀ?]{in}
   exteras gentes Legatorum jus temerasset {Hist. 3. c. 80.}³ 4 Ins.
   {153.}⁴ Speaks of Amb[assad]ors Leagues & Truces synonymously
   &c as **sacred**.}

[*in left margin:*] {Stat[ute]s of Conserv[at]ors of Truces &c}[5] {Cartel—}
Read him in [Coro[nation]?]. {besides Truces relax the Rigour of War
&c.}

2. Two Characters united in Publick Messengers A Representative & his
   [pro][per].   The first not forf[eite]d or destroyd by any Act of the
   latter— Unless malum in se jure gentium as Treason Felony &c contra
   jus gentium & then he may be pun[ishe]d here & Curtesy to remit him:
   but Vide Grot[ius] as quoted 10 Mod. 4.[6] Who knew Laws of
   Nat[ion]s better th[at] Rex a quoa & not ad quem[7] must punish.[8]
       Cokes **contra jus gentium** must mean hostile Acts & not barely
   th[in]gs [pro]hibited by Laws of Nations—& so it is explained in
   Puf[endor]f 151.[9] "Amb[assad]ors are inviolable Unless Spies or
   engaged in some **hostile** design. but Grot[ius] says even then to be
   remitted.   So Neutral Vessels sacred & safe while carry[in]g
   Enemies Goods—but liable when carry[in]g Contraband for that an
   Act of hostility. [*page break*]

3. This trust exists so strongly it cannot be destroyd— It woud be
   destroy[in]g all order—sett[in]g the Serv[an]t above the Master &
   giv[in]g a private Man Authority to revoke publick Acts.   This
   someth[in]g like Case of Ex[ecut]ors at Common Law whose Goods
   as Ex[ecut]or not liable to his own debts—but much stronger of a
   p[ub]lick Trust {as here}.

4. So "if You exceed the Limits of a private Comm[issi]on You are bound
   but not he that sent You.["] Cod[e]. 4. [3]5. 12. Wood 253.[10] {here a
   publick Com[missi]on.}   But the French King[11] will be bound with a
   Witness here if Vessel detaind.

5. But say they "Goods of Accession[12] only are free["]— Grant it— Is not
   the Vessel & Men & [Pro]visions & enough to fit out & pay the
   Men—Goods of Accession? Not one book says Goods of Accession
   are liable on any Acco[un]t   Why this Silence?

6. We have heard a good deal of Goods of Accession— What is the Law
   ab[ou]t them? Not th[at] ~~they~~ {all other Goods} may be seizd—but
   that other Goods are liable to their Debts—by Implic[ati]on[.]
   {However the Ship &c Goods of Accession &c}

> Now all his Goods are Accessions or some are & some are not—
> What are to be done with those th[at] are not— By Impl[icati]on from
> the Books—they are liable to his Debts—but does any {book} say
> they are to be seizd at his Com[in]g or if they were—how coud they be
> liable to his debts contracted afterw[ar]ds—so far from Seiz[in]g th[at]
> Puf[endor]f says. [b]. 8. c. 9. §. 12. n. 1. that no reprizals shall be made
> on them.[13]

7. The Flag of Truce lawful humane commendable—the bring[in]g so
large a Cargo it is said unlawful—but our Law a bond for some things
lawf[ul] & others not good for the first.

Ms (PPL-JDFP)

---

[1] Hull: "The body or frame of a ship, apart from the masts, sails, and rigging." (*OED*).

[2] Hom. *Od.* 22:381–82. The full line, as translated in Pope, *Odyssey* (5:128), is: "A deed like this is thy future fame would wrong. / For dear to Gods and Men is sacred song."

[3] Lat. the dignity of the ambassador, respected even by foreign nations, would have been profaned. The complete phrase is "et ni dato a duce praesidio defensi forent, sacrum etiam inter exteras gentis legatorum ius ante ipsa patriae moenia civilis rabies usque in exitium temerasset" or, "had they not been protected by an escort provided by the general, the dignity of the ambassador, respected even by foreign nations, would have been profaned with fatal violence by the madness of Roman citizens before the very walls of their Country." Tac. *Hist.* 3.80.

[4] 4 Coke, *Institutes* 153, is part of c. 26, titled, "And incidently of the office, authority, and priviledge of Ambassadors, And of Leagues, Treaties, and Truces." Coke writes, "of ancient time Ambassadours were called *Oratores* [Lat. orators, or speakers] . . . . And afterwards they were called *Legati à legando* [Lat. commissioners (or deputies) from commissioning (or deputizing)], *Nuntii à nuntiando* [Lat. messengers from announcing], and afterwards *Ambassiatores* or *Embassiotores*, and sometimes Agents."

[5] Conservator of Truce: "An officer appointed to ensure the king's truces and safe conducts for foreign merchants and others were observed on the high seas and in English ports" (*OED*). Statutes such as 2 Hen. 5, c. 6 (1414): "Breaking of Truce and Safe Conduct Shall be High Treason: In Every Port There Shall be a Conservator of the Peace and Safe Conduct," gave conservators the power to "inquire of all such treasons and offences to be done against the truce and safe conducts upon the main sea."

[6] 10 *Modern* 4: "The goods of an ambassador not liable to distress, *a fortiori*, not his person. An ambassador must be intreated, and upon refusal sent back to his master. If an ambassador commit a crime of a transcendant nature, the king *a quo, non ad quem* [Lat. by whom, not to whom] must punish him." This passage is attributed to Grotius in the marginalia, but it is not a direct quotation as JD suggests. Rather, it generally tracks the line of thinking in Grotius, *Rights* (1738) 380: "There are others of Opinion that Violence is never to be offered to an Ambassador, unless he be found to act against the Government or the Dignity of the Potentate, to whom he is sent; though some think even this to be of dangerous Consequence, that Complaint should rather be made to his Principal, and that it should be left to him, to punish his Ambassador according to his pleasure."

---

[7] That is, the crimes of ambassadors are to be punished by the ones who sent them, not the ones to whom they were sent.

[8] 10 *Modern* 4–5, "The Case of Andrew Artemonowitz Mattueof, Ambassador of Muscovy," Trin. 8 Ann., B.R. (1709). During the trial, Attorney General James Montagu (1666–1723) argued that the "person of an ambassador has ever been held scared and inviolable, by the law of nations. . . . My Lord Coke says, *legatos violari contra jus gentium* [Lat. ambassadors were assaulted against the law of nations]; nor does he add, as certainly he would, had he thought so, that though this be so in civil law, it is not so in ours."

[9] Pufendorf 151: "Among the chief Heads of that *voluntary Law of Nations* which *Grotius* maintains, he reckons the Law of Embassies. Now as to this Point it is our Opinion, that the Persons of Embassadors are sacred and inviolable, even amongst Enemies, by the meer Law of Nature; provided they do not come purely as Spies, nor enter into any hostile Design against the Person to whom they are sent; altho' in the ordinary Course of Business, and of Treaties, they prefer their Master's Interest to all others."

[10] Just. Code 4.35.12: "As you assert that you stated what should be done with reference to certain business which you wished to be transacted, it is proper that your attorney should comply with your directions in good faith. Therefore, if, contrary to the terms of the mandate, he sold the tract of land belonging to you, and you did not subsequently ratify the sale, you cannot be deprived of the ownership of the property."

Wood 253: "If you exceed the limits of your *Commission* you yourself are bound, but not he that employ'd you."

[11] Louis XV (1710–1774) reigned from 1715 to 1774.

[12] Accession: "A method of acquiring property whereby a property owner is entitled to that which his property produces, or to that which is naturally or artificially added to or incorporated with it. Also: addition to property in this manner" (*OED*).

[13] Pufendorf 863. Jurist and translator Jean Barbeyrac (1674–1744) added the following note: "As for [the ambassador's] Goods, we cannot seize upon them for any Debt by way of Justice; for that would suppose a taking away from the Jurisdiction of the Sovereign to whom his Ambassy is made: But if he refuses to pay his Debt, we must take the same Measures with him, as we have already observ'd, are to be used in obtaining Satisfaction for the Damage and Injury he has done us."

61

Notes for *Levy & Hart v. Unknown*, [n.d.]

These notes relate to a proceeding that challenged forfeiture of an unidentified ship that had been commissioned as a flag of truce. The arguments resemble those JD made in other flag-of-truce trade cases and in his "Reflections on the Flag of Truce Trade in America" (doc. 2:34). It is unclear, however, what specific legal issue was involved in the proceeding; it may have been whether the ship was subject to forfeiture when it had not attempted to land its cargo.

All the Sta[tutes] of Forf[eiture] mention

Lawful for Neutral Nations   Landing &c

Spirit of Laws. 20
Book
6 Chapter.[1]

Mess[ieu]rs Levy & Hart ⎫ English Flag of Truce taken
    v   ⎬
             ⎭

1. More benefit to England by exporting to foreign Marke[ts], than to France by purchasing the Sugars at a low price   3d.[s2]
{Provisions wanted by the French Islands & not money}
{Gold not to be eaten.}
[*in left margin:*] {1~~2~~. We have no Sugars enough for Our own Col[ony] on the Continent[.] Then We reap the Adv[antage] of the French, & dont interfere with our own Col[ony] in the West Indies.}
{Postlethwaite 23 remarkable.}[3]

2. Privateers or Letters of Marque no Right to seize but his Majesty's Officers as Collectors Comptrollers &c   Vide Commission of Privateers.
{If anybody the King for breach of Comm[issi]on & the 6 G. 2. c. [13].[4] for imposing Duties on French Sugars. Gen[eral] Treat[ise] 428. 429. very strong. 2 Strange 952. {Malloy 471. Spir[it] of Laws {Book 20. c. 1[3].}}}[5]

3. Difference between this Case & the Flag of Truce condemnd here before—because She was smuggling in the River—& came into an other Port.

{ 3. Meaning of the word **Trade**. {Molloy's App[endix] 9. Sir W[illiam] Jones' Op[inion]} {Vaugh[an][6] 4. We have registerd. Should be glad to know at what Critical Minute it shoud be done.}

4. Case of a Flag of Truce in Boston & Russel the Judge[7] sent for the Admiralty's Directions at home.

5. Vide the Act imposing Duties on French Sugars &c   6. G. 2. c. 1[3]. General Treatise 428.[8]

[*cont. in lower left margin:*]
6. Want of a Register not material on a Redemption from the Reason of the thing
{Vide 7 & 8 W. 3.[9] Our ransoming the Ship a benefit to the publick [designd?] by the Act.}

{V[ide] General Treatise 419.[10] {1.} "Lading or unlading &c" 2. We did not come here voluntarily {never within an English Port till then.}.

7. Forfeitures odious in Equity wh[ich] governd by the same Rules as Admiralty Courts— The Nature & Design of Punishments.

8. No Supposition to be made of a fraud. Vaughan 169.[11] & uncharitable. {We have enterd the Sugars.}

9. One or 2 Instances (if they coud be quoted) of no great weight. [i]bidem.

10. Trading with the Spanish West Indies allowd in time of War.
{[B?][*illegible words; torn along lower edge*]}

11. ~~By this We~~ What more coud be desire than to grind them down to labour for [~~illegible~~]{Us}?}

[*cont. in middle left margin:*]
12. We get the French Sugars at a less Expence than by fitting ou[t] Privateers & taking them.
{Vide the Declaration of War.}[12]

13. Supp[ose] We coud oblige the French to send all their Commodities in our [bott]oms.[13]
{Postleth[wayt] 260. 185. &c}[14]

[*cont. in upper left margin:*]
{14.} Molloy's General Treatise 667. in Point.   2 Ins. 58. 28.[15]
{Magna Charta direct "only by way of Reprisals".}

{15.} We have enterd the Sugars.

16. Laws of Rhode Island[16] complied with & well known that Flags of Truce are not paid [*page break*]

The barely [pro]hibiting the taking Arms &c is a tacit License for taking every thing else—especially as Flags of Truce are not paid
Difference between Our taking the Sugars & the Dutch carrying them because the [Pro][per]ty continues French—& it is to their Advantage they are sold in Foreign Markets, but here the Ballance settles with Us.

[*in lower half of page, rotated 180°:*]

Contract with the Customhouse Off[ice][r] to pay Customs for 2000 Quintals[17] when there were more Quintals Good. 1 Vol. of Gen[era]l Treat. 197.[18]

Case of Reneger & Focassa—Plow. 2̶{1}.[19]

==

No Custom due till Landing. 1 Vol. ib[idem] 199. Holton & Raworth's Case. Ha[rdress]. 358.[20]

==

In action of Trover it was held that if Goods are landed & pay Custom, & are carried over Land or Sea to another Port—they shall not pay Custom there

Even Condemnation on an Inform[ati]on in the Exchequer will not always justify the **converting** them. 1 Vol. Gen[era]l Treat. 199. Case of Bruen & Roe. Sid. 264.[21]

==

{The} **Libel repugnant & contradictory**— It rises up in Jud[gmen]t ag[ains]t itself—

"Out of thy own mouth shalt thou be condemned."[22]

Ms (PHi-Logan)

---

[1] Montesquieu, XX, 6 is titled, "The Spirit of England, with respect to commerce."

[2] Symbol for French deniers or British pence.

[3] Postlethwayt, *System* 23: "But when our Traders shall be converted into mere domestic Money-Shufflers, most of the current Coin of the Kingdom will be turned out of the Channels of Trade, and the Heads of its Merchants and Traders off their proper business. . . It hath changed honest Commerce into bubbling; our Traders into Projectors; Industry into Tricking; and Applause is earned when the Pillory is deserved. . . There is nothing left to be done, but for all honest Men to join Heads, Hearts, and Hands, to find Means, not only to prevent the Encrease of Public Debt, but to think, even in the time of War, of laying the Foundation, gradually to lessen our public Burthens."

[4] 6 Geo. 2, c. 13 (1733): "An Act for the Better Securing and Encouraging Trade of his Majesty's Sugar Colonies in *America*."

[5] Justice 428–29, *Durado v. Gregory*, Trin. 21 Car. 2., B.R. (1669): The cause concerned "a Contract at *Malaga* [a port city in Southern Spain] concerning Lading of a Ship, and for breach of this, which was said to be upon Sea, *viz.* That the Master would not receive 40 Butts [casks] of Wine into the Ship according to the Agreement; there was a Libel in the Foreign Admiralty, and the Sentence that the Wine should be receiv'd into the Ship; which being refused, another Libel was Commenc'd in the Admiralty here in *England*, reciting the former Sentence, and charging the Defendant with the Breach of it, and a Prohibition was pray'd, because it appears the Contract was made upon the Land."

2 Strange 952, *Horne v. Boosey*, Trin. 6 Geo. 2. (1732): an action of trover concerning Boosey, a tidesman [an "officer appointed to inspect the loading and unloading ships to

prevent contraband transactions" (*OED*)], who seized brandy without a permit and carried it to the king's warehouse. Boosey did not have the authority to make such a seizure because he "could not enter a house without a writ of assistance and a peace officer, the words of his warrant being so retrained." The "jury found *pro quer[ente]* [Lat. for the plaintiff] for brandy and casks."

Justice 471: "The use of Privateers to endamage an Enemy's Trade is not perhaps very ancient . . . yet that they are lawful none can question."

Montesquieu, XX, 13: "The laws of commerce concerning confiscation of merchandises."

[6] Justice 9: "I am of the Opinion, that a Ship bought beyond Seas by one of His Majesty's Subjects, and brought into a Port of *England*, ought not to pay Custom: For tho' in a larger sense, Ships may be said to be Goods, yet the Word Goods is coupled with Merchandize, and no Man doth understand a Ship under the Word Merchandize, but rather such Goods or Commodities as are exported or imported in Ships." Justice notes in the marginalia that this is "*Sir* Will. Jones's *Opinion.*"

It is unclear exactly to what JD is referring in Vaughan, but it may be the following section from *Thomas v. Sorrell*, a case he cites below (see doc. 1:63, n. 22): "If Exportation, Importation of a Commodity, or the exercise of a Trade be prohibited generally by Parliament, and no cause expressed of the Prohibition, a license may be granted to one or more without *limitation* to Export or Import, or to exercise the Trade (Vaughan 345).

[7] Chambers Russell (1713–1767) was a judge on both the Superior Court and the Vice Admiralty Court for the colonies of Massachusetts Bay, New Hampshire, and Rhode Island.

[8] 2 *General* 428: "By *6 Geo. 2. cap. 13.* the Planters of the Sugar Colonies in *America* having fallen under great Discouragements, so as to be unable to improve or carry on the Sugar Trade upon an equal Footing with the foreign Sugar Colonies, without some Advantage or Relief given to them from *Great Britain*; it is enacted, that there shall be paid to his Majesty for all Sugar and Paneles ["Brown unpurified sugar from the Caribbean" (*OED*)] of the Product of any Plantations in *America*, not under the Dominions of his Majesty, which shall be imported into any of his Majesty's Plantations, the Sum of *5 s.* for every hundred Weight; and for all Rum or Spirits of foreign Produce. *9 d.* for every Gallon; and for Melasses or Syrups, of such foreign Produce *6 d. per* Gallon."

[9] Specifically 7 & 8 Will. 3, c. 22 (1696): "An Act for Preventing Frauds, and Regulating Abuses in the Plantation Trade."

[10] 2 *General* 419: "All Ships, whether the King's or Merchants Ships, lading [i.e., loading] or unlading Goods at any of the Plantations aforesaid, the Masters and Commanders thereof shall be subject to the same Rules, Visitations, Searches, Penalties and Forfeitures, as Ships and their Ladings, and the Commanders and Masters are subject and liable to in this Kingdom, by Virtue of 14 *Car. 2. cap.* 11. [1662]." This law was titled, "An Act for Preventing Frauds, and Regulating Abuses in His Majesty's Customs."

[11] Vaughan 169, *Edmund Sheppard, Jr., v. George Gosnold, William Booth, William Haygard,* and *Henry Heringold,* Hill. 23 & 24 Car. 2, B.C. (1671). The defendants pled not culpable to forcibly taking and detaining Sheppard's goods until he paid them forty-nine shillings. They argued that they were officers duly appointed to collect poundage on goods, even those that had been intended for export and then returned to England after a shipwreck. Sheppard objected to the suggestion that he was engaged in fraud by casting his goods overboard to avoid paying poundage: "This supposal [of fraud] is remote, and cannot be of some Wrecks possible; as, of Wrecks of derelicted Goods, or of Goods cast into the Sea to unburden a Ship."

[12] *His Majesty's Declaration of War against the French King* (New York: J. Parker, 1756): "That whatever Ship or Vessel shall be met withal, transporting or carrying Soldiers, Arms, Powder, Ammunition, or any other Contraband Goods, to any of the Territories, Lands,

Plantations, or Countries of the said French King, the same, being taken, shall be condemned as good and lawful Prize."

[13] Bottom: "A ship, boat, or other vessel" (*OED*).

[14] Postlethwayt, *System*, regarding "the Trade of the *French* Sugar Islands, and that of their *North-American* Colonies" (258). Postlethwayt discusses French efforts to stop contraband trade (260), and asserts that "it is possible, that *Britons* can thus expose themselves to such a Nation as *France*, that is immoderately bent on enlarging her Traffic" (185).

[15] Justice 667: "As to the present Circumstances of our Trade, and the State of Commerce in general, since the breaking out of the War, the World may remember how solicitous the *English* Parliament was at the beginning of it to prevent all Traffick, and even all manner of Correspondence, not only between her Majesty's Dominions and the Enemies Countries, but also between our Allies the *Dutch* and they; but it having since appeared that the *Dutch* would not be easily persuaded to continue those severe Prohibitions, the *English* wisely began to consider, that besides the present want of the usual Supplies of *Spanish* Bullion for our Manufactures, if thro' our Obstinancy not to Trade with the Queen's Enemies in time of War, the *Dutch* should get the knack of serving them both with our Manufactures and with *East India* Goods, it would not be easy for us to retrieve that Loss in time of Peace."

2 Coke, *Institutes* 58, is an exposition of c. 30 of Magna Carta (1225), which reads: "All merchants, unless they have before been publicly prohibited beforehand, shall be able to go out of and come into England safely and securely and stay and travel throughout England."

2 Coke, *Institutes* 28, is an exposition of c. 14 of Magna Carta (1225), which reads: "A free-man shall not be amerced [given an arbitrary fine] for a trivial offence, except in accordance with the degree of the offence and for a grave offence in accordance with its gravity, yet saving his way of living."

[16] For Rhode Island's abuse of flag-of-truce trade, and its reformation under the guidance of the Board of Trade, see below, doc. 1:62, n. 8 and 9.

[17] Quintal: "A unit of weight equal to one hundredweight, originally 100 lb" (*OED*).

[18] 1 *General* 197: "A Merchant beyond Sea shipped 4500 Quintals of Woad [indigo dye] for England, and a Tempest arising the Master of the Ship and Mariners threw great part of it into the Sea to save their Lives; after this ship arrived at *Southampton*, and the Master not knowing how much remain'd, but believing there might be 2000 Quintals left, agreed with the Custom-house Officer to pay the Duty for so much."

[19] Plowden, 1–20, *Reniger v. Fogossa*, Pasch. 4 Edw. 6, Cam. Scacc. (1550). Robert Reniger was comptroller of the Custom and Subsidy in Southampton who seized the cargo of Anthony Fogossa, a Portuguese merchant, because Fogossa had not paid the requisite duties. Fogossa claimed he only docked in Southampton to avoid a storm, and successfully argued that necessity demanded an exception to the law requiring him to pay. He may have broken "the words of the law," the court noted, but not "the law itself" (20).

[20] 1 *General* 198–99: "But in an Information upon a Seizure of Canary Wines, against a Merchant for not paying Custom, it was made a Question, whether Custom was due upon Importation, and adjudged that it was not due before landing, because Goods may be imported by Stress of Weather, or for want of Water or Victuals, and not by way of Merchandize. . . . 'Tis likewise due, according to the true Estimate of the Quantity landed, and not according to the Vessel in which it is contained."

Hardress 358–64, *Holton v. Raworth*, Hill. 15 & 16 Car. 2, Scacc. (1663). The case concerned 58 tons of canary wines that leaked so badly on the voyage from the Canary Islands to London that only 52 tons were left. "[T]he sole question was, whether or no twelve pounds per cent, which the act allows for leakage, shall be allowed for these 52 ton; the act directing 12 l. per cent to be allowed upon due entry made" (358). Holton argued that it should not be allowed because tonnage was due upon importation with an allowance for leakage then and not later. Raworth argued that duty was due upon unlading. The court "concluded for the King, and judgment was given accordingly" (499).

[21] Conversion: "The action of (illegally) converting or applying something to one's own use" (*OED*).

Siderfin 264, *Bruen v. Roe*, Trin. 17 Car. 2, B.R. (1665): "Et le condemnacion de eux en le Exchequer sur Informacion pur le Roy sur le dit Stat pur nient paiant de Customes ne poet salve le Defendant de conversion al jour precendent" [LFr. And the condemnation of them in the Exchequer upon Information of the King upon the said statute for not paying customs is not able to save the defendant from conversion on the previous day]. The case defined what a conversion was, establishing that to be convicted of that crime, the defendant had to either find the goods or they had to be delivered to him, and then he had to refuse to give them up when requested to by the plaintiff.

[22] This quotation could be an adaptation of several passages from scripture, but it seems to be taken verbatim from William Chillingworth, "The Third Sermon," in *The Works of William Chillingworth*, 10th ed. (London: D. Midwinter, A. Ward, et al., 1742), 32.

62
Draft One of Notes for *Spring & Kemp v. Ospray & Elizabeth*, [c. 1758]

This set of notes appears to be a preliminary draft of the following set (doc. 1:63). Both relate to a proceeding in the Vice Admiralty Court seeking forfeiture of a vessel, the *Ospray*, which was commissioned as a flag of truce by Rhode Island to carry French sugar from Port-au-Prince. JD made two arguments against the forfeiture: first, the *Ospray* had done nothing illegal and had complied with English and Rhode Island law regulating flag-of-truce trade; and second, those seeking the forfeiture had no right to seize the *Ospray* because an Admiralty Court could not order forfeiture of an English subject's property without a statute explicitly authorizing it to do so. These notes were the basis for JD's lengthy essay, "Reflections on the Flag of Truce Trade in America" (doc. 2:34).

Evidence indicates that the event that precipitated this court proceeding may have occurred before 1759. Although the case itself might well have taken a year or two to make it into court, with no other date indicated, we have grouped these two documents with other flag-of-truce cases.

Capt[ai]n Benja[min] Spring &
Captain John Kemp & Al[ia]
Owners &
Comp[an]ies of the Spry &
Speedwell Privateers[1]
v.
The Brig Ospray &
The Schooner Elizabeth

Libel in the Admiralty ag[ains]t the Ospray an English Flag of Truce from Rhode Island for taking on board French Sugars at Port Au Prince in Hispaniola   And ag[ains]t the Elizabeth & Cargo as French Property.

The Case.

It appears from Capt[ai]n Rodman's[2] Deposition that he bought these Sugars for light Pistoles—[3] And that the Elizabeth was an English Vessel taken & condemnd by the French;[4] & that he bought her & her Cargo with light Pistoles likewise.

Two Points.

No Instance of Cond[iti][ons] of a flag of Truce.

1.[st] That the Ospray has done nothing unlawful upon this Occasion.

2.[ly] If She has, that the Libellants have no Right or Authority to seize upon, or ~~demand~~ {[pro]ceed ag[ains]t} her as Prize, here.

Three Reasons to [pro]ve the first point.

First Reason. That She has strictly obeyd the Comm[issi]on She was chargd with.　　She has not taken one single Article that was [pro]hibited— She has complied with the Laws of the **Colony** relating to Flags of Truce.

==

* The [Pro][pri]ety of their call[in]g Us to an Acco[un]t be consid[ere]d hereafter.

This Offence is chargd as a Breach of the Comm[issi]on. Where is that **Breach**?{*}　　The Inj[uncti?]on of not taking **Military** Stores &c plainly means in going out: or Absurdity woud follow.

==

The forbidding these Acts is a plain & tacit Allowance of those not forbidden.　　Well known **Axiom**, "That the Exclusion of **Generals** is by **general Terms**, but the [pro]hibiting **particulars** extends only to those [pro]hibited."[5] "Qui omne dicit, nihil excludit." 2 Ins. 81. Th[at] all Widows may devise their Corn.[6]　　Adam woud have been culpable if nothing but the Tree of Knowledge had been [pro]hibited.[7] ~~Everything~~

==

Especially here—Where the Legislature of Rhode Island[8] & the Gov[ern]or[9] knew there was no pay to **Flags of truce**: [*page break*]

It was an Employm[en]t under the Gov[ernmen]t— They were our Superiors　　They directed—We obeyd.　　They knew We had no benefit {no motive} but this & did not forbid it—{but sent Us} Therefore they allowd it.

==

By Virtue of th[at] Comm[issi]on We went. It was our Instructions. By th[at] Compass We were to sail.   The Gov[ern]or had such Power— He is to blame—if he allowd Us to do wrong—Not **We**.

The Charge unsupported then as We have obeyd our Comm[issi]on & {therefore} noth[in]g illegal.   We have neither supplied the Enemy with [Pro]visions nor Arms— But it is said We supply them with Money the Sinews of War.[10]

Second reason. No Injury done to England.
Some Benefit to France.   More to England.   Bought at 8^s a h[undre]d say 10^s.   Sold at 30^s in foreign Markets— We receive th[at] 10^s & [~~thir~~?]{twen}ty shillings more.   The 10^s reimburses Us & puts Us on an Equality   The [3?]{2}0^s is clear Gains & a Superiority.

Little Arithmetick or Understand[in]g necessary for this. It is giv[in]g Names w[ith]out meaning then to call this Aiding our Enemies

If they rise one foot & We that one, & two more—We gain a Superiority We had not before.   The **Ballance** in our favour. {& th[at] a **Ballance** of Power. Gr[eat] Brit[ain's] true System 185.}[11]
[*in left margin:*] {**Objection**. We dont design to export—but run & defr[au]d the King. Answer. Uncharitable Supp[ositi]on   Of Universal Extent if allowd here. Void of a single Circumst[ance] to support it. Suff[icien]t Advantage by export[in]g   Besides **Entered** here. The Coll[ecto]r has accepted th[at] Entrance. King's Off[ice]r sworn as careful as a Privateer.   Great good learned Judge Vaugh[an][12] 169. Woods Ins. Civ. Law 350.}[13]

==

But suppose it is not **exported**— Here is a vast Duty to the King's Revenue—for the **public Good**—Wh[ich] is supposd to be <u>Equivalent</u> to the Disadvantage of Trading with <u>France</u>.   Natural Rivalship— Natural Enmity between France & England   ~~W~~ {P}eace & War much the same— Always undermining   In peace   they acquire Power to carry on War.

Therefore our Trade with them laid under such {so to be carried on in our bottoms. Deny &c.} Regulations as compensate for all the Benefit accru[in]g to the[m].   It woud not be allowd in time of Peace if these Regul[ati]ons did not answer these Ends.

Greater Benefit to Us theref[ore] in time of War   As We give less for their Sugars.   **Besides** recov[erin]g **our Subjects**.

==

If the **King** cant suffer then by this **Trade**: At least cant suffer in this [par][ticu]lar Case—By the Entries made & Securities given.

What other Injury is sufferd?

We dont interfere with Our Mother Country at all.

We dont interfere with Our Col[onie]s {Mr. Francis's[14] Opinion on this Act of Parl[iamen]t} more th[an] in time of Peace: theref[ore] as {Crim[ina]l then.}

The unjust Act in their fav[ou]r like the Papal Prærog[ative] of furnish[in]g Corn, from the Popes Granaries.[15] Carried by a Corrupt Min[iste][r] Who[~~illegible~~]{a}ttempted the Excise Act. [*page break*]

X French Trade embargo[e]d. Agreed V[ide] here.

==

Buy 1000 Vessels as well when of no Use & rotting there. Answ[er] Then cheap but this an Engl[ish] Vessel. {Can She be} Forfeited because recov[ere]d to the former Owners?

{X} What greater Advantages coud We desire from the most successful War, than th[at] the French shoud labour toil & sweat for Us at the Pittance of 7 or 8^s a hundred?

And We have the double Benefit of encreasing Our Shipping by the **Carriage** & gather[in]g all the **Sweets** of their Labour

Woud Humanity wish shoud be pound down lower? Our Slaves?   Could Avarice desire they   Coud they be more

==

This different from the Dutch carry[in]g the~~ir~~{fr}ench Commodities—

There the [Pro][per]ty & Emolument French. Here Ours. therefore diametrically opposite.

==

No Doubt **Privateer[in]g** lawful. Advant[age]   Successful   We get the Sugars at less Expense this way than by Priv[a]t[eerin]g

They are brought down to our own terms   Adv[an]t[a]g[e]ous. What an **Absurdity** to say it would be <u>lawful</u> to attack a French Sugar Ship & take her at the Expence of the **Lives** of **50** or **60** of his <u>Majesty's Subj[ec]ts</u>   but that it is **unlawful** to take her at the Expence of a few <u>Dollars</u>~~-~~ or Pistoles.   Compare these 2 Methods Shoud be glad to know if the **Lives** of Sailors [~~is?~~]{are} not valuable.

Vain to attempt to prevent it~~?~~{!} If blood is necessary **A Stratagem.** Knock 2 or 3 people on the head

All is fair   just   proper   Legal.

Third Reason. From the Spirit of the English Commerce & its Laws.
<u>Nature</u> designd the Engl[ish] for Merch[an]ts
Commerce her Strength   Glory   Safety
Whatever tends to cramp th[at] Commerce   dangerous

==

Monopolies only to be erected by Parl[iamen]t

==

King formerly (Vide Coke) might [pro]hibit Trade with Infidels[16]
But denied in Sand's & Child's Case 2 Lev. 312.[17]   Infidels worse
than Enemies.

==

Merch[an]ts may go out of the Realm 5 Rich. 2. c. 2.[18] w[ith]out Leave
Gen[era]l Treat[ise] of Trade & Commerce Vol. 1. pa. 5.[19] [*page
break*]

English Nation extremely Jealous of their Commerce. 2 Ins. 61.[20]

==

Whatever affects th[at] Commerce   must be plain   positive Laws
Not constructive Offences by the thinspun Arg[umen]ts of the Barr.
Engl[and] too wise to leave any part unguarded   All the Laws of
Trade clear. {No Argumentative Crimes.[21] So in the Civil
Law. Wood's Ins. 115.}[22]

This comes in {again} postea}[23] under 2.ᵈ Title.

Where Customs necessary—imposd. On paym[en]t the Merch[an]t safe   Montisquieu Bo[ok] 20. c. 6. & c. 12[24] very strong to shew how free the English Commerce is.   ~~Chapter 13~~ {Nothing to do but to settle with the Kings Off[ice]rs} This confirmd by 3 H. 6. c. 3[25] Wh[ich] forbids any Searcher or Customer to keep a Ship

Very Rem[arka]ble (says Montisquieu Bo[ok] 20. c. 13. Th[at] the
Engl[ish] make the **Freedom of foreign Merch[an]ts** One Article of
their Liberty.

Their Goods not to be seizd but by way of <u>Reprizals</u>[26]   on
break[in]g War out. If such Tenderness for Foreigners   Much more
for Englishmen.

==

Of Antient time 3 people priviledgd in War. Clericus Agricola
Mercator {2 Ins. 58.}[27]

Such the **Gen[era]l Spirit** of the **English** Commerce.

No Law appears ag[ains]t Us.

But to place this Action of Ours in the strongest **Light**—tis said

X War may
be w[ith]out
[Pro]clam[ati]on.
H.H.P.C. 144.[28]

It furnishes Our Enemies with the Sinews of War & is contrary to the King's {[X]}**Proclamation** &c

==

The first mere words {If they are embargo[e]d So will the money be &c}   for no Injury app[ea]rs as before {Crimes [Per] Accidens[29] dang[e]rous 10 Mod. 108.}[30]—& it is plain from a similar Instance not to be **unlawful**   for

By the Law of Nations   Neutral Powers {not to **aid** or **assist** En[emie]s & yet} may carry anything but **warlike Stores** or **[Pro]visions** to a place besieged. So th[at] no Trade but th[at] is lookd upon by th[at] Law to **aid & assist** Enemies

θ Instance 1 Vent.
173. Of Bellicos
Apparatus.[31]

{θ} Surely We woud not stre[n]gthen our Trade to encrease theirs

Besides Vide Grotius Bo[ok] 3. c. 22. § 4 & 5. What Acts lawful with Enemies.[32]

==

This shews the Sense of the Civil Law on this point   Now as to **Proclamation**. {It may declare War—but not make new Laws.} Shoud be glad to know its **force**. Vide 2 Ins. 61.   3 Ins. 162. says [Pro]clam[ati]ons founded on Law are of Great force.[33] Keilw {116.}[34] This **strongly** confirmd by the Conduct of the Parl[iamen]t[s?] at the break[in]g out of the ~~2 last~~ Wars. {in King W[illia]m's time.}[35] All Trade with France [*remainder missing*]

Ms (PHi-Logan)

---

[1] The *Speedwell*, a privateer from the island of New Providence in the Bahamas, captured numerous vessels in the Caribbean in 1758, 1761, and 1762 (*PG*, April 20, 1758, April 23, 1761, July 15, 1762; *Boston News-Letter*, Sept. 20, 1758; *Boston News-Letter*, Aug. 26, 1762). The ship's captain was apparently either John Kemp (c. 1695–1777), of that island, or his son John Kemp (c. 1717–1790). The younger John Kemp was later accused of assisting American privateers making use of the harbor on New Providence during the Revolutionary War ("The Taking of the Bahamas by the Continental Navy in 1776," *PMHB* 49 [1925], 349–66, at 357).

[2] Probably William Rodman, who departed Philadelphia for the French island of Guadeloupe in January 1761. See *PG*, Jan. 1, 1761.

[3] Pistole: "A Spanish gold double-escudo dating from the 1530s and surviving into the 19th cent.; (also) any of various coins derived from or resembling this from the 17th and 18th centuries, esp. the louis d'or issued in 1640 (during the reign of Louis XIII), an Irish coin issued

in 1642–43 (in the reign of Charles [II]), and the Scottish twelve pound piece issued in 1701 (during the reign of William III)" (*OED*). In a 1723 petition to the Pennsylvania Assembly on a pending paper credit bill, Isaac Norris I (1671–1735) and James Logan (1674–1751) noted that "when their [New York's] Silver brings from *Nine to Ten Shillings per* Ounce, and their light Pistoles pass at *Twenty-eight Shillings*, or higher, then [paper] Bills are truly so much fallen in Value as the others are advanced" (*Votes*, supp. [1753], 2:340).

[4] *BG*, March 30, 1761, reports "Rodman from Philadelphia" in a "List of Vessels taken by the French and carried into Martineco [Martinique] from the 1st of Jan. to the 15th Feb."

[5] See for example Siderfin 401, *Barns qui tam v. Hughes*, 20 & 21 Car. 2, B.R. (1668): "les General parols ne voent aver exclude luy & ascun doubt ad estre de ceo particular exclusion" [LFr. the general words will not have excluded him and any doubt had to be of this particular exclusion].

[6] 2 Coke, *Institutes* 81: Lat. he who says everything, excludes nothing; and "[t]enant in Dower may devise her Corn growing upon the Land at the time of her death."

[7] A reference to the story of Adam and Eve, and specifically Gen. 2:16–17: "And the Lord God commanded the man, saying, Of every tree of the garden thou mayest freely eat: But of the tree of the knowledge of good and evil, thou shalt not eat of it: for in the day that thou eatest thereof thou shalt surely die."

[8] The Board of Trade urged Rhode Island to establish a committee to inspect flag-of-truce ships in order to reduce illegal trading and put an end to the corruption, which was practiced all the way up to the governor's office. In June 1757, the Assembly resolved "that all masters and owners of all and every flag and flags of truce, that may proceed out of this colony, shall give bond in the secretary's office, unto the King, in the penal sum of £1,000 sterling money of Great Britain, that no goods, wares or merchandise, of any sort, have been, or shall be laden, put, or taken on board any of his or their flag or flags of truce, contrary to law, before, at, or after such inspection and examination." John Russell Bartlett, ed., *Records of the Colony of Rhode Island and Providence Plantations, in New England*, 10 vols. (Providence, R.I.: A.C. Green et al., 1856–65) 6: 93.

[9] Stephen Hopkins (1707–1785) served as governor of Rhode Island in 1755–57, 1758–62, 1763–65, and 1767–68. Prior to the establishment of the 1757 committee, Hopkins charged £500 to any merchant wishing to embark on a flag-of-truce voyage, and pocketed the money himself. After 1758, flag-of-truce missions were no longer lucrative. See William McLoughlin, *Rhode Island: A History*, The States and the Nation Series (New York: W. W. Norton & Co., 1986), 67–68.

[10] "What else is that but supplying an enemy with all the arms necessary for civil war: first of all with the sinews of war, money in abundance?" Cic. *Phil.* 5.2.

[11] Postlethwayt, *System* 185: "[C]an *Britons* thus expose themselves to any Potentate, who is convinced by Experience that the *Ballance of Trade*, wherever it centers, must secure the *Balance of Power*, and whose unbounded Ambition when this supported, shall temp him to contend for universal Empire?"

[12] Sir John Vaughan (1603–1674) was chief justice of the Court of Common Pleas from 1668 to 1674. He is best known as the presiding judge in Bushel's Case (1670), or *The King v. William Penn and William Mead*, which established the precedent that a jury cannot be forced to change a verdict when the judge disapproves of it. This case also confirmed that the Court of Common Pleas could issue a writ of habeas corpus in ordinary criminal cases.

[13] Wood 350: "It is always observ'd, that the proof lies upon him that alledges and *affirms*, whether Plaintiff or Defendant. *For a Negative Proposition there can be no direct proof.*"

[14] Possibly Tench Francis.

[15] This is a reference to the arbitrary power of the pope to bestow or withhold beneficia at his pleasure.

[16] Possibly a reference to Coke's exposition of the Magna Carta's prohibition on trade with "Merchant strangers, whose Sovereign is in War with the King of England." See 2 Coke, *Institutes* 57. JD might also have been thinking of a 1609 case on which Coke ruled as chief justice of the Court of Common Pleas, *Michelbourne* v. *Michelbourne*, Hill. 7 Jac. 1, C.B. (1609): "It was said by the Lord *Coke*, that no Subject of the King, trade with any Realm of Infidels, without license of the King." See 2 Brownlow 296.

[17] *Sands qui tam, &c. v. Sir Josiah Child, Franklin and Leach*, Pasch. 5 W & M., B.R. (1693). 3 Levinz 351–55. Sands was about to sail his ship, *The Commerce of London*, when the defendants "prosecuted a Suit in the Admiralty for Stay on the said Ship, 'till Security given that they should not go traffick with Infidels within the Limits of the Charter of the *East-India* Company" (351). Sands then sued Child for wrongfully suing him. The court awarded him £1,500 in damages and double costs under 2 Hen. 4, c. 11 (1400): "A Remedy for Him Who is Wrongfully Pursued in the Court of Admiralty."

[18] 5 Rich. 2, c. 2 (1382): "Woolfels [wool skins] and Leather May be Carried Into Any Country by Aliens or Denizens, Saving Into France, Until Michelmas Come Twelvemonth." The act mandated "the passage of wools, leather, and woolfels be open to all manner of merchants and other, as well foreigners as denizens" to "carry and bring them towards what parts they will choose beyond the sea, without impediment of impeachment, *except to the realm of* France."

[19] 1 *General* 5: "It has been formerly held, that no *English* Subjects may Trade to and with a Nation of *Infidels* without the King's Leave, because of the Danger of relinquishing Christianity; and it was said by the Lord Chief Justice *Coke*, that he had seen a License from one of our Kings . . . . But Merchants are not generally restrained from leaving the Kingdom, . . . they being excepted out of the Statute *5 Rich. 2. chap. 2.*"

[20] 2 Coke, *Institutes* 61: "No imposition or charge, &c. shall be set without assent of Parliament. . . . And where imposts, or impositions, be generally named in divers Acts of Parliament, the same are to be intended of lawful impositions, as of Tunnage and Poundage, or other Subsidies imposed by Parliament, but none of those Acts or any other do give the King power at his pleasure to impose."

[21] A constructive crime is one "built up by the court with the aid of inference and implication" (*BLD*). An argumentative crime is one proved only by inferential or circumstantial rather than direct evidence.

[22] Wood 115: "All Rules ought to be known, or at least so expos'd to the publick view of the World, that no Person can act contrary to it with Impunity under pretence of Ignorance."

[23] Postea: "The record of the trial proceedings and the verdict in a civil process" (*OED*).

[24] Montesquieu, XX, 12 is titled, "What it is that destroys this Liberty."

[25] The correct statute is 20 Hen. 6, c. 5 (1442): "No Customer, &c. Shall Have a Ship of His Own, Use Merchandise, Keep a Wharf or Inn, or be a Factor." JD obtained the citation from the broader discussion of customs in 1 *General* 176–77, which in one note cites the following: 3 Hen. 6, c. 3 (1424): "The Penalty of a Customer, &c. Concealing the King's Custom"; 11 Hen. 6, c. 15 (1433): "A Customer Shall Discharge the Merchant That Hath Paid His Custom"; and 20 Hen. 6, c. 5.

[26] Montesquieu, XX, 13: "The Magna Charta of England forbids the seizing and confiscating, in case of war, the effects of foreign merchants; except by way of reprisals. It is very remarkable, that the English have made this one of the articles of their liberty."

[27] Lat. clergymen, husbandmen, merchants, a paraphrasing of 2 Coke, *Institutes* 58: "Clericus et agricola et mercator, tempore belli, ut oret, colat, et commutet, pace fruuntur," or "Clergymen, husbandmen, and merchants, in order that they may preach, cultivate, and trade, enjoy peace in time of war."

---

[28] Hale, *Pleas* 144, Sir John Oldcastle's Case (c. 1413–1417): "for levying war against the king," upon which Hale remarks: "Altho this indictment in not expressly upon this clause of levying of war, for that is not the principal charge of the indictment, but compassing [plotting] the king's death, yet the marching with a great army to St. *Giles's modo guerrino arraiati* [Lat. in warlike fashion] was an express levying of war, tho there were no blow yet struck."

[29] Lat. by chance or accident.

[30] 10 *Modern* 108, *Stennil v. Brown*, Mich. 11 Ann. B.R. (1712): "A Condemnation of a ship as prize, in the admiralty court of *France*, was attempted to be proved by *a copy* of the condemnation, subscribed by the officer of the court. But Parker, *Chief Justice*, who tried the cause, would admit of no evidence, but an *exemplification* [copy] of the condemnation under the seal of the court."

[31] 1 Ventris 173, *Radly and Delbow v. Eglesfield and Whital*, Mich. 23 Car. 2, B.R. (1671): a ship, the *Malmoise*, seized by the defendant, was determined to be a lawful prize because it carried *bellicos apparatus* (i.e., contraband goods) in the Second Anglo-Dutch War, 1665–67.

[32] The citation to this section of Grotius, *Rights* (1738) 727–28, does not seem relevant, treating as it does a sovereign being bound by acts of his commissioner. JD may have meant to cite a different part of the same source, bk. 3, c. 1, § V.1–3 (pp. 518–19), which asks, "[W]hat we may lawfully do to those, who are not our Enemies, nor are willing to be thought so, and yet supply our Enemies with certain Things." Grotius distinguishes among things used only in war, things of no use in war, and things used in both war and peace. He finds that if the first things are provided, "he is to be reputed as siding with the Enemy, who supplies him with Things necessary for War. As to the second Sort of Things, there is no just Cause of Complaint." He explains further that to categorize things as in the third sort, it is necessary to determine the present state of the war and to what extent a person incurs damages by the trade. To that degree, he is justified in "deal[ing] with him agreeably to his Offence."

[33] 3 Coke, *Institutes* 162: "Note. Proclamations are of great force, which are grounded upon the laws of the Realme."

[34] Keilway 116: "[E]n ceux cases chescun home deins le countie est tenus per prendre notice per force de tiel proclamacion, car ceo est done per course de ley [LFr. In these cases each man within the county is held to take notice by force of such proclamation, because this is done in the course of law].

[35] King William's War (1688–97), known as the Nine Years' War in North America, was the first of six colonial wars between the English and the French, with their respective Indian allies. Trade with France was prohibited under 1 W. & M., c. 34 (1688): "An Act Prohibiting All Trade and Commerce with France"; 2 W. & M., sess. 2., c. 14 (1690): "An Act for the More Effectual Putting in Execution an Act, intitled, *An Act for Prohibiting All Trade and Commerce with* France"; and 4 & 5 W. & M., c. 25 (1692): "An Act for Continuing the Acts for Prohibiting All Trade and Commerce with France, and for the Encouragement of Privateers."

63

Draft Two of Notes for *Spring & Kemp v. Ospray & Elizabeth*, [c. 1758]

Capt[ai]n Spring & Al[ia]
Comm[ande]r & Owners of
the Spry Privateer

v

The Brig Ospray
& Cargo—

Libel ag[ains]t the Ospray an English Flag
of Truce for taking on board French
Sugars at Port Au Prince.

The Disadvantage of being **accusd**—
Prejudices will arise.{,} {difficult
even for Innocence to conquer.}
{==}
Expected some **new** arg[umen]ts to
support this **new** [Pro]cedure—but
find only the old Dutch Complaint of
aiding our Enemies[1] joind with some
terrible words that are freq[uen]tly
usd in our Common Law Courts

This trite Obj[ecti]on & these solemn words are to
support this surprizing Declaration of War made in his
Mag{j}esty's name ag[ains]t his Mag{j}esty's
Subj[ec]ts.

" In **verbis** Res & Ratio quærendæ est."[3]

2 Points.

1.{st.} That the Brig Ospray has done nothing unlawful
upon this occasion.

2.{ly.} That if She has, The Comm[ande]r & Officers
of the Spry Privateer have no Authority or Right to
seize upon or demand her as Prize.

*

It shoud be
[pro]secuted for the
King & not for the
Whole as prize but
for a punish[men]t
Vide postea.[2]
This Offence is
chargd as a breach
of the Flag of
Truce. Where is the
breach?
θ The forbidd[in]g
to carry Arms &c is
a **tacit** Allow[ance]
of things not
[pro]hibited—
Especially as it was
known Flags of
Truce were not
paid.

As to the **first** point—The Ospray has complied with
the **Laws** of the Colony She saild from—& with the
express Tenor of the Commission—for the Injunction
of not taking "military Stores &c contrary to Law"
means plainly in her ~~sw~~{go}ing out   Shew these &c.

{{Tacit Allowance of every other Act not
[pro]hibited.

The Legislature of Rhode Island knowing there was
no pay {has regulated Flags of Truce}— The
Gov[ern]or knowing there was no pay has allowd
them & leaves them the little advantages they may
make by the friendly Office.{θ} {{{Diff[erence]
between this Case & the Flag of Truce condemnd—
for She was in the wrong port & smuggling.}

~~The French Gov[ern]or's Sense of this Act   his
Reward by [Per]mit[s?].~~

"Incidit in Scyllam, qui tentat vitare Charybdem."[4]

We have neither supplied the Enemy with [Pro]visions nor Military Stores: But it is said We supply them with Money the Sinews of War.

No Law quoted against [~~illegible~~]{Us}.

No Injury to England.

1st [Pro]of of the 1st Point.   Some Benefit to France   more to England   bought at 8s   sold at 30s in foreign Markets.   Suppose a 3.dWe receive that 10s & 20s more—the 10s reimburses Us & puts us on an Equality—the 20s is clear Gains & a Superiority—little Arithmetick or Understanding necessary for this—   It is giving Names without **meaning** then—to call this **aiding** our Enemies— for if they [*page break*]

rise one foot—& We rise one foot—& then 2 feet more—We acquire a Superiority We had not before.

The <u>Ballance</u> of this Trade then surely in our favour—& Madness to think of Our being displeasd at it.

Ballance of Trade, Ballance of Power. Great Brit[ain's] true Syst[em] 185.

==

Is it to be imagind the French Gov[ernmen]t woud allow this Trade to any Degree?— Observe how the Gov[ern]or of Port Au Prince particularizes the **Reasons** of such a <u>favour</u>.

==

Objection. We dont design to export, but to run these Sugars & defraud the King.

Answer. This Supposition founded on the Wickedness of Mankind in General—A Suppos[iti]on void of a single Circumstance to induce a [Pro]bability of such a Design in Us—Of Universal Extent if allowd in this Case.   Uncharitable.

Many Circumst[ance]s in our favour.   Suff[icien]t Advantage tho[ugh] We ~~pay the Duty~~, Enter.   We have actually <u>enterd</u>, & the Coll[ecto]r of his Majesty's Custom has accepted the Entrance.   We have given [pro][per] Security—[pro]bable that the King's Officer sworn to his Duty will take as much Care of his Majesty's Interest as a Captain of a Privateer.

What the great good & learned L[or]d Chief Justice Vaughan says of these Suppositions of Frauds. page 169. Woods Ins. Civ. Law. 356.

==

If then the King is not to suffer by this Trade—at least cannot suffer in this [par][ticu]lar Case from the Entries made Security given &c
What other Injury is sufferd?
==

We dont interfere with our Colonies—for they dont make more than Sugars enough to serve Us. The unjust Act past by their Influence like the Papal Prærogative of furnishing from the Pope's Granaries.
==

What greater Advantages coud We desire from most successful War than that the French shoud labour toil & sweat for Us at the pittance of 7 or 8ˢ a hundred—& We have the double benefit of increasing our Shipping [*page break*] by the **Carriage**, & gathering all the sweets of their fatigue—

Woud Humanity wish—nay coud Avarice desire they shoud be ground lower   Coud they be more our Slaves?
==

This diff[eren]t from the <u>Dutch</u> carrying these Commodities for there the [Pro][per]ty & Emolument is French—here ours **therefore** diametrically opposite.
==

We take French Sugars by Privateers—th[at] counted advantageous & successful— We take them with less Expence of blood & Money in this Way than by **privateering**
They are reducd they are brought down to our own **Terms** & more advantageous ones We can hardly desire—

Not a
General
Trade   What an **absurdity** to say it woud be lawful to attack a french {Sugar} Ship & take her at the <u>Expence</u> of the **Lives** of fifty of his Majesty's **<u>Subjects</u>**—but that it is
unlawful to take her at the <u>Expence</u> of a few **<u>Dollars</u>**.

It appears then We reap the Benefit of this Trade.
2. [Pro]of of the 1ˢᵗ point. Vide Margin.

From the Spirit
of the English
Commerce & its
Laws.
      Nature designed the English for Merchants—
Commerce is her Strength, Safety, Glory.
Whatever cramps that Commerce
disadvantageous— & there must be plain & positive Laws for it—
Monopolies erected by Acts of Parl[iamen]t   [Pro][per] Customs

imposd—if these Complied with the Merc[h.ᵗ]{ha}nt is safe—; In this Case Duties by 6 G. 2.

==

{Not to be harrassd by Seizures on the High Se[as] & therefore [pro]vided by 3 H. 6. c. 3. th[at] no Customer Searcher &c shall keep a [Shi]p &c. Spanish Guarda Costas.[5]   1 Vol. Gen[era]l Treatise 177.}[6]

From the earliest Ages the English Nation Jealous of the Freedom of its Commerce. Magna Charta. c. 14. "Salva Merchand[isa] sua."[7] Montisquieu B. 20. c. 6. ~~& c. 12.~~   Magna Charta c. 30. makes it one Article of their **Liberty**, that foreign Merch[an]ts Goods shoud not be seizd but by way of <u>Reprizals</u>   on break[in]g out of War.

If such Case of foreign Merchants—surely more of Englishmen [*page break*]

King's [Pro]clamation cannot affect [Pro][per]ty th[at] always sacred {— King enabled by 3 G. 1.[8] to [pro]hibit Import[ati]on & Export[ati]on from Sweden. Gen[eral] Treat[ise] 4.}[9]
=={but   Drap[ier's] Letters}[10] An Offender punishable for an unlawful Act

==

Goods <u>unjustly</u> acquird Yet the [Pro][per]ty vested Instances of Engrossing & {buying [pretensd] Rights of Land ag[ains]t Statute of H. 8.} Gaming. Q[uære] Of Extortion.[11]

==

Trad[in]g with an Enemy contrary to Proclam[atio]n   No Offence unless injurious to the Community & then Not expressly forbidden.

==

Then no Arbitrary power in the Judge to condemn. Conf[essi]on must be free & w[ith]out Compulsion. Wood Civ. Law. 355. no[r] A Witn[ess] to accuse himself 362. 2. Ab. Ca. in Eq. Vern.[12]
No arbitrary power in the Judge to condemn a whole Cargo— Let it be punishd as a Crime

& if unlawful to seize on their Goods—but as Satisf[acti]on, tis impossible ~~En~~{su}ch Goods belonging to Englishmen can be lawfully seizd on—because that Reason in this Case can never exist.

"Of Antient time 3 people were priviledgd in time of War   Clericus, Agricola & Mercator." 2 Ins. 58

If Enemies when Merch[an]ts were sacred— & still allowd to be so in Flags of Truce— tho[ugh] generally restraind—how absurd is it to say that Act is unlawful wh[ich] is done in Consequence of this Law

==

~~Molloy's General Treatise   667. in Point.~~ {By the 3 J. 1. c. 6.[13] All the King's Subj[ec]ts are to have a free Trade to & from France Spain & Portugal.}
By the Law of Nations it is lawful for a Neutral Nation to trade with our Enemies— except as to furnishing them with [Pro]visions & Military Stores—th[at] is to buy their Goods—{&} sell them their own & these Goods so bought are not liable to be seizd
But they are not to **aid & assist** our Enemies to carry on the War ag[ains]t Us—   This

{what gives this Court Jurisd[icti]on—Surely the Comm[issi]on}: but no Law says this shall be a **forfeiture** of the whole

==

Goods of a Subject cannot be prize. 1 L[or]d Raym[ond] 271.[14]

==

{ Law Courts woud be preferrd. Penalties odious by Civil Law. Chanc[ery] to [pre]vent [Use]

proves therefore that <u>all</u> trading with our Enemies does not assist them to carry on the War

==

Our Subj[ec]ts have the same Priv[ilege]s with Neutral Nations & theref[ore] **lawful** for them.

{Crimes [per] Accidens dangerous. shoud be plainly so, 20 H. 6. c. 1.[15] Gen[eral] Treat[ise] 283[16] very strong}

==

Molloy's General Treatise 667. in point. {Trade with France [pro]hibited by 1 W. & M. c. 34. during the War—but repeald by 9 Ann c. 8}[17]
{Stat[ute] 13. G. 2. c. 27.[18] [pro]hibits all Trade with Spain.}

==

Instance of Russel the Judge sending over to England for the Admiralty's Direction.

==

The **Damage** of trading with the French cannot be great because they [ca]nt do it w[ith]out a Comm[issi]on of Truce wh[ich] may be restraind. Absurd to cutt off a Limb, that may be gently cur[e]d.

{ {**England** ensured French [Pro][per]ty in last War.} }
The Laws to affect an Englishman in Life Liberty or [Pro][per]ty must be plain & positive—not constructive by thinspun Arg[umen]ts of the Quib[b]l[in]g barr.

==

By the Comm[issi]on of Truce—the War ends as to this Vessel & like Merchants ment[ione]d in Coke's Inst[itutes] Proclam[ation] of War made it unlawful even to go.

==

This Off[ence] not pun[isha]ble by the Law of Nat[ure] & Nations—then by Municipal Law—but where does the English Law vest such power in one man

==

You are to say Prize or not—but not to inflict arbitrary Penalties for th[at] woud be the Case as this is English Property. Great Caution of the English Laws.

==

Magna Charta says "Salva Merchandiza sua." [*page break*]

{Formerly Trade with Infidels might be [pro]hibited. 2 Ins. 58. But denied in Sands & Child's Case 3 Lev. So here Act of Parl[iamen]t} {Repeald by 9 Ann c. 8.} {prohibited by 1 W[illiam] & Mary, c. 34.} {& All Trade with Spain by 13 G. 2. c. 27.}

Even in time of War.

==

Gr[an]t it a Crime.
θ [Pro]clam[ati]on dont say shall be **forfeit**.

Here was a Law to found the King's [Pro]clam[ati]on upon, wh[ich] enacted the penalty.   {Hear a Lawyer say King's {θ}[Pro]clam[ati]on can affect [Pro][per]ty— Unl[ess] Act is punishable.
No such th[in]g this War— Why? Plain & strong Reason wh[ich] clearly shews the Law. Molloy's Gen[era]l Treat[ise] 667. in point.

==

θ So Contracts for Ransoms valid
Much of the same Nature—viz for the Recovery of Subjects.

Noth[in]g more now necessary   {θ}However one more Instance

England ensurd French [Pro][per]ty all the **last War**. & Parl[iamen]t approvd of it. {Exchange alarmd on tak[in]g french fleete} That Universal   but this Trade may be Restraind {Absurd to cutt off a Limb th[at] may be gently curd.}   for Flags of Truce may be denied

And if it is better to let our Subj[ec]ts rot on Gaols—will be denied.   This Advant[age] instead of pay by the King for bring[in]g back his Subj[ec]ts.

Theref[ore] Trad[in]g with an Enemy not unlawful.

==

The Q[ues]tion of Ensurance **doubtful**—

but if any Disadv[antage] better to [per]mit it—than lay Restraints. Took our Saviour's Advice. Matt. 13. 29. "Gather not up the Tares lest You root up also the Wheat with them."

L[or]d Chesterfields Expressions on the Liberty of Press applicable to the Liberty of Commerce.

==

Hales H[istory] [of the] P[leas] [to the] C[rown] 159. 160. Ubi bellum non est Pax est.[19]

* Trade will be Gen[era]l Answer th[at] dep[en]ds on the Gov[ernmen]t [& the] P[oin]ts by the [Stat[ute]?].

{*}**The present Question** not of such a Trade in Gen[era]l but by **Flags of Truce**. Grant[in]g then the utmost force to [Pro]clam[ati]ons Procl[amati]on dont affect this Case—for as unlawful to go there as to trade   The War ceases as to the Flag   And [she is?] in Peace. The Gov[ernmen]t may impose what Cond[iti]ons it pleases on the Messenger. Gov[ernmen]t lead Us into this Error.

If it was lawful to go to Port Au Prince notw[ithstandin]g the [Pro]clam[ati]on it was lawful to trade notw[ithstandin]g the [Pro]clam[ati]on.   for surely

The Merch[an]t is as sacred then   as formerly in the time[*illegible*]{s m}ent[ione]d {by Coke.} If greater Disadv[antage] than Adv[antage]   may be restraind   but **Absurd** to cutt off a Limb   th[at] may be gently cur[e]d.

Adhering to Enemies High Treason & surely when Legisl[ature] about they made suff[icien]t [Pro]vision.

This [Pro]clam[ati]on Gen[era]l   but this an Exception. Wood's Ins. Civil Law. 114.[20] {How absurd to call this Act a Breach of the Comm[issi]on wh[ich] is done in Consequence of it.}   We ought to have some Recompe[nse] for Regain[in]g his Majestys Subjects or attempting it. [*page break*]

Second General Point. If the Ospray has done any th[in]g wrong—The Libell[an]ts have no Right or Authority to seize upon or [pro]ceed ag[ains]t her as Prize here.

[Pro][per]ty Alterd
Ent[ere]d with Coll[ecto]r

This Crime chargd as Breach of the Comm[issi]on—but not supported. How absurd &c.

However the Libel does not say the [Pro][per]ty of the Sugars was French at the <u>time</u> of Caption

X Carth. 252.[21] Ag[ains]t Act of Parl[iamen]t {with Penalty.} {Contr[ac]ts void.}
* We acknowledge We have broken the Comm[issi]on **tho[ugh]** We have not {broken it.} We acknowl[edge] our Action unlawful **tho[ugh]** it is not unlawful We achnowl[edge] it to be injurious **tho[ugh]** it is not injurious We acknowl[edge] A [Pro]clam[ati]on to have the same force as Stat[ute] tho[ugh] &c
  But We deny their Right or Authority to condemn here.

Theref[ore] the poss[essi]on be[in]g English the [Pro][per]ty is English. Viner title [Pro][per]ty. 71.[22] Poss[essi]on good but ag[ains]t very Right. & after in same pa. Strong.

{ {[x]}Finch's Law [octavo] 210[23] Tresp[assing] alters [Pro][per]ty. So in Engross[in]g. So in buy[in]g Pretencd Titles ag[ains]t Stat. of H. 8. Nay, [Pro][per]ty changd tho[ugh] Act of Piracy.[24] {Hob. 78.}[25]

{Co. Litt. 2. b. Fort[e]s[cue] 329. b.} {King shall have it.}}[26]

═══

But the [Pro][per]ty [pro]vd to be English beyond Doubt by the Depos[iti]ons. Then these Q[ues]tions arise Whether An English Subj[ec]t's Goods can be <u>seizd</u> by the Lib[e]ll[an]ts or <u>condemnd</u> by this Court.

No Express Law to this [Pur]pose only Constructive Arg[umen]tative Crime. Vide pa. 4. ante.[27] The first impossible. Then Vide the Privateer's Comm[issi]on as set forth. Harrassing of Trade. as ante 4.

═══

Privateers only in time of War & designd only ag[ains]t Enemies Moll. 471[28]

═══

θ Montis[quieu] ante 4. Every th[ing] managd by Kings Officers.

═══

If any forf[eiture]s his.

═══

No Inst[ance] of Subject claim[in]g a forf[eiture] but where given by Stat[ute].

═══

This Act out of their Comm[issi]on. {[θ]}

═══ { {This Action belongs only to the King. {Not any Subject.}Vaugh 335. 6. 342.[29] }} {Sid. 264. Bruen & Roe.}[30]

  {*}**Then** as to the Court's Authority. No Express Law. No Instance of a Flag of Truce be[in]g cond[emne]d Forf[eiture] **odious** to Law—Espec[ial]ly to the Civil Law Th[at] calld in to aid Com[mon] Law

Here the King's Off[ice]r has allowd of the Trade has adm[inistere]d Entrance {==} Stat[ute] of Trade w[ith]out penalites only directory.}}}} Vaugh 345.[31] and surely the King's [Pro]clam[ati]on not of more force th[an] a Statute. **Licenses**. ib[idem] & th[at] **Gov[ern]ors** may grant such Licenses. Vaugh 354.}[32]

I appeal to the Court—if ever A forf[eiture] was decreed by the Adm[iral]ty— Unless it was so orderd by Statute Never It coud not {be}.

{**Penalties** Juris positivi & not Juris naturalis.[33] Hale 13.}

{Crown shall have penalties 10 Mod. 121. {358. 364.}}[34] Strong Case in 2 Strange 952.[35]

==

An Engl[ishman] not to be stript of his [Pro][per]ty (tho[ugh] unj[us]tly acquird) but by plain positive Laws Espe[cial]ly in **Trade**.

==

Diff[erence] between determin[in]g Prize or not Prize {taken or not from Our Enemies} And inflicting Arbitrary Penalties on Subj[ec]ts for th[at] now the Case.

==

It appears manif[es]tly from Grotius as before And the Case of Neutral Vessels th[at] this Act is not contrary to the Law of Nations. What Law gives this Power to the Adm[iral]ty to condemn whole {Cargos.} [*page break*]

Gent[lema]n on the other Side. I shall consider Man in the State of Nature.
Answer. I shall consider an Englishman in his present State.
Surely the C[our]ts of Common Law woud be preferrd.

All this rel[ates] to diff[erence] ==

By the same Reason {Misera servitus ubi Jus vagum aut incertum.}[38] other unknown Mines may be sprung up ag[ains]t the English Trade—for this never crim[ina]l before.

Adher[in]g to Enemies H[igh] Treason: & surely the Legisl[ature] when about woud have [pro]vided in this Case. V[ide] H. H. P. C. 166.[36] Strong Case. Chew[37] says it is **Aiding &**

==

Suppos[in]g it an Offence ag[ains]t the Community {It is not malum in Se. Vaugh 358.}[39]— It is punishable in the Kings Courts but never can come into the Admiralty. 7 Mod. 99.[40]

==

The Offender is liable to punishm[en]t but never to be ruind & cannot be judgd of in the Adm[iral]ty.

Assist[in]g.

To conclude this point   I Call on the G[entle]men to shew th[at] ever a forf[eiture] was given by the Adm[ira]lty but where directed by Stat[ute].

Magna Charta c. 14.

12 Rep. 104. 105. 13 Rep. 53.[41]

Th[at] the Adm[ira]lty is no Court of Record   Can only amerce

And not to make A forf[eiture] of a Man's Merchandize

Sum up the Whole. We have done noth[in]g unlawful.

1.[st]   Because We have strictly complied with our Commission. & this Offence chargd as a Breach of it.   Some benefit surely designd to <u>Us</u> by the Gov[ernmen]t   {[O]}**As they did not pay**   for recov[erin]g their {Subj[ec]ts.}

O Eye on this

2.[ly]   Because no Injury to England—As We greatest Gainers—By Export[ati]on   or The vast Encrease of the King's **Revenue**

θ   Th[at]   Statute never repeald

The Wisdom of the Legisl[ature] thought the {[θ]}**duty** a suff[icien]t Recompense.

Peace & War the same with France.

less Expensive than Privateer[in]g.

3.[ly] Spirit of Engl[ish] Commerce & its Laws.   Great Care to [pre]serve Freedom of Trade.   No Arg[umen]tative Offences in Trade.   Trad[in]g with Enemies not unl[awful] from Inst[ance]s of {1.} **Ransoming** {2.} **Insuring** 3. **Prohibitory Statutes**. 4. **Molloy** ~~471.~~ {667.}

This **confirmd by Civil Law**. Grotius Bo. 3. c. 22. S. 4 & 5. & Instance of Neutral Vessels.

Th[at] We are not in a worse Case by King's [Pro]clam[ati]on   That dont affect [Pro][per]ty Even when grounded on Law   but [*page break*]

w[ith]out some Law for Support is nothing. {No Vestige here.} Inst[ance] in Will[iam]'s time.

[postea?]. No ~~Inst[ance]~~ of forf[eiture] on Stat[ute] w[ith]out ~~say[in]g~~ so {Stat[ute] w[ith]out Pen[alty?] ~~only directory~~ Vaugh[an] 345.}—but [Pro]clam[ati]on dont say **forfeit**   {Not ~~greater~~ than Stat[ute].} Besides   this ~~Case~~ a **License** {Exception} [out] of it & {Gov[ern]ors may grant such. Vaugh 354.}

2.^d **General point**. If We have done an Unlawful Act   We are irreg[ular]ly [pro]secuted.   Breach of Comm[issi]on alledgd   but unsuppor[ted?].

English [Pro][per]ty [pro]vd   Uncommon Q[ues]tion if Engl[ish] [Pro][per]ty can be lawful prize to Engl[ish] Subjects.

{1.} Inconsistent with [Pri]vateers Comm[issi]ons   {2.} Harrassing of Trade.   {3.} Engl[ish] Subj[ec]ts noth[in]g to do but to settle with the King's Off[ice]rs pa. 4. ante. {4.} If any penalties—belong to the King. Vaugh 34[0?]{2}. {3[0?]}{3}5. 6.} 10 Mod. 121. 358. {5.} Here the King's Off[ice]r contented who sworn & knows his Duty. 2 Strange 952. {No Instance of Forf[eiture] on Stat[ute] w[ith]out saying so. [Pro]clam[ati]on dont say **forfeit**. Not stronger th[an] Stat[ute].}

As to Court's Authority

{**Besides** a **License** here, wh[ich] Gov[ern]ors may grant. Vaugh 354.}
At most this is but a Misdem[eano]r & the Off[ice]r pun[isha]ble.
No Express Law   {&} Laws should be publick. Wood 115. {plain & positive in Trade.}   Forf[eiture] odious   [No Inst[ance]?] of Forf[eiture] in Adm[iral]ty but where directed.   All Stat[ute]s w[ith]out penalties only directory in Trade. Vaugh 345.

No arbitrary Power here to inflict [pun[ishment]] on Subjects.
Confirmd by Magna Charta c. 14. "Salva Merchandiza sua."

[bottom of page, exterior of folded document:]
No Instance of a forf[eiture] ag[ains]t an English Subjects w[ith]out an Express Statute: For carry[in]g Arms or Military Stores is ag[ains]t the Statute of Edw[ar]d 3.

Subj[ec]t's Goods cant be prize   Carth. 32 Bend [&c?] [20]. 12 Co. 75[42] [Pro]clam[ati]on cant make a penalty incertain

==

Alien Enemy may [pur]chase {Lands.}

==

Ms (PHi-Logan)

---

[1] England and the Dutch Republic were old maritime rivals, but each also considered France, a Catholic country, the greater enemy. Thus when Britain and France were at war, the Dutch were especially bitter when the British persisted in trade with France. For example, an editorial in a London paper, purportedly a letter from a Dutchman, sought to convince the English to give up that trade. "There is no way left us to maintain good friendship with Great

Britain," wrote J. Van K–ple, "and to put the Republic beyond the reach of the power of France, but to reject the temporary expedients, which our Merchants and Navigators propose, to enrich themselves by, under the privilege of a neutrality; and to take part in the war against France." *The Universal Chronicle, or Weekly Gazette* (London), Feb. 24–March 3, 1759.

[2] Lat. see later.

[3] Lat. In phrasing, the substance and rationale, not the words, is sought. The complete phrase is: *In verbis non verba sed res et ratio quaerenda est.*

[4] Lat. He stumbles into Scylla, who tries to avoid Charybdis. Hom. *Od.* 12.73.

[5] That is, Spanish privateers.

[6] 1 *General* 76–77: "And no Customer, Comptroller, Searcher, Surveyor, or their Clerks, Deputies, Ministers, or Servants, shall have any Ships of their own, or freight Ships . . . on pain of 40*l.* to be divided between the King and Prosecutor. *Stat. 3. Hen 6. c. 3. 11 H. 6. c. 15. and 20 H. 6 c. 5.*"

[7] Lat. saving to the trader his merchandise. See 2 *CLE* 378: "that no man shall have an amercement imposed upon him than his circumstances will bear." Amercement: "A discretionary penalty or fine; (originally) spec. one imposed on an offender at the discretion of the court of his or her lord, as opposed to a statutory fine. Formerly also: the income from such penalties or fines" (*OED*).

[8] 3 Geo. 1, c. 1 (1716): "An Act to Enable His Majesty Effectually to Prohibit or Restrain Commerce with Sweden."

[9] 1 *General* 4: "In the third Year of King *George* the First, by an Act of Parliament then made, the King was enabled by Proclamation to prohibit all Trade both Exportation and Importation with Sweden, on the intended Invasion of this Kingdom by the late King of *Sweden*: this being only a Temporary Statute in expired with the apprehended danger."

[10] The *Drapier's Letters* was the collective name for a series of seven pamphlets written by "M.B. Drapier" (Jonathan Swift; Dublin: J. Harding, 1724–25). Swift wrote them to raise awareness among the Irish people of a privately minted copper coinage that Swift believed was licensed through a corrupt process. He urged the Irish to resist the imposition of the currency through a boycott, which resulted in the patent's revocation. The *Letters* were ultimately an indictment of English rule over Ireland.

[11] To engross: "To gain or keep exclusive possession of; to concentrate (property, trade, privileges, functions) in one's own possession (often with the notion of unfairness or injury to others); to 'monopolize'" (*OED*). Possibly related to property obtained under false pretenses—some statute of 33 Hen. 8 (1541).

Possibly 33 Hen. 8, c. 1 (1541): "The Erection of the Court of Surveyors of the King's Lands, the Names of the Officers There, and Their Authority," which states "That if any person or persons shall make or pretend any claim, right, title, interest or possession in or to any manors, lands, tenements or hereditaments, bargained, sold or exchanged or hereafter to be bargained, sold or exchanged by the King our sovereign lord, to any person or persons in fee-simple or fee-tail, by his Highness letters patents, made or to be made thereof under the great seal of *England*, upon which letters patents there is or shall be reserved any annual rents or farms payable to the King's highness, his heirs or successors, in his said court of augmentations."

[12] Wood 328, 355, 362: "The Judge has not an arbitrary and extraordinary Power to condemn or absolve at his Pleasure; but *such* an arbitrary Power is entrusted with him that he may *lessen* or *encrease* the Punishment when he sees Reason for it, and when a particular Punishment is not assign'd by the Law"; "It ought to be free and without compulsion or torture, unless he confirms afterwards when free and at liberty"; "When the Witness deposes, let the Judge take notice, whether with an air of Sincerity he gives his

Evidence, or with exactness and Judgment. Yet the Witness ought not to answer Questions to accuse himself of any Crime."

It is unclear to what JD is referring. The citation suggests 2 Bacon, *Cases*. It is possible he is referring generally to chapter 38 (pp. 395–419), titled "Evidence and Witnesses."

It is unclear exactly to what JD is referring in Vernon. Both volumes include a section titled "Witness" in the index, though self-incrimination is not listed as a subtopic.

[13] 3 Jac., c. 6 (1605): "An Act to Enable All His Majesty's Loving Subjects of England and Wales, to Trade Freely Into the Domains of Spain, Portugal and France."

[14] 1 Raymond, *Cases* 271: Mich. Term 9 Will. 3 *Shermoulin v. Sands* (1697): Shermouline libeled in the Admiralty Court for a ship allegedly taken unlawfully. The "question there was, whether the capture . . . altered the property." The plaintiff cited Broom's Case (Trin. 9 Will. 3). "In the same manner here, the question being, prize or no prize." Chief Justice Holt argued that "[i]t is not alleged in the libel, that the capture was *super altum mare* [Lat. on the high seas]; so that nothing appears, to give jurisdiction in the admiralty."

[15] 20 Hen. 6, c. 1 (1442): "All Letters of Safe Conducts Shall be Inrolled in the Chancery." Sec. 3: "And moreover, if hereafter any goods or merchandises be taken by the said subjects of our lord the King upon the sea, or the coasts of the same, charged in any ship or other vessel, which is belonging to the enemies of adversaries of our lord the King for the time being, not having sufficient letters of safe conduct inrolled . . . , that they which so shall take the same goods and merchandises shall enjoy them without any restitution thereof to be made in any wise, to whatsoever person the same goods and merchandises so taken, at the time of the taking of the same, or before, were belonging."

[16] 1 *General* 282–83: "Where any Vessell of fifty Tons, or under, laden with customable or prohibited Goods, shall be found hovering on the Coasts . . . any Officer of the Customs may go on board, and take Account of the Lading, and demand Security of the Master, by Bond with Conditions, that such Vessel shall proceed regularly in her Voyage, and land the Goods in some foreign Port; and if such Master, &c. shall refuse . . . then all the foreign goods on board the Vessel may by any Officer of the Customs . . . be taken out of the said Ship, and brought on shore and secured; and if such Goods are customable, the Customs shall be paid."

[17] 9 Ann., c. 8 (1710): "An Act to Repeal the Act of the Third and Fourth Year of Her Majesty's Reign, Intituled, *An Act for Prohibiting All Trade and Commerce With France*; So Far As It Relates to the Prohibiting the Importation of French Wines."

[18] 13 Geo. 2, c. 27 (1740): "An Act for Prohibiting Commerce With Spain."

[19] 1 Hale, *Pleas* 159–60: In "Chap. XV: Concerning *treason* in adhering to the king's enemies *within the land or without*," he writes, "A peace, which is only a negation or absence of war, is that which I call a negative peace, because it is only an absence or negation of war, there intervening no league nor articles of peace, nor yet any denunciation of war, for it is regularly truce, *ubi bellum non est, pax est* [Lat. where there is peace, there is no war], tho neither prince is under any capitulation or contract; for there are divers princes in the world, that never capitulate one with another, and yet there is no state of war between them."

[20] Wood 114: "Exceptions are Rules which limit the extent of other Rules, and order matters otherwise by particular considerations, which render either just or unjust, that which the Rule understood without exception would have render'd on the contrary either unjust or just."

[21] Carthew 252, *Bartlett v. Vinor*, Mich. 4 W. & M., B.R. (1692): Bartlett brought an action against Vinor for £600, asserting that Vinor had agreed to pay him that sum after he "procure[d] 15000*l.* to be lent to the King, &c. upon an Act of Parliament for the Pound-Rate, in the name of the Defendant." Justice Holt ruled for the plaintiff, rejecting the argument that the arrangement was "extortive and usurious, and by Consequence unlawful,"

but noted that "every Contract made for or about any Matter or Thing which is prohibited and made unlawful by any Statute, is a void Contract, tho' the Statute it self doth not mention that it shall be so, but only inflicts a Penalty on the Offender, because a Penalty implies a Prohibition, tho' there are no prohibitory Words in the Statute."

[22] Viner. The volumes are not numbered but arranged alphabetically. The entry on Property is on 63–78 in the appropriate volume. It is likely JD was interested in sec. E, "Property Given, Alter'd, or Transferred; By What Act. *Fraud* &c.," which asserts that "Tho' a Trespassor gains Property *by the taking of Goods* . . . yet the Owner may affirm the Property to remain in him" (69).

[23] Finch 210: "Stealth is the wrongful taking of goods without pretence of title: and therefore altereth not the property, as a trespass doth, so as upon an appeal the party shall re-have them."

[24] 11 Will. 3, c. 7 (1698): "Piracy Act."

[25] Hobart 78, *Don Diego Serviento de Acuna v. Iolliff Tuckeri and Sire Richard Bingley* (n.d.): Diego Serventio de Acuna, a Spanish ambassador, libeled Tucker and Bingley in the Admiralty Court for taking goods belonging to the king of Spain. Bingley asked for a prohibition, but the king's serjeant ruled that "he could not sue for their goods at Common Law, because they were not proprietary," and because "[p]iracy did not change property, no more then left at land."

[26] 1 Coke, *Institutes* 2 b.: "And so it is if the Alien doth purchase land and die, the law doth cast the freehold and inheritance upon the King. If an alien purchase any estate of freehold in houses, lands, tenements, or hereditaments, the King upon office found shall have them. If an alien be made Denizen and purchase land, and die without issue, the Lord of the fee shall have the escheat and not the King. But as to a lease for years, there is a diversity between a lease for years and a house for the habitation of a merchant stranger being an alien, whose King is in league with ours, and a lease for years of lands, meadows, pastures, woods, and the like. For if he take a lease for years of land, meadows, &c. upon office found, the King shall have it."

1 Strange 328, *Shadford v. Houstoun*, Trin. 6 Geo., B.R. (1719): Judge John Fortescue (c. 1394–1479) argued, "There is a difference between a disability by act of Parliament, and a disability at common law; yet considering this as a disability at common law, the law never throws any interest upon a person disabled. If an alien purchases lands to him and his heirs, albeit he can have no heir; yet he is of capacity to take, but not to hold, for upon office found, the King shall have it. If a man be attainted, he is of capacity to purchase, but not to hold; for he can only purchase for the benefit of the King; he can neither have an heir nor be heir to any man, for by the attainder his blood is corrupted. 1 *Inst. 2. b.*"

[27] Lat. before.

[28] Justice 471: "[I]f War is lawful, Privateers are certainly so."

[29] Vaughan discusses nuisances (i.e., injury or harm), stating, "the parties particularly damaged by a Nusance, have their Actions on the Case for their damage, whereof the King cannot deprive them by his Dispensation" (335). If an "Act of Parliament can call an offence a Nusance, from which no particular damage can arise to a particular person, to have his Action, the King may dispense with such a nominal Nusance as with an offence against a penal Law, for which a man can have no Action for his particular damage" (336). Relatedly, "As if Transportation of Wooll, Mony, Corn, Horses, Bell-metal, Beer, or the like, be penally prohibited by Acts of Parliament, no Subject can derive a particular damage to himself for having an Action against the Offender. Secondly, If one might have an Action for such offenses, every man might have the like, therefore such offences are only to the Kings damage in his publique Capacity of Supreme Governour" (342).

[30] See doc. 1:61, n. 22, above.

[31] Vaughan 330–59, *Edward Thomas v. Thomas Sorrell, Cam. Scacc.* (1673), an important case for alcohol licensing law. Edward Thomas prosecuted Thomas Sorrell for selling wine at

his tavern without a license from the claimant, the Company of Vintners. Chief Justice John Vaughan ruled in favor of the claimant. Vaughan 345: "So if the King will, *ex speciali gratia* [Lat. from special favor], licence a Mortmain ["an instrument conveying the permission of the monarch to alienate property in mortmain" (*OED*)], the Chancellor need not issue any *Ad quod damnum* [Lat. according to the harm], for the King without words of *Non obstante* [Lat. notwithstanding], is sufficiently appris'd by asking for his *licence* to do a thing, which at *Common Law* might be done without it, that now it cannot be done without it. And that is all the use of a *Non obstante*."

[32] It is unclear exactly to what JD is referring. Vaughan provides a list "Other Presidents of Licenses to Corporations" (352–54). The only mention of governors is the observation that the king did not govern "in person" but rather through "Governours . . . in the Plantations of the Western Islands" (354).

[33] Lat. positive law and natural law, respectively.

[34] 10 *Modern* 121, *Thornby v. Fleetwood*, Hill. 11 Ann., C.B. (1712): The case concerned the settlement of the Duchess of Hamilton's estate. The defense argued that "where any act gives a penalty, but does not say to whom, there the crown shall have it." Judgment was for the defendant, resulting in a writ of error being brought to the King's Bench.

10 *Modern* 356–67, *Thornby v. Fleetwood*, Hill. 3 Geo. 1, B.R. (1716): The plaintiff's lawyer argued that, "to the objection, that by interpretation of law, the crown is to have the profits during non-conformity, it may answered, that the rule laid down by them [the defense] must be admitted for law: *viz.* that in penal statutes, when the act is silent to whom the penalty is forfeited, the crown shall have it" (358). The defense argued that their construction of the statute in question "was most consonant to the rules of common law, where no particular direction is given . . . there the law always throws it upon the king" (364).

[35] See doc. 1:61, n. 6, above.

[36] Hale, *Pleas* 165–66, is part of Chap. 15, entitled, "Concerning *Treason* in Adhering to the King's Enemies *Within the* Land *or Without*." "If there be a war between the king of *England* and *France*," Hale writes, "and then a temporary truce is made, and within the time of that truce an *Englishman* goes into *France*, and stays there and returns before the truce expired, this is not an adherence to an enemy within this statute."

[37] Possibly Benjamin Chew.

[38] Lat. It is a miserable slavery where the law is vague or uncertain.

[39] Vaughan 358: "Public Nusances are not *mala in se*, but *mala politica & introducta* [Lat. evils in themselves, but political and introduced evils]."

[40] 7 *Modern* 99, *Domina Regina v. Sturney*, Mich. 1 Ann., B.R. (1702): "He was convicted in a summary Manner on the Statute of the *13 & 14 Car. 2.* for a fraud in a Custom; and the Conviction being removed here, was quashed on Motion. For *per Cur.* The Statute directs no particular way of Trial, but only that the Offender shall be fined at the Sessions; and whenever an Act of Parliament makes an Offence, and is silent on the Manner of trying it, it shall be intended to be a Trial *per Pais* [Lat. by the country, or by a jury] according to *Magna Charta*."

[41] 12 Coke, *Reports* 104–05, *Thomlinson v. Philips*, Hill. 2 Jac. 1 (1604): Thomlinson "had brought an Action of Account for Goods against one *Philips* in the Common Pleas, and thereupon *Philips* sued *Thomlinson* in the Court of the Admiralty, supposing the Goods to have been received in foreign parts beyond the Seas." The Court of Common Pleas heard the case, arguing that the Admiralty "hath no Cognizance of Things done beyond the Sea, and this appears plainly by the Statute of 13 *Rich. 2. cap. 5*" ([1389]: "With What Things the Admiral and His Deputy Shall Meddle."). The court also argued that "the Proceedings in the Court of the Admiralty are according to the Course of the Civil Law, and therefore the Court is not of Record."

---

13 Coke, *Reports* 53, "The Case of the Admiralty," Trin. 7 Jac. 1 (1609): The case concerned Sir Richard Hawkins (1562–1622), vice admiral for Devon, aiding and abetting notorious pirate, William Hull (d. 1643). The court observed that "the Court of Admiralty is not a Court of Record," and that it could "amerce the Defendant for his Default by their Discretion."

[42] Carthew 31–32, *Beak v. Tyrell*, Pasch. 1 W. & M., B.R. (1688): an action of trover for a ship the defendant seized as a prize. The plaintiff argued that "the Goods of one Subject cannot be a Prize to another Subject; because a Prize is properly something taken on the High Sea from a common Enemy against whom War is declared."

12 Coke, *Reports* 75: "Note; The King by his Proclamation, or other Ways, cannot change any part of the Common Law, or Statute Law, or the Customs of the Realm."

64
Notes for *John Campbell v. The Owners of The Spry*, [c. 1758]

By the late 1750s, the Royal Navy had severely hampered the illicit and lucrative trade taking place as flag-of-truce missions. As JD notes in doc. 2:34, public opinion had turned against the flag-of-truce trade, seeing it as both treasonous and illegal. JD did support the trade as constitutional, but he did not support dealings in contraband goods, which violated the terms of the trade and were in fact illegal.

This and the following three documents (docs. 1:65, 1:66, and 1:67) form a subset in the flag-of-truce-trade cases. They relate to JD's representation in the Vice Admiralty Court of the owners of a ship called the *Spry*, who were apparently being sued for unlawfully intercepting John Campbell, commander of the *Prussian Hero*, an English snow.[1] The *Pennsylvania Gazette* reported that the *Prussian Hero* had "mounted 18 Guns, and had above 50 Hands on board; her Cargo Provisions, Dry Goods, &c. and was designed for Port-au-Prince from St. Eustatia. They threw overboard several Chests of Arms, some of which were fished up again. She is Prize to the Spry and Knowles Privateers of this Place, and the Hawk of New-York."[2] The question at hand was whether Campbell intended to trade in contraband arms with the French in the Caribbean.

Owners of [*blank*]
v
The Spry Privateer }

1.[st] The Vessel lost by the Act of God[3]— wh[ich] shall not injure any one by the Laws of Eq[uity] & Reason— "No one to answer for an Inevitable Chance—w[ith]out an Agreem[en]t Woods Ins. 28.[4]

2[ly]—The same Accident might have happ[ene]d if We had not seizd her.

3^{ly}—If there was suff[icien]t cause for Suspicion—it was suff[icien]t to justify Us—from Want of Papers &c Answ[er] of Engl[ish] Lawyers 12–13.[5]   [Per]haps If she had been brought in—&c even aquitted— She might not have been entitled to Costs & absurd to make us liable for the Conseq[uence]s when the Beginning of the action was justifiable—

4^{ly}—Discouragm[en]t of the Vigilance of Privateers wh[ich] the Gov[erno]r so much encourages by giv[in]g up by sev[era]l Stat[ute]s all the Benefit of the Captures to them.

5^{ly}—If they have been g[ui]lty of a Fault in acting in such a manner as to incur a Susp[ici]on—they ought to suffer for it—

"Quod quis ex culpa sua Damnum sentil, non intellig[itur] sentire." Dig. 50. 17. 203.[6] So "Non debit quis negligentiam suam ad alienam injuriam referre." Dig. 2. 15. 3.[7]

Wood's Ins. 26.[8]

Ms (PHi-Logan)

---

[1] Snow: "A small sailing-vessel resembling a brig, carrying a main and fore mast and a supplementary trysail mast close behind the main mast; formerly employed as a warship" (*OED*).

[2] *PG*, Sept. 14, 1758.

[3] Act of God: "orig. *Law* the operation of uncontrollable natural forces; an instance or result of such forces; frequently in the context of insurance" (*OED*).

[4] Wood 28: "All Persons in all Cases are to be answerable for *Deceit*, notwithstanding a contrary Agreement; but no one in any Case for inevitable *Chance*, unless there is an *Agreement* to answer it."

[5] Newcastle, 12–13: "[I]f there be false or colourable Papers; if any Papers be thrown overboard; if the Master and Officers examined in *Preparatorio* grossly prevaricate; if the proper Ship's Papers are not on Board; or of the Master and Crew can't say, whether the Ship or Cargo be the Property of a Friend or Enemy, the Law of Nations allows, according to the different Degrees of Misbehaviour, or Suspicion, arising from the Fault of the Ship taken, and other Circumstances of the Case, Costs to be paid, or not to be received, by the Claimant, in Case of Acquittal and Restitution."

[6] Lat. "He who sustains any damage through his own fault is not considered to have been injured." Just. Digest, 50.17.203. This quotation appears in a footnote to the following passage from Wood 26: "That an Act should be *regular* and *legal*, *Diligence* is necessary; for a *Fault* or *Neglect* is discountenanced, and every one is answerable for it."

[7] Lat. "He ought not permit his negligence to give injury to another." Just. Digest, 2.15.3.

[8] See n. 6, above.

65

Depositions for *John Campbell v. The Owners of The Spry*, [c. 1758]

The following depositions were not, it seems, originally for the present case but rather for an earlier one involving the same parties. In doc. 1:67, however, JD insists they must be used in this case and read first by the court since many of the men deposed had since left Philadelphia. We therefore place them in the *Campbell v. Spry* series, followed by notes on the plaintiff's arguments (doc. 1:66) and, finally, the fullest version of JD's arguments (doc. 1:67).

W[illia]m Campbell's {Nephew of John C[ampbell]} Depos[iti]on. John
Cambell being haild said he came from St. Kitts
✓   bound to to Jam[aic]a   Did not shew ~~French~~ {Dutch} Snows Papers
Danish Vessels a Blind.[1]   Shipt after the Vessel was Laden
Believes C[ampbell] intended to supply the French.

Dennis Walker.	Heard C[ampbell] acknowl[edge] the throw[in]g the Arms overboard— Shipt after the Vessel was laden. C[ampbell] refusd to come to ✓ Philad[elphi]a tho[ugh] requested.
James Preston.	All the Crew sign'd Articles for Jam[aic]a {To touch at Tortola[2] or any Neutral Port.} A Dutch Pilot. 1̶5̶{4} Chests of Arms—4 of them for Ship's Use 2 or 3 Tons of Cannon ball {from 6 to 2 pounders}. Arms thrown overboard by Campbell's orders. Signd the Bills of ✓ Lading for Monti Christi {& Savannah La Mar}[3]—but Campb[ell] coverd them with his hand. C[ampbell] desired to go on Shore at
Arms taken up [pro]vd by all—	M[onte] Christi— Discov[ere]d w[ith] Chests of Arms on board after at Sea. C[ampbell] said he intended them for the Pr[i]v[at]eers at Jamaica. C[ampbell] desird they wo[ul]d not be so illn[ature]d as to put him on board a man of War
Walter Burke.	C[ampbell] refusd to come to Philad[elphi]a tho[ugh] requested. C[ampbell] acknowl[edge]d his order[in]g the arms to be thrown overboard {out of the 14 Chests.}. 36 Musketts & some Cutlasses in each Chest. Bro[ugh]t to to the Leeward of the Line—
	C[ampbell] has a Brother living at Port Dauphine.[4] Twenty six French Books to be make pres[en]ts of at Port Dauphine.
//////	Blind Believes C[ampbell] intended to supply the French with Arms.
	C[ampbell] made him first Offer of going

Henry Jones.[Pro][of?] Master— "We say to Jam[aic]a Isle of Man & Liverpool—but give your word to go Ill let You into Whole Scheme of the Voy[age] wh[ich] will be most advantageous &c["]
Believes some Contraband Trade designd.

Rich[ar]d Linchey [Pro][of?]
W[illia]m King
  Made the crew drunk.

Shipt to Jam[aic]a Isle of Man & Liverpool— Cannon Ball loose & in Hog[s]h[ea]ds— Ship mounted with 16 Guns— Saw C[ampbell] throw[in]g the Arms overboard— Did not see any other Goods but Bricks. Capt[ai]n Spring[5] calld Campb[ell] Rogue for carry[in]g Arms {C[ampbell]} Answ[ere]d when haild "From St. Kitts.["]

Dav[i]d Sullivan. C[ampbell] answ[ere]d when haild "From St. Kitts.["] Great Quant[ity] of Cannon Ball Shipt for Jam[aic]a Isle of Man & Liverpool.

John Falcon. ✓ Shipt same Voyage. But cert[ain]ly knew not the Cargo as he says he never saw more than 4 chests of Arms

Peter Buchanan. ✓ Never heard C[ampbell] desire to come to Philad[elphi]a   Same Voy[age] with rest. Shipt after Vessel was laden.   C[ampbell] answ[ere]d from "St. Kitts."

John Quin. ✓ Same Voy[age] to Jam[aic]a &c Vessel laden before he was shipt

{Only} {Spring on d[esign?][in]g [*illegible*]{for} Arms & bringing them up—said he Saw no Arms but 4 chests for the Ship's use—from day to day [*illegible*] to be hangd.

W[illia]m Phelps. ✓— Vessel was laden before he was shipt.

Geo[rge] Buckmaster. Heard C[ampbell] say he designd with a Load of Sugars from M[onte] Christi to London.

John Maddock. A Great Number of Cannon Ball &c &c [*page break*]

From W[illia]m Campbell's Depos[iti]on in the 1.[st] Cause it app[ea]rs every thing was kept a Secret from him— He was not taken as Master till the Vessel was laden—

From James Preston's Depos[iti]on— The same Reserve— John
　　　Campb[ell] made him sign the 2 Bills of Lading for Monto
　　　Christo tho[ugh] coverd by his hand— And he tho[ugh] Purser did
　　　not know of ten chests of Arms that were on board—till they got
　　　to Sea.
{From Henry Jones's Depos[iti]on.}
{From all the Mariners Depos[iti]ons <u>but one</u> th[at] they knew nothing of
　　　Loading the Vessel.}
From Ja[me]s Bo[urkes?] Depos[iti]on— It app[ea]rs th[at] Campbell has
　　　a Brother living at Port Dauphine but 2 or 3 Leagues[6] from
　　　M[onte] C[risti]
　　　The Vessel brought to Anchor within the French Territories to the
　　　Leeward of the Dividing Line.
　　　Twenty six new French Books.
　　　==
　　　　　　　　　　　　　　　　{Gent. Magazine Vol. 13. pa 162}[7]
　　　　　　　　　　　　　　　　　　{Moll. 210. 211.}[8]

1. Constant Usage—nay y[ou]r
Ho[nou]r's Condemn[ati]on in this
very Cause
2. The Nature of the Adm[iral]ty
constituted for Maritime Affairs

[Pro]hibitions to the Adm[iral]ty
not fav[ore]d as [Pro]hib[itions] to
the Ecclesiastical Courts. 213[9]
Nor the same Reason[s].

3. The King's Just Præerog[ative]
maint[aine]d by the Adm[iral]ty <u>in</u>
<u>time of War</u>
4. Adm[iral]ty's Jurisd[icti]on
allowd of even in {some} Civil
Causes
{5. But clearly in all Criminal
Causes some little Alter[ati]on made
by 28 H. 8.}[10]
==

==

The former Despos[iti]ons must be
Evid[ence] because 1.[st] the Judge
cant divest his Conscience of the
Knowl[edge] he now has
2.[ly] Because {Right &
conseq[uent]ly} our Defence is
founded on those Depos[iti]ons.
==

From Jos[eph] Buckmaster's Depos[iti]on
　　　[Pro] Quer[ente][11] it appears John
　　　Campbell intended to go from Monto
　　　<u>Christi</u> to <u>London</u> quite contrary to the
　　　Voyage agreed on with the Sailors—And
　　　that he was loaded with Dry Goods—
　　　wh[ich] was false {& contrad[icte]d by

◎ Judges are to observe
the Stat[ute]s Not to
form imag[ina]ry
Offences—but to
observe what are created
so by the Laws of the
Land.

Campb[ell's] own Claim.   What a **Sea Rover**.[12]
So Campbell in his Claim says he was <u>bound</u> from Statia[13] to M[onte]
Christi & from thence to Jamaica when not a single Sailor was shipt
for that Voyage. [*page break*]

The Intention punishable equally with the Fact in High Treason. 4 Rep. 16.
11 Rep. 98.[14]
Q[uære]. If an Attempt to convey Arms to an Enemy is not an Overt Act.
     Vide 1 Ins. 261. 3 Ins. 10. 11. Hawk. P. C. 14. H. H. P. C.[15]
==

The same Inj[ur]y to Englishmen to be tried for Pirates as this Trial.

==

1. Obj[ecti]on. [Par][ticu]lar Priv[ateer] of Englishmen to be tried [per]
     pares—[16] Answ[er]. above
2.[d] Obj[ecti]on. No Crime yet committed.
==

His Alleg[ation] cant be annulld
==

If a Dutchman he had no Right to furnish Arms—
==

Campbell in his Claim says—the Arms &c were designd for his Ship's
Use— But too many for her—
        18 = 8
        14—
         3— 1— 6
        12———
        14—15—
         7
        ————————
        ~~70~~{69} = 4 = 6 [*page break*]

Begin with the Orig[ina]l [*blank*] D[ense?] [*blank*] then State Campb[ell]s
Walkers Preston's & Burke's Depos[iti]ons
==

Then class John C[ampbell]'s Depos[iti]ons   How far contrad[ict] how
far confirm.   First the Voy[age] a Secret to all— They agree as to
C[ampbell]'s Answer when haild— They agree as to Arms thrown
overboard   His own {Witn[esse]s fix the time after th[at] for the ill
Usage}   They agree that they never heard C[ampbell] request to come to
Philad[elphi]a except {X}Quin [*in left margin:*] {The only contrad[icti]on

& th[at] they never heard C[ampbell] say he intended for a french port. As to the Line— Answ[er]. Not contrad[icte]d by any but [Dewar?] & th[at] only as to Port Dauphine {5 Le[a]gues distant.} However only matter of Opinion that: does that impeach his Testim[ony] as to facts?}   Who is contra[dicte?]d by Register by C[ampbell]'s own Nephew Walker a Surgeon & Burke a Captain— Agree as to Cannon Ball & Arms.   His own Witn[esse]s [pro]ve the Load[in]g a Secret   Then our Testimon[ials?] Jones King & Linchey

==

I apprehend they shoud have [pro]vd what **Expressly** those Arms were for how he got them from St. Kitts   Cleard up the Contrad[icti]ons in former Trial as Art[icle]s for Jam[aic]a & Bills of Lad[in]g for M[onte] Christi Keep[in]g it a [Secret]

Flags of Truce

Ms (PHi-Logan)

---

[1] Blind: Also known as a "spritsail," a term for a square-rigged sail below the bowsprit of a large ship, which blocks the forward view when set.

[2] Tortola, one of the largest islands in the Caribbean and a main port in the sugar trade, was taken from the Dutch by the English in 1672.

[3] Savanna-la-Mar in Jamaica was an important port of trade for sugar and slaves.

[4] Port Dauphin was on Hispaniola, an hour's sail from Monte Cristi (see doc. 1:67 below).

[5] Capt. Benjamin Spring.

[6] League: "An itinerary measure of distance, varying in different countries, but usually estimated roughly at about 3 miles" (*OED*).

[7] The edition for March 1743 contains a report of an Admiralty case concerning the seizure of beef and pork. JD quotes the report in its entirely in doc. 1:67, p. 350.

[8] Justice 210–11 is part of c. 4, entitled, "Containing A Discourse of the Jurisdiction of the Admiralty in England." These specific pages are part of an extended excerpt reprinted from John Godolphin, *Synēgoros Thalassios, A View of the Admiral Jurisdiction* (London: W. Godbid, 1661), which outlines the extent of the court's jurisdiction.

[9] Justice explains that "the Writ, which in our Law is called a *Prohibition*," is a method "by which this Jurisdiction [of the Admiralty] is sometimes interrupted . . . . And indeed it does not seem very reasonable to grant Prohibitions against that Court, if due Consideration be had of the first Intent of awarding Prohibitions, which certainly was for the Preservation of Royal Rights and Prerogatives of the Crown: For which I shall vouch the Testimony of that Learned Civilian, *D. Cowel*, who speaking of Prohibitions, says, *That tho' they might have been of use to preserve the Rights of the Crown, when the Ecclesiastical and Secular Jurisdiction acknowledged two Separate Heads: now that the King is own'd to be the Sovereign Head of the Church as well as of the Laity, they are becoming unnecessary and grievous*" (211, 213).

[10] 28 Hen. 8, c. 15 (1536): "An Act for Punishment of Pirates and Robbers on the Sea."

[11] Lat. for the plaintiff.

[12] That is, a pirate.

[13] St. Eustatius, a Dutch possession in the northern Leeward Islands.

---

[14] 4 Coke, *Reports* 16 b., *Eaton v. Allen*, Trin. 40 E., C.B. (1597): "Words [are] not actionable: For the Purpose or Intent of a Man without Act is not punishable by Law."

11 Coke *Reports* 98 b., "James Bagg's Case," Trin. 13 Jac. 1, B.R. (1615): "They who have Offices of Trust and Confidence shall not forfeit them by Endeavours and Intentions to do Acts, although they declare them by express Words, unless the Act itself shall Ensue."

[15] 1 Coke, *Institutes* 261: "The Statute of 25 E. 3. *De proditionibus*, doth declare, that it is Treason by the Common Law to adhere to the enemies of the King within the Realm, or without; if he be thereof proveablement attaint of overt fact, and that he shall forfeit all his lands, &c."

3 Coke *Institutes* 10–11, is part of c. 1, titled, "Of High Treason." An edition of Hawkins to match JD's citation was not found, but Hawkins (1739), c. 17, entitled "Of High Treason," runs from p. 33 to 46.

1 Hale, *Pleas* 58. The discussion of high treason is c. 10.

[16] Lat. by one's peers.

66

Notes on the Plaintiffs' Arguments in *John Campbell v. The Owners of The Spry*, [c. 1758]

Campbell's lawyers, John Ross and Joseph Galloway, seem to have experimented with several arguments on his behalf, including that the depositions in the "Orig[ina]l Cause" should be dismissed, the court not having jurisdiction, and claiming that Campbell was not an Englishman. JD's answers, sketched roughly here, are expanded in doc. 1:67 below.

ProQuerente

Ross [Pro] Querente.

> The Depos[iti]ons in the Orig[ina]l Cause dont support the Libel [*illegible*] th[at] C[ampbell] was bound to a french Port—   Answ[er]. Y[ou]r hon[ou]r thou[gh]t the Libel suff[icient]ly [pro]vd—& either thou[gh]t C[ampbell] was bound to a french port   or th[at] being bound to M[onte] Christi with his Intentions was the same thing.
>
> ==
>
> No Dutch no french Passports Answ[er]. They did not desire to be lookd on as Dutch—tho[ugh] they had taken in th[in]gs at Statia they w[oul]d not take in at St. Kitts w[ith]out a Bond to del[ive]r at some Engl[ish] port & then no inj[ury] coud be done the publick
>
> ==

Galloway [Pro] Querente.   The Prussian Hero was at Statia. {St. Kitts.}

342

Answ[er]. Jones's Depos[iti]on. All the Seamen never say a word of it

But grant it—then how coud they bring th[ese] Arms w[ith]out a Clearance—

==

[Pro]digious Cruelty   threats   Hardship &c

==

Gen[era]l Report at M[onte] Christi & Quin's Depos[iti]on that C[ampbell] woud have come to Philad[elphi]a   Answ[er]. he waited till our Witn[esse]s gone   He might know from depos[iti]ons th[at] his Design was not fully discoverd.

==

His [Per]son shoud [~~not~~] have been arrested   But not his [Pro][per]ty   If vested in any body   vested in the King Answ[er].   This overthrows y[ou]r hon[ou]r's Determ[inati]on. Vide all the Author[ities] cited in Arg[umen]t

Lawful to trade from one Neutral Port to ano[the]r Answ[er]. Is C[ampbell] to be lookd on as a Dutchm[an] or Englishm[an]— Ross says as an Engli[shman] Gall[oway] says as an English{Dutch}man.
== {If his Intent was to supply Arms by means of the Span[iar]ds—was that Legal}
As to Treason—acknowl[edged] not to be Treason unless arms sold—then no Com[mon] Law courts can punish for Stat[ute] of H[enry] 8.[1] wh[ich] app[oin]ts a Court for try[in]g Treasons & Felonies directs how they shall be tried—
All other Off[ence]s left at Law to Adm[ira]lty.

==

He went w[ith]out french [Pro]tections— Answ[er]. If they had taken him—woud they have had any more.

Great Expence of fitting out his Vessel. Answ[er]. for his own [Pro]tections—He might have had a flag of Truce Answ[er]. Then he must have returnd to St. Kitts or the place he went from [*page break*]

He said French Vessels— Answ[er]. [h?]{H}e was obligd to take
something—woud he suffer the poor Negroes to inform.
==

C[ampbell]'s com[in]g here [pro]ves his Innoc{ence.} Answ[er].
It [pro]ves his Assurance for such I must think it &c.

Fear does things so like a Witch
We cannot tell which is which.   A Play[2]

3 Ins. 12.[3] Provable [merits?]. Answ[er]. This was in
Treason & a Com[mon] Law Case. 1 H. H. P. 6. 86.[4]
Circumst[ance]s surely y[ou]r hon[ou]r thinks some
Evid[ence]. 2 Hawk. 222.[5]   That is of Treasons
Misprisions of Treasons &c 1 Hale H. P. 6. 367.[6]

Ms (PHi-Logan)

---

[1] 35 Hen. 8. c. 2 (1543): "An Act Concering the Trial of Treasons Committed out of the King's Majesty's Dominions."

[2] "For fear does things so like a witch, / 'Tis hard t'unriddle which is which." From Samuel Butler, *Hudibras. In Three Parts* (London: W. Rogers, 1684), 174.

[3] 3 Coke, *Institutes* 12: "[High treason] must be provably, by an open act, which must be manifestly proved."

[4] 1 Hale, *Pleas* 6, discusses Roman homicide law and explains if someone killed another person "merely by misfortune it was not punished."

    1 Hale, *Pleas* 86: "Now although the crime of high treason is the greatest crime against faith, duty, and human society . . . there should be some fixed and settled boundary for this great crime . . . and of what great importance the statute of 25 *E.* 3 was, in order to that end."

[5] 2 Hawkins 222 specifically treats "Treasons, Felonies, and Robberies, &c upon the Sea" within the chapter's broader discussion of indictments: "It is enacted by 35 *H.* 8. 2. That all manner of Offences . . . [declared] to be Treasons, [or] Misprisions of Treasons . . . shall be from thenceforth inquired, heard and determined before the King's Justices of his Bench."

[6] Misprision of treason is the offense at common law of not reporting treason to the proper authority.

    1 Hale, *Pleas* 367–68: "Lastly, touching execution of judgements of treason, they are directed by the judgement, whereof before. There be nevertheless some things, that accidentally happen, that suspend or abate the execution."

67

Arguments for *John Campbell v. The Owners of The Spry*, [1761]

In these detailed notes, JD argues that the depositions (doc. 1:65) from "the former Trial" should be admitted now because it would be "cruel" to deprive his clients of the benefit of testimony by persons who were no longer available because of Campbell's "Artifice" in staying away until they were gone. He also argues that the testimony—of which the presiding judge obviously had knowledge—should be in the record of the proceeding in any appeal of the judge's decision to a higher court.

He then addresses the two most substantive claims, first, that the Vice Admiralty Court did not have jurisdiction; and second, that there was insufficient proof of arms dealing. To the first point, JD countered that it was customary for the court to restrain illegal trade even more in time of war, and that if the court did not have jurisdiction, the proper remedy would have been an action at common law. To the second point, JD reviewed the testimony in the earlier proceeding and argued that, contrary to Ross and Galloway's contentions, it was sufficient to support a determination that Campbell's intent was to supply arms to the French, notwithstanding that the *Prussian Hero* was purportedly sailing from one neutral port, the Dutch island of St. Eustatius, to another, the Spanish port of Monte Cristi on Hispaniola. JD cited several circumstances that revealed Campbell's intent, including his secrecy about the vessel's cargo and destinations, his sailing from port to port, his various misstatements and conflicting statements, and his throwing the arms overboard. In this document, the notes follow the columns.

---

(1)

John Campbell Claimant

v

The Owners & Comp[anies?] of the Private Ship of War The Spry & Others—

In the Admiralty

John Campbell claims the Snow Prussian Hero taken by the Spry in the Harbour of Monti Christi about a year ago—& condemnd here for carrying on a Contraband Trade.

The Depos[iti]ons taken at the former Trial ought to be read. 1.st Because The Judge who is to determine accord[in]g to Conscience cant divest his Consc[ience] of the Knowledge he now has. 2.^{ly} If he coud—yet it woud be cruel to deprive Us of that Benefit by the Artifice of the Claimant Who staid till they were gone before he appeard. 3.^{ly} Because our Right to the Prussian Hero—& consequently our Defence is founded on those Depos[iti]ons.{X} 4.^{ly} Because these are but one Action, & the Decree now made is only **in possessorio**[1]—Vide Moll. Dom. 208. Clarke's

X If obj[ecte]d th[at] We fil[e]d Interrog[atories] Answ[er]. They

were gen[era]l &
the [Per]sons
belongd to the Ship

Pract. 63.[2]   And if an Appeal shoud be made in the [pre]sent Cause—All the [Pro]ceed[in]gs must be sent home—& it woud be absurd to repeal {reject Evid[ence] here on wh[ich]} the Sentence of this Court on Evid[ence] not allowd in this Court, {may be repeald} in a Superior Court. So in 1 Strange 35.[3] In the Court of Delegates[4] Depos[iti]ons taken by a Surrogate tho[ugh] no Cause in Court allowd to be read in Conf[essi]on of other Evid[ence]. So in 1 Strange 69.[5] Coroner's Inquest allowd to be given in Evid[ence] on an issue from Chanc[ery] being **Ad inform[ia]m conscientiam**.[6]

2 Points

First   Whether this Court has Jurisdiction in the present Cause—tho[ugh] Campbell actually intended to supply the French with Arms by the way of Monti Christi.

2ly   If this Court has Jurisd[icti]on in the present cause—Whether there is suff[icien]t [Pro]of that Campbell intended to supply the French with Arms.

As to the first Point.

H. H. P. C. 12 &c.[7]   The Com[mon] Law of Engl[an]d as to Crim[ina]l matters extends only to the Land—from whence Juries may come for the Trial

==

Laws of Oleron
observd [at this]
Day tho[ugh] made
by R[ichard] 1.[8]

But as Eng[lan]d has long been a trad[in]g Nation surro[unde]d with Seas—many Off[ence]s comm[itte]d at Sea   And theref[ore] the Adm[iral]ty erected in very early Ages— My L[or]d Coke. ~~3~~{4} Ins. [*blank*] says it existed long before Ed[ward] 3 time[15]

==

X Interest Rei
P[ub]licæ ut ne sint
Crimina
impunita—[9]

No other Jurisd[icti]on {X} for trying Crimes at Sea but this {28. H. 8.}[16]—& in all the Disputes between the King's Courts & the Adm[iral]ty V[ide] ~~3~~{4} Ins.[17] [*blank*] no doubt ever made of their Author[ity] in Crim[ina]l matters.   Some in Civil Causes. [*page break*]

(2)

Diff[erence]
betw[een] this Case
& Hart's[10] flag of
Truce for lawful to
trade with French
but not to assist
them.

If Adm[ira]lty cant Seize—no others can—then if
they can authorize to seize—they are authorizd to
condemn for every Incidence must follow— Sid.
Saund. Keb. 12 Mod.
The Adm[iral]ty instituted for the publick Good—
& never regarded with that Jealous Eye that other
Civil Law Courts were. Moll. Dom. 213.[18]
[Pro]hib[iti]ons to Adm[iral]ty not fav[ore]d nor
the same Reason.

1.[st]

This is not a Civil
but a Crim[ina]l
Cause.

~~That the Adm[iral]ty has Author[ity] in this [par][ticu]lar Case. Moll. Dom. 210. 211. Carth. 30. 31.~~

If this Co[ur]t has no Jurisd[icti]on
they are wrong to endeavour to [pro]cure a 2.[d]
Extraj[udicia]l Act— {Their [pro][per] Remedy
wo[ul]d be at Common Law as the Jud[gmen]t of
this Court must be cor[am] non Judice.[19]
Contrad[icti]on to alledge Want of Jurisd[icti]on
when they are Pl[ainti]ff's.}

2.[ly]

Constant Custom for Adm[iral]ty to restrain illegal
Trade in time of War.   The Condemnation in this
very Cause.{θ} ~~A Monti Christi Trader~~ condemnd
lately at York—   The trade there broke up. {{θ}I
dare say the Author[ity] of this Court was well
consid[ere]d before the former Cond[iti]on.   The
only po[in]t now disputable is Whether Claim[an]t
is guilty of the Fact— And not the Law on that
fact—wh[ich] last strikes at y[ou]r honours
Jud[gmen]t in the Law.}

3[ly]

4{3}[ly]

Salus populi Suprema Lex—[20]

{Consider the ~~[par][ticu]lar Nature of C[ampbell]'s
Offence.~~}

By the Laws of our Country Campbell was engagd
in a treas[ona]ble Act— 25 E. 3.[21]   This Court
must observe the Stat[ute]s 4 Ins. 143.[22]   Shall
not now enquire Whether the sail[in]g on this
Design amo[un]ts to an Overt act of Treason—as
held that Cruis[in]g[23] does Sal. 635.[24]   Supp[ose]
it not Treason till the Off[ence] comm[itte]d
then no other Court can punish the Attempt or

θ If not lawful then Cataline & Manlius Captains were unjustly punishd.[11] Apply that here. Love of Country a beautiful Arg[umen]t but mera verba.[12] **Salus populi &c** More tender to a Community than an Individual. X For in some Ages Piracy was hon[ora]ble— Homer—but no Age or Country ever allowd of Rebellion. By the Valerian Law[13] Enemies to the State might be put to death w[ith]out Trial by [pri]vate [Per]sons— V[ide] pa. 8 [po[s]t[ea]?][14] 4[ly]

[pre]vent it but this   {**1 Hawk. 65.**}[25] {X} {2 Hawk. 77. Woods Ins. Civ. Law 299.}[26] Punish[in]g Attempts not contrary to Reason or Justice. 1 Str. 196.[27] Att[emp]t to pick a pockett punishd.

An Indubitable Maxim in {X} Law {θ} Politicks {θ The Act the same as {if assisted—}}[28] & Morality th[at] Every not only has a Right but ought to prevent every dangerous or Wicked Act— {As to Law V[ide] X.}   So far has the Maritime Law gone th[at] the [Pro][per]ty of a Pirates Vessel being taken immed[iate]ly vests in the Captors— w[ith]out Cond[iti]on. Treat[ise] of Comm[erce] 2 Vol. 265. 6.[29]

This {X}   worse   than   Pirat[ica]l   Act—a treas[ona]ble Act. {Our Capture is a kindness to C[ampbell] as he wo[ul]d have forf[eite]d Life & Fortune both if his Act had been accomplishd. But he thought himself secure by living at Statia.}

▣[30] The Crime however not being accomplishd [pro]duces a new kind of Arg[umen]t—Wh[ich] is the same as to say—We sho[ul]d suffer the Inj[ur]y to be done & then punish—Sed præst[?] Caut[?] quam &c.[31] {Go to Brest & then ruin You for it}[32]
==

If convey[in]g Arms to an Enemy was not thought suff[icient]ly [pro]vided ag[ains]t Woud it have been omitted out of the severe Act about [Pro]visions.[33] By the Answ[er] of the Engl[ish] Lawyers pa. 11. unlawful for Neutral Nations to furnish Arms—[34] Absurd if Lawful for Subjects [*page break*]

Pistoles Gov[ern]ors of
Governors.
{Neutral[ity] not violated in
seiz[in]g Rebellious Subjects &c}
Treat[ise] of Nav[al] Law &c
2. Vol. 235. 6.
Answ[er] of Engl[ish] Lawy[ers]
19.
Lex Merc[atori]a 29. 30.
Moll. Dom. 472.[35]

(3) {Read Carth. 31.
first.
Vent. 1. 173 a Vessel
condemnd for
carrying bellicos
Apparatus.}[36]

{1 H. P. C. 65.
Woods Ins. C L.
120.[37] The
forf[eiture] here no
doubt the same as if
accomplishd—&
trial at Com[mon]
Law.}

5[ly] Remarkable Case before Sir Henry Penrice[38] in last War. Gent. Magazine for March 1743 pa. 162.[39] {2 Ins. 51}[40] {Molloy's Dom of the Sea 210— 211— Carth. 30. 31. to shew Subj[ec]ts Goods may be Prize[41]   12 Mod. 134.[42] The Com[mon] Law gave Way to the Adm[iral]ty Law.}

6[ly]

A.

This
comes in
next page
at letter **C.**

As to C[amp]bell's sailing from one Neutral Port to ano[the]r that cannot dissolve his Allegiance. Multitude of Author[ities] at Com[mon] Law. Wood's Ins. Civ. Law. pa. 70.[43] Besides his Crew were all Eng[lish] & his Comm[issi]on English. {He calls himself an Engl[ish] Subj[ec]t of St. Kitts: So when hail[ed]}   But gr[an]t[in]g this Amphibious Gentleman to be a Dutchman Surely no Treaties allow them to furnish our Enemies with Arms they exp[ress]ly forbid it. V[ide] Treaty 1674.[44]

7[ly]

❖

θ [C?]an it be
denied th[at]
Adm[iral]ty has
Power to try
Engl[ish]men for
Offences &c
  This not a
civil but a
criminal Cause.}

Obj[ecti]on. That Englishmen ought not to lose their [Pro][per]ty w[ith]out Express Laws— Gr[an]t it— Here is the Stat. of 25 E. 3.[45]   But It is {θ}surely as great a hards[hi]p for Engli[sh]men to be tried for ~~Pirates~~ {Offences} or lose their Vessels as above without express Law.

{The Crime shoud be Evid[en]t
ag[ains]t a Subject &
So it is by the 25 E. 3.}

If the Adm[iral]ty has Jurisd[icti]on in the Cause as undoubtedly It has   It is absurd to talk of the hardships an Englishman suffers from the penalties   for wherever Adm[iral]ty has Jurisd[icti]on   their Law [pre]vails tho[ugh] contrary to Com[mon] Law— So in 2 Vol.

Treat[ise] of Commerce Goods of Pirates vest in Captors w[ith]out Cond[iti]on— Al[ia?] by Com[mon] Law—So in 12 Mod. 184. 5.[46] Of Goods not brought infra Praesidia &c &c.   Who is best entitled We th[at] prevented or he th[at] woud have [a][ttemp?]ted a Treason. Gentlemans Magazine for March 1743—page 162.

Thursday 24.[th]

"Came on, before Sir Henry Penrice, Judge of the High court of Adm[ira]lty, a cause concerning a Seizure made by John Love Esqr. Collector of the Customs at Cork in Ireland, of 800 barrels of Beef and 400 Barrels of Pork, loaden on board the Vertue, Capt[ain] Gains, of Yarmouth; and contracted for by Timothy and James Macnamara, Irish Merchants residing at Malaga, for the King of Spain's Gallies;[47] it appearing upon trial that Capt[ain] Gains had a Spanish Pass, the Court were of opinion they were a legal Prize.["]

B. this comes in next pa. at letter **C.**

Civ[il] Law pun[ishe]s what is contrary to their Design. Wood 120.
Mens facit esse reum[48]
Here was a g[uil]ty Intention coupled with a lawful Act—

Ingenious Arg[umen]ts

It is the <u>mind</u> {Affectio tua imponit &c.}[49] that Constitutes Vice or Virtue—{seem[in]gly} Charitable or pious Actions are <u>Crimes</u> when done with sinister Views— The Patriot may [pro]mote publick Good—from little [pri]vate motives **fixit legis**["][50] &c

Tho[ugh] lawful to go to M[onte] Christi—it might be on an unlawful Errand

A thing Lawful in itself may be done in such manner to shew an unlawful design.
This the Mean[in]g of Timothy 1 Ch. 8 verse[51]
The Law is good—if a man use it lawfully.—
{He only carried the [*page break*]

Arms to M[onte] Christi—the Spaniar[ds] supplied the French— Coud not the Arms be movd from thence? Yes but the Span[iar]ds &c. Answer. This is handl[in]g High Treason with &c}

(4)

Second Point. Whether there is suff[icien]t [Pro]of that C[ampbell] intended to supply the French with Arms,{?}

==

{We speak to Conscience.} If Evid[ence] enough to <u>convince</u>—enough to <u>condemn</u>.

==

Express Evid[ence] cannot be expected in such a transaction therefore The 6th Interrog[atory] on C[ampbell]'s behalf appeard a little singular

==

The Master of a Family never lights a Candle & puts it under a Bushel—[57] But the Thief will put it there—if he finds it.

==

Our Pr[o]ofs arise from Circumst[ance]s wh[ich] C[ampbell] coud not help disclos[in]g &c They are neither slight nor single &c

Shall not aggravate them but lay them in order before the Court in order They will explain themselves.

==

I have always thought the Paths of <u>Honesty</u> streight & plain— No Wind[in]gs or Intricasies— One may [per]ceive the Traveller at a Dist[ance] but in the crooked Walks of <u>Cunning</u>—He is almost always hid—at most but a Glimpse—& then lost again

==

The honest man discovers every th[in]g because <u>he has noth[in]g to</u> conceal— The Cunning man discovers th[in]gs by his very <u>Care to conceal them</u>.

{Such is the Case here— So much

C.   Pains

taken to keep a Secret—th[at] it is evident that Secret must be a bad one.}

First— It may be [pro][per] to take Notice of the great Stress laid on C[ampbell]'s sail[in]g from one Neutral port to ano[the]r {V[ide] pa. [illegible]}{**A.**

Arms were **English** therefore must come from an Engl[ish] port & shou[d] have a Clearance.

1.ˢᵗ Circumstance.

////////// w[ith]out Bond

Arms not to be ~~shipt~~} Their being found w[ith]out an Account—suff[icien]t Reason to condemn. Arms were not [per]mitted to come from N[ew] York to Philad[elphi]a last War—

And Sir Peter Warren[52] condemnd a french Vessel only for having Naval Stores last War.

B.}} He has indeed tried every Shape—but he must be an Englishman or a Dutchman.

This very Double Deal[in]g shews someth[in]g unlawful was designd. C[ampbell] in his Claim acknowl[edges] the Wines to be French Prize Wines wh[ich] must be bro[ugh]t from an Engl[ish] Port— He went to ~~Jam[aic]a~~ {St. Kitts} carried men from there—his **Commission**. Q[uære] Regist[er?]

==

Comm[issi]on from ~~Statia~~ {Kitts} for a Vessel at St. {ta} ~~Kitts~~ {tia}:   Why did he not sail from St. Kitts— Answ[er]. His trade not fit for an Englishman

Why not a Clearance from St. Kitts as well as Comm[issi]on

Answ[er]. He coud not get one for a Cargo of Warlike Stores.

==

[X?] First obs[ervation] this Comm[issi]on was not intended ag[ains]t our Enemies from his Complaisance to Dutch Vessels.

◎ 2.ˡʸ Designd as a Cover for the Master of the Vessel never knew of it till at Sea & then fo[un]d himself superseded— What is the mean[in]g &c.

2.ᵈ Circumst[ance].

Obj[ecti]on. The Comm[issi]on of Marque covers the <u>Arms</u> ~~wh[ich] were for the Ships Use~~? Answ[er]. {X}Not more than for the Ship's Use—

These Comm[issi]ons are to <u>cruise</u> & not to <u>trade</u>— But Evid[en]t th[at] C[ampbell] intended to trade with these Arms for he confessd to [*blank*]

(Vide his Depos[iti]on) th[at] he intended them for the Priv[a]teers at Jamaica.

Confirms the 1.ˢᵗ   The great Care to keep the <u>Cargo</u> & <u>Voyage</u> Secret from the Men. Vide Abstract of Depos[iti]ons. [*page break*]

(5)

The first effected by shipp[in]g the Men after the Vessel was laden. Some surprizd at discov[erin]g them at Sea.

The 2.^d By Articles for Jam[aic]a Isle of Man & Liverpool

{When by his own Claim his Voyage was for M[onte] Christi—what did [*illegible*] Several remarkable things in managing this diff[icul]t {Point}}

First. Conceal[in]g the Bills of Lad[in]g {for M[onte] Christi} wh[ich] Ja[me]s Preston signd

Secondly. Conv[ersati]on with Henry Jones.

He knew his Design too iniquitous for honest Sailors {Conscience} {Press these—}

Why shoud he conceal if his Design was lawful.

This Circumst[ance] of **concealing** joind with the Bills of Lading signd by Preston— C[ampbell]'s own Claim & his Declar[ati]on to Buckmaster [*blank*] & to [*blank*] th[at] the Arms were for Privateers at Jam[aic]a shew th[at] he orig[inal]ly intended the Arms for Monti Christi—

His answer[in]g when haild—"that he came from St. Kitts." At that time he was will[in]g to forf[ei]t his Dutch [Pro]tection Quilibet potest renunciare &c[58] The Privateers acted in Conseq[uence] of that Renunciation.

Why shoud C[ampbell] deviate from Truth.— But from his Suspicions Shall I say G{C}unning or Guilt?

Mean[in]g of Sea Rovers

"Not going the intended Voyage a Crime" Moll. 211. {Case of the Wool Ship.}[59] Surely then &c Such Prevarication strong Evid[ence] of ~~the~~ {a} Crime here—

Depos[iti]ons. So of the Negroes being shipt in Statia &c. C[ampbell]'s Contrad[icti]ons of himself {about these Arms &c.}. Frequent—palpable &c

---

Obj[ecti]on. This Trade was very [pro]fitable—& theref[ore] C[ampbell] conceald it. Answ[er]. above 30 Vessels there then Men of War began to take Vessels the[re]

3.^d Circumst[ance]. Ships shoud be [pro]vided with [pro][per] Pa[pers] Answ[er] of Engl[ish] Lawy[ers] Moll. Dom. 449.[53] {Case in Magaz[ine]}[54] Heaven seems to make Art discover Art.

4.th Circumst[ance]. Not com[in]g to Philad[elphi]a before—His being impr[is][one]d[55] until contrad[icte]d by Burkes & other

4.th Circumst[ance].

Q[uære]. If he said they were designd for Tortola?

Men engagd in **unlawful designs** shoud have good Memories.

I call upon C[ampbell] to say what he designd to do with these Arms?   If intended for th[i?]{e} [~~illegible~~] {Spaniards}—{X} Why did he not acknowledge this at once? Why fearful of tell[in]g Truth? {Why say for the Privateers at Jamaica?} This shews they were not intended for the Span[iar]ds

==

Why shoud he carry Arms to those at peace &c.
X Why such indirect means usd as tak[in]g Danish Vessels Pretence of Water &c.

First. C[ampbell] has not denied his intend[in]g these Arms for the French—& has artfully sl[urr]d over the Quantity.

◎ This directly contrary to the Articles with the Sailors.

Well—but{!} he did not chuse to tell **every thing**: I believe it.   He says to [*blank*] that they were intended for the Privateers at Jam[aic]a   Once more I believe C[ampbell]

But how happend it th[at] the Bills of Lading <u>for **them**</u> are for M[onte] Christi—Obtaind by a <u>Trick</u> too

Or how does this agree with his Conf[essi]on to Buckm[aste]r that he designd to go to {◎}London with a Load of Sugars

== Then he must miss the Jam[aic]a Privateers [*page break*]

(6)

If your Hon[ou]r has Patience   I will make one more   Suppos[iti]on   for   this   unfortunate G[entle]man.

In his **Claim** he says the Arms were for the Ship's use.

This is expressly contrad[icte]d by the Bills of Lad[in]g & by his Declar[ati]on that they were for the Priv[at]eers at Jam[aic]a

==

Vide Acco[un]t Sales Shot too big for Guns

To sum up these Contrad[icti]ons. If his Design was lawful—he woud have declard it— But he has not declard it because one part of his words contrad[ic]ts the Rest   **therefore** his Design was unlawful—   If unlawful—   noth[in]g so but supply[in]g the French—therefore his design to supply the French

==

~~In short~~ {{**Or** to bring this arg[umen]t in}to {a narrower Compass by} make{ing} an Inductive Syllogism,}[60] he did not intend these arms for the Span[iar]ds because he told [*blank*] they were for the Priv[at]eers at Jam[aic]a

He did not intend them for the Priv[at]eers at Jam[aic]a because In his Claim he says they were for his own Use—And he did not intend them for his own use—because by the Bills of Lad[in]g they were for M[onte] Christ & by his Declar[ati]on to [*blank*] for the Priv[at]eers at Jam[aic]a

Not com[in]g to Philad[elphi]a

With Submission then do I go too far when I say they were for an unlawful purpose—or speak any thing but what y[ou]r honour thinks when I say they were for the French at Port Dauphine

26 French Books for Presents

A Brother &c

{26 French Books &c. Burke's Depos[iti]on. {Burke was a Capt[ai]n & a man of Credit.}}

Throw[in]g the Arms overboard. Quest[ion] is Whether he did it in Consequence of Capt[ai]n Spring's threats—or the Dictates of his own fear

5th Circumst[ance].

==

No reason for believ[in]g the first—for not the least Evid[ence] of threats nor one angry word **before** the Arms were thrown overboard.

Besides th[at] very Act done in Night—the <u>first</u> Night [pro]ves th[at] he expected the Arms were undiscov[ere]d by the Priv[at]eers—for it woud have been Stupid Stupidity indeed to throw them over <u>after</u> they were <u>seen</u>.

Time of threat[e]n[in]g & throw[in]g overboard very material. App[ea]rs from Quin his own Witn[ess] that he was calld Rascal after the Arms were gotten up. So from Linchey's Evid[ence]. Every th[in]g hon[ora]ble that was gainful &c X Servetur ad imum Qualis ab incepto [pro]cesserit; & sibi constet.[56]

==

A Regular plan of

{{Answ[er] of Engl[ish] Lawyers [11?][61]
Throw[in]g Papers overboard}}

First Obs[ervati]on—to be made is the {X}Agreem[en]t of this Act with C[ampbell]'s whole Cond[uc]t

The conc[ea]l[in]g these Arms— The men ignorant of the Lad[in]g   Nay the Purser sign[in]g w[ith]out knowing [*blank*] Stowd in the Bottom of the

Cunn[in]g formd [pro]secuted & concluded with the same artful consistency throughout.

Let us imagine the Action now [per]form[in]g— At midnight Every mortal at rest—but this wakeful G[entle]man begins to bustle in the hold: All Darkn[ess] but what one little Candle afforded &c Suppose one had calld out

Vessel— When Eyes of Hon[es]ty look [then?] plungd to the Bottom of the Sea   But accord[in]g to old [Pro]verb **Truth** lies at the Bottom.[62] [*page break*]

(7)

But **Truth** shall spring out of the **Earth** says David. &c.[63]

==

And these {dreaded dripping} drowned Witn[esse]s shall t[illegible] {give} silent but strong Evidence Why throw these Arms **overboard**? They are for your own Use: You are a L[ette]r of Marque: There are Priv[at]eers at Jam[aic]a in great want of Arms &c   Noth[in]g can save them &c

All these Cons[i]d[erati]ons vanish like Morn[in]g Clouds— Guilt is alarm[in]g.
    "**Thus** Conscience does make Cowards of Us All"—[64]
This Advent[ure] accomplishd   The trembl[in]g fit was succeeded by a viol[en]t Heat. He [mo[p]s?] the Deck   A Storm ensues &c   The mighty cause The Cable too short in **calm** water {Caius &c.}[65] The Arms thrown out behind   The Cable lengthend   C[ampbell] became an easy innocent man.

==

Have they removd the found[ati]on of y[ou]r hon[ou]r's Condemn[ati]on?

This cause of the utmost Consequence— The French Trade ruind   So they cant supply their Colonies with Arms—
    The Dutch will not venture as they know the very find[in]g them aboard woud condemn them
    Theref[ore] the greatest part of their Priv[at]eers fitted out by these Rebels to their Country &c. M[onte] Christi an hour's Sail from Port Dauphine that if no Vessel had appeard in Sight might have

[slipt in?].

==

If determ[inati]on ag[ains]t Us—It will be
impossible to convict of Assisting the Enemy—

Must rely on y[ou]r ho[nou]r's Human[ity] &
tenderness more than the Justice of their cause.
[*page break*]

"Nunquam in hac urbe ii, qui a Republica
defecerunt, civium jura tenuerunt.["]
{Cic. in Catal.}[66]
Scipio Nasica killd Gracchus   Ahala killd Spurius
Melius
Scæva the Slave of Q[uintus] Croto killd
Saturninus[67]

Ms (PHi-Logan)

---

[1] Lat. in possessory.

[2] Justice 208: "[In] the Admiralty of *England*, are comprehended all Affairs relating to any manner to Navigation. The Judicial Proceedings wherein are summary; . . . Remission of the Cause to the Judge *a Quo* [Lat. from which], Decree for Execution, and Sentence executed Accordingly: Besides the other Way of Proceeding by Arrest of Goods, or of Goods in other Mens Hands, and so to a *Primum Decretum* [Lat. first decree, or a provisional order] (as to the Possession)."

Clerke 63: "39. *Of the manner of Proceeding in a Petitory Suit* [i.e., a suit of ownership established by means of a petition to a court]: The person who is put in Possession of the aforesaid Goods by the Judge's Sentence, of his adversary will continue to dispute and proceed in *Petitorio*, and prove that the Goods belong to him, is obliged before he is put in real Possession of them, to give Security to answer the Plaintiff *in Petitorio*; that is, to restore the aforesaid Goods and not to embezzle them, to abide the Determination of the Court, to pay the Costs, and approve of and confirm what his Proctor does in his behalf, in case the Plaintiff gets better, and the Goods are, by the Judge's Decree, to be appraized according to their just Value by skilled and honest Persons."

[3] 1 Strange 35, *Sacheverell v. Sacheverell*, Hill. 3 Geo. (1716): "The widow produced an *affidavit* of the intestate's, made by him before a surrogate of *Doctor's Commons*, that he was married to her; which affidavit agreed with the register, and referred to it."

[4] Court of Delegates: "great court of appeal in ecclesiastical and Admiralty causes" (*OED*).

[5] 1 Strange 69, *Dominus Rex v. Wakefield*, Mich. 4 Geo. (1717): "The defendant was coroner of Litchfield, and as such took an inquisition *super visum corporis* [Lat. upon a view of the body] if a man that hanged himself, whereby he was found felo de se [Lat. felon of himself, i.e., had committed suicide]."

[6] Lat. to inform the conscience.

[7] 1 Hale, *Pleas* 12: "And although at this day it is commonly received, that the courts at the common law have no jurisdiction of felonies committed upon the high sea, yet most certainly the king's bench had usually cognizance of felonies and treasons done upon the

narrow seas, tho out of the bodies of counties." Here JD seems to mean "circa 12" (as opposed to chapter 12), because several of the following pages discuss common law jurisdiction for felonies committed on or near water.

[8] Richard I, son of Eleanor of Aquitaine (1122–1204), introduced the Laws of Oleron in England around 1190.

[9] Lat. it concerns the state that crimes do not go unpunished.

[10] Possibly *Hart &. Levy v. Unknown,* [n.d.], doc. 1:61.

[11] Lucius Sergius Catalina's 63 BC plot to overthrow the Roman republic resulted in the execution of five leading conspirators without a trial.

[12] Lat. only words.

[13] The first Valerian law (509 BC) allowed Roman citizens to resist by force any man who tried to establish a tyranny by not resigning his magistracy at the appointed time.

[14] Although there are only seven numbered pages in the present document, there are eight leaves, suggesting the possibility that JD anticipated writing more.

[15] 4 Coke, *Institutes* 142 (marginalia): "The Antiquity of the Court of Admiralty long before the reign of E. 3. in whose days some have dreamed it began."

[16] 28 Hen. 8, c. 15 (1536): "For Pirates."

[17] Chap. 22 is entitled "The Court of the Admiralty Proceeding According to the Civill Law." See 4 Coke, *Institutes* 134–47.

[18] See above, doc. 1:65, n. 8.

[19] Lat. not before a judge.

[20] Lat. the good of the people shall be the supreme law.

[21] 25 Edw. 3, stat. 5 (1350): "A Statute of Purveyors."

[22] 4 Coke, *Institutes* 143: "Et come le maistre de Niefs du dit roialme d'Englitere in absence de dits Admirals eussent este en paisible possession de conustre et juger des touts faits en la dite mier entre touts manere de gents selon les lois estatuts et les defenses, franchises and customes" [LFr. And as the master of ships of the realm of England in absence of the said Admirals having been in peaceable possession to know and to judge all deeds on the said sea among all manner of people according to the laws, statutes, and the defenses, franchises, and customs]. The page discusses the powers of the Admiral and the Court of Admiralty and that, in the absence of these, the king is the master of all ships. In this light, the king's courts would be required to follow the king's laws.

[23] Cruising: "To sail to and fro over some part of the sea without making for a particular port or landing-place, on the look out for ships, for the protection of commerce in time of war, for plunder" (*OED*).

[24] 2 Salkeld 635: "Cruising is a sufficient Overt Act of Adhering, Comforting and Aiding."

[25] 1 Hawkins 65: "Felony is said to be included in High Treason, and consequently a Pardon of Felony discharges and Indictment of High Treason, if it want the Word *Proditorie*" [Lat. treasonably].

[26] 2 Hawkins 77: "As to the arresting of Offenders by private Persons of their own Authority, permitted by Law for the Prevention of Treason or Felony only intended to be done; it seems that any one may lawfully lay hold on another, who he shall see upon the Point of committing a Treason or Felony."

Wood 299: "The *endeavor* only to commit this Crime is Treason, if it can be prov'd by open act, contrary to the common Rule, *viz. That an endeavour to commit an Offense or Trespass is not punishable.*"

[27] 1 Strange 196, *Dominus Rex v. Kinnersley and Moore,* Trin. 5 Geo. (1719). The defendants were accused of trying to extort money from Lord Sunderland by threatening to accuse him of attempted sodomy with Moore if he did not pay. The defense objected that there was no overt act to punish but "the whole court were unanimous in over-ruling all the

exceptions. And *Powys* J. quoted a case in *Godb.* Where a man was punished for an attempt to pick a pocket."

[28] Possibly the Roman legal maxim *vigilantibus et non dormientibus jura subveniunt*: Lat. the law assists those who are vigilant with their rights, and not those who sleep on their rights.

[29] 2 *General* 265–66: "And therefore if a Ship shall be on a Voyage to *America*, &c. and on her way she is attacked by a Pirate, but in the Attempt the Pirate is overcome; by the Law Marine the Vessel immediately becomes the Captors, and the Pirates may be forthwith executed without any Solemnity of Condemnation."

[30] Sibling symbol not found.

[31] Although the intended expansions of these Latin words are unclear, the meaning is most likely "take care how."

[32] Possible reference to the Battle of Camaret Bay at the French port of Brest on June 18, 1694, part of the Nine Years' War. The Anglo-Dutch fleet suffered a resounding defeat, after which the English scapegoated the duke of Marlborough, John Churchill, accusing him of sending a letter of warning to deposed monarch James II, who had fled to France.

[33] The Flour (or Provisions) Act, which received the royal assent on Feb. 15, 1757, was the only piece of parliamentary legislation passed to regulate trade during the French and Indian War. Directed specifically at the North American colonies, the bill prohibited the export of provisions such as flour, grain, bread, and salted meats to any port except Irish- or British-owned ports. See Thomas M. Truxes, *Defying Empire: Trading with the Enemy in Colonial New York* (New Haven, Conn.: Yale University Press, 2008), 68.

[34] Newcastle, 11: "That Contraband Goods, going to the Enemy, tho' the Property of a Friend, may be taken as Prize; because supplying the Enemy, with what enables him better to carry on the War, is a Departure from Neutrality."

[35] 2 *General* 235–36: "If part of the Cargo of a Ship taken by a Privateer be prohibited Goods, and the other part not prohibited . . . the Goods prohibited only shall be adjudged Prize . . . : But if a Ship be wholly laden with contraband Goods, both the Ship and Goods may be Prize . . . . And if any such Ship shall be attacked in order to be examined, on their refusing to submit, they may be assaulted; and if the Persons on board to not surrender themselves, the Ships may be entered by Force, and the Persons resisting be slain."

Newcastle, 19: "The Ships could not be intitles to Costs, because the Cargoes, or Part of them, being lawful Prize, the Ships were rightly brought in."

It is unclear to what JD is referring to in *Lex Merc.*, 29–30, which is in a section entitled, "Weights for Monies, and their correspondence for most places of Traffique."

Justice 472: "If Part of a Cargo is taken by a Privateer be prohibited Goods, and the other Part be not prohibited, but such as according to the Necessity of the War shall be so deemed, that may draw on a consequential Condemnation of the Ship as well as Lading . . . : [I]f any Privateer willfully commits any Spoil on the Ships of Friends or Neuters, or on the Ships of their Fellow Subjects, according as the Circumstances of the Crime are more or less heinous, he is liable to be punished by Death or otherwise, and the Ship to be forfeited."

[36] For Carthew, see doc. 1:63, n. 42; for Ventris, see doc. 1:62, n. 29.

[37] It is unclear to what JD is referring. The citation suggests 1 Hale, *Pleas* 65, which discusses oaths of fidelity within a chapter on high treason.

Wood 120: "If the Law forbids, either in general to all Persons, or in particular some sort of Persons, some kind of Agreements, a certain Commerce, or makes any other Prohibition whatsoever, everything done contrary to these Prohibitions, shall either be annull'd or restrain'd, according to the nature of the Prohibition, and the Violation of it, altho' the Law does not expressly declare the Nullity, and leaves the other Penalties undtermin'd."

[38] Sir Henry Penrice (d. 1752) served as a judge of the Admiralty Court, 1715–51.

[39] See block quote below on p. 350.

[40] 2 Coke, *Institutes* 51: "If any injury, robbery, felony, or other offence be done upon the high Sea, *Lex terrae* [Lat. the law of the land] extendeth not to it, therefore the Admiral hath conusance thereof, and may proceed according to the marine Law by imprisonment of the body, and other proceedings, as have been allowed by the Laws of the Realm."

[41] See above, doc. 1:65, n. 7.

JD most likely means Carthew 31–32, *Beak v. Tyrell*, Pasch. 1 W & M, B.R. (1688). See doc. 1:63, n. 42.

[42] 12 *Modern* 134, *King v. Broom*, Trin. 9 W. 3, B.R. (1697). Broom was authorized "under *African* Company (who, by the King's Letters Patent, had Orders to take the Ships of Enemies, and dispose of them as they pleased)." He took a French ship "into a River beyond Sea" and sold it and its goods and kept the proceeds. The king's proctor then successfully exhibited a libel against him in the Admiralty Court for embezzlement. Broom tried to transfer the case to the King's Bench but the Admiralty Court denied his request because the crime originated on the high seas and thus was under its jurisdiction. See also above, doc. 1:58.

[43] Wood 70: "A *Subject* is he that is under the *Power* and *Protection* of the Prince. And is either so by *Birth*, which Relation he can never put off, no not by swearing Allegiance to another Prince; or by *Residency* under such a Prince, which is temporary only, and ceases when le leaves that Prince's Territories."

[44] Treaty of Westminster (1674) ended the Third Dutch-Anglo War.

[45] Specifically c. 4, "None Shall be Condemned Upon Suggestion Without Lawful Presentment."

[46] It is possible that JD means 12 *Modern* 134–35. See above, n. 41.

[47] Galley: "A low flat-built sea-going vessel with one deck, propelled by sails and oars, formerly in common use in the Mediterranean" (*OED*).

[48] Lat. intent makes the deed. It seems JD is working from the maxim, "actus non facit reum, nisi mens sit rea" [Lat. An act does not make (the doer of it) guilty, unless the mind be guilty].

[49] Lat. "your intention gives character to your work." The complete phrase is "affectio tua nomen imponit operi tuo."

[50] Lat. he fixed by law.

[51] 1 Tim. 1:8: "But we know that the law is good, if a man use it lawfully."

[52] Sir Peter Warren (1703–1752) was a naval officer who served at the failed siege of St. Augustine, Fla., in 1740, and the successful siege of Louisbourg, Canada, in 1745. His defeat of a French squadron off Cape Ortegal, Spain, in May 1747 earned him promotion to vice admiral.

[53] See doc. 1:64, n. 5, above.

Justice 449: "He [the master of the ship] must not carry any Counterfeit Cocquets [customs seals], or other fictitious and colourable [fraudulent] Ship-Papers, to involve the Goods of the Innocent with the Nocent [guilty]."

---

[54] See pp. 349–50 and doc. 1:65, p. 339, above.

[55] Or impr[es][se]d.

[56] Lat. "Let it be preserved to the last such as it set out at the beginning, and be consistent with itself." Hor. *Ars P.* 126–27.

[57] Matt. 5:51: "Neither do men light a candle, and put it under a bushel, but on a candlestick; and it giveth light unto all that are in the house."

[58] Lat. "Any one may renounce a law introduced for his own benefit. To this rule there are some exceptions." The complete phrase is: *Quilibet potest renunciare juri pro se inducto.*

[59] It is possible JD means Justice 211. The long list provided of matters under the Admiralty's jurisdiction includes the "Exportation of Goods to prohibited Ports; or the Places not designed." It is unclear what the "Case of the Wool Ship" is.

[60] "And all teaching is based on what is already known, as we have stated in the *Analytics*; some teaching proceeds by induction and some by syllogism. Now, induction is the starting point for knowledge, of the universal as well as the particular, while syllogism proceeds *from* universals. Consequently, there are starting-points or principles from which a syllogism proceeds and which are themselves not arrived at by a syllogism. It is, therefore, induction that attains them. Accordingly, scientific knowledge is a capacity for demonstration and has, in addition, all the other qualities we have specified in the *Analytics*. When a man believes something in the way there specified, and when the starting points or principles on which his beliefs rest are known to him, then he had scientific knowledge; unless he knows the starting point or principles better than the conclusion, he will have scientific knowledge only incidentally." Arist. *EN*, VI.3, 27–35, trans. Oswald.

[61] See n. 33, above.

[62] "Truth lies at the bottom of a well." This proverb comes from a phrase attributed to Democritus: "We know nothing certainly, for truth lies in the deep." See *Oxford Dictionary of Proverbs*, ed. Jennifer Speake, 6th ed. (Oxford: Oxford University Press, 2015), 327.

[63] Ps. 85:11: "Truth shall spring out of the earth; and righteousness shall look down from heaven."

[64] *Hamlet*, 3.1.

[65] Caius or Gaius a Latin prenom for many Roman leaders and the name of characters in several Shakespearean plays. It is unknown which JD intended.

[66] Lat. "But in this city those who have rebelled against the republic have never had the rights of citizens." Cic. *Cat.* 1.11.28.

[67] Publius Cornelius Scipio Nasica Serapio (c. 183–132 BC) was a consul of the Roman Republic in 138 BC. He assassinated Tiberius Gracchus during the 133 BC elections. Gaius Servillus Ahala was a 5th c. Roman politician to whom Roman writers like Cincius Alimentus attributed the murder of Spurius Maelius. Spurius Maelius (d. 439 BC) was a wealthy Roman plebeian whose attempt to buy popular support and make himself king led to his murder. As Cicero writes, "Indeed, if freedom was bestowed upon Scæva, Quintus Croto's slave who killed Lucius Saturninus, what reward would have been fittingly bestowed upon a Roman knight?" Cicero, *Oratio Pro C. Rabirio Perduellionis Reo*, 31.

****

68
Interrogatories in the Vice Admiralty Court on Behalf of
Captain John Macpherson, et al., [1758]

According to shipping news in the *Pennsylvania Gazette*, the snow *Desire*, a 35-ton vessel, was captured on February 23, 1758, by French privateers on her journey from Surinam to Rhode Island. She was then retaken on February 26 by the English privateer *Britannia*, piloted by Captain John Macpherson. The captain's recent success was also newsworthy: after his capture of the *Desire*, he was reported to have taken six other vessels of various sorts before March 23.[1]

In the case for which these interrogatories were written, Macpherson was bringing suit against the owners of the *Desire*, Oswell Eve and Samuel Oldman of Philadelphia, to obtain the prize from the French subjects. In the Admiralty Court, after the claimant, or libellant, filed his complaint, or libel, the second step was the questioning of the witnesses, which is what JD has prepared here. The ship registers for the Port of Philadelphia reveal that Macpherson prevailed.[2]

Interrogatories to be administred to Witnesses to be producd sworn & examined in the Court of Vice Admiralty held for the Province of Pennsylvania on the part of {John McPherson}[3] in behalf of himself & others the Owners of the Private Ship of War called the {Britiannia}[4] and the Company belonging to the said ship against one Snow called the Desire with the{i}r Guns Apparel Tackle & Furniture of the same Snow— and the Cargo & Lading of the same Snow—

Interrogatory 1st   Do you know the Snow called the Desire [*blank*] now residing at Anchor in the Port of Philadelphia? Did you ever sail in the said Snow [*blank*]? If Yea Were You in any office or employment on board the said Snow [*blank*] at the time of your sailing in her what was that Office or Employment? Was the said snow [*blank*] at any time when You were sailing in her taken as Prize by any English Privateer Ship or Vessel? About what time & where was such Caption? What was the said Privateer Ship or Vessel called & who was the Captain or Commander of that Privateer{&c} at the time the said Snow did sail from before the time of her Caption & Whither was She at that time bound? What King or Prince State or Potentate[5] were the [*page break*] Commander[6] & Mariners that navigated the said Snow [*blank*] at the time of her Caption the Subjects of? Was the said Snow [*blank*] at the time of her Caption laden with any Goods Wares or Merchandizes?

{And of what sort they were?} Declare the Truth of your Knowledge or belief therein fully & at large with the Reasons of your Belief—

Interrogatory 2.^d   Who was or were the Owner or Owners of the said Snow at the time of her said Caption? What King or Prince State or Polentate was or were such Owner or Owners the Subjects of at the time of the said Caption of the said Snow [*blank*] {*}? Where did such Owner or Owners of the said Snow at the time of such Caption reside or dwell? {θ} [*in left margin*:] {θ How d{d}id such Owner or Owners obtain possession or property of the said Snow ~~Whether~~ by Capture ~~or by Purchase~~? If ~~by Capture~~ {Yea then about what time & where was such Capture made? What was the {French} Privateer Ship or Vessel that made the said Capture calld? And who was the Captain of the said Privateer Ship or Vessel at the time of the said Caption? How long did the said Snow remain in the possession of the French Captors before She [*cont. on next page*:] She was retaken by the English? ^O ~~If the Owner or Owners~~ [*in left margin*:] {Was any Alteration or Addition made in {or} to the Tackle Apparel or Furniture of the said Snow after She was taken by the French & before She was retain by the English & what such Alteration or Addition was?} What person or persons was or were Owner or Owners of the said Goods Wares or Merchandizes at the time of the Caption of them as aforesaid? What King or Prince State or Potentate was or were such Owner or Owners of the said Goods wares or Merchandizes the Subjects of at the time of the same Caption? Were did such Owner or Owners of the same Goods Wares or Merchandizes at the time of such Caption reside or dwell? {*} [*on next page*:] {* Did the Owner or Owners of the said Goods Wares or Merchandizes obtain possession or Property of the same by Capture? If Yea then when & how they were taken & Whether in the said Snow and how long they were in the Possession or the French Captors before they were taken?} Declare the Truth of your Knowledge or Belief therein fully & at large with the Reasons of your belief—

Interrogatory 3.^d   Do You know of any other matter or thing or have You heard or can You say any thing touching the matters in question that may tend to the Benefit or Advantage of the Libellants in this Cause besides what You have been before interrogated unto? Declare the same fully & at large as if You had been thereunto particularly interrogated.

John Dickinson Proctor for the Libellants.

---

[1] *PG*, May 4, 1758.

[2] See "Ship Registers for the Port of Philadelphia, 1726–1775," *PMHB* 26, no. 1 (1902): 126–43, at 136. The *Providence Gaz.* reported the loss on Jan. 14, 1764.

[3] Capt. John Macpherson (1726–1792), born in Edinburgh, Scotland, became a captain in 1750 and profited significantly as a privateer during the Seven Years' War. With his fortune he acquired property in Philadelphia and built Mount Pleasant in 1761. He became known among merchants as the publisher of the first trade magazine, the *Philadelphia Price Current*, and among the Philadelphia elite for his science experiments and lectures on natural philosophy. His relationship with JD was varied and colorful. His son, John Macpherson, Jr., (1754–1775) became JD's law clerk and in 1767 copied the *Farmer's Letters*. The senior Macpherson was an admirer of JD's, even publishing a poem in tribute to him, until he apparently had a bout with mental illness in 1771, at which time he wrote bitter invectives against JD from his forced confinement, for which he blamed JD. See John Macpherson's poem to JD as the Farmer in *PG*, April 28, 1768, signed "A Mariner," in Volume 4 of the present edition; *Macpherson's Letters &c.* (Philadelphia: W. Evitt, 1770); *A Pennsylvania Sailor's Letters, alias the Farmer's Fall* (Philadelphia: R. Bell, 1771), both included in Volume 5 of the present edition.

[4] As of 1757, the *Britannia* had ten carriage guns and several swivels mounted, and carried a crew of forty men. See *PG*, July 28, 1757.

[5] Potentate: "A powerful city, state, or institution" (*OED*).

[6] Capt. Rufus Hopkins (1727–1812) of Providence, R.I., was the son of Gov. Stephen Hopkins. In addition to his maritime duties, he was a jurist, politician, and founder of Hope Furnace, the iron forge that cast ammunition for the Continental Army during the Revolution. See Ellery Bicknell Crane, *Historic Homes and Institutions and Genealogical and Personal Memoirs of Worcester County, Massachusetts.* 4 vols. (New York: Lewis Publishing Co., 1907), 1:419–20.

69
To Robert McKean, 175[8]

This is the only known letter JD drafted in Latin; its racy content may have been his impetus for using a language few would have known. A translation with annotation is offered immediately below.

Vir Amate,

Me multis negotiis occupatum silere, noverit mirandum; sed cui causæ ditior, quod obliviscaris Amici tui amantissimi. Dulce est Absentiam relevare, absentiam reminiscendo; & absentibus quid magis placet quam reminisci?

Non parvi honoris mihi est, quod in ~~strepite~~ deliciarum {diversitate}, vociferatione forensi & incantationibus incantantibus, horam tibique amicitiæque seponar—

Exemplum moveat; & B— a deabus, Nymphisque Rasitoniis relictis, magnanime recedens, dic mihi quodvivis & valeas. Onus crudele si hoc tibi {si} videatur, {Indicam tabulam, & Loquacitatulam otiosissimam relinquere} te [*illegible*] ignoscendum habebo, quamvis de Liliis Rosisque, pectoribus niveis oculisque nigris {et cæteris,} nil nisi dicas: Cum enim epistola tua ad meas manus perveniat, hoc erit pro certo, ~~quod~~ {jam} jam dubitandum, tenor esse provectum,

"Quo Numa devenit & Ancus."

Magno me gaudio afficiat, te pro desideris locatum esse. Novistine fratrem tuum mecum, sodalibusque aliis in animo habere, te, cum erit annus formosissimus, visere. Hoc volo, hoc precor, quocumque tempore te videam, ~~t[u?]~~ te videam beatum: Quod in sano corpore, mente sana fruaris, & Fortuna et Puellæ, dulci decorique arrideant.

Habes neminem tui observantissimum

vel amantissimum quam [*in left margin:*] dum tempus pretiosum ad amicum scribendo consumo. [*page break*]

Written to Rob[er]t McKean[1] 1758—
3 P. Will. 464. Sid. 269— Cro Car. 343.[2]

Beloved Man,

Busy with many tasks, I have been surprisingly quiet; but I have been productive for this reason, as you have forgotten your most beloved friend. It is sweet to uncover Absence, by remembering absence; and what is more pleasant than remembering those absent?

It is no small honor for me that among the ~~crowd~~ {variety} of delights, the clamor of the courts, and other enchanting charms, I may set aside some time for you and our friendship—

Let me give an example; even B___ retiring nobly among the goddesses, nymphs and the rest of the shaved-heads,[3] tell me how you live and how well you may be. If this should seem to you a cruel burden, you may ignore this request and my leisurely chatter, and I will forgive you, unless you say nothing about the Lilies and Roses, pale breasts and dark eyes {and other things}: For when your letter shall reach my hands, this, ~~which is~~ now doubtful, will be for certain: that the course was taken,

"Where Numa and Ancus have already gone."[4]

It be a great delight for me for you to be occupied according to your own wishes. Did you know that your brother wished to visit you, with me and some of his other companions, when the weather would be pleasant. I desire this, I pray this, that I may see you sometime, and that I may see you prosperous: That you may enjoy a healthy body, healthy mind, and that Fortune and Girls may smile upon sweet and decorous [you].

You have no one so attentive

or so loving of you than [*in left margin:*] when I spend precious time writing to my friend.

ALS (PPL-JDFP)

---

[1] Robert McKean (1732–1767) was the younger brother of Thomas McKean.

[2] These citations do not appear to be related to the letter.

3 Peere 464 is a page from the report on *Dominus Rex v. Thomam Burridge*, Mich. 9 Geo. 2, B.R. (1735), a case in which Burridge was accused of helping a felon escape from prison.

It is unclear to what JD is specifically referring. Siderfin 269 reports on three cases, *Plaier v. Pettit, Clark v. Mullineaux*, and *Lumbuty & sa Feme v. Tailor*, all from Trin. 17 Car. 2, B.R. (1665).

3 Croke 343 reports on two cases: *Brett v. Reed*, Hill. 9 Car. 1, B.R. (1633), a case concerning a debt for unpaid rent, and *Lord Hastings v. Sir Archibald Douglass*, Trin. 8 Car. 1, B.R. (1632), a case concerning stolen jewels.

[3] A reference to the common belief that prostitutes in Corinth had shaved heads, sometimes based on 1 Cor. 11:5: "But every woman that prayeth or prophesieth with her head uncovered dishonoureth her head: for that is even all one as if she were shaven."

[4] The quotation is: "Ire tamen restat, Numa quo devenit et Ancus." Q. Horatii Flacci, *Ep. Lib.* 1.6.27. Numa Pompilius (753–637 BC) was the second king of Rome and his grandson, Ancus Marcius (c. 677–617 BC), was the fourth king of Rome. Addressed to Horace's (65–8 BC) patron Numicius, the letter prescribes a formula for happiness. The preceding lines strike a satirical note as they encourage the reader to pursue worldly ambitions, while reminding him that we all go to the grave eventually. Horace ultimately concludes that the only thing worth pursuing is virtue.

APPENDIX

Secondary Works on John Dickinson

This chronological bibliography contains known scholarly works on JD, including books, book chapters, essays in collections, articles, and PhD theses. It excludes MA theses, dictionary and encyclopedia entries, documentary collections, children's literature, and visual media.

1800s

Armor, William C. "John Dickinson." In *Lives of the Governors of Pennsylvania, with the Incidental History of the State, from 1609 to 1872*, 234–50. Philadelphia: James K. Simon, 1872.

Dickinson, Wharton. "John Dickinson, LL.D: the Great Colonial Essayist." *Magazine of American History* 10 (1883): 223–34.

Cook, Frank Gaylord. "John Dickinson." *Atlantic Monthly* 65, no. 388 (1890): 70–83.

Moore, George H. *Suum Cuique: John Dickinson, the Author of the Declaration on Taking Up Arms in 1775*. New York: Printed for the author, 1890.

Stillé, Charles J. *The Life and Times of John Dickinson, 1732–1808*. Philadelphia: Historical Society of Pennsylvania, 1891.

Campbell, John H. "John Dickinson, 1771." In *History of the Friendly Sons of St. Patrick and of the Hibernian Society for the Relief of Emigrants from Ireland*, 143. Philadelphia: Hibernian Society, 1892.

1900s–1920s

Richards, Robert H. *The Life and Character of John Dickinson*. Wilmington, Del.: Historical Society of Delaware, 1901.

———. "The Life and Character of John Dickinson." *Papers of the Historical Society of Delaware* 30 (1901): 3–26.

Himes, Charles F. "The True John Dickinson: A Paper Read February 23, 1912, before The Hamilton Library Association, Carlisle, Pa." Carlisle, Pa.: Historical Society of Cumberland Co., 1912.

Sharpless, Isaac. "John Dickinson." In *Political Leaders of Provincial Pennsylvania*, 224–43. New York: Macmillan Co., 1919.

Shilling, D.C. "John Dickinson, Statesman and Patriot." *The Historical Outlook* 11 (1920): 174–76.

1930s

Frank, Will P. "John Dickinson, Who Refused to Sign." *Dickinson Alumnus* 9, no. 4 (1932): 11–15.

Snyder, Edmund S. "A Glimpse of John Dickinson." *Dickinson Alumnus* 10, no. 2 (1932): 22–24.

Dickinson, John. "The Political Thought of John Dickinson." *Dickinson Law Review* 39 (1934): 1–14.

Powell, John H. "John Dickinson and the Constitution." *PMHB* 60, no. 1 (1936): 1–14.

———. "John Dickinson: Character of a Revolutionist." *Friends in Wilmington, 1738–1938*. Wilmington, Del., 1938, 87–95.

———. "John Dickinson, Penman of the American Revolution," PhD diss., University of Iowa, 1938.

1940s

Powell, John H. "Speech of John Dickinson Opposing Independence, 1 July, 1776." *PMHB* 65, no. 4 (1941): 458–81.

Jensen, Merrill. "The Dickinson Draft of the Confederation." In *The Articles of Confederation: An Interpretation of the Social-Constitutional History of the American Revolution, 1774–1781*. Madison, Wis.: University of Wisconsin Press, 1940.

Hooker, Richard J. "John Dickinson on Church and State." *AL* 16, no. 2 (1944): 82–98.

Powell, John H. "John Dickinson, President of the Delaware State, 1781–1782." *DH* (1945): 1:1–54; (1946): 111–33.

1950s

Powell, John H. "The Debate on American Independence, July 1, 1776." *Delaware Notes* (1950): 37–62.

DeValinger, Leon, Jr. "John Dickinson's Handwriting." *Autograph Collectors' Journal* 3, no. 4 (1951): 2–6.

———. *The John Dickinson Mansion*. [Dover, Del.?: Delaware State Museum, 1953?].

Soler, William G. "Some Important Influences upon John Dickinson's Thought: Chiefly Bacon, Locke, and Pope." PhD diss., Temple University, 1953.

———. "John Dickinson's 'Ode, on the French Revolution.'" *AL* 25, no. 3 (1953): 287–92.

———. "A Reattribution: John Dickinson's Authorship of the Pamphlet 'A Caution,' 1798." *PMHB* 77, no. 1 (1953): 24–31.

Powell, John H. *The House on Jones Neck: The Dickinson Mansion*. Dover, Del.: Friends of the John Dickinson Mansion, 1954.

Soler, William G. "John Dickinson's Attitude Toward the French, 1797–1801." *DH* 6, no. 4 (1955): 294–98.

———. "A Note on John Dickinson's Pamphlet, 'A Caution.'" *PMHB* 79, no. 1 (1955): 100–01.

Gummere, Richard M. "John Dickinson, the Classical Penman of the Revolution." *The Classical Journal* 52, no. 2 (1956): 81–88.

Tolles, Frederick B. "John Dickinson and the Quakers." In *"John and Mary's College": The Boyd Lee Spahr Lectures In Americana 1951–1956*, 67–88. Westwood, N.J.: Fleming H. Revell Co., 1956.

Tunnell, James Miller, Jr. "John Dickinson and the Federal Constitution." In *"John and Mary's College": The Boyd Lee Spahr Lectures In Americana 1951–1956*, 60–66. Westwood, N.J.: Fleming H. Revell Co., 1956.

Rodney, Richard S. "John Dickinson: An Address." Dover, Del.: s.n., 1958.

Colbourn, H. Trevor. "John Dickinson, Historical Revolutionary." *PMHB* 86, nos. 3 & 4 (1959): 271–92; 417–53.

Jacobson, David L. "John Dickinson and Joseph Galloway, 1764–1776: A Study in Contrasts." PhD diss., Princeton University, 1959.

1960s

Powell, John H. "John Dickinson as President of Pennsylvania." *PH* 28, no. 3 (1961): 254–67.

Colbourn, H. Trevor. "A Pennsylvania Farmer at the Court of King George: John Dickinson's London Letters, 1754–1756." *PMHB* 86, no. 3 (1962): 241–86.

———. "A Pennsylvania Farmer at the Court of King George: John Dickinson's London Letters, 1754–1756." *PMHB* 86, no. 4 (1962): 417–53.

Jacobson, David L. "John Dickinson's Fight Against Royal Government, 1764." *WMQ* 19, no. 1 (1962): 64–85.

Colbourn, H. Trevor. "The Historical Perspective of John Dickinson." In *Early Dickinsoniana: The Boyd Lee Spahr Lectures In Americana 1957–1961*, 3–37. Harrisburg: Telegraph Press, 1961.

Powell, John H. "'A Certain Great Fortune and Piddling Genius.'" In *Early Dickinsoniana: The Boyd Lee Spahr Lectures In Americana 1957–1961*, 41–72. Harrisburg: Telegraph Press, 1961.

Knollenberg, Bernhard. "John Dickinson vs. John Adams: 1774–1776." *PAPS* 107, no. 2 (1963): 138–44.

Jacobson, David L. "The Puzzle of 'Pacificus.'" *PH* 31, no. 4 (1964): 406–18.

———. *John Dickinson and the Revolution in Pennsylvania, 1764–1776.* Berkeley: University of California Press, 1965.

Wolf, Edwin, 2nd. "The Authorship of the 1774 Address to the King Restudied." *WMQ* 22, no. 2 (1965): 189–224.

———. *John Dickinson: Forgotten Patriot.* [Wilmington, Del.: Friends of the John Dickinson Mansion, 1967].

Kaestle, Carl F. "The Public Reaction to John Dickinson's Farmer's Letters." *Proceedings of the American Antiquarian Society* 78 (1968): 323–59.

1970s

Power, M. Susan. "John Dickinson After 1776: The Fabius Letters." *Modern Age* 16, no. 4 (1972): 387–97.

———. "John Dickinson: Freedom, Protest, and Change." *Susquehanna Studies* 9, no. 2 (1972): 99–121.

Johannesen, Stanley K. "Constitution and Empire in the Life and Thought of John Dickinson." PhD diss., University of Missouri, 1973.

Fredman, Lionel E. *John Dickinson: American Revolutionary Statesman.* Charlotteville, N.Y.: SamHar Press, 1974.

Johannesen, Stanley K. "John Dickinson and the American Revolution." *Historical Reflections/Réflexions Historiques* 2, no. 1 (1975): 29–49.

Aldridge, A. Owen. "Paine and Dickinson." *EAL* 11, no. 2 (1976): 125–38.

Flower, Milton E. "John Dickinson: Delawarian." *DH* 17, no. 1 (1976): 12–20.

Holder, Jean. "The Historical Misrepresentation of John Dickinson." *Journal of Historical Studies* 1, no. 2 (1976): 1–20.

Slotten, Martha Calvert. "John Dickinson on Independence, July 25, 1776." *Manuscripts* 28, no. 3 (1976): 188–94.

Bradford, M.E. "A Better Guide than Reason: The Politics of John Dickinson." *Modern Age* 21, no. 1 (1977): 39–49.

Marambaud, Pierre. "Dickinson's *Letters from a Farmer in Pennsylvania* as Political Discourse: Ideology, Imagery, and Rhetoric." *EAL* 12, no. 1 (1977): 63–72.

1980s

The Centinel: Warnings of a Revolution, edited by Elizabeth I. Nybakken. Newark, Del.: University of Delaware Press, 1980.

Hynes, Sandra Sarkela. "The Political Rhetoric of John Dickinson, 1764–1776." PhD diss., University of Massachusetts, 1982.

Flower, Milton E. *John Dickinson, Conservative Revolutionary*. Charlottesville, Va.: University Press of Virginia, 1983.

Hutson, James H. "John Dickinson at the Federal Constitutional Convention." *WMQ* 40, no. 2 (1983): 256–82.

Power, M. Susan. *Before the Convention: Religion and the Founders*. Lanham, Md.: University Press of America, 1984.

DeValinger, Leon, Jr. "John Dickinson and the Federal Constitution." *DH* 22, no. 4 (1987): 299–308.

Wright, Robert K., Jr., and Morris J. MacGregor, Jr. "John Dickinson." In *Soldier-Statesmen of the Constitution*, 82–84. Washington, DC: Center of Military History, 1987.

McDonald, Forrest. "John Dickinson and the Constitution." *Requiem: Variations on Eighteenth-Century Themes*, 85–103. Lawrence, Kans.: University Press of Kansas, 1988.

McDonald, Forrest, and Ellen Shapiro McDonald. "John Dickinson, Founding Father." *DH* 23, no. 1 (1988): 24–38.

Bastian, Peter. "'To Secure the Approbation of the Worthy': The Political Journey of John Dickinson." *Australasian Journal of American Studies* 8, no. 1 (1989): 1–11.

1990s

Browne, Stephen H. "The Pastoral Voice in John Dickinson's *First Letter from a Farmer in Pennsylvania*." *Quarterly Journal of Speech* 76, no. 1 (1990): 46–57.

Bell, Robert R. "Profile 2: John Dickinson (1732–1808)." In *The Philadelphia Lawyer: A History, 1735–1945*, 49–54. Selinsgrove, Pa.: Susquehanna University Press, 1992.

Lawson, Karol Ann Peard. "Charles Willson Peale's *John Dickinson*: An American Landscape as Political Allegory." *PAPS* 136, no. 4 (1992): 455–86.

Willson, John. *John Dickinson: The Letters of Fabius*. Hillsdale, Mich.: Hillsdale College Press, 1992.

Bradford, M.E. "Delaware: John Dickinson." In *Founding Fathers: Brief Lives of the Framers of the United States Constitution*, 99–104. 2nd ed. Lawrence, Kans.: University Press of Kansas, 1994.

Ahern, Gregory Stephen. "'Experience Must Be Our Only Guide': John Dickinson and the Spirit of American Republicanism." PhD diss., Catholic University of America, 1997.

Bell, Whitfield J., Jr. "John Dickinson (1732–1808): American Society: 19 January 1768." In *Patriot-Improvers: Biographical Sketches of Members of the American Philosophical Society*. Vol. 1, 383–90. Philadelphia: American Philosophical Society, 1997.

Ahern, Gregory Stephen. "The Spirit of American Constitutionalism: John Dickinson's Fabius Letters." *Humanitas* 11, no. 2 (1998): 57–76.

Heisey, Daniel J. *Marginal Notes: Essays Here and There*. Carlisle, Pa.: New Loudon Press, 1999.

2000s

Natelson, Robert G. "The Constitutional Contributions of John Dickinson." *Penn State Law Review* 108, no. 2 (2003): 415–77.

Harris, Matthew L. "'Experience Must Be Our Guide': John Dickinson and the Origins of American Federalism, 1754–1808." PhD diss., Syracuse University, 2004.

Morton, Joseph C. "John Dickinson (1732–1808)." In *Shapers of the Constitutional Convention of 1787: A Biographical Dictionary*, 66–82. Westport, Conn.: Greenwood Press, 2006.

Calvert, Jane E. "America's Forgotten Founder: John Dickinson and the American Revolution." *History Compass* 5, no. 3 (2007): 1002–12.

———. "Liberty without Tumult: Understanding the Politics of John Dickinson." *PMHB* 131, no. 3 (2007): 233–62.

Holland, Randy J. and Eric Stockdale. "American Students at Middle Temple." *Middle Temple Lawyers and the American Revolution*, 39–70. Eagan, Minn.: Thomson West, 2007.

Howard, Hugh. "John Dickinson's Poplar Hall." In *Houses of the Founding Fathers: The Men Who Made America and the Way They Lived*, 24–35. New York: Artisan, 2007.

Lubert, Howard L. "John Dickinson (1732–1808)." In *America's Forgotten Founders*, edited by Gary L. Gregg II and Mark David Hall, 90–101. Louisville: Butler Books, 2008.

Calvert, Jane E. *Quaker Constitutionalism and the Political Thought of John Dickinson*. New York: Cambridge University Press, 2009.

2010s

Calvert, Jane E. "'The Character of an Author': A Note on the Attribution and Misattribution of the Writings of John Dickinson." *Papers of the Bibliographical Society of America* 104, no. 3 (2010): 341–46.

———. "Letter to Farmers in Pennsylvania: John Dickinson Writes to the Paxton Boys." *PMHB* 136, no. 4 (2012): 475–77.

Bastian, Peter. "Forgotten Founder: Revolutionary Memory and John Dickinson's Reputation." In *Remembering the Revolution: Memory, History, and Nation Making from Independence to the Civil War*, edited by Michael A. McDonnell et al., 58–74. Amherst, Mass.: University of Massachusetts Press, 2013.

Vile, John R. "John Dickinson (1732–1808): Delaware." In *The Men Who Made the Constitution: Lives of the Delegates to the Constitutional Convention of 1787*, 48–60. Plymouth, UK: Scarecrow Press, 2013.

Calvert, Jane E. "The 'Documentary Democracy' of the Writings of John Dickinson, Then and Now." *Scholarly Editing* 34 (2013), http://www.scholarlyediting.org/2013/essays/essay.calvert.html.

Murchison, William P. *The Cost of Liberty: The Life of John Dickinson.* Wilmington, Del.: ISI Books, 2013.

Calvert, Jane E. "John Dickinson's Quaker Contributions to the Creation of the American Republic." In *Faith and the Founders of the American Republic*, edited by Daniel L. Dreisbach and Mark David Hall, 277–304. New York: Oxford University Press, 2014.

———. "Myth-Making and Myth-Breaking in the Historiography on John Dickinson." *Journal of the Early Republic* 34, no. 3 (2014): 467–80.

Hutchins, Zachary McLeod. "The Slave Narrative and the Stamp Act, or Letters from Two American Farmers in Pennsylvania." *EAL* 50, no. 3 (2015): 645–80.

McWilliams, Susan. "Finding Foundings: The Case of Fabius." *Polity* 47, no. 4, Resistance to Domination (2015): 542–49.

Calvert, Jane E. "An Expansive Conception of Rights: The Quakerly Abolitionism of John Dickinson." In *"When in the Course of Human Events": 1776 at Home, Abroad, and in American Memory*, edited by Will R. Jordan, 21–54. Macon, Ga.: Mercer University Press, 2018.

Delaware's John Dickinson: The Constant Watchman of Liberty, edited by John Sweeney. Dover, Del.: Friends of the John Dickinson Mansion, 2018.

Calvert, Jane E. "The Friendly Jurisprudence and Early Feminism of John Dickinson." In *Great Christian Jurists in American History*, edited by Daniel L. Dreisbach and Mark David Hall, 72–89. New York: Cambridge University Press, 2019.

INDEX

Page numbers in roman type indicate primary documents and spans of entire documents, including editorial notes. Page numbers in *italic* type indicate headnotes and endnotes. When a page contains items in both the primary document and the editorial apparatus, the number is in roman type. Page numbers in **bold** type indicate person identifications. Information on legislation and court cases, including JD's, follow this portion of the index, and are cross-referenced in **bold**. The Appendix, "Secondary Works on John Dickinson," has not been included in the index.

A

Abhorrers, 186, *193*

Act of Settlement (1751). *See*
Legislation: Acts of Parliament: 24
Geo. 2 c. 24

Adams, John, xxv, xxxv–xxxvi

Adams Papers, xxiv

Admiralty Courts: in the Bahamas,
316; *Beaux Enfants*, 298–302;
Broom's Case, 294–95, *332*; *John
Campbell v. The Owners of The
Spry*, 335–61; cases in, xxxiv, lii–
liii; in the East Indies, *359*;
establishment of, lii, *293*, 346–47,
358; foreign, *294*, 295, *297*, *308*,
319; judges of, lv, 306, *309*, 323–24,
331–32, 339, 345, 347, 350, *357–58*,
360; jurisdiction of, lii, 295, *299*,
324, 327–*35*, 339, *341–43*, 345–47,
349–50, *357*, *360–61*; *Levy & Hart
v. Unknown*, 305–11; libels in, liii,
297, 298–335, 342, *360*, 362–64;
lords of, *73*, 89, *301*, *334*; in New
England, *309*; Office of, *132*; in
Pennsylvania, xxxiv, lv–lvi, lii, *293*,
298–99, 311–12, *318*, 324, 327–30,
335–36, 339, *341–43*, 345–47, 349–
50, *362–64*; process in, liii, *298*,
306–07, *311*, 324, 346, *362*, *357*;
Purviance et al. v. Angus, lvi; and
religion, 315, *318*, 325; seal of, *297*,
319; *Spring & Kemp v. Ospray &
Elizabeth*, 311–35; *Talbot qui tam
&c. v. the Commanders and Owners
of Three Brigs*, lv. *See also* flag-of-
truce trade; punishments and
penalties

Æsop's *Fables*, 60, *62*, *158*, 229, *232*

Acuna, Diego Serventio de, *333*

Africa, 294

African Company, 294, *360*

afterlife, 2, 17, 56, 88, *209*. *See also*
eternity; heaven and hell

agriculture: corn, *11*, *19*, *117*, 312,
314, *317*, *334*; in Delaware, 25–26,
88; farmers, 65, *149*, 315, *318*, 323;
fruit trees, 25–26, 68; grain and
granaries, 82, *117*, 314, 322, *359*; in
New Jersey, *117*; in Pennsylvania,
117; planters, *1*, *3*, *6*, *10*, *15*, *19*, *55*,
149, *309*; vineyards, *231*; weather
affects, 29. *See also* sugar; tobacco;
weather

Agrippa, Asinius, *231*

Ahab (biblical figure), *231*

Ahala, Gaius Servillus, 357, **361**

alcohol, xxxv; beer, *334*;
drunkenness, li, 32, 144–46, *149*,
338; and laws, *113–14*, *308–10*,
328, *332–33*; as metaphor, 28, 67;
spirits, liv, 2, *49*, *113*, *309*; wine,
49, *308*, *310*, *332–33*, 352. *See
also* food and drink

Aldborough, Yorkshire Co., England,
32, *132*

Alexander the Great, king of Macedon,
58–**59**

Alimentus, Cincius, **361**

Allen, Margaret Hamilton, 128, **129**

Aristotle: *Nicomachean Ethics*, 355, *361*

Armbrüster (Armbruster), Anton (Anthony), *152*, **201–02**; as witness in William Smith Libel Trial, *194–95*, 198, 215, 221–22, 237, 248–49, *267*, 287

Aroas (Seneca warrior), **114**

art and architecture, 57–*59*, 63, 68–69

Articles of Confederation (1776), xxxvii, lxxxiii

Aston Township, Chester Co. (now Delaware Co.), Pa., *149*

Augsburg, Germany, 104, *116*

Augusta Frederica, Princess, 78, **80**

Augusta of Saxe-Gotha-Altenburg, Princess, 71, **72**, *73*, 78, *80*

Augustus, **231**

Avon River, *136*

B

Bacon, Anthony, 13, **15**, 33–34, 48, 136

Bacon, Francis: *A Collection of Some Principall Rules*, 65, *67*; *Lord Bacon's Law Tracts*, 67

Bacon, Matthew: *General Abridgment of Cases in Equity*, 323, *332*

Bahamas, *316*

bail, 227, 229, 241, 279, 288; and common law, 164, 182, 203, 226, 262, 265, 283; and habeas corpus, *165*, *167*, 181, 206–07, 212, 226, 262, 265

Bailyn, Bernard, xxiii, xxv

Baker, Mary Worrilow. *See* Taylor, Mary Worrilow Baker

Baltimore, Frederick Calvert, sixth baron, 71–**72**

Baltimore family, 71–*72*

Bancroft, George, xx

banks, xxxviii, 12, *15*, *24*, *90*

Barbados, xxxv

Barbé-Marbois, François, lvi

Barbeyrac, Jean, **305**

Barclay, David, 23–**24**, 46, 78, 120; family of, *3*, 77. *See also* David Barclay & Sons

Barnard, Anna Hanbury (1732–1792), **15**, 36, *38*

Barnard, Thomas, **15**

Barnardiston, Samuel, **172**

Bath, William Pulteney, first earl of, 131, **133**

Battle of Blenheim (1704), *70*, *80*

Battle of Culloden (1746), *73*

Battle of Lauffeld (1747), *73*

Battle of Zama (202 BC), *230*

Baynton, John, *2*, 201–**02**

Beachy Head, East Sussex Co., England, 5–7

Bedford, John Russell, fourth duke of, 71, **73**, *133*

Bell, Mr., 14, 23, 68, 124–25

Berks Co., Pa., *116*, *156*, *231*

Berkshire Co., England, *72*

Besaw River, 294

Bible, 58, 224, 228, *311*; in argument, 222, 224, 296, *298*, 312, *317*, 326, 350–51, 356, *360–61*; Dickinson family, xxxiv, *5–6*; as interpreted by Quakers, xlv, 105; and law, xlv, *298*

NEW TESTAMENT: 69, 105; 1 Cor., *365–66*; Matt., 56, *59*, 296, *298*, 326, 351, *361*; 1 Tim., 350, *360*

OLD TESTAMENT: Ex., 296, *298*; Gen., 13, *15*, 312, *317*; Lev., 222; 1 Kgs., 224, *231*; Ps., 30–*32*, 66, 69–*70*, 356, *361*

Bill of Rights (1689), 207, 212, 226, *229*

Birmingham Township, Chester Co., Pa., *149*

birthdays, 77–*80*

Blackstone, William, *172*, *267*

Blackwall (London), 7, *10*

Blackwell, Mr., 45

Blair, John, **37**

Blakeney, William, **125**, *133*, 138

Bland, Elias, 13, **15**

Church of England, *cont.*
Anglicanism; churches; ministers (religious)
churches: bells for, *24*; Christ Church, Philadelphia, *24*; St. Michael's Church, St. Albans, 57, *59*; St. Paul's Cathedral, London, *51*; Temple-Church, London, 34, 50
Cibber, Colley, *80*
Cicero, Marcus Tullius, xxxv, 69–**70**, 82; *Catiline*, 357, *361*; *De Officiis*, *70*; *Philippics*, 313, *317*
citizens, xxxvii, xxxix–xl, *297*; in London, 25, *27*, 53; in Rome (ancient), 243, 260, *304*, *358*, *361*
civility, 30, 39, 242, 259. *See also* manners; politeness
civil liberties, xvii, xxxv–xxxvii, xl, 261. *See also* freedom of speech; habeas corpus; law (practice of); liberty of the press; religious liberty; rights
Clapham, Lambeth (borough), England, 25, 44–45, *49*
Clarendon, first earl of: Edward Hyde as, 100, **116**; and Philip Yorke, 29–*30*
Clarke, Thomas, 42–**43**
clergy, 92, 229, 247, 287, 315, *318*, 323. *See also* ministers (religious)
Clerke, Francis: *Practice of the Court of Admiralty of England*, 345–46, *357*
Cleveland, Yorkshire Co., England, *49*
clothing, 22, 38, 41, 44–47, 65, 75, 77, 79
coaches, 16, *27*, 44–48, 66, 78
coal, 48–49, 102
Cockpit (at Whitehall Palace, London), 21, *23*, 94, *210*
Codrington, Christopher, **69**
coffeehouses, 8, 45–48
Coke, Edward, 20, **23**, 82, 138, 186, 238, *305*, 326; *Abridgement of the First Part of Ld. Coke's Institutes*, 44, *48–49*; *Institutes of the Laws of*

England, 23, 66–*67*, 123, *167*, 182, *192*, 295, *297–98*, 300–*01*, 302–*04*, 307, *310*, 312, 315–*19*, 324, 327, *333*, 340, *342*, 344, 346–47, 349, *358*, *360*; *Reports of Sir Edward Coke*, 73, 147–49, *166*, 216, 222, *230–31*, 329–30, *334–35*, 340, *342*
Colbourn, H. Trevor, xxi–xxiii
College of New Jersey, lxxxii
College of Philadelphia, *151*, *166*, 275, 281
Colpeper (Colepeper), William, 164, **167**–*68*, 212, 228, 235. *See also* Kentish Petition (1701)
Colpeper's Case, *167–68*, 186–88, 203, 207–08, 212, 228, 235
Comdr. Thomas MacDonough House. *See* The Trap, New Castle Co., Del.
common law, xlv; action of trover, 295, *297*, 308–*09*, 355; Admiralty Courts based on, lii; and bail, 164, 182, 203, 226, 262, 265, 283; and John Campbell (ship captain), *342*–47, 349–50, *357*; and Coke's *Institutes*, *67*; in colonial America, xlvi; convictions under, 240; courts of, xlvii, xlix, li, lii, *43*, *83*, 137, *142*, 163–64, *173*, 183–84, 186–87, 190, 203, 207, 211–12, 217–18, 227, 234–35, 240, 263, 276–77, 283–84, *290*, 320, 328, *333–34*, *342*–45, 347, 349, *358*; Courts of Quarter Sessions as, li; disability at, 327, *333*; and *Doctrina Placitandi*, xl, *83*, *123*; and equity, li, *83*, 137–38; forms and procedures, xlvii, 272; harshness of, li, *83*, 137; indictments under, 184; judges of, lii, *43*; jurisdiction of, *153*, *157*, *172*, 190, 212, 235, 263, 283–84, 290, *345*, *347*, *358*; king cannot alter, *335*; maxims of, l; pleading, xxxix, *123*; and precedent, xlv; protects the wealthy, xlvii; and punishments, 186–87, 190, *192*, 207, 211, 328, 235, 343, 303; and Quakers, xlv, xlvii; as reason, *123*;

DICKINSON, JOHN

Books and Reading

CLASSICAL: Æsop, 60, 62, 155, 228–29; Aristotle, 355; Cicero, 69, *70*, 82, 313, 329, 361; Dionysius II, 120, 137; Quintus Horatius Flaccus, 365; Aelius Galenus, 66; Hippocrates, 66; Homer, 23; Horace, 137, 355; Just. Digest, 336; Plutarch, 296; Tacitus, 220, 228, *230, 231*; *230–32*, 240, 260, *266, 268*, 302, *304*; Virgil, 75, *89–90*

HABITS: "a different Way of Reading," 118; purchases coffeehouse pamphlets, 46; subscriptions, 46

LAW: Francis Bacon, 65, *67*; Matthew Bacon, 323, *332*; Carthew, 327, 330, 349, *360*; chancery reports, 82, 137–38; Chandler, 227; Clerke, 345–46; Coke, 20, 44, *48–49*, 82, 123, 138, 182, 217, 222, *231*, 295, 303, 315, 316, *318*, 327, 333, 340, 344, 346, 347, 349; Croke, *366*; *Doctrina Placitandi*, 83, 123; Dyer, 162, 171, 209; Finch, 327; *General*, 308, 323, 324, 348, 349; Gilbert, 206; Grotius, 303, 316, 329; Hale, 316, 326, 328, 340, 344, 346, *359*; Hardress, 308; Hawkins, 44, 163, *167*, 170, 206, 217, 222, 340, 344, 348; Hobart, 327; Justice, 306, 307, 324, 329, 339, 345–46, 347, 349, 353, *361*; Keble, 162, *165–66*, 169, 171, 209; Keilway, 316; Levinz, 162, 169, 171, 184, 189, 209, 315; *Lex Merc.*, 349, *359*; *Lex Parl.*, 163, 169, 170, *172*, 182; Littleton, 74, 188; *Modern*, 206, 295, 296, 299, 303, 316, 328, 330, 349, 350, *360*; Moore, 132, 222; Newcastle, 296, 336, 348, 349; Plowden, 20, 74, 138, 171, 209, 308; Postlethwayt, 306, 307, 313; Pufendorf, 300, *302*, 303, 304; Raymond, 162, 163, *167*, 169, 170, 217, 295, 296, 323, 324; Salkeld, 138, 296, 347; Sallust, 32, 136; Saunders, 162, 171, 209; Siderfin, 162, 171, 209, 308, 312, 327, 365, *366*; Strange, 306, 328, 330, 346, 348; Vaughan, 306, 307, *309*, 313, 321, 327, 328, 329, 330, *334*; Ventris, 138, 316; Vernon, 323, *332*; Viner, 327; Wood, 296, 303, 313, 315, 321, 323, 326, *332*, 335, 336, 348, 349

LIBRARY OF: xxvii, xxxviii, xl, lxxxiv, lxxxv, 9, 20, 39, 41, 44, 46, 47, 48–*49*, 53, 74, *76*, 82, 123, 135, 137–*39*

LITERATURE: Samuel Butler, 344; Miguel de Cervantes, 87–88; Abraham Cowley, 23; Thomas Gray, 56; Murdoch McLennan, 130; William Mason, 75, *76*; Milton, 127, *128*; Alexander Pope, 17, 20, 56, 57, *59*, 69; Paul de Rapin, 127; Shakespeare, 205, 356; Edward Young, 223

NEWSPAPERS AND MAGAZINES: 118, 130, 132, 135, 339, 349, 353

POLITICAL: Bolingbroke, 128; *His Majesty's Declaration of War*, 127, *128*, 130, 307, *309–10*; Montesquieu, 48, 306, 315, 323; Jonathan Swift, 323; Algernon Sydney, 173, 206, 217

RELIGION: Bible, *6*, 13, 31, *32*, 56, 58, *59*, 69, 79, 85, 224, *231*, 296, 312, 326, 350, 351, 356, 365; Edward VI, 69, *70*

Domestic Life

aunts and uncles of, *6*, 15–17, 53, 75, 94, 120; children of, xxviii, lxxxii–lxxxiv; cousins of, xxxi, 37, 80; and Mary Norris Dickinson, xxviii, xxxvi, lxxxii, lxxxvi; filial

Elymas (biblical figure), *59*
emoluments, xxxix, 65, 314, 322
Empson, Martha Taylor, **148**
Empson, William, 142, 145, **148**
England: Americans in, liii, 7–8, *10*,
12–13, *15*–16, 35, *37–38*, 40, 49–52,
54, 60–61, 63–64, 69, 74–77, 84–*85*,
87–88, 120–*122*, 128, 131, *132*,
135; Civil War (1642–51), *23*, *70*,
116, 128, *173*; climate of, 16, 40, 54,
75; colonies of, xxxii, 12, 36, *38*, 61,
64, 95, 104, 120, *122*, *154*, *158*;
constitution of, 95, 98, 103–04, 106,
109, 127–28, 131, *158*, 169, 171,
173, 182–83, 203, 221, 226–27, 247,
260, 276, 282, *293*; countryside, 16,
35, 53, 63, 135; court (royal), 42, 54,
70, 77–79; debt of, *59*, 104; JD's
arrival in and departure from, *3*, *4*, 5,
7–8, 9, 18, 22, 25–26, 30, 35–36, 38,
39–41, 82, 117–118, 127, 132, 135;
JD's opinion of, 8, 11–13, 16–18,
25, 27–28, 35–36, 39–40, 53–54, 61,
66, 68, 77, 81, 86, 92, 120, 129;
JD's reviewers in, xxxi; elections in,
4, 23–*24*, 32, 42–*43*, 72–*73*; and
foreign troops, 131; gardens, 36, *38*,
44, 47; government of *3*, *4*, 22–*24*,
29–*30*, 71, *86*, *90*, 93–117, 120, *122*,
133, *139*, *172*, 308, *310*, *311*, *317*;
history of, *154*; holidays in, 12, *43*,
53, 75, *91*, 120, *151*, 196; invasion
of, *133*; laws of, xlv–xlvi, li–lii, 99,
109, 128, 137, *153*, 170, *172*, 182,
192, 208, *231–32*, 253, 261, 263,
267, *292*, *319*, 324–25, 329, 339,
347, *360*; liberties of, *173*, 182, 207,
212, 235, 243; medical training in,
176; merchants of, *3*, *6*, 9, 14–*15*,
23–*24*, 28–*29*, 33, 42–*43*, 49, 62, *64*,
66, 91, *122*, *301*, *308*, *310*, 315, *318*,
322, 324, *331*; newspapers in, *30*,
43, *64*, *80*, 85, 120, 132, *134*, *151*,
198, *229*, 278, 286–87, *330–31*;
Nore (in Thames River), 63–*64*;
people of, 22, 53–54, 61, 66, 77–79,
80–81, 132, 187, *193*, 207, 212, 235;
persecution of dissenters in, xlvi, l,
104, 110–11; Quakers in, xlv–xlvi,
xlviii, l, *3*, 5–9, 12, 14–*15*, 18, 23–
26, 36, *38*, 42–*43*, 46, 52, 62, *64*,
75, 77–78, 81, 85, 88–89, 95, 104,
110–11, *115*, 120, 132, *134*;
relations with Holland, 321, *332*,
342, 350, *361*; and Rome (ancient),
267; Society for Promoting
Religious Knowledge and the
English Language Among the
German Emigrants in Pennsylvania,
202, 221, 247–49, *267*, 278–79,
286; trade, *3*, *43*, 72, 107, *293*, *308–
09*, *311*, 306–07, 313–16, *318–26*,
328–30, *331–33*, *359*; travel and
sightseeing in, 5, 7, 11–12, 16–17,
25, 36, *38*, 44–45, 47, *49*, 53, 57–
59, 62–*64*, 68–*72*, 77, *80*, 123, 135;
troops in, 118, 127. *See also names
of individual monarchs*; Anglicans
and Anglicanism; cabinet (Engl.);
Church of England; courts (of law);
flag-of-truce trade; French and
Indian War (1754–63); London,
England; Magna Carta (1215);
Middle Temple; Parliament; rights;
Royal Navy; Seven Years' War
(1756–63); trade. **Legislation**: Acts
of Parliament
English Merchant (JD pseudonym),
xvii. *See also* **DICKINSON, JOHN**:
Writings
equality: and equity, lii; social, 60; in
trade, 313, 321. *See also* Great
Chain of Being; hierarchy (social)
equity, lii, 185, 296, *298*. *See also*
courts (of law)
Essex Co., England, 63
eternity, 17, 60, 93
Ethiopia, *158*
Eure (Evers), Sampson (Samson),
123; *Doctrina Placitandi, ou L'Art
et Science de Bon Pleading*, xl, *83*,
123

French and Indian War (1754–63),
cont.
forts and fortifications; military and
militia; Pennsylvania Assembly;
Seven Years' War (1756–63)
French Navy, *4*, 89, 119, *125*, 127,
130, *133*, *136*, *139*, 325, *360*
French Revolution, lxxxv
friends and friendship, 32, 163, 302;
ally in wartime, 300, 330, 336, *359*;
of Rebecca Anderson, 120–21, 128;
and JD, xxxi, xxxiii, xxxv, xxxviii,
lv, *1–4*, 7–9, 12–13, 16, 18, 20, 27,
31, 35–*38*, 40–41, 43, 49–52, 54,
62–63, 69, 74–78, 80–81, 84–85,
87–89, 110, 121, 127–28, 140–41,
364–66; of Mary Cadwalader
Dickinson, 121, 128; of Sampson
Eure, *123*; and good morals, 8–9,
17, 27–28; of Indians and British,
101; of Indians and Quakers, *113*; of
Henry Ireton, 100; joys of, 219, 242,
261; of William Moore, 244, 280,
291; of William Smith, 163, 205–
06, 218–19, 237, 240–42, 259–60,
265, 286; of Algernon Sydney, *193*;
of Elizabeth Taylor, 146, *149*; wives
as, 26
Friends of the John Dickinson
Mansion, xxiii–xxiv
Frome River, *136*
furniture: aboard ship, 362–63; beds, 2,
7–8, 219, 243, 261; chairs, 25, 57,
74, 79, 143, *158*; desks, xlvii, 92,
118; JD acquires, 25, 48; tables, 67,
69, 25, 143
Fust, Johann, **70**
future, xxxi, 56–57, 104, 185, 246,
304; JD's, xx, xl, 15–16, 18, 31, 36,
39, 41, 60, 89, 137

G

Gains, Capt., 350
Gale, Mr., 14, 23
Galenus (Galen), Aelius, 66, **67**

Gallatin, Albert, xxiv
Galloway, John, *19*
Galloway, Joseph, **192**; and 1764
campaign for royal government,
156, *269*; in flag-of-truce trade
cases, *293*, 342–43, *345*; as lawyer,
liv, *269*, *293*, 342–43, *345*; as
loyalist, *269*; rivalry with JD, lxxxi,
232, 250, 252, 254–56, *267*, 269–
73; in William Smith Libel Trial,
153–54, 179, 185–86, 190–91, 200,
238, 250–52, 254–56, *266*, 268–70,
273, *290–91*
Galloway, Mary. *See* Chew, Mary
Galloway
Garrick, David, 12, **14**
Gaspee Affair, xxxvi
General Society of Colonial Wars,
xxvii
*General Treatise of Naval Trade and
Commerce*, 306–*10*, 315, *318*, 323–
24, *331–32*, 348, *359*
Gentleman's Magazine (London), *229*
George I, king of England, *80*, *129*,
133, *331*
George II, king of England, **19**, 33, 50;
addresses and petitions to, 86, 94;
birthday celebration, 77–*80*; bonds
to, *317*; and colonial defense
dispute, *86*, *94*, 105, 112–*14*, *121*,
135; colonial opposition to, 103; and
customs, 324; and William Denny,
133; JD's trust in, 128; English of,
144; family of, 63, *72–73*, *80*; and
foreign troops, 127; in Hanover, 28–
30, *90*; at Kensington Palace, *30*;
and lotteries, 89–*90*, 119; and
Parliament, 42, 119, *122*; and St.
James's Palace, *14*, *132*; and ship
launch, 63; and taxation, 84; at the
theater, 18–*19*; and Treaty of
Westminster (1756) *122*; and war
with France, *3*, 119, *122*, 129–30,
132, *266*, *309*. *See also* Crown of
England; executive power

law (practice of), *cont.*
xxxviii, xlv, liv–lv, 127, *153*, *165*, 218, 235, 240, *294–95*, *317*; presumptive evidence, 239, *266*; purposes of, 57, 74; settlements, l, *73*, 87, 296, 315, 330, *334*; testimony, *142*, *156*, 191, *202*, 214, 216, *229*–30, 237, 239–41, 243, 247, 251, 257, 259–60, *266*, *268*, 288, *341*, *344–45*; warrants, 140–*4*, *152*, *154*, *165*, 183, 263, *268*, 281, 289, 290, *291*, *309*; wills, 142–48; witnesses, l, lv, 140, 143, *156*, *158*, *162*, 171, 174–76, 188, 191, 194–202, 214–15, 217–18, 221, 233, 235–37, 239–41, 244, 248, 250, 258–59, *268*, 270, 272–75, 277, 280, 283–85, *291*, 303, 323, *331–32*, 340–41, 343, 355–56, 362; writs, *83*, *154*, 163, *165*, *167*, 169, *192*, *193*, 203, 265, *309*, *317*, *334*, *341*. *See also* bail; crimes; debts and debtors; flag-of-truce trade; handwriting; lawyers; punishments and penalties; rights; trials; William Smith Libel Trial

law (types), xliv–xlv; affecting rights, 324, 329, 349; of appropriation, 160; arbitrary, xlvii, 325; Babylonian, 296, *298*; Chancery, 137; civil, xxx, 135, *172*, *210*, 295–96, *305*, 315–16, *318*, 324, 327, 329, *334*, 339, 346–47, 349–50, *358*; common, xl, xlv–xlvii, li, lii, *67*, *83*, *123*, 137, *142*, *153*, *157*, *172*, 184, *192*, 212, 234–35, 240, 259, 272, 283, 290, *297*, 303, 327, *333–35*, *342*, 344–*45*, 346–47, 349–50, *357*; criminal, l–li, *157*, 159–*62*, 206–07, *210*, *230*, 276, 283, *291*, 347, 349; divine, xlv, xlvi, 97, 207, 227, 296, *298*; Egyptian (ancient), 163, *167*, 169, 171, 209, 215, 220, 246; of Embassies, *305*; English, xlv–xlvi, li–lii, 99, 109, 128, 137, *153*, 170, *172*, 182, *192*, 208, *231–32*, 253, 261, 263, *267*,

292, *319*, 324–25, 329, 339, 347, *360*; of equity, xlix, li–lii, *83*, 296, *298*, 335; eternal, xlv; of evidence, 206, 216–17; fundamental, xlv; of the land, 34, 50, 170, *172*, 182–83, *192*, *232*, 295, *298*, *319*, *335*, 349, *360*; maritime, xxx, lii, lv, 339, 348, *360*; municipal, 325; of nations (*ius/jus gentium*), xxxviii, xlv, lii, lvi, *293*, 296, *298*, 302–03, *305*, 316, 323, 325, 328, *336*; natural, xlv, li, 95, 107, *192*, 296, *302*, *305*, 325, 329, *334*; of Oleron, 346, *358*; of Parliament, 186, *192*; penal, l, 171, 209, 221, *334*, *341*; positive law, xlv, 182, *192*, 276, 282, 315, 322, 324, 328, 330, *334*; of reason, *123*, *192*, 247, 254, 296, 335, 348; of restitution, 295, *332*; of retaliation (*lex talonis*), 296, *298*; of Rhode Island, 307, *311*, *317*; Roman (ancient), xlv, *4*, 136, 220, *231*, 247, *344*, 348, 350, *358–59*; of society, 102, 107; statute, xliii, xlv, lv, *24*, 99, 104, 111, 160, *162*, *166*, 182–83, 188–89, *193*, 208, 213, 295–96, 303–*04*, *311*, *318*, 323–24, 326–*31*, *333*–36, 339, *342*, 343, *344*, 347, 349, *358*; of treason (*lex læse majestatis*), 220, 228, *230–31*, 228, 236, 243, 260, *268*; Valerian, 348, *358*. *See also* Admiralty Courts; courts (of law); crimes; law (general); law (Pennsylvania); law (practice of); punishments and penalties; **Legislation**

lawyers, *94*, 148, 188, *210*, 215–17, 224, 237, 274, 280–81, 325; barristers, liii, *3*, *24*, 40, *43*, 83, *116*; in Delaware, 65, 82; Doctors' Commons, *357*; duties of, 57, 65, 180, 227, 233, 261, 273–74; English, liii, 20–21, 40, 296, 300, 336, 348–49, 353, 355; honesty of, liii, 81–82; king's counsel, xxxiv, lxxxi, *3*, 83–*84*, *152*, *230*; in

Middle Temple, *cont.*
  JD AT: xxii, xxxiv, liii, lxxxi, 2–*4*,
    17, *153*, *294*; attends courts of
    law, 9, 21–22, 31, 41, 47–48, 71–
    72, 81–83, 92; bond of, 33–35;
    call to the bar, 41, 140; chambers
    at, 7–8, *10*, 13, 16, 25, 38, 91;
    degree from, 41–42, 140; enrolls
    in, 7, *10*; excitement about, 2;
    expenses at, 8, *10*, 25, 27, 38–39,
    40–41, 44–49, 86, 88; extends
    stay at, 35, 39–41, 71; life at, *4*, 8–
    9, 20, 25, 27, 35, 60, 71, 87;
    lodges at Kingston-upon-Thames,
    77, 85–88, 90; lodges in Clapham,
    25, 44–45, *49*; materials from,
    xxii, xxxviii, xl, 48, 82–*83*, *94*,
    123, *142*, *294*; study habits and
    methods, 5, 9, 20, 27, 31, 35, 39–
    41, 57–58, 60, 71, 73, 82, 85, 89,
    90–92, 118, 123–24, 125–26, 135,
    137. *See also* books; courts (of
    law); **DICKINSON, JOHN**;
    Dickinson, Mary Norris (wife);
    Dickinson, Samuel (1689–1760;
    father); England; law (practice
    of); lawyers; leisure; London,
    England
Middleton, Mary. *See* Ridgely, Mary
  Middleton
Middletown Township, Bucks Co.,
  Pa., *149*
military and militia, xxx, *15*, 129;
  avoidance of duty, 98, 102–03; in
  Delaware, xxxvii, lxxxiv; as
  "Democratical Army," 103, 106; in
  England, 118, 127, 131; First
  Philadelphia Battalion of
  Associators, xxxvi, lxxxiii; funds
  for, *86*, *93*–99, 101–09, 111–*14*,
  118–*22*, 124, 132–*34*, *266*; militia
  bill (Engl., 1755–56), 131, *133*;
  militia bill (Pa., 1755), *44*, 97–98,
  102–03, 106–07, 109, 111, *114–15*,
  121, *136*, *151*, *156*; militia laws, *44*,
  97–99, 102–03, 106, 107, 109, 111,
  114–15, *121*, 131, *133*, *136*, *151*,
  156, *267*; monarch and, 98, 103,
  107, 111, *117*; in New Jersey, *6*; and
  pacifists, 98, 102; in Pennsylvania,
  xxxvi–xxxvii, lxxxiii, *4*, 44, *94*, 98,
  104, 106–07, 109, 111, *114–15*, *121*,
  151–52, *166*; regulation of, xvii,
  102, *115*, *151*–52; in Rome
  (ancient), 220, *230*; in Scotland,
  121, 131; servants enlisting in, 98,
  115; standing army, *168*; stores and
  supplies, *112*, 124, 312, 320–21,
  323, 330; strategy, 124. *See also*
  names of individual wars; British
  Army; Pennsylvania Assembly;
  Quaker party; Royal Navy
Miller, Samuel, xxxix
Milo of Croton (Kroton), 51, **55**
Milton, John: *Paradise Lost*, 127–**28**
mineral springs, *49*
ministers (religious): Anglican, *16*, *55*,
  88, 110, *117*, *151*, 163, *166*, 168,
  171–*72*, 209, 215, 221, 224, 229–*30*,
  247, *279*, 287, 289; German
  Reformed, *267*; Lutheran, *201*;
  Presbyterian, xxxix; Quaker, *149*.
  See also Trial of Seven Bishops
  (1688)
ministers and magistrates, xxxvi, *115–*
  16, *192*, 206, 214, *331*;
  accountability of, 220, 246–47;
  assemblyman, xvii, *149*, 179, 185–
  86, *202*, 213; beloved, 29; duties of,
  103; misbehavior of, 103, 200, 214,
  217, 244, *358*; speakers, lxxxi, *1*, *19*,
  23–*24*, 32, *38*, *113*, *161*, *166*, 177–
  80, 184–86, 189, *191–92*, 221, 233–
  42, 244, 247, 249–59, 262, *268–70*,
  272, 286, 288–89, *291*. *See also*
  names of individual ministers;
  ambassadors; Parliament;
  Pennsylvania Assembly
Minorca, Spain, 124–*25*, 130–31 *133*,
  135–36, *138*
Modern Cases in Law and Equity, 206,
  210

Seven Years' War (1756–63), *cont.*
Indian War (1754–63); military and
militia; Royal Navy; weapons
Shakespeare, William: *Hamlet*, 205–
06, *209*, 356, *361*
Sharpe, Peter, **55**
Sharp's Island, Talbot Co., Md., 52,
55, 71–*72*
Sheerness, Isle of Sheppey, England,
63–*64*
Sherlock, Thomas, **117**, *279*
ship captains, 348, *359*; as
ambassadors, *294*–95, 298–305;
carry letters and supplies, 13, 22, *24*,
26–27, *29*–30, 38, *43*, 51, 54–*55*,
60–*61*, 65–*66*, 77, 79, 81, *83–86*,
129, 137; in lawsuits, lv–lvi, *292*–
93, 298–302, 311–63; in military,
63–*64*, *133*; transport JD, 7, 13–14,
30, 74, 77
NAMES OF: Richard Budden, *24*, 27,
65–*66*, 77, 81, *83*; Walter Burke,
337, 340–41, 353, 355; John
Campbell, 335–61; Coward, 13,
22, *24*, 38; Gains, 350; Gordon,
129; William Hamilton, 38, *43*;
Charles Hargrave, 85–*86*; Hewet,
298–99; Hill, 7, *10*, 14, 26, 30, 46,
54, 74, 79, 84–*85*; Rufus Hopkins,
364; John Kemp (c. 1695–1775),
311, *319*; John Kemp (c. 1717–
1790), *316*; John Macpherson,
362–64; Stephen Mesnard, 27, *29*,
51, *55*; Peter Reeve, 60–*61*; John
Richey, 13, *15*, 27, 38; William
Rodman, 312, *316*, *317*; James
Shirley, 27, *29*–30, 38, 88;
Benjamin Spring, *298*–99, *301*,
311–35, 338, *341*, 355; Edward
Vaughan, 137, *138*; White, 81,
83. See also flag-of-truce trade;
occupations and offices; ships and
shipping
Shippen, Edward, Jr., **279**
ships and shipping, xxxvi, 7, *10*, 37,
39, 52, 54, 92, 124–25, 128, *133*,
292; barks, 95, *112*; blinds, 337,
341; bottoms, 307, *310*, 313;
building of, 63; capture of, 132,
134, 294–95, *297*, *299*, *317*, *332*,
345, *359*, 363; condemned, 295–
97, *301*, 349, *306*, 308, *311*–12,
316, *319*–20, 323, 327, 328, 339,
345, 347, 349, 351–52, 356, *359*–
60; and contraband, 296, *298*, *319*–
21, 323, 330, *335*–61, 300–*01*,
303, *309*–*10*, 312, *317*; cruising,
90, 347, 352, *358*; and customs
seals, 300, *302*, *360*; Danish, 337,
354; Dutch, *293*, 295, *297*, 307,
314, 322, 337, 352, *359*; English,
295, *297*, 306, 311–12, 320, 335,
362; flags of truce, *294*, *298–302*,
305–06, 311–35, 345; forfeiture of,
lii, 296, 305–35, *342*, 349, *359*;
French, 119, *134*, 138, 294–95,
298, *301*, 326, 344, 352, *360*, 363;
gallies, 350, *360*; impressed, 353,
361; laws on, 306–07, *309*, *332*,
359; and letters of marque (mart),
lv, 294, *297*, 306, *308*, 352, 356;
papers of, 336–37, 355, *360*;
pirates, 348–49, 351, *359*; and
prisoners of war, *298*–99, 302,
316; ransomed, 306, 325; tackle,
362–63; taken as prizes, 294–*97*,
300–*01*, 312, *319*–20, 324–26,
328, 330, *332*, *335*, 349–50, 352,
359–*60*, 362–64; wrecks, 22, *309*
NAMES OF: *Ann Galley* (ship), *43*;
Beaux Enfants (ship), *298*–99,
301–02; *Beulah* (ship), 13, *15*;
Britannia (privateer), *362*, *364*;
Carolina (ship), *29*; *Centurion*,
HMS, 63–*64*; *Desire* (snow),
362–64; *Dunkirk* (man of war),
64; *Elizabeth* (schooner), 311–
35; *Hawk* (privateer), *335*;
Hibernia (brigantine), lvi;
Integrity (ship), *24*; *Intrepid*
(ship), 138; *Ipswich*, HMS, *125*;
Knowles (privateer), *335*; *Little*

Spithead, Hampshire Co., England, 89–*90*

Spring, Benjamin, *298*–99, **301**, 311–35, 338, *341*, 355

Stafford, William Howard, first viscount of, 163, *167*, 169

Stafford, Staffordshire Co., England, *34*

Stamp Act (1765): Congress, xvii, xxxv, lxxxiii, *2. See also* **Legislation**: Acts of Parliament: 5 Geo. 3, c. 12

Stewart, James, xxiv

Stillé, Charles J.: *Life and Writings of John Dickinson*, xx, xxiv

Strange, John, 33–**34**, 42–*43*, 49, *51*; *Reports of Adjudged Cases in the Courts of Chancery, King's Bench, Common Pleas and Exchequer*, *302*, 306, *308–09*, 328, *333*, 346, 348, *357–59*

Style, William: *Narrationes Modernæ*, 148, *150*

sugar: act (1764), *293*, 323, *331*; as colonies, *308–10*, *331*, *341*, *362*; and JD, 44, 47; and health, *49*; molasses, *293*, 306, *308–09*, 323; trade, *43*, *49*, *134*, *292*, *299*, *301*, 306–14, 320–22, 327, *331*, 338, *341*, 354. *See also* flag-of-truce trade; food and drink

suicide, *231*, *357*

Sullivan, David, 338

Surinam, *362*

Susquehanna River, *121*

Sussex Co., Del., xxxv, *15*, *19*, *141*, *161*

Sweden, 119, *331*

Swift, Jonathan, **14**, *331*; *Drapier's Letters*, 323, *331*

Sydney, Algernon, 163, **167**, *193*, 206, 217, *230*, *268*; *Discourses Concerning Government*, *167*

Syracuse, Greece, *122*

T

Tacitus, Publius Cornelius, 135, **136**; *Annales*, 220, *230*, *231*; *230–32*, 240, *266*, 302, *304*; on civil liberties, 242; *Historiæ*, 228, 260, *268*, 302, *304*; on lex lesæ majestatis, 220, 243, 260, *268*

Talbot, Hannah Baker, 147–48, **149**

Talbot, Joseph, 144, 147, **149**

Talbot, William, **133**

Talbot Co., Md., xxxiv, lxxxi, *6*, *15*, *55*, *76*, *122*, *128*

Tangier, Morocco, 127, *129*

taverns and inns, xxxvi, 8, 45–*49*, 79, *149*, *333*

taxes and taxation: colonial, xvii, lxxxii, *6*, *15*, 108, 132, *269*, *293*; customs duties, 300, *302*, 306–*11*, 313, 315, *318*, 321–23, 329, *331–32*, *334–35*, 350, *358*, *361*; customs seals, 300, *302*, *360*; exchequer, 22, *24*; French, 119; of proprietary estate, *43–44*, *86*, 97, 101, 105, *114*, *121*, *134*; revenue from, *24*, 313, 329

Taylor, Elizabeth, 142–45, **148**

Taylor, Jacob, **149**

Taylor, John, 142–43, 147, **148–49**

Taylor, John, Jr., **149**

Taylor, Martha. *See* Empson, Martha Taylor

Taylor, Mary Worrilow Baker, **149**

Taylor, Philip, 143, **149**

Taylors Island, Md., 71–72

Temple University, xxiv

textiles, *43*, 75; broadcloth, 77, 79; linen, *61*; silk, 45

Thames River, *6*, *10*, *38*, *43*, *49*, *51*, 58–*59*, 62, *64*, 77, *80*, 86–88

theater, 12, *14*, 18–*19*, 45, 48

Theodosius I, **231**

theology, xxxix, xlv

Third Anglo-Dutch War (1672–74), *297*, *360*

water (bodies of), *cont.*

HARBORS AND PORTS: *36*, 341–42, *359*; Irish, *359*; London, *83*, *132–33*, *138*, *154*, *310*, 338–39, 354; Malaga, *308*, 350; Monte Cristi, *293*, 337–43, 345–47, 350, 353–56; neutral, *292–93*, 337, 343, *345*, 349, 351; New York, 300; Oxford, Md., 52, *55*; Philadelphia, *24*, 26, 29, *43*, *61*, 66, 72, *83*, 86–87, 91–92, 125, 138, 145, *293*, *316–17*, 337, 343–44, 353, 355, 362; Port-au-Prince, 311, 320–21, 326, *335*; Port Dauphin, 337, 339, *341*, 355–56; Port Mahon, 124–*25*, 130–31, *133*, 138; Port of Sally, *359*; Portsmouth, *90*, *125*; Savanna-la-Mar, 337, *341*; Tortola, 337, *341*, 354; Toulon, 124–*25*, 131

OCEANS AND SEAS: 9, 25, *341*; Atlantic, xxxii, *3*, 5, 77, 119, *125*, *134*; crimes on, 323, 325–26, *332*, *344*, 346, 353, *357–60*; JD travels by, 7, 14, 118; goods carried by, 308; goods taken at, *332*, *335*; goods thrown into, *309–10*; Mediterranean, *4*, 124–25, 131, *133*, 135–36; metaphorical, 36, *70*, 190, 356; Pacific, *64*; and war, 89–*90*, 119, 124, 127, 130, *297*; weather on, 5, 7, 13, 25, 29, 36, *132*, *298*, 300–*01*, *310*, 356

RIVERS: 306, *360*; Avon, *136*; Besaw, 294; Choptank, *6*, *55*; Elizabeth, *15*; Frome, *136*; James, *15*; Medway, 63–*64*, 77; Ohio, *113*; Serpentine, 16; Susquehanna, *121*; Thames, *6*, *10*, *38*, *43*, *49*, *51*, 58–*59*, 62, *64*, 77, *80*, 86–88. *See also* Admiralty Courts; flag-of-truce trade; Royal Navy; ship captains; ships and shipping

Wayne, Isaac, **151**

wealth, 20, 22, 31, 53, 56, 348, *361*, *364*; of JD, xxxiv, liii, *3*, 74; of lawyers, *83*; of merchants, *15*, *122*, *316*; of Alexander Pope, 62; of Quakers, xlvii, 107–10, *141*, *149*; of women, *43*, *85*, 87. *See also* debts and debtors; money

weapons: ammunition, 135, *309*, *364*; arms, 109, 121, 124, 307, *309*, 313, *317*, 320, 330, *335*, 337–41, 343, *345*–46, 348–56, 362; artillery, 63–64, 119, *125*, *298*, *335*, 337–38, 341, *364*; guns, *94*, 354, 362; as metaphor, 126; muskets, 121, 337; powder, *309*; swords, 126, *132*, 337; taking up of, xx, xxxvi, xxxvii, lxxxiii, 96, 101–02, 109, *115*, 121, 337; thrown overboard, 336, 337–40, *345*, 355–56, *309*; trade in, 307, *309–10*, 313, *317*, 320, 330–61. *See also* flag-of-truce trade; military and militia; pacifism; war

weather: acts of God, 337; cold, 42–*43*, 73; farmwork affected by, 29; fine, 16, 42, 123, 365; fog, 7, 16; foul, 5, 12, 16, 26, 42, 74, 92; heat, 356; as metaphor, 25, 36, 74; storm, *310*, 356; wind, 5, 13, 130, *132*. *See also* agriculture; seasons; water (bodies of)

West Indies, *113*, 124, *301*, 306–07. *See also names of individual islands*

West Looe, Cornwall Co., England, *34*

Westtown Friends School, xxxix, lxxxvi

Wharton, Samuel, **2**; JD's letter to, 2–3

whigs (historians), xviii, xx

Whigs (political faction), xl, *4*, *129*, *167*

White, Capt., 81, *83*

Whitechapel, England, *24*

Whiting, Charles, 49–50

Willes, John, 41, **43**

William III, king of England, **59**, *161*, *230*, *317*; and double returns, 189, *193*, 203; and Hampton Court

Palace, 58–59; and Kentish Petition (1701), *168*; painting of, 58–*59*
William Nelson Cromwell Foundation, xxvii
William Smith Libel Trial, xxxiv; Address of Pa. Assembly to governor, 214, 220, 244–45, 275, 277, 280–81, 284; and ancient law, 164, 171, 209, 220, 247, 260; and *Ashby v. White*, 183, *192*, 228; bail, 164–*65, 167*, 181–82, 203, 206–07, 212, 226–27, *229*, 241, 262, 265, 279, 283, 288; and civil liberties, *154*, 203, 217, 223–24, 251–53, 261, 264, 279, 287; and Colpeper's Case, *167–68*, 186–88, 203, 207–08, 212, 228, 235; conclusion of, *153, 154*, 162, 171, 181, 207, 263, 274, 287–90; contempt in, 160, 162, 164–*65*, 168–70, *172–73*, 183, 187, 190, *192–93, 202*–03, 208, 235, *266*, 276–77, 283–84, 290; deferment requested, *202, 204*; JD as counsel in, *153, 177*, 179–80; JD introduces self, 204, 210–11; JD maligned by assemblymen, *232*, 234–35, 247, 250–52, 254–56, 263–64, 269–74; JD's health during, 229, 233, 257; JD's preparation for, 204–05, 211; JD threatened with arrest, 256; due process in, *153*, 170, *173*, 177–181, 190–91, 213, 234, 226, 262, 275, 277, 282, 284–85; and George II, *154*, 190, 224, 262, 274, 278–79, 287–89; and habeas corpus, *152, 154*, 162, 169–70, *173*, 181–83, *192*, 206–07, *210*, 212, 226, 235, 262, 265; and history of Pennsylvania, 158–62; jurisdiction of Pa. Assembly in, *152, 158–59, 161–62*, 164, 168–70, 177–80, 182–87, 189–91, 194, 203–05, 207–09, 211–13, 218, 226–28, 235–36, 260, 263, *266–67*, 275–77, 280–85, 289–*92*; justice in, 162, 171, 179, 181, 183–84, 189, 205, 207–09, 211–12, 214–

15, 218, 220, 226–28, 234–35, 237, 241, 244–46, 263–64, 272–73, 277–78, 283–84, 286, 288–88; and Kentish Petitioners, *167–68*, 208, 212, 235; and Lamb's Case, 216, 222, *230–31*, 238; libel defined in, *152–54, 157*, 162–63, *165–66*, 170–71, *173*, 178, 184, 208–09, 213–14, 216, 220, 242–44, 259, 275, 277, 284–86, 289; and liberty of the press, *154, 156–57*, 200–201, 223–24, 251–53, 258, 261, *267*, 278–79, 287; Onslow's Case in, 189, *193*; Pa. Assembly consented to publication of William Moore's "Address," 221–22, 224, 227, *231*, 250–51, 255–57, 275, 278, 286–87; Pa. Assembly judges in own case, 164, 178, 181, 202, 205, 207, *210*–12, 219, 223–25, 227, 233, 278, 286–87; precedent for resolves in, 178–79, 182–83, 185–86, 188, 212, 285; public opinion of, *154, 158*, 179, 181, 220, 245, 279, 288; resolves of Pa. Assembly in, *152–53*, 177–78, 187, 190, *192*, 208, 226, 234, 264, 275–76, 282–85; and Richmond Park affair, 215, *229*; and Algernon Sydney, 163, *167, 193*, 206, 217, *230, 268*; testimony in, *156*, 191, *194–95*, 198–*202*, 214, 216, 218, *229–31*, 237, 239–41, 243, 247, 250–57, 259, *267–74*, 278–79, 286–87; trial in, *152–53*, 170, *172*, 182, 184, 190, 226, 263, 276, 283; and Trial of Seven Bishops, 163, 168, 171–*72*, 209, 215, 221, *230*; votes in Pa. Assembly, 201, 206–08, 213, 223, 227, *230*, 236, 243, *268*; and Isaac Wayne, *151*; witnesses in, *156, 158, 162*, 171, 174–76, 188, 191, 194–202, 214–15, 217–18, 221, 233, 235–37, 239–41, 244, 248, 250, 258–59, 272–75, 277, 280, 283–85, *291*